Readings In The Analysis Of Survey Data

Readings In The Analysis Of Survey Data

Robert Ferber
University of Illinois-Urbana

AMERICAN MARKETING ASSOCIATION
222 South Riverside Plaza - Chicago, Illinois 60606 - (312) 648-0536

Printed in the U. S. A.

Cover Design by Mary Jo Krysinski

Library of Congress Cataloging in Publication Data

Main entry under title:

Readings in the analysis of survey data.

1. Marketing research--Statistical methods--Addresses, essays, lectures. 2. Market surveys--Addresses, essays, lectures. 3. Marketing--Mathematical models--Addresses, essays, lectures. I. Ferber, Robert.
HF5415.2.R34 658.8'3'028 80-12975
ISBN 0-87757-140-6

414/1000/480

Contents

Introduction

The rapid growth of the survey technique in marketing and other fields, plus the growing sophistication of researchers in analyzing these data, has led to widespread interest in the applications of multivariate and related techniques to survey data. At the same time, marketing and other researchers have come forth with a number of new and innovative approaches to the analysis of survey data. These techniques are widely used and the references on them are frequently sought in practical work only to be forgotten or misplaced. The purpose of this volume is to ameliorate this problem by bringing together some of the key references in the marketing literature dealing with the analysis of survey data as well as with such key problems as the treatment of missing data.

While the focus of this volume is on relatively recent references dealing with the analysis of survey data, it nevertheless includes some of the "classics" in this subject area, such as the article by Don Morrison on the meaning of discriminant analysis. The principal emphasis, however, is on the more recent references, and particularly on the methods that have come to fruition only in the last five to ten years, such as logit analysis, confirmatory factor analysis and the application of econometric techniques to the analysis of panel data.

Of particular value to the applied researcher will be the opening pair of references dealing with the treatment of missing data. This is a topic which most textbooks, even advanced ones, and most articles on multivariate analysis seem to ignore. Most of these sources simply assume that the data sets are complete and that the only problem faced by the researcher is what analytical technique to apply to the data to obtain a given objective. In practice, however, nothing is further from the truth. Many observations may be missing; values for some variables may be missing; and more often than not a key problem, and a very time-consuming one, is to decide how to treat these missing values. Should estimates be made of the missing values? If so, how? When should observations with missing values be retained? In many instances the answers to these questions may have a more profound influence on the later results than the particular analytical technique that is employed. The references provided in the opening section of this volume should aid considerably in the resolution of these problems.

The readings in this book are divided into six sections. The opening section contains two papers dealing with the treatment of missing data. The first paper, by Kim and Curry, provides a general overview of the topic, discussing among other things how to decide whether missing data is a serious problem, and then indicating some general approaches to either data deletion or data replacement. The paper by Chapman focuses on various ways of imputing missing data in large data sets, especially imputation for item nonresponse by the "hot deck" procedure. In addition, this article discusses means of imputing missing values for an entire questionnaire, that is, adjusting for nonresponse.

The second part of this volume contains four articles dealing with some of the newer aspects of regressions and canonical techniques. The question of the statistical robustness of different regression procedures is covered in the article by Robert Hogg, which provides a good overview of the relatively recent methods of robust regression, methods which have so far found little application in marketing. An overview of a different type of analysis, canonical regression, is provided in the second article, by Claes Fornell. Three different approaches to canonical regression are covered in this article, and the different applications to marketing problems are clearly illustrated.

The third article provides some useful, cautionary information on a widely used technique, AID. As Doyle and Fenwick point out, this technique is commonly misused and misinterpreted, and the authors illustrate why and show what can be done about it. The final article in this section, by Richard Lutz, brings out the flexibility of regression analysis, showing how a general hypothesis can be tested within the framework of a system of equations, and also how the analysis of variance can be carried out on the data as part of the same model.

Discriminant analysis is the subject of the third set of papers in this volume. The first article in this section is one of the "classics" in the multivariate analysis of marketing data. This article, by Don Morrison, provides a very clear and simple introduction of discriminant analysis and the pitfalls involved in its application. The second article, by Crask and Perreault, deals with one of the major such pitfalls, that is, how to validate the results of a discriminant analysis.

Various modifications to deal with shortcomings of discriminant analysis are considered in the remaining articles in this section. Thus, different approaches to the multinomial classification problem are considered in the article by Dillon, Goldstein and Schiffman. In addition to comparing different multinomial classification procedures with each other, including linear discriminant analysis, the authors present a sequential variable selection procedure which helps to select not only key variables but also key levels of measurement. Another alternative to multiple discriminant analysis is presented in the article by Gitlow. This technique, multivariate nominal scale analysis, is shown to be a useful alternative to multiple discriminant analysis, although it does not have the ability of discriminant analysis to identify statistically significant variables.

The application of the concept of the jackknife to a variety of marketing problems, including discriminant analysis, is illustrated in the final article in this section, by Ian Fenwick. As Fenwick demonstrates, the jackknife technique is a highly versatile tool, which applies not only to the validation of discriminant functions but to coping more generally with the problems of biases in survey data.

The fourth section of this volume covers logit and log-linear models. In the first of the articles in this section, Flath and Leonard contrast two different logit models, and show how they fit into the overall framework of multivariate (qualitative) data analysis. They suggest a maximum likelihood form of logit model which has the advantage of not requiring grouping of data or multiple observations per cell. A comparison between the logit approach and the multiple regression approach is provided in the article by Gensch and Recker, in which they point out the theoretical advantages of the logit approach for studying choice behavior and illustrate these advantages by means of an example relating to store preference.

An interesting example of the joint use of two multivariate approaches is provided in the article by Green. In this article he shows how preliminary results obtained from the AID technique may be used as input into the formulation of a logit model, which then serves to supply explicit parameterization of the problem.

The last article in this section builds on the article by Green and takes up the problem of, given the formulation of a general framework for a model, how does one select which variables to include at all? The approach by Dillon is simple and is very efficient from a statistical point of view, though others may criticize it because of its pure reliance on statistical considerations.

The analysis of models that involve unobservable variables is the subject of the fifth section of this volume. Such unobservable variables may exist partly because of the conceptual approach taken in the formulation of the model and partly because the variables being measured are subject to unknown errors. Undoubtedly, the most popular approach for dealing with unobservable variables is factor analysis, and the first two articles deal with this approach. In the first of these articles, Hauser and Koppelman compare factor analysis to discriminant analysis and the similarity judgment approach. and find it superior to these other two techniques for purposes of perceptual mapping.

The factor analytic method described by Heeler. Whipple and Hustad in the second article in this section is very different from the traditional approach. Contrary to this traditional method of exploratory analysis in which no restrictions are imposed on the data or the relationships. this newer "confirmatory factory analysis" involves the application of prior knowledge or theory to specify certain hypotheses about the underlying structure of the model, and then to test this structure by the factor analytic approach. A comparison of both approaches is provided in this article. and the pros and cons of each are discussed.

A second approach to dealing with unobservable variables is the subject of the third article in this section, by Aaker and Bagozzi. They show how the econometric approach of structural equation models can be used to deal with this situation. drawing an interesting parallel between this method and that of factor analysis. They also illustrate how alternative hypotheses can be tested within the general framework of structural equation models.

A broad overall view of different approaches to the measurement of consumer preferences, subsumed under the general heading of conjoint analysis. is discussed in the article by Green and Srinivasan. Defining these terms to include "models and techniques that emphasize the transformation of subjective responses into estimated parameters," they review the steps involved in carrying out this type of study, the pros and cons of alternative techniques, and the evaluation of results.

A different means of dealing with unobservable variables is illustrated in the article by Don Morrison. In this article. which involves the transformation of purchase intention data into predictions of later purchases, Morrison shows how errors in the intentions variables, whatever the source of the errors, can be incorporated into the model and the predictions adjusted accordingly.

The final section of this volume focuses on the analysis of panel data. With the growing reliance on panels to trace changes in consumer and market behavior over time. there is a concomitant increase in the need for more powerful methods of analyzing such data. The proper analysis of such data can be difficult at times because such analysis may present all the problems of analyzing both cross-section data and of analyzing time series data. As a result. fairly sophisticated econometric and other techniques are required, and a few such techniques are explained in these articles. In the first one, several of the econometric approaches to analyzing panel data are covered in detail by Bass and Wittink. In addition to providing illustrative examples, this article also raises the question of when cross-section data should be pooled and under what circumstances.

The second and third articles in this section illustrate techniques in the analysis of panel data, both relating to the analysis of variance. Winter shows how dummy variables can be used in conjunction with the analysis of covariance to allow for behavioral differences among households. On their part, Farley and his colleagues make use of the multivariate analysis of variance to track the impact of a new brand of car, and to detect what attributes of the car account for differences.

The final article by Kasulis, Lusch and Stafford presents a different approach as applied to a very different sort of problem, namely, the use of Guttman scalogram analysis for determining the order of acquisition of durable goods, a question of considerable relevance to market planners as well as economists. This technique, incidentally, does not necessarily require panel data.

The articles in this volume represent only a small selection of the flood of material that is starting to appear using sophisticated methods to analyze marketing survey data. A relatively small set of articles such as this cannot encompass all the techniques that are available. However. they should provide an idea of the diversity of material on this subject, and hopefully stimulate the reader to consult the references in the bibliographies of these articles as well as textbooks on the topic.

Procedures for treating missing data in the statistical analysis of survey data are reviewed. The main topics covered are: (1) how to assess the nature of missing data especially with regard to randomness, (2) a comparison of listwise and pairwise deletion, and (3) methods for using maximum information to estimate (a) parameters or (b) missing values.

THE TREATMENT OF MISSING DATA IN MULTIVARIATE ANALYSIS

JAE-ON KIM
JAMES CURRY
University of Iowa

For any large data set it is unlikely that complete information will be present for all the cases. In surveys which rely on respondents' reports of behavior and attitudes, it is almost certain that some information is either missing or in an unusable form. Although statisticians have long appreciated that the existence of such missing information can change an ordinarily simple statistical analysis into a complex one (e.g., Orchard and Woodbury, 1972) and responded to this challenge by producing enormous amounts of literature (see, for example, Afifi and Elashoff, 1966; Hartley and Hocking, 1971; Orchard and Woodbury, 1972; Press and Scott, 1974), there is little indication that survey researchers have paid much attention to the literature. When faced with such missing-data problems, most survey researchers are likely to choose either a listwise deletion or pairwise deletion, and then proceed to interpret the resulting statistics as usual.[1]

The primary objective of this paper is to review and organize the procedures for handling missing data, having in mind the practical needs of survey researchers with a relatively complex analysis problem but with little statistical sophistication. To make the task manageable, we will confine our discussion mostly to the situation in which variables are measured at least on an interval scale. Other situations will be dealt with only when such excursion is simple and does not interrupt the flow of the presentation. For researchers with specific problems not discussed in this paper, a brief bibliographical note is included.

Reprinted with permission from *Sociological Methods & Research,* **6 (November 1977), 215-40, copyright ©Sage Publications Inc.**

MISSING DATA PROBLEMS: A PRACTICAL OVERVIEW

There are many different ways to categorize the treatment of missing data problems. From the practical point of view, however, the most important question is when and under what conditions can one safely consider the problem of missing information to be trivial. This much is obvious: the smaller the relative proportion of missing information, the larger the sample, and the more random the missing information, the less troublesome the missing data problems.

If the sample size is large, as is usually the case in survey research, and the proportion of missing data relatively small, probably the first options to consider for handling missing data are the simplest ones: listwise deletion or pairwise deletion. If the problem can be handled safely by either of these options, the missing-data problem may be considered trivial. But when is the proportion of missing data considered relatively small? The overall loss of data for a given analysis depends on several factors: the proportion of missing observations on each variable, the number of variables under consideration, the degree to which missing observations are clustered, and the choice of procedures for handling missing data.

Although listwise deletion is the simplest, there is an inherent conflict in the often recommended requirements for its use in that for a fixed number of variables and a given proportion of missing cases for each variable, the number of deleted cases increases as the pattern of missing information becomes more random. To illustrate, if only 2% of the cases contain missing values on each variable and the pattern of missing values is random, the listwise procedure will delete 18.3% of the cases in an analysis using 10 variables. As the overlap of missing values increases, the loss due to listwise deletion will decrease, in the extreme to 2% of the cases. Pairwise deletion is an attractive alternative when the number of missing cases on each variable is small relative to the total sample size, the pattern of missing values is random, and the number of variables involved is large.

The problem with the use of listwise deletion is the relatively greater loss of data, whereas the problem with the pairwise deletion is the potential inconsistency of the covariance matrix in a multivariate context.[2] There is an approach which tries to overcome the limitations of these two simple procedures. The basic strategy of this approach is to estimate in the first step the missing *values* (not parameters) from the available information and then proceed to the estimation of parameters. The drawback of this approach is that except for very simple situations it depends on iterative numerical solutions, making it out of reach of most survey researchers (at least until ready-made computer programs are more widely available.) But the advantages of this approach are too compelling not to consider its adoption: (1) the parameter estimation is more efficient because a greater amount of available information is used and (2) it allows at the same time the use of estimated values for index construction, thereby preventing a severe data loss in complex analyses.

Keeping in mind, however, the varied needs of researchers, we will organize our discussion around the following three practical issues: (1) how to evaluate whether or not observations are randomly missing and how to live with a potentially serious missing data problem, (2) if missing data are trivial, what are the factors to consider in choosing between listwise and pairwise deletion, and (3) when these simpler methods are inappropriate what are the general techniques available in the literature.

ASSESSING THE NATURE OF MISSING DATA

Almost all the techniques suggested in the literature assume that information is missing randomly (see Buck, 1960; Hartley and Hocking, 1971; Orchard and Woodbury, 1972; Beale and Little, 1974). But the simple dichotomy—random versus nonrandom—is often not sufficient. We begin therefore with a brief examination of various patterns of missing data.

TYPES OF MISSING DATA

Because the most important aspect of missing data is whether and to what extent the missing information may be considered random, the following categorization is chiefly based on the pattern of randomness.

(1) Missing data is randomly produced. That is, whether information is missing or not on a given variable is unrelated to the values of that variable or to the values of other variables in the data set. As the sample size increases, it is expected not only that the mean and variance of each variable and the covariance between any two variables will be affected less by the existence of missing data but

also that the pattern of missing data will exhibit such randomness. By the pattern of missing data we mean the frequency distribution of different categories of missing patterns such as missing only on X_1, missing on both X_1 and X_2, and so on.

(2) Missing data on a given variable X_1 is dependent on the value of another variable X_2. The differentiating characteristic of this pattern is whether information is missing on a given variable X_1 is not dependent on the value of X_1 but rather on its underlying relationship with another variable X_2. Therefore, whether or not information is missing on X_1 is independent of the values of X_1 given values of X_2. This represents an important class of missing data which is not completely random but allows simple factorization of maximum likelihood (e.g., see Little, 1976a; 1976b). An example of this type of missing data problem can be found in the situation in which respondents are asked whether they voted in previous elections but some were ineligible to vote because of age.[3] Or, in a panel study, a whole set of information may be missing from the later waves for some respondents who were not available. The missing data pattern will be systematic, but the cause of the missing data may be independent of the values of the variables under consideration (Rubin, 1976).

(3) Underlying values not observed in a given data set may determine whether information is missing or not. For example, in an attitudinal survey, a respondent with low cognitive skills may refuse or be unable to give usable answers to many questions. In this case, the pattern of missing data will exhibit clustering. The difference between this case and (2) above is that here the variable which determines the pattern of missing data is not included in the survey. The practical difference is that in case (2) the missing information can be made conditionally independent of its underlying values by controlling for the differences in the determining factor (e.g., age). Such a control is usually impossible in the present example. But the difference between cases (2) and (3) is not an absolute one; there may exist variables such as education and other measures of cognitive ability with which the underlying syndrome may be approximated and factored out.

(4) Whether information is missing on a given variable X_1 is dependent on the values of itself, that is, X_1. For example, respondents with excessively high income may be reluctant to reveal their level of income. In this type of missing data problem, the mean and variance of the variable is affected by the existence of missing information. The degree to which the missing information can be estimated from the existing data will depend on the degree to which the variable is related to other variables in the data set, but unless the determination

is complete, completely eliminating the effects of missing data is not possible. In addition, an examination of the pattern of missing data alone may not provide clues to the nature of this type of missing data.

(5) Missing data is a product of a particular combination of two or more variables. For instance, people with *high* education may be less inclined to reveal their *low* income, or people with high income may be unwilling to reveal their low education. In this type of situation, any effort to recover the missing information from the relationship between the variables in existing data would be misleading.

TESTING FOR A RANDOM PATTERN

A simple test for the randomness of missing values can be devised if missing values are relatively large and many variables are involved in the analysis. The strategy is to consider the (K + 2) patterns of missing data where K is the number of variables with a substantial number of missing cases (say, 20 or over). The pattern to consider is: (M_1), (M_2), . . . (M_k), (MM—missing on two or more variables), and (NM—none missing) where M_i stands for cases on which information is missing only on the variable X_i. To illustrate, if there are three variables, X_1, X_2, and X_3, the categories involved and the expected frequencies under the assumption of randomness are given as follows:

$$M_1 = (Q_1P_2P_3)N$$
$$M_2 = (Q_2P_1P_3)N$$
$$M_3 = (Q_3P_2P_3)N$$
$$MM = (1 - P_1P_2P_3)\ N - M_1 - M_2 - M_3$$
$$NM - (P_1P_2P_3)N$$

where Q_i and P_i stand respectively for the proportion of missing and nonmissing cases of variable i. The significance of the deviation of the observed frequencies from the expected frequencies can be evaluated by the ordinary χ^2 test with degrees of freedom equal to the (K + 1) number of variables involved.[4]

If such tests indicated that the missing data can be assumed random, then many techniques suggested in the literature are available. In particular, the adoption of either pairwise or listwise deletion may be seriously considered. But it should be noted that this test is of no use if missing information exists on only one variable or there is nonrandomness such that (as in case [5]) the examination of the pattern alone is not sufficient.

USE OF INDICATOR VARIABLES

As suggested by Cohen and Cohen (1975), it is convenient to represent the existence of missing data with dummy indicator variables. Following their lead, we will illustrate the use of indicator variables in the context of bivariate regression. They argue that in a (bivariate) regression it is convenient to delete cases with missing information on the dependent variable (Y) from the analysis. If one follows their suggestion, one will have the following simple pattern of missing data:

$$\begin{array}{l} Y\!: y_1\ y_2 \ldots y_m\ y_{m+1}\ y_{m+2} \ldots y_n \\ X\!: x_1\ x_2 \ldots x_m \end{array} \qquad \text{(Pattern A)}$$

We assume that cases are rearranged such that cases missing on the independent variable (X) are placed at the end so that $m < N$.

If the missing information on X is missing randomly, we would expect that the mean of Y for the first m cases would be similar to the mean of Y for the last $(N - m)$ cases. The simplest way to test whether such an expectation is met in the data is to create a dummy indicator variable X_a (assigning 1 if the information is missing and O otherwise) and then regress Y on X_a. The constant a in the regression equation $Y = a + bX_a$ will represent the mean of Y for the first m (compete) cases and the coefficient *b* will represent the difference between the mean of the missing cases and that of the nonmissing cases. The test for the significance of b will serve as a test for the randomness of the missing data.

Furthermore, if one inserts any arbitrary constant in the place of the missing X values and regresses Y on both X and X_a, then the partial regression coefficient associated with X will be equivalent to the simple b that would be obtained from the complete data of the m cases. The data pattern would then be:

$$\begin{array}{l} Y\!: y_1\ y_2 \ldots\ldots\ldots\ldots\ldots\ldots\ldots\ldots\ldots\ldots\ldots\ldots\ldots\ldots y_n \\ X\!: x_1\ x_2 \ldots\ldots\ldots\ldots\ldots\ldots\ldots\ldots\ldots x_n\ c\ c \ldots\ldots\ldots\ldots c \\ X_a\!: 0\ 0 \ldots\ldots\ldots\ldots\ldots\ldots\ldots\ldots\ldots 0\ 1\ 1 \ldots\ldots\ldots\ldots 1 \end{array}$$

The increment in R^2 due to X from the dummy regression is equivalent to the simple r^2 that would exist for the first m cases. The complete analysis calls for a hierarchical regression. If, on the other hand, the missing values on X are replaced by the mean of X (for the m cases), then the regression of Y on X and X_a need not be made in a hierarchical fashion; the partial b's associated with X and X_a are then equivalent to simple b's (see Cohen and Cohen, 1975, for more illustrations and uses of different coding methods).

The use of dummy indicator variables can be easily extended to the situation in which X is a categorical variable. The only adjustment necessary is to regress Y on the missing data indicator variable X_a first and then on both X_a and other dummy variables representing (K - 1) categories of X. Cohen and Cohen therefore argue that it is not only unnecessary to assume randomness in missing data but also unwise to do so when such easy means of handling missing data are available (1975: 288).

It must be noted, however, that their suggestion is of limited value in most survey research where many variables are examined in a complex manner as in path analysis. In path analysis, a variable is often considered a dependent variable in one context, but an independent variable in another context. Nevertheless, the use of a dummy indicator variable is very convenient in testing whether the type (4) situation exists. If information is missing on Y because of the underlying values of Y itself (type [4]), one would look for another variable (Z) that is closely related to Y. Then one would regress Z on Y_a (the indicator variable) and test whether the b associated with Y_a is significant. One must be cautious, however, in interpreting a result from such a bivariate case. Even if the missing cases have different means on some variables, it does not mean that the pattern belongs to case (4); the case (2) can produce significant differences if the bivariate association between the two variables is strong. As will be shown later, such situations can be exploited as means of obtaining extra information about the missing data.

Another method suggested by Cohen and Cohen (1975: 286f) is to examine the relationships among the missing data indicator variables to see if there is any significant clustering. Although applying factor analysis to dichotomous variables in not fully justified, such an application may still provide means of identifying important underlying dimensions of the clustering of missing values when the correlations are moderate (Kim et al., 1977). Such examination of clustering may help identify the underlying causes of missing data. Even if the nature of missing data remains obscure, one can at least control for the unknown effects of missing data more efficiently by including missing value scales along with other independent variables in a multivariate analysis (Cohen and Cohen, 1975: 286f.).

An examination of the correlation matrix for the set of missing-data indicator variables can also serve as a quick way of ascertaining whether there is any unusual clustering between missing values of two variables. Noting that the correlation between dichotomous variables (r_{ij}) is equivalent to ϕ, and that $\phi^2 = \chi^2/N$, one may consult the χ^2 table with $\chi^2 = \phi^2 (N)$ and degrees of freedom = 1 (Cramer, 1946: 441-445).[5]

As may have been obvious from the discussion in this section, the researcher really does not have much recourse in assessing the nature of the missing data. The final assessment should be based on substantive knowledge about the content and the circumstances under which the data were collected.

LISTWISE AND PAIRWISE DELETION

If one is willing to assume (or the test for randomness shows) that the pattern of missing data does not deviate significantly from the random model, the easiest options to consider are listwise and pairwise deletion of missing cases.

As noted earlier, the disadvantage of listwise deletion is the relatively greater loss of data. Its advantages are that it always generates consistent covariance and correlation matrices and that test statistics used with the complete data can be used without modification. The advantages and disadvantages of pairwise deletion are complementary to those of listwise deletion. The matrix generated by pairwise deletion may not be consistent (not positive-definite), especially when the missing data pattern is not random or when the total sample size is small.[6] Furthermore, the sampling distribution of estimates based on pairwise deletion usually contains nuisance parameters which are not readily computable (Haitovsky, 1968).

The choice between the two methods, even in trivial situations, is not clearly indicated in the literature. Using the matrix based on pairwise deletion may be close to the spirit of maximum likelihood solutions proposed for missing data problems (e.g., see Haitovsky, 1968: for a summary of earlier literature of maximum likelihood solutions, see Anderson, 1957). A specific comparison between the two methods was first attempted (as far as we know) by Buck (1960) in his examination of several methods for handling missing data. He compared the estimated coefficients using various methods of handling missing data to those based on the complete (74 cases) data (Buck, 1960: 305). Among other things, he showed that listwise deletion produced results closer to the complete data than pairwise deletion. Because his conclusion is based on the examination of a single data set (containing 72 cases and 4 variables from which he randomly deleted a few cases from each variable resulting in a total loss of 34 cases) and *a single* simulation, his conclusion should not be taken seriously.

Glasser (1964) argued that the efficiency of pairwise deletion over listwise deletion improves as the overall correlation among the independent variables decreases, and may become better when the sample is large and correlations are below a certain level, given a fixed pattern of missing values. For example, for the situation where there are two independent variables and the proportion of missing values is uniform, the efficiency of estimating partial b's from the covariance matrix based on the pairwise deletion is in general better than that based on the listwise deletion if the magnitude of correlation between the two variables is less than .58 (Glasser, 1964: 839).

As far as we know, Haitovsky (1968), through the use of computer simulation, has performed the most systematic and extensive comparisons between the two methods. His finding is fairly conclusive: listwise deletion is in general superior to pairwise deletion in the estimation of partial regression coefficients. He summarizes his finding as follows: "In almost all the cases which were investigated the former method [ordinary least squares applied only to complete observations] is judged superior. However, when the proportion of incomplete observations is high or when the pattern of the missing entries is highly non-random, it seems plausible that one of the many methods of assigning values to the missing entries should be applied" (Haitovsky, 1968: 67). Later publications based on simulations do not consider the pairwise deletion partly on the basis of evidence presented by Haitovsky (e.g., Timm, 1970; Beale and Little, 1974).

After carefully examining Haitovsky's simulation model, however, we conclude that he does not have a model typical of sociological data, which usually contains only moderate bivariate correlations and a multiple R usually not beyond .7. Furthermore, it is not clear at what point the proportion of missing observations should be considered to be high. Partly for these reasons, we have made our own simulations using Blau and Duncan's correlation matrix among status-attainment variables as the model (Blau and Duncan, 1967: 169).

More specifically, we have simulated sampling 1,000 cases from a multivariate-normal population with a correlation matrix equal to Blau and Duncan's matrix, and we deleted randomly about 10% of the cases from each variable.[7] Such sampling was repeated 10 times, and the resulting sample correlations and covariance matrixes were compared with the population model. The results are present in Table 1.

TABLE 1

Simulation Results, Using Blau-Duncan's Correlation Matrix as the Model, Sample of 1000, Replicated 10 Times, from Multivariate Normal Population, and 10% of Cases are made Missing Randomly from Each Variable

		Mean Deviation from the Model			
		Correlations		Covariances	
	Blau-Duncan Model	List-Wise Deletions	Pair-Wise Deletions	List-Wise Deletions	Pair-Wise Deletions
YW	.541	.0285	.0248	.0453	.0331
YU	.596	.0320	.0202	.0548	.0369
YX	.405	.0311	.0272	.0418	.0366
YV	.322	<u>.0266</u>	<u>.0271</u>	<u>.0306</u>	<u>.0327</u>
WU	.538	.0259	.0223	.0436	.0379
WX	.417	.0228	.0203	.0267	.0263
WV	.332	.0354	.0334	.0526	.0452
UX	.438	.0355	.0254	.0540	.0386
UV	.453	.0287	.0279	.0447	.0378
XV	.516	.0292	.0262	.0460	.0424
Overall Deviation Index		.0296	.0258	.0449	.0371

Legends:
Y: 1962 Occupational Status
W: First Job Status
U: Education
X: Father's Occupational Status
V: Father's Education

a. Deviation index is given by: $d_i = \sqrt{\sum_j (M_i - S_{ij})^2/10}$

Where i refers to the bivariate relationships indicated in column one; M_i refers to the underlying value from the Blau-Duncan Model; S_{ij} refers to the corresponding sample estimate where j stands for 10 different samplings.

b. Overall Deviation Index = $\sqrt{\sum_i \sum_j (M_i - S_{ij})^2/100}$

Source of the model: (Blau- and Duncan, 1967: 169.)

In contrast to Haitovsky's findings, our simulations indicate that the pairwise deletion performs better than listwise deletion, at least for the present model. Pairwise deletion produces less mean deviation from the model with respect to not only the whole matrix but also every individual coefficient but one (the exception is underlined in Table 1). The result is about the same whether we consider the sample correlation matrices or covariance matrices. To evaluate the fit between

TABLE 2
Sampling Variability as Measured by the Mean Deviation of Sample Coefficients from Population Values, When There is No Missing Data[a]

Bivariate Relation	Mean Deviation from the Model: Correlations	Covariances
YW	.0216	.0333
YU	.0163	.0350
YX	.0219	.0320
YU	.0238	.0295
WU	.0194	.0348
WX	.0201	.0293
WV	.0258	.0398
UX	.0285	.0423
UV	.0236	.0391
XV	.0283	.0462
Overall	.0232	.0361

a. Based on the same samples as presented in Table 1, except that coefficients are calculated before some information is made randomly missing.

the model and the sample covariance matrix, one may also include variance terms in the calculation of the index. Since such an inclusion produces similar results, we have not included them in Table 1.

The deviation indices in Table 1 alone do not provide full information about the effects of employing these two methods of handling missing data. We also need the sampling variability of the same size samples with no missing data. Table 2 contains information from samples without missing data. Sample correlations and covariances from samples without missing data deviate from the model to almost the same extent as the sample coefficients based on pairwise deletions Compare, for instance, .0258 from the third column of Table 1, to .0232 from Table 2. In other words, most of the variability observed

TABLE 3

Simulation Results Using the Blau-Duncan Correlation Matrix: 10 Samples of 1000 Cases Each from a Multivariate Normal Population Where 10% of the Cases are Missing Randomly From Each Variable: Unstandardized Path Coefficients[a]

Path Coefficient		Mean Deviation from the Model	
		Listwise Deletion	Pairwise Deletion
YW	.2881	.0271	.0308
YU	.3983	.0348	.0270
·YX	.1205	.0298	.0282
YV	-.0139	.0378	.0277
WU	.4326	.0333	.0256
WX	.2144	.0440	.0398
WV	.0254	.0467	.0416
UX	.2784	.0364	.0351
UV	.3094	.0393	.0369
XV	.5160	.0365	.0315
Overall Index		.0370	.0328

Where Y is regressed on W, U X and U; W is regressed U,X and V; U is regressed on X and V; X on V for convenience.

a. See Table 1 for source and legends for the variables.

in Table 1 is due to the general sampling variability and not to the problem of missing data.

Since Haitovsky's findings were based on the examination of the unstandardized regression coefficients, we thought it prudent to examine such regression coefficients as well. In Table 3, we present results based on the direct examination of regression coefficients, representing the values of the presumed population model. Then the sample path coefficients (unstandardized)[8] are compared to these

TABLE 4
Mean Deviations of Sample Covariances from Population covariances for 10 Samples of 1000 Cases, Each Based on the Blau-Duncan Correlation Matrix by Percent Randomly Missing[a]

% of Missing from each Variable	1% Missing	2% Missing	5% Missing	10% Missing
Listwise	.0383	.0394	.0426	.0449
Pairwise	.0363	.0376	.0378	.0371

a. See Table 1 for source of data and description of deviation indexes.

underlying values. The conclusion is the same; pairwise deletion still fares better than listwise deletion.

In order to check whether our findings are due to the excessive amount of missing data, we repeated the simulations while decreasing the proportion of missing observations on each variable. Note that listwise deletion would retain only about 590 cases while pairwise deletion will retain about 810 cases when 10% of the cases are randomly missing on each variable. As shown in Table 4, however, pairwise deletion maintains its superiority as the proportion of missing values on a variable is decreased to about 1%.

The sample size differences between a pairwise deletion and a listwise deletion is greatly affected by the number of variables involved. With 10% missing on each variable (randomly), listwise deletion with a five-variable data set would lose about 410 cases out of 1000, but would lose only 270 cases with a three-variable data set. In contrast, pairwise deletion would retain a data base of 810 cases regardless of the number of variables involved. Table 5 illustrates the effects of such changes in the data base as we decrease the number of variables. As expected from the result of Table 4, pairwise deletion performs better.

Although we cannot generalize our finding because it is based on a fixed (large) sample size (1000 cases) and a fixed (moderate) correlation matrix, it is clear that the use of pairwise deletion can be better than the use of listwise deletion for a certain type of data and that it is premature to preclude the issue on the basis of Haitovsky's simulations.[9] For survey researchers with a relatively large data set, where the strengths of the bivariate associations are moderate, pairwise

TABLE 5

Overall Mean Deviation of Sample Covariances, when the Number of Variables Are Reduced (10% missing from each variable.)[a]

	2 Variables	3 Variables	4 Variables	5 Variables
Listwise Deletion	.0376[b]	.0433	.0393	.0453
Pairwise Deletion	.0376[c]	.0373	.0370	.0375

a. See Table 1 for source of data and description of deviation indexes.
b. The variables used in these simulations are: Y and U; Y, U, and W; Y, X, U, W; and all five.
c. The two methods are equivalent.

deletion should remain a viable option provided the observations are missing randomly. But if one is interested in retaining as many cases as possible as in index construction, the use of pairwise deletion in the stage of parameter estimation (such as factor loadings) will not be of much help. One must find ways of removing missing values before constructing a composite index, otherwise the data loss will be as severe as in the case of listwise deletion.

ESTIMATING MISSING VALUES

There are three main reasons why a researcher might consider replacing missing information with some estimate: (1) to simplify calculation of statistics, (2) to improve parameter estimations, or (3) to retain as many cases as possible in constructing scales out of many variables.

The first reason has become trivial as researchers rely increasingly on computers for their calculations. But there are situations in which ease of presentation and/or interpretation may justify using such a method even with a computer (Draper and Stoneman, 1964). An example in point has already been given in the section on the use of dummy indicator variables; when the mean values are used in the place of the missing values of X, the partial regression coefficients for the indicator variables X, and X′ (with mean replaced for missing values) become equivalent to simple regression coefficients. Of course, it also implies that a simple regression of Y on X′ will be equivalent to a regression based on the m cases only. Wilks, 1932; also see Afifi and Elashof, 1966; Cohen and Cohen, 1975. But this does not mean that the correlation between the two for the m cases will be the same because the variance of X′ will be less than the variance of X for the first m cases.[10]

Another example is found when the orthogonality of an experimental design is destroyed by the existence of some missing data and the use of neutral values can simplify the calculation and presentation of the result (Cochran and Cox, 1957).

MAXIMUM UTILIZATION OF INFORMATION

Reexamination of the pattern A (below will reveal that neither listwise deletion nor pairwise deletion uses all the available information. For the estimation of a covariance, both procedures use the same data base and therefore are equivalent in this case. If there is some relationship between Y and X,

$$X: x_1, x_2, \ldots x_m \ldots x_N \qquad \text{(Pattern A)}$$
$$Y: y_1, y_2, \ldots y_m$$

and missing values are independent of the values of Y given the values of X—therefore, the observed covariation between Y and X is unaffected in the long run by the existence of missing values in Y—then the X values for the last (N − m) cases contain some information about the possible values of the missing Ys.[11]

Estimates based on the utilization of all the available data are given by (Wilks, 1932; Anderson, 1957).

$$m_x = \Sigma X_i / N \qquad (i = 1, 2, \ldots N)$$
$$m_y = m_y^* + b_{yx}(m_x - m_x^*)$$
$$V_x = \Sigma(X_i - m_m)^2 / N \qquad (i = 1, 2, \ldots N)$$
$$V_y = b_{yx} V_x + V_{y \cdot x}$$
$$V_{yx} = b_{yx} V_x$$

where

$$m_y^* = \Sigma Y_i / m \qquad (i = 1\ 2, \ldots m)$$
$$m_x^* = \Sigma X_i / m \qquad (i = 1\ 2, \ldots m)$$
$$b_{yx} = \Sigma \left\{ (X_i - m_x^*)(Y_i - M_y^*) \right\} / \Sigma(X_i - m_x)^2 \qquad (i = 1, 2, \ldots m)$$
$$V_{y \cdot x} = \Sigma (Y_i - m_y^*) / m - b_{yx} V_x$$

In other words, estimates of the mean and variance of Y can be improved if information on X and the relationships between Y and X are utilized. The solutions above are derived using the least-squares principle, but they will be maximum-likelihood solutions if the underlying population distribution is bivariate normal and these estimates are in general more efficient than estimates based on only the first m cases (e.g., Wilks, 1932; Anderson, 1957).

It must be noted that if there is no underlying association between Y and X, no information would be gained by following this type of strategy and as the association between the two variables gets stronger the greater will be the gain in efficiency (see Little, 1976b).

In arriving at the more efficient estimates of parameters, the values of missing Ys are not actually replaced by the estimated values. Such estimation of parameters is possible only because the missing data pattern A is extremely simple. We turn now to a more complex pattern of missing data.

ESTIMATION OF MISSING VALUES AND ITERATIVE SOLUTIONS

Consider now two relatively more complex missing data patterns, B and C. In pattern B:

$$\begin{aligned} X&: x_1, x_2, \ldots x_m, y_{m+1}, \ldots x_{m+n}, *, \ldots *, ** \\ Y&: y_1, y_2, \ldots y_m, *, \ldots *, y_{m+n}, \ldots y_{N=m+n+w}, ** \end{aligned} \qquad \text{(Pattern B)}$$

(* represents missing data)

missing values are present on both X and Y. We would normally delete the cases with no valid information and consider only the first N cases. In pattern C, we present only abbreviated data:

Types:	1	2	3	4	5	6	7	8
X:	/	/	/	*	/	*	*	*
Y:	/	/	*	/	*	/	*	*
Z:	/	*	/	/	*	*	/	*

(Pattern C)

(/ indicates nonmissing data; * indicates missing data)

There are 2^p (where p = number of variables and $2^3 = 8$) types of data. Out of these potential types only the last one does not contain any information. Therefore, we would normally consider only the first (8 - 1) types, deleting the last type out of analysis. In particular note that type 7 would have been deleted in bivariate context, and that in general, the greater the number of variables under consideration (provided they are all associated with each other to some extent), the greater the utilization of existing information.

Returning to pattern B, and extending the strategies used in dealing with the A data, we may try to estimate underlying parameters from the examination of the two different combinations of data. (1) Use the first (m + n) cases to retrieve the lost information due to n missing values on Y, and (2) use (m + w) cases to retrieve the lost information due to missing values on X. But the resulting estimates are likely to disagree. A general solution to deal with situations like B, as well as C, is as follows (Beale and Little, 1974):

(1) Use available information to estimate missing values;

(2) after replacing the missing values with estimated values, estimate the parameters from the data containing estimated values (with proper adjustment);

(3) reestimate the missing values, using the estimated parameters given in step (2);

(4) repeat the process (1) through (3) until the estimated values converge.

More specifically, the steps are:

(1) Estimate regression coefficients for each type of missing data, while using all the available information. Then insert the predicted values based on the regression in the place of missing data (for convenience, one can use the covariance matrix based on listwise deletion for the initial estimation of missing values).

(2) Then estimate the parameters—mean (m_j), variance, and covariance (v_{jk})—by:

$$m_j = \Sigma X_{ij} / N$$
$$V_{jk} = \Sigma \left\{ (X_{ij} - m_j)(X_{ik} - m_k) + V_{jk \cdot P_i} \right\} / N, \quad (i = 1,2, \ldots N)$$

where $v_{jk \cdot P_i}$ refers to the partial covariance between variable j and k while P_i represents the other variables in the set with valid information on case i—(X_{ij} is the observed value if not missing).

(3) Repeat the process until convergence. The only aspect requiring comment is the adjustment term $V_{jk \cdot P_i}$ in step (2). This is the term that

vanishes unless information is missing on both variables j and k (which implies, of course, in calculating variance [v_{jj}] the term must appear whenever information is missing on one variable). This adjustment term is necessary because the estimated values reduce the variance of a variable and reduce or increase the covariance depending upon the direction of partial relationship between j and k (see, e.g., Buck, 1960; Beale and Little, 1974).

For the demonstration that such a solution leads to the maximum likelihood solution proposed by Orchard and Woodbury (1972) when multivariate normality is assumed and that this iterated solution is in general superior to other methods, Beale and Little (1974) should be consulted. Among the methods Beale and Little (1974) examine are (1) ordinary regression solutions based on listwise deletion and (2) the method of using regression estimates of missing values by Buck (1960). Unfortunately, they did not consider the regression solution based on pairwise deletion, relying partly on the evidence presented by Haitovsky (1968). On the basis of our simulation presented earlier, we must consider for now that the relative merits of pairwise deletion and the iterative solution are unknown for a large sample with moderate correlations.[12]

ESTIMATION OF MISSING VALUES WITHOUT ITERATION

For those who have no access to custom computer programming, we will mention a few other procedures of estimating missing values and parameters:

(1) Assigning regression estimates to missing values and estimating parameters with some adjustments (Buck, 1960);

(2) assigning regression estimates and random component with equal-expected variance as the residual variance ($v_{yx \cdot P_i}$), then estimating parameters using ordinary regression routines;

(3) estimating the missing values by using principal component transformation, then estimating parameters (by Dear, cited in Afifi and Elashof, 1966; and Timm, 1970).

The first procedure above is to use regression estimates as one would do in the first step of iterative solution but without iterations.

The accuracy of the first estimate is more critical in this method than in the iterative solution. Therefore, one may not use the matrix based on listwise deletion but should use a different matrix for every type of missing value pattern. This method was found to be generally superior to assigning means to missing values or to Dear's method, but not in every case (see Timm, 1970). One point needing special attention is that variances and covariances calculated from the variables (with estimated values replacing the missing values) have to be corrected for bias (as was the case in iterative solutions).

The second procedure is a modification of Buck's. Instead of replacing the missing values with regression estimates, this method replaces them with regression estimates plus a random component in order to simulate the degree of residual variance existing in the data:

$$\text{Value to use in the place of the missing value on } X_{ij} = \hat{X}_{ij} + (\text{error of estimate})\ (\text{random normal number})$$

Because the random component reintroduces the expected residual variation in the predicted data, one can use ordinary regression algorithms to estimate various parameters. That is, it obviates the need for adjustment in the estimation of parameters. At least one popular statistical package, SPSS (Nie et al., 1975), allows the generation of random numbers to be used in such situations along with the variables under consideration.

The third procedure applies principal-components analysis to the correlation matrix based on listwise deletion. The principal components for the missing values are then estimated from the existing data, using the weights given by the principal-components analysis. Next, the principal components are transformed back to raw data. Then the raw data (with the estimated values included) are used for parameter estimation (see Afifi and Elashoff, 1966; and Timm, 1970). Timm's (1970) simulations do support this solution as preferable to Buck's only when the number of variables is relatively large in relation to the sample size, correlations are not moderate, and the missing information is substantial. Overall, however, he finds that this procedure is inferior to Buck's.

Finally, although all the procedures for estimating missing values involve considerably more complex computations, they have one

TABLE 6

Overall Comparison of Various Methods, Using the Blau-Duncan Matrix as Model: 10 Samples of 1000 Cases, 10% Missing on Each Variable

	Mean Deviations from the Model				
Method	(1)	(2)	(3)	(4)	(5)
Correlation Matrix	.0497	.0296	.0258	.0286	.0232
Covariance Matrix	.0891	.0449	.0371	.0388	.0361

Legends:
(1) Means assigned to missing values
(2) Listwise deletion of missing data
(3) Pairwise deletion of missing data
(4) Regression estimate and random component in the place of missing values
(5) Complete Sample

definite advantage over simple solutions such as pairwise and listwise deletion: in constructing scales out of many variables, the estimated values can be used in the place of missing values. Furthermore, the estimated values are based on a more refined use of the available information than simply replacing missing values with the mean as is found as an option in at least one packaged program for scale construction (Nie et al., 1975).

To recapitulate some salient points from various computer simulations, Buck (1960) and Haitovsky (1968) find listwise deletion preferable to pairwise deletion. Timm (1970) finds that Buck's (1960) regression solution is superior in general to the regression solution based on listwise deletion; Beale and Little (1974) find the iterative maximum likelihood solution superior to Buck's regression solution; assigning means to missing values does not fare well in comparison with any of the other solutions mentioned above and Dear's principal components solution appears to lag behind Buck's regression solution. Against this background, we find that for a large data set with moderate correlations, the pairwise deletion performs better than the listwise deletion. It is obvious that we need additional studies comparing these various methods using sociological data.

Some preliminary results from our own simulations are presented in Table 6.[13] Most of the data presented in Table 6 are from earlier tables. The only new information is the performance of the regression method with a random component compared with other standard procedures. We find that replacing missing values by this method does not do as well as pairwise deletion but is superior to listwise deletion. More importantly, parameter estimates based on pairwise deletion and the regression-random component method are fairly close in their efficiency to the estimates based on the complete samples with no missing data.

CONCLUSION

We have tried to abstain from making general assertions as to the superiority of one method over another because convenience and feasibility must also be considered in making the final decision. Furthermore, when the sample size is very large (say 1000 or more), the choice may not make very much difference (Beale and Little, 1974). It is our hope that the preceding discussion alerts survey researchers to possible complications arising from missing data and to the fact that they may be using less than an optimal solution to the problem.

Since we have confined our discussion largely to the multivariate case where variables are measured on at least an interval scale and are considered to be random variables, a few words are in order concerning other situations not covered in this paper.

First, in least-squares regression and analysis of variance, it is customary to consider the independent variables as fixed constants. When one deals with survey data, however, there is no compelling reason to consider the independent variables as fixed constants other than the fact that such an assumption (although not very realistic) can simplify the derivation of the sampling distributions of parameter estimates (Johnston, 1972). On the other hand, if one has a data set with genuinely fixed independent variables as in an experimental design, the researcher should consult specialized sources (e.g., Hartley and Hocking, 1971).

For situations in which some variables are categorical, see Hartley and Hocking (1971), Jackson (1969), and Chan and Dunn (1974).

See also Hertel (1976) and the report of the U.S. Bureau of the Census for a description of the "hot-deck" procedure which is especially suited for large data sets such as the national census. Either because of their reviews of the literature or their generality of scope, the following sources are especially valuable: Afifi and Elashoff, (1966, 1967, 1969); Hartley and Hocking (1971); Orchard and Woodbury (1972); Beale and Little (1974); Cohen and Cohen (1975); and Rubin (1976). Orchard and Woodbury (1972) contains a classified bibliography. See also Press and Scott (1974; 1976) for an introduction to the growing literature on the Bayesian approach. A few recent materials dealing with specialized topics are included in the bibliography without comment.

NOTES

1. Computer packages, such as SPSS (Nie et al., 1975), have made it easy for a researcher to choose either a *listwise* deletion or a *pairwise* deletion of missing data by making them standard options in various multivariate analysis. A *pairwise* deletion estimates bivariate relationships on the basis of cases for which information is complete for the two variables only, and then constructs a synthetic multivariate data matrix from the bivariate matrix.

2. When the correlation or covariance matrix is not consistent, one may get regression results in which the multiple correlation is greater than one or less than zero. The statistical results from such a matrix would be meaningless (see Cohen and Cohen) for an illustration of the problem, 1975).

3. In this case, the existence of missing data on the variable of interest, voting, is due simply to the fact that the respondent was too young to vote. We may thus view the legal-age restriction on voting as essentially unrelated to the respondent's overall propensity for political participation. Yet, at the same time, a prime research objective may be to construct a general index of political participation such that complete information on voting behavior is necessary.

4. We do not examine all the possible patterns of missing data because, in most instances, the expected frequencies for some of the categories such as $(M_1M_2M_3)$, will be too small to be used for x^2 testing. For the same reason, variables with too small a number of cases, producing M less than 5 cases, may be dropped from the test.

5. One may further refine x^2 tests by introducing Yate's correction for continuity if the expected frequencies are relatively small (Cramer, 1946: 445), or may use Fisher's exact test.

6. See note 2 above.

7. For the generation of random numbers see Newman and Odel (1971), and for the generation of population correlation matrices see Kaiser and Dickman (1962). We

have generated random-normal numbers using the "Super-Duper" program (from Duke University). After creating samples with a given population correlation matrix according to Kaiser and Dickman's method, we augmented the data set with an equal number of variables using the random-uniform number generator provided by SPSS. The proportion of cases made "missing" on a given variable was determined by the range of the associated random-uniform variable. For this reason, the proportion of missing observations is not fixed but fluctuates slightly from sample to sample.

8. We assume the basic model in the population to be multivariate normal with mean = 0, and variance = 1. However, samples from such a population would not necessarily have a mean of 0, and a variance of 1. Therefore, the sample variance and covariance would be different, although they should be equivalent in our population model.

9. We hope to report on further comparisons of these two options as well as other procedures which we are currently investigating with the support of NIMH Grant #30407-01.

10. Hertel (1976) illustrates this point and advocates the replacement of regression estimates instead of the mean for the missing values. But regression estimates also introduce biases into the calculation of variances and covariances. These points are discussed in a later section of the text.

11. Cases (1) and (2) of the missing data patterns would qualify. On the other hand, if the missing data are produced by the process described in (5), an attempt to retrieve information would be erroneous. Other patterns, such as (3) and (4), would allow one to retrieve some information from the available data but would not allow unbiased estimation (see Little, 1976b; Rubin, 1976).

12. This and other problems of missing data are now under investigation (NIMH Grant #30407-01); we will report the result in the near future.

13. Due to special programming chores required to evaluate Buck's regression method and the iterative method, we do not yet have results comparing the two methods but we hope to report them soon (see note 12).

REFERENCES

AFIFI, A. A. and R. M. ELASHOFF (1969) "Missing observations in multivariate statistics IV: a note on simple linear regression." Amer. Statistical Association 64 (March): 359-365.

——— (1969) "Missing observations in multivariate statistics III: large sample analysis of simple linear regression." Amer. Statistical Association 64 (March): 337-358.

——— (1967) "Missing observations in multivariate statistics II. Point estimation in simple linear regression." Amer. Statistical Association 62 (March): 10-29.

——— (1966) "Missing observations in multivariate statistics I. Review of the literature." Amer. Statistical Association 61: 595-604.

ANDERSON, T. W. (1957) "Maximum likelihood estimates for a multivariate normal distribution when some observations are missing." Amer. Statistical Association 52: 200-203.

BEALE, E. M. and R.J.A. LITTLE (1974) "Missing values in multivariate analysis." J. of the Royal Statistical Society, London 37.

BLAU, P. M. and O. D. DUNCAN (1967) The American Occupational Structure. New York: John Wiley.

BLOOMFIELD, P. (1970) "Spectral analysis with randomly missing observations." Royal Statistical Society, London B, 32: 369-380.

BOX, M. J., N. R. DRAPER, and W. G. HUNTER (1970) "Missing values in multi-response non-linear model fitting." Technometrics, 12 (August): 613-320.

BUCK, S. F. (1960) "A method of estimation of missing values in multivariate data suitable for use with an electronic computer." Royal Statistical Society, London B, 22: 302-306.

CHAN, L. S. and O. J. DUNN (1974) "A note on the asymptotic aspect of the treatment of missing values in discriminant analysis." J. of the Amer. Statistical Association 69 (September): 672-673.

CHOW, G. C. and AN-LOH LIN (1976) "Best linear unbiased estimation of missing observations in an economic time series." J. of the Amer. Statistical Association 71 (September): 719-721.

COCHRAN, W. G. and G. M. COX (1957) Experimental Designs. New York: John Wiley.

COHEN, J. and P. COHEN (1975) Applied Multiple Regression/Correlation Analysis. New York: Erlbaum.

CRAMER, H. (1946) Mathematical Methods of Statistics. Princeton: Princeton Univ. Press.

DAGENAIS, M. G. (1974) "Multiple regression analysis with incomplete observations, from a Bayesian viewpoint." Stud. in Bayesian Econometrics and Statistics.

——— (1971) "Utilization of incomplete observations in regression analysis." J. of the Amer. Statistical Association 66 (March): 93-98.

DRAPER, N. R. and D. M. STONEMAN (1964) "Estimating missing values in unreplicated two-level factorial and fractional factorial designs." Biometrics 20 (September): 443-458.

GLASSER, M. (1964) "Linear regression analysis with missing observations among the independent variables." J. of the Amer. Statistical Association 59: 834-844.

GOODMAN, L. A. (1968) "The analysis of cross-classified data: independence, quasi-independence and interactions in contingency tables with or without missing entries." J. of the Amer. Statistical Association, 63 (December): 1091-1131.

FIENBERG, S. E. (1970) "Quasi-independence and maximum likelihood estimation in incomplete contingency tables." J. of the Amer. Statistical Association 65 (December): 1610-1616.

HAITOVSKY, Y. (1968) "Missing data in regression analysis." Royal Statistical Society. London, B, 30: 67-82.

HARTLEY, H. O. and R.R. HOCKING (1971) "The analysis of incomplete data," Biometrics, 27 (December): 783-823.

HARTWELL, T. D. and D. W. GAYLOR (1973) "Estimating variance components for two-way disproportionate data with missing cells by method of unweighted means." J. of the Amer. Statistical Association 68 (June): 379-383.

HERTEL, B. R. (1976) "Minimizing error variance introduced by missing data routines in survey analysis." Soc. Methods and Research 4 (May): 459-474.

HOCKING, R. R. and H. H. OXSPRING (1971) "Maximum likelihood estimation with incomplete observations in regression analysis." J. of the Amer. Statistical Association 66 (March): 65-70.

HOCKING, R. R. and W. B. SMITH (1968) "Estimation of parameters in the multivariate normal distribution with missing observations." J. of the Amer. Statistical Association 63 (March): 159-173.

JACKSON, E. C. (1968) "Missing values in linear multiple discriminant analysis." Biometrics 24 (December): 835-844.

JOHNSTON, J. (1972) Econometric Methods. New York: McGraw-Hill.

KAISER, H. F. and K. DICKMAN (1962) "Sample and population score matrices and sample correlation matrices from an arbitrary population correlation matrix." Psychometrika 27: 179-182.

KELEJIAN, H. H. (1969) "Missing observations in multivariate regression: efficiency of a first-order method." Amer. Statistical Association 64 1609-1616.

KIM, JAE-ON, N. H. NIE, and S. VERBA, (1977) "A note on factor analyzing dichotomous variables: the case of political participation." Pol. Methodology (Spring): 39-62.

LIN, PI-ERH (1973) "Procedures for testing the difference of means with incomplete data." J. of the Amer. Statistical Association 68 (September): 699-703.

——— (1971) "Estimation procedures for difference of means with missing data." J. of the Amer. Statistical Association 66 (September): 634-636.

——— and L. E. STIVERS (1975) "Testing for equality of means with incomplete data on one variable: a Monte Carlo study." J. of the Amer. Soc. Association 70 (March): 190-193.

LITTLE, R.J.A. (1976a) "Comments on paper by D. B. Rubin." Biometrika 63, 3: 590-591.

——— (1976b) "Inference about means from incomplete multivariate data." Biometrika 63: 593-604.

McDONALD, L.(1971) "On the estimation of missing data in the multivariate linear model." Biometrics 27 (September): 535-543.

MEHTA, J. S. and P.A.V.B. SWAMY (1973) "Bayesian analysis of a bivariate normal distribution with incomplete observations." J. of the Amer. Soc. Association 68 (December): 922-927.

MORRISON, D. F. (1971) "Expectations and variances of maximum likelihood estimates of multivariate normal distribution parameters with missing data." J. of the Amer. Soc. Association 66 (September): 602-604.

NEWMAN, T. G. and P. L. ODELL (1971) The Generation of Random Variates. New York: Hafner Publishing.

NIE, N. H., C. H. HULL, J. G. JENKINS, K. STEINBRENNER, and D. H. BENT (1975) Statistical Package for the Social Sciences. New York: McGraw-Hill.

ORCHARD, T. and M. A. WOODBURY (1972) "A missing information principle: theory and applications." Proceedings of the sixth Berkeley Symposium on Mathematical Statistics and Probability, Theory of Statistics, Univ. of California Press.

PRESS, S. J. and A. J. SCOTT (1976) "Missing variables in Bayesian regression, II." J. of the Amer. Soc. Association 71 (June): 366-369.

——— (1974) "Missing variables in Bayesian regression." Studies in Bayesian Econometrics and Statistics. Amsterdam: North Holland: 259-272.

RUBIN, D. B. (1976) "Comparing regressions when some predictor values are missing." Technometrics 23 (May): 201-205.

——— (1976) "Inference and missing data." Biometrika 63, 3: 581-592.

———(1974) "Characterizing the estimation of parameters in incomplete-data problems." J. of the Amer. Statistical Association 69, 346: 467-474.

TIMM, N. H. (1970) "The estimation of variance-covariance and correlation matrices from incomplete data." Psychometrika 35 (December): 417-437.

U.S. Bureau of the Census (1970) 1970 Census User's Guide. 1: 26-28.

WILKS, S. S. (1932) "Moments and distributions of population parameters from fragmentary samples." Annals of Mathematical Statistics 3 (August), 163-195.

WOODBURY, M. A. (1971) "Discussion of paper by Hartley and Hocking." Biometrics 27 (December): 808-823.

Jae-On Kim is Associate Professor of Sociology at the University of Iowa. His areas of interest are political sociology, social stratification, and quantitative methodology.

James Curry is a Ph.D. candidate in Sociology at the University of Iowa. He is interested in social stratification and quantitative methodology.

Errata

Page 5, the last equation should read:

$$NM = (P_1 P_2 P_3)\ N,$$

instead of

$$NM - (P_1 P_2 P_3)\ N.$$

On the same page, the last sentence of the second paragraph should read:

"The significance of the deviation of the observed frequencies can be evaluated by the ordinary X^2-test with degrees of freedom equal to 1."

instead of

"...with degrees of freedom equal to the (K+1) number of variables involved."

A SURVEY OF NONRESPONSE IMPUTATION PROCEDURES [1]

David W. Chapman, Westat, Inc.

1. Introduction - A good sampling plan for a sample survey will include an extensive effort, whenever necessary, to obtain a usable response for each unit selected into the sample. Various aspects of the design, such as clustering and allocation of resources, are adapted to make this feasible and practical. However, in spite of such efforts there will always be some nonresponse in large-scale surveys. Furthermore, as indicated in a report on methodology for the Current Population Survey (12,p.53), there are no known unbiased or even consistent methods of imputing for nonresponse (unless special assumptions are made regarding the nature of the nonresponse.)

Rather than imputing for nonresponse at the time survey tabulations are prepared, tabulations could be presented with the amounts of nonresponse reported in a nonresponse category. This would allow users of the data to select their own method of making nonresponse imputations. However, the additional burden of having to compute nonresponse adjustments may not be worth having the choice of imputation method. Furthermore, users would have to make imputations from the tabulated data, and some of the related information available at the tabulation stage could not be used in these imputation procedures. It therefore appears to be more appropriate to make imputations at the time tabulations are prepared, thus eliminating the nonresponse category from the tables (except perhaps to allow for item nonresponse). If nonresponse adjustments are made, the level of nonresponse should always be reported when presenting survey results.

Pritzker, Ogus, and Hansen (10,p.445) indicate that, based on extensive experience, if the survey nonresponse rate is less than five percent, any plausible method of nonresponse imputation will probably provide acceptable results. However, in many sample surveys, nonresponse rates are substantially higher than five percent. Even with interviewer surveys which include several call-backs to households and telephone followup efforts, nonresponse rates will sometimes equal or exceed 20 percent.

In such cases, the method of nonresponse imputation can have a substantial effect on the values and biases of the survey estimates. Much research has been carried out in an attempt to discover imputation methods which reduce or minimize the nonresponse bias.

In this paper an attempt will be made to summarize some of the procedures which have been used. These procedures will be discussed in two sections: one dealing with item nonresponse, and the other dealing with total (questionnaire) nonresponse.

2. Imputation for Item Nonresponse - In most surveys some of the respondents refuse, neglect, or are unable to complete one or more questionnaire items even though they do complete most of the items. (For example, income is sometimes not supplied in a household survey.) Item nonresponse also arises when a response is received which, on the basis of the editing procedures, is determined to be unacceptable. For respondents with missing items, the information available from the completed items can be used to help impute responses for the incomplete items. In fact, sometimes there is redundant information in the questionnaire and a missing item can be inferred appropriately from other responses. In other instances, an approximate value for a missing item may be obtained by considering the general relationship between this item and another item. For example, for purchases of homes, closing costs might be estimated as a percentage of the price of the home.

Two procedures which have been used by the Bureau of Census (among others) to impute for missing values or presumably incorrect values are the "cold-deck" and "hot-deck" methods. These two procedures will be discussed in this section.

2.1 The Cold-Deck Procedure for Imputation[2] - Basically, the cold-deck procedure uses values from some prior distribution to substitute for missing responses. The distribution used is usually obtained from a previous survey taken from essentially the same population. For example, for the Census an appropriate distribution would be obtained from the previous Census, or a recent household survey.

To use a distribution of prior responses for imputation, the responses are classified by one variable or jointly by two or more variables that are reported. An attempt is made to define cross-categories (or cells) in such a way that responses will be relatively homogeneous within cells and heterogeneous between cells. There must be at least one response in each cell available for imputation. The responses in each cell are stored in the memory of the computer. A cold-deck distribution is prepared in advance for each cell.

For each missing item for a particular respondent to the current survey, the values of the appropriate completed items are noted to identify the relevant cell. The respondent is associated with the cell corresponding to the values of the items. A value is then selected from the responses in the cold deck included in the same cell. This value is usually selected at random or systematically.

As an example, suppose that the age of a respondent could be placed in a cell determined by sex and household relationship, and perhaps by the age of another member of the household. Then the age of one of the cold-deck respondents selected at random from the same cell would be inserted for the missing age.

2.2 The Hot-Deck Procedure for Imputation [3] - An objection to the cold-deck procedure is that it does not utilize data obtained from the current survey. The hot-deck procedure does use the current responses to substitute for missing items.

As with the cold-deck procedure, crossclassifications (or cells) are identified by one or more relevant variables. Initial values for each cell must be supplied from a cold deck to initiate the procedure. Then new responses are supplied for each cell from the new (or hot) deck as they appear in a pass through the file. The file may be arranged in order based on relevant variables before the procedure begins. A response remains in a cell until another respondent appears who has the same characteristicts (i.e., is in the same cell) and has a response for the particular item.

Whenever an item is missing for a respondent, he is first identified with the appropriate cell, based on the responses he does supply. Then the value retained in that cell is imputed to the respondent with the missing value. As an example, suppose that age, sex, race, household relationship, and level of education were used to define cells for imputing income values. A respondent whose income is not provided is placed into the appropriate cell as determined by his responses to the above items. The value of income in that cell (ie., the income of the respondent having the same characteristics and appearing most recently in the file sequence) would be taken as the missing income. In order to avoid using the same income value repeatedly, several income values could be stored in a cell and these values could be used in rotation, if necessary.

The method described above of imputing the preceding value for a missing item is better than using a random selection from all those in the sample falling into the same cell. This is because there is usually some special ordering of the respondents which indicates that an imputed value from a respondent close in the file would be better than one picked at random from the cell. Also, it is a more convenient procedure for computer processing.

There are some possible variations on the use of the hot-deck procedure. One would be to use as an imputed value one obtained from a regression of the particular item on several of the other items. A regression equation could be developed from either a hot deck or a cold deck.

Another variation would be to use a moving average of values in a cell to substitute for a missing value. This procedure would prevent extreme values from being duplicated and would therefore reduce slightly the variances of the estimates. However, if the ordering of the respondents were important, such a procedure would contain slightly more nonresponse bias.

3. Imputation for Total Questionnaire) Nonresponse - The hot-deck procedure described above for imputing missing items could also be used to impute values for an entire questionnaire to survey nonrespondents. As described by Pritzker, Ogus and Hansen (10,p.460), this was done in the 1960 Census by substituting for a nonresponding household the questionnaire responses of the previously listed responding household. This procedure amounts to doubling the weight[4] of the respondents whose records are duplicated. Such a procedure can yield somewhat larger variances of the survey estimates than would the procedure of weight adjustment discussed below. Hansen, Hurwitz, and Madow (3,pp.232-233) show that the maximum increase in variance is about 12 percent for the method of duplicating records.

In many surveys imputation for nonresponse is carried out by adjusting the weights of the respondents in some way to account for the nonrespondents. Alternate methods of making weight adjustments plus other methods of imputation for survey respondents will be discussed in the following sections.

3.1 The Use of a Single Weight Adjustment to Account for Nonresponse - The simplest type of nonresponse adjustment is to make one overall weight adjustment. This adjustment would be equal to the sum of the initial weights of all units selected into the sample divided by the sum of the weights of the respondents. Such an adjustment "weights up" the respondents to the total sample. (If all units selected have the same initial weights, this adjustment would equal the sample size divided by the number of respondents.)

The nonresponse bias associated with this procedure can be derived in a simple case. Suppose that a simple random sample of n units is selected from the N units in the population. The basic sampling weight for each unit selected is N/n (ie, the inverse of the selection probability). Let n_1 represent the number of the n sample units that respond to the survey. If one overall weight adjustment is used in this case, it would be n/n_1 since all sample units have the same basic weight. Also, assuming no other weight adjustments are used, each of the n_1 respondents would have the same final weight, $(N/n)(n/n_1)$.

The basic formula for estimating a population mean from weighted data is the following:

$$\bar{x} = \sum_{j=1}^{n_1} w_j x_j \Big/ \sum_{j=1}^{n_1} w_j \qquad (1)$$

where

n_1 = the number of respondents,

w_j = the final weight assigned to the jth respondent,

x_j = the value of the variable (item) for the jth respondent.

In this case, since the weights of the respondents are all equal, the estimated mean in equation 1 reduces to a simple unweighted mean of the n_1 respondents.

In this case the expected value of $\bar{x}$ is equal to $\bar{X}_{.1}$, the mean of the variable for all those in the population who would respond if selected for the survey.

The bias of $\bar{x}$ for this case can be written as follows:

$$\text{bias}(\bar{x}) = E(\bar{x}) - \bar{X} = \bar{X}_{\cdot 1} - [R\bar{X}_{\cdot 1} + (1-R)\bar{X}_{\cdot 2}]$$
$$= (1 - R)(\bar{X}_{\cdot 1} - \bar{X}_{\cdot 2}) \qquad (2)$$

where

R = the population response rate (ie, the proportion of the N population units that would respond if selected for the survey),

$\bar{X}_{\cdot 2}$ = The mean of the variable for all those in the population who would not respond if selected.

As expected, the bias of $\bar{x}$ depends on two factors: (1) the population nonresponse rate, $1 - R$, which is a function of the data collection procedures; and (2) the difference between the population mean for respondents and the mean for nonrespondents, $\bar{X}_{\cdot 1} - \bar{X}_{\cdot 2}$.

In an attempt to reduce the nonresponse bias of this simple adjustment procedure, weighting classes are often defined based on the characteristics available for both respondents and nonrespondents. Separate nonresponse weighting adjustments are made within each weighting class. This procedure is discussed in the next section.

3.2 <u>The Use of Weighting Classes to Make Nonresponse Adjustments</u> - Suppose that the population is partitioned into c classes, based on the values of one or more survey items. Let $P_1, P_2, \ldots P_c$ represent the proportions of the population members contained in each of these classes. Also, let $R_1, R_2, \ldots R_c$ be the proportions of the units in these weighting classes that would respond if selected for the survey.

As in the previous case, suppose that a simple random sample of n units is selected from the N population units. Let $n_1, n_2, \ldots n_c$ be the number of sampling units falling into each of the classes. Of course, the n_i values are random variables and their sum must equal n. Also, let $n_{11}, n_{21}, n_{31}, \ldots, n_{c1}$ represent the number of survey respondents in the c classes. The basic sampling weight (ie, inverse of the selection probability) would be (N/n) for each sample unit (as in the previous case). However, the nonresponse adjustments would vary from class to class. For each respondent in the ith class this adjustment would equal (n_i/n_{i1}), which is the sum of the sampling weights of all sampling units falling into the ith cell divided by the sum of the sampling weights of all respondents falling into the ith cell.

The estimate, $\bar{x}_1$, of the mean would then be computed as

$$\bar{x}_1 = \frac{\sum_{i=1}^{c} \sum_{j=1}^{n_{i1}} (N/n)(n_i/n_{i1}) x_{ij}}{\sum_{i=1}^{c} \sum_{j=1}^{n_{i1}} (N/n)(n_i/n_{i1})} = \sum_{i=1}^{c} p_i \bar{x}_{i1}, \qquad (3)$$

where

$\bar{x}_{i1}$ = the sample mean among respondents in the ith weighting class,

p_i = the proportion of the sample falling into the ith weighting class.

The expected value of $\bar{x}_1$ is the following:

$$E(\bar{x}_1) = \sum_{i=1}^{c} P_i \bar{X}_{i1} \qquad (4)$$

where

$\bar{X}_{i1}$ = the mean of the variable for all those in the population contained in the ith weighting class who would respond if selected for the survey.

The bias of $\bar{x}_1$ can be written as follows:

$$\text{bias}(\bar{x}_1) = \sum_{i=1}^{c} P_i(1 - R_i)(\bar{X}_{i1} - \bar{X}_{i2}). \qquad (5)$$

It is useful to compare the bias of $\bar{x}_1$ given in equation 5 to that of $\bar{x}$ given in equation 2. If for each of the c weighting classes $(\bar{X}_{i1} - \bar{X}_{i2})$ equals $\bar{X}_{\cdot 1} - \bar{X}_{\cdot 2}$, the biases of $\bar{x}$ and $\bar{x}_1$ are identical. Also, the bias of $\bar{x}_1$ is equal to that of $\bar{x}$ if all the class response rates, $R_1, R_2, \ldots, R_c$, are equal to the overall nonresponse rate, R.

However, if the $\bar{X}_{i1} - \bar{X}_{i2}$ values tend to be less (in absolute value) than $\bar{X}_{\cdot 1} - \bar{X}_{\cdot 2}$ and the response rates (ie, the R_i values) vary from class to class, the nonresponse bias will be reduced by the use of the weighting classes to make nonresponse adjustments. Therefore, the successful application of this procedure requires the identification of survey characteristics which will define weighting classes which vary both with respect to response rates and survey estimates. Furthermore, the characteristics used to define weighting classes must be available for both the respondents and nonrespondents. This requirement will, in many surveys, severely limit the choices of variables to use to define weighting classes.

There are many surveys in which the procedure discussed above is used to impute for nonrespondents. Among them are the Health Examination Survey (8,p.6) and the Current Population Survey (12,p.53). In Cycle I of the Health Examination Survey, seven age-sex weighting classes were defined within each of 42 primary sampling units (PSU's) for a total of 294 separate cells. Nearly half of the 294 nonresponse adjustments were between 1 and 1.10 and the three largest estimates were between 2.01 and 2.10. In the CPS, the PSU's are grouped together based on the population and labor-force characteristics of the strata from which the PSU's were selected. Within groups of PSU's respondents are placed in six cells based on race-residence characteristics.

In some cases the total number of members in each weighting class is known (or a good estimate is available) and used in the nonresponse adjustment. In such cases, the weights of respondents in a cell are weighted up to the "known" total. This procedure is closely related to stratification after sampling, discussed by Hansen, Hurwitz and Madow (3,p.232; 4, pp. 138-139). The bias of the estimate of the mean using this procedure is the same as that given in equation 5 for $\bar{x}_1$, assuming the population totals are known exactly. However, the variance and therefore the mean square error would be less for the procedure based on known totals.

Care must be taken in the application of these two imputation procedures. As demonstrated in Hansen, Hurwitz and Madow (4,pp.138-139), the variance of the estimated mean can be increased by weighting up to cell totals if the number of respondents in the cells is small. As a rule of thumb, a minimum of 20 respondents is used for the weighting cells in the CPS (12,p.53). Furthermore, for the CPS a maximum of 2.0 is taken for the nonresponse adjustment factor. In cases in which the adjustment exceeds 2, cells are combined to the extent necessary to reduce the adjustment to 2.0 or less.[5] In the Health Examination Survey (8,p.6), the 294 weighting cells average about 25 respondents each.

The choices of which variables to use to define weighting classes are usually based on which variables have the higher correlations with the zero-one response variable and with the characteristics for which survey estimates are made. It is assumed that variables which show a high correlation among respondents for survey characteristics to be estimated would show high correlations among survey nonrespondents. If so, then the use of such variables to define weighting classes would presumably minimize the nonresponse bias. The decisions on priorities of the use of variables to define weighting classes are largely subjective. These decisions involve choices as to which variables to collapse whenever weighting cells have to be combined to provide adequate numbers of respondents per cell.

A procedure which can be used to determine weighting classes objectively from a pool of possible weighting variables is the AID programmed procedure. One way this can be done is discussed in the next subsection.

3.3 <u>The Use of the AID Programmed Procedure to Define Weighting Classes</u> - The AID programmed procedure can be used to select which variables to use in weighting classes and also to specify which crossclassifications of these variables should be used to define weighting classes.[6] Using this procedure the sample would be divided sequentially into subgroups in a way to maximize the amount of variability explained in some dependent variable. The dependent variable used could be the zero-one response variable, or a survey questionnaire item. As a first step, the sample would be split in half based on the categories of a single variable. The variable selected from the pool of variables is the one which provides for the maximum amount of explained variance by a division into two groups. Next, one of these two groups is split again in such a way as to maximize the explained variance in the dependent variable. This procedure of defining new subgroups to account for the maximum amount of variance is repeated until the weighting classes become as small as is allowed in the specifications, or until it is no longer possible to explain meaningful proportions of remaining variance.

There has been very little investigation of the use of AID in this capacity. In a report prepared for NCHS by Chapman (2,pp.10-20), the use of AID was tested on data collected in the Health and Nutrition Examination Survey. The basic conclusion from this investigation was that the use of AID to define specific weighting classes for nonresponse adjustments does not appear to be feasible. The specific classes identified by AID can be very complex and would probably be rather awkward to work with in practice. Also, some of the classes contained a very small number of respondents, which can increase the variance (as discussed earlier). Finally, there is no easy way of merging an AID analysis based on the zero-one response variable as the dependent variable with that based on one or more survey items as dependent variables.

Perhaps the most useful information from the AID results is obtained by noting which independent variables are used most often in defining "optimal" splits in the sample subgroups. These independent variables would probably be most useful in defining weighting classes of the type discussed earlier in Section 3.2.

3.4 <u>The "Raking" or "Balancing" Procedure for Nonresponse Imputation</u>[7] - The "raking" procedure is one which allows the use of a large number of variables to define weighting classes simultaneously, without being concerned about the number of respondents in crossclassifications.

This method utilizes known marginal totals for the categories of two or more characteristics selected for weighting variables. These characteristics must, as before, be known for nonrespondents as well as respondents. First, the weights of the survey respondents are blown up to the given marginal totals for one of the variables. Next, the weights of the respondents, as adjusted in the prior step, are further adjusted to add to the given marginal totals for one of the other variables. This procedure is repeated for each of the variables used for the raking procedure. At this point, only the last variable dealt with will be sure to have desired marginal weight totals. However, the procedure can be repeated and the marginal totals converge to the desired numbers for all variables. The convergence proof is due to Ireland and S. Kullback(5).

The resulting adjustment applied to a particular respondent is the product of the adjustments made for the marginal total for each variable for each iteration. Estimation based on these weights has a justification in statistical information theory.[8]

As an example of the raking procedure, suppose that two variables are used in the adjustment process. Let the given marginal total for the ith category of the row variable be denoted as $N_{i.}$, and let the known total for the jth category of the column variable be noted as $N_{.j}$. Also, let $n_{i.}$, $n_{.j}$, and n_{ij} represent marginal sample size for the ith category of the row variable, the marginal sample size for the jth category of the column variable, and the sample size for the ijth cell. (These sample sizes can be taken to be sums of respondent weights.) Then, adjusting the row totals first, the new frequency (or sum of weights) of the respondents in the ijth cell is the following:

$$N_{ij}^{(1)} = (N_{i.} / n_{i.})n_{ij} \qquad (6)$$

Next, the cell frequency $N_{ij}^{(1)}$ is replaced by the following value:

$$N_{ij}^{(2)} = N_{ij}^{(1)} (N_{.j} / N_{.j}^{(1)}) \qquad (7)$$

where

$N_{.j}^{(1)}$ = the marginal total for the jth column after the first adjustment is made using equation 6.

Repeated iterations of this process can be made until the desired level of convergence on the marginal totals is reached.

3.5 The Use of Regression in Weighting Adjustments - A procedure using multiple regression in nonresponse imputation has been used by Astin and Molm (1) for a follow-up survey of college freshmen. Basically, the zero-one response variable is regressed on some set of independent variables which are available for both respondents and nonrespondents. The value of the regression equation for each respondent is the estimated response rate or probability of responding for population members with the same values of the independent variables. The nonresponse weight adjustment for each respondent is taken as the inverse of the value of the regression equation.

In the application of this technique the multiple correlation coefficient was less than .25. Since this indicates that only about six percent of the variation in the zero-one response variable was explained by the regression equation, there is some doubt regarding the use of this procedure. However, to compare this procedure with the weighting-class-type procedure, corresponding measures of the explained variance for the zero-one response variable would have to be observed. The low proportion of explained variation may be a result of the linearity assumption underlying the regression model which was used. The implications of the linearity assumptions are discussed for a simple case by Chapman (2,pp.60-61). A nonlinear regression model may lead to higher proportions of explained variation in the zero-one response variable. If this is the case, this method of nonresponse imputation may be more appropriate for nonlinear regression.

There are other ways that regression could be used in imputation. For example, each survey item could be regressed on the variables that are available for both respondents and nonrespondents. Of course, estimates of the regression coefficients would have to come from the respondent sample. Imputed values for the questionnaire items would be obtained for a nonrespondent from the regression equations.

A difficulty with this procedure would be the need for a large number of regression equations -- one for each questionnaire item. Another problem would be the limited information that is available for nonrespondents. That is, there may not be enough meaningful independent variables available for the regressions to be worthwhile. Perhaps this procedure would be more useful in the case of imputation for item nonresponse since a larger number of independent variables would be available in that situation.

3.6 The Use in Imputation of the Amount of Effort Needed to Obtain Response - If whether or not an individual selected for a sample survey participates in the survey is correlated to the measurements taken, then it seems plausible that the number of calls required to obtain participation would also be correlated to the measurements taken. If so, the number of calls required per respondent could be useful in nonresponse imputation.

One way that the number of calls could be used would be to make nonresponse weight adjustments among only those respondents who agreed to participate after several calls. Weighting classes would be defined among the nonrespondents and the "late cooperators". The late cooperators would receive weight adjustments computed in a way similar to those discussed in Section 3.2.

This procedure would minimize the bias if, indeed, the survey characteristics of the nonrespondents were more alike those of the late cooperators than those for all survey respondents. However, the validity of this assumption is questionable. It might hold for some surveys and not for others. With regard to the CPS, Waksberg and Pearl (14,p.232) indicate that there is no support for the hypothesis that the characteristics of the nonrespondents become more like the respondents as the number of visits required for interview increases. This statement was based on results from an intensive follow-up of CPS nonrespondents in which about 40 percent of the original nonrespondents were interviewed.

This procedure can have an undesirable effect on the variances of survey estimates. If the number of late cooperators is not considerably larger than the number of nonrespondents, the nonresponse weight adjustments could be relatively large. If so, the variances of survey estimates would be increased substantially.

In the imputation process another method of using the number of calls needed to complete the interview would be to try to project a mean response for nonrespondents. That is, for a particular survey item, a mean response would first be computed among respondents requiring only one call. The corresponding mean would also be computed among those requiring two calls, among those requiring three calls, etc. If the mean responses were plotted against the number of calls, a trend might be apparent.

This procedure was investigated by Chapman (2,pp.51-59) for data collected in the Health and Nutrition Examination Survey. In this case there were many different patterns observed for the various survey items. It was not possible to determine a general trend. Also for most items, the trend of mean response as a function of the number of calls was not evident enough to even attempt to project a mean value for the nonrespondents. Even for the few items for which the trend was apparent, the method appropriate to extrapolate to the nonrespondents is unclear. Consequently, the use of degree of persuasion in the imputation process for that survey did not appear to be feasible.

3.7 Imputation by Substitution of Additional Selections from the Population - For surveys in which it is feasible, imputations for nonrespondents are sometimes made by selecting substitute units from the population to take the place of the nonrespondents. For such cases an attempt is made to obtain a substitute with characteristics which are similar to those of the nonrespondent. This may be done by selecting an additional sampling unit at random from the same stratum or cluster as the unit which did not respond, or may involve a substitute picked on a subjective basis to appropriately "represent" the nonrespondent, such as a neighbor. When such a substitute sampling unit is obtained for the sample, the substitute unit is weighted as though it had been initially selected.

A possible difficulty with a substitution procedure of this type is that the effort put forth to obtain a response from each of the originally selected sampling units may not be as strong as it would have been if no substitution procedure were used. This is a serious problem since the only satisfactory way to deal with nonresponse is to keep it to a low level. Therefore every effort should be made to obtain usable responses from those units originally selected before substitutions are made.

Also, when substitutes are used, it is important to keep in mind that the total sample (ie., original respondents plus substitutes) is not equivalent to a probability sample of the same total size from the population. This is because of the bias introduced due to the use of substitutes in place of some of the originally selected units. Therefore, when this procedure is used, the amount of substitution involved should be reported.

If the above problems are taken into account and kept under reasonable control, then the substitution procedure is good if adequate substitutions are made. In particular, it has the advantage over the weighting-class method in that it does not involve any inflation of weights which causes some increase in the variances of the estimates. Also, it does provide more respondent data than the other procedures.

Of course, it is usually not possible to obtain a substitute for each nonrespondent. Therefore, even when substitution is used, one of the previous methods of adjusting weights must also be used to some extent.

As an example, Westat Research was a subcontractor to the Educational Testing Service to help design a sample of 448 elementary schools in which to administer achievement tests. The test design required exactly 448 schools. Therefore substitutes had to be obtained for each of the nonresponding schools.

The first level substitute for a nonresponding school was taken to be that school, if any, located in the same district, having the same grade structure, and having similar levels of enrollment, mean income of the surrounding community, and percent minority of the students. If such a substitute was not available, no other school in the same district was allowed as a substitute. For the second, third, fourth and fifth priority level substitutes, schools were selected at random from the same stratum as the nonresponding school.

As a result of a superb effort on the part of ETS personnel (Western Office), all 448 slots were presumably filled. Unfortunately, improper test administration forced three of these schools out of the respondent group, leaving a total of 445 responding schools. Weight adjustments using classes defined by strata were used to impute for the three missing schools.

FOOTNOTES

[1] I would like to express my sincere appreciation to Morris H. Hansen and Sidney A. Jaffe for their many helpful suggestions regarding the content of this paper. They also read over the first draft and made many useful comments.

[2] The discussion of the cold-deck imputation procedure given here is based on a description of the procedure given by Svein Nordbotten (9,pp. 26-27).

[3] The discussion of the hot-deck imputation procedure is based primarily on descriptions by Svein Nordbotten (9,pp.28-29) and the Bureau of the Census (13,pp.22-23).

[4] The weight of a respondent is a quantity which is used to give the respondent his appropriate representation in the calculation of the survey estimates. This weight consists of the product of (1) the inverse of the selection probability, (2) any ratio adjustments to known totals, and (3) nonresponse adjustments.

[5] This use of 2.0 as a maximum weight is based, to a large extent, on the overall CPS nonresponse rate of only 5 percent. In surveys with higher nonresponse rates, the maximum adjustment allowed is probably higher.

[6] A detailed description of the AID programmed procedure is given by Morgan and Sonquist (7).

[7] The general description of the raking procedure given here is based on a description by Rosenblatt (11, especially pp.4-6).

[8] This is discussed by Rosenblatt (11,p.5) and is covered in detail by Kullback (6).

REFERENCES:

1. Astin, Alexander W. and Linda D. Molm, Correcting for Nonresponse Bias in Follow-up Surveys, 1972. An unpublished manuscript available from the Office of Research of the American Council on Education, 1 Dupont Circle, Washington, D. C.
2. Chapman, David W., "An Investigation of Nonresponse Imputation Procedures for the Health and Nutrition Examination Survey," prepared for the Division of Health Examination Statistics, National Center for Health Statistics, HEW, by Westat, Inc., 1974.
3. Hansen, M.H., W.N. Hurwitz, and W.G. Madow, Sample Survey Methods and Theory, Vol. I,

New York: John Wiley and Sons, Inc., 1953.

4. Hansen, M.H., W.N. Hurwitz, and W.G. Madow, Sample Survey Methods and Theory, Vol. II, New York: John Wiley and Sons, Inc., 1953.
5. Ireland and Kullback, S., "Contingency Tables with Given Marginals," Biometrika, Vol. 55, No. 1 (March 1968), pp.179-188.
6. Kullback, S., Information Theory and Statistics, New York: John Wiley and Sons, 1959; Dover Press, 1968.
7. Morgan, James N. and John A. Sonquist, "Problems in the Analysis of Survey Data, and a Proposal", Journal of the American Statistical Association, 58 (June 1963), pp.415-435.
8. National Center for Health Statistics: Cycle I of the Health Examination Survey: Sample and Response, United States, 1960-1962. Vital and Health Statistics. PHS Pub. No. 1000 - Series 11 - No. 1 Public Health Service. Washington: U. S. Govt. Printing Office, April 1964.
9. Nordbotten, Svein, "Automatic Editing of Individual Statistical Observations", Conference on European Statisticians, Statistical Studies, No. 2, United Nations, New York, 1963.
10. Pritzker, L., J. Ogus and M.H. Hansen, "Computer Editing Methods - Some Applications and Results", Bulletin of the International Statistical Institute Preceedings of the 35th Session, Belgrade 41 (September 1965), pp. 417-441.
11. Rosenblatt, Harry M., "Study of Proposed Ratio Estimators for 1970 Census". Prepared for Census History, Statistical Research Division of the U. S. Bureau of the Census, March 11, 1971.
12. U. S. Bureau of the Census, The Current Population Survey - A Report on Methodology. Technical Paper No. 7, U. S. Government Printing Office, Washington, D. C., 1963.
13. U. S. Bureau of the Census, United States Censuses of Population and Housing, 1960: Processing the Data. Washington, D. C.,1962.
14. Waksberg, Joseph and Robert Pearl, "New Methodological Research on Labor Force Measurements". Proceedings of the American Statistical Association, Social Statistics Section, 1965, pp. 227-237.

Statistical Robustness: One View of Its Use in Applications Today

ROBERT V. HOGG*

Users of statistical packages need to be aware of the influence that outlying data points can have on their statistical analyses. Robust procedures provide formal methods to spot these outliers and reduce their influence. Although a few robust procedures are mentioned in this article, one is emphasized; it is motivated by maximum likelihood estimation to make it seem more natural. Use of this procedure in regression problems is considered in some detail, and an approximate error structure is stated for the robust estimates of the regression coefficients. A few examples are given. A suggestion of how these techniques should be implemented in practice is included.

KEY WORDS: *M* estimator; Outliers; Robustness; Robust regression.

1. INTRODUCTION

The method of least squares and generalizations of it have served us well for many years. It is recognized, however, that outliers, which arise from heavy-tailed distributions or are simply bad data points due to errors, have an unusually large influence on the least squares estimators. That is, the outliers pull the least squares "fit" toward them too much, and a resulting examination of the residuals is misleading because then the residuals look more like normal ones. Accordingly, robust methods have been created to modify least squares procedures so that the outliers have much less influence on the final estimates.

Since Box (1953) coined the term *robustness*, an enormous amount of material has been published on the subject. Tukey's (1962) comments on spotty data have spurred on these investigations. Perhaps the greatest contributions have been those of Huber. His fundamental article (1964), his Wald lectures, and the review articles (1972, 1973) based on these talks are milestones in this development. Hampel's use of the influence curve in robust estimation is also central, but beyond the scope of this article. The interested reader is referred to Hampel (1974).

Thus, today's statisticians can find plenty of material on *M, R,* and *L* estimators and various generalizations, including adaptive versions of them. One survey of some of these procedures is that of Hogg (1974). In addition, a new paperback by Huber (1977) provides an excellent summary of many of the mathematical aspects of robustness.

With all these existing robust methods, we might think that the applications would be flooded with their use. But clearly this is not the case! Of course, some use of robust methods has been made in practice, but most persons continue to use only least squares techniques (or generalizations of least squares) that are associated with usual normal assumptions. Yet if one studies the literature on robustness, it does seem as if there is some place for these newer techniques. Seemingly, today we should seriously question the dogma of normality in each analysis under consideration and truly be concerned about the influence of outliers and bad data points on our inferential statistics. This concern should range from simple cases with data that are not clearly out of line to multivariate situations in which it is extremely difficult to detect spotty data. Thus, we need formal procedures—like robust methods—to help find those outlying points and eliminate or reduce their effects.

Why is it that robust methods are not used more frequently today? Possibly there are too many robust schemes, and the applied statistician simply does not know where to start. If so, it seems to me that the "robustniks" should agree to support certain basic and understandable robust procedures and then try to sell them to the statistical community. I do not mean to imply that all research in this exciting area should be stopped. On the contrary, research should be encouraged and stimulated, with the understanding that recommendations made in future years will quite likely be different from those of today. But we should try to make a significant start in the introduction of robust estimation in statistical practice now.

Hence, the major purpose in writing this article is to generate some interest in robustness among statistical users by considering a limited number of procedures and concentrating on only one of them. The procedure that is emphasized is one that, with some adaptations, can be used whenever least squares (or generalizations of it) is used: regression, analysis of variance (ANOVA), multivariate analysis, discrimination, and so on. This proposed method is a reasonable approach and involves fairly easy computations. Thus, I believe it should be the major robust method in use today.

In this article, I will try to provide some background, beginning with maximum likelihood estimation of one parameter, that I hope will make robust estimation seem natural and rather easy. Some approximate sampling distribution theory will be stated for these robust estimators, providing information about the error structure so that statistical inferences can be made. Finally, I must emphasize here that I am not going to recommend that we discontinue using the method of least squares and all the computer packages

* Robert V. Hogg is Professor and Chairman of the Department of Statistics, University of Iowa, Iowa City, IA 52242. This work was supported in part by National Institutes of Health Grant GM 22271-02. The author wishes to thank John Tukey, T. DeWet, R.K. Zeigler, the editor, an associate editor, and two referees for making generous suggestions that substantially improved this article.

associated with it and its generalizations. On the contrary, I urge that we continue to use these methods with which we are so familiar. But I also urge that, along with each such analysis, a robust analysis should be made. If the two procedures are in essential agreement, that fact, together with the usual (least squares) summary of the analysis, should be reported. If, however, substantial differences exist in the two analyses, another hard look at the data must be taken, searching in particular for outliers or bad data points. The robust procedures will, for all practical purposes, detect these spotty data points by recording low weights for large residuals from the robust fit.

2. THE LOCATION PARAMETER

In a distribution described by the density $f(x)$, let us introduce an unknown location (slippage) parameter θ, obtaining the density $f(x - \theta)$, $-\infty < \theta < \infty$. If $X_1, X_2, \ldots, X_n$ represents a random sample from this distribution, one popular method of estimating θ is that of maximum likelihood. The logarithm of the likelihood function $L(\theta)$ is

$$\ln L(\theta) = \sum_{i=1}^{n} \ln f(x_i - \theta) = -\sum_{i=1}^{n} \rho(x_i - \theta),$$

where $\rho(x) = -\ln f(x)$. If we can maximize by differentiating, we have

$$\frac{d[\ln L(\theta)]}{d\theta} = -\sum_{i=1}^{n} \frac{f'(x_i - \theta)}{f(x_i - \theta)} = \sum_{i=1}^{n} \psi(x_i - \theta),$$

where $\rho'(x) = \psi(x)$. The solution of

$$\sum_{i=1}^{n} \psi(x_i - \theta) = 0$$

that maximizes $L(\theta)$ is called the maximum likelihood estimator of θ and is frequently denoted by $\hat{\theta}$.

Three typical classroom examples of this process are given by the following distributions, the first of which provides the least squares estimate and the second, the least absolute values estimate.

1. *Normal*: $\rho(x) = x^2/2 + c$, $\psi(x) = x$, $\sum_{i=1}^{n} (x_i - \theta) = 0$ yields $\hat{\theta} = \bar{x}$.
2. *Double exponential*: $\rho(x) = |x| + c$, $\psi(x) = -1$, $x < 0$, and $\psi(x) = 1, x > 0$, $\sum_{i=1}^{n} \psi(x_i - \theta) = 0$ yields $\hat{\theta} =$ sample median.
3. *Cauchy*: $\rho(x) = \ln(1 + x^2) + c$, $\psi(x) = 2x/(1 + x^2)$, $\sum_{i=1}^{n} \psi(x_i - \theta) = 0$ is solved by iterative methods.

It is interesting to note that the ψ functions of examples (2.) and (3.) are bounded and that of (3.) even redescends and approaches zero asymptotically. We note that the solutions in (2.) and (3.) are not influenced much by outliers. On the other hand, the least squares estimator $\bar{X}$ of (1.) is greatly influenced by extreme values. That is, it is well known that the least squares estimator $\bar{X}$ is not extremely good in situations in which the underlying distribution has long tails, for example, in the Cauchy case. Therefore, in robust estimation, we look for estimators that are quite efficient (usually around 90 to 95 percent) if the underlying distribution is normal but are also very efficient even though the underlying distribution has long tails. Sometimes the amount of efficiency lost under normal assumptions, say 5 percent, is referred to as the premium that we pay for the protection that we get in case we actually have a distribution that has longer tails than the normal one.

For a certain theoretical reason (actually minimizing the maximum asymptotic variance of the estimators associated with a certain class of distributions), Huber (1964) proposed that we use for our robust estimator the maximum likelihood estimator of the location parameter associated with a density that is like a normal in the middle but like a double exponential in the tails. In particular, Huber's ρ function is (except for an additive constant)

$$\begin{aligned} \rho(x) &= x^2/2, & |x| \le k, \\ &= k|x| - k^2/2, & k < |x|, \end{aligned}$$

so that the ψ function is

$$\begin{aligned} \psi(x) &= -k, & x < -k, \\ &= x, & -k \le x \le k, \\ &= k, & k < x. \end{aligned}$$

Of course, with this ψ function, the equation

$$\sum_{i=1}^{n} \psi(x_i - \theta) = 0$$

must be solved by iterative methods. An estimator of this type (not necessarily using this particular ψ function) is denoted by $\hat{\theta}$ and called an M estimator, M for maximum likelihood.

There is another feature of this M estimator on which we should comment. Suppose a solution $\hat{\theta}$ were found for a particular sample $x_1, x_2, \ldots, x_n$, and then these items were replaced by some in which the deviations from $\hat{\theta}$ were tripled, for example. The new solution $\hat{\theta}$, using this modified sample, would not necessarily be the same. That is, the estimator would not be scale invariant. To obtain a scale-invariant version of this estimator, we could solve

$$\sum_{i=1}^{n} \psi[(x_i - \theta)/d] = 0,$$

where now d is a robust estimate of scale. Although ad hoc, a popular statistic d used in this solution is

$$d = \text{median}\,|x_i - \text{median}\,(x_i)|/(.6745).$$

(Sometimes the numerator of d is called the MAD, the median of the absolute deviations.) The divisor .6745 is used because then $d \approx \sigma$ if n is large and if the sample actually arises from a normal distribution. Usually the sample standard deviation s is not used as a d value since it is influenced too much by outliers and thus is not robust.

This particular scheme of selecting d suggests appropriate values of the "tuning" constant k so that the efficiency of $\hat{\theta}$ will be high if the underlying distribution is actually normal. In the normal situation, we would want most of the items to satisfy the inequality

$$|(x_i - \theta)/d| \leq k$$

because then

$$\psi[(x_i - \theta)/d] = (x_i - \theta)/d.$$

As a matter of fact, if all items enjoyed this inequality, then $\hat{\theta} = \bar{X}$, which is the desired estimator in the normal case. Because $d \approx \sigma$, k is usually taken to be some number close to 1.5. When $k = 1.5$, we refer to this procedure (or the corresponding estimator) as a (1.5)Huber procedure (estimator). If σ is known (i.e., d is known), the asymptotic efficiency of it, under normal assumptions, is greater than 95 percent (Huber 1964), and, in most heavy-tailed situations, it performs extremely well (Andrews et al. 1972). Thus, our premium is small for much protection in nonnormal cases; however, σ is usually unknown and it must be estimated; this does reduce that efficiency only a very little when $n \geq 10$ (see Andrews et al. 1972).

Other ψ functions that are commonly used are the following, along with suggested values of the respective tuning constants.

1. (a,b,c) *Hampel*

$$\psi(x) = (\text{sign } x)\begin{cases} |x|, & 0 \leq |x| < a, \\ a, & a \leq |x| < b, \\ a\,\dfrac{c - |x|}{c - b}, & b \leq |x| < c, \\ 0, & c \leq |x|. \end{cases}$$

Reasonably good values of the constants are $a = 1.7$, $b = 3.4$, and $c = 8.5$.

2. (k) *Wave of Andrews*

$$\psi(x) = \sin(x/k), \quad |x| \leq k\pi,$$
$$= 0, \quad |x| > k\pi,$$

with $k = 1.5$ or 2.0. Actually if the scale is known, $k = 1.339$ requires a premium of 5 percent.

3. (k) *Biweight of Tukey*

$$\psi(x) = x[1 - (x/k)^2]^2, \quad |x| \leq k,$$
$$= 0, \quad |x| > k,$$

with $k = 5.0$ or 6.0. If the scale is known, $k = 4.685$ implies a premium of 5 percent.

It should be noted that the wave and biweight procedures are very similar and are reasonable substitutes for each other. Because the ρ functions associated with these three redescending ψ functions are not convex, there could be certain convergence problems in the iterative procedures, although this situation is not too likely. That is, these have been successful procedures and should be used, but with some care.

Suppose, by an iterative numerical method, we find the solution $\hat{\theta}$ to our equation; that is, let $\hat{\theta}$ be the M estimator so that $\sum \psi[(X_i - \hat{\theta})/d] = 0$, for any bounded ψ function that is odd. It is easy to approximate this last equation by replacing the left member by two terms of Taylor's series, expanded about the true parameter value θ. From this approximation, when $d = \sigma$, it is a straightforward exercise to show

$$\sqrt{n}(\hat{\theta} - \theta) \approx \frac{\sigma\left[\sum \psi\left(\dfrac{X_i - \theta}{\sigma}\right)\right]\Big/\sqrt{n}}{\left[\sum \psi'\left(\dfrac{X_i - \theta}{\sigma}\right)\right]\Big/n},$$

and this expression has a limiting normal distribution with mean zero and variance

$$\frac{\sigma^2 E\left[\psi^2\left(\dfrac{X - \theta}{\sigma}\right)\right]}{\left\{E\left[\psi'\left(\dfrac{X - \theta}{\sigma}\right)\right]\right\}^2}.$$

Of course, because we do not know the underlying density, we must, in practice, approximate the expected values and the σ that appear in this asymptotic variance. One approximation to the variance of $\sqrt{n}(\hat{\theta} - \theta)$ is given by

$$s_1^2 = \frac{d^2\{(1/n) \sum_{i=1}^{n} \psi^2[(x_i - \hat{\theta})/d]\}}{\{(1/n) \sum_{i=1}^{n} \psi'[(x_i - \hat{\theta})/d]\}^2}.$$

That is, for large n, $\sqrt{n}(\hat{\theta} - \theta)/s_1$ has an approximate standardized normal distribution. An even better approximating distribution to $(n - 1)^{1/2}(\hat{\theta} - \theta)/s_1$ can be found by using one member of the t family, possibly one with $n - 1$ degrees of freedom (or even one with somewhat smaller degrees of freedom than $n - 1$; see Huber 1970). With one of these approximate distributions, we can make statistical inferences about the unknown θ. Gross (1976) explores confidence intervals based on this idea as well as those resulting from other schemes, and he finds robustness of validity (maintaining the 95 percent confidence coefficient) and of efficiency (establishing relatively short intervals).

3. ROBUST REGRESSION

Suppose that we have the linear model

$$\mathbf{Y} = \mathbf{X}\boldsymbol{\beta} + \mathbf{E}$$

where $\mathbf{Y}$ is an $n \times 1$ random vector, $\mathbf{X}$ is an $n \times p$ design matrix of known constants such that $\mathbf{X}'\mathbf{X}$ is of full rank, $\boldsymbol{\beta}$ is a $p \times 1$ vector of unknown parameters, and $\mathbf{E}$ is an $n \times 1$ random vector, whose elements are like a random sample from a distribution that is symmetric (but not necessarily normal) about zero. To parallel the approach used with the location parameter, we wish to minimize, with a robust ρ function, the summation

$$\sum_{i=1}^{n} \rho[(y_i - \mathbf{x}_i\boldsymbol{\beta})/d]$$

where y_i is the ith element of $\mathbf{Y}$, $\mathbf{x}_i$ is the ith row of $\mathbf{X}$, and d is an estimate of the scale of the distribution associated with $\mathbf{E}$. Equating the first partial derivatives with respect to the elements of $\boldsymbol{\beta}$, say β_j, equal to zero, we see that this is equivalent to finding the maximizing solution associated with the p equations

$$\sum_{i=1}^{n} x_{ij}\psi[(y_i - \mathbf{x}_i\boldsymbol{\beta})/d] = 0, \quad j = 1, 2, \ldots, p,$$

where x_{ij} is the element in the ith row and jth column of $\mathbf{X}$.

Let us first concern ourselves with an initial estimate $\boldsymbol{\beta}_0$ of $\boldsymbol{\beta}$; this is needed for two things: a robust estimate d of scale and a "start" in the iteration to find $\hat{\boldsymbol{\beta}}$. If it is easy to find the L_1 (least absolute values) estimators for the regression coefficients, these would be good and something like the median in the single-sample case. Moreover, for the estimate of scale, we would then use the median of the absolute values of the nonzero residuals divided by .6745, as in the location case. Many statisticians, however, find it inconvenient to determine L_1 estimators, and therefore let us consider an algorithm of Dutter (1977) for estimating $\boldsymbol{\beta}$ and scale simultaneously. The algorithm is described here only for the ψ function of Huber. This method, as will be seen, is then very close to least squares (and is only one of several suggestions listed in Dutter's article).

Let us begin with some initial estimates, $\boldsymbol{\beta}_0$ and d_0, which might very well be the usual estimates of $\boldsymbol{\beta}$ and scale. We proceed as follows:

1. Compute the residuals $z_i = y_i - \mathbf{x}_i\boldsymbol{\beta}_0$, $i = 1, 2, \ldots, n$.
2. Find a new estimate of scale

$$d_1^2 = \frac{1}{(n-p)E(\psi^2)} \sum_{i=1}^{n} [\psi(z_i/d_0)]^2 d_0^2,$$

where $E(\psi^2)$ is the expected value of Huber's $\psi^2(W)$ and where W is a standardized normal random variable. For illustration, $E(\psi^2) = .7785$ in the (1.5)Huber procedure.

3. "Winsorize" the residuals; that is, determine

$$\Delta_i = \psi(z_i/d_1)d_1, \quad i = 1, 2, \ldots, n.$$

Of course, the Winsorized residual $\psi(z_i/d_1)d_1$ equals z_i if $|z_i/d_1| \le k$ but is equal to kd_1 $(-kd_1)$ if $kd_1 < z_i$ $(z_i < -kd_1)$. For more on the general concept of Winsorizing, see Dixon and Tukey (1968).

4. Find the least squares estimates of the regression coefficients as if the Winsorized residuals were the observations, namely,

$$\hat{\boldsymbol{\zeta}}_0 = (\mathbf{X}'\mathbf{X})^{-1}\mathbf{X}'\boldsymbol{\Delta}_0$$

where $\boldsymbol{\Delta}_0$ is the $p \times 1$ column vector of $\Delta_1, \Delta_2, \ldots, \Delta_n$.

5. Compute a new estimate of $\boldsymbol{\beta}$, namely

$$\boldsymbol{\beta}_1 = \boldsymbol{\beta}_0 + q\hat{\boldsymbol{\zeta}}_0$$

Dutter found that a suitable choice of the factor q is

$$q = \min\left[\frac{1}{\Phi(k) - \Phi(-k)}, 1.9\right],$$

where Φ is the standardized normal distribution function.

With the new estimates, $\boldsymbol{\beta}_1$ and d_1, as the starting values, repeat steps 1 through 5. Continue this iteration process until (on the mth iteration), for all $i = 1, 2, \ldots, p$,

$$|q\hat{\zeta}_m^i| < \epsilon d_{m+1}\sqrt{x_{ii}} \quad \text{and} \quad |d_{m+1} - d_m| < \epsilon d_{m+1},$$

where $\epsilon > 0$ is an appropriate tolerance level, $\hat{\zeta}_m^i$ is the ith component of $\hat{\boldsymbol{\zeta}}_m$, and x_{ii} is the ith diagonal element of $(\mathbf{X}'\mathbf{X})^{-1}$. At that point, stop the iterations and estimate $\boldsymbol{\beta}$ and the scale parameter by using $\boldsymbol{\beta}_{m+1}$ and d_{m+1}, respectively.

The reader should note exactly how close this procedure is to least squares. Of course, step 4 is least squares on the Winsorized residuals, step 5 would provide the least square estimate of $\boldsymbol{\beta}$ in case $q = 1$, and $\boldsymbol{\Delta}_0$ equals the vector of actual residuals (not Winsorized) for any initial estimate $\boldsymbol{\beta}_0$. It is also of interest to observe that $(\mathbf{X}'\mathbf{X})^{-1}$ needs to be computed only once in the iterative process, and this is a definite computational saving.

After obtaining good robust estimates of $\boldsymbol{\beta}$ and scale by using Dutter's algorithm, least absolute values, or another scheme (some nonparametric methods might be quite suitable), we could treat outliers more severely by using these robust estimates as new "starts," say $\tilde{\boldsymbol{\beta}}_0$ and $\tilde{d}_0$, with a redescending ψ function such as a wave or biweight. In those cases, a weighted least squares procedure is a good algorithm to use. In this method we replace the p equations

$$\sum_{i=1}^{n} x_{ij}\psi[(y_i - \mathbf{x}_i\boldsymbol{\beta})/d] = 0, \quad j = 1, 2, \ldots, p,$$

or, equivalently when $y_i - \mathbf{x}_i\boldsymbol{\beta} \neq 0$,

$$\sum_{i=1}^{n} x_{ij} \frac{\psi[(y_i - \mathbf{x}_i\boldsymbol{\beta})/d]}{(y_i - \mathbf{x}_i\boldsymbol{\beta})/d} (y_i - \mathbf{x}_i\boldsymbol{\beta}) = 0,$$

by the approximations

$$\sum_{i=1}^{n} x_{ij}(w_{i0})(y_i - \mathbf{x}_i\boldsymbol{\beta}) \approx 0, \quad j = 1, 2, \ldots, p,$$

where

$$w_{i0} = \frac{\psi[(y_i - \mathbf{x}_i\tilde{\boldsymbol{\beta}}_0)/\tilde{d}_0]}{(y_i - \mathbf{x}_i\tilde{\boldsymbol{\beta}}_0)/\tilde{d}_0}, \quad y_i \neq \mathbf{x}_i\tilde{\boldsymbol{\beta}}_0,$$

and $w_{i0} = 1$, when $y_i = \mathbf{x}_i\tilde{\boldsymbol{\beta}}_0$. In matrix notation, in which $\mathbf{W}_0$ is the $n \times n$ diagonal matrix with $w_{10}, w_{20}, \ldots, w_{n0}$ on the principal diagonal, the one-step estimator is

$$\tilde{\boldsymbol{\beta}}_{1W} = (\mathbf{X}'\mathbf{W}_0\mathbf{X})^{-1}\mathbf{X}'\mathbf{W}_0\mathbf{Y}.$$

The iteration requires that, on each step, we recompute the weights and thus the inverse $(\mathbf{X}'\mathbf{W}_j\mathbf{X})^{-1}$, $j = 0, 1, 2, \ldots$. With good estimates $\tilde{\boldsymbol{\beta}}_0$ and $\tilde{d}_0$ resulting from Dutter's procedure, however, only a few iterations are usually needed to obtain good redescending ψ estimates.

What should be used for the error structure associated with the final estimate $\hat{\boldsymbol{\beta}}$? It is true (Huber 1973) that under certain reasonable conditions (one is a known spread $d = \sigma$), $\hat{\boldsymbol{\beta}}$ has an approximate normal distribution with mean $\boldsymbol{\beta}$ and variance-covariance matrix

$$\frac{\sigma^2 E[\psi^2(Z/\sigma)](\mathbf{X}'\mathbf{X})^{-1}}{\{E[\psi'(Z/\sigma)]\}^2},$$

where Z represents an element of the random vector $\mathbf{E}$. An approximation to this variance-covariance matrix is

$$\frac{(nd^2)\{(1/n) \sum \psi^2[(y_i - \mathbf{x}_i\hat{\boldsymbol{\beta}})/d]\}(\mathbf{X}'\mathbf{X})^{-1}}{(n - p)\{(1/n) \sum \psi'[(y_i - \mathbf{x}_i\hat{\boldsymbol{\beta}})/d]\}^2}.$$

Of course, the weighted least squares program also automatically provides another estimate of this variance-covariance matrix. Two other suggestions are given by Welsch (1975), but there is not general agreement on which of these approximations is best. Nevertheless, whichever one we choose, we do have some idea about the error structure of $\hat{\boldsymbol{\beta}}$, and we can thus make some approximate statistical inferences about $\boldsymbol{\beta}$ by using the usual normal theory.

Let us close this section on regression with a remark about the procedure in which we do not have a linear model, but $\mathbf{Y} = h(\boldsymbol{\beta}) + \mathbf{E}$, $h(\cdot)$ is a nonlinear function of $\boldsymbol{\beta}$. Let $h_i(\boldsymbol{\beta})$ be $h(\boldsymbol{\beta})$, which is associated with Y_i. We wish to minimize

$$\sum_{i=1}^{n} \rho\left(\frac{y_i - h_i(\boldsymbol{\beta})}{d}\right)$$

where an estimate d of spread can be found by using a preliminary estimate $\tilde{\boldsymbol{\beta}}_0$. Equating the first partial derivatives to zero, we have

$$\sum_{i=1}^{n} \frac{\partial h_i(\boldsymbol{\beta})}{\partial \beta_j} \psi\left(\frac{y_i - h_i(\boldsymbol{\beta})}{d}\right) = 0,$$

$$j = 1, 2, \ldots, p.$$

With the preliminary estimate $\tilde{\boldsymbol{\beta}}_0$ and a weighted nonlinear least squares package, it is easy to solve

$$\sum_{i=1}^{n} \frac{\partial h_i(\boldsymbol{\beta})}{\partial \beta_j} (w_{i0})[y_i - h_i(\boldsymbol{\beta})] = 0, \quad j = 1, 2, \ldots, p,$$

where

$$w_{i0} = \frac{\psi[(y_i - h_i(\tilde{\boldsymbol{\beta}}_0))/d]}{[y_i - h_i(\tilde{\boldsymbol{\beta}}_0)]/d}, \quad y_i \neq h_i(\tilde{\boldsymbol{\beta}}_0)$$

and $w_{i0} = 1$, when $y_i = h_i(\tilde{\boldsymbol{\beta}}_0)$, $i = 1, 2, \ldots, n$. In the nonlinear case, the weighted least squares algorithm seems to be easiest although Dutter's algorithm can be modified with $\partial h_i / \partial \beta_j$ replacing x_{ij}.

Holland and Welsch (1977) compare robust estimates resulting from eight ψ functions. They also note that a semiportable subroutine library (including these eight ψ functions) called ROSEPACK (RObust Statistical Estimation PACKage) has been developed at the Computer Research Center of the National Bureau of Economic Research, Inc., in Cambridge, Massachusetts. For example, from their report, a "tuning constant" of $k = 1.5$ seems to be appropriate for the wave estimate because then it would have an efficiency greater than 95 percent, provided that $d = \sigma$ is known and the underlying distribution is normal. One desirable feature of a redescending ψ function, like that of Andrew's wave or Tukey's biweight, is that the extreme outliers are treated much more harshly than in Huber's procedure; many times, in practice, we find that zero weight has been assigned to an outlier or bad data point.

Of course, whenever least squares procedures (or generalizations of them) are used, it seemingly would be possible to use robust procedures with some type of adaptation. These include ANOVA, regression, time series, splines, multivariate analysis, and discrimination. For example, Lenth (1977) has produced some robust splines that give excellent fits to data points for which the usual (least squares) splines fail. Also, Randles et al. (1977) have found robust estimates of mean vectors and variance-covariance matrices that are used in discrimination problems. Robust ANOVA procedures are reported on by Schrader and McKean (1977). From these studies it is clear that, with the necessary imagination, appropriate adaptations can be made; one hopes that much more will be done in the future.

4. *L* ESTIMATION

Let us first consider the simple case of a random sample from a distribution of the continuous type that has a location parameter θ. Say the order statistics of the sample are $X_{(1)} \leq X_{(2)} \leq \ldots \leq X_{(n)}$. An L estimator is one that is a linear combination of these order statistics. Examples of L estimators are

1. Sample median;
2. An α-trimmed mean $\bar{X}_\alpha = \sum_i X_{(i)}/(n - 2[n\alpha])$, where the summation is over $i = [n\alpha] + 1, \ldots, n - [n\alpha]$;
3. Gastwirth's estimator, which is a weighted average of the 33⅓rd, 50th, and 66⅔rd percentiles with respective weights .3, .4, and .3; and
4. Tukey's trimean, which is a weighted average of the first, second, and third quartiles with respective weights ¼, ½, and ¼.

These and other L estimators are also described by Andrews et al. (1972).

The generalization of L estimators to the regression situation is not clear as in the case of M estimators. Because the use of the ρ function, $\rho(x) = |x|$, yields the median as an estimator (and the median plane or surface in the regression situation), this could easily be modified to get other percentiles. That is, the ρ function

$$\rho(x) = -(1-p)x, \quad x < 0,$$
$$= px, \qquad x \geq 0,$$

yields the $(100p)$th percentile in the single-sample case and thus estimates of the $(100p)$th percentile plane or surface in the regression situation (see Koenker and Bassett 1978). Clearly, generalizations of estimates like those of Gastwirth and Tukey could now be constructed in regression problems. Moreover, it seems as if in many situations (e.g., educational data involving prediction of college performance from high school rank and SAT or ACT scores) we would be interested in estimates of some percentiles other than those of the middle. Thus, percentile estimates could stand on their own as well as in combination with others to predict a middle plane or surface.

5. *R* ESTIMATION

R estimation is a nonparametric method resulting from ranking when the sample arises from a continuous-type distribution. *R* estimation can easily be extended to regression. Consider the linear model and modify least squares by replacing one factor in $(y_i - \mathbf{x}_i\boldsymbol{\beta})^2$ by the rank of $y_i - \mathbf{x}_i\boldsymbol{\beta}$, say R_i. The rank R_i is clearly a function of $\boldsymbol{\beta}$. Hence we wish to minimize $\sum_{i=1}^{n} (y_i - \mathbf{x}_i\boldsymbol{\beta})R_i$. This, in turn, can be generalized by replacing the ranks 1, 2, . . . , n by the "scores" $a(1) \leq a(2) \leq \ldots \leq a(n)$. Thus, in this generalized setting, we wish to minimize $\sum_{i=1}^{n} (y_i - \mathbf{x}_i\boldsymbol{\beta})a(R_i)$. Of course, two examples of scores are (a) Wilcoxon scores: $a(i) = i$ or ranks, and (b) median scores: $a(i) = -1, i < (n+1)/2$, and $a(i) = 1, i > (n+1)/2$.

Jaeckel (1972) proved that this minimization is equivalent to solving the p equations

$$\sum_{i=1}^{n} x_{ij}a(R_i) = 0, \quad j = 1, 2, \ldots, p,$$

that must be solved approximately because of the discontinuities in $a(\cdot)$ and R_i. Moreover, it is well known that "good" (having certain asymptotic properties) scores are those given by

$$a(i) = \phi[i/(n+1)],$$

where

$$\phi(t) = -f'[F^{-1}(t)]/f[F^{-1}(t)].$$

Examples of this are

1. *f normal* produces $\phi(t) = \Phi^{-1}(t)$, $0 < t < 1$, that gives normal scores;
2. *f double exponential* produces $\phi(t) = -1$, $0 < t < ½$, and $\phi(t) = 1$, $½ < t < 1$, that gives median scores; and
3. *f logistic* produces $\phi(t) = 2t - 1$, $0 < t < 1$, that gives Wilcoxon scores.

Jurečková (1977) proved that, with certain scores $a(\cdot)$ and ψ functions, the *R* estimators and *M* estimators are asymptotically equivalent. Among other conditions we need that

$$\phi(t) = c_1\psi[F^{-1}(t)] + c_2,$$

where c_1 and c_2 are constants, for this equivalence. In light of this result, it seems more reasonable to use *M* estimators because the computations are easier, at least at this time.

6. ADAPTIVE ESTIMATORS

Only brief note is made here of adaptive estimators. The reader interested in more background is referred to an expository article on the subject (Hogg 1974). The basic idea of adapting is the selection of the estimation procedure after observing the data. Thus, for example, the tuning constants or the amounts of trimming could be dictated by the sample. As a matter of fact, even the forms of the function $\psi(\cdot)$ and the score function $a(\cdot)$ could be selected after observing the sample.

Of course, asymptotically, we can select the "best" $\psi(\cdot)$ or $a(\cdot)$, but most of the time we are working with sample sizes like 20, 30, or 50, not infinity. Hence we must find some reasonable procedures for those very limited sample sizes. One such scheme is to select a small class of underlying distributions that span a large collection of possible distributions. Then determine a good procedure for each member of that class. Finally, let the observations select (through analysis of residuals, plots, etc.) which procedure will actually be used by taking that distribution seemingly closest to what was observed. Incidentally, there is no objection to analyzing with all the procedures: If they say the same thing, that is the answer; if they differ, then the selection procedure is critical and it is most important that it be done well.

There has been some evidence (Hogg 1974) that adaptive procedures are of value. After all, if the "Hubers, Hampels, waves, biweights, . . ." are good, wouldn't adaptive ones be better (particularly because the former are included in the latter)? Moreover, it seems as if the applied statisticians would find adaptation very appealing (they do it all the time anyway), which gives us a chance to bring theory and applications closer together.

7. EXAMPLES

1. *Linear regression*. Andrews (1974) reports on a set of data that had been analyzed by Daniel and Wood (1971). There were 21 observations and three independent variables. After some astute observations, Daniel and Wood were able to set aside 4 of these 21 observations because of unusual behavior. At the end of their analysis, they did use a model different from

$$E(Y) = \beta_0 + \beta_1x_1 + \beta_2x_2 + \beta_3x_3.$$

Andrews notes, however, that "most researchers do not have the insight and perseverance of these authors" (p. 530). Hence he simply summarizes three fits to this model: (a) least squares on all 21 points, (b) least squares on 17 points after discarding those 4 points, and (c) robust estimates using the Andrews's ψ function with $k = 1.5$ on all 21 points (the estimated standard errors are in parentheses).

Method	β_1	β_2	β_3
a	.72(.17)	1.30(.37)	−.15(.16)
b	.80(.07)	.58(.17)	−.07(.06)
c	.82(.05)	.52(.12)	−.07(.04)

It is very impressive to note that the robust method on all 21 points provides essentially the same estimates as does least squares using the 17 observations, with the 4 bad points set aside. This means that an investigator could have used least squares (a) and the robust scheme (c) and found the four spotty points and the better estimates without having the "insight and perseverance" of Daniel and Wood.

2. *Half-life of plutonium-241.* Zeigler and Ferris (1973) reported that each of six laboratories had a sample of plutonium containing ^{238}Pu, ^{239}Pu, ^{240}Pu, ^{241}Pu, and ^{242}Pu. To determine the half-life of ^{241}Pu, the ratio (say Y) of the contents of ^{241}Pu to that of ^{239}Pu was reported by each of six laboratories every four months. These reports were continued longer than three years until more than 70 data points were collected. The problem was to fit the nonlinear function $E(Y) = \beta_0 e^{-\beta_1 t}$. At a later date and with additional data, Zeigler used, along with least squares, a robust scheme based on Andrews's wave. The two estimates of half-life were 14.84 and 14.70 years, respectively. The most interesting part of this analysis, however, was that, with Andrews's weighting function, there were 6 data points with weights of zero, all 6 of which were reported incorrectly by the same laboratory because of a technical error (that has since been corrected).

3. *Splines.* Lenth (1977) considered 51 observations that were simulated from a Cauchy distribution such that the median of each was on the curve sin $(2\pi e^{-x^2})$, where the 51 x values ranged from 0 to 2.5. The conventional least squares spline fit with six knots ($x = 0$, .3, .7, 1.2, 1.8, and 2.5) was compared with two robust spline fits: (1.1)Huber and (1.2)wave. The latter two produced much better fits than the one by least squares. Of course, the Andrews's wave fit was somewhat better than that of Huber because a redescending M estimate is more appropriate with the underlying Cauchy distribution.

4. *Automated data reduction.* Agee and Turner (1978) note that grossly erroneous measurements, when undetected, "completely destroyed automated data reduction" at the U.S. Army White Sands Missile Range. The application of M estimation (primarily with Hampel's ψ) has been highly successful in dealing with these problems that occur in data preprocessing, instrument calibration, N-station cinetheodolites, N-station radar situations, and filtering.

8. SUMMARY

Good applied statisticians have always been on guard for outliers or bad data points, discarding them or investigating them further as is appropriate. In complicated data sets, however, spotting some of these extreme points is most difficult. But a formal robust procedure can definitely help us in this regard. Hence it is recommended that in our statistical investigations we do the following:

1. Perform the usual (least squares or a generalization of it) analyses.
2. Also use a robust procedure. Ideally, this might be (1.5)Huber for several iterations followed by the (1.5)wave or (5.0)biweight for two or three iterations. At the minimum, however, the one-step wave or biweight estimator (i.e., one step of an iterative process) should be found, and one should note which weights are starting to decrease substantially from the number one.
3. If estimates from methods (1.) and (2.) are in essential agreement, report that agreement and the usual statistical summaries associated with method (1.).
4. If the estimates from methods (1.) and (2.) do not agree very well, take another hard look at the data. In particular, look at those points with low weights or large residuals from the robust fit (the weights and residuals of the points should always be displayed on the last iteration). Then the usual questions can be asked about these points: from "Has someone made a simple recording error?" to "Is this outlier trying to tell us something significant about our experiment?"

If a robust element is added to our present methods, we will detect many simple, and not so simple, errors. These procedures have been used very successfully (e.g., Los Alamos Scientific Laboratory has the option of using them in all regression problems and this option is exercised frequently). Many interesting things have been discovered through use of these procedures. My hope is that by 1980 almost all statistical investigations will include a robust aspect. And, by that time, the researchers in robust methods will have other new and better procedures to propose to the statistical community.

[*Received January 1978. Revised February 1979.*]

REFERENCES

Agee, William S., and Turner, Robert H. (1978), "Application of Robust Statistical Methods to Data Reduction," Technical Report No. 65, White Sands Missile Range, N. Mex.

Andrews, D.F. (1974), "A Robust Method for Multiple Linear Regression," *Technometrics*, 16, 523–531.

———, Bickel, P.J., Hampel, F.R., Huber, P.J., Rogers, W.H., and Tukey, J.W. (1972), *Robust Estimates of Location*, Princeton, N.J.: Princeton University Press.

Box, George E.P. (1953), "Non-Normality and Tests on Variances," *Biometrika*, 40, 318–335.

Daniel, Cuthbert, and Wood, Fred S. (1971), *Fitting Equations to Data*, New York: Wiley-Interscience.

Dixon, W.J., and Tukey, John W. (1968), "Approximate Behavior of the Distribution of Winsorized *t* (Trimming/Winsorization 2)," *Technometrics*, 10, 83–98.

Dutter, Rudoft (1977), "Numerical Solution of Robust Regression Problems: Computational Aspects, a Comparison," *Journal of Statistical Computation and Simulation*, 5, 207–238.

Gross, Alan M. (1976), "Confidence Interval Robustness With Long-tailed Symmetric Distributions," *Journal of the American Statistical Association*, 71, 409–416.

Hampel, Frank R. (1974), "The Influence Curve and Its Role in Robust Estimation," *Journal of the American Statistical Association*, 69, 383–393.

Hogg, Robert V. (1974), "Adaptive Robust Procedures: A Partial Review and Some Suggestions for Future Applications and Theory," *Journal of the American Statistical Association*, 69, 909–927.

Holland, Paul W., and Welsch, Roy E. (1977), "Robust Regression Using Iteratively Reweighted Least-Squares," *Communications in Statistics*, A6, 813–828.

Huber, Peter J. (1964), "Robust Estimation of a Location Parameter," *Annals of Mathematical Statistics*, 35, 73–101.

——— (1970), "Studentizing Robust Estimates," in *Nonparametric Techniques in Statistical Inference*, ed. M.L. Puri, London: Cambridge University Press, 435–463.

——— (1972), "Robust Statistics: A Review," *Annals of Mathematical Statistics*, 43, 1041–1067.

——— (1973), "Robust Regression: Asymptotics, Conjectures, and Monte Carlo," *Annals of Statistics*, 1, 799–821.

——— (1977), *Robust Statistical Procedures*, Philadelphia: Society of Industrial and Applied Mathematics.

Jaeckel, L.A. (1972), "Estimating Regression Coefficients by Minimizing the Dispersion of the Residuals," *Annals of Mathematical Statistics*, 43, 1449–1458.

Jurečková, J. (1977), "Asymptotic Relations of *M*-estimates and *R*-estimates in Linear Regression Models," *Annals of Statistics*, 5, 464–472.

Koenker, Roger, and Bassett, Gilbert (1978), "Regression Quantities," *Econometrics*, 46, 33–50.

Lenth, Russell V. (1977), "Robust Splines," *Communications in Statistics*, A6, 847–854.

Randles, Ronald H., Broffitt, James D., Ramberg, John S., and Hogg, Robert V. (1978), "Generalized Linear and Quadratic Discriminant Functions Using Robust Estimates," *Journal of the American Statistical Association*, 73, 564–568.

Schrader, Ronald M., and McKean, Joseph W. (1977), "Robust Analysis of Variance," *Communications in Statistics*, A6, 879–894.

Tukey, John W. (1962), "The Future of Data Analysis," *Annals of Mathematical Statistics*, 33, 1–67.

Welsch, Roy E. (1975), "Confidence Regions for Robust Regression," Working Paper No. 111, National Bureau of Economic Research, Cambridge, Mass.

Zeigler, R.K., and Ferris, Yvonne (1973), "Half-Life of Plutonium-241," *Journal of Inorganic Nuclear Chemistry*, 35, 3417–3418.

Three approaches to canonical analysis

Claes Fornell
Northwestern University

Abstract

Canonical analysis is increasingly being applied in marketing research. While canonical analysis has the capability to handle complex multidimensional relationships for both criterion and explanatory variables, it is also a complex method to use. There are several unresolved problems, most of which have simply been ignored in many marketing applications. When interpretative or statistical problems have been addressed, researchers have been guided by empirical considerations such as multicollinearity, stability, and significance.

This article presents a framework designed to facilitate comprehension and application of canonical analysis. It is argued that the choice of interpretative statistics should not be dictated by empirical considerations only. A more basic issue concerns the logical conformity between the type and objective of analysis, and the statistics employed. Canonical correlation, canonical variate analysis, and canonical regression represent three different approaches to canonical analysis, each pursuing a separate objective and requiring its own set of statistics.

Introduction

As multivariate statistical methods have become increasingly popular, gaining a position as indispensible tools in the multidimensional world of the social sciences, even the most complex methods are now finding application in marketing research. Many of these methods come neatly packaged in standard computer programs easily available to most researchers. Since they appear to make the long and mazy road of analysis much shorter, the multivariate methods are the racing machines of analysis. Like most sophisticated racing vehicles, they are extremely sensitive to chance variation, demanding a thorough understanding of their delicate machinery in order to give top performance and to avoid possible contretemps. Unfortunately, the great potential of multivariate analysis has been marred by inept usage. The fervid rush into application has all too often prevented sufficient analysis of the methods themselves and their appropriateness for solving the research problem at hand.

The use, and mis-use, of canonical analysis indicate that this particular method is poorly understood (Fornell). The purpose of this article is

---

Reprinted with permission from the *Journal of the Market Research Society,* **20 (July 1978), 166-81, copyright ©Claes Fornell.**

to clarify some aspects of canonical analysis by relating it to more familiar techniques of data analysis. Rather than focusing on its mathematical construction, it is the conceptual logic and the interpretation of canonical analysis that will be discussed.

While canonical analysis might look simple and straightforward at first glance, there are a multitude of unresolved issues associated with it. Consequently, there is a host of pitfalls, some of which have been discussed in recent marketing literature (Alpert & Peterson, 1972; Fornell; Lambert & Durand, 1975). It is clear that many issues are in need of further exploration and that both theoretical and empirical inquiries into the very structure of canonical analysis are called for. In this article it is suggested that the comprehension of canonical analysis will be facilitated if one understands that canonical analysis can be viewed as several related techniques, each with a somewhat different logic and a different established practice.

The flexibility of canonical analysis

Social phenomena may not easily lend themselves to one-dimensional conceptualization, nor to one-dimensional measurement. Indeed, many social objects may not be subject to direct measurement at all. A multivariate approach to analysis is a logical concatenation to a multidimensional approach to observing. If the objective is to describe, predict, or to explain a complex phenomenon (expressed as a set of observed variables) via its relation to other phenomenona (expressed as individual variables or as sets of variables), we have multivariance in both criterion and predictor variables. Canonical analysis is a general method designed to handle this type of variable association. Through the use of dummy variables, canonical analysis can be applied in experimental settings where MANOVA or ANOVA normally are employed, or in classification studies that ordinarily belong to the domain of discriminant analysis.

The canonical solution is the maximum correlation between pairs of linear composites of variables. The objective is to find pairs of variable combinations (canonical variates), so that the correlation between them is maximized. Subject to the restriction of variate orthogonality, new pairs can be formed from residual variances with the maximum number of pairs being equal to the number of variables in the smaller of the two sets. Hence each canonical variate is a constructed, unobserved variable, regressed on the observed variables within that set.

Because of its generality, it is not surprising that canonical analysis is beginning to find increasing application in the social sciences. Although there have been several applications in marketing, they are still comparatively few in contrast to regression and correlation studies. They have also been rather limited in scope. The bulk of canonical analyses in marketing has been concerned with the relationship between personality and purchase behaviour (Alpert, 1971, 1972; Baumgarten & Ring, 1971; Kernan, 1968; Sparks & Tucker, 1971; Worthing *et al*, 1971). As shown by Lambert and Durand (1975), one can seriously question both the validity and reliability of the results presented and the propriety of the conclusions drawn in several of these studies.

The typical analysis regarding canonical solutions begins with an examination of the size of the canonical correlations; then a decision is made on (often on the basis of a statistical test) how many variate pairs should enter the analysis; and thirdly, an interpretation of the meaning of the variates and/or an assessment of variable 'importance' from the relative size of the standardized canonical weights is attempted. This pathway of analysis has been followed rather indiscriminantly and without regard to research objectives. Such a mechanical procedure is no substitute for rigorous method and serves no useful purpose; it can only add more confusion and contribute to further mis-use and misunderstanding of canonical analysis.

Writers in multivariate statistics acknowledge that canonical results can be extremely difficult to interpret, but they have been more inclined to explain the mathematical nature of the technique and less interested in providing guidance for interpretation. Tatsuoka (1971), for example, considers it quite natural that seemingly nonsense results do not hamper the potential value of canonical analysis. It only implies that the mathematical formulation may not be susceptible to 'meaningful verbal descriptions of our intuitive everyday concepts'.

Canonical analysis is not as rigid an approach to data analysis as its mathematics and typical application indicate. In fact, much of the confusion and misunderstanding may stem from the conception of canonical analysis as a single technique. Multiple regression, MANOVA and ANOVA, and multiple discriminant analysis can all be shown to be special cases of canonical analysis. Principal components analysis is also in the inner family circle. The difference is that in canonical analysis variates are extracted so as to maximally correlate, whereas in principal components variates are constructed from one set of variables so as to retain as much variance as possible. In both cases we obtain composite variables consisting of linear weighted averages of the observed original variables.

Consequently, canonical analysis can be depicted as consisting of several inter-related techniques. In this study, we will view canonical analysis as an approach to, rather than as a technique of, data analysis. Within this approach we will explore several techniques in an attempt to compose coherent methodologies for canonical analysis. In education and psychological research it is not uncommon to use techniques such as analysis of variance (Pruzek, 1971) and discriminant analysis (Maxwell, 1961) within the context of canonical correlations. Here we will discusss canonical analysis as: (a) a tool for examining covariation among variables (canonical correlaton analysis); (b) a device for factor identification and interpretation (canonical variate analysis); (c) a regression method with several dependent variables (canonical regresson). Based on this structure, we will present a framework that can be useful in tackling many of the problematical issues in canonical analysis.

Canonical correlation analysis

Canonical correlation analysis, as defined here, applies to the examination of the overall significance and magnitude of relationships between two sets of variables. The canonical correlation is symmetric and there is no causation implied. The objectives of canonical correlation analysis are to determine the complexity of the relationship, and to provide information about the overall nature of that relationship.

Canonical correlation may be expressed as:

$$\begin{array}{ll} Y_1 = w_{y11}y_1 + \ldots + w_{y1n}y_n & X_1 = w_{x11}x_1 + \ldots + w_{x1m}x_m \\ \vdots & \vdots \\ Y_d = w_{yd1}y_1 + \ldots + w_{ydn}y_n & X_d = w_{xd1}x_1 + \ldots + w_{xdm}x_m \end{array} \qquad (1\text{–}1)$$

Y = Standardized canonical variates for variables y_1 to y_n
X = Standardized canonical variates for variables x_1 to x_m
w_y = Canonical weights in the Y-variates
w_x = Canonical weights in the X-variates
x = Standardized variables of the X-set
y = Standardized variables of the Y-set
d = The number of canonical correlations

The complexity of the relationship is reflected in the number of canonical correlations (d). The first canonical correlation is, by definition, the largest and hence represents the most substantial relationship; the second one is the second largest and so forth. The decision on when to stop extracting variate pairs is, in the final analysis, up to the subjective judgment of the researcher. One may set a criterion for the size of the canonical correlation, below which the remaining covariation is ignored; similarly, one may choose to ignore a variate that accounts for less than a predetermined percentage of the variance in those observed variables of which it is composed; one may use various statistical tests; or one may choose to rely on the proportion of redundant variance associated with a given canonical relationship.

These ways to determine the number of relevant dimensions are not mutually exclusive. Instead they can often be used in a complementary fashion. Even though one may demote the import of statistical significance, there is seldom a good reason for interpreting relationships that are below a reasonable statistical significance.

A commonly used test for the statistical significance of the canonical correlations is Bartlett's (1941) chi-square approximation of Wilk's Lambda. The null hypothesis states that there is no residual linear association between the sets following the extraction of preceding variates. That is, according to the null hypothesis there is no more than k canonical correlations. Normally, the testing procedure starts with $k=0$ and if the hypothesis is rejected, the value of k is increased by one and the test repeated until the hypothesis can no longer be rejected.

Since canonical correlations show relations between composites of variables and not direct associations between observed variables the statistical significance may have little *practical significance*.

Another method to determine the number of canonical correlatons is to look at the proportion of redundant variance (Stewart & Love, 1968) associated with a given relationship. The squared k : th canonical correlation ($R^2_{c\,k}$) multiplied by the average squared product moment correlation ($\bar{r}^2_{Y_K \cdot y_j}$) between the canonical variate Y_k and its corresponding original variables y_1 to y_n, divided by the total proportion of the intersection (redundancy) between the variable sets, gives the proportion of total redundancy (V_k) in the Y-set (given the X-set) that is associated with variate k.

$$\bar{R}^2_{(y/x)} = R^2_{ck}\left[\sum_{j=1}^{n}\frac{(r^2_{Y_K \cdot y_j})}{n}\right] \qquad (1\text{–}2)$$

$$V_{k_{(y\,x)}} = \frac{\bar{R}^2_{(y\,x)}}{\sum_{i=1}^{d}\bar{R}^2_{(y\,x)_i}} \qquad (1\text{–}3)$$

where n is the number of variables in the Y-set and d is the number of canonical relations. We can also compute the proportion of total redundancy in the X-set, given the Y-set, by using the average squared correlation between the variate X_k and its corresponding variables x_1 to x_m, multiplied by the same squared canonical correlation R^2_{ck}.

An illustration

A canonical correlation applied to the simultaneous analysis of a Y-set, consisting of eight variables, and its association with an X-set consisting of 14 variables, produced the following results.

In Table 1, there are three statistically significant canonical relations, two beyond the .001 level and a third beyond the .05 level. Thus, the following of the criterion that the relationships should be significantly different from zero implies that these three canonical correlations are deemed relevant and therefore subject to further analysis.

The measures of redundancy provide a somewhat different picture. The redundancy in the Y-set, given the X-set, is .26 for the first canonical correlation, .07 for the next, and only .03 for the third. The contribution of the third variate is a mere 8% of the total redundancy in the Y-set. As for redundancy in the X-set, given the Y-set, the third dimension accounts for a redundancy of .02 which is equivalent to a contribution to overall redundancy of 8%. So, in comparison with the proportion of total redundancy associated with the first canonical root (which is around 70%), and also relative to the second root (which has a proportion of redundancy of around 20%), the contribution of the third is meagre. Consequently, despite a statistically significant relationship, there is a strong case for ignoring the third canonical correlation in the interpretation of the results. As to the variance of the observed variables that is retained by the respective variates, the canonical loadings and the communalities will have to be inspected. We will return to this issue in the following section.

In canonical correlation we are interested in the *overall* association between sets of variables or in the *non-complex relationship* between observed variables. Since the variates are left uninterpreted, this type of analysis is less complicated than canonical regression or canonical variate analysis. Through the correlation between the uninterpreted variates, the relationships between the observed variables in the sets are assessed. In the first canonical correlation in Table 1, variables 04 and 08 are chiefly related to variables 13 and 16, while several variables in the Y-set do not exhibit strong association with the X-variate, and most variables in the X-set show weak relationships with the corresponding variables of the other set.

On the other hand, in the second correlation we see that several variables are relatively strongly related. In the Y-set, variables 04 and 08

Table 1 Canonical results

Canonical correlation (R_c)	.85	.72	.58
Canonical root (R_c^2)	.71	.51	.34
Significance	$p<.001$	$p<.001$	$p=.016$
Redundancy ($\bar{R}^2_{(y\ x)}$)	.26	.07	.03
Proportion of redundancy ($V_{(y\ x)}$)	.73	.20	.08
Redundancy ($\bar{R}^2_{(x\ y)}$)	.17	.05	.02
Proportion of redundancy ($V_{(x\ y)}$)	.71	.21	.08
Y-set	*Standardized weights*		
var 01	.14	−.38	−.65
var 02	−.02	−.19	.85
var 03	.07	−.41	−.08
var 04	.43	−.38	.01
var 05	.16	−.14	−.72
var 06	.00	−.02	.28
var 07	.22	.44	−.01
var 08	.43	.61	.34
X-set			
var 09	.06	−.31	.08
var 10	.08	−.30	.33
var 11	.02	.12	−.08
var 12	.11	−.07	.49
var 13	.34	−.63	.27
var 14	.17	−.17	−.88
var 15	.24	.46	.64
var 16	.28	.04	.23
var 17	.08	.21	.13
var 18	.00	−.12	.11
var 19	.25	−.03	−.14
var 20	−.04	.28	−.08
var 21	.09	.19	−.62
var 22	−.10	.18	.04

are not dominant to the same extent as in the first dimension, a fact which seems to make the second variate correlated to more variables in the *X*-set. There is no doubt that variable 13 is the one variable in the *X*-set that is more closely associated with the variates of the *Y*-set, and thus with most of the variables in the *Y*-set. Similarly, variables 04, 07 and 08 are closely related to most variables in the *X*-set.

It is a mistake to interpret pairs of variable associations as if they were independent of each other. The fact that the variate pairs are statistically unrelated does not mean that they are independent from an interpretation point of view. On the contrary, each variable relationship has to be considered simultaneously in all variates. That is, the *complexity* of the variable relationship has to be explored if the association is to be accurately assessed. Consider the following example from our illustration.

In the first canonical correlation we have positive relations between the major variables, but in the second, variables 07 and 08 which are significant in the first correlation, show a positive association with their composite, while the major variable coefficient 13 is strongly negatively related to its corresponding variate. So, while we may find positive relations between two or more variables in one canonical correlation, we may discover the opposite to be true in the next correlation; something that nullifies the relationship if it is to be described as a one-dimensional association.

Consider the relationship between variables 08 and 13. These two variables have a strong positive relationship in the first canonical correlation and a negative one in the second. In order to explain the nature of this relationship adequately, one-dimensional analysis does not suffice. Just as ordinary product moment correlation restricts analysis to one-dimensional relationships, canonical correlation analysis does the same if it is not extended to include variate analysis as well. That is, when the complexity of a variable relationship exceeds one, we cannot focus on individual variables only, but must also consider the structure of the composite, unobserved variables. Without reference to what the variates represent it is difficult to describe conflicting variable relationships. If more than one canonical correlation is allowed to enter the analysis, we deal with several dimensions of relationships. In cases where the directionality of variable associations differs between variate pairs, the dimensions have to be interpreted before one can turn to the examination of those associations. Thus, we are talking about two aspects of canonical dimensions. One is the problem of determining the number of *canonical correlations*; the other is the dimensionality of *variable relationships*.

Before discussing the interpretation of canonical dimensions where the complexity of variable relationships exceeds one, it should be pointed out that there is at least one alternative to the weight statistic in canonical correlation. Cross-correlations between the variate Y and the original variables x_1 to x_m are bivariate but more direct measures of the between-set associations. While weights indicate the individual contribution of each variable x to the variance of the composite variable X, cross-correlations reflect the variance shared by a composite Y and each individual variable x, without simultaneously considering the influence of the other x-variables. Consequently, cross-correlation may be particularly useful when there is high multicollinearity.

Canonical variate analysis

Canonical variate analysis differs from canonical correlation analysis in much the same way as factor analysis differs from simple correlation analysis. To factor analyze in the most general sense means to express a variable as linear combinations of other variables. If 'Canonical Factor analysis' had not been coined by Rao (1955) as a method of factoring, it would have been an appropriate label for the type of analysis we will now discuss.

Instead of moving directly to the examination of covariation between variables, canonical variate analysis begins with focusing on the within-structure of the variates. The objective of canonical variate analysis is to identify and, ultimately, label relevant dimensions in a multivariate domain, so that the original number of variables is reduced to a few meaningful constructs. This is a very different form of analysis from canonical correlation. In lieu of assessing the covariation between observed variables via the correlation of their composites, or through cross-correlation, the unobserved composites are examined via their direct relationship with the observed within-set variables. The determination of dimensionality, ie how many canonical correlations should be retained, may follow any of the procedures mentioned in canonical correlation analysis.

Because the purpose of variate analysis is different from that of canonical correlation, the statistics for interpreting the results are not identical either. In applications, however, canonical weights have been used both to examine covariation of observed variables and to identify the unobserved constructs. This is true for canonical analysis in marketing (Baumgarten & Ring, 1971; Kernan, 1968; Sparks & Tucker, 1971; Worthing *et al*, 1971) and also in other behavioural sciences (Darlington *et al*, 1973). But the heavy reliance on weights has not been completely unchallanged. Recent articles in the marketing literature (Alpert & Peterson, 1972; Lambert & Durand, 1975) discuss some pitfalls of canonical analysis by the indiscriminatory use of weights as a basis for variate interpretation. Chiefly on empirical grounds, the validity of the weight statistic has been questioned. Meredith (1964) states flatly that when there is even moderate multicollinearity within the sets, the possibility of interpreting canonical variates from variable weights is practically nil.

Canonical weights are equivalent to beta weights in regression. Although beta weights are not without ambiquity, they are usually interpreted as the independent contribution of each explanatory variable to the variance of a criterion variable. By analogy, the canonical weights reveal the independent contributions of each variable to the variance of the within-set composite variable. This variable is not, as in regression, an observed phenomenon which is operationally defined through its measurement. Instead, it is subject to interpretation following the canonical solution since it is undefined prior to the analysis. Thus, it is difficult to find a rationale for using weights in canonical variate analysis, for this type of analysis resembles factor analysis more than it does regression analysis. Rather than relying on the independent variable contributions to the variances of the canonical composites to identify the underlying constructs, the focus of variate analysis is on the *structure of the composites* as manifested by their product moment correlations with the observed variables. Akin to factor analysis, these correlations are called loadings—canonical loadings—reflecting the degree to which a variable is represented by a canonical variate. In canonical variate analysis the observed variables can be written:

$$z_{ij} = Y_{i1}(r_{y_j \cdot Y_1}) + \ldots + Y_{id}(r_{y_j \cdot Y_d}) + e_{ij} \quad (1\text{–}4)$$

where z_{ij} is the standardized value of variable j for individual i, and e_{ij} is the residual variance. In Table 2, which is based on the same data as Table 1, we find the canonical loadings for the Y set of the first two canonical relations.

Table 2 Canonical loadings and communalities

	$r_{Y_1 \cdot y_j}$	$r_{Y_2 \cdot y_j}$	*Communality*
var 01	.48	−.41	.40
var 02	.29	−.46	.30
var 03	.60	−.41	.53
var 04	.71	−.46	.72
var 05	.52	−.07	.28
var 06	.54	−.13	.31
var 07	.71	.41	.67
var 08	.81	.39	.81
Mean squared loading and average communality	.36	.14	.50

Although weights and loadings produce a rather congruous overall picture, variables 05 and 06 in the first dimension are strongly associated with the composite variable according to loadings. This is not the case if weights are used for interpretation. In the second canonical correlation these two variables are insignificant, but instead a minor variable 02 (according to weights) becomes a major one.

As in factor analysis, the sum of squared loadings divided by the number of variables is a measure of how well the composite variables retain the variance of the observed variables. The redundancy index (1-2) is based on this measure and the size of the canonical correlation coefficient. Likewise, it is often useful, though almost never done, to compute communalities in canonical variate analysis. Communalities show the percentage of variance that is summarized by the canonical composites. Together, the composites in Table 2 retain 50% of the variance in the data.

Because canonical variate analysis is very close to factor analysis—indeed it is a type of factor analysis—there is no reason why the same interpretative devices could not be used. Should the canonical variates be difficult to comprehend in terms of general factors, the loadings can be rotated.

The possibility of rotating canonical variates has not been fully explored, however. In view of the often delicate task of interpretation, it would seem that rotation is worth further research. One may, for example, rotate to maximize the number of high or low loadings, or to minimize the number of variates with which a variable is associated. Of course, canonical variate analysis with rotation does not, unlike ordinary canonical correlation, produce a unique solution. Different rotation procedures may reveal different variate structures. These structures were always present in the data, but could perhaps not have been discovered without rotation. According to Darlington *et al* (1973) canonical variates may be rotated without regard to their corresponding variate pairs. But this would mean abandoning the idea of analyzing the relationships *between* the sets of variables. A more useful approach would probably involve a simultaneous rotation of the sets, so that the original properties of the canonical solution (ie the sum of squared canonical correlations) are retained.

Canonical regression analysis

Thus far, we have discussed canonical analysis without partitioning the data matrix into explanatory and criterion sets. Rotation of canonical solutions may also be useful in the analysis of dependence, where the criterion canonical variates are interpreted as factors.

Canonical regression analysis differs from both canonical correlation and canonical variate analysis. It applies to the same situations as ordinary regression with the exception that the dependent variable is multidimensional. In both cases the independent variables consist of observed phenomenona which, through simultaneous analysis, explain or predict the dependent variable. In canonical regression, the dependent variable is an index composed of a linear combination of observed dependent variables. Depending on the number of relevant dimensions necessary to adequately describe the relationships, there may be more than one such index. These indices cannot be interpreted *a priori*. They are identified during the course of analysis. The problem of comprehending the dependent variables in canonical regression is identical to interpreting the variates in canonical variate analysis.

Once the multivariate dependent variables have been interpreted and labelled, the analysis proceeds as in ordinary multiple regression: each criterion construct is regressed on the observed explanatory variables.

$$Y_1 = w_{y11}y_1 + \ldots + w_{y1n}y_n = (w_{x11} \,.\, R_{c1})x_1 + \ldots + (w_{x1m} \,.\, R_{c1})x_m + e \quad (1\text{–}5)$$

The standardized regression coefficients are proportional to the standardized canonical weights. Each canonical correlation weight is multiplied by a constant—the canonical correlation coefficient (R_c) of that dimension. Since the dependent construct Y is a standardized variable, the beta coefficients are equal to the unstandardized regression weights multiplied by the standard deviation of the observed variable. R^2 is of course identical to the canonical root (eigenvalue).

Canonical regression falls in between canonical variate analysis and canonical correlation analysis. The interpretation of dependent variable structure is based on loadings (1–4), and the assessment of individual variable contribution to the variance of the dependent construct is based on the relative size of the weights.

The transformation of canonical analysis into a regression has considerable practical advantages. Not only is regression more well-known and better understood, but it is also routinely accompanied by a larger set of potentially helpful statistics and extensions that are not found in standard computer packages for canonical analysis. It might, for example, be very useful to inspect each individual variable contribution to changes in R^2, as well as the standard error of regression coefficients. Various stepwise methods may also be used.

Explained variance in canonical regression

If a regression program with the canonical composites as dependent variables is used, one must keep in mind that the measures of standard error and R^2 pertain to the unobserved canonical variates. Whether R^2 should be used as a measure of explanatory power or not depends on how well the criterion constructs reflect the phenomenon under study. It has been argued by several (Alpert & Peterson, 1972; Darlington *et al*, 1973; Lambert & Durand, 1975; Stewart & Love, 1968) that the canonical root is a highly inflated measure of explained variance, because the canonical solution operates so as to find optimal weights for the observed variables in order to maximize the correlation between the composites, and does not pay any attention to the loadings. That is, the squared canonical correlation reflects the explained variance of two maximally correlated vectors. Naturally, if one is interested in the explanatory power of a set of variables on the observed individual dependent variables, and not in the explanation of the constructed dependent variables, this estimate will be overly optimistic.

Stewart and Love's (1968) redundancy index (1-2) has been proposed as an estimate of explained variance that takes the observed variables into account. This index is the mean squared loading multiplied by the corresponding canonical root summed over the canonical dimensions. Using the first two variates, we note that 33%* of the variance in the *Y*-set is accounted for by the variance in the *X*-set.

This is considerably lower than the measure of shared variance between the *composites*.

Since the redundancy index is computed by multiplying the mean squared loadings of a canonical vector correlation of the corresponding vector

$$\bar{r}^2_{Y_K \cdot y_j} \cdot \bar{R}^2_{ck} = \bar{R}^2_{(y/x)} \tag{1–6}$$

$$\text{where } \bar{r}^2_{Y_k \cdot y_j}, \bar{R}^2_{ck} \leq 1$$

it follows that $\bar{R}^2_{(y/x)} \leq R^2_{ck}$

and in most practical situations. $\bar{R}^2_{(y/x)}$ will be much lower than R^2_{ck}. Even though the redundancy index has some interesting features, such as being non-symmetric, it is nevertheless a rather crude summary statistic of the average similarity between two sets of variables. There may be cases where this statistic can be misleading. If, for example, a composite retains a great deal of the variance in the observed variables, but is poorly explained by a majority of the variables in the other set, only a few of the observed variables would determine the structure and interpretation of the composites, and a single measure of average associations makes little sense.

As yet, there is no single 'best' measure of explained variance in the observed dependent variables in canonical regression. A good deal can, however, be learned by inspecting communalities, mean squared loadings, canonical roots, the redundancy index and individual variable effect on R^2. One may also compare these to simple correlations and to the multiple correlation coefficients when the observed dependent variables are used in separate regressions.

*$(.36 \times .71) + (.14 \times .51) = .33$

Any attempt to account for the omitted variance from the original variables is bound to be extremely problematical. Actually, one may ask if it is really worthwhile or very useful to try to do this in all situations. Is it not possible that the unobserved, composite variables may better portray the phenomenon under study than the observed variables? The decision on whether to assess explained variance on R^2's and canonical roots, or on redundancy indices and simple correlations, depends on the confidence one has in the consructed variables: to what extent do they accurately reflect the phenomenon under study?

Loadings and communalities show how well the observed variables are represented by the composites: if the structure of the canonical variates is meaningful and if the variates account for a large proportion of the variance in the original data, the canonical root may be interpreted as R^2 in ordinary multiple regression. Hence, loadings and communalites are internal validation indices for canonical variates.

Confidence in canonical constructs could also, and often more effectively, be obtained (or lost) through external indices. If, for example, a variate is labelled 'propensity to act' and proves to be a better correlate to that action than any of the original variables, the variate is the superior criterion variable.

Should quantitative external indices be difficult to find, there are other ways to examine the validity of canonical constructs. For example, Fornell (1976) compared non-quantitative case descriptions of respondents with their scores on the composite canonical variables. To avoid unconscious bias, it is important that such case studies are conducted independently and without knowledge of the canonical results.

Summary and conclusions

It has been the objective of this article to provide a framework for the application of canonical analysis. In particular it was a concern to show the flexibility of canonical analysis and its wide applicability for different types of data analysis. The viewing of the method from various, and somewhat different, analytical perspectives demonstrated that the question of weights versus loadings is essentially a logical one.

1 In canonical correlation analysis *weights* or *cross-correlations* are used to examine variable relationships.

2 In canonical variate analysis the *loadings* are used to identify 'meaningful' constructs from the variate structure.

3 In canonical regression analysis both *weights* and *loadings* are used:

loadings for the comprehension of variate structure in the criterion variables and weights to estimate the regression for predictor variables.

Canonical correlation analysis is the simplest and the most limited type of analysis. It cannot fully handle multivariate relationships between sets of variables. Whenever we deal with several dimensions, their relationships are very difficult to describe without an understanding of what the dimensions represent. Canonical variate analysis is designed to help such understanding. It is a form of external factor analysis and, as such, the factor structure (canonical loadings) is used for interpretation. As in factor analysis, the loadings may be rotated. In canonical regression the weights are used for estimation. Naturally, the usefulness of canonical weights can be questioned on the same grounds as beta weights in regression.*

The concept of explained variance poses a special problem in canonical analysis. Since the (significant) canonical variates rarely retain all the original variance of the observed variables, there is a question of whether or not this should be taken into account by the estimate of explained variance. If it is ignored, it might be argued that the estimate (canonical root) is misleading and inflated. On the other hand, one may choose to explain the variance of the composites on the grounds that omitted variance was error variance and that the composites thus reflect the object under study more accurately. Then, of course, it is perfectly rational to use the canonical root in the same way as R^2 in regression.

Judging from the literature, researchers seldom realize that there are several avenues to canonical analysis. Weights and canonical roots are used without regard to the objective and type of analysis. In those rare instances when there has actually been a choice between weights and loadings, the decision has been dictated by empirical considerations. While the importance of such things as multicollinearity, sample size, standard errors and stability of estimates should not be demoted, there is a significant theoretical dimension that ought to be considered as well.

*If all the variables that affect the criterion variable are either included or uncorrelated with those that are included, and if the direction of causality and the functional form of the equation are correctly specified, beta weights are the superior estimates of the true regression (Darlington, 1968).

References

ALPERT, MARK I (1971) 'A canonical analysis of personality and the determinants of automobile choice', *Combined Proceedings*. Chicago: American Marketing Association, pp 312–6.

ALPERT, MARK I (1972) 'Personality and the determinants of product choice', *Journal of Marketing Research*, **9**, 1, pp 89–92.

ALPERT, MARK I and PETERSON, ROBERT A (1972) 'On the interpretation of canonical analysis', *Journal of Marketing Research*, **9,** pp 187–92.
BARTLETT, M S (1941) 'The statistical significance of canonical correlations', *Biometrika*, **32,** pp 29–38.
BAUMGARTEN, STEVEN A and RING, L WINSTON (1971) 'An evaluation of media readership constructs and audience profiles by use of canonical correlation analysis', *Combined Proceedings*, Chicago: American Marketing Association, pp 584–8.
DARLINGTON, RICHARD B (1968) 'Multiple regression in psychological research and practice', *Psychological Bulletin*, **69,** 3, pp 161–82.
DARLINGTON, RICHARD B; WEINBERG, SHARON L and WALBERG, HERBERT J (1973) 'Canonical variate analysis and related techniques', *Review of Educational Research*, **43,** 4, pp 433–54.
FORNELL, CLAES (1976) *Consumer Input for Marketing Decisions: A Study of Corporate Departments for Consumer Affairs*. New York: Praeger.
FORNELL, CLAES. 'Problems in the interpretation of canonical analysis: The case of power in distributive channels', *Journal of Marketing Research*, Forthcoming.
GREEN, PAUL, E; HALBERT, MICHAEL H and ROBINSON, PATRICK J (1966) 'Canonical analysis: An exposition and illustrative application', *Journal of Marketing Research*, **3,** 1, pp 32–9.
GREEN, PAUL E and TULL, DONALD S (1975) *Research for Marketing Decisions*, New Jersey: Prentice-Hall.
KERNAN, JEROME B (1968) 'Choice criteria, decision behaviour and personality', *Journal of Marketing Research*, **5,** 2, pp 155–65.
LAMBERT, ZARREL V and DURAND, RICHARD M (1975) 'Some precautions in using canonical analysis', *Journal of Marketing Research*, **12,** 4, pp 468–75.
MAXWELL, A E (1961) 'Canonical variate analysis when the variables are dichotomous', *Educational and Psychological Measurement*, **XXI,** 2, pp 259–71.
MEREDITH, WILLIAM, (1964) 'Canonical correlations with fallible data', *Psychometrika*, **29,** pp 55–6.
PRUZEK, ROBERT M (1971) 'Methods and problems in the analysis of multivariate data', *Review of Educational Research*, **41,** pp 163–90.
RAO, C RADHAKRISHNA (1955) 'Estimation and tests of significance in factor analysis', *Psychometrika*, **20,** pp 93–111.
SPARKS, DAVID L and TUCKER, W T (1971) 'A multivariate analysis of personality and product use', *Journal of Marketing Research*, **8,** 1, 67–70.
STEWART, DOUGLAS and LOVE, WILLIAM (1968) 'A general canonical correlation index', *Psychological Bulletin*, **70,** 3, pp 160–63.
TATSUOKA, MAURICE M (1971) *Multivariate Analysis: Techniques for Educational and Psychological Research*, New York: John Wiley & Sons.
WORTHING, PARKER M; VENKATESAN, M and SMITH, STEVE (1971) 'A modified approach to the exploration of personality and product use', *Combined Proceedings*, Chicago: American Marketing Association, pp 363–7.

PETER DOYLE and IAN FENWICK*

AID is commonly misused and misinterpreted. A complete application of the methodology illustrates the nature of the inevitable problems of the technique and the necessity of validation procedures.

The Pitfalls of AID Analysis

The Automatic Interaction Detector (AID), proposed formally by Morgan and Sonquist [9] in 1964, has become widely used in the analysis of survey data. The purpose of this study is to evaluate the use of this technique. Our investigations suggest that, as prevalently employed and interpreted, AID is both misleading and unreliable to an unexpected degree. Further, even when used correctly at a preliminary stage of data analysis it is subject to considerable bias and its use without validation tests can never be justified. In this article a more critical use of AID and similar programs is encouraged.

THE DATA ANALYZED

The analysis is based upon a 1972 study of the Sunday reading habits of a representative sample of over 2000 adults in the United Kingdom. In personal interviews, respondents provided information about media usage, attitudes, and a large number of socioeconomic characteristics. This article relates to one aspect of media usage—time spent reading newspapers. Heavy readers are important to publishers and advertisers because such readers have a higher probability of seeing an advertisement. They are also likely to have a stronger commitment to the vehicle, thus reading time may indicate the degree to which editorial content influences the effectiveness of an advertisement [5]. A goal of the research reported here was to determine the characteristics of these readers.

ALTERNATIVE ANALYSIS METHODS

Formally our problem relates to studying a relationship of the form:

$$y = f(x_1, \dots x_n) + e \qquad (1)$$

where y is readership time; $x_1, \dots x_n$ are the predictors or correlates of y, and e is an error term. A good model is a formulation of (1) which includes the most significant correlates and combines the variables in an accurate structural form. Prior knowledge or theory will usually suggest an approach to selecting the variables, but in general, the functional form; nonlinear effects and interactions among the independent variables will be more difficult [9]. An incorrectly specified model will lead to a greater unexplained variance, and bias the estimates of the effects of the predictors.

Nonlinearities can usually be identified through straightforward graphical procedures or transformations. Interactions have presented a more complex problem. An interaction exists where the effects of one predictor depend upon the value of another. For instance, education may affect time spent reading among men but not among women. Graphically this is represented by the two slopes in Figure 1. If this interaction is ignored, the effect of education will be underestimated. Morgan and Sonquist [9, 11, 12] have shown that such interactions are common in social research.

The advantage of *cross-classification* tables is that such interactions can be isolated [10]. This feature plus their general simplicity have made them the most widely used method of presenting the results of a survey analysis. The main problem with cross-classification tables is that it is difficult to extend the analysis beyond two predictors: the analysis becomes too cumbersome and the sample is soon segmented into subgroups too small for study [7]. If significant predictors have to be left out, then the model will fail to explain a significant proportion of the variance. If the predictors are correlated, omission of one or more will also lead to biased estimates of the effects of those included.

Regression analysis permits these multiple predic-

*Peter Doyle is Professor of Marketing and Ian Fenwick is Lecturer in Marketing, University of Bradford Management Centre, England. They wish to thank the Surveys Division of the International Publishing Corporation for providing the data on which this study is based.

Reprinted from *Journal of Marketing Research,* 12 (November 1975), 408-13, published by the American Marketing Association.

Figure 1
INTERACTION BETWEEN EDUCATION AND SEX IN PREDICTING SUNDAY READING

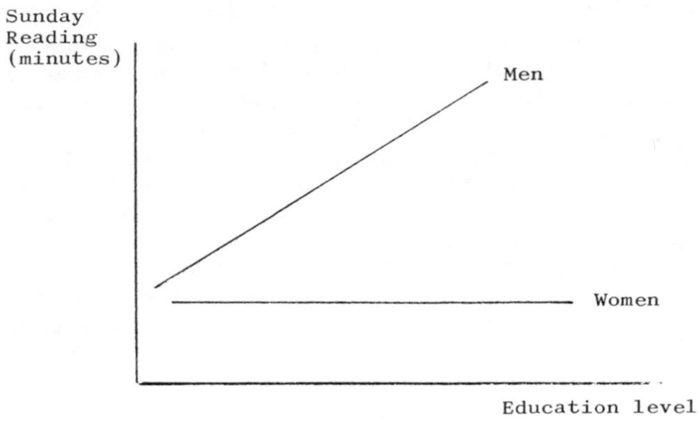

tors to be handled and their significance levels and partial contributions to be estimated. However, this gain is made at the expense of more restrictions as to the form of the model. Frequently, this means assuming that the effects of the independent variables are linear and additive. While nonlinearities and interactions can be estimated, it is necessary that these be specified a priori. A second problem, persuasively argued by Bass, Tigert, and Lonsdale [4], is that regression analysis is commonly unsuitable as a technique for predicting behavior. In general one is interested in identifying groups with significant differences in behavior. Regression analysis, however, uses the individual rather than the group as the unit of observation, and within-group rather than between-group variation as the criterion for fitting the model. Consequently, regression coefficients may not reflect important differences between grouped data.

Assael [3] and others offer AID as a method of overcoming these problems. It permits multiple predictors to be handled in the explanation of group behavior, and at the same time avoids restrictive assumptions about the structure of the model.

THE AID TECHNIQUE

The comparisons of AID with cross-classification and especially regression analysis [3, 8, 12] have been more misleading than helpful. The objective of AID is not to solve the problem represented by (1), but simply to delineate its structure. Unlike regression analysis, AID provides no reliable information about the relative importance or the statistical significance of the predictors. Its prime function is to search for the nature of the relations between variables—whether they are additive or interactive. As such, it is clearly a *preliminary* to a regression formulation or some similar technique [11].

The basic strategy employed by AID is to divide the total sample into the most homogeneous groupings in terms of the dependent variable. All independent variables are treated as categorical, the user specifying the number of categories and their range for each variable. The algorithm considers each variable in turn as the possible basis for dichotomizing the sample. Thus for each variable that partition is found which maximizes between-group sum of squares:

$$BSS_i = N_1 \bar{Y}_1^2 + N_2 \bar{Y}_2^2 - N_i \bar{Y}_i^2$$

where Y is the dependent variable and subscripts 1 and 2 refer to split subgroups and i to the parent group. The program then splits the sample on that variable affording the largest such between sum of squares.

The two groups so formed become themselves candidates for splitting. The output can conveniently be represented by a tree, each branch bifurcating until terminated by one of three stopping rules: (1) a group becomes so small as to cease to be of interest; (2) a group becomes so homogeneous that further division is unnecessary; (3) there is no possible division that significantly reduces BSS.

Limitations of AID

The intuitive and visual appeal, no doubt, accounts for the popularity of AID, but many applications have failed to recognize some of the severe limitations of AID:

Sample size. Since the group rather than the individual is the unit of analysis, large sample sizes are required. Songuist, Baker, and Morgan [12] advise at least 1000 cases if meaningful results are to be obtained. Even this is an underestimate since search techniques should always be validated. If a split-sample analysis is used, then 2000 cases are required for useful results.

Intercorrelated predictors. Unlike multivariate techniques, AID takes no account of intercorrelated predictors. As is illustrated below, where correlated predictors are present, one of them is likely to be chosen exclusively. Not only will one of the variables have to be chosen "first," but having been chosen, its correlates will be less likely to be selected. Thus order of appearance of variables is no indication of relative importance, and exclusion does not necessarily imply insignificance. This last caveat makes the simple and prevalent interpretation of the AID tree extremely foolhardy.

Skewed variables. If the *dependent* variable is heavily skewed, the program may tend repeatedly to split off small groups. Sonquist [11] reports that skewedness in *predictors* reduces their power to increase BSS making their appearance in the AID tree unlikely. In fact, the effect on BSS is dependent on the direction of skew—if the predictor is skewed toward high values of the dependent variable, BSS can be greatly increased by splits on the skewed variable. However, the program refuses splits generating groups with fewer than, in our case, 25 members. Thus heavily skewed variables tend to be eliminated particularly in the later stages of analysis. In both cases a log or square root transformation can sometimes help.

Noise. Both correlated predictors and noise in the data make it unlikely that the same tree will be obtained from different samples from the same population. Sonquist [11] finds the composition of end groups to be stable even though the order of appearance of variables changes. However, Doyle [6], working with correlated predictors, finds problems of unstable trees. Tree stability can be tested by noting for each split that variable offering the next best BSS, the program can then be re-run forcing this variable to appear. If the resulting trees are unstable, the analyst can either purge his data of intercorrelations by factor analysis, or the overall structure suggested by the set of trees can be incorporated into the final regression equation.

Significance tests. Although early versions of AID give a significance test for splits, they ignore the basic search strategy followed by the algorithm. Sonquist, Baker, and Morgan admit "because of the large number of possible splits examined there is no point asking about statistical significance" [12, p. 10].

Interactions. Despite the explicit goal of identifying structure, AID is found to be insensitive to various forms of interaction. Since AID only examines the immediate effect of a predictor on BSS and not future possible splits, any interactions which are not "one-stage" will not be identified. Thus if $E(Y/X_1 \& X_2) \neq E(Y/\bar{X}_1 \& \bar{X}_2)$ where X_1 denotes presence and $\bar{X}_1$ absence of a characteristic, but $E(Y/X_1) = E(Y/\bar{X}_1)$ and $E(Y/X_2) = E(Y/\bar{X}_2)$, then although X_1 and X_2 interact and affect Y, neither will appear in the AID analysis because they have no individual effect. In the latest versions of AID, (AID-III), a look-ahead option is available which does examine some of these interactions, but this facility greatly increases computer time.

Stopping rules. Because of the problems caused by correlated predictors, the decision concerning the specification of stopping rules becomes important. If the rules lead to an early truncation of the tree, then important variables may not be used. On the other hand, with low stopping rules, there is an increased probability of noise leading to spurious splits.

AID as a Preliminary to Regression Analysis

These problems mean that the use of AID alone in data analysis cannot be justified. Despite the occasional recognition of this fact [7, 11] virtually all previous applications have concentrated on the AID tree alone without proceeding to the regression stage [3, 13], or even used AID *after* stepwise regression analysis [8]. Validation, too, has been the exception rather than the rule. As a preliminary to regression or multiple classification analysis [2], AID serves to identify interactions which can be incorporated into an equation linear in coefficients by the use of dummy variables.

Interactions may be indicated in three ways:

1. The structure of the tree: variables entering one branch and not another give a crude indication of interaction.
2. The profile of means: as illustrated below, for each predictor at each split attempt, the mean value of the dependent variable can be plotted for each predictor category. If the predictor has only additive effects then profiles will be similar, marked divergence from congruence then indicates interactions.
3. The BSS/TSS ratio: the ratio of between to total sum of squares for each predictor at each split attempt shows the proportion of the total variation explained by such a split. Sharp changes in this ratio indicate interactions.

A visual inspection of the tree is therefore inadequate. The regression analysis which incorporates identifiable interactions has three significant uses: (1) variables need not be categorized—their effects may be estimated throughout their range of values and not simply by a dichotomy; (2) multicollinearity, unless severe, can be handled by the estimators; (3) the variables may be assigned importance, either in terms of significance or from the relative size of their effects. None of these results are, of course, possible from AID alone.

ANALYSIS

The dependent variable was the respondent's estimate of minutes spent reading the major popular Sunday papers (i.e., *News of the World, Sunday Mirror, Sunday Express, Sunday People*). The attitudinal data measuring interest in 25 topics covered by the media were factor analyzed to remove extreme multicollinearity. Six factors were found with eigenvalues greater than 1, explaining 65% of the total variance (an underestimate in that the data are strictly ordinal). Table 1 shows the factor interpretations after varimax rotation.

An initial AID run was performed to examine the characteristics of the data and to eliminate variables lacking a useful causal interpretation [11, pp. 191-201]. Low parameter values were used on the algorithm to extract the maximum information. The six factors and six other variables shown in Table 2 were retained for further analysis.

As noted above AID is particularly subject to upward bias due to sampling error and to the nature of the search procedure. Consequently, it is essential to build in a validation procedure. Here the sample was randomly halved to give just over 1000 respondents each for analysis and validation. Figure 2 shows the final tree derived from the analysis sample. The stopping rules were: where group size fell below 100; where

Table 1

FACTOR ANALYSIS OF INTEREST RATINGS

Factor number	*High variable loading*	*Factor interpretation*
F1	Articles on film personalities	People
	Advice and help	
	Stories and gossip	
	Letters	
	Horoscope	
	TV guide	
F2	Local news	News
	UK news	
	Political news	
	International events	
	News comment	
	Exposes	
F3	Ads and shopping news	Home and leisure
	Fashion advice	
	Women's items	
	Furniture and home	
	Holiday advice	
F4	Cars and motoring	Male interests
	Pictures of girls	
	Cartoons	
	News pictures	
F5	Crosswords	Puzzles
	Competitions	
F6	Football	Sport
	Horse-racing	

group variance was below .01% of total variance; or where no split led to BSS of above .001% of total variance.

The heaviest readers are older males, are heavy watchers of ITV, and have strong "male interests." By contrast, younger women who were low ITV viewers and interested in articles about "people" read on average little more than one tenth of the time spent by the heaviest readers. The characteristics of various reading categories can easily be identified.

Table 2

VARIABLES USED IN AID ANALYSIS

Variable	*Description*
Age	14–65+ in 7 categories
Sex	Male, female
Social class	5 categories
	A: Upper middle class (3% of UK adults)
	B: Middle class (9%)
	C1: Lower middle class (22%)
	C2: Skilled working class (31%)
	D: Working class (26%)
	E: Lowest Level (9%)
BBC 1 viewing	Average Sunday viewing (minutes) 0–210+ in 6 categories
BBC 2 viewing	Average Sunday viewing (minutes) 0–94+ in 6 categories
ITV viewing	Average Sunday viewing (minutes) 0–400+ in 6 categories
6 factors	See Table 1, each in 3 categories

Figure 2

CORRELATES OF READERSHIP: THE AID TREE

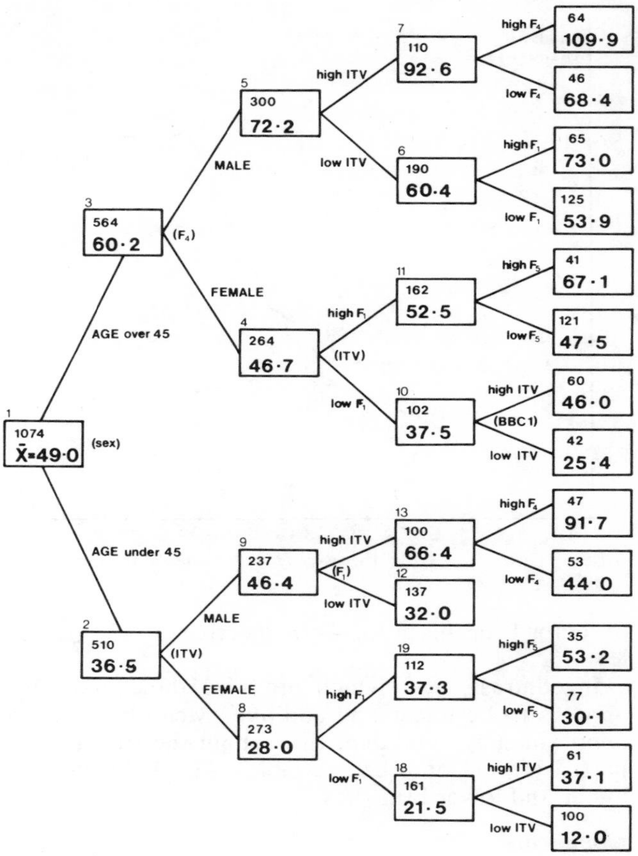

Moving from description to the prime goal of formulating structural relationships, several interactions were identified from the output of the program. Sex, although entering both branches with similar profiles, interacts with those variables following it. Thus for males television viewing is important, whereas it only affects females with low scores on factor 1. Figure 3 shows the profile of mean readership levels against ITV viewing categories for group 4 (females aged 45+) and group 5 (males aged 45+). The divergence in profiles clearly indicates the sex/TV interaction. A more complex interaction is shown in Figure 4 which plots the explanatory power of factor 1 for three routes through the AID tree. The route to group 7 (males aged 45+, with high ITV viewing) shows factor 1 as a relatively unimportant variable. However that to group 6 (males aged 45+, with low ITV viewing) shows a sharp rise in the power of factor 1. Thus factor 1 only acquires significance for males if they are low ITV viewers. The plot for group 4 (females aged 45+), on the other hand, indicates the importance

Figure 3
MEAN PROFILE FOR ITV VIEWING FOR GROUPS 4 AND 5

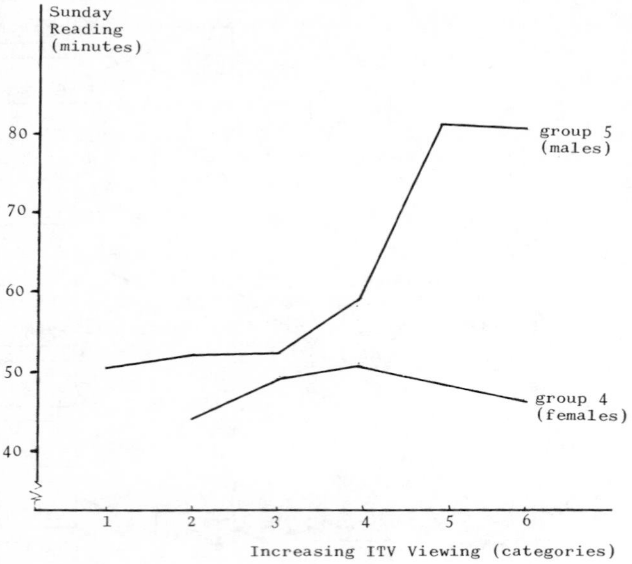

of factor 1 for this group—irrespective of ITV viewing level.

In contrast, age, which provides the initial split, appears to be linear and additive. Mean profiles are approximately congruent throughout the tree and the partial effects of other variables are about equal in upper and lower branches.

Comments

The AID output immediately reveals a number of the difficulties discussed earlier. To illustrate the problem caused by correlated predictors, where a rival variable produced a BSS close to that selected, this variable is shown in parentheses in Figure 2. In many

Figure 4
EXPLANATORY POWER OF FACTOR 1

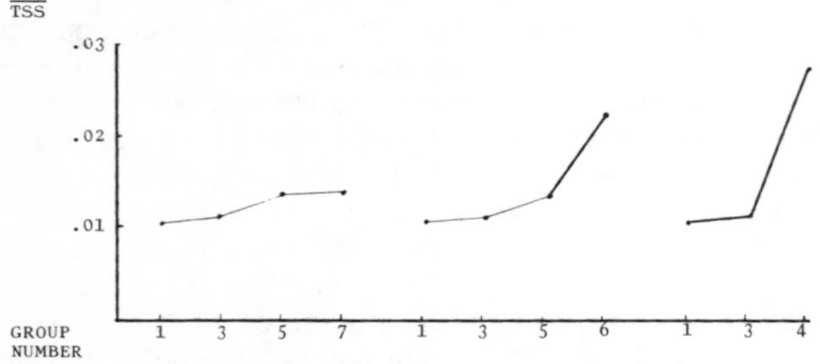

For a description of group composition see Figure 2

cases, rival candidates (BSS within 1% of the selected variable) did exist. For example, F1 was almost chosen in group 9, but finally did not even appear in this branch. The stopping rules exacerbated this problem; several significant variables did not appear at all in the tree.

Another important point concerning interactions which has not previously been recognized is illustrated in the tree. Some interactions turn out to be spurious on distributional grounds. Factor 4, for example—"male interests"—is skewed because only males score highly on it. This results in the effect of the Interaction being underestimated. By contrast, F4 only appears for high ITV viewers within the male branch; this is a genuine rather than a distributional interaction.

Regression Analysis

The regression equation was specified to reflect the structure discovered in the AID analysis. For example the effect of ITV viewing is estimated separately for males (group 5) and for females with a low score on F1 (group 10). As a check on the effectiveness of AID in identifying significant predictors, the effect of F4 was estimated not only for group 7 but also for the rest of the sample, even though the AID analysis made no use of F4 in the latter. Factor F5 was checked in a similar way.

The first equation was fitted to the same data used in the AID analysis:

$$\begin{aligned} y = {} & -18.5 + \underset{(1.0)}{8.5D_5} + \underset{(3.3)}{0.08D_5 * ITV} + \underset{(4.6)}{13.9D_7 * F_4} \\ & + \underset{(3.7)}{11.7D_6 * F_1} + \underset{(1.6)}{5.6(1 - D_5) * F_1} + \underset{(0.4)}{0.01D_{10} * ITV} \\ & + \underset{(3.1)}{7.8D_{11} * F_5} + \underset{(1.1)}{2.2(1 - D_7) * F_4} \\ & + \underset{(1.4)}{3.2(1 - D_{11}) * F_5} + \underset{(8.5)}{6.7 \text{ Age}} \end{aligned}$$

$$\bar{R}^2 = 0.52$$

where $D_i = 1.0$ if respondent is in group i, 0 otherwise. The t-statistics are shown in parentheses. Four out of the six true interactions are significant and contribute to explained variation, and the two "test" interactions are insignificant at the 5 percent level.[1] Overall the equation is not unsatisfactory, accounting for about 50% of the variation in reading time.

VALIDATION

The significance of the regression equation is, however, not an adequate test of the bias and limitations of AID described earlier, all of which lead to

[1] A linear form of the model, ignoring interactions, had an $\bar{R}^2 = 0.21$.

an overestimate of the power of the model. A true test of the predictive power of the model must be based upon validation. One method is to compare the tree from the analysis sample (Figure 2) with that generated from the validation sample. The model fails this test. The new tree looks very different from the original. A different age split occurs and the variable no longer enters in a simple additive form; sex is only used in one branch and there are substantial differences in the structure of the terminal groups. Precise replication is, however, unlikely. Intercorrelated predictors, sampling error, and arbitrary stopping rules all make replication unlikely. A more appropriate test is one of the *predictive* value of the model. This can be performed by using the analysis equation to generate readership levels for the validation sample. This reduced the coefficient of determination by 50% ($\bar{R}^2 = 0.25$)—a reduction much greater than can be attributed to chance (see [1, p. 76]). The search procedure, therefore, greatly overestimates the predictive power of the AID-regression model.

Further insight into the robustness of the interaction terms generated by AID can be obtained by *fitting* the original equation structure to the validation sample:

$$
\begin{aligned}
y = {} & -24.3 + \underset{(1.5)}{16.6D_5} + \underset{(4.6)}{0.14D_5 * \text{ITV}} + \underset{(0.7)}{3.13D_7 * F_4} \\
& + \underset{(4.3)}{16.2D_6 * F_1} + \underset{(2.4)}{10.3(1 - D_5) * F_1} + \underset{(0.7)}{0.02D_{10} * ITV} \\
& + \underset{(2.1)}{6.19D_{11} * F_5} + \underset{(1.7)}{1.6(1 - D_7) * F_4} + \underset{(2.0)}{4.2(1 - D_{11})F_5} \\
& + \underset{(7.3)}{6.9\ \text{Age}}
\end{aligned}
$$

$$\bar{R}^2 = 0.40$$

The coefficients are very different from the analysis sample, although not all these differences are statistically significant. In addition, the two "test" interactions now turn out to be significant. These results confirm that AID leads to upward bias in prediction and that the search procedure tends to generate artificial interaction terms.

CONCLUSIONS

As a widely available technique AID is extraordinarily prone to misuse. The authors are unaware of any previous article in the marketing literature which illustrates the construction of the regression formulation from the AID model and effectively validates the results. Yet without these stages, AID is virtually useless!

Even when used correctly as a simple descriptive device or as a preliminary to regression, AID is still easily misinterpreted. This is caused by two related factors: the inability of the technique to handle correlated predictors and the lack of restrictive assumptions in the model which make its interpretation prone to idiosyncrasies caused by sampling and measurement errors. Little trust therefore can be placed on results which are not validated.

REFERENCES

1. Anderson, T. W. *An Introduction to Multivariate Statistical Analysis.* New York: Wiley, 1958.
2. Andrews, F. M., James N. Morgan, and John A. Sonquist. *Multiple Classification Analysis.* Ann Arbor: Survey Research Center, University of Michigan, 1967.
3. Assael, Henry. "Segmenting Markets by Group Purchasing Behavior: An Application of the AID Technique," *Journal of Marketing Research,* 7 (May 1970), 153-8.
4. Bass, Frank M., Douglas J. Tigert, and Ronald T. Lonsdale. "Market Segmentation: Group Versus Individual Behavior," *Journal of Marketing Research,* 5 (August 1968), 264-70.
5. Brown, Michael, "Print Media Research Objectives and Applications," in Robert M. Worcester, ed., *Consumer Market Research Handbook.* London: McGraw-Hill, 1972, 548-76.
6. Doyle, Peter. "The Use of AID and Similar Search Procedures," *Operational Research Quarterly,* 24 (September 1973), 465-7.
7. Frank, Ronald E., William F. Massy, and Y. Wind. *Market Segmentation.* Englewood Cliffs, N.J.: Prentice Hall, 1972.
8. Heald, Gordon I. "The Application of AID and Multiple Regression Techniques to the Assessment of Store Performance and Site Selection," *Operational Research Quarterly,* 23 (June 1972), 445-54.
9. Morgan, James N. and John A. Sonquist. "Problems in the Analysis of Survey Data and a Proposal," *Journal of the American Statistical Association,* 58 (September 1963), 415-34.
10. Moser, C. A. and G. Kalton. *Survey Methods in Social Investigation.* London: Heinemann, 1971.
11. Sonquist, John A. *Multivariate Model Building.* Ann Arbor: Survey Research Center, University of Michigan, 1970.
12. ———, Elizabeth L. Baker, and James N. Morgan. *Searching for Structure.* Ann Arbor: Survey Research Center, University of Michigan, 1971.
13. Staelin, Richard A. "Another Look at AID," *Journal of Advertising Research,* 11 (October 1971), 23-8.

An Experimental Investigation of Causal Relations Among Cognitions, Affect, and Behavioral Intention

RICHARD J. LUTZ*

The effects of messages designed to change belief and evaluation components of cognitive structure are investigated within the context of the Extended Fishbein Model. Using a general linear model, causal patterns among cognitive and affective response variables are found to support the flow of effects generally hypothesized to operate in such situations.

To date, the several studies in consumer behavior which have examined the so-called Extended Fishbein Model have been characterized by a static, correlational paradigm that allows no investigation of causal patterns among the constructs in the model (Wilson, Mathews and Monoky, 1972; Lutz, 1973; Bonfield, 1974; Harrell and Bennett, 1974; Weddle and Bettman, 1974). One of the more recent of these studies concludes with a call for "further examination of the *BI* model . . . in a laboratory context to establish causal relationships . . ." (Wilson, Mathews and Harvey, 1975, p. 47). The purpose of this paper is to report the results of two laboratory-type experiments designed to investigate causal relationships within the Fishbein Model, thus providing empirical evidence regarding the explanatory power of the model. As is the case with the familiar multi-attribute attitude model, the considerable potential diagnostic virtues of the Extended Fishbein Model remain untapped until it has been demonstrated that *changes* in the model's explanatory (predictor) variables lead to *changes* in the criterion variables (Lutz, 1975a). Only then can the model be used with confidence by policy-makers to effect desired behavioral changes.

* Richard J. Lutz is Assistant Professor of Marketing in the Graduate School of Management, University of California, Los Angeles. He gratefully acknowledges the support of the Procter and Gamble Company in the data collection phase of this study. Appreciation is also expressed to Olli T. Ahtola, Gordon Bechtel, James R. Bettman, Joel B. Cohen, Paul E. Green, Harold H. Kassarjian, Masao Nakanishi, Michael J. Ryan, and Paul R. Winn, who commented on an earlier version of this manuscript.

THE MODEL

The Extended Fishbein Model is essentially a modification of Dulany's theory of propositional control (Dulany, 1968; Fishbein, 1967) and is designed to allow the prediction, explanation, and modification of a specific behavior. In one of its recent forms the model can be represented by the following two equations:[1]

$$Aact = \sum_{i=1}^{n} B_i a_i \qquad (1)$$

$$B \sim BI = W_1(Aact) + W_2\left(\sum_{j=1}^{m} NB_j Mc_j\right) \qquad (2)$$

where B is a specific action or behavior; BI is the individual's intention to perform that action (behavioral intention); $Aact$ is the individual's attitude toward (affect for or against) performing the behavior; B_i is the belief (probability) that performing the behavior will lead to consequence i; a_i is the individual's evaluation of consequence i; n is the total number of consequences salient to the individual with respect to the behavior; NB_j is the individual's perception of the expectations of referent j with respect to the behavior (normative belief); Mc_j is the individual's motivation to comply with referent j's expectations; m is the total number of salient referents; and W_1, W_2 are empirically derived weights.

[1] In their recent book, Fishbein and Ajzen (1975) have introduced a new notation to represent the constructs in the model. As the present study was conducted prior to the publication of that book, the notation used herein is consistent with Fishbein (1967).

Reprinted with permission from *Journal of Consumer Research,* 3 (March 1977), 197-208.

Examination of equation (1) above reveals that the theoretical conceptualization of attitude under the Extended Fishbein Model conforms to a general expectancy-value formulation, in that *Aact* is conceived of as being composed of a person's expectations of the consequences of performing the act, weighted by his evaluation of each of these consequences. In precise congruence with Fishbein's (1963) earlier (A_0) model, *Aact* and a_i are measured on an affective dimension, while B_i is measured on a probability dimension.

Turning now to equation (2), the tilde between *B* and *BI* indicates that behavioral intention is approximately equivalent to overt behavior. To obtain the best possible behavioral prediction through the use of this model, the *BI* measure should be situation specific and should be quite close temporally to the overt behavior. In addition, the behavior must be one over which the individual has a high degree of volitional control.

Unlike most other attitude-behavior models, the Extended Fishbein Model considers other possible explanations for a person's behavior with respect to a given object. In addition to the attitude component, Fishbein includes a normative component which attempts to assess the person's perceptions of how others think he should act in a given situation. These norms can be with respect to any person, group, or even society as a whole, depending on its salience to the individual. Tempering the effects of others' expectations (NB_j) are the person's desires to conform (Mc_j) with these expectations.

The two empirically determined weights in equation (2) are estimated through multiple regression procedures and are used to determine if a particular action is under attitudinal or normative control. This is a crucial distinction, particularly for the policy maker interested in behavior change, because it provides direction for the types of promotional appeals (i.e., attitudinal or normative) which are most likely to be successful.

Beyond its potential usefulness to the policy maker as an aid in strategy formulation, the Extended Fishbein Model also has direct relevance to marketing theory. In studies of advertising effectiveness, for example, the notion of "hierarchy of effects" has generated considerable interest and some controversy (Lavidge and Steiner, 1961; Palda, 1966). More recently, consumer behavior theory has embraced a "decision process" model that incorporates distinct cognitive, evaluative and behavioral stages in a formal representation of the consumer's purchase decision (Engel, Kollat and Blackwell, 1973).

Underlying both the hierarchy of effects and decision process models are assumptions of causal relationships among the constructs in the model. Specifically, it is assumed that certain cognitive elements (e.g., beliefs about a brand) combine in some manner to produce affect for the brand, which in turn leads to behavior with respect to the brand. A similar causal flow is postulated in the Extended Fishbein Model, which, in addition, includes operational definitions of the constructs in the model. Therefore, the Extended Fishbein Model provides a framework for precise empirical testing of some important concepts in the body of current marketing theory.

Recent reviews of research utilizing the Extended Fishbein Model have appeared in both the social psychology (Ajzen and Fishbein, 1973) and the consumer behavior literature (Ryan and Bonfield, 1975). Both reviews conclude that the model offers satisfactory predictive validity; i.e., it is possible to predict behavioral intentions with a relatively high degree of accuracy from a linear combination of the attitudinal and normative components of the model. Further, three recent studies in psychology (Ajzen, 1971; Ajzen and Fishbein, 1972; McArdle, 1972) have shown a reasonable degree of support for the model's ability to predict *changes* in intentions. However, there is presently no evidence for the model's explanatory power in a consumer behavior context.

METHODOLOGICAL ISSUES

To provide support for the explanatory power of the Extended Fishbein Model, it must be empirically demonstrated that a *change* in cognitive structure ($\Sigma B_i a_i$) leads to a *change* in attitude; and that a change in *either* attitude or the normative component leads to a change in intentions. Finally, a change in intentions should be shown to lead to a change in overt behavior. Providing empirical evidence regarding such a process is not an easy matter—several research issues must be confronted before that task can be accomplished.

Response—Response Paradigm

The traditional approach to establishing causal relations between two variables has been experimentation, in which one or more antecedent variables, or stimuli (*S*), are systematically manipulated and the effects upon a response (*R*) variable measured. This traditional *S-R* paradigm has seen considerable use in consumer research. However, an *S-R* approach is not appropriate for examining the validity of the Extended Fishbein Model, which posits a series of relationships among responses—i.e., beliefs, attitude, intention. Rather, a *Response-Response (R-R) paradigm* is dictated for investigation of this model (Dulany, 1968).

Basically an *R-R* paradigm can be thought of as an experiment in which several interrelated dependent variables are measured. However, the main features of the data which are of interest are not cell-to-cell differences in a classic ANOVA sense, but rather the *strengths of the relationships among the dependent variables*. For instance, suppose that a researcher is interested in determining the effects of humor in advertising on sales response. He creates three commercials, with high, moderate and low degrees of humor, runs a test market, and observes sales. If he simply analyzes his data via a one-way ANOVA, then he is using an *S-R* model. The three commercials are designated as stimuli varying in humor, and sales responses are compared across the three ads.

However, within an *R-R* framework, the researcher would view his data differently. First of all, humor would be treated as a *mediating* variable which intervenes between the commercial stimuli and sales response. Since there is likely to be within-cell heterogeneity in subjects' reactions to the humorous appeals, measurement of the *degree of humor perceived by each subject* provides important data. For example, a subject in the high degree of humor condition may not perceive the commercial as humorous and is not induced to buy the product. Assuming that the true underlying relationship between humor and sales is direct and positive, this subject's data would appear in the *S-R* analysis as error variance (i.e., a person in the high humor cell who does not purchase). Yet, when viewed from the *R-R* perspective, this subject fits the pattern perfectly—he did not perceive the commercial to be humorous, and he did not purchase. Thus, one of the primary advantages of an *R-R* paradigm is that "what is error variance in *S-R* relations may become nonerror variance in *R-R* relations" (Dulany, 1968, p. 371). Note that in this example, an *S-R* analysis would still be the appropriate means for determining the humorousness of the various commercials.

Typically, *R-R* experiments are not particularly advantageous unless there is a fairly rich theoretical network of constructs being tested. The hypothetical example discussed above would probably not meet this criterion, as only two variables were under investigation. However, the Extended Fishbein Model does contain a theoretical network of constructs and should, therefore, be examined via an *R-R* paradigm.

Causal Inferences from Correlations

Adoption of an *R-R* paradigm means that correlational measures of the strength of relationships among variables become the basic data of the investigation. However, it is well known that correlation does not imply causation. How, then, may statements be made regarding causal relationships within the Extended Fishbein Model? Recent developments in the analysis of correlational data (e.g., path analysis) make it possible to derive causal inferences from non-experimental

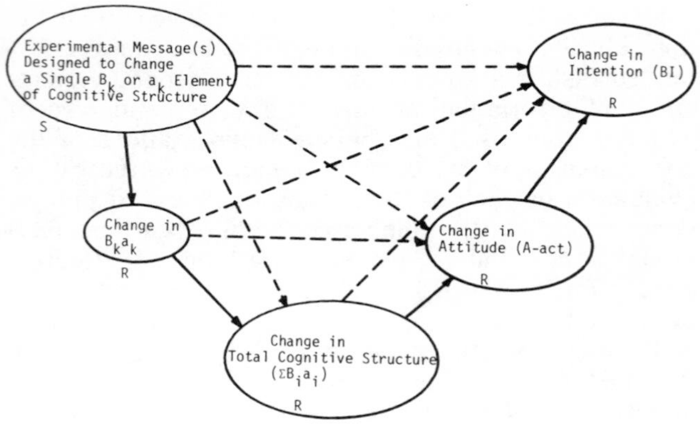

FIGURE 1
Hypothesized Causal Flows Resulting from Belief Change and Evaluation Change Messages

data (Blalock, 1964). These procedures are also quite appropriate for testing *R-R* relations *within an experimental setting*.

In Figure 1 the heavy black arrows indicate the hypothesized causal flow of effects within the Extended Fishbein Model following experimental treatments designed to modify single *belief* (B_k) or *evaluation* (a_k) elements of cognitive structure. The message is seen as a stimulus which produces a response in the form of a change in a single *belief-evaluation compound* ($B_k a_k$). This response, in turn, produces a change in total cognitive structure, and so forth. Thus, a linear chain of effects is postulated, such that each construct has a direct causal impact on the construct immediately following it in the proposed flow, and no direct causal impact on any other variable in the system. The dashed arrows in the Figure illustrate the latter phenomenon. For instance, the experimental messages are expected to have no direct causal impact on $\Sigma B_i a_i$, *Aact*, or *BI*; all the message effects should be manifest in $B_k a_k$ only.[2] By testing for the existence of the relationships represented by both the solid and dashed arrows, a stronger test of the Fishbein Model is obtained.

Specifically, the following two global research hypotheses can be formulated:

H1: Relationships represented by solid arrows in Figure 1 are statistically significant and reasonably strong in terms of variance explained.

H2: Relationships represented by dashed arrows in

---

[2] In Figure 1, the belief-evaluation compound is used as the first hypothesized effect, rather than simply B_k and a_k. The reason for this is the bipolar scaling used to operationalize both B_k and a_k (Bettman, *et al.*, 1975). Since the valence of either element can be reversed by multiplication with the other, it is necessary to perform the multiplication before relating the single cognitive element to subsequent response measures in the model.

TABLE 1

EXPERIMENTAL DESIGN: EXPERIMENT ONE

	Critical Attribute Evaluation (a_k)							
	Positive (Effective in all water temps)				Negative (Costly to use)			
Initial Critical B_k Position (Formation)	Positive ("very high")		Negative ("very low")		Positive ("very high")		Negative ("very low")	
Advocated Critical B_k Position (Change)	Negative ("low")	Control[a]	Positive ("high")	Control[a]	Negative ("low")	Control[a]	Positive ("high")	Control[a]
Hypothesized Sign of $B_k a_k$	−	+	+	−	+	−	−	+
Cell Number	1	2	3	4	5	6	7	8
n	62	62	62	61	61	61	61	61

[a] Control conditions received no additional information regarding B_k.

Figure 1 are near zero when the effects of intervening variables have been removed.

METHOD[3]

Overview

Two experiments were conducted, one of which dealt with changes in B_i elements of cognitive structure, the other with changes in a_i elements. Both experiments utilized the same general format: Subjects were asked to read "prepublication" releases from *Consumer Reports* which were reporting on the merits of a new (actually fictitious) laundry detergent, Brand M.[4] Ratings of the brand on several predetermined salient attributes were the central focus of the articles. Thus, the *CR* articles were used to allow subjects to form beliefs, attitudes and intentions with respect to Brand M.

Following the initial *CR* article, subjects in the experimental (Change) conditions read a page of "Additional Information" which purported to be reporting updated findings that reversed some aspect of the initial article.[5] For example, subjects in one B_i change condition read that while Brand M was previously thought to be "very high" in cost of use, new evidence showed that it was, in fact, "very low" in cost of use. Subjects in control (Formation) conditions received no "Additional Information." In the final stage of the experiments, subjects provided ratings of Brand M corresponding to each of the constructs in the Extended Fishbein Model (except behavior). Thus, although no pretest was employed, changes in the model's constructs could be inferred by comparison of experimental and control groups in a posttest only control group design (Campbell and Stanley, 1963). Specific features of the two experimental designs are now presented.

Design of Experiment 1: B_i Change

Table 1 shows the 2 × 2 × 2 factorial design used in Experiment 1 to investigate the effects of changes in B_i elements of cognitive structure. The first factor, Critical Attribute Evaluation, refers to whether the *CR* article dealt with a positive or negative attribute in its "Additional Information" message designed to change B_k. The positive attribute was "effective in all water temperatures;" the negative attribute was "costly to use." Both were selected on the basis of pilot test results.

The second factor, Initial Critical Belief Position, manipulated the "ratings" of the two critical attributes through messages which stated that Brand M was either "very high" (positive) or "very low" (negative) in the attribute. Characterization of the belief position in terms of "positive" and "negative" was done in recognition of the −3 to +3 scales typically used to operationalize this construct in the Fishbein Model. Ratings of all other attributes—"above average" in cleaning power, "average" in safety of use, and "very low" in pollutant content—were held constant across all conditions.

[3] A complete description of the method employed in this study is available elsewhere (Lutz, 1975a). In the interest of brevity only a summary will be included here. The interested reader is encouraged to consult the earlier study for full details.

[4] The cooperation of Consumers Union in consenting to the use of the *Consumer Reports* name in this research is gratefully acknowledged.

[5] One could argue that beliefs about the detergent were not really "formed" by the initial article and then "changed" by the additional information, but were simply formed after the receipt of both messages. In the absence of some form of cognitive response measurement (Wright, 1973), there can be no direct resolution of this issue. However, since subjects in the control conditions responded quite consistently to the B_i measures, and since at least 2–3 minutes intervened between the first presentation of an attribute and its subsequent reversal for the experimental subjects, the present interpretation will be couched in terms of belief change.

TABLE 2

EXPERIMENTAL DESIGN: EXPERIMENT TWO

Critical B_k Position	Positive (High Sudsiness)			Negative (Low Sudsiness)		
Advocated a_k Position	Positive (suds good)	Control[a]	Negative (suds bad)	Positive (suds good)	Control[a]	Negative (suds bad)
Hypothesized Sign of $B_k a_k$	+	Neutral	−	−	Neutral	+
Cell Number	9	11	10	12	14	13
n	17	10	18	17	9	19

[a] The initial evaluation (a_k) was neutral in all six cells.

The third factor is best thought of as a Formation vs. Change manipulation. The four control, or Formation, groups received no B_k change message. The four experimental, or Change, groups received messages attempting to reverse the "sign" of the critical attribute's likelihood. As shown in the Table, all three factors combined to yield an hypothesized sign of the critical attribute's belief-evaluation compound, $B_k a_k$. For instance, in Cell No. 5, $B_k a_k$ was expected to be positive, based on the algebraic combination of a negative a_k and a negative B_k, which had been reversed from its initial positive position. Translated into what the subject read: "Brand M is very high in cost of use." The additional information then read (in part): "Brand M is very low in cost of use." By comparing the mean of B_k in Cell No. 5 with the B_k mean in Cell No. 6, the effectiveness of the manipulation could be determined. Similar logic applies to the other three pairs of conditions in Table 1.

Since all three factors in the design were expected to interact in determining final $B_k a_k$ ratings provided by subjects, the only significant effect expected from a 2 × 2 × 2 ANOVA was the third order interaction term, with the cell means conforming roughly to the pattern hypothesized in Table 1.

Design of Experiment 2: a_i Change

Table 2 shows the 2 × 3 factorial design used in attempting to create changes in the evaluation (a_k) of the critical attribute. In this experiment, which was designed to investigate the effects of a_i change on the other constructs shown in Figure 1, an initially neutral attribute, sudsiness, was the focus. A neutral attribute was selected for the attempted manipulation in the belief that a more highly polarized attribute evaluation would be difficult to influence. The first factor, Critical Belief (B_k) Position, was designed to manipulate subjects' beliefs about the level of sudsiness in Brand M. Subjects in "Positive" cells read that Brand M was "very high" in sudsiness, while "Negative" cell subjects were informed that it was "very low" in sudsiness.

The second factor, Advocated Evaluation Position, had three levels: "Positive," in which subjects read "Additional Information" to the effect that high sudsiness was a desirable feature in a detergent; "Negative" in which the "Additional Information" condemned high sudsiness; and "Control," in which no "Additional Information" was presented.

The two factors were expected to interact to affect subjects' ratings of the belief-evaluation compound, $B_k a_k$. Hypothesized signs for each cell are shown in Table 2.

Measures

Following the experimental messages, subjects completed a questionnaire measuring all the constructs shown in Equations 1 and 2. First, evaluations (a_i) of nine attributes of laundry detergent were addressed via 7-point scales ranging from "extremely good" (+3) to "extremely bad" (−3). Next, perceptions of the likelihood (B_i) that Brand M possessed each of the nine attributes were measured on 7-point scales ranging from "extremely likely" (+3) to "extremely unlikely" (−3). The nine resultant $B_i a_i$ terms were summed to yield the index of cognitive structure ($\Sigma B_i a_i$).

Next, subjects were asked to estimate the normative influences which would impinge upon their decision to try Brand M. Pretests had shown that the normative factor was not likely to be strong in the decision to purchase a new detergent, but in the interest of completeness and in case of an unanticipated relationship between the experimental treatments and the normative component, it was felt that measures of the normative component should be included in the analysis. Accordingly, normative beliefs (NB_j) were measured for each of the three reference groups (family, friends, neighbors) on scales of the following form:

When Brand M detergent is introduced onto the market in this area,

(+3) (−3)
My family would __:__:__:__:__:__:__ would not expect me to try Brand M.

TABLE 3

RECURSIVE SYSTEM OF EQUATIONS FOR EXPERIMENT ONE

$$B_k a_k = \beta_{11}X_1 + \beta_{12}X_2 + \beta_{13}X_3 + \beta_{14}X_1X_2 + \beta_{15}X_1X_3 + \beta_{16}X_2X_3 + \beta_{17}X_1X_2X_3 + e_1$$

$$\Sigma B_i a_i = \beta_{21}X_1 + \beta_{22}X_2 + \beta_{23}X_3 + \beta_{24}X_1X_2 + \beta_{25}X_1X_3 + \beta_{26}X_2X_3 + \beta_{27}X_1X_2X_3 + \beta_{28}B_k a_k + e_2$$

$$A\text{-}act = \beta_{31}X_1 + \beta_{32}X_2 + \beta_{33}X_3 + \beta_{34}X_1X_2 + \beta_{35}X_1X_3 + \beta_{36}X_2X_3 + \beta_{37}X_1X_2X_3 + \beta_{38}B_k a_k + \beta_{39}\Sigma B_i a_i + e_3$$

$$BI = \beta_{41}X_1 + \beta_{42}X_2 + \beta_{43}X_3 + \beta_{44}X_1X_2 + \beta_{45}X_1X_3 + \beta_{46}X_2X_3 + \beta_{47}X_1X_2X_3 + \beta_{48}B_k a_k + \beta_{49}\Sigma B_i a_i + \beta_{410}A\text{-}act + \beta_{411}\Sigma NB_j Mc_j + e_4$$

Motivation to comply (Mc_j) was then measured on scales of this form:

With respect to my choice of laundry detergent,

(+3) (−3)
I want to __:__:__:__:__:__:__ do not want to do what my family expects me to do.[6]

The three NB_jMc_j terms were summed to yield the normative component measure.

Finally, attitude toward the use of Brand M was represented by the sum of four evaluative items which were included in an 8-item semantic differential, and behavioral intention was measured on three semantic differential scales (likely-unlikely, probable-improbable, possible-impossible), which were summed to yield the final measure of *BI*.

Subjects and Procedures

The sample for Experiment 1 consisted of 491 housewives in the Tampa area who were members of the Procter and Gamble product testing panel. Treatments were administered in the form of booklets titled "Consumer Information Study," the ostensive purpose of which was to obtain consumers' evaluations of the *Consumer Reports* article described earlier. All subjects were randomly assigned to one of the eight cells in the experiment, and they were run in groups of four to eight. As they left the panel site, they were given written debriefing notices.

Subjects in Experiment 2 were 90 members of a women's club in Urbana, Illinois. The author randomly administered treatment booklets similar to the ones described above to all subjects at a regular monthly meeting of the organization. After collecting all treatment booklets, subjects were debriefed verbally. None of the participants had suspected the true purpose of the study, thus lending credence to the effectiveness of the cover story.

ANALYSIS AND RESULTS

As was previously illustrated in Figure 1, the causal flow under examination in the present study consists of one *S-R* relation and several *R-R* relations. In order to parsimoniously test the strengths of all these relationships, the general linear model was selected as the appropriate analytic tool (Cohen, 1968). Using categorical variables to represent experimental treatment combinations and continuous variables to represent constructs in the Extended Fishbein Model, the general linear model can perform both ANOVA and correlational analyses within a unified framework (Kerlinger and Pedhazur, 1973).

Experiment One

To perform the $2 \times 2 \times 2$ ANOVA specified in the design of the first experiment (See Table 1), it was first necessary to create variables representing the experimental treatment conditions for inclusion in the regression model. Accordingly, the first factor—Critical Attribute Evaluation—was designated as variable X_1 and coded +1 if a_k was positive (i.e., effective in all temperatures) and −1 if a_k was negative (costly to use). Similarly, Initial Critical Belief Position became variable X_2, coded +1 for "high" likelihood conditions and −1 for "low" likelihood conditions. Finally, the Advocated Critical Belief Position (Formation-Change) factor (X_3) was coded +1 for Change conditions and −1 for Formation Conditions. These three variables thus represented the three main effects in the experiment, and each subject in the study was characterized by a +1 or −1 on each variable. This procedure is known as *contrast coding* (Cohen, 1968) and provides an ANOVA within the linear model. Multiplication of the three coded variables yielded the appropriate two-way (X_1X_2, X_1X_3, X_2X_3) and three-way ($X_1X_2X_3$) interaction terms for entry into the linear model. Thus, the first equation in Table 3 represents a $2 \times 2 \times 2$ factorial ANOVA performed on the B_ka_k compound, which is the construct hypothesized as the first in the causal flow of effects. This equation also corresponds to the first solid arrow in Figure 1, i.e., the relationship between experimental messages and B_ka_k. Taken together, then, the seven predictor variables in the equation should explain a major portion of the variance in B_ka_k, with the three-way interaction ($X_1X_2X_3$) the only variable expected to attain a significant regression weight.

The second equation in Table 3 specifies an 8-variable regression for the prediction of ΣB_ia_i. The first seven variables are identical to the predictor variables in the first equation (i.e., the experimental

[6] Recently Fishbein and Ajzen (1975) have suggested that more appropriate scale endpoints for Mc_j would be "I want to do" and "I want not to do," rather than the wording employed in this study.

TABLE 4

REGRESSION RESULTS FOR EXPERIMENT ONE*

Dependent Variable	Standardized Regression Coefficients**													
	X_1	X_2	X_3	X_1X_2	X_1X_3	X_2X_3	$X_1X_2X_3$	B_ka_k	ΣB_ia_i	A-act	ΣNB_jMc_j	R	R^2	F_{ADD}
B_ka_k	16[a]	−02	−10[a]	04	05	−03	−59[a] (−59[a])	—	—	—	—	.625[a] (.590[a])	.390 (.348)	5.6[a]
ΣB_ia_i	−12[a]	08[b]	−03	−03	−00	02	−02	48[a] (47[a])	—	—	—	.497[a] (.472[a])	.247 (.222)	2.3[b]
Aact	−01	−04	−04	−05	02	−01	−07	05	40[a] (45[a])	—	—	.462[a] (.445[a])	.214 (.198)	1.2
BI	06	04	01	04	−01	−01	−02	05	−03	69[a] (69[a])	04 (04)	.706[a] (.698[a])	.499 (.488)	1.2

* Numbers in parentheses are regression results for models including only hypothesized mediating variables.
** Decimals omitted
[a] $p < .01$.
[b] $p < .05$.

treatments), while the final variable, B_ka_k, was the dependent variable in the previous equation. Referring to Figure 1, it can be seen that B_ka_k should be the only variable to reach significance (solid arrow), with all of the treatment effects expected to be zero (dashed arrow). Similarly, ΣB_ia_i is expected to be the only significant predictor of *Aact*.

Finally, *BI* should be explained only by *Aact*, although the normative component is included in the fourth equation for the sake of completeness. Since the present study dealt with manipulations of the attitudinal component, changes in ΣNB_jMc_j were expected to be mininal and not causally related to *BI*.

The best way to test the set of equations specified in Table 3 is to compare alternative models for each equation taken separately. Specifically, in each equation, one term is hypothesized as the *only* significant predictor. Accordingly, the appropriate test is to run one analysis with only that variable as a predictor and then run a second analysis which includes that variable together with *all* other predictor variables. By comparing the results of these two regressions, the contribution of the variables not hypothesized to be causally related to the dependent variable can be determined, *for the entire set*. This test is important, for while none of the variables may be significant when taken in isolation, the group of variables, taken together, may be statistically significant predictors.

Therefore, in order to test the equations shown in Table 3, a total of eight regressions were performed, two for each equation in the model.[7] For each equation, the two regressions were compared via the F_{ADD} statistic:

$$F_{ADD} = \frac{(R_{TOT}^2 - R_{HYP}^2)/(k_T - k_H)}{(1 - R_{TOT}^2)/(N - k_T - 1)}$$

where R^2_{TOT} is the variance explained by the regression using all predictor variables; R^2_{HYP} is the variance explained by the regression containing only the hypothesized mediating variable(s); k_T is the total number of predictor variables; k_H is the total number of hypothesized mediating variables; and N is the number of observations. F_{ADD} is distributed as an F distribution with k_T-k_H and N-k_T-1 degrees of freedom (Kerlinger and Pedhazur, 1973, p. 178). In the model to be tested, it is hypothesized that the F_{ADD} statistic for all four equations in Table 3 is nonsignificant. In essence, this pattern of results would indicate that changes in the dependent variable of interest are mediated by the construct immediately preceding it in the proposed causal flow of effects. The effects of a variable on another construct farther down the hypothesized flow should be near zero, as intervening variables should be performing the mediating function. Any deviation from this pattern would be evidence contrary to the Extended Fishbein Model. By analyzing the weights attached to particular variables, possible insights can be gained into the sources of discrepancies between the model's predictions and the observed results.

Table 4 presents the results of the first experiment (B_i change). All equations were statistically significant, and in general the relationships were reasonably strong. The F_{ADD} statistic revealed that for each of the first two equations, there were unanticipated relationships between certain predictors and the dependent variable of interest. The first equation shows that most of the variance in B_ka_k was controlled

[7] Taken together, the four equations in Table 3 form a recursive system, such that each successive equation can be analyzed meaningfully from a causal standpoint only if the equations preceding it have been considered and the error terms of the four equations have been assumed to be independent (Blalock, 1964).

by the three-way interaction term, as expected. However, two small main effects were detected for Critical Attribute Evaluation and Formation-Change. These relatively minor deviations from the expected pattern of results in the first equation have no consequence on the causal ordering among the constructs in the model, but they do show that the experimental manipulations were not entirely successful in creating the exact levels of $B_k a_k$ called for by the experimental design. In particular, the groups receiving information about the positive attribute (all temperature effectiveness) tended to have higher scores for $B_k a_k$ ($\bar{X} = 1.76$) than did the groups receiving information on cost of use ($\bar{X} = -0.55$), a negatively valued attribute. This effect seemed primarily due to the fact that the evaluative aspect (a_i) of "effective in all temperatures" was more polarized ($\bar{X} = 2.66$) than was the a_i for "costly to use" ($\bar{X} = -1.79$). Additionally, the small main effect for X_3 (Formation-Change) resulted from greater polarization ($\bar{X} = -1.31$) in the Formation groups than in the Change groups ($\bar{X} = -0.10$). Presumably, this effect may have been due to a decrease in the credibility of the *CR* article when it was accompanied by the contradictory "Additional Information." This possible difference in credibility could have led to relatively greater belief strength in the Formation groups, as reflected in the higher polarization in their $B_k a_k$ scores.

The second equation in Table 4 shows that $B_k a_k$ controlled virtually all of the explained variance in total cognitive structure.[8] The three-way interaction term, which had been a heavy contributor to $B_k a_k$ variance, dropped to nonsignificance. Two small main effects lingered, one for Critical Attribute Evaluation and the other for Initial Critical Belief Position. These effects were not expected and should have been mediated by $B_k a_k$. Therefore, from a pure statistical significance viewpoint, these coefficients must be considered evidence against the sole mediating effect of $B_k a_k$. However, taken together, the two effects controlled only two percent of the variance in $\Sigma B_i a_i$, so the deviations from expectations were quite small. For instance, the main effect for X_1 (Critical Attribute Evaluation) showed that the groups receiving information on all-temperature effectiveness had $\Sigma B_i a_i$ scores slightly lower ($\bar{X} = 32.46$) than did the cost of use groups ($\bar{X} = 32.59$). An even smaller effect was observed for X_2 (Initial Critical Belief Position). Here, the mean for the groups for which B_k was initially "high" ($\bar{X} = 35.25$) was slightly greater than the mean for the "low" groups ($\bar{X} = 31.80$).

Total cognitive structure ($\Sigma B_i a_i$) was the only significant predictor of *Aact* in the third equation. While the total amount of variance explained by the equation is somewhat smaller than in previous studies using the Fishbein Model, it must be borne in mind that the present study involved manipulations designed to change specific elements in cognitive structure. No conclusion was stated regarding the desired attitudinal effect; subjects were left to form the relationship between cognitions and affect themselves. Under these conditions, it is not too surprising that the relationship between $\Sigma B_i a_i$ and *Aact* was somewhat smaller than in survey designs where well-established attitudes and beliefs are measured. In any event, $\Sigma B_i a_i$ appeared as the only significant mediator of changes in *Aact*, a result in accord with the hypotheses.

Finally, *Aact* emerged as the only significant explanatory variable in the *BI* equation; no other variable even approached significance. The strength of the relationship is quite encouraging and suggests that attitudes are closely related to purchase intentions. (Under what conditions individuals translate their intentions into overt behavior remains an important question for future research.)[9]

In sum, the results of Experiment 1 provide strong support for the flow of effects hypothesized by the Extended Fishbein Model. Significant and substantial proportions of variance in the model's constructs were explained by mediating constructs within the model. Contributions of variables hypothesized to be unrelated to particular constructs were generally quite low and often zero. There was some indication, however, that the relationships within the model are not as strong under conditions of change than have been found previously under more static research paradigms.

Experiment Two

Table 5 shows the set of equations used to analyze the data from the second experiment. In order to represent the 2 × 3 ANOVA outlined earlier (Table 2), five categorical variables were necessary. Variable X_1 was coded +1 for "high" likelihood conditions and −1 for "low" likelihood conditions to represent

[8] Technically speaking, the causal impact of $B_k a_k$ on $\Sigma B_i a_i$ is tautological, since the single $B_k a_k$ element is included in the overall cognitive structure index ($\Sigma B_i a_i$). But $B_k a_k$ is not necessarily that *strong* of an influence on $\Sigma B_i a_i$, as demonstrated by Lutz (1975b). Therefore, it seemed appropriate to investigate the influence of the single element on total cognitive structure. Ideally, an independent measure of cognitive structure which did not use the same $B_k a_k$ data would be constructed. It is not immediately apparent, however, exactly how this index could be formulated.

[9] It should be noted that although the normative component was included in the intention equation, it was not expected to carry any weight, due to the design employed in the study. Under more natural conditions, and with respect to a more socially visible behavior, the normative component could be expected to contribute to the explanation of intentions (e.g., Wilson, Mathews and Harvey, 1975).

the first factor, Critical Belief Position. The second factor, Advocated Evaluation Position, required two coded vectors to represent its main effect. Variable X_2 was coded +1, 0, and −1 for the Positive, Neutral, and Negative conditions, respectively, while variable X_3 was coded 0, +1, and −1 for the same conditions. Finally, the interaction term in the design was also represented by two coded vectors, derived by multiplying variable X_1 by both X_2 and X_3. Thus, the weights associated with variables X_1X_2 and X_1X_3 became the key features in examining the *S-R* relation posited in Table 2. The remaining equations in Table 5 correspond directly to the equations in Table 3 and are designed to test the causal flows in the *R-R* relations within the Extended Fishbein Model under conditions of a_i change.

Table 6 summarizes the results of Experiment 2. The F_{ADD} statistic revealed that the first equation did not conform precisely with expectations. While most of the explained variance was controlled by the interaction term, as shown by the large beta weights for X_1X_2 and X_1X_3, the first factor—Critical Belief Position—showed a main effect as well. The "high" B_k groups ($\bar{X} = -1.31$) differed from the low B_k groups ($\bar{X} = 2.82$) primarily because the manipulation of a_k was not entirely successful. It was intended that the initial position of a_k be near zero; however, it was substantially negative ($\bar{X} = -1.15$ for the two control groups). B_k scores, when multiplied with this polarized a_k score, led to the main effect on B_ka_k. This deviation from the original design of the experiment was not too damaging, however, as there was still ample room for a_k to change in both positive and negative directions (Lutz, 1975a).

Turning to the second equation, B_ka_k dominates in the explanation of variance in total cognitive structure. Again, the relationship is quite strong, more than double that found in Experiment 1. However, despite the fact that the F_{ADD} statistic failed to reach significance for the entire set of variables, there is an unexpectedly significant main effect due to the second factor—Advocated Evaluation Position.[10] Analysis of cell means revealed that the groups receiving the message favoring high sudsiness ($\bar{X} = 8.62$) were substantially lower than both the control groups ($\bar{X} = 17.68$) and the groups receiving the message condemning high sudsiness ($\bar{X} = 20.78$). There were virtually no differences among the three groups on B_ka_k scores, so most of this unexpected effect was due to differences in the other, unattacked, attributes. Just why these differences occurred is

TABLE 5

RECURSIVE SYSTEM OF EQUATIONS FOR EXPERIMENT TWO

$$B_ka_k = \beta_{11}X_1 + \beta_{12}X_2 + \beta_{13}X_3 + \beta_{14}X_1X_2 + \beta_{15}X_1X_3 + e_1$$

$$\Sigma B_ia_i = \beta_{21}X_1 + \beta_{22}X_2 + \beta_{23}X_3 + \beta_{24}X_1X_2 + \beta_{25}X_1X_3 + \beta_{26}B_ka_k + e_2$$

$$A\text{-}act = \beta_{31}X_1 + \beta_{32}X_2 + \beta_{33}X_3 + \beta_{34}X_1X_2 + \beta_{35}X_1X_3 + \beta_{36}B_ka_k + \beta_{37}\Sigma B_ia_i + e_3$$

$$BI = \beta_{41}X_1 + \beta_{42}X_2 + \beta_{43}X_3 + \beta_{44}X_1X_2 + \beta_{45}X_1X_3 + \beta_{46}B_ka_k + \beta_{47}\Sigma B_ia_i + \beta_{48}A\text{-}act + \beta_{49}\Sigma NB_jMc_j + e_4$$

[10] This discrepancy in results was due to the fact that almost all of the variance attributable to nonhypothesized variables was concentrated in X_2, and the difference in degrees of freedom was enough to allow the single variable to be statistically significant while the entire set was not.

TABLE 6

REGRESSION RESULTS FOR EXPERIMENT TWO*

Dependent Variable	Standardized Regression Coefficients**											
	X_1	X_2	X_3	X_1X_2	X_1X_3	B_ka_k	ΣB_ia_i	$Aact$	ΣNB_jMc_j	R	R^2	F_{ADD}
B_ka_k	−32[a]	−02	03	65[a]	−50[a]	—	—	—	—	.733[a]	.537	
				(84[a])	(−71[a])					(.663)	(.440)	5.9[a]
ΣB_ia_i	−02	−20[b]	13	09	12	63[a]	—	—	—	.758[a]	.574	
						(72[a])				(.724[a])	(.524)	1.9
$Aact$	−15	15	−12	22	−23	−30	30	—	—	.354	.125	
							(22)			(.223)	(.050)	1.2
BI	−07	−03	−07	19	−11	−02	−05	61[a]	−09	.656[b]	.431	
								(64[a])	(−07)	(.633[a])	(.401)	0.6

* Numbers in parentheses are regression results for models including only hypothesized mediating variables.
** Decimals omitted
[a] $p < .01$
[b] $p < .05$

not clear. Perhaps there were some non-obvious interrelationships among the various attributes that led to a "haloing" effect in the $\Sigma B_i a_i$ ratings. Another possibility is that, with the rather small sample sizes in Experiment 2, the results are statistical artifacts. In either case, the effect is quite small in comparison with the size of the beta weight for $B_k a_k$; nevertheless, the most conservative interpretation of this result is that it is evidence contradictory to the flow of effects postulated in Figure 1.

Somewhat more damaging evidence for the Extended Fishbein Model is found in the third equation, where $\Sigma B_i a_i$ fails to attain statistical significance in the prediction of *Aact*. It is only partially comforting that no other variable is significant in that equation. This result, taken together with the rather weak relationship observed between $\Sigma B_i a_i$ and *Aact* in Experment 1, may point to a weakness in the proposed causal chain. Numerous studies have demonstrated relatively strong relationships between the two constructs. Yet, in both experiments reported here, the relationship was severely attenuated.

Perhaps, as has been suggested by Rosenberg (1968) the assumption of a simple linear relationship between cognitive change and attitude change is an oversimplification. This linearity assumption can be seen as an outgrowth of the "information processing" approach to attitude change; Rosenberg suggests that a cognitive consistency approach to attitude change would possibly show up as a "step function" relationship between cognitive change and attitude change, such that a certain threshhold in the amount of cognitive change would have to be crossed for attitude change to occur. The present data suggest that this area is worthy of further investigation. If more than one single a_i element had been under attack, perhaps the hypothesized relationship would have been observed. Alternatively, the present results may be spurious, due to inadequate measurement of cognitive structure, or any number of other factors. In any event, more evidence pertaining to the strength of the $\Sigma B_i a_i$—*Aact* relationship in dynamic situations is needed before the model can be used with confidence in generating attitude change strategies.

Finally, the fourth equation in Table 6 provides relatively strong support for the power of *Aact* in determining intentions. It appears likely that changes in attitude will manifest themselves on intentions in situations where behavior is under attitudinal control. In general, the magnitudes of the hypothesized coefficients in Experiment 2 were similar to those in Experiment 1. Thus, except for the failure of $\Sigma B_i a_i$ to predict *Aact* in the a_i change situation, the conclusions drawn from the two sets of analyses are basically the same: There is reasonably strong support for the postulated causal flow of effects within the Extended Fishbein Model.

DISCUSSION

Despite the generally favorable findings of this study, several considerations must be taken into account which have implications for both the theoretician and the practitioner.

First of all, the present research was somewhat limited methodologically. A laboratory-type experimental setting was employed, the stimulus brand was a hypothetical one, and no behavioral criterion was employed. Each of these features should be overcome in subsequent tests of the model in field situations before concluding that the model is a reasonably valid one for marketing decision makers. On the positive side of the ledger, the present research is the first reported in the marketing literature which has investigated potential attitude change strategies within the Extended Fishbein Model, a step which has been advocated by other researchers in the area. Thus this study fills a need in moving from static, correlational designs to laboratory experimentation, and sets the stage for more sophisticated and complex tests of the model in the marketplace.

There is a clear need for more investigation of the normative component in the model, and research should be undertaken to determine under what conditions normatively-based change strategies can influence intentions and behavior. Ryan (1975) has recently reported initial work on the normative component. At the present time, this component remains the most serious threat to the validity of the overall model, so careful attention should be devoted to it.

From a managerial perspective, the weakness of the relationship between cognitive change and attitude change is disturbing. It is difficult to justify the construction of promotional strategies based on findings of this magnitude. Several tactics for enhancing the size of the relationship, and hence the usefulness of the model, are available however. First, persuasive messages can employ an explicit conclusion, rather than the implicit conclusion used in this research. Use of an explicit conclusion, particularly in the mass media, should help reduce discrepancies between cognitions and affect.

Second, the threshold concept mentioned by Rosenberg (1968) may be seen as applying to several issues. His argument was that multiple beliefs, or attributes, should be attacked in a persuasive message to arouse cognitive inconsistency beyond some threshold level. Similarly, the use of repeated exposures to messages may be seen as playing on a threshold concept: The more exposures, the more likely it is that attitudes and beliefs will be brought into close congruence. Finally, even without repeated exposures, the passage of time may lead to greater consistency between cognitions and affect. The present study was conducted at one point in time. Perhaps a delayed posttest would have revealed a stronger relationship between $\Sigma B_i a_i$ and *Aact*.

A third tactic of possible use to the policy maker in enhancing attitude change is to take advantage of the interrelationships among elements of cognitive structure. In Experiment 1, elements of cognitive structure which were not attacked in the attitude change message had more influence on change in total cognitive structure than did the elements included in the persuasive appeals. By determining in advance some of the likely "second order effects" of a message, the marketer can either build upon them or explicitly argue against them if they are unfavorable to his position (Lutz, 1975b).

For the marketing theorist, the present results are encouraging. There is strong support for the hierarchy of effects notion, which has managed to avoid empirical verification for several years. Similarly, the idea of a decision process model is supported by the present data; however, there is some indication that simple flow chart models and linear relationships may not adequately account for the motivation of buyers to process information in making their purchase decisions (Katz, 1960; Rosenberg, 1968).

In closing, it must be underscored that the present study represents only a small portion of the evidence necessary to fully examine the Extended Fishbein Model. What is needed is a body of literature similar to that which has accumulated surrounding the multi-attribute attitude model. For instance, the present results shed some new light on the ability of the multi-attribute model to predict attitude under attitude change conditions. Only through further study utilizing a variety of methodological approaches can similar insights be gained into the causal patterns among cognitions, affect and behavioral intentions.

REFERENCES

Ajzen, Icek. "Attitudinal vs. Normative Messages: An Investigation of the Differential Effects of Persuasive Communications on Behavior," *Sociometry*, 34 (1971), 263–80.

Ajzen, Icek, and Martin Fishbein. "Attitudes and Normative Beliefs as Factors Influencing Behavioral Intentions," *Journal of Personality and Social Psychology*, 21 (1972), 1–9.

———. "Attitudinal and Normative Variables as Predictors of Specific Behaviors," *Journal of Personality and Social Psychology*, 27 (1973), 41–57.

Bettman, James R., Noel Capon and Richard J. Lutz. "Cognitive Algebra in Multi-Attribute Attitude Models," *Journal of Marketing Research*, 12 (May 1975), 151–64.

Blalock, Hubert M., Jr. *Causal Inferences in Non-Experimental Research*. Chapel Hill: University of North Carolina Press, 1964.

Bonfield, E. H. "Attitude, Social Influence, Personal Norms, and Intention Interactions as Related to Brand Purchase Behavior," *Journal of Marketing Research*, 11 (November 1974), 379–89.

Campbell, Donald T., and Julian C. Stanley. "Experimental and Quasi-Experimental Designs for Research," in N. L. Gage, ed. *Handbook of Research on Teaching*. Chicago: Rand McNally, 1963, 171–246.

Cohen, Jacob. "Multiple Regression as a General Data-Analytic System," *Psychological Bulletin*, 70 (1968), 426–43.

Dulany, Don E. "Awareness, Rules, and Propositional Control: A Confrontation with S-R Behavior Theory," in Theodore R. Dixon and David L. Horton, Eds. *Verbal Behavior and General Behavior Theory*. Englewood Cliffs, N.J.: Prentice-Hall, 1968, 340–87.

Engel, James F., David T. Kollat and Roger D. Blackwell. *Consumer Behavior*, Second Edition. New York: Holt, Rinehart and Winston, 1973.

Fishbein, Martin. "An Investigation of the Relationships Between Beliefs About an Object and the Attitude Toward That Object," *Human Relations*, 16 (1963), 233–40.

———. "Attitudes and the Prediction of Behavior," in Martin Fishbein, ed. *Readings in Attitude Theory and Measurement*. New York: Wiley, 477–92.

Fishbein, Martin and Icek Ajzen. *Belief, Attitude, Intention and Behavior: An Introduction to Theory and Research*. Reading, Mass.: Addison-Wesley, 1975.

Harrell, Gilbert D., and Peter D. Bennett. "An Evaluation of the Expectancy Value Model of Attitude Measurement for Physician Prescribing Behavior," *Journal of Marketing Research*, 11 (August 1975), 269–78.

Katz, Daniel. "The Functional Approach to the Study of Attitudes," *Public Opinion Quarterly*, 24 (Summer 1960), 163–204.

Kerlinger, Fred N., and Elazar J. Pedhazur. *Multiple Regression in Behavioral Research*. New York: Holt, Rinehart and Winston, 1973.

Lavidge, Robert J., and Gary A. Steiner. "A Model for Predictive Measurements of Advertising Effectiveness," *Journal of Marketing*, 25 (October 1961), 59–62.

Lutz, Richard J. "A Comparison of Two Alternative Models of the Attitude-Behavior Relationship," in *Proceedings*, 81st Annual Convention of the American Psychological Association, 1973, 927–8.

———. "Changing Brand Attitudes Through Modification of Cognitive Structure," *Journal of Consumer Research*, 1 (March 1975a), 49–59.

———. "First-Order and Second-Order Cognitive Effects in Attitude Change," *Communications Research*, 2 (July 1975b), 289–99.

McArdle, Judy. "Positive and Negative Communications and Subsequent Attitude and Behavior Change in Alcoholics," unpublished doctoral dissertation, Department of Psychology, University of Illinois, Urbana-Champaign, 1972.

Palda, Kristian S. "The Hypothesis of a Hierarchy of Effects: A Partial Evaluation," *Journal of Marketing Research*, 3 (February 1966), 13–24.

Rosenberg, Milton J. "Cognitive Structure and Attitudinal Affect," *Journal of Abnormal and Social Psychology*, 53 (1956), 367–72.

———. "Discussion: Impression Processing and the Evaluation of New and Old Objects," in Robert

P. Abelson, *et al.*, Eds. *Theories of Cognitive Consistency: A Sourcebook.* Chicago: Rand McNally, 1968, 763–8.

Ryan, Michael J. "A Test of Associations in a Causal Chain Derived from Fishbein's Behavioral Intention Model," unpublished paper, University of Alabama, 1975.

Ryan, Michael J., and E. H. Bonfield. "The Fishbein Extended Model and Consumer Behavior," *Journal of Consumer Research*, 2 (September 1975), 18–36.

Weddle, David E., and James R. Bettman. "Marketing Underground: An Investigation of Fishbein's Behavioral Intention Model," in Scott Ward and Peter Wright, Eds., *Advances in Consumer Research, Vol. I.* Urbana, Ill.: Association for Consumer Research, 1974, 310–8.

Wilson, David T., H. Lee Mathews and John F. Monoky. "Attitude as a Predictor of Behavior in a Buyer-Seller Bargaining Situation: An Experimental Approach," in *Combined Proceedings*, American Marketing Association, 1972, 390–5.

Wilson, David T., H. Lee Mathews and James W. Harvey. "An Empirical Test of the Fishbein Behavioral Intention Model," *Journal of Consumer Research*, 1 (March 1975), 39–48.

Wright, Peter L. "The Cognitive Processes Mediating Acceptance of Advertising." *Journal of Marketing Research*, 10 (February 1973), 53–62.

DONALD G. MORRISON*

With the availability of "canned" computer programs, it is extremely easy to run complex multivariate statistical analyses. However, it is not as easy to interpret the output of these programs. This article offers some comments about the well-known technique of linear discriminant analysis; potential pitfalls are also mentioned.

On the Interpretation of Discriminant Analysis

BACKGROUND

Many theoretical- and applications-oriented articles have been written on the multivariate statistical technique of linear discriminant analysis. However, on a practical level little has been written on how to evaluate results of a discriminant analysis—at least in managerial, as opposed to statistical, terminology. This article looks at the problem of evaluation from various viewpoints and thus highlights some features pertaining to other statistical techniques.

Overview of Discriminant Analysis

The objective of a discriminant analysis is to classify objects, by a set of independent variables, into one of two or more mutually exclusive and exhaustive categories. For example, on the basis of an applicant's age, income, length of time at present home, etc., a credit manager wishes to classify this person as either a good or poor credit risk. For expository purposes we will limit this discussion to two classifications; later we will comment on n-group discriminant analysis.

For notation, let

- X_{ji} be the *ith* individual's value of the *jth* independent variable
- b_j be the discriminant coefficient for the *jth* variable
- Z_i be the *ith* individual's discriminant score
- $z_{\text{crit.}}$ be the critical value for the discriminant score.

Linear Classification Procedure

Let each individual's discriminant score Z_i be a linear function of the independent variables. That is,

$$(1)\quad Z_i = b_0 + b_1X_{1i} + b_2X_{2i} + \cdots + b_nX_{ni}.$$

* Donald G. Morrison is associate professor of business, Columbia University.

The classification procedure follows:

if $Z_i > z_{\text{crit.}}$, classify Individual i as belonging to Group 1;
if $Z_i < z_{\text{crit.}}$, classify Individual i as belonging to Group 2.

The classification boundary will then be the locus of points,
where

$$b_0 + b_1X_{1i} + \cdots + b_nX_{ni} = z_{\text{crit.}}$$

When n (the number of independent variables) $= 2$, the classification boundary is a straight line. Every individual on one side of the line is classified as Group 1; on the other side, as Group 2. When $n = 3$, the classification boundary is a two-dimensional plane in 3-dimensional space; the classification boundary is generally an $n - 1$ dimensional hyperplane in n space.

Advantages of a Linear Classification Procedure

The particularly simple form of (1) allows a clear interpretation of the effect of each of the independent variables. Suppose the independent variable X_1 is income, and the classification procedure is if $Z_i > z_{\text{crit.}}$, classify the individual as being a good credit risk, i.e., the higher the value of Z_i, the more likely the individual is a good credit risk. If the sign of b_1 is positive, then higher income implies a better credit risk, and the larger the size of b_1, the more important variable X_1 is in discriminating between Group 1 and Group 2 individuals. Clearly, if $b_1 = 0$, then X_1 has no effect.

If we had a more complex discriminant function, we could not isolate the effect of each variable so easily. Suppose we had a nonlinear discriminant function, say

$$Z_i' = a + bX_i + cX_i^2 + dY_i + eY_i^2 + fX_iY_i.$$

Reprinted from *Journal of Marketing Research,* 6 (May 1969), 156-63, published by the American Marketing Association.

The effect on Z_i' of increasing X_i by one unit depends on the value of X, b, c, f, and even Y.[1]

Hence, for interpretation, a linear discriminant function is highly desirable. This raises the following question.

When is a Linear Classification Procedure Valid?

The technical details of this section are in the appendix. However, the essence of these details can be easily expressed. A linear classification procedure is optimal if the spreads (variance) of the independent variables (the X's) in Group 1 are the same as the spreads in Group 2 and if the interrelations (correlations) among the independent variables in Group 1 are the same as the interrelations in Group 2. Really we are saying that the covariance matrices of Group 1 and Group 2 are equal.

The appendix also gives a brief example of the kind of nonlinear classification region that can arise when the assumption of equal covariance matrices is not true.

Next is the discussion of evaluating the results after a discriminant analysis has been run.

STATISTICAL SIGNIFICANCE

Distance between Groups

One of the standard quantities that appears on the output of a discriminant analysis is a distance measure, the Mahalanobis D^2 statistic, between the two groups.[2] After a transformation this D^2 statistic becomes an F statistic, which is then used to see if the two groups are *statistically* different from each other. In fact this test is simply the multidimensional analog of the familiar t test for the statistical significance of the difference between one sample mean $\bar{x}_1$ and another sample mean $\bar{x}_2$. The D^2 (or transformed F) statistic tests the difference between the n-dimensional mean vector $\bar{x}_1$ for Group 1 and the corresponding n-dimensional mean vector $\bar{x}_2$ for Group 2. However, the statistical significance per se of the D^2 statistic means very little.

Suppose the two groups are significantly different at the .01 level. With large enough sample sizes, $\bar{x}_1$ could be virtually identical to $\bar{x}_2$, and we would still have statistical significance. In short, the D^2 statistic (or any of its transformed statistics) suffers the same drawbacks of all classical tests of hypotheses. The statistical significance of the D^2 statistic is a very poor indicator of the efficacy with which the independent variables can discriminate between Group 1 individuals and those in Group 2.

PERCENTAGE CORRECTLY CLASSIFIED

A Bias Exists in Many "Canned" Programs

One common source of misinterpretation of discriminant analysis results comes from the way in which most of the "canned" computer programs construct the classification table (sometimes called the confusion matrix). The computer will print out the following table:

		Classified Group 1	*Classified* Group 2	
Actually	Group 1	n_{11}	n_{12}	$n_{1.}$
	Group 2	n_{21}	n_{22}	$n_{2.}$
		$n_{.1}$	$n_{.2}$	n

The entry n_{ij} is the number of individuals who are actually in Group i, but were classified under Group j. Then $(n_{11} + n_{22})/n$ is the proportion of individuals correctly classified. However, the typical canned program uses all n observations to calculate the discriminant function and then classifies these *same n* individuals with this function. Frank, Massy, and Morrison [3] discuss in detail the upward biases that can occur in classification tables constructed in this way. One method of avoiding this bias is to fit a discriminant function to part of the data and then use this function to classify the remaining individuals. It is the classification table for these last individuals that we will discuss now.

Percent Correctly Classified by Chance

Suppose a researcher is interested in determining the socioeconomic variables that distinguish adopters of a new product from nonadopters. His "fresh" second half of the split sample contains 30 adopters and 70 nonadopters. He applies his discriminant function obtained in the first half of the split sample to this second

---

1 Some of the variables may have little influence on the discrimination, i.e., the b's associated with these variables are very close to zero. The main part of the discrimination will then occur in a space of lower dimensionality.

2 The Mahalanobis D^2 statistic can be considered as a generalized distance between two groups, where each group is characterized by the same set of n variables and the variance-covariance structure is identical for both groups. Each group can be further characterized by its n-dimensional mean vector. In the special case where all n variables are mutually independent, D^2 is merely the square of the usual Euclidean distance between the two mean vectors, where the orthogonal coordinate system is normalized by the standard deviation of each variable. If the variables are collinear, the coordinate axes are also rotated so that the cosine of the angle between the two axes is equal to the correlation between the two variables associated with these axes.

Let μ_1 be the mean vector for Group I and μ_2 be the mean vector for Group II. If $(\mathbf{V})$ is the common covariance matrix, the Mahalanobis D^2 statistic is

$$(\mu_1 - \mu_2)\mathbf{V}^{-1}(\mu_1 - \mu_2)'.$$

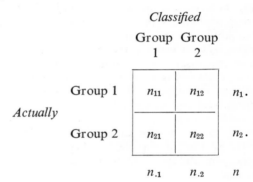

half and gets 70 percent correct classifications. He then says, "By chance I could get 70 percent correct classifications; therefore, my discriminant function is not effective in separating adopters from nonadopters." Notice that the chance model has not been explicitly stated. The remainder of this section will develop a more appropriate chance model that will show that in a statistical sense this hypothetical researcher is being overly pessimistic.

Assume that there exists a population with only two types of individuals, Type I and Type II. Let p be the proportion of the population that is Type I, and $1 - p$ the proportion that is Type II. If the variables (age, income, etc.) actually have no effect on discriminating I's from II's, we can expect to get a proportion p correctly classified *if we classify everyone as Type I.* Hence, if $p > 1/2$, we would classify everyone as Type I; if $p < 1/2$, would classify everyone as Type II.

Our hypothetical researcher wishes to identify adopters. However, since his sample has only 30 percent adopters and 70 percent nonadopters, he defies the pure chance odds if he classifies an individual as an adopter. This is true because any individual has an a priori .7 probability of being a nonadopter and only a .3 probability of being an adopter. But what if the researcher says, "I want to try to identify the adopters. I believe my discriminant function has some merit; therefore, I am going to classify 30 percent of the individuals as adopters." Given this outlook, what is the appropriate chance model?

Let

p be the true proportion of Type I individuals,

α be the proportion classified as Type I.

Then the probability of an individual being classified correctly is

$$P(\text{Correct}) = P(\text{Correct} \mid \text{Classified Type I})P(\text{Classified Type I}) + P(\text{Correct} \mid \text{Classified Type II})P(\text{Classified Type II})$$

$$(2) \qquad P(\text{Correct}) = p\alpha + (1 - p)(1 - \alpha).$$

For our researcher, $p = \alpha = 0.3$. Hence the chance proportion correctly classified is $(0.3)^2 + (0.7)^2 = .58$. *Note that when $p = .5$, i.e., two groups of equal size, $P(\text{Correct}) = .50$ regardless of the value of α.*[3]

More formally this *proportional chance criterion is*

$$(3) \qquad C_{\text{pro.}} = \alpha^2 + (1 - \alpha)^2,$$

where

α is the proportion of individuals in Group 1

$1 - \alpha$ is the proportion of individuals in Group 2.

The researcher who said, "By chance I could get 70 percent correct," was using the *maximum* chance criterion,

$$(4) \qquad C_{\text{max.}} = \max(\alpha, 1 - \alpha),$$

where $\max(\alpha, 1 - \alpha)$ is read, "the larger of α or $1 - \alpha$." For example, $\max(.3, .7) = .7$.

Situations Where $C_{\text{pro.}}$ and $C_{\text{max.}}$ Should Be Used

If the sole objective of the discriminant analysis is to maximize the percentage correctly classified, then clearly $C_{\text{max.}}$ is the appropriate chance criterion. If the discriminant function cannot do better than $C_{\text{max.}}$, you are wiser to disregard it and merely classify everyone as belonging to the larger of the two groups. Obviously, this is rarely true for a marketing research study. Usually a discriminant analysis is run because someone wishes to correctly identify members of *both* groups. As indicated, the discriminant function defies the odds by classifying an individual in the smaller group. The chance criterion should take this into account. Therefore, in most situations $C_{\text{pro.}}$ should be used. Recall that our discussion on chance models applies to individuals not used in calculating the discriminant function. If the individuals were used in calculating it, then some upward adjustment must be made on $C_{\text{pro.}}$ or $C_{\text{max.}}$. Frank, Massy, and Morrison [3] give methods for estimating these biases.

Analogy with Regression

Perhaps an analogy with regression will clarify these concepts. We have all read articles in which the author has found "significant" relations; however, he has "explained" only four percent of the variance, i.e., $R^2 = 0.04$. But since the sample size is large, this sample R^2 is statistically significantly different from zero. In discriminant analysis, the percentage correctly classified is somewhat analogous to R^2. One tells how well we classified the individual; the other tells how much variance we explained. Statistical significance of the R^2 is analogous to the statistical significance of the D^2 statistic. Clearly, with a large enough sample size in discriminant analysis we could classify 52 percent correctly (when chance was 50 percent) and yet have a statistically significant difference (distance) between the two groups.

EVALUATION CRITERIA FOR DISCRIMINANT ANALYSIS

When results of a discriminant analysis are obtained, there are three basic questions to ask: (1) Which independent variables are good discriminators? (2)

[3] A generalization of (1) for N groups with n individuals in Group i, $i = 1, \cdots, N$ is found in [5]. This excellent article is worthwhile reading for anyone working with discriminant analysis or any other classification techniques. These more general results will be necessary for multiple discriminant analysis when the number of groups (or types) is greater than two.

How well do these independent variables discriminate among the two groups? (3) What decision rule should be used for classifying individuals? We have already discussed the first two questions; the third one obviously involves economic considerations. More complete answers to these questions require a synopsis of the theoretical derivation of the discriminant function.[4]

Deriving the Discriminant Function

Let us look at Individual i and observe his values of the n independent variables. That is, we see

$$x_i = (x_{1i}, x_{2i}, \cdots, x_{ni}).$$

Let

$P(I)$ be the unconditional (prior) probability that an individual belongs to Group 1

$P(I \mid x_i)$ be the conditional (posterior) probability that an individual belongs to Group 1, given we have observed x_i

$l(x_i \mid I)$ be the likelihood that an individual has the vector of values x_i, given that he belongs to Group 1.

Analogous definitions hold for Group 2. From Bayes Theorem we have

$$\frac{P(I \mid x_i)}{P(II \mid x_i)} = \frac{l(x_i \mid I)}{l(x_i \mid II)} \cdot \frac{P(I)}{P(II)}.$$

Or,

(5) Posterior Odds = Likelihood Ratio × Prior Odds.

The classification procedure will then be as follows. If the odds are strongly enough in favor of Group 1, classify the individual as belonging to Group 1. (If the odds were 3 to 1 in favor of Group 1, this would mean a probability of .75 that the individual belongs to Group 1.) We may also use the logarithm of the odds as a criterion. For example, odds greater than one (a probability greater than .5) is equivalent to the logarithm of the odds being greater than zero. We may write (5) as

(6) $$\log(\text{posterior odds}) = \log(\text{likelihood ratio}) + \log(\text{prior odds}).$$

If the assumptions of normality and equal covariance matrices discussed earlier are true, the logarithm of the likelihood ratio is of the form,

(7) $$\log(\text{likelihood ratio}) = b_0 + b_1 X_1 + \cdots + b_n X_n .$$

This is the discriminant function. When the two groups are of equal size, each group's prior probabilities are equal. The prior odds are then one, and the posterior odds are merely the likelihood ratio. When the prior odds are different from one, then

$$\log(\text{posterior odds}) = b_0 + b_1 X_{1i} + \cdots + b_n X_{ni} + \log(\text{prior odds}).$$

However, since the prior odds contain none of the independent variables, this quantity is a constant, and the discriminant function is

$$b_0' + b_1 X_{1i} + \cdots + b_n X_{ni},$$

where

(8) $$b_0' = b_0 + \log(\text{prior odds}).$$

An understanding of the foregoing nonmathematical material is sufficient to answer the three basic questions.

Determining the Effect of Independent Variables

The sign and size of the b_j's determine the effect of the independent variables X_j. The size of the coefficient b_j in the discriminant function,

$$Z_i = b_0 + b_1 X_{1i} + \cdots + b_j X_{ji} + \cdots + b_n X_{ni},$$

will clearly be influenced by the scale that we use for X_j. Suppose X_j is family income. A change of X_j from \$6,000 to \$7,000 will have the same effect on Z_i whether or not X_j is scaled in dollars or thousands of dollars. Therefore if X_j is measured in thousands of dollars, b_j will be one thousand times larger than if the units of X_j are in dollars. However, if we normalized (divided) each variable by its standard deviation, the original units become irrelevant. As units are scaled by a factor k, the standard deviation is also scaled by the same factor k. That is, if the standard deviation of X_j is σ_j, then the standard deviation of kX_j is $k\sigma_j$. Then since $X_j/\sigma_j = kX_j/k\sigma_j$, we need not worry about the scale of X_j.

Let b_j^* be the discriminant coefficient that results when the standardized variables $X_j^* = X_j/\sigma_j$ are used.[5] Suppose $|b_j^*| > |b_k^*|$. Then variable X_j is a better discriminator between Group 1 and Group 2 than variable X_k. A unit change in X_j^* has more effect on Z_i than a unit change in X_k^*. The more a variable affects Z_i, the better it discriminates. We are justified in normalizing our variables by their standard deviations, since we are discriminating on the basis of *statistical* distance between the two groups and statistical distances are measured in units of standard deviations.[6]

If the discriminant analysis is run with nonstandardized variables, it is extremely easy to obtain b_j^*

[4] Mathematical details on this derivation are in [1, Chapter 6].

[5] We assume that the variables form at least an interval scale. That is, any variable X can be transformed to a new variable $Y = a + bX$, where a and b are arbitrary constants, without affecting the analysis. The standardized coefficients b^* will remain unaffected by these linear transformations of the data. Some of the other multivariate methods, e.g., some cluster analysis techniques, do not require such strict assumptions about the scale of the independent variables.

[6] See [3] for a detailed discussion of distance concepts.

from b_j. We have seen that

$$b_jX_j = b_j^*X_j^* = b_j^* \frac{X_j}{\sigma_j}.$$

Hence,

(9) $$b_j^* = b_j\sigma_j.$$

Recall that the sign of b_j^*, which is the same as that of b_j, determines the direction of the effect of X_j. If b_j^* is positive, as X_j increases, Z_i increases; the larger Z_i, the more likely that Individual i belongs to Group 1.

We want to obtain the best possible estimates b_j. As in all statistical estimation, the larger the sample size (assuming it is a representative sample), the better the estimates. Suppose we have 900 individuals in Group 1 and 100 individuals in Group 2. If we use only 100 of Group 1 individuals in calculating the discriminant function, the prior probability of an individual belonging to Group 1 is 0.5. But if we use all 900 members of Group 1, this prior probability drops to 0.1. Does this affect any of the b_j's of interest? No. Recall from (8) that the prior probabilities affect only b_0 and have no effect on $b_1, b_2, \cdots, b_n$. Therefore, in determining which variables are the best discriminators, we should use all the data. (By this we mean all individuals and not necessarily all available independent variables. As in any multivariate technique, if X_j and X_k are highly correlated, they are measuring almost the same thing. The coefficients b_j and b_k will be unstable and hard to interpret.)

The advisability of using all data in calculating the b_j's is not surprising; in fact it is intuitively obvious. However, in assessing the discriminant function's performance, we may not want to use all the data.

How Well Do the Variables Discriminate?

To answer this question we need to use the classification table and an appropriate chance criterion. Throughout this discussion we will assume that we either have fresh data or that we have adjusted for "fitting-the-discriminant-function-to-data" bias. The question of how to use the data arises when the two groups are of greatly unequal size.

We saw from (6) that when the two groups are of equal size, the likelihood ratio (which contains all sample information) completely determines the discriminant function. However, when the prior probabilities are unequal, this influences the classification procedure. If the groups are greatly unequal, the term log(prior odds) can completely dominate the term log(likelihood ratio). Here we cannot determine how well the independent variables discriminate. We would obtain the clearest picture if the prior odds were equal and, hence, did not affect the classification.

Assume that we were attempting to discriminate adopters of a new product from nonadopters. If we had a sample of 1,000 people, a result of 50 adopters and 950 nonadopters would not be unusual. If we attempted to classify all 1,000 individuals, we might get a classification table like the following:

		Classified 1	2	
Actual	1	7	43	50
	2	13	937	950
		20	980	1,000

Here we classified 944 (or 94.4 percent) individuals correctly. The proportional chance criterion is (see (2))

$$C_{\text{pro.}} = (.05)^2 + (.95)^2 = .907.$$

However, given that we classified 98 percent as Group 2, the outcome should have been

$$(.98)(.95) + (.02)(.05) = .932,$$

or 93.2 percent correctly classified.

The maximum chance criterion is

$$C_{\text{max.}} = .95.$$

Therefore our 94.4 percent correct classification is not too impressive. However, of the 20 individuals classified as Group 1, seven were correct. This is 35 percent compared with a chance percentage of 5. This last result is fairly impressive.

Now let us change the hypothetical classification slightly.

		Classified 1	2	
Actual	1	1	49	50
	2	9	941	950
		10	990	1,000

Here, we still classified slightly over 94 percent correctly; however, only one in ten was correct for Group 1 classifications.

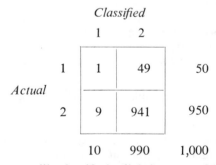

In summary, when one group is much larger than the other, almost all individuals are classified as the larger group. This means several will automatically be correctly classified. When we allow the posterior odds to classify the individuals—see (5)—we usually get even fewer classified in the smaller group than actually belong in it. There is often more interest in the smaller group, and classification tables like the preceding two are not the best way to assess the discrimination power of the independent variables.

One possibility is to rank all 1,000 individuals by their Z values and put the 50 highest in Group 1. This assures that a sufficient number will be classified as Group 1. We can now see how well we classified these individuals.

Another method would be to randomly divide the 950 Group 2 individuals into 19 groups, each with 50 members. We could construct 19 classification tables; the same 50 Group 1 members and the 19 different Group 2's. Then we could see on the average how well we did. This procedure has the advantage that the chance model is unambiguously 50 percent. Working with 50 percent chance models also makes interpretation easier. It is clear that correctly classifying 75 percent when chance is 50 percent is a good classification. (Of the 50 percent by which we could improve chance, we got half or 25 percent.) When the sample sizes were 50 and 950, the proportional chance criterion was 90 percent. Suppose we again obtain half of that remaining after chance and classify 95 percent correctly. This could occur by doing well with Group 1 individuals or by merely classifying everyone as Group 2. However, the interpretation is not as clear.

In summary we can say that (a) when the groups are of greatly unequal size, it may be difficult to interpret the classification table, and (b) regardless of the total sample size, the effective sample size (for determining ability to discriminate) is governed by the *smaller* of the two groups.

This last point is particularly relevant in the planning stages of a research project. A large total sample size is of little comfort without a sufficient number of individuals in each group.

Classification Decision

The last two sections dealt with which variables are good discriminators and their ability to discriminate. However, if the discriminant function is used to classify individuals, then clearly the misclassification costs must enter the decision.

As before, let

$P(I \mid x_i)$ be the posterior probability that an individual belongs to Group 1, given that we observed his vector of independent variables x_i

$P(II \mid x_i)$ be analogous definition for Group 2

C_{12} be the opportunity cost of classifying an individual in Group 2 when he actually belongs in Group 1

C_{21} be the opportunity cost of classifying an individual in Group 1 when he actually belongs in Group 2.

Any rational cost structure would have $C_{11} = C_{22} = 0$.

If we classify Individual i as Group 1, the expected opportunity cost is

$$K_i(I) = P(II \mid x_i)C_{21} .$$

Similarly, if we classify him as Group 2, the expected opportunity cost is

$$K_i(II) = P(I \mid x_i)C_{12} .$$

The classification procedure becomes: if $K_i(I) < K_i(II)$, we classify Individual i as belonging in Group 1 and vice versa.

By the same reasoning used to examine the effect of prior probabilities on the discriminant function, it is clear that C_{12} and C_{21} affect only the b_0 term of the discriminant function (or equivalently it simply changes the $z_{crit.}$ value).

Let the logarithm of the likelihood ratio—see (6)—be

$$\log(\text{likelihood ratio}) = b_0 + b_1X_{1i} + b_2X_{2i} + \cdots + b_nX_{ni} .$$

The classification rule is then:

classify Individual i as Group 1 if

$$b_0 + b_1X_{1i} + b_2X_{2i} + \cdots + b_nX_{ni} > \log k. \quad (10a)$$

Classify Individual i as Group 2 if

$$b_0 + b_1X_{1i} + b_2X_{2i} + \cdots + b_nX_{ni} < \log k, \quad (10b)$$

where

$$k = \frac{P(II)C_{21}}{P(I)C_{12}} . \quad (11)$$

In a real application, the difficult problem will be obtaining good estimates for the opportunity costs C_{12} and C_{21}.

IMPLEMENTATION OF THE RESULTS

One of the first successful business applications of discriminant analysis was in credit selection. Good credit risks were separated from poor credit risks on the basis of demographic and socioeconomic variables. Since on the credit application the individual fills in information on these same demographic and socioeconomic variables, the discriminant function can be applied directly to his application. The classification procedure (10a) and (10b) is then used to determine whether the applicant is to be given credit.

A main problem with this kind of project is obtaining representative past data. Chances are that the company only has data on individuals accepted as good credit risks. Of these previously screened individuals, some were actually good credit risks, others were not. However, this sample is not representative of the applicants applying for credit. In other words, the discriminant function for past data may not be the best for discriminating among current applicants. Of course, there is always the problem that the past discriminant function is outdated. Time or the competitive situation has changed the environment enough to make old results inapplicable. But at least for credit selection the variables used to discriminate were operational; the independent variables were used in decision making. This is not always true.

Suppose a researcher were able to discriminate adopters of a new product from nonadopters on the basis of demographic characteristics. If the product is sold through supermarkets and advertised in the mass media, it may be difficult to direct in-store displays and ads specifically at the likely adopters. However, if cents-off coupons are mailed, it may be relatively easy to direct this mailing to the more likely adopters. If a discriminant analysis is to be considered a decision-making aid (as opposed to a strictly research-oriented study), management needs a clear idea how the results will be implemented before the project is undertaken.

When the independent variables are obtained by personal interviews, there is a whole new set of problems.[7] It may be particularly hard to get comparability across interviewers.

High degrees of collinearity (high correlations) among the independent variables should be avoided. The resulting discriminant coefficients will be unstable, and it will be more difficult to interpret the contribution of each independent variable. Hence, if two independent variables are highly correlated, e.g., $r = .95$, only one of these variables should be included in the analysis. Otherwise the variances of the b's (the discriminant coefficients) will be unnecessarily large.

DISCUSSION

In summary, some considerations follow:

1. A linear discriminant function is appropriate only when the groups' covariance matrices are equal (or nearly equal).
2. The D^2 statistic (which may be transformed to an F statistic) only tests the statistical significance of the difference between groups. Recall the effect of the sample size on statistical significance.
3. Beware of the upward bias that results from classifying the same individuals used to calculate the discriminant function.
4. Beware of the different chance models that can result when groups have different sizes. Remember that greatly unequal-sized groups make interpretation of the classification table difficult.
5. The effective sample size is really governed by the smaller group.
6. Have the discriminant coefficients been normalized by the standard deviations of the independent variables?
7. In forming the classification decision, be sure that prior probabilities and opportunity costs of misclassification have been considered.
8. Will the independent variables used for discrimination be operational?

All of these apply to multiple discriminant analysis, i.e., when we are classifying individuals into more than two groups. The only main difference is that it is not as easy to assess the effect of the independent variables in discriminating among the groups. For example, variable j might be the best discriminator for Group 1 and Group 2, but variable k is best between Group 2 and Group 3. Strictly speaking, all eight points also apply to discriminant analysis for more than two groups.

[7] Ferber discusses these problems in detail in [2, pp. 251–9].

APPENDIX

Conditions Required for Optimal Linear Classification

Let

μ_{j1} be the mean of the jth variable for individuals who belong to Group 1

σ^1_{jk} be the covariance between variables j and k for individuals who belong to Group 1.

The mean vector μ_1 is formed as follows:

$$\mu_1 = (\mu_{11}, \mu_{21}, \cdots, \mu_{n1}).$$

The covariance matrix $\mathbf{V}_1$ is

$$\mathbf{V}_1 = \begin{bmatrix} \sigma^1_{11} & \sigma^1_{12} & \cdots & \sigma^1_{1n} \\ \sigma^1_{12} & \sigma^1_{22} & \cdots & \sigma^1_{2n} \\ \vdots & \vdots & & \vdots \\ \sigma^1_{1n} & \sigma^1_{2n} & \cdots & \sigma^1_{nn} \end{bmatrix}.$$

σ^1_{11} is merely the variance of X_1. The covariance between X_j and X_k is equal to the covariance between X_k and X_j; hence, the matrix is symmetrical. Finally, the covariance is related to the simple correlation between two variables. Letting r_{jk} be the correlation between variables X_j and X_k, we have

$$r_{jk} = \frac{\sigma_{jk}}{\sqrt{\sigma_{jj}\sigma_{kk}}}.$$

Analogous definitions hold for the mean vector μ_2 and covariance matrix $\mathbf{V}_2$. With these preliminaries we can now state the conditions for optimality of a linear classification procedure.

A linear classification procedure is optimal if: (a) the independent variables in Groups 1 and 2 are multivariate normal with mean vectors μ_1 and μ_2 and covariance matrices $\mathbf{V}_1$ and $\mathbf{V}_2$, respectively, and (b) $\mathbf{V}_1 = \mathbf{V}_2$.

We will now illustrate how unequal covariance matrices can lead to nonlinear classification boundaries. Suppose we are classifying two groups on the basis of two variables X_1 and X_2. Assume that the mean vectors μ_1 and μ_2 are equal, but that the covariance matrices are of the form,

$$\mathbf{V}_1 = \begin{bmatrix} \sigma_{11} & 0 \\ 0 & \sigma_{22} \end{bmatrix}$$

$$\mathbf{V}_2 = \begin{bmatrix} \alpha\sigma_{11} & 0 \\ 0 & \alpha\sigma_{22} \end{bmatrix},$$

where

$$\alpha > 1.$$

Then intuitively, the farther an individual's x_i is from the common mean vector μ, the more likely it is that he belongs to Group 2. Mathematically we would calculate the distance from μ at which the likelihood functions for both groups were equal. Because the covariance matrices are symmetrical, the locus of such points will be a circle with μ as the center. The classification boundary will be this circle. If the prior probabilities favor Group 1, the radius of the circle will increase and vice versa.

Interpretation of the variables is very difficult (or at least not simple). An increase in X_1 may increase or decrease the likelihood of an individual belonging to Group 1; it depends on the previous values of X_1 and X_2.

REFERENCES

1. T. W. Anderson, *Introduction to Multivariate Statistical Analysis,* John Wiley & Sons, Inc., 1958.
2. Robert Ferber, *The Reliability of Consumer Reports of Financial Assets,* Studies in Consumer Savings No. 6, Urbana, Ill.: Bureau of Economic and Business Research, University of Illinois, 1966.
3. Ronald E. Frank, William F. Massy and Donald G. Morrison, "Bias in Multiple Discriminant Analysis," *Journal of Marketing Research,* 2 (August 1965), 250–8.
4. Donald G. Morrison, "Measurement Problems in Cluster Analysis," *Management Science,* 13 (August 1967), B775–80.
5. Frederick Mosteller and Robert R. Bush, "Selective Quantitative Techniques," *Handbook of Social Psychology,* Vol. 1, in Gardner Lindzey, ed., Reading, Mass.: Addison-Wesley, 1954.

MELVIN R. CRASK and WILLIAM D. PERREAULT, JR.*

The validation problems inherent in small-sample discriminant analysis are examined. Two recently developed alternatives to the more traditional methods are explained and illustrated in the context of a salesman-selection problem. Concluding discussion covers the applicability of these approaches to other areas of marketing research in which validation is a problem.

Validation of Discriminant Analysis in Marketing Research

INTRODUCTION

Since marketing researchers first were introduced to discriminant analysis nearly 20 years ago [1, 10, 16], it has become a widely used analytical tool [4-6, 18, 21, 23, 28, 31-33, 35, 36, 38]. The adoption of discriminant function analysis (DFA) techniques has been rapid because marketing researchers and managers alike frequently are concerned with the nature and strength of the relationship between group membership (for example, different market segments) and individual characteristics (such as life style measures). Furthermore, the widespread availability of easy-to-use discriminant analysis computer programs has facilitated implementation of these techniques [7, 8, 26]. The use of DFA in marketing research has proved most beneficial for three major purposes: (1) developing predictive models to *classify* individuals into groups [5, 28, 31, 32], (2) "*profiling*" characteristics of groups which are most dominant in terms of discrimination [4, 6, 21, 27, 33], and/or (3) identifying the major underlying *dimensions* (i.e., discriminant functions) which differentiate among groups [1, 10, 16, 18, 23].

The general applicability of DFA and the ease of computation, however, pose a question which all too often is ignored by marketers who use DFA in sample-based research. How valid are sample-based discriminant analysis results with respect to the broader population of interest? The issue of validity can be raised for each of the purposes of DFA. First, is actual classification potential as high as sample estimates indicate? Second, are the true population profiles what they appear to be from the sample results? Third, are the underlying sample-based dimensions generalizable to the population? The implications of a negative response to any of these questions are evident; no marketing manager wants to commit the resources of his firm on the basis of possibly inaccurate results, and scholars do not wish to misdirect the body of knowledge in an area by reporting sample-specific findings. Although validation problems are not restricted to small-sample research, the issue becomes critical as the sample size is decreased. However, marketing researchers often are forced to use small samples which severely limit their ability to answer the aforementioned questions affirmatively. Thus, the purpose of this report is to discuss the validation of small-sample discriminant analysis results in marketing research.

Toward this objective, a brief review of previous work in this area is provided. Two recently proposed improved alternatives are discussed, and their advantages and limitations examined. The proposed methods of validation are illustrated in the context of a salesman-selection problem. Finally, the operational necessities for using these methods are discussed and other areas of marketing research where the techniques could be applied are considered.

APPROACHES TO VALIDATION

As with other optimizing procedures, the ability of DFA to "find" strong relationships is the cause of the concern over the results obtained because the procedure may simply be capitalizing on relationships that exist as an artifact of the sample. Obviously,

*Melvin R. Crask is Assistant Professor of Marketing, University of Georgia, and William D. Perreault is Assistant Professor of Business Administration, University of North Carolina.

Reprinted from *Journal of Marketing Research,* 14 (February 1977), 60-68, published by the American Marketing Association.

the smaller the sample the greater the chance that such spurious relationships will influence the generalizability of the results.

The potential for bias in the use of small samples in discriminant analysis long has been realized in the marketing literature [11, 14, 23, 24]. Several discussions of alternative approaches to validating results have been presented [11, 23, 24], although most have focused on the bias in the error rates of classification. Montgomery [23] recently provided an excellent and concise critique of these approaches. They are reviewed only briefly here to examine their shortcomings and thus give a clearer concept of what a good validation technique should provide.

The most frequently suggested validation approach is the holdout method, in which the sample is randomly split. One of the subsamples is used to develop estimates of the discriminant coefficients, and these coefficients are applied to the observations in the other subsample for classification purposes. With a large data base this approach may be appropriate. In small-sample research its use is impractical because splitting an already small sample makes the derived coefficients even less reliable; the error rates in classification may not be representative of the function which would be derived with the total sample. Furthermore, as typically applied this approach is only useful in considering classification and does not help in determining the validity of the profiles or the underlying dimensions.

Monté Carlo simulations also have been suggested as a mechanism for evaluating discriminant results [11]. Synthetic data are generated and discriminant functions are derived with the same degrees of freedom as the original data. This approach is very useful when the predictors are independent, but this is usually not the case with marketing data. When the predictors are not independent the problem is straightforward: in generating synthetic data it is impossible to model the covariance structure between the predictor variables [23, p. 259]. This method holds great potential if the problems of generating data can be overcome, but until that time results from this approach do not adequately address the problems of marketers.[1]

In a recent study, Montgomery [23] used another method of evaluating the classification results of discriminant analysis. He randomly assigned observations to groups and computed discriminant scores. By repeating this procedure several times, one can compare the results of these classifications with the true group results. By use of the actual data instead of synthetic data, the interrelationships among the sample data are preserved. This approach is interesting and the writers have found it a useful method for evaluating classification results. However, one must question the comparisons being made. Researchers typically are interested in how well the DFA performs in an absolute sense rather than how it performs in comparison with a similar random chance model. Furthermore, like the holdout method, this procedure does not provide a means of evaluating the validity of the DFA results used to define differences between groups.

At a basic level, the validity of DFA results resides in the stability of the coefficients derived. Classifying, profiling, and evaluating the underlying discriminant dimensions all are based directly or indirectly on these coefficients. Considering this fact in light of the foregoing review, marketing researchers would like a validation procedure which provides a mechanism that uses all of the information in the sample data for evaluating the stability of parameter estimates while allowing unbiased estimation of error rates.

Recently, independent research efforts directed toward these criteria have generated two very similar alternatives for validation of DFA. One of these, known as the U-method [19], focuses on the issue of classification errors. The other, generally referred to as "jackknife analysis" [25, 34], focuses on coefficient stability. When the two methods are applied simultaneously, a very useful validation procedure evolves. In fact, the researcher is able to evaluate not only classification rates and coefficient stability, but also the expected classification error rates regardless of sample size. A marketing research example is used to illustrate these approaches after a review of the logic upon which they are based.

Validation: The Jackknife and the U-Method

The jackknife statistic is a general method for reducing the bias in an estimator while providing a measure of the variance of the resulting estimator by sample reuse. The result of the procedure is an unbiased, or nearly unbiased, estimator and its associated approximate confidence interval. Because of the versatility of the technique, it is named after another tool of many uses, the Boy Scout's jackknife [34].

The essence of the jackknife approach is to partition out the impact or effect of a particular subset of the data (e.g., a single case) on an estimate derived from the total sample. Before considering the jackknife as applied in discriminant analysis, it is useful to review its general form.

Suppose that a random sample of size N is under consideration, and that there is an observed variable X for each of the N sampling units. Let the sample be partitioned into k subsets of size M (i.e., $kM = N$), so that a new random sample can be formed by arbitrarily deleting one of the subsets from the original sample. Let θ' be defined as an estimator

[1] If the predictor variables are factor scores or similar independent, normally distributed measures, the Monté Carlo method remains a useful alternative.

using *all* the sample values of X, and θ_i' an estimator defined on only those values of X which remain after the "i^{th}" subset of size M has been deleted from the total sample.

The first step in computing the jackknifed estimator is to compute k different *pseudovalues* [29], which are weighted combinations of the θ' and θ_i' values. Specifically, the pseudovalues are:

$$(1) \qquad J_i(\theta') = k\theta' - (k-1)\theta_i', \quad i = 1, \ldots, k.$$

Then the jackknife statistic is:

$$(2) \qquad J(\theta') = \left[\sum_{i=1}^{k} J_i(\theta')\right] \bigg/ k = k\theta' - (k-1)\bar{\theta}_i';$$

thus, the jackknife is simply the average of the pseudovalues.

The logic of the partitioning process by which the pseudovalues are computed (equation 1) is clarified by considering a simplified example. Suppose that a sample of size 5 provides values of 3, 2, 1, 5, and 4. By use of the pseudovalue equation, the impact of the first observation on an estimator, the sample mean, can be eliminated by substituting into equation 1 and computing

$$5\,[(3+2+1+5+4)/5] - 4\,[(2+1+5+4)/4] = 3.$$

If this process is repeated, with systematic deletion of a different subset (observation) each time, and the computed pseudovalues are averaged, the resulting statistic is the jackknifed mean on the sample.

Computing the jackknife for a mean as in the example illustrates the logic of the pseudovalue derivation but is of little consequence. However, when applied to more complex estimators (e.g., discriminant function coefficients), the pseudovalues and subsequent jackknife estimators have important properties. In particular, the pseudovalues can be treated as independent, identically distributed random variables, and hence can be used to obtain approximate confidence intervals for the jackknife estimate. The confidence intervals can be tested with Student's t having $k - 1$ degrees of freedom [25, 34]. Moreover, when applied to linear estimators, the jackknife is important in itself because the bias in the jackknife estimate has been shown to be *less than* the bias in the original sample estimate, θ', and frequently approaches zero [14].[2] Furthermore, little efficiency is lost by structuring the subsamples to be very small. Thus the jackknife is very useful in determining the stability of the estimates in many situations where marketing researchers use statistics and particularly in discriminant analysis.

The generalized forms for the computation of pseudovalues (equation 1) and for the jackknife statistic (equation 2) are directly applicable to each of the discriminant coefficients of a discriminant analysis. The procedure is briefly here outlined and clarified further by an illustration.

Step 1. To use jackknife procedures in discriminant analysis, the researcher partitions his sample into k subsamples. The standard discriminant function is computed by combining all of the subsamples.

Step 2. Then, a discriminant function is computed by using $k - 1$ of the subsamples (i.e., holding out one subsample). This step provides estimates corresponding to the θ_i' and is repeated k times, with a different subsample omitted each time. The pseudovalues, as indicated in equation 1, are derived by weighting and subtracting these coefficients from the estimates of step 1.

Step 3. The jackknifed coefficients are computed from the averaged pseudovalues as indicated in equation 2. The use and interpretation of the jackknifed coefficients are discussed in the next section. The main benefit of this type of analysis is that it provides a foundation for evaluating the *stability* of the coefficients.

If, however, estimation of *error rates* in classification is the principal concern, Lachenbruch and Mickey [19] have proposed a similar sample reuse procedure, the U-method. To apply the U-method, one observation is omitted from the sample and a discriminant function is computed by using the remaining observations. This function is used to determine the group membership of the omitted observation. By repeating this procedure for all observations in the sample, an estimate of misclassification can be obtained for each group by totalling the number of misclassifications in the group and dividing by the total number of cases in the group. Although it might appear that a complete new discriminant analysis would be required for each omitted observation, Bartlett [2] describes a procedure in which only one explicit matrix inversion is required; in fact the U-method is named for this inversion procedure.

By the U-method, there is no effective way to determine the stability of the coefficients of the discriminant function because the U-method does not have the bias reduction properties of the jackknife.[3] However, the procedures used for the jackknife and for the U-method are very similar in that both involve an efficient partitioning of the sample. It is therefore possible to combine the procedures simultaneously

[2] More specifically, the jackknife *completely* eliminates biases which are inversely proportioned to sample size [20, p. 570]. Miller [22], however, has pointed out that in some nonlinear estimation situations the jackknife does not reduce bias; his caveats are useful to researchers who wish to apply the jackknife in situations dissimilar to those discussed in this article.

[3] The bias reduction properties of the jackknife are a function of the weighting procedure used in its calculation. These weights are not applied in the U-method.

to achieve both estimates of the error rates of classification and stability of the coefficients, as shown in the following example.

THE RESEARCH PROBLEM

The data for this example were provided by a major manufacturer of consumer goods and concern the selection of salesmen for intermediate markets. Through an outside agency, the company administers personnel tests to new salesmen. After acquiring on-the-job experience, each salesmen is classified by his sales manager as a high or low performer. This illustration is based on a two-group (high versus low performers) discriminant analysis using six personnel test scores as predictors. Data for 24 salesmen are used in the analysis. This situation was chosen as an illustration for several reasons. First, a two-group discriminant analysis, in contrast to a k-group case, allows easier understanding of the techniques presented here; this is not to imply that these procedures are not useful with the k-group case. Instead, with two groups of equal size the issue of classification errors can be evaluated directly by examining discriminant function scores, rather than Mahalanobis' D-square. Second, the use of few cases (salesmen) in relation to the number of variables results in the type of bias which is of concern in discriminant analysis and allows a rather complete presentation of results to facilitate understanding. Finally, the situation is typical of the type of application where the sample is not large enough for traditional holdout methods but where there is very real managerial and legal [15] concern for validation of results.[4]

ANALYSIS

When a standard discriminant analysis is computed with the sample, *all* of the salesmen are classified correctly. Most researchers would question the validity of such results and their applicability to the broader population of sales applicants. Thus, let us evaluate the validity of the discriminant results in three stages. First, the U-method is used to classify salesmen. Second, the jackknifed discriminant functions are computed and their stability evaluated. Third, the two approaches are integrated to evaluate coefficient stability, classification error rates, and expected classification results if an infinite sample were available.

U-Method Results. As mentioned, developing a discriminant function using all of the subjects and then classifying the same salesmen with this function yielded perfect classification. This result can be expected because, with a small number of observations, each subject has significant impact upon the coefficients of the function. With the U-method, any given observation has no effect upon the coefficients of the function used to classify that observation.

To apply the U-method, the salesmen were grouped randomly into 12 pairs, each pair containing a high and a low performer. By holding out one pair, a discriminant function was computed with the remaining 11 pairs and the pair held out was classified by use of this function. Repeating this process for each pair allowed each salesman to be classified by a discriminant function in which his test scores had no influence upon the coefficients. Table 1 presents the results. Three salesmen (12.5%) are misclassified by the U-method whereas none was misclassified by a standard discriminant analysis. Thus, in this case, the U-method provides a more conservative (higher) estimate of classification error than that observed by use of the total sample. In a Monté Carlo study, Lachenbruch and Mickey [19] found a similar pattern of classification errors, and suggest that the more conservative (U-method) estimates are a better estimate of the error than can be achieved by use of the total sample.

Jackknife Results. The U-method results have provided a basis for evaluating the classification model derived from the discriminant analysis. If the researcher is concerned instead with characterizing between-group profiles or the underlying dimensions which discriminate between groups, the jackknife method would be used. For the salesman-selection problem, the first step is to compute the pseudovalues for the discriminant coefficients. These values are computed according to equation 1, by use of each of the 12 discriminant equations derived from the U-method (Table 2) and the equation which results from the analysis on the total sample. The jackknifed coefficients (which yield the jackknifed discriminant function) are computed as the averages of the pseudovalues; the jackknifed values are presented in Table 2.

The stability of the jackknifed discriminant coefficients is evaluated directly by computing the traditional standard errors for each set of pseudovalue coefficients (computation of the jackknife standard error follows the traditional calculation of the standard error of the mean). Because the jackknifed coefficients approximate the t distribution [25], each coefficient can be divided by its associated standard error (shown in parentheses under the jackknifed equation in Table 2) to give a t-value; the degrees of freedom for the t-value are based on the number of partitions of the sample (pseudovalues) minus 1, or 11 in this case. In this analysis, only the t-value for the coefficient of test 6 exceeds the critical value, and thus it may be the only true discriminator between the salesman performance groups.

[4] With regard to the legal requirements of the salesman selection problem, it should be noted that this analysis is based only on salesmen who actually were hired; for strict predictive validity, all *applicants* should be hired, and *then* the relationship between test scores and performance evaluated.

Table 1
CLASSIFICATION OF SALESMEN BY STANDARD DISCRIMINANT ANALYSIS, *U*-METHOD, AND JACKKNIFE

Salesman pair "i"	*Salesman discriminant scores*					
	Total sample results		*U-method results*		*Jackknife results*	
	High performers	*Low performers*	*High performers*	*Low performers*	*High performers*	*Low performers*
1	0.8601	0.4895	0.6467	0.4364	1.0595	0.6533[a]
2	1.1621	0.2152	1.2877	0.2071	1.2048	0.3818
3	1.0689	0.0772	1.0853	0.0773	0.9929	0.1488
4	1.2396	0.1209	1.4907	0.1712	1.1281	0.2961
5	1.2199	0.0649	1.2904	0.0568	1.1539	0.1425
6	0.5657	0.0722	0.4566[a]	0.0761	0.6671	0.0692
7	0.9454	−0.0143	0.9001	−0.0138	0.9530	0.1168
8	0.8295	0.0988	0.7885	0.0795	0.8325	0.1619
9	1.0819	0.0499	1.2948	0.0452	0.9122	0.1090
10	0.5137	0.1702	0.4119[a]	0.1489	0.5883	0.1744
11	0.5126	0.0343	0.4541[a]	−0.0073	0.4988[a]	0.1492
12	0.6683	−0.0522	0.6363	0.0662	0.6643	0.0479
Discriminant score average	0.8898	0.1106	0.8936	0.1009	0.8880	0.2042

[a]These scores result in misclassification of the associated salesman.

Although the jackknife approach is used mainly for evaluating stability of coefficients, the resulting equations can be used to compute discriminant scores on which the salesmen can be classified. The jackknife classification in this problem results in two misclassifications (see Table 1).

The jackknife provides a basis on which the strength of classification, not just the number classified, can be evaluated. Specifically, confidence intervals about the jackknife discriminant score for a salesman can be computed from the standard errors of the scores obtained from the pseudovalue equations. The larger the confidence interval which is possible without containing the cutpoint between groups, the more securely a salesman is classified. Six salesmen were found to have discriminant scores more than two deviations from the cutpoint, and four other salesmen have values more than 1.6 deviations from the cutpoint. The rest were not so securely classified.

A Combined U-Method/Jackknife Approach. The foregoing approaches are valid if the researcher is interested in either stability *or* error classification. If it is desirable to evaluate both simultaneously, a combined approach must be used because of bias

Table 2
ADJUSTED DISCRIMINANT AND JACKKNIFE COEFFICIENTS FOR SALESMAN DISCRIMINANT ANALYSIS

Salesman pair omitted for pseudovalues	*Discriminant coefficients*						
	Test 1	*Test 2*	*Test 3*	*Test 4*	*Test 5*	*Test 6*	*Constant*
(none)	0.03420	0.00317	−0.00915	−0.00295	−0.00194	−0.01413	−0.83552
1	0.04023	0.00337	−0.00665	−0.00225	−0.00355	−0.01370	−1.63210
2	0.02726	0.00310	−0.00535	−0.00311	0.00051	−0.01245	−0.58232
3	0.03515	0.00304	−0.00946	−0.00322	−0.00191	−0.01420	−0.85930
4	0.05743	0.00511	−0.01741	0.00073	−0.00713	−0.01467	−2.31195
5	0.03845	0.00385	−0.01061	−0.00288	−0.00255	−0.01445	−1.08386
6	0.04356	0.00574	−0.01179	−0.00290	−0.00270	−0.01279	−1.72382
7	0.03457	0.00367	−0.00952	−0.00330	−0.00153	−0.01369	−0.90551
8	0.03321	0.00246	−0.00971	−0.00365	−0.00198	−0.01380	−0.60924
9	0.03452	0.00285	−0.00860	−0.00679	−0.00138	−0.01358	−0.63029
10	0.03059	0.00083	−0.00604	−0.00344	−0.00177	−0.01488	−0.55750
11	0.02813	0.00209	−0.00866	−0.00382	0.00004	−0.01443	−0.30358
12	0.03452	0.00296	−0.01052	−0.00256	−0.00266	−0.01395	−0.73444
Jackknife coefficients	.009	.002	−0.005	−0.001	−0.001	−0.014	.913
Standard error of coefficient	(.026)	(.004)	(.010)	(.005)	(.006)	(.002)	(1.890)

introduced when both issues are evaluated simultaneously by only one of the methods. A combined approach, suggested in [25], is illustrated and an extension which may be very important in pretest research is discussed.

Suppose each of the 12 salesmen in one group is paired with a salesman in the other group. Holding out one of these pairs and performing a complete jackknife analysis on the remaining 11 pairs yields 11 pseudovalue equations and the resulting jackknifed equation. The pair held out then can be classified by use of each of the 11 pseudovalue equations as well as by the jackknifed equation. Twelve legitimate cross-validations thus are provided for each member of this pair and the pair *was not influential* in the determination of any of the equations. Repeating this procedure for each of the 12 pairs provides a total of 288 cross-validations, and thus yields a good measure of the performance of the variables. In the salesman-selection problem, an average error rate of 13.6% was obtained for these 288 cross-validations, although the error rates for individual salesmen ranged from 4.5 to 45%. These extremes indicate a tremendous influence by the individual salesmen upon the discriminant function.

The pseudovalues also can be used to calculate confidence intervals on the coefficients, as in the foregoing simple jackknife situation. The average coefficient values and their associated confidence intervals yield the equation:

$$D'_j = -4.728 + 0.069T_1 + 0.006T_2 - 0.008T_3 + 0.002T_4 - 0.004T_5 - 0.015T_6.$$

(1.162) (.016) (.002) (.005) (.003) (.004) (.001)

Tests 1, 2, and 6 all can be considered discriminators from this result, whereas in the original jackknifed equation, D_j (Table 2), only test 6 yielded a significant coefficient. However, D'_j should provide much more accurate coefficient estimation because this estimation is based on more than six times the number of observations used in the first equation.

The literature in the area of error rates in classification suggests yet another possible extension when these two methods are used simultaneously [25]. In general, this extension seeks to answer the question, "What error rate in classification might be expected if the researcher had available an infinite population rather than a limited sample?" Even if these six tests were perfect predictors of high and low performers, dispersion around the population centroids would occur because of the variances of these population means. Depending upon the magnitude of these variances, some error in classification may occur regardless of the sample size. Finding this error rate is analogous to a determination of the probability of making a Type 1 error. In the foregoing analyses, the researcher knows from the sample results that approximately a 13% error rate is expected. Although this rate is much better than the 50% error rate one would expect if there were no discriminatory power, management might desire a function which would perform at some specified level (e.g., yield no more than 10% error). The researcher or manager would like to know, in effect, whether or not these six tests would meet this criterion if the sample size were increased. The following discussion illustrates how this problem can be attacked.

The population centroids are known to be zero and one, and variation around these centroids can be attributed to two sources: the population standard error and the sample size used. The larger the sample size, the smaller this effect will become. Total variation as well as the variation due to the sample size can be calculated and used to estimate the population standard error. This standard error then can be used to estimate the lower limit of the error rates one might expect.

The total variation is measured by the variation in the mean estimates (the jackknifed estimates). Because grouped data were used, a pooled estimate of the total variation must be obtained by (1) calculating the variance of each group of salesmen (the average of the sum of squared deviations of the mean estimates of the salesmen from their group centroid), (2) adding the variances of both groups, and (3) averaging this sum to obtain a pooled estimate of the total variation.

The variation caused by the sample size is captured by the dispersion of the pseudovalues around the mean estimates. This variation can be derived by (1) calculating the variance of the mean estimate of each salesman (the average of the sum of squared deviations of the salesman's pseudovalues from his mean estimate, or jackknifed value), (2) summing the variances of all salesmen, and (3) averaging this sum to obtain a measure of the variation due to the sample size. The population standard error then can be calculated by subtracting the variation due to the sample from the total variation.

By this procedure the population standard error obtained is 0.2369. Though not exact, this estimate indicates that both population means are approximately two standard deviations from the cutpoint. Depending upon the assumed distribution, one can estimate the error rate expected regardless of the sample size. For example, the expected error rate for this problem is approximately 5% if a normal distribution is assumed.

Thus, this extension uses small-sample results to develop an estimate of the classification rates that might be expected with much larger samples. This information would be most useful in market pretest research where data collection is very expensive. The researcher can evaluate the results of a small-sample analysis and have a more complete basis for determining whether the expense of collecting data on a large sample would be warranted. It should be emphasized that such "infinite sample" estimates are, in a practical sense, limited to the two-group discriminant case. Though there has been some work to generalize this type of analysis to the multiple-group situation [12], operational solutions have not been developed.

DISCUSSION AND IMPLICATIONS

Stability

The researcher interested in validating the stability of discriminant coefficients quickly confronts the problem that "canned" computer programs are not available to implement the jackknife method. To compute the jackknife equations with present software requires many successive computer runs, each with selective deletion of subsamples from the analysis. This process becomes cumbersome (and expensive) when many subsamples are used.

This is not to suggest that coefficient stability should be ignored. Because the stability of the jackknife can be computed with relative ease and accuracy from relatively few pseudovalues, the researcher can divide his sample randomly into a few *nonoverlapping* subgroups. Pseudovalues and the jackknifed equation can be computed by systematically holding out one sample subgroup and computing the pseudo-equations. The confidence intervals on the coefficients (or the discriminant scores) then would be computed as described. Although this type of partitioning of the data is not as "efficient" as holding out individual observations, it is a relatively simple way to evaluate the stability of the coefficients and the general validity of the results of the research.

Classification

In an ideal sense the best estimates of classification accuracy of sample results would be based on the combined jackknife/U-method. Here again good computer software is not available. However, in the salesman performance example, the U-method provided nearly the same error rate estimation alone as it did in combination with the jackknife. The writers have found this similarity of performance to be typical.

Computationally, the U-method can be implemented very easily on the computer. Very flexible discriminant analysis computer programs recently have become available which provide this analysis as an option [8, 9]; one of these [8] is widely available as a program in the BMDP series. Because the classification is based on a jackknifed Mahalanobis' D-square, the researcher can (1) prespecify the prior probabilities of group membership (as when the researcher knows that his sample is not stratified in the same proportion as the total market), (2) use more than two groups, and (3) use different sample sizes for each group.

When the estimate of error classification rates is computed as suggested heretofore, cost is not prohibitive. For example, to provide cost data which might be illustrative of a typical marketing research situation, a four group/six predictor variable discriminant analysis was computed for 100 cases by use of the program described in [8, p. 411-51]. The analysis, including classification based on sample reuse, cost less than three dollars when run on an IBM 360 computer. In short, the incremental cost of the extended analysis is minor.

Other Jackknife Applications

The jackknife approach has been discussed in the context of bias estimation in discriminant analysis. Several other areas where the jackknife has potential for marketing researchers are worth noting briefly.

In general, if an unbiased estimator exists, the jackknife will yield such an estimator. For example, Brillinger [3] has advocated the jackknife in developing estimates of the mean and variance of response variables in market surveys. More specifically, the jackknife is appropriate in any research situation where the analysis procedures (and test statistics) assume normality but the data seriously violate this assumption. This situation is common in marketing research applications of (multivariate) linear statistics, especially when stratified sampling procedures have been used. In this regard, Ireland and Uselton [17] demonstrate the superiority of the jackknifed F-statistic over the conventional F-statistics under conditions of nonnormal data in regression analysis; the jackknife was more robust to violations of the normality assumptions. Similarly, Mantel [20] has discussed the applicability of the jackknife in other estimation situations where it is not advantageous to assume a form of the distribution for a parameter.

It also has been suggested that the jackknife may be very useful with ratio estimators. For example, consider the case of a company which would like to introduce a product in select test markets and, on the basis of test market sales, to estimate sales levels which might be expected if the product received national distribution. One approach might be to evaluate the ratio of sales to population in the test markets, and then to extrapolate to the total population. There is a major problem, however, because the ratio will vary substantially, introducing bias, depending on which test markets are chosen and any spurious forces in those markets. The jackknife is well applied in such situations to reduce bias in estimation. Raj [30] and Gray and Schucany [13] provide detailed discussion and illustration of the use of jackknife approaches to ratio estimators of this type.

It also has been suggested that the jackknife may be useful in research models based on stochastic processes. There is typically substantial bias in the estimates derived by stochastic models in marketing and consumer behavior research, and in many circumstances this bias can be reduced with the jackknife [37].

The foregoing discussion is not intended to serve as an exhaustive listing of jackknife applications, but rather to emphasize that marketing researchers may find it a useful tool in many situations where bias in results can lead to costly mistakes in marketing strategy.

SUMMARY

This report has addressed the issue of validity in sample-based marketing research, with particular emphasis on problems which arise in applications of discriminant analysis. Two approaches to the validation problem, the U-method and the jackknife, are discussed and illustrated in the context of a marketing research problem. Operational procedures for implementing these methods are suggested, as well as other areas of marketing research where these methods may be valuable aids in analysis and decision making.

REFERENCES

1. Banks, Seymour. "Why People Buy Particular Brands," *in* Robert Ferber and Hugh G. Wales, eds., *Motivation and Market Research.* Homewood, Illinois: Richard D. Irwin, Inc., 1958, 277-93.
2. Bartlett, Maurice S. "An Inverse Matrix Adjustment Arising in Discriminant Analysis," *Annals of Mathematical Statistics*, 22 (March 1952), 167.
3. Brillinger, David R. "The Application of the Jackknife to the Analysis of Sample Surveys," *Journal of the Market Research Society*, 8 (April 1966), 74-80.
4. Brody, Robert P. and Scott M. Cunningham. "Personality Variables and the Consumer Decision Process," *Journal of Marketing Research*, 5 (February 1968), 50-7.
5. Churchill, Gilbert A., Jr., Neil M. Ford and Urban B. Ozanne. "An Analysis of Price Aggressiveness in Gasoline Marketing," *Journal of Marketing Research*, 7 (February 1970), 36-42.
6. Claycamp, Henry J. "Characteristics of Thrift Deposit Owners," *Journal of Marketing Research*, 2 (May 1965), 163-70.
7. Dixon, Wilfred J., ed. *BMD: Biomedical Computer Programs.* Berkeley: University of California Press, 1973, 211-54.
8. ———. *BMDP: Biomedical Computer Programs.* Berkeley: University of California Press, 1975, 411-52.
9. Eisenbeis, Robert A. and Robert B. Avery. *Discriminant Analysis and Classification Procedures.* Lexington, Massachusetts: Heath, 1972.
10. Evans, Franklin B. "Psychological and Objective Factors in the Prediction of Brand Choice: Ford versus Chevrolet," *Journal of Business*, 32 (October 1959), 340-69.
11. Frank, Ronald E., William F. Massey and Donald G. Morrison. "Bias in Multiple Discriminant Analysis," *Journal of Marketing Research*, 2 (August 1965), 250-8.
12. Glick, Ned. "Sample-Based Classification Procedures Derived from Density Estimates," *Journal of the American Statistical Association*, 67 (March 1972), 116-22.
13. Gray, Henry L. and W. R. Schucany. *The Generalized Jackknife Statistic.* New York: Marcel Dekker, Inc., 1972.
14. Green, Paul E. "Bayesian Classification Procedures in Analyzing Customer Characteristics," *Journal of Marketing Research*, 1 (May 1964), 44-50.
15. *Guidelines on Employment Selection Procedures.* Washington, D.C.: Equal Employment Opportunity Commission, August 1970.
16. Harvey, John R. "What Makes a Best Seller," *in* Robert Ferber and Hugh G. Wales, eds., *Motivation and Market Research.* Homewood, Illinois: Richard D. Irwin, Inc., 1958, 361-81.
17. Ireland, M. Edward and Gene C. Uselton. "A Distribution Free Statistic for Management Scientists," *in* W. W. Menke and C. H. Whitehurst, eds., *Proceedings*, Eleventh Annual Meeting of the Southeastern Chapter, The Institute of Management Science, October 1975, 25-6.
18. King, William R. "Marketing Expansion—A Statistical Analysis," *Management Science*, 9 (July 1963), 563-73.
19. Lachenbruch, Peter A. and M. Ray Mickey. "Estimation of Error Rates in Discriminant Analysis," *Technometrics*, 10 (February 1968), 1-11.
20. Mantel, Nathan. "Assumption-Free Estimators Using U-Statistics and a Relationship to the Jackknife Method," *Biometrics*, 23 (September 1967), 567-71.
21. Massy, William F. "Discriminant Analysis of Audience Characteristics," *Journal of Advertising Research*, 5 (March 1965), 39-48.
22. Miller, Rupert G. "A Trustworthy Jackknife," *Annals of Mathematical Statistics*, 35 (December 1964), 1594-605.
23. Montgomery, David B. "New Product Distribution: An Analysis of Supermarket Buyer Decisions," *Journal of Marketing Research*, 12 (August 1975), 255-64.
24. Morrison, Donald G. "On the Interpretation of Discriminant Analysis," *Journal of Marketing Research*, 6 (May 1969), 156-63.
25. Mosteller, Frederick and John W. Tukey. "Data Analysis, Including Statistics," *in* G. Lindsey and E. Aronson, eds., *The Handbook of Social Psychology*, Vol. 2. Reading, Massachusetts: Addison-Wesley, 1968, 80-203.
26. Nie, Norman H., D. Hadlai Hull, Jean G. Jenkins, Karin Steinbrenner and Dale H. Brent, eds. *SPSS: Statistical Package for the Social Sciences.* Englewood Cliffs, New Jersey: McGraw-Hill Book Co., Inc., 1975.
27. Perreault, William D., Jr. and William R. Darden. "GRAFIT: Computer Based Graphics for the Interpretation of Multivariate Analysis," *Journal of Marketing Research*, 12 (August 1975), 343-5.
28. Pessemier, Edgar A., Philip C. Burger and Douglas J. Tigert. "Can New Product Buyers Be Identified?" *Journal of Marketing Research*, 4 (November 1967), 349-54.
29. Quenouille, M. H. "Notes on Bias in Estimation," *Biometrika*, 43 (December 1956), 353-60.
30. Raj, Deg. *Sampling Theory.* New York: McGraw-Hill Book Co., Inc., 1968.
31. Rao, Tanniru R. "Is Brand Loyalty a Criterion for Marketing Segmentation: Discriminant Analysis," *Decision Sciences*, 4 (July 1973), 395-404.
32. Robertson, Thomas S. and John N. Kennedy. "Prediction of Consumer Innovations: Application of Multiple Discriminant Analysis," *Journal of Marketing Research*,

5 (February 1968), 64-9.
33. Shuchman, Abe and Peter C. Riesz. "Correlates of Persuasibility: The Crest Case," *Journal of Marketing Research*, 12 (February 1975), 7-11.
34. Tukey, John W. "Bias and Confidence in Not-Quite Large Samples" (abstract), *Annals of Mathematical Statistics*, 29 (June 1958), 614.
35. Uhl, Kenneth, Roman Andrus and Lance Poulsen. "How Are Laggards Different? An Empirical Inquiry," *Journal of Marketing Research*, 7 (February 1970), 51-4.
36. Utterback, James M. "Successful Industrial Innovations: A Multivariate Analysis," *Decision Sciences*, 6 (January 1975), 65-77.
37. Watkins, T. A. "Jackknifing Stochastic Process," unpublished Ph.D. dissertation, Texas Tech University, 1971.
38. Wind, Yoram. "Industrial Source Loyalty," *Journal of Marketing Research*, 7 (November 1970), 450-7.

WILLIAM R. DILLON, MATTHEW GOLDSTEIN, and LEON G. SCHIFFMAN*

Buyer usage behavior data are used to compare the relative performance of a linear discriminant analysis and several multinomial classification methods. The potential shortcomings of each of the procedures investigated are cited, and a new method for determining the contribution of a variable to discrimination in the context of the multinomial classification problem also is presented.

Appropriateness of Linear Discriminant and Multinomial Classification Analysis in Marketing Research

INTRODUCTION

Although many of the data collected in marketing research studies are of a qualitative or categorical nature, the treatment of such data has received scant attention in the marketing literature. Consequently, a tendency in analyzing data composed wholly or partly of nominal and ordinal variables has been to ignore their discrete nature and to proceed with continuous variable techniques. In the case of classification or discrimination this approach leads to the use of a linear discriminant function, which was first derived by Fisher [12].

The use of this discriminant function (hereafter referred to as Fisher's LDF) in marketing research studies has been, by any standards, extensive. Among the many applications of this procedure are studies of innovator profiles [6, 26, 30], relevant criteria for segmenting markets [3, 10, 24], and consumer brand preference behavior [1, 11, 29]. Though far from exhaustive, this list is sufficient to illustrate the general class of marketing problems that are amenable to discriminant analysis. However, with the exception of [13, 24, 28], few studies have addressed the design and interpretation difficulties associated with discriminant analysis. Furthermore, though the original derivation of Fisher's LDF was from a distribution-free standpoint, its use nevertheless cannot be justified in the sense of minimizing the Bayes risk unless multivariate normality and equal covariance matrices are assumed present. In effect, Fisher's LDF is one approach to the classification problem and although, for example, it does not require normality, its justification in the likelihood ratio sense certainly does.

Problems of this nature have led to research in classification procedures whereby the underlying distributions are discrete, and in particular multinomial.[1] In multinomial classification the data are qualitative in the sense that each variable assumes only a finite and usually small number of values. However, contrary to the growing interest in the analysis of qualitative data by multidimensional contingency tables and log-linear models [see 2, 19], little mention or use of discrete discrimination techniques is found in the marketing literature.[2]

Because the theoretical properties of the sample-based Fisher LDF tend to be very complex, knowledge of the population parameters is needed to report global statements as to the superiority of one procedure over another. For this reason many of the researchers attempting to compare the performance of Fisher's

*William R. Dillon is Assistant Professor of Marketing, School of Business Administration, University of Massachusetts. Matthew Goldstein is Professor of Statistics and Leon G. Schiffman is Associate Professor of Marketing, Bernard M. Baruch College, City University of New York. The authors thank the reviewers for the valuable comments which led to improvements in the original draft.

[1]Articles in the statistical literature of fundamental importance and interest with regard to multinomial classification include [4, 7, 14, 15, 20, 27].

[2]With the exception of [9, 18], the authors are not aware of any marketing studies either using or investigating the use of multinomial classification rules.

Reprinted from *Journal of Marketing Research,* 15 (February 1978), 103-12, published by the American Marketing Association.

LDF on nonnormal data have used a Monté Carlo sampling framework. However, a question of major importance to the practitioner is how well Fisher's LDF will perform, in relation to alternative techniques, on real data not satisfying the normality assumption. Therefore, the proposed multinomial classification methods, as well as Fisher's LDF, are illustrated on a marketing-related set of data[3] rather than by Monté Carlo sampling experiments.

Specifically, the purpose of the present study is threefold. First, reasons are presented why practitioners should take a closer look at the classification problem in situations where the available data are qualitative, rather than simply assuming multivariate normality and then proceeding to use some variant of Fisher's LDF. Second, several multinomial classification methods are described, and their performance along with Fisher's LDF is assessed on an illustrative set of data on consumption behavior for a major household service product. Finally, one of the most serious problems plaguing multinomial classification analysis is discussed and a potential remedy is described which takes the form of a new method for selecting good discriminatory variables.

DATA ANALYZED

The data used for analysis were collected in a 1975 study designed to examine the consumption behavior for a major household service product. Respondents were selected from three geographically dispersed areas in which the sponsoring company offered its services. The dependent (grouping) variable considered was extent of customer usage of a specific service provided by the firm. Customer usage was in terms of actual dollar expenditures for a fixed time period. Of a total of 464 respondents, 234 were identified as "heavy users" and the remaining 230 were identified as "light users." The distinction between heavy and light users conformed to the firm's general experience based on extensive market segmentation research. For purposes of this study, nine socioeconomic and demographic variables were selected to form the basis for classification; a description of the variables is given in Table 1.

WHY EXAMINE ALTERNATIVE PROCEDURES?

If the assumptions of normality and identical covariance matrices are satisfied, then there is no reason to examine alternatives to Fisher's LDF. However, in situations in which the available data are qualitative, application of this procedure is likely to introduce a certain amount of distortion by treating the categorical variables as though they were continuous. Moreover, when the applicability of Fisher's LDF is suspect because of the availability of categorical variables, the practitioner should *at least* consider the use of multinomial classification methods for the following reasons.

Evidence from Monté Carlo sampling experiments. Several researchers [7, 14, 27] have attempted to compare the performance of a number of classifica-

[3]This is not to imply that Monté Carlo sampling studies are of no value to the practitioner. On the contrary, it is not difficult to extrapolate from Monté Carlo simulations to a real data environment if data structures are first analyzed. Further, one of the purposes of this article is to alert the practitioner to the fact that improvements in discrimination may be realized if data structures are analyzed before a technique is chosen.

Table 1
VARIABLE DESCRIPTIONS

Variable	*Descriptions*
Home ownership	Own, rent
Number of rooms in home	Less than 5 rooms; at least 5 rooms
Length of residency	Less than 5 years; at least 5 years
Location of previous home	5 categories: Within this same city or town Outside of this city but in same county Outside of this county but in same state In another state but within the U.S.A. Outside U.S.A.
Marital status	3 categories: married, single, and widowed, separated or divorced
Head of household's occupation[a]	10 categories: Professional, technical Manager, official, or proprietor Sales or clerical worker Craftsman or foreman Operator Laborer Service worker Housewife Student Retired
Head of household's education	Some grade school—Master's degree+ in 8 categories
Family income	Under \$3,000–\$30,000+ in 11 categories
Stage in family lifecycle	6 categories: Head of household less than 55 years old, single (widowed, separated or divorced), no children Head of household less than 55 years old, married, no children Head of household less than 55 years old, with children (none teenagers) Head of household less than 55 years old with children (at least one teenager) Head of household at least 55 years old, employed Head of household at least 55 years old, unemployed

[a]Respondents were given illustrations of the types of jobs associated with each category.

tion procedures, including Fisher's LDF, on binary data by Monté Carlo sampling experiments. Although the general consensus appears to be that Fisher's LDF is fairly robust for binary variables, there are clear indications that it cannot satisfactorily cope with more complex phenomena. For example, Moore [27] concluded that Fisher's LDF should not be used in population structures in which disordinal interactions are present. (In Moore's language, disordinal interactions are called *reversals* because they reflect a nonmonotonicity of the likelihood ratio.) In a more recent Monté Carlo study, Dillon and Goldstein [7] examined trends in performance resulting from increasing (decreasing) correlational values and found Fisher's LDF to perform reasonably well in population structures characterized by low-to-moderate correlations (i.e., $\leq |.20|$). However, large (absolute) correlations in the predictor variable set were shown to affect its performance adversely. In particular, especially poor performance resulted with the use of Fisher's LDF in population structures for which all of the predictor variables had intercorrelations of about $|.30|$. Note that the presence of large (absolute) correlations in the predictor variable set translates into the probable presence of disordinal interactions.

In light of these results it would be useful to know how frequently disordinal interactions are found in real data. In certain fields such as marketing research, it is reasonable to suspect they may occur frequently given the kinds of variables generally analyzed.

Convergence rates. It is well known that the *apparent error rate*—the error rate obtained when the set of data used to construct the classification rule is also used to evaluate its performance—is an optimistically biased estimate of the true (optimum) error rate of classification. Several authors have attepted to get a fix on the asymptotic convergence rate of the apparent error to the optimum error [see 15, 16]. In particular, Glick [15] showed that for the case of qualitative variables with multinomial distributions the sample-based classification rule had error rates which converged to the optimum rate more rapidly than those of the multivariate normal classification rule. Hence, superior convergence rates adds credence for the investigation of multinomial classification methods.

Another interesting point can be made from this result. Though it appears to be common practice to treat the qualitative variables as though they were continuous, some authors have advocated the reverse procedure, namely, converting the available data (regardless of its form) into categoric data to take advantage of the superior convergence speeds resulting from the use of multinomial classification methods [4, 15, 23]. Obviously, a question of some importance is how much information is lost by discretizing more or less continuous variables such as respondent age or family income. Clearly, dichotomization of such continuous variables is a drastic action which in general will cause considerable loss of information. If continuous measurements are not available, however, dichotomizing categorical data representing class intervals appears more reasonable and may allow the practitioner the opportunity to take advantage of the superior convergence rates resulting from the use of multinomial classification methods.

Measurement considerations. In practice, because many of the predictor variables are qualitative, coding them raises several important problems. However, these problems are generally bypassed by assigning numerical scores to the k levels of each variable (e.g., 1,2, ..., k), or by dichotomizing each level such that $k - 1$ zero-one dummy variables are created for each original variable. In the context of Fisher's LDF, application of either one of these coding schemes appears to have three drawbacks.

1. Fictitious information is introduced in the form of metrics on such qualitative variables as marital status, sex, or religion.
2. The assignment of numerical scores may, by its very nature, create either illusory linearities in the data, or, perhaps, introduce nonlinearities which cause variables to have signs opposite (in the linear discriminant) those expected on the basis of prior knowledge.[4]
3. To analyze qualitative variables by statistical methods originally intended for continuous variables only subjects the statistical results to certain vagaries.

Hence, if the available data are qualitative and depart from anything resembling normality, it may be more natural to examine multinomial classification methods which capture the distributional properties which generate the data.

MULTINOMIAL CLASSIFICATION METHODS

To prepare the data for multinomial classification analysis, the researcher has several alternatives. Ideally, the most suitable approach if the variables are categorical or qualitative is to use the actual sample distributions to define the classification rule. That is, if the predictor variables are sex, marital status, and stage in family life-cycle, having two, three, and six categories respectively, then each individual is characterized by his responses to those questions. In total, there are 36 ($2 \times 3 \times 6$) possible response patterns (or states), and each individual is represented by one and only one pattern. In any reasonable application, however, the number of possible response patterns in relation to the total number of sample observations available will be large, and hence the estimates of the multinomial densities are likely to very unreliable.

[4]Montgomery cites the rather arbitrary method of coding categorical variables as a possible cause of sign reversals for three of the independent variables used in his study of supermarket buyer decisions [26, p. 258–9].

Table 2
VARIABLE CODINGS AND DESCRIPTIONS

Variable	Descriptions: Coding 1	Descriptions: Coding 0
Home ownership (X_1)	Own	Rent
Number of rooms in house (X_2)	At least 5 rooms	Less than 5 rooms
Length of residence (X_3)	At least 5 years	Less than 5 years
Location of previous home (X_4)	Outside of county, state or U.S.A.	Within the same town or county
Marital status (X_5)	Married	Single, widowed, or divorced
Head of household's occupation (X_6)	Professional or manager	Sales, craftsman, clerical worker (or below)
Head of household's education (X_7)	Some college or above	No college
Family income (X_8)	At least \$11,000 a year	Less than \$11,000 a year
Stage in family lifecycle (X_9)	55 years or older, employed or unemployed	Less than 55 years old

For example, as originally defined, the nine categorical variables (see Table 1) ranged from 2 levels for x_1 (home ownership) to 11 levels for x_8 (family income). Therefore, if all levels are maintained an immense number of states in relation to the sample size would be generated. In general, then, state sparseness will prohibit the use of the actual multinomial sample distributions in determination of the classification rule.

Another possible coding procedure open to the researcher is to dichotomize the categories of each variable. By this approach, $k-1$ dummy variables are created for each variable having k categories. However, in the present case the use of this approach would increase the number of variables to 49, without effecting a reduction in the dimensionality of the problem.

At this point a coding procedure still is needed in which the resulting number of possible states will be at least manageable. To illustrate the simple, practical approach taken let x_j^* represent the cutoff point where the difference between the *relative cumulative frequencies* for each group is a maximum, and let $s_i(x_j)$ be the percentage of individuals in group i with the jth variable less than or equal to x_j. Now the cutoff point x_j^* is given by

$$x_j^* = \operatorname*{Max}_x |S_1(\cdot) - S_2(\cdot)|. \quad (1)$$

Choosing x_j^* in this way maximizes the difference between the marginal probabilities p_{ij}, i = 1, 2; $j = 1, 2, \ldots, p$ where

$$p_{ij} = P(X_j = 1|G_i). \quad (2)$$

Hence, this approach involves use of a pseudodistributional distance and seeks a critical category for each variable such that the distributions above and below that category across the two groups have maximum separation.[5] Each variable now takes on a value of zero or one and in total there are 2^9 (512) possible response patterns or states. A description of the coding for each variable is presented in Table 2.

Methods of Analysis

The methods used for analysis in this section belong to the class of procedures in which underlying multinomial structures are assumed. To allocate an individual to one of two groups, G_1 or G_2, one observes p-discrete random variables each assuming at most a finite number of distinct values 0, 1, ..., s_p, where the random vector $\mathbf{X} = (X_1, X_2, \ldots, X_p)$ is multinomial. For example, assuming that each variable is dichotomous, then there are $s = 2^p$ states, where a particular realization of the vector $\mathbf{X}$ called a response pattern is denoted by $\mathbf{x}$.

In theory, a simple Bayes rule leads to the most effective classification rule because it permits the estimation of the posterior probability of an individual belonging to G_1 or G_2 given both the prior probability and the observation. To illustrate, if $P(G_i|\mathbf{x})$ is the posterior probability, then $P(G_i|\mathbf{x}) = P(G_i) P(\mathbf{x}|G_i)/P(\mathbf{x})$ where $P(\mathbf{x}) = \Sigma_i P(G_i)P(\mathbf{x}|G_i)$ and $\mathbf{x} = (X_1, X_2, \ldots, X_p)$ is the vector of observations. The $P(\mathbf{x}|G_i)$ are the likelihoods or conditional joint probabilities, and the $P(G_i)$ and $P(\mathbf{x})$ are the prior and marginal probabilities, respectively. The major problems with this approach are obtaining good estimates of the $P(\mathbf{x}|G_i)$—the likelihoods—and knowing the $P(G_i)$—the prior probabilities. If these are available, then the Bayes decision rule is to allocate an individual with response pattern $\mathbf{x}$ to G_1 if $P(G_1|\mathbf{x}) > P(G_2|\mathbf{x})$. In terms of the likelihoods ratio $\beta_x = P(\mathbf{x}|G_2)/P(\mathbf{x}|G_1)$, this implies allocating an individual to G_1 if $\beta_x < \beta_o$ and to G_2 if otherwise, where $\beta_o = P(G_1)/P(G_2)$.

In practice, neither the likelihoods—$P(\mathbf{x}|G_i)$—nor the prior probabilities—$P(G_i)$—will be known. However, suppose in a random sample of size n drawn from a mixed population (G_1 and G_2 combined), all of the observations can be correctly classified. The

[5]Another possible approach to splitting each variable would be to use a higher dimensionality. That is, in the spirit of a multivariate problem, critical cutoff points for each variable could be determined simultaneously.

prior probabilities can be estimated by $\hat{P}(G_i) = N_i/n$, where N_i denotes the number of observations in the sample from G_i, $i = 1, 2$. With respect to the likelihoods or posterior probabilities, five methods for their estimation are considered.

1. *Full multinomial.* This procedure is based on estimating the multinomial densities for each of the $s = 2^p$ states by $\hat{P}(\mathbf{x}|G_i) = N_i(\mathbf{x})/N_i$, where $N_i(\mathbf{x})$ is the number of individuals in a sample of N_i from the ith population having response pattern $\mathbf{x}$. In general, unless the sample size is large in relation to the number of states the estimates will be unstable; therefore, they may tend to be poor estimates on which to base an allocation rule.
2. *First-order independence.* This procedure assumes independence among the variables. It has the simplification of fewer parameters to be estimated but in many applications it may be unrealistic. There are $2p$ parameters to be estimated, namely $P(X_j = 1|G_i)$ for $j = 1, 2, \ldots, p$ and $i = 1, 2$. These are given by

$$\hat{P}(X_j = 1|G_i) = \Sigma_{s_j} N_i(\mathbf{x})/N_i, \tag{3}$$

where s_j is the set of responses $\mathbf{x}$ which have $X_j = 1$. The multinomial densities are then estimated by

$$\hat{P}(\mathbf{x}|G_i) = \prod_{j=1}^{p} P(X_j = 1|G_i)^{x_j} (1 - P(X_j = 1|G_i))^{1-x_j}, \tag{4}$$

for $i = 1, 2$. Because only the marginal distribution of each X_j is used, the independence method leads to linear likelihoods and, therefore, its performance should be rather similar to that of Fisher's LDF.
3. *Distance method.* By this method, proposed by Dillon and Goldstein [7], a distributional distance measure [25] is used to construct a sample-based classification rule. To illustrate, let $(n_1, n_2, \ldots, n_s)$ and $(m_1, m_2, \ldots, m_s)$ be the respective state frequencies based on samples of size n and m. Now, the distance between the empirical distributions s_n and s_m generated by these frequencies is given by

$$||s_n - s_m||^2 = \sum_{i=1}^{s} (\sqrt{n_i/n} - \sqrt{m_i/m})^2. \tag{5}$$

The rule for assigning a future observation $\mathbf{x}$ assumes the following form:

$$\text{Classify } \mathbf{X} \text{ into } G_1 \text{ if } ||S_{n+1} - S_m|| > ||S_n - S_{m+1}||,$$
$$\text{Classify } \mathbf{X} \text{ into } G_2 \text{ if } ||S_{n+1} - S_m|| < ||S_n - S_{m+1}||, \tag{6}$$
$$\text{Randomly allocate if } ||S_{n+1} - S_m|| = ||S_n - S_{m+1}||,$$

where S_{n+1} is the empirical distribution function based upon $n + 1$ observations; similarly for S_{m+1}. The rationale for this rule is simply that if assigning $\mathbf{x}$ to G_1 results in greater sample-based distributional distance than if $\mathbf{x}$ is assigned to G_2, then $\mathbf{x}$ should be classified into G_1.

After some algebra, it is easy to see that the rule given in (6) has an equivalent representation with the first inequality replaced by

$$\sqrt{m_j(n_j + 1)/m(n + 1)} + \Sigma_{i\neq j} \sqrt{m_i n_i/m(n + 1)} < \sqrt{n_j(m_j + 1)/n(m + 1)} + \Sigma_{i\neq j} \sqrt{n_i m_i/n(m + 1)}. \tag{7}$$

Note that when $n = m$, the distance and full multinomial methods are equivalent. However, when $n \neq m$ the rules are different, and it is in these cases that the distance method has been shown to have advantages over other available methods [7].
4. *Nearest-neighbor procedures.* This set of procedures has the advantage that the estimated likelihood ratios will be, in general, less subject to sampling variability; however, they are not necessarily consistent. In constructing a nearest-neighbor rule of order k for a particular response pattern the likelihood ratio is estimated by including all individuals with response patterns differing in up to k responses ($k = 0, 1, \ldots, p$). Therefore, the estimated likelihoods are given by

$$\hat{\beta}_{\mathbf{x}} = (\Sigma_{s_j} N_2(\mathbf{x})/N_2)/(\Sigma_{s_j} N_1(\mathbf{x})/N_1), \tag{8}$$

where s_j is the set of response patterns $\mathbf{x}_j$ such that they differ from $\mathbf{x}$ in no more than k responses. The nearest-neighbor rule of order 0 corresponds to the full multinomial, whereas the rule of order p degenerates to $\beta_{\mathbf{x}} = 1$. In this study only a nearest-neighbor rule of order 1 is considered.
5. *Linear discriminant function.* The last procedure considered is Fisher's well-known LDF. Recall, though the original derivation of Fisher's LDF was from a distribution-free standpoint, it may be unsuitable for allocating a new individual when the underlying assumptions for optimality do not hold as in the case of binary variables.

Multinomial Classification Analysis: Results

Because an inflated estimate of the percentage hits is obtained when the set of data used to construct the classification rule is also used to assess performance, a subset of individuals from each group is used to compute the rule, and the remaining individuals are used to estimate the error rates. In this study the classification rule is constructed from a 70% analysis sample, and the remaining holdout observations (30%) are used for validation.

Table 3 shows the results of the comparative study in the two sets of data. The methods have been ranked by their estimated actual error rates as given in the seventh column. It is surprising to note the relatively poor performance of the nearest-neighbor procedure (order 1). Interestingly, this procedure is expected

Table 3

PERCENTAGE MISCLASSIFICATIONS WITH MULTINOMIAL RULES

Method	*Analysis sample (70%)* Heavy	Light	Total	*Holdout sample (30%)* Heavy	Light	Total	Rank
Full multinomial	22	31	27	28[a]	35[a]	31[a]	1
First-order independence	32	41	37	39	40	40	3.5
Distance method	23	31	27	42	27	34	2
Nearest-neighbor procedure (order 1)	33	40	36	41	46	43	5
Linear discriminant	31	45	38	41	39	40	3.5

[a]These percentages are based on a reduced sample size (108) because three are 31 individuals for whom there is no information in the analyzed data set for forming an allocation rule by the full multinomial method (see text).

to reduce the sampling errors of the estimated likelihood ratios by including for any given response pattern those individuals differing in only one response. It might be that a higher order nearest neighbor would yield better results, or possibly its poor performance is somehow an artifact of the data.

As in the findings reported by Moore [27], the first-order independence method and Fisher's LDF give comparable results and, though comparing favorably with the nearest-neighbor procedure, they do not fare as well as either the full multinomial or distance method. Although not shown because of space constraints, the intercorrelations in the predictor variable set provide some explanation for the relatively poor performance of the linear methods (first-order independence method and Fisher's LDF). The presence of large (absolute) correlations can perhaps be a signal that any linear procedure will not be able satisfactorily to characterize the underlying population structures. Indeed, an inspection of the correlation matrix revealed that more than one-fourth of the intercorrelations exceeded $|.35|$.

The full multinomial and distance methods which yield the smallest apparent errors (27%) also produce the smallest error rates in the holdout sample. However, a major limitation associated with the use of the full multinomial is that a number of individuals in the holdout sample are unclassifiable. With a total sample size of 325 observations in the analyzed data set, a majority (410) of the 512 possible states are empty, containing responses from neither heavy nor light product users. For these states $\hat{\beta}_x = 0/0$, and so individuals in the holdout sample with these particular response patterns cannot be classified. In fact, 15 of the 69 heavy product users and 16 of the 70 light product users had one of these response patterns. Hence, although a 31% error rate compares favorably, no good rule is given for 31 (22%) of the individuals in the holdout sample.

In general, unless both analysis and holdout samples are relatively large, state sparseness is likely to result in a number of unclassifiable observations. A split-sample validation technique seems particularly insensitive to this problem because more often than not the researcher is confronted with samples of moderate size and, depending on how the total sample is split, the credibility of either the estimated classification rule or its performance will be suspect. It would be desirable, therefore, to use a validation technique which makes use of all the available sample observations yet does not yield severely optimistically biased estimates of the error rate. Lachenbruch and Mickey [22] suggest just such a technique which they call the U-method. The U-method recently has been described in some detail in [5], and the method is sketched briefly as follows.

> Denoting the probabilities of misclassification based on N_1 and N_2 observations by $E_1(N_1, N_2)$ and $E_2(N_1, N_2)$, the U-method obtains estimates of $E_1(N_1 - 1, N_2)$ and $E_2(N_1, N_2 - 1)$. In words, this approach translates into computing the classification rule for each of the possible samples of size $N_1 - 1$ and N_2 obtained by omitting one observation from G_1 and recording for each of these rules whether the omitted observation is misclassified. Next, one computes the rule for each of the possible samples of size N_1 and $N_2 - 1$ obtained by omitting one observation from G_2 and records whether each omitted observation is misclassified. If M_1 and M_2 are the numbers of observations misclassified, estimates of E_1 and E_2 are given by M_1/N_1 and M_2/N_2. Note that the estimated error rates are *unbiased* for the probabilities of misclassification for a rule based on $N_1 - 1$ and N_2 observations and N_1 and $N_2 - 1$ observations, respectively. Furthermore, in the multinomial case the estimated error rates are rather easy to compute because it is only necessary to consider those states for which the allocation rule changes when one observation is removed. However, a number of individuals still may be unclassifiable but they should represent a smaller percentage of the observations than in the holdout sample approach.

As expected, the U-method results in a reduction in the number of sample observations having response patterns which cannot be classified. In fact, with this approach only slightly more than 10% of the observations can be allocated to neither of the two groups. The estimate of the probability of misclassification obtained is 33%, which compares favorably with that of the other procedures.

THE NAGGING PROBLEM OF SPARSENESS

In practice the most severe limitation with the use of the full multinomial rule is state sparseness. Even a few variables each assuming a small number of distinct levels can result in a proliferation of possible states making analysis very difficult especially with small sample sizes. As in the case of large contingency analysis, state sparseness is a troublesome problem with no easy solutions. However, the problem is clearly one of dimensionality reduction and, therefore, a potentially useful approach might consist of using some desirable subset of the p variables. This would yield a classification rule based only on variables with good discriminative ability, thus restricting the number of variables used which reduces the number of states multiplicitively, thereby reducing the number of empty states. It should be remembered, however, that the tradeoff for throwing away variables is a possible loss of discriminatory power.

The basis of any stepwise selection procedure should be a test statistic with known distribution properties which provides a measure of the relative contribution of each variable so that the most important variables can be selected. For discrete variables each assuming a small number of distinct values, a finer tuning of the selection process is possible because one can look at the contribution of a new variable in the presence of each of the levels of those variables already in the system. In the stepwise selection procedure discussed here, recently proposed by Goldstein and Dillon [17], the distributional properties of a Kullback [21] minimum discrimination divergence statistic are used to determine the contribution of new variables given the levels of those variables already included, and to provide stopping rules for the inclusion of new variables.[6] The data given in Table 2 illustrate the technique; however, the procedure has extensions to the r group problem and to the case in which the levels for the variables are in excess of two.

A Sequential Variable Selection Procedure

To demonstrate this technique consider the p-dichotomous random variables $X_1, X_2, \ldots, X_p$ which generate 2^p multinomial states within the two groups G_1 and G_2. In each group G_i, $i = 1, 2$, the state probabilities will be denoted by p_{ij}, $i = 1, 2$; $j = 1, 2, \ldots, s$, where $s = 2^p$. Suppose that two random samples of size N_1 and N_2 are taken from G_1 and G_2 respectively, and denote the observed state frequencies by $(\mathbf{f}_1) = (f_{11}, f_{12}, \ldots, f_{1s})$, $(\mathbf{f}_2) = (f_{21}, f_{22}, \ldots, f_{2s})$, where $\Sigma f_{1j} = N_1$ and $\Sigma f_{2j} = N_2$. Now, consider the following hypotheses:

H_1: The samples are from different populations.

$(\mathbf{p}_1) = (p_{11}, p_{12}, \ldots, p_{1s})$, $(\mathbf{p}_2) = (p_{21}, p_{22}, \ldots, p_{2s})$.

H_2: The samples are from the same population.

$(\mathbf{p}_o) = (p_{o1}, p_{o2}, \ldots, p_{os})$, $p_{1j} = p_{oj}$, $j = 1, 2, \ldots, s$.

Following Kullback [21], define a measure of the divergence between the two groups by

$$J(1{:}2) = \sum_{j=1}^{s} (p_{1j} - p_{2j}) \log \frac{p_{1j}}{p_{2j}} \tag{9}$$

Large values of J in an absolute sense point to potential discrimination. It follows that the information in favor of H_1 as opposed to H_2 can be expressed in terms of J where, if the parameters are replaced by their respective estimates, the estimate of the error component of the divergence is given by:

$$\hat{J} = N_1 \Sigma \left(\frac{f_{1j}}{N_1} - \frac{f_{1j} + f_{2j}}{N_1 + N_2} \right) \log \frac{(N_1 + N_2) f_{1j}}{N_1 (f_{1j} + f_{2j})} + N_2 \Sigma \left(\frac{f_{2j}}{N_2} - \frac{f_{1j} + f_{2j}}{N_1 + N_2} \right) \log \frac{(N_1 + N_2) f_{2j}}{N_2 (f_{1j} + f_{2j})}. \tag{10}$$

Note that (10) is under H_2 asymptotically chi square with $s - 1$ degrees of freedom. In addition, the estimated divergence $\hat{J}(X_k | X_1 = j_1, X_2 = j_2, \ldots, X_{k-1} = j_{k-1})$ computed from the conditional distribution of X_k given X_1 is at level j_1, X_2 is at level j_2, ..., and X_{k-1} is at level j_{k-1} is also asymptotically chi square but with one degree of freedom.

The stepwise selection procedure suggested translates in practice into the following steps.

1. On the basis of the magnitude of all the individually calculated divergences, select that variable X_j with the largest value of $\hat{J}$; i.e., $\hat{J}(X_j) = \max_{1 \le j \le p} \hat{J}(X_p)$.
2. Consider the best pair which includes X_j so that $\hat{J}(X_1 X_j) = \max \hat{J}(X_i X_j)$. Under the hypothesis that the four-state multinomial distribution induced by $(X_i X_j)$ are identical, $\hat{J}(X_i X_j)$ is asymptotically chi square with three degrees of freedom. If this is significant compute $\hat{J}(X_i | X_j = 0)$ and $\hat{J}(X_i | X_j = 1)$, otherwise stop. Both these conditional divergences have asymptotic chi square distributions with one degree of freedom. If, for example, $\hat{J}(X_k | X_j = 1)$ is significant but not $\hat{J}(X_1 | X_j = 0)$, then observe X_i only if $X_j = 1$.
3. Observe the best triplet including both X_i and X_j such that $\hat{J}(X_k X_i X_j) = \max_{k \ne i \ne j} \hat{J}(X_k X_i X_j)$ and if significant when compared to chi square with seven degrees of freedom compute the four conditional divergences $\hat{J}(X_k | X_i\ (0, 1), X_j\ (0, 1))$. Variable X_k is then only observed with those levels of X_i and X_j for which the computed conditional divergences are significant.

[6]The stepwise procedure presented here is similar in a sense to one proposed by Hills [20]. The principal difference, however, is that whereas Hills uses the divergence statistic only to rank variables for entry, this procedure utilizes the distributional properties of a minimum discrimination divergence statistic to test whether the inclusion of a new variable yields a result consistent with the hypothesis that multinomial distributions so induced in the two groups are identical.

Table 4

VARIABLES SELECTED BY USE OF GROUP DIVERGENCE RULE

Step at which variable is selected	*Variables included*	$\hat{J}$	*d.f.*	*Critical value (.01)*	*Apparent error (%)*
Family income	X_8	34.92	1	6.6	37
Head of household's occupation	$X_6 X_8$	43.23	3	11.3	37
Location of previous home	$X_4 X_6 X_8$	51.15	7	18.5	36
Stage in family lifecycle	$X_9 X_4 X_6 X_8$	61.83	15	30.6	34
Marital status	$X_5 X_9 X_4 X_6 X_8$	86.00	31	52.4	32
Stop					

4. The procedure continues in a similar fashion. The selection process terminates at the rth stage if the next variable considered x_r yields a value of $\hat{J}(X_r, \ldots, X_k, X_i, X_j)$ which is nonsignificant. Therefore, the conditional divergences computed up through state $r - 1$ indicate whether a new variable is worthy of entry on the basis of the levels of those previously observed.

This procedure not only reduces the number of variables to be considered but also indicates whether or not a new variable should be entered given the levels of those variables already selected. The logic for not including a variable is that it is reasonable to assume that discriminatory power will not be increased sufficiently if the divergence is not large enough to reject the hypothesis that at a given state the two groups have identical multinomial distributions. It should be noted that although the term "stepwise" is used to describe this procedure, it is really a forward procedure in that no provision is made for deletion of a variable once it has been entered. Furthermore, in some instances the stepwise procedure after a number of variables have entered will probably have to be slightly amended because of state sparseness. The authors have developed a computer program which, in addition to proceeding through the stepwise process as delineated, prints out the various frequency distributions so that the practitioner can make a judgment with respect to the credibility of the calculations.[7] A more detailed description of the computer program can be found in [8].

To illustrate the stepwise selection procedure the authors chose to use all of the available sample observations. Tables 4 and 5 show summary results. From Table 4 note that the procedure begins by entering X_8 (family income). The procedure continues by entering X_6 (head of household's occupation) and because this is significant ($\alpha = .01$) the two conditional divergences $\hat{J}(X_6|X_8 = 0)$ and $\hat{J}(X_6|X_8 = 1)$ are computed with values 17.8 and 4.3, respectively (see Table 5). Both statistics are significant ($\alpha = .05$), and hence head of household's occupation is important in the presence of family income at both its levels. Variable X_4 (location of previous home) is selected next; however, note from Table 5 that this variable

[7]As a general statement, care must be exercised in using any stepwise procedure. This is especially true with multinomial discrimination because state sparseness can become a problem very early in the selection process. Therefore, the authors suggest that the frequency distributions be examined at each stage so that the credibility of the computed divergences can be assessed.

Table 5

LEVELS OF VARIABLES ENTERING WITH CONDITIONAL DIVERGENCE STOPPING RULE

Variable selected given previous levels	$\hat{J}$	*d.f.*	*Critical value (.05)*
$Z_6 \| Z_8 = 0$	17.80	1	3.84
$Z_6 \| Z_8 = 1$	4.30	1	3.84
$Z_4 \| Z_6 = 0, Z_8 = 0$	10.80	1	3.84
$Z_4 \| Z_6 = 0, Z_8 = 1$	13.50	1	3.84
$Z_4 \| Z_6 = 1, Z_8 = 0$	1.17	1	3.84
$Z_4 \| Z_6 = 1, Z_8 = 1$	5.10	1	3.84
$Z_9 \| Z_4 = 0, Z_6 = 0, Z_8 = 0$	14.50	1	3.84
$Z_9 \| Z_4 = 0, Z_6 = 0, Z_8 = 1$	16.00	1	3.84
$Z_9 \| Z_4 = 0, Z_6 = 1, Z_8 = 1$	1.50	1	3.84
$Z_9 \| Z_4 = 1, Z_6 = 0, Z_8 = 0$	48.50	1	3.84
$Z_9 \| Z_4 = 1, Z_6 = 0, Z_8 = 1$	11.67	1	3.84
$Z_9 \| Z_4 = 1, Z_6 = 1, Z_8 = 1$	23.70	1	3.84
$Z_5 \| Z_4 = 0, Z_6 = 0, Z_8 = 0, Z_9 = 0$	85.37	1	3.84
$Z_5 \| Z_4 = 0, Z_6 = 0, Z_8 = 0, Z_9 = 1$	99.57	1	3.84
$Z_5 \| Z_4 = 0, Z_6 = 0, Z_8 = 1, Z_9 = 1$	3.28	1	3.84
$Z_5 \| Z_4 = 1, Z_6 = 0, Z_8 = 1, Z_9 = 1$	.03	1	3.84

does not contribute enough divergence in the presence of $X_6 = 1$ and $X_8 = 0$ to warrant its inclusion for discrimination. In other words, no significant amount of discriminatory information is obtained from examining responses to the location of previous home question if the head of household's occupation is known to be either professional or manager and if family income is less that $11,000 a year.

The procedure eventually terminates after entering variable X_9 (family lifecycle) followed by variable X_5 (marital status).[8] The apparent errors given in Table 4 were computed by use of the full multinomial method. If all nine variables are used the apparent error evaluates to 25% compared with 32% if only the five selected variables are used. Note that the conditional divergences of X_9 given $X_4 = (0, 1)$, $X_6 = 1$, and $X_8 = 0$ are not shown because at the previous stage the conditional divergences for patterns ($X_4 = 0$, $X_6 = 1$, $X_8 = 0$) and ($X_4 = 1$, $X_6 = 1$, $X_8 = 0$) were nonsignificant. Several divergences computed from the conditional distributions of X_5 for given patterns of X_4, X_6, X_8, and X_9 are also not included in Table 5 for similar reasons. In addition, there are five patterns which are not shown because of state sparseness. In short, the stepwise selection procedure reduces the number of variables from nine to five and, more dramatically, one now needs to consider only those 24 states which provide significant divergences instead of the original 512.

CONCLUDING REMARKS

The authors have considered the classification problem in situations in which the available data are qualitative. Several multinomial classification methods are discussed and illustrated in the context of a marketing-related problem, with particular emphasis on the problems likely to arise in their application. Further, a new multinomial stepwise selection procedure is discussed which will allow the practitioner the opportunity not only to select good subsets of variables, but also to identify those levels which need measurement.

In conclusion, several points should be noted. First, though the authors have argued for the recognition of multinomial classification methods, the intention has not been to discourage the use of Fisher's LDF in general. On the contrary, when the data reasonably satisfy the assumptions underlying its optimality, Fisher's LDF has considerable advantage over other classification procedures because of its widespread assessibility. The results of this study suggest that it would also be useful to compare the performance of the full multinomial and distance procedures in other situations such as in the presence of disproportionate sample sizes, or where the available sample sizes are large enough to allow the predictor variables to assume more than two values. Finally, it would be interesting to study whether any advantages are obtained by modifying the multinomial classification methods discussed herein to take account of any ordering among the levels of the qualitative variables.

[8]The authors chose to use a more conservative significance level for the group divergences than for the conditional divergences. If a critical α of .05 were employed, the stepwise procedure would have included x_2 number of rooms in home and then terminated.

REFERENCES

1. Banks, Seymour. "The Relationship Between Preference and Purchase of Brands," *Journal of Marketing*, 15 (October 1951), 145–57.
2. Bishop, Yvonne M. M., Stephen E. Fienberg, and Paul W. Holland. *Discrete Multivariate Analysis: Theory and Practice.* Cambridge, Massachusetts: The MIT Press, 1975.
3. Claycamp, Henry R. "Characteristics of Owners of Thrift Deposits in Commercial Banks and Savings and Loan Associations," *Journal of Marketing Research*, 2 (May 1965), 163–79.
4. Cochran, William G. and Carl E. Hopkins. "Some Classification Problems with Multivariate Qualitative Data," *Biometrics*, 17 (March 1961), 10–32.
5. Crask, Melvin R. and William D. Perreault, Jr. "Validation of Discriminant Analysis in Marketing Research," *Journal of Marketing Research*, 14 (February 1977), 60–8.
6. Darden, William R. and Fred D. Reynolds. "Backward Profiling of Male Innovators," *Journal of Marketing Research*, 11 (February 1974), 79.
7. Dillon, William R. and Matthew Goldstein. "On the Performance of Some Multinomial Classification Rules," *Journal of the American Statistical Association*, forthcoming.
8. ——— and ———. "VARSEL: A Stepwise Discrete Variable Selection Program," *Journal of Marketing Research*, 14 (August 1977), 419–20.
9. Dolan, Robert J. "Market Segmentation Via Alternative Discriminant Procedures," *Combined Proceedings*, American Marketing Association, 1975, 132–6.
10. Etzel, Michael J. "Using Multiple Discriminant Analysis to Segment the Consumer Credit Market," *Combined Proceedings*, American Marketing Association, 1974, 35–40.
11. Evans, Frank B. "Psychological and Objective Factors in the Prediction of Brand Choice: Ford versus Chevrolet," *Journal of Business*, 31 (October 1959), 340–69.
12. Fisher, R. A. "The Use of Measurements in Taxonomic Problems," *Annals of Eugenics*, 7 (1936), 176–84.
13. Frank, Ronald E., William F. Massy, and Donald G. Morrison. "Bias in Multiple Discriminant Analysis," *Journal of Marketing Research*, 2 (August 1965), 250–8.
14. Gilbert, Ethel S. "On Discrimination Using Qualitative Variables," *Journal of American Statistical Association*, 63 (December 1968), 116–22.
15. Glick, Ned. "Sample-Based, Multinomial Classification," *Biometrics*, 29 (June 1973), 241–56.
16. Goldstein, Matthew and Edward Wolf. "On the Problem of Bias in Multinomial Classification," *Biometrics*, 33 (June 1977), 325–31.
17. ——— and William R. Dillon. "A Stepwise Discrete Variable Selection Procedure," *Communications in Statistics*, forthcoming.

18. Green, Paul E. "Bayesian Classification Procedures in Analyzing Customer Characteristics," *Journal of Marketing Research,* 1 (May 1964), 44–50.
19. ———, Frank J. Carmone, and David P. Wachspress. "On the Analysis of Qualitative Data in Marketing Research," *Journal of Marketing Research,* 14 (February 1977), 52–9.
20. Hills, M. "Discrimination and Allocation with Discrete Data," *Journal of the Royal Statistical Society*, Series C, 16, No. 3 (1967), 237–50.
21. Kullback, S. *Information Theory and Statistics.* New York: John Wiley and Sons, Inc., 1959.
22. Lachenbruch, Peter A. and M. Ray Mickey. "Estimation of Error Rates in Discriminant Analysis," *Technometrics*, 10 (1968), 1–9.
23. Linhart, H. "Techniques for Discriminant Analysis with Discrete Variables." *Metrika*, 2 (May 1959), 138–49.
24. Massy, William R. "On Methods: Discriminant Analysis of Audience Characteristics," *Journal of Advertising Research,* 5 (March 1965), 39–45.
25. Matusita, Kameo. "Decision Rule, Based on Distance, for the Classification Problem," *Annual Institute of Statistical Mathematics*, 8 (1956), 67–77.
26. Montgomery, David B. "New Product Diffusion—An Analysis of Supermarket Buyer Decision," *Journal of Marketing Research*, 12 (August 1965), 255–65.
27. Moore, Dan H., II. "Evaluation of Five Discrimination Procedures for Binary Variables," *Journal of the American Statistical Association*, 68 (June 1973), 399–404.
28. Morrison, Donald G. "On Interpretation in Discriminant Analysis," *Journal of Marketing Research,* 6 (May 1969), 156–63.
29. Perry, Michael. "Discriminant Analysis of Relations Between Consumer's Attitude Behavior and Intention," *Journal of Advertising Research,* 9 (1969), 34–9.
30. Robertson, Thomas S. and James N. Kennedy. "Prediction of Consumer Innovators: Application of Multiple Discriminant Analysis," *Journal of Marketing Research*, 5 (February 1968), 64–9.

HOWARD S. GITLOW*

The author compares two discrimination procedures used for analyzing nominally scaled data sets, dummy variable multiple discriminant function analysis and multivariate nominal scale analysis. Both procedures are illustrated on an in-home consumption data base.

Discrimination Procedures for the Analysis of Nominally Scaled Data Sets

Much marketing literature has been devoted to discriminant analysis, but only scant attention has been given to discrimination problems where all of the independent variables are nominally scaled. The author discusses and compares two discrimination procedures which are applicable when all independent variables are nominally scaled, dummy variable multiple discriminant function analysis (MDF) and multivariate nominal scale analysis (MNA).

DUMMY VARIABLE MULTIPLE DISCRIMINANT FUNCTION ANALYSIS

The most widely known multivariate technique for analyzing nominally scaled dependent variables, when the independent variables are all nominally scaled, is dummy variable MDF. However, dummy variable MDF has not received much attention in the literature.

The dummy variable multiple discriminant function (MDF) model is:

$$Y_{k\ell} = B_{\ell o} + \sum_{i=1}^{P} \sum_{j=1}^{C_i - 1} b_{ij\ell} x_{ijk} \qquad \text{for all } \ell = 1 \text{ to } G$$

where:

$Y_{k\ell}$ = individual k^s group membership, e.g., $Y_{k\ell} = 2$ if individual k is a member of group $2(\ell = 2)$,

G = the number of groups,

$B_{\ell o}$ = a constant term for the ℓth group,

P = the number of original independent variables,

$C_i - 1$ = the number of dummy variables needed to represent the C_i categories of the ith original independent variable,

$b_{ij\ell}$ = the MDF coefficient for the dummy variable formed from the jth category of the ith original independent variable, for group ℓ; and

$$x_{ijk} = \begin{cases} 1 \text{ if individual } k \text{ exhibits the characteristic represented by the } j^{\text{th}} \text{ category of the } i^{\text{th}} \text{ independent variable,} \\ 0 \text{ otherwise.} \end{cases}$$

MULTIVARIATE NOMINAL SCALE ANALYSIS

Multivariate nominal scale analysis (MNA) is a technique designed for problems where (1) the dependent variable is nominal and must have three or more categories, (2) the independent variables are nominally scaled, and (3) an additive model is appropriate to represent the data set.

The literature on multivariate nominal scale analysis is scant. Andrews and Messenger (1973) discuss the theoretical underpinning of MNA. Sheth (1974) discussed MNA in a *JMR* book review and Andrews, Morgan, and Messenger (1974) commented on Sheth's review.

The MNA model is:

$$Y_{k\ell} = \bar{Y}_{\ell} + \sum_{i=1}^{P} \sum_{j=1}^{C_i} (a_{ij\ell} x_{ijk}) \qquad \text{for all } \ell = 1 \text{ to } G$$

$$Y_{k\ell} = \begin{cases} 1 \text{ if individual } k \text{ is a member of group } \ell \text{, and} \\ 0 \text{ otherwise,} \end{cases}$$

G = the number of groups,

*Howard S. Gitlow is Associate Professor of Management Science and Marketing, University of Miami, Coral Gables. The author acknowledges the aid and guidance of Leon Schiffman (Professor of Marketing, Rutgers University), William Dillon (Assistant Professor of Marketing, University of Massachusetts), and two unknown reviewers.

Reprinted from *Journal of Marketing Research,* **16 (August 1979), 387-93, published by the American Marketing Association.**

$\bar{Y}_\ell$ = the percentage of individuals in group ℓ,
P = the number of independent variables,
C_i = the number of categories in the ith independent variable,
$a_{ij\ell}$ = the MNA coefficient indicating the percentage deviation from the overall percentage of individuals in group ℓ caused by category j of the ith independent variable (see Andrews and Messenger 1973 for the derivation of the $a_{ij\ell}$), and

$$x_{ijk} = \begin{cases} 1 \text{ if individual } k \text{ has the characteristic represented by category } j \text{ of the } i^{th} \\ \text{independent variable, 0 otherwise.} \end{cases}$$

Three basic statistics are used to measure the strength of the bivariate relationship between group membership and each independent variable: (1) the one-way analysis of variance *eta* squared statistics ($\eta_{i\ell}^2$), which are summarized in the generalized *eta* squared statistic (η_i^2); (2) the bivariate *theta* statistics (θ_i); and (3) the category-specific *beta* squared statistics ($\beta_{i\ell}^2$).

The *eta* squared statistic (Hays 1963) measures the percentage of variation in the ℓth group explained by the ith independent variable. The generalized *eta* squared statistic is a variance weighted average of the *eta* squared statistics and measures the percentage of variation in all groups explained by the ith independent variable.

The bivariate *theta* statistic (Messenger and Mandell 1972) is the percentage of the sample which is correctly grouped using only the ith independent variable. It is helpful to compute ($\theta_i - \max_\ell \bar{Y}_\ell$) for each independent variable. This quantity indicates the increase (if positive) or decrease (if negative) in explanatory power gained over classifying all individuals into the largest group, named C_{max} by Morrison (1969), by including the ith independent variable in the analysis.

The *beta* squared statistics are helpful in indicating: (1) the relative predictive power of different independent variables with respect to a given group and (2) the relative predictive power of a given independent variable with respect to the different groups, in both cases within the context of "holding other variables constant" (see Andrews and Messenger 1963, p. 80).

The interpretability of the *beta* squared statistics arises from the notion that large $a_{ij\ell}$, in general, indicate the most important categories of the most important variables, for a given group and across groups.

Beta squared statistics are still in the experimental stage and should be used cautiously. They should not be used in terms of percentage of variance explained because

$$\sum_{i=1}^{P} \beta^2_{i\ell} \neq 1,$$

unless all other independent variables are uncorrelated and multivariate analysis is not needed.

Two statistics are used to measure multivariate strength of association in MNA, R^2_ℓ (which generalizes into $\mathbb{R}^2$) and θ. R^2_ℓ is the percentage of variation in the ℓth group explained by all of the independent variables. $\mathbb{R}^2$ (generalized squared multiple correlation coefficient) combines the R^2_ℓ statistics and measures the percentage of variation in all groups explained by the entire set of independent variables.

θ is the percentage of individuals grouped correctly using all of the independent variables. θ is the multivariate extension of the bivariate θ_i. It may be helpful for the researcher to compute ($\theta - \max_\ell \bar{Y}_\ell$). This quantity represents the percentage increase (if positive) or decrease (if negative) in explanatory power gained over classifying all individuals into the largest group by including all independent variables in the analysis.

EVALUATING THE RELATIVE EFFICIENCY OF MNA AND DUMMY VARIABLE MDF

Two methods are available for comparing the ability of MNA and dummy variable MDF to predict an individual's group membership, classification matrices and Press' *Q*-statistic. A classification matrix is a $G \times G$ matrix whose margins are labeled "actual group membership" and "predicted group membership," whose diagonal elements denote correct classifications, and whose off-diagonal elements denote misclassifications (Frank, Massy, and Morrison 1965; Morrison 1969).

Press' *Q*-statistic can be used to test the null hypothesis that the discrimination model did not do better than chance versus the alternative hypothesis that the discrimination model did do better than chance. The *Q*-statistic is distributed χ^2 with one degree of freedom (Frank, Massy, and Morrison 1965; Morrison 1969).

Table 1 is a comparison of MNA and dummy variable MDF in terms of features, statistical bases, types and numbers of allowable variables, permissible statistics, and computer program restrictions.

MDF is inappropriate for many data structures, for example, if group covariance matrices are not equal. MNA lacks a statistical base; consequently, it is not known for what data structures MNA is appropriate. Both of these facts may lead to a wide variety of situations in which MNA is preferable to MDF.

AN EXAMPLE

An in-home consumption data base provides a means of demonstrating and comparing dummy variable MDF and MNA. The data base was constructed by drawing a systematic random sample from the mailing list of a firm which distributes women's clothing and accessories.

A model for profiling in-home consumption is:

Table 1
COMPARISON OF DUMMY VARIABLE MDF AND MNA

Features of classification procedures	*MNA*	*Dummy variable MDF*	
Model features			
1. Additive (no interactions)[a]	Yes	Yes	
2. Linear	Yes	Yes	
3. Form	$Y_{k\ell} = \bar{Y}_\ell + \sum_{i=1}^{P} \sum_{j=1}^{C_i} a_{ij\ell} x_{ijk}$	$Y_{k\ell} = B_{\ell o} + \sum_{i=1}^{P} \sum_{j=1}^{C_i - 1} b_{ij\ell} x_{ijk}$	
4. Type	Conceptual	Predictive	
5. Purpose	Measures magnitude of relationships	Determines statistical significance	
6. Interpretability	High	Low	
Statistical base			
1. Has distribution theory underpinning	No	Yes	
2. Homogeneity of variance required	No	Yes	
3. Type of estimators generated	Least squares and maximum likelihood	Least squares and maximum likelihood	
4. Procedure for residual analysis	Intuitive procedure	Statistical procedure	
Types and numbers of variables			
1. Scale of dependent variable	Multichotomous nominal	Nominal	
2. Scale of independent variables	Nominal	Dummyized nominal (binary), interval, or ratio	
3. Number of independent variables	$C = \sum_{i=1}^{P} C_i$	$R = C - P$ (if all independent variables are dummyized)	
Permissible statistics			
1. Bivariate	$\eta^2_{i\ell}, \eta^2_i, \theta_i, \beta^2_{i\ell}, R^2_i$	None	
2. Multivariate	$\theta, I\!R^2, Q$	D^2, V, Q	
Program restrictions	OSIRIS—MNA	BMD05M	BMD07M
1. Restrictions on the number of dependent variable categories	$3 \le G \le 10$	$2 \le G \le 5$	$2 \le G \le 80$
2. Restrictions on the total number of independent variable codes after dummyizing	$1 \le C \le 100$	None	None
3. Restrictions on the number of categories in each independent variable	$C_i \le 20$ for all i	None	None
4. Restrictions on the total number of independent variables after dummyization	None	$G \le R \le 25$	$1 \le R \le 80$
5. Data base restrictions	$N \le 1{,}000{,}000$	Groups size $\le$ 175 per group	None

[a]Both models can deal with interactions by collapsing variables (see Richards 1973, 1975).

$$Y = f(X_1, X_2, \ldots, X_{12})$$

where Y is mail order expenditures in 1976 (small, medium, large), and the X_i are defined in Table 2.

The following frequency distribution was constructed from the survey of consumer expenditures on women's clothing and accessories in 1976.

Category		*Frequency*	*Percent*
Under \$50.00	(small)	181	54.85
\$50.00 to \$100.00	(medium)	39	11.82
Over \$100.00	(large)	110	33.33
Total		330	100.00

(All individuals included in the "small" group purchased at least one item.)

By classifying all individuals as "small" in-home consumers one would be assured of correct classification 54.85% of the time. It now remains to be seen how much better (or worse) than 54.85% the dummy variable MDF and MNA models predict group membership.

MNA

The MNA coefficients indicate (see Table 2):

1. "Small" in-home consumers feel in-home shopping is less satisfying than in-store shopping (a_{431} = 18.72), have a low educational attainment (a_{911} = 12.83), and are young (a_{811} = 10.92).
2. "Medium" in-home consumers are not so confident in their own ability to shop (a_{732} = 13.97) and feel in-home shopping is as satisfying as in-store shopping (a_{422} = 13.97).
3. "Large" in-home consumers feel in-home shopping is more satisfying than in-store shopping (a_{413} = 39.69 and a_{423} = 12.55), feel their friends view mail-order items as being of higher quality than in-store items (a_{513} = 10.92), and are older (a_{843} = 9.44).

Satisfaction toward in-home shopping is the independent variable which is most strongly associated with each level of in-home consumption (in Table 2, η^2_i and β^2_i statistics are highest for satisfaction toward in-home shopping) and globally with in-home consumption (η^2_4 = .2171).

Table 2
MNA STATISTICS

VARIABLES		Small (ℓ=1)	Medium (ℓ=2)	Large (ℓ=3)
(X_1) Attitude toward in-store shopping				
1. enjoyable	$a_{11\ell}$	-2.30	1.90	0.40
2. neutral	$a_{12\ell}$	4.02	-2.28	-1.74
3. not enjoyable	$a_{13\ell}$	1.65	-3.68	2.03
$\eta^2_1 = .0219$	$\eta^2_{1\ell}$	.0289	.0015	.0235
$\theta_1 = .5667$	$\beta_{1\ell}$	.0033	.0051	.0007
(X_2) Satisfaction with local stores				
1. satisfied	$a_{21\ell}$	-0.72	-2.45	3.17
2. neutral	$a_{22\ell}$	-1.62	0.58	1.04
3. not satisfied	$a_{23\ell}$	3.49	2.98	-6.47
$\eta^2_2 = .0092$	$\eta^2_{2\ell}$	.0140	.0061	.0052
$\theta_2 = .5485$	$\beta_{2\ell}$	.0017	.0045	.0066
(X_3) Time available for in-store shopping				
1. adequate	$a_{31\ell}$	1.14	-1.23	0.10
2. inadequate	$a_{32\ell}$	-2.37	2.57	-0.21
$\eta^2_3 = .0065$	$\eta^2_{3\ell}$	.0100	.0076	.0021
$\theta_3 = .5475$	$\beta_{3\ell}$	.0011	.0030	.0000
(X_4) Satisfaction toward in-home shopping				
1. more satisfactory than in-store shopping	$a_{41\ell}$	-35.48	-4.21	39.69
2. as satisfactory as in-store shopping	$a_{42\ell}$	-26.32	13.77	12.55
3. less satisfactory than in-store shopping	$a_{43\ell}$	18.72	-5.26	-13.46
$\eta^2_5 = .2171$	$\eta^2_{4\ell}$	.2879	.0698	.2073
$\theta_5 = .6909$	$\beta_{4\ell}$	.2232	.0673	.1547
(X_5) Friends expectation of mail-order item's quality				
1. better in quality than in-store items	$a_{51\ell}$	-9.02	-1.89	10.92
2. same in quality as in-store items	$a_{52\ell}$	-0.66	0.06	0.60
3. lower in quality than in-store items	$a_{53\ell}$	4.47	0.26	-4.73
$\eta^2_5 = .0497$	$\eta^2_{5\ell}$	.0630	.0034	.0566
$\theta_5 = .5727$	$\beta_{5\ell}$	.0037	.0002	.0052
(X_6) Cautious shopper				
1. sees item in mail order catalog and orders it	$a_{61\ell}$	-6.52	0.63	5.89
2. sees item in mail order catalog and tries to find item in local store	$a_{62\ell}$	6.29	-0.61	-5.68
$\eta^2_6 = .0850$	$\eta^2_{6\ell}$	.1151	.0083	.0857
$\theta_6 = .5970$	$\beta_{6\ell}$	.0166	.0004	.0151
(X_7) Confidence in own ability to shop				
1. always confident	$a_{71\ell}$	2.64	-2.71	0.07
2. usually confident	$a_{72\ell}$	-2.09	1.47	0.62
3. not so confident	$a_{73\ell}$	-7.50	13.97	-6.47
$\eta^2_7 = .0037$	$\eta^2_{7\ell}$	.0041	.0104	.0002
$\theta_7 = .5485$	$\beta_{7\ell}$	.0033	.0135	.0010
(X_8) Age				
1. less than 30	$a_{81\ell}$	10.92	-1.37	-9.55
2. 30 to 39	$a_{82\ell}$	6.89	1.97	-8.86
3. 40 to 49	$a_{83\ell}$	-4.08	-1.80	5.88

Table 2
(CONTINUED)

4. 50 and over	$a_{84\ell}$	-10.41	0.97	9.44
$\eta^2_8 = .0508$	$\eta^2_{8\ell}$	.0609	.0042	.0613
$\theta_8 = .5545$	$\beta_{8\ell}$	.0303	.0023	.0334
(X_9) Education				
1. high school or less	$a_{91\ell}$	12.83	-3.23	-9.60
2. at least some college	$a_{92\ell}$	-3.21	0.81	2.40
$\eta^2_9 = .0024$	$\eta^2_{9\ell}$	.0033	.0004	.0023
$\theta_9 = .5485$	$\beta_{9\ell}$	.0166	.0025	.0104
(X_{10}) Income				
1. less than $15,000	$a_{10,1\ell}$	3.97	1.94	-5.91
2. $15,000 and more	$a_{10,2\ell}$	-2.24	-1.09	3.33
$\eta^2_{10} = .0415$	$\eta^2_{10\ell}$	.0152	.0003	.0204
$\theta_{10} = .5485$	$\beta_{10\ell}$	.0036	.0020	.0089
(X_{11}) Marital Status				
1. married	$a_{11,1\ell}$	1.69	-0.28	-1.41
2. other	$a_{11,2\ell}$	-3.62	0.61	3.01
$\eta^2_{11} = .0010$	$\eta^2_{11\ell}$	.0003	.0010	.0017
$\theta_{11} = .5485$	$\beta_{11\ell}$	.0025	.0002	.0019
(X_{12}) Employment Status				
1. employed	$a_{12,1\ell}$	0.76	-0.04	-0.73
2. not employed	$a_{12,2\ell}$	-1.17	0.06	1.12
$\eta^2_{12} = .0016$	$\eta^2_{12\ell}$	.0017	.0000	.0023
$\theta_{12} = .5485$	$\beta_{12\ell}$	.0004	.0000	.0004
Constant Term		54.85	11.82	33.33

The full MNA model explained:

- —28.57% of the variation present in the levels of in-home consumption ($I\!R^2 = .2857$),
- —36.45% of the variation present among "small" in-home consumers ($R_1^2 = .3645$),
- —9.43% of the variation present among "medium" in-home consumers ($R_2^2 = .0943$), and
- —28.90% of the variation present among "large" in-home consumers ($R_3^2 = .2890$).

Further, the MNA model classified 70.91% of all in-home consumers correctly ($\theta = .7091$). This figure represents an increase in predictive power of 16.06 percentage points over classifying all in-home shoppers as "small" in-home shoppers (.7091 − .5485). The full MNA model predicted the correct classification for in-home consumers only 1.82% better than a model using only the consequences component of risk variable.

MDF

The dummy variable MDF coefficients indicate (see Table 3) that "confidence in one's own ability to shop" (dummy variables 11 and 12 and original variable 7), "friends' expectation of mail-order item's quality" (dummy variables 8 and 9 and original variable 5), and "employment" (dummy variable 19 and original variable 12) contribute most to the classification of an individual into all categories of in-home consumption.

Both the Mahalanobis D^2 statistic and Bartlett's V statistic are significant at the .001 level; hence, the full dummy variable MDF model can be used to discriminate among the three levels of in-home consumption. The dummy variable MDF model classified 70.91% of all in-home consumers correctly ($\theta = .7091$), a 16.06% increase over classifying all individuals as "small" in-home consumers.

It is interesting to note that both procedures generated identical θ statistics; however, the profiles generated were very different. Both θ statistics were significantly greater than C_{max} at the .001 level of significance. C_{max} is the percentage of correct classifications obtained by classifying all in-home consumers into the "small" category ($C_{max} = .5485$).

Comparison

The MNA classification matrix indicates (see Table 4) that:

Table 3
DUMMY VARIABLE MDF STATISTICS

Original variable	Dummyized variables	Small purchases	Ranked importance	Medium purchases	Ranked importance	Large purchases	Ranked importance
	0. Constant	30.20056		29.98569		28.79021	
1	1. Enjoyable attitude/not enjoyable attitude	4.15825	7	4.79876	6	4.25559	8
	2. Neutral attitude/not neutral attitude	5.47982	6	5.51349	7	5.25350	7
2	3. Satisfied/not satisfied	2.70783	15	2.69031	14	3.177349	13
	4. Neutral/not neutral	0.55967	19	0.24620	19	1.07026	18
4	5. More satisfactory than in-store shopping/not more satisfactory than in-store shopping	4.67703	12	5.89274	9	3.34029	14
	6. As satisfactory as in-store shopping/not satisfactory as in-store shopping	4.57141	13	2.46535	17	0.60489	19
3	7. Adequate time/inadequate time	3.77147	11	3.31183	13	3.65239	12
5	8. Better in quality than in-store item/not better in quality than in-store item	15.08612	3	14.94413	3	14.39655	3
	9. Same in quality as in-store item/not same in quality as in-store item	14.61817	4	14.30262	4	13.54207	4
6	10. Sees item in mail order catalog and orders it/sees item in mail order catalog and tries to find item in local store	2.81529	16	2.23197	16	1.91429	17
7	11. Always confident/not always confident	18.33965	2	16.52025	2	18.20261	2
	12. Usually confident/not usually confident	19.58740	1	18.30481	1	19.64645	1
8	13. Less than 30/30 or more	4.78317	10	5.22187	11	4.95851	11
	14. 30 to 39/not 30 to 39	3.98048	14	4.50110	12	5.10527	9
	15. 40 to 49/not 40 to 49	4.14799	9	5.14388	8	5.63889	6
9	16. High school or less/at least some college	2.14001	18	3.08560	15	3.17721	16
10	17. Less than $15,000/$15,000 or more	1.75469	17	1.72348	18	2.32517	15
11	18. Married/other	4.57063	8	4.29587	10	4.21076	10
12	19. Employed/not employed	5.15570	5	5.07589	5	5.01620	5

1. "Small" in-home consumers have a strongly differentiated profile.
2. It is difficult to differentiate between "medium" in-home consumers and "small" or "large" in-home consumers.
3. "Large" in-home consumers have a distinct profile but are frequently confused with "small" in-home consumers.

The dummy variable MDF classification matrix indicates (see Table 4) the same basic patterns as the MNA analysis except that "medium" in-home consumers are predicted correctly about 25% of the time and there is more confusion in predicting "small" or "large" in-home consumers. In summary, the dummy variable MDF model gains some predictive ability among the "medium" in-home consumers but loses predictive ability among the "small" and "large" in-home consumers.

Table 4
CLASSIFICATION MATRICES

	Small purchases		*Medium purchases*		*Large purchases*	
	MNA	*MDF*	*MNA*	*MDF*	*MNA*	*MDF*
Small						
Classification matrix	162	158	0	5	19	18
Holdout sample's classification matrix	84	66	1	25	10	4
Medium						
Classification matrix	18	14	0	10	21	15
Holdout sample's classification matrix	8	9	0	4	11	6
Large						
Classification matrix	38	37	0	7	72	66
Holdout sample's classification matrix	21	14	0	22	34	19

Holdout Sample

The discriminatory power of both profile generation techniques was tested on a holdout sample (see Table 4). The MNA profile performed much better than the dummy variable MDF profile, 69.8% correct classifications versus 52.7% correct classifications. Further, there is much less confusion among misclassified individuals in the MNA profile; for example, all misclassified "large" in-home consumers are classed as "small" in-home consumers whereas in the dummy variable MDF profile, misclassified "large" in-home consumers were classed as both "small" and "medium" in-home consumers.

Press' Q statistic indicates that the procedures have equal predictive ability ($Q = 209.67$ for both MNA and dummy variable MDF) for in-home consumption on the main sample classification matrices. However, MNA's predictive ability is far superior to that of dummy variable MDF in the holdout sample; $Q = 101.26$ for MNA and $Q = 28.41$ for MDF, or 118 versus 89 correct classifications. Further, a chi square test indicates that classification ability is related to the discriminatory procedure used at the .01 level of significance. Thus the MNA profile is more representative of the true profile of in-home consumption than is the dummy variable MDF profile.

CONCLUSION

Multivariate analyses of nominally scaled data sets are filled with problems for the marketing researcher. The author discusses and compares two procedures for handling nominally scaled data sets when there is one dependent variable and two or more independent variables. MNA is a relatively new and untested procedure and deserves attention as a potential avenue for the analysis of nominally scaled data sets. An expanded version of this article is available from the author on request.

REFERENCES

Andrews, F. M. and R. C. Messenger (1973), *Multivariate Nominal Scale Analysis: A Report on a New Analysis Technique and a Computer Program,* Survey Research Letter, Institute for Social Research, The University of Michigan, Ann Arbor, Michigan, 1973.

——— J. N. Morgan, and R. C. Messenger (1974), "Comments on Reviews by Jagdish N. Sheth of MNA and THAID," *Journal of Marketing Research,* 11 (November) 473–5.

Frank, R. E., W. F. Massey, and D. G. Morrison, "Bias in Multiple Discriminant Analysis," *Journal of Marketing Research,* 2 (August 1965), 250–258.

Green, P. E. and D. S. Tull (1975), *Research for Marketing Decisions,* 3rd edition. Englewood Cliffs, New Jersey: Prentice-Hall, Inc.

Hays, William Lee (1963), *Statistics for Psychologists.* New York: Holt, Rinehart and Winston.

Messenger, R. and L. Mandell (1972), "A Modal Search Technique for Predictive Nominal Scale Multivariate Analysis," *Journal of the American Statistical Association,* 67 (December).

Morrison, D. F. (1969), "On the Interpretation of Discriminant Analysis," *Journal of Marketing Research,* 6 (May), 156–63.

O'Malley, P. M. (1972), "An Empirical Composition of MNA and MDF," unpublished paper, Department of Psychology, University of Michigan.

Richards, L. E. (1975), "Detection and Incorporation of Interactive Effects in Discriminant Analysis," *Decision Sciences,* 6 (July), 508–12.

——— (1973), "Detection of Unexplained Joint Effects Through an Analysis of Residuals," *Decision Sciences,* 4 (January), 40–3.

Sheth, J. N. (1974), Book review of *Multivariate Nominal Scale Analysis* by Frank Andrews and Robert C. Messenger, *Journal of Marketing Research,* 11 (May), 228–32.

Suits, Daniel (1957), "Use of Dummy Variables in Regression Equations," *Journal of the American Statistical Association,* 52 (December), 548–51.

IAN FENWICK*

The "jackknife" technique developed by Tukey (1958), although rarely used in marketing, promises to be widely applicable. The very name of the technique was chosen to express its versatility. The jackknife offers the researcher the opportunity to reduce bias, perform significance tests, and assess the validity and stability of analyses without requiring a large sample. The author describes the jackknife method, applies the method to an analysis of international marketing effectiveness, and discusses some of its unresolved problems.

Techniques in Market Measurement: The Jackknife

The market researcher is frequently constrained in the choice of analysis method by the size of the sample and is forced either to forego the more sophisticated techniques or else, straining the available degrees of freedom, to produce results of questionable value. The jackknife method developed by Tukey (1958) from previous research by Quenouille (1949, 1956) and Jones (1956) enables an assessment to be made of the stability and significance of results *without* requiring a large sample. The method therefore should be very useful in a wide range of marketing analyses.

THE GENERALIZED JACKKNIFE

In its most generalized form (Gray and Schucany 1972) the jackknife is simply a method of combining two estimators. Thus if $\hat{p}_1$ and $\hat{p}_2$ are both estimators of a parameter p, the generalized jackknife, $G(\hat{p})$, is defined as:

$$G(\hat{p}) = \frac{\hat{p}_1 - R\hat{p}_2}{1 - R} \qquad (1)$$

where R is a weighting factor.

The importance of the method lies in the choice of R. If $\hat{p}_1$ and $\hat{p}_2$ are both biased estimators and R is set equal to the ratio of their biases,[1] the jackknife, $G(\hat{p})$, will itself be unbiased. Furthermore, if the bias in $\hat{p}_1$ and $\hat{p}_2$ has a number of components and R is set equal to the ratio of even some of these components, then although $G(\hat{p})$ will retain some bias, it will in many cases be less biased than *either* of the original estimators.

In practice, one particular form of the jackknife is applied. Its aim is to remove completely that bias

*Ian Fenwick is Associate Professor of Marketing, Dalhousie University School of Business Administration, Halifax, Nova Scotia.

[1]Clearly it is necessary to assume $R \neq 1$, i.e., the estimators are not identically biased.

Reprinted from *Journal of Marketing Research,* 16 (August 1979), 410-14, published by the American Marketing Association.

which is inversely proportional to sample size, a major component of the bias of many estimators (particularly maximum likelihood estimators).

THE JACKKNIFE

For any analysis method, the normal jackknife procedure obtains one estimator by applying the analysis to the entire sample; call it $\hat{p}_{\text{all}}$. The other estimator is obtained by splitting the sample into N arbitrary, equal-sized subsets and forming N "new" samples by omitting each subset in turn. Applying the particular analysis under consideration to each of these "new" samples yields a set of estimates $\hat{p}_i$, $i = 1, N$. The mean of these $\hat{p}_i$, $\bar{\hat{p}}$ forms the second estimator. Finally R is set equal to $(N - 1)/N$.

As biases inversely proportional to sample size are terms in $1/N$ for $\hat{p}_{\text{all}}$ and in $1/(N - 1)$ for $\bar{\hat{p}}$ (as $\bar{\hat{p}}$ is based on a sample omitting one of the N subsets), and R has been set equal to $(N - 1)/N$, i.e., the ratio of the estimators' biases, this form of the jackknife will indeed remove that bias inversely proportional to sample size. Furthermore, it has been shown that this bias reduction is likely to be accompanied by only a modest increase in estimator variance (Quenouille 1949), and in some cases the jackknife may actually reduce variance along with bias (Durbin 1959).

The normal jackknife, $J(\hat{p})$, can then be written:

$$J(\hat{p}) = \frac{\hat{p}_{\text{all}} - \frac{N-1}{N}\bar{\hat{p}}}{1 - (N-1)/N} = N\hat{p}_{\text{all}} - (N-1)\bar{\hat{p}}. \tag{2}$$

In the following discussion and throughout the literature, "the jackknife" refers to the method just described and $J(\hat{p})$ is called the jackknife estimate. It should be noted that the jackknife cannot always be counted on to reduce bias (e.g., if there is no $1/N$ term in the bias, but say a $1/N^2$ term[2]), and for some nonlinear estimators, the jackknife could actually increase bias (e.g., in estimating the population maximum by the sample maximum, the jackknife will produce an unwarranted reduction in the estimate). However, the jackknife procedure has three other properties that may be of more practical importance for marketing applications.

1. *Significance testing.* Tukey's contribution to the jackknife method (Mosteller and Tukey 1967; Tukey 1958) was the observation that the estimators $\hat{p}_i$, calculated from the sample omitting the subset i, could themselves be useful. He proposed that "pseudovalues," $P(\hat{p})$, be calculated by applying the jackknife formula for each $\hat{p}_i$, i.e.:

$$P(\hat{p}_i) = N\hat{p}_{\text{all}} - (N-1)\hat{p}_i,\ \hat{\imath} = 1, N. \tag{3}$$

The jackknife estimator, $J(\hat{p})$, is simply the mean of these pseudovalues. Tukey suggested that the pseudovalues could be treated as having approximately independent normal distributions, thus it would be reasonable to regard $J(\hat{p})$ as a sample mean and S_p (the standard deviation of the pseudovalues) as a sample standard deviation, giving the statistic

$$\frac{J(\hat{p}) - p}{S_p/\sqrt{N}}$$

approximately a t-distribution with $N - 1$ degrees of freedom.[3]

That the pseudovalues are asymptotically independent normal is attested by Gray and Schucany (1972, p. 138–62). However they admit the advisability in practice of adjusting the "t" statistic for possible interdependence between the pseudovalues. If the correlation (intraclass correlation) between pseudovalues is equal to r, the t-statistic should be calculated as:

$$\frac{J(\hat{p}) - p}{S_p/\sqrt{N}} \times \sqrt{\frac{1-r}{1+(N-1)r}}\,. \tag{4}$$

Although the true correlation of the pseudovalues will vary, depending on the estimator being jackknifed and the underlying distribution, Gray and Schucany suggest that the use of $r = 1/N$, giving

$$\frac{J(\hat{p}) - p}{S_p/\sqrt{N}} \times \sqrt{\frac{N-1}{2N-1}}\,, \tag{5}$$

will be "probably conservative" (1972, p. 166).

This offers the opportunity to apply significance tests both in situations where the usual assumptions for such tests are not satisfied (e.g., discriminant analysis using predictors that are not multivariate normal) and where tests are not usually available (e.g., for the individual coefficients in a canonical correlation).

2. *Stability.* Even if the researcher is not willing to accept the t-test, the pseudovalues offer direct evidence of the stability of the analysis. Inspection will show the extent to which intersample differences affect results and can be diagnostically useful in identifying observations which are out of line with the rest of the sample. Although frequently traceable to transcription or punching errors, such pathological cases can suggest new hypotheses for testing or new variables to be examined.

[2]Although Mantel (1967) suggests terms in $1/N^2$ may also be removed by a two-tier jackknifing, i.e., exclusion of *two* subsets from the sample and the application of the jackknife to already jackknifed estimators.

[3]If the estimation process of $P(\hat{p}_i)$ is such that they cannot attain N distinct values, the degrees of freedom should be reduced to the number of distinct values less one (Mosteller and Tukey 1967). For example, in estimating the median, and using subsets of size one, only two distinct values for $\hat{p}_i$ are possible (depending on whether the omitted observation is above or below the overall median); in this case, only one degree of freedom is available.

3. Validation. Given marketing's frequent use of search techniques supported by little in the way of prior hypotheses, it is particularly important that analyses be validated (see, for example, Doyle and Fenwick 1975). The jackknife offers a useful framework for validation with the key advantage that it does not require a large sample. Thus the analysis applied to the sample omitting a particular subset can be validated against that subset. For example, in the application presented hereafter, a discriminant function is used to classify those cases *not used in its estimation* and thus the normal bias problems (Morrison 1969) are avoided. It basically represents a gearing-up of the usual split-half or hold-out validation methods, which tend to require larger samples than are available in many marketing research situations.

The benefits of the jackknife method are well illustrated by the following application in an international marketing study.

EXPORT MARKETING PERFORMANCE IN THE U.K. CLOTHING INDUSTRY

Despite continuing emphasis on the importance of export sales, and the necessity for the U.K. to boost its share of world trade, there has been surprisingly little systematic analysis of the factors associated with companies' export performance. The study outlined here was based on a sample of companies in the U.K. clothing industry and was designed as the pilot stage of a wider multi-industry study (for a full description see Fenwick and Amine 1977).

Detailed information was collected on companies' export strategies and exporting performance by means of a combination of mail questionnaires and personal interviews with senior executives; 48 usable returns were obtained. The volume of information and the high level of management cooperation required necessitated the small sample size. Stratification, however, ensured the sample covered the full range of export involvement, and sample members were responsible for 10% of total texile exports. Nonetheless, conventional analysis would be limited to cross-tabulations or, at best, highly speculative multivariate analyses. Clearly the jackknife could be usefully applied here.

Predictors used in the study are shown in Table 1. They are a set of dummy variables designed to reflect important differences in export strategy, the measures used being based on an extensive literature review (Fenwick and Amine 1977). The major analysis performed was a discriminant analysis aiming to distinguish companies with an above-average export ratio for their industry sector.

RESULTS

The standardized coefficients of the discriminant function are shown in Table 2; this function correctly classified 79% of the total sample. However, as most

Table 1
EXPORT POLICY MEASURES

Variable	*Conditions for companies to score 1 on this variable*
Attitude and commitment to exporting	
X_1	Pursuing targeted export expansion plan; export orders given priority as a matter of policy.
X_2	Export market entry and export product policy decisions taken at board level.
X_3	Separate export department; annual export budget; ad/sales ratio in export markets > domestic.
Market selection	
X_4	Alternative markets considered and researched before making latest market entry.
X_5	Stipulation of a minimum export order size; export market plans for > 6mth horizon; specific market targets set.
Marketing mix	
X_6	Flexible pricing policy allowing sterling or foreign currency quotes as required.
X_7	No product adaptation at home or for export ("world range").
X_8	Products adapted at buyer's request both home and abroad ("matched adaptation").
X_9	Distribution system in export markets matched to home distribution system.
Company characteristics	
X_{10}	Years of exporting experience.
X_{11}	Number of export markets.
X_{12}	Change in percentage of total exports going to top three markets, 1972–75.

Table 2
JACKKNIFED DISCRIMINANT FUNCTION

Variable[a]	*Analysis applied to entire sample*	*Jackknifed estimates*	*Standard error of the jackknifed estimates*
X_1	.39	.47[b]	.22
X_2	−.32	−.37	.64
X_3	.11	.098	.27
X_4	−.040	.25	.38
X_5	−.27	.33	.33
X_6	.69	.90	.47
X_7	.23	.20	.33
X_8	−.77	−.84[b]	.42
X_9	−.26	−.19	.63
X_{10}	.95	1.19[b]	.47
X_{11}	−.37	−1.53	1.09
X_{12}	.083	.18	.25

[a]For definitions see Table 1.
[b]Significant at 5% level.

of the predictors are dummy variables, conventional significance tests are inapplicable, and the bias in the classification rate is well known (Morrison 1969).

To apply the jackknife the sample was split into 24 subsets (each containing one company with an above-average and one with a below-average export ratio) and 24 further discriminant analyses were conducted, a different subset being omitted for each. Thus for each coefficient of the discriminant function, 24 pseudovalues could be calculated by applying equation 2. For each coefficient Table 2 shows the mean of these pseudovalues (the jackknifed estimate) and their standard error ($S/\sqrt{n}$).

Although in most cases the jackknifed estimates are close to those obtained by the single analysis on the whole sample, only three of the coefficients are significant at the 95% level: X_1, a measure of attitude and commitment, X_8, product adaptation, and X_{10}, years of export experience. The jackknife procedure shows that the other coefficients, although in some cases large, are unstable against changes in sample composition.

Validation analysis was performed by using each of the discriminant functions to classify those companies that had not been used in its estimation. This step produced 48 individual validations (24 discriminant functions each used to classify two companies) of which 32 were correctly classified—a "genuine" success rate of 66%.[4]

PROBLEMS IN USE

Working with the jackknife technique shows it to be a powerful tool, but there are a number of unanswered questions about its use; three are particularly important.

1. *What is the effect of altering the size of the omitted subset?* The only guidance available here is the comment by Mosteller and Tukey (1967) that the size of the omitted subset might be adjusted to ensure the estimation process yields a number of different values for $P(\hat{p}_i)$. Otherwise, the size of subsets seems to be determined only by the cost of computation of the N jackknives. However, limited experimentation shows that subset size can affect the significance of results—in the case investigated the omission of larger subsets reduced coefficients' significance.

Another point when subsets are of size greater than one is whether all combinations of cases should be omitted, or just whole subsets. In the example, fixed pairs of companies were omitted (e.g., company 1 was always paired with company 12); one could argue that it would be better to omit every possible combination of two companies in turn (i.e., produce 1128 pseudovalues rather than 24). Quenouille (1956) suggests this latter approach.

2. *What is the effect of multitiered jackknifing?* An alternative to the straight jackknife is to lay one subset of the data completely aside and apply the jackknife to the remaining cases (producing $N - 1$ pseudovalues). Repeating this process for each subset laid aside in turn (producing $N(N - 1)$ pseudovalues) constitutes a two-tier jackknife, originally suggested as a validation tool (Mosteller and Tukey 1967).

However, Crask and Perreault (1977) find a two-tier jackknife greatly improves significance levels, mainly by producing much larger jackknifed estimates rather than smaller standard errors. There is clearly a tradeoff in computation costs between employing fewer larger subsets and a multitiered jackknife and using smaller subsets in a simple jackknife. Evidence on relative merits of these two procedures is badly needed.

3. *If the results of an analysis are to be transformed before use, should the jackknife be applied before or after the transformation?* For example, if the estimates obtained are to be fed into some objective function, should one simply use the final jackknifed estimates, or should the objective function be evaluated for each pseudovalue and averaged? Except for linear functions, results will differ for the two approaches. Conceptually, it seems more attractive to recalculate the objective for each pseudovalue, and obtain both the mean value of the function and its variability, but arguments undoubtedly could be advanced for the alternative approach.

Finally, the basic point must be remembered: the jackknife merely makes more intensive use of a sample; the relevance of its results depends on the representativeness of the sample. Similarly, the lack of significant values under a jackknife analysis shows that the sample used is too varied to support the relationship, not that a larger sample would not produce significant results. Despite all these reservations, the jackknife does offer unique advantages to the researcher forced to work with small samples, and will undoubtedly attain wider use in marketing analyses.

[4]Multitiered jackknifing can vastly increase the available validations, e.g., the entire jackknifing procedure could be applied to the sample omitting two companies; the 23 discriminant functions obtained could then be used to classify those two omitted companies. Repeating the entire process for every pair of companies yields $24 \times 23 \times 2 = 1104$ independent validations. Additional tiers of jackknifing would expand even more the validations available.

REFERENCES

Crask, M. R. and W. D. Perreault (1977), "Validation of Discriminant Analysis in Marketing Research," *Journal of Marketing Research,* 14 (February), 60–8.

Doyle, P. and I. Fenwick (1975), "Pitfalls of A.I.D. Analysis," *Journal of Marketing Research,* 12 (November), 408–13.

Durbin, J. (1959), "A Note on the Application of Quenouille's Method of Bias Reduction to the Estimation of Ratios," *Biometrika,* 46, 477–80.

Fenwick, I. and L. Amine (1977), "Export Marketing Strategies and Market Performance," paper presented at the

Association for International Business, U.K. Annual Conference.
Gray, H. L. and W. R. Schucany (1972), *The Generalized Jackknife Statistic*. New York: Marcel Dekker.
Jones, H. L. (1956), "Investigating the Properties of a Sample Mean by Employing Random Subsample Means," *Journal of the American Statistical Association*, 51 (March), 54–83.
Mantel, N. (1967), "Assumption-free Estimators Using U-Statistics and a Relationship to the Jackknife Method," *Biometrics*, 23 (September), 567–71.
Miller, R. (1964), "A Trustworthy Jackknife," *Annals of Mathematical Statistics*, 35 (December), 1594–605.
——— (1968), "Jackknifing Variances," *Annals of Mathematical Statistics*, 39 (April), 567–82.
Morrison, D. G. (1969), "On the Interpretation of Discriminant Analysis," *Journal of Marketing Research*, 6 (May), 156–63.
Mosteller, F. and J. W. Tukey (1967), "Data Analysis, Including Statistics," in *Handbook of Social Psychology*, G. Lindzey and E. Aronson, eds. Reading, Massachusetts: Addison-Wesley.
Quenouille, M. (1949), "Approximate Tests of Correlation in Time Series," *Journal of the Royal Statistical Society, Series B*, 11, 68–84.
——— (1956), "Notes on Bias in Estimation," *Biometrika*, 43, 647–9.
Tukey, J. W. (1958), "Bias and Confidence in Not-Quite Large Samples" (abstract), *Annals of Mathematical Statistics*, 29 (June), 614.

DAVID FLATH and E. W. LEONARD*

The authors compare the application of two logit models for the analysis of qualitative marketing data. A weighted least squares logit model is compared with a maximum likelihood logit model different from that mentioned by Green et al. Empirical applications are used to compare the models. Suggestions are presented for interpreting and reporting the results of logit-type models, with special attention to interaction effects.

A Comparison of Two Logit Models in the Analysis of Qualitative Marketing Data

Increasing attention is being directed to statistical models for explaining categorical choices by survey respondents, such as their adoption or nonadoption of a new service. These choices are represented mathematically by qualitative variables which assume one of only two possible values. "Logit"-type models have been shown to be appropriate for analysis of such data and their mathematical properties have been well studied, first by Berkson (1955) and more recently by Nerlove and Press (1973). But practitioners of marketing research are not yet fully informed of these results, despite a fine start by Green, Carmone, and Wachspress (1977). The following discussion is intended to further that effort.

A maximum likelihood logit model is described and shown to be superior to a logit-type model presented by Green, Carmone, and Wachspress (1977), the "weighted least squares logit."[1] Also, interpretation of results of logit-type models is discussed, with special attention to interaction effects.

AN EXAMPLE

The estimation problems here addressed are understood best in the context of a specific example. The results of a randomized survey conducted by Leonard (1978) are shown in Table 1. Retail bank customers were surveyed as to characteristics thought related to probability of their having adopted a recently introduced automatic teller service. From the responses, qualitative variables were constructed:

$$\text{ADOPT} = \begin{cases} 1, \text{ if adopted automatic teller service} \\ 0, \text{ otherwise} \end{cases}$$

$$\text{AGE} = \begin{cases} 1, \text{ if older than 35 years} \\ 0, \text{ otherwise} \end{cases}$$

$$\text{INCOME} = \begin{cases} 1, \text{ if annual income greater than \$15,000} \\ 0, \text{ otherwise} \end{cases}$$

$$\text{MOBILITY} = \begin{cases} 1, \text{ if lived in at least 3 different cities in last 10 years} \\ 0, \text{ otherwise} \end{cases}$$

"ADOPT" is the criterion variable in a dependence structure with "AGE," "INCOME," and "MOBILITY" as predictors.

The traditional marketing approach to analyzing data sets like these is first to group observations into cells. A statistical model then is defined which is based on the means of observations in each cell. An alterna-

[1] The maximum likelihood logit model discussed here is slightly different from the model Green et al. identify as a "log-linear maximum likelihood" logit model. The difference between the two maximum likelihood models is their parameterization. Here a regression format is adopted rather than the ANOVA structure of the Green et al. "log-linear" logit model. The advantages here of the regression-type model are that it (1) facilitates direct comparison with the weighted least squares logit model and (2) highlights an important feature of the maximum likelihood approach: its reliance on individual rather than grouped observations. See Nerlove and Press (1973, p. 41–5) for an extensive discussion of the relation between the ANOVA (log-linear) ML logit model and the regression ML logit model.

*David Flath is Assistant Professor of Economics and Business, North Carolina State University. E. W. Leonard is Assistant Professor of Marketing, Emory University.

Reprinted from *Journal of Marketing Research,* 16 (November 1979), 533-8, published by the American Marketing Association.

tive approach is to base the statistical model on the individual observations themselves, rather than on the cells of observations. In the example used here, the traditional approach leads to a weighted least squares regression procedure, whereas the latter implies maximum likelihood estimation. In either case the criterion variable is "probability of adoption."

LOGIT-TYPE MODELS

If the criterion variable is constrained to lie between zero and one, use of a linear or log-linear function is precluded. In this case, the response function is a probability function by definition. Two functions which have been used in models with qualitative dependent variables are the normal and the logistic. The first defines the "probit" class of models and the other the "logit" models. Because the logit models present much simpler computation problems, attention in this article is restricted to that class.[2]

The logistic *cdf* is defined:

$$y = f(\mathbf{x}) = \frac{1}{1 + e^{-\boldsymbol{\beta}\mathbf{x}}} \tag{1}$$

where:

$$\boldsymbol{\beta}\mathbf{x} = \beta_0 + \beta_1 X_1 + \ldots + \beta_k X_k.$$

The function represents an S-shaped surface with inflection always occurring at $Y = 1/2$. Changes in β_0 shift the surface laterally whereas changes in β_1, . . ., β_k affect its dispersion (see Figures 1 and 2). The logistic function can represent a fairly close approximation to the normal, which is (heuristically)

Figure 1
EFFECT OF CHANGE IN THE CONSTANT PARAMETER ON THE MAPPING OF LOGISTIC FUNCTION

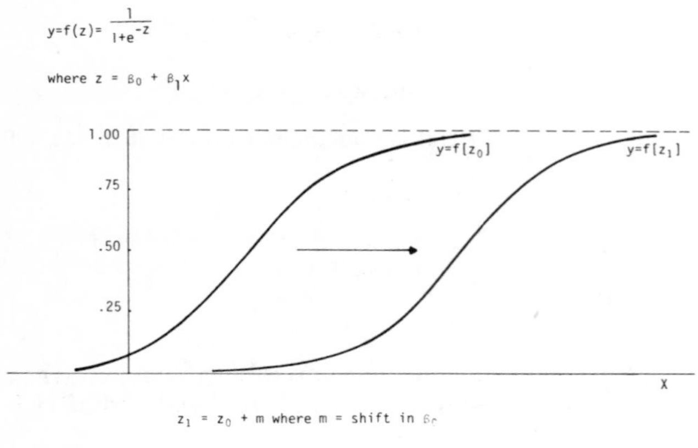

[2]The normal function entails more complex and therefore costly computation. For the maximum likelihood estimator described hereafter, the cost of using the logit formulation was less than one dollar. With probit analysis, the cost of maximum likelihood estimates was greater, but the results were very close.

Figure 2
EFFECT OF CHANGE IN A SLOPE PARAMETER ON THE MAPPING OF LOGISTIC FUNCTION

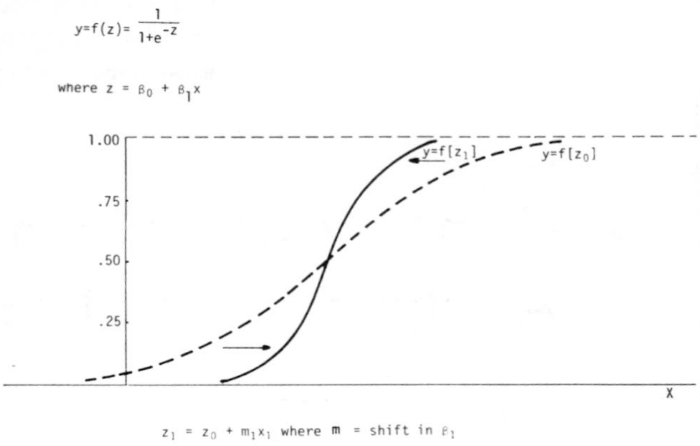

an advantage. If y falls in the closed interval [0, 1], equation 1 can be rewritten:

$$\log \frac{y}{1 - y} = \boldsymbol{\beta}\mathbf{x}. \tag{1'}$$

The left side of equation 1′ is called the "logit" of y. All logit-type models share this general form and its considerable advantages over ANOVA, cross-tabulation, or other conventional techniques. In logit models, the predicted values of the criterion variable have intuitive appeal as probability estimates, and estimates of the coefficient vector ($\boldsymbol{\beta}$) can be used in calculating direction and magnitude of marginal effects.

Weighted Least Squares Logit

A weighted least squares logit (WLS logit) model has been defined by Berkson (1955) and applied to marketing data by Green, Carmone, and Wachspress (1977). Let "P_j" represent the proportion of positive responses in the jth cell and let "$\mathbf{X}_j$" be the vector of predictor variables in the jth cell. The Berkson model postulates the relation:

$$P_j = \frac{1}{1 + e^{-\boldsymbol{\beta}\mathbf{x}_j - \xi_j}} \tag{2}$$

Note that if $0 < p_j < 1$ for every cell, this is equivalent to

$$\log \frac{P_j}{1 - P_j} = \boldsymbol{\beta}\mathbf{x}_j + \xi_j \tag{2'}$$

Linear regression techniques can be applied to equation 2′. To calculate efficient estimates of $\boldsymbol{\beta}$ requires knowledge of the distribution of ξ. It can be shown that

Table 1

PROPORTION OF RESPONDENTS ADOPTING AUTOMATIC TELLER SERVICE, RELATED TO AGE, INCOME, AND MOBILITY

(sample size = 100)

	Age ≤ 35 years		*Age > 35 years*	
Income	*Nonmobile*	*Mobile*	*Nonmobile*	*Mobile*
≤$15,000/yr.	0.222 (9)	0.692 (13)	0.000 (11)	1.000 (1)
>$15,000/yr.	0.500 (12)	0.809 (21)	0.500 (28)	0.200 (5)

Note: Number of observations in each cell is shown in parentheses. The original data set included many more cells than the eight shown here. For a discussion and analysis of the complete set, see Leonard (1978).

$$\xi_j \sim N(0, n_j \Pi_j (1 - \Pi_j))$$

where:

n_j = number of observations in the cell and
Π_j = probability of a positive response in the jth cell.

The unknown probabilities (Π_j) can be estimated by the proportions of positive responses (P_j) in each cell and a weighted least squares estimate of β calculated.[3] Because the efficient estimator is only approximated by this procedure, *t*-statistics are true only asymptotically. This WLS logit model was applied to the Leonard data and the results are reported in the first line of Table 2.

WLS logit requires more than one observation per cell, preferably many observations per cell, for its reliability depends on accurate estimates of the cell probabilities (Π_j). Furthermore, because the logit transformation is not defined for cells in which $P_j = 0$ or $P_j = 1$, the WLS logit model may require elimination of observations (even if the overall sample size is very large). Both of these considerations severely prejudice results in the example used here. Two of the eight cells had to be deleted, one because $P_j = 0$ and the other because $P_j = 1$.

Berkson (1968, p. 153) suggests an adjustment which precludes the necessity of deleting cells. P_j is replaced by P_j':

$$P_j' = \frac{n_{j,1} + 1/2}{n_j + 1} \tag{4}$$

where:

$n_{j,1}$ = number of positive responses in the jth cell and
n_j = the total number of observations in the jth cell.

Note that $\log \dfrac{P_j'}{1 + P_j'}$ is defined for virtually every cell and furthermore for $n_j \rightarrow \infty$, P_j' will be extremely close to P_j. WLS logit with the Berkson adjustment was applied to the Leonard data set and the results are reported in the second line of Table 2. Inclusion of the two cells which were originally deleted dramatically improves statistics. But the results still suffer from the small overall sample size, and are now further prejudiced by application of an admittedly *ad hoc* adjustment. A different approach can be used to avoid these problems.

Maximum Likelihood Logit

Rather than grouping observations into cells, one could define a response function for each individual:

$$\Pi_i = F(\beta \mathbf{x}_i) = \frac{1}{1 + e^{-\beta \mathbf{x}_j}} \qquad i = 1, \ldots, n \tag{5}$$

where Π_i = true probability that i^{th} respondent is positive. This relation can be used to define a likelihood function (L) on the observations:

$$L(y_1, \ldots, y_n; x_1, \ldots, x_n)$$

$$= \prod_{i-1}^{n} F(\beta \mathbf{x}_i)^{y_i} [1 - F(\beta \mathbf{x}_i)]^{(1-y_i)} \tag{6}$$

where:

y_i = 0, 1 response variable and
$\mathbf{x}_i$ = vector of observations on predictor variables.

[3] If variances in error terms are not uniform, the OLS estimator is not efficient (meaning that another linear unbiased estimator has less variance). For cases in which residual variances are known (or known up to a scalar constant), a simple transformation of the data (Aitken transformation) restores efficient estimation. This transformation is equivalent to dividing observations by the standard deviations in their respective error terms. Suppose that (in matrix notation),

$$y_j = \mathbf{x}_j' \beta + \xi_j$$

and

$$\text{variance } (\xi_j) = \frac{\sigma^2}{\omega_j}.$$

Then the Aitken transformation yields:

$$y_j \sqrt{\omega_j} = \mathbf{x}_j' \sqrt{\omega_j} \cdot \beta + \xi_j \sqrt{\omega_j}.$$

See that residual variances in the equation are uniform:

$$\text{variance } [\xi_j \sqrt{\omega_j}] = \sigma^2.$$

When OLS is applied to the weighted data, estimation is efficient.

Table 2
PROBABILITY OF ADOPTING AUTOMATIC TELLER SERVICE
(sample size = 100)

Type of logit model used	*Intercept*	*Age*	*Income*	*Mobility*	*F*	χ^2	R^2	λ
	Coefficients on explanatory variables, with asymptotic t-statistics							
Weighted least squares, empty cells deleted	−0.580 (−0.584)	−0.471 (−0.485)	0.805 (0.770)	1.013 (1.102)	0.752		0.530	
Weighted least squares, Berkson adjustment	−0.710 (−0.992)	−0.582 (−0.842)	0.971 (1.350)	1.030 (1.523)	1.734		0.565	
Maximum likelihood	−0.880 (−1.733)[a]	0.822 (−1.621)	1.216 (2.468)[a]	1.129 (2.223)		18.915		0.000

Note: See text for discussion of models and definition of variables. λ is the likelihood ratio for the hypothesis $\beta = 0$, and is a measure of "goodness of fit." $\chi^2 = -2 \log \lambda$.
[a]Significant at 5% level.

Maximum likelihood estimators (ML logit) can be calculated at relatively low cost, using an iterative computer routine such as the one developed by Nerlove and Press (1973). Asymptotic standard errors in these estimates can be used in calculating asymptotic *t*-statistics. The *F*-statistic of the WLS logit procedure has a counterpart in the likelihood ratio test statistic $= -2 \log \lambda \sim \chi^2$, where λ = likelihood ratio for $H_0: \beta = 0$.

The likelihood ratio (λ) ranges in value from 1 to 0, having smaller values as the goodness of fit improves. It is therefore a possible analog to the coefficient of determination (R^2) in the WLS logit model.

Because the ML logit procedure does not require many observations per cell, what was a "small' sample for weighted least squares may be adequate for maximum likelihood. This feature is evidenced by the dramatic improvement in test statistics with application of the latter (see the third line of Table 2).

One would expect less difference in results between the WLS logit model and the ML logit model if the sample size were very large. Green, Carmone, and Wachspress (1977) report results of WLS logit estimation of a three-variable, eight-cell model with 10,524 observations. These are replicated in the first line of Table 3, and test statistics have been calculated in the same manner as was done for the Leonard data set. ML logit estimates for the Green et al. data set are shown in the second line of Table 3.

Coefficient estimates are very close for both procedures but, interestingly, test statistics are more significant with ML logit, even for this large sample. However, it is clear that difference between WLS logit and ML logit is much related to sample size—minimal for large samples, very pronounced for small samples.

INTERPRETATION OF LOGIT COEFFICIENTS

One way of presenting results of logit-type models (either WLS or ML) is to calculate predicted probability of a positive response for each cell. These estimates will be superior to the simple proportions in each cell in the sense that they are based on a wider set of information (in logit-type estimation, unlike the simple procedure of calculating cell proportions, sam-

Table 3
PROBABILITY OF ADOPTING A NEW TELECOMMUNICATIONS SERVICE
(sample size = 10,524)

Type of logit model used	*Intercept*	*Education*	*Income*	*Mobility*	*F*	χ^2	R^2	λ
	Coefficients on explanatory variables, with asymptotic t-statistics							
Weighted least squares	−0.903 (−9.417)[a]	−0.164 (−1.428)	−0.438 (−3.764)[a]	−0.986 (−8.716)[a]	30.884		0.959	
Maximum likelihood	−0.902 (−19.073)[a]	−0.161 (−2.772)[a]	−0.444 (−7.709)[a]	−0.992 (−17.610)[a]		411.526		0.000

Note: Data are from Green, Carmone, and Wachspress (1977).
[a]Significant at 1% level.

ple points in all cells influence estimated probabilities in any one cell).

In addition to predictions for each cell the researcher may be interested in the marginal effect of changes in each predictor variable. For example, what is the change in probability of adoption implied by increase in income from category 0 to category 1? Define Π^0 as the subject's initial probability of a positive response, and Π^1 as the probability after the change in predictor. Then the induced change in probability is:

$$\Delta\Pi = \Pi^1 - \Pi^0 = \frac{1}{1 + e^{-\beta x^1}} - \frac{1}{1 + e^{-\beta x^0}}. \tag{7}$$

By use of the ML logit estimates for the Leonard data set, these marginal effects are calculated for unit changes in each predictor, for arbitrarily selected initial probabilities of adoption. These figures are reported in Table 4.

Notice that the magnitude of the marginal effects is influenced in each case by the initial probability of adoption. This indicates a type of interaction among predictor variables, implicit in the logistic function. If one assumes for the moment that predictors are continuous, the partial derivatives of equation 1 are:

$$\frac{\partial y}{\partial x_j} = y(1 - y)\beta_j \qquad J = 1, \ldots, k. \tag{8}$$

Because y is itself a function of all the predictors ($x_1, \ldots, x_k$), so are the partial derivatives, and this is one meaning of "interaction." This result is generalizable to the case of categorical predictor variables.

Calculations like those in Table 4 can be especially informative if the number of cells is large. In these cases, rather than selecting arbitrary values for initial probability of a positive response, the researcher might select the quartiles of the predicted probabilities. Marginal effects reported would then be descriptive for the actual sample population.

If the interaction implicit in the logistic function were thought not to capture the full interaction effects, variables could be defined such as:

$$x_{k+1} = \begin{cases} 1, \text{ if } x_1 = 1 \text{ and } x_2 = 1 \\ 0, \text{ otherwise} \end{cases}$$

$$x_{k+2} = \begin{cases} 1, \text{ if } x_1 = 1 \text{ and } x_2 = 1 \\ 0, \text{ otherwise} \end{cases}$$

$\vdots$

etc.

Inclusion in model 1 of variables like these would alter the partial derivatives in a way which could be said to represent *additional* interaction effects. Note that including all possible interaction effects would be tedious and that the addition of a large number of interaction terms should be weighed against the reduction in the number of degrees of freedom available in estimation.

Suppose that instead of a single dependent variable there were several qualitative dependent variables presumed to be interrelated—e.g., probability of adopting push-button phone service, probability of adopting color phones, and probability of adopting princess style may all be subjects of study and thought interrelated. In such a case a multivariate logistic function is the appropriate mathematical model. To capture interaction effects among the separate but related *dependent* variables it is necessary to include interaction terms (in this instance bivariate and/or trivariate) indicating coincidence of adoption of the different services. *This* interaction would not be implicit in separate estimation of marginal logistic functions for each of the three dependent variables unless the extra terms were added.[4]

Table 4

PREDICTED EFFECTS OF CHANGES IN EXPLANATORY VARIABLES ON PROBABILITY OF ADOPTING AUTOMATIC TELLER SERVICES, BASED ON MAXIMUM LIKELIHOOD ESTIMATES

Initial probability of adoption = Π	$\Delta\Pi$ / Δ *age*	$\Delta\Pi$ / Δ *income*	$\Delta\Pi$ / Δ *mobility*
.25	−0.123	0.279	0.258
.5	−0.195	0.271	0.256
.75	−0.181	0.160	0.153

Note: Estimates are based on maximum likelihood estimates of coefficients, reported in Table 2. See text for discussion of calculation procedure.

CONCLUSIONS

Many conceptual models can be formulated as probability functions. An efficient and economical technique for estimating such functions is therefore a valuable tool of analysis. The maximum likelihood logit procedure is shown here to be such a technique.

The WLS logit model requires many observations per cell. With survey data, it therefore entails categorization. (With experimental data as in the biological sciences, it need not entail categorization.) The ML logit procedure is based on individual observations,

[4]The number of separate logit equations implied by a multivalued criterion is equal, in each case, to the number of independent binary distinctions. If the criterion variable assumes K possible *mutually exclusive* values, the response is completely represented as K-1 binary choices. In the telephone example given in the text, the three phone characteristics are not mutually exclusive, and therefore entail three independent binary choices. In this instance three separate logit equations would be required. See Nerlove and Press (1973) for a complete discussion of multivariate qualitative models.

and therefore can be used with categorical *or* continuous data.

The WLS logit model requires *ad hoc* adjustment if cells include all positive responses or no positive responses. The ML logit model does not require any such adjustments.

The WLS logit model produces less precise estimates than the ML logit. Sample size may be "too small" for use of the WLS logit model but adequate for ML logit.

Interaction effects are implicit in all logit-type models, and should be taken into consideration in presenting results of these models.

Berkson, the coiner of the term "logit" more than 20 years ago, compared the properties of ML logit and WLS logit estimates (1955, 1968). Using experimental data with many observations per cell, Berkson found little difference between WLS logit (he called it "minimum logit χ^2" . . .) and ML logit estimates. But he argued for use of the former on the basis of its relative ease of computation. For marketing research this verdict should now be reversed for two reasons. First, in some marketing applications (unlike experimental biology applications) there will necessarily be few observations per cell, maybe even only one per cell. Second, the computer revolution has significantly lowered the relative costs of numerical calculations. There is no longer any reason to prefer WLS logit over ML logit for marketing applications.

REFERENCES

Berkson, J. (1955), "Maximum Likelihood and Minimum χ^2 Estimates of the Logistic Function," *Journal of the American Statistical Association,* 50 (March).

——— (1968), "Application of Minimum Logit χ^2 Estimate to a Problem of Grizzle with a Notation on the Problem of 'The Interaction,' " *Biometrics,* 24, 75–96.

Green, Paul E., Frank J. Carmone, and David P. Wachspress (1977), "On the Analysis of Qualitative Data in Marketing Research," *Journal of Marketing Research,* 14 (February), 52–9.

Leonard, E. W. (1978), "Life Style Measures and Segmentation in Retail Banking: An Empirical Examination Applied to Automated Tellers," unpublished Ph.D. dissertation, Oklahoma State University.

Nerlove, Marc and James S. Press (1973), *Univariate and Multivariate Log-Linear and Logistic Models.* Santa Monica: Rand Corporation (December).

DENNIS H. GENSCH and WILFRED W. RECKER*

The authors argue that for the cross-sectional multiattribute approach to choice modeling, the multinomial logit is theoretically and empirically superior to the more commonly used regression approach. Other choice methodologies also are discussed briefly in relation to logit. The difference between individual level (where regression is appropriate) and cross-sectional analysis is recognized. Most marketing managers, because of their research goals, will be using a cross-sectional approach. The derivation of the logit from an underlying model of choice is illustrated. It is this underlying behavioral model of choice that provides logit with several conceptual advantages for modeling a multiattribute choice structure.

The Multinomial, Multiattribute Logit Choice Model

The concept of evaluating a decision, product, or service as a function of its attributes is a rather universally accepted approach which has been implemented in such fields as economics (Fishburn, 1967, 1968; McFadden, 1973; McGuire and Weiss, 1976; Theil, 1970), engineering (Gustafson et al., 1971; Huber 1968; Turban and Metersky, 1971), finance (Slovic et al., 1972), medicine (Huber et al., 1969), and social psychology (Dawes, 1971; Fishbein, 1972, MacCrimmon, 1973; Rosenberg, 1956). Readers need only refer to an extensive review article (Wilkie and Pessemier, 1973) and past issues of this journal to see the prominence of the multiattribute approach in current marketing research. Marketing practitioners are now attempting to implement the multiattribute approach for their specific problems.

The goals of the research determine whether an individual or cross-sectional multiattribute analysis is appropriate. Major uses of the individual approach involve trying to understand the information processing done by particular individuals making a decision (Bettman et al., 1975) or predicting the actual choice of particular individuals (Keeley and Doherty, 1972; Slovic et al., 1972). Because the analysis is by individual rather than by alternative, regression has been successfully and correctly used for situations in which the number of alternatives exceeds the number of attributes.

Marketing practitioners usually are more interested in statistics indicating group tendencies or preferences than in sets of unique statistics for each individual. The desire for aggregate statistics implies cross-sectional rather than individual analyses. When they are attempting to predict the choice distribution of a population or when their interest centers on the diagnostic information about an attribute's relative influence on preference for the *total population,* cross-sectional analysis is appropriate. However, when analyzing the crucial diagnostic information in a cross-sectional multiattribute study in which the dependent variable is a rank or intervally scaled measure of the preference for an alternative, the practitioner observes that the statistical technique most used in marketing research, often with reservations, is regression (Bass and Wilkie, 1973; Sheth and Talarzyk, 1972). One thus might conclude that regression, despite its limitations, is perhaps the best or only technique available.

The authors attempt to show that, for the purpose of deriving diagnostic information from multiattribute hypotheses, a reasonable model is one in which individuals compare pairs of choice alternatives on the basis of their *perceived differences* in satisfaction on

*Dennis H. Gensch is Professor, School of Business Administration, University of Wisconsin at Milwaukee. Wilfred W. Recker is Visiting Senior Analyst, Transportation and Urban Analysis Department, Research Laboratories, General Motors Corporation.

Reprinted from *Journal of Marketing Research,* 16 (February 1979), 124-32, published by the American Marketing Association.

those attributes possessed by all alternatives adjusted by absolute levels of satisfaction on attributes specific to one alternative. For example, consider the comparison of two grocery stores. Both have the same set of attributes with the one exception that store 1 does not have a meat counter and store 2 does. For the attribute "quality of meat" an absolute value is added to the preference score of store 2. The rest of the preference score for store 2 and the entire preference score for store 1 consist of perceived differences in satisfaction on the common attributes. Such a conceptualization considers multiattribute model specfications in which evaluations between alternatives are treated as differences between attribute scores (Bass and Wilkie, 1973). The method also allows each individual in the sample to have a *different* set of available or feasible alternatives.

The purpose of this article is to illustrate the usefulness of the logit model in a real-world situation in which a set of consumers are asked to rate the grocery stores they frequent most. As in many real-world studies, the researcher is faced with the prospect of individuals having different sets of stores (alternatives) from which they make a choice; also, each of the stores can have a different set of relevant attributes. Because the logit model is derived from an underlying behavioral model of choice, the logit is suited to choice situations that present problems for other covariance techniques such as regression, discriminant analysis, and factor analysis which are often used in choice modeling. In addition, the authors argue that, because of the underlying choice model from which the logit is derived, the diagnostic information such as the elasticities of the attributes provides more meaningful measures of reality than the diagnostic information from other covariance choice models.

In the following sections, the logit model's derivation from an underlying behavioral model of choice is presented briefly, the basic approaches to choice modeling are categorized and logit is discussed in relation to other covariance approaches, the actual application of the logit to real-world data and a comparison with a regression model on the same data are provided, and finally an interpretation of the diagnostic information provided by the logit model is discussed. In conclusion, a summary is given of the basic features of the logit model that make it particularly well suited for a covariance analysis of the choice process with cross-sectional data.

Multinomial Logit Method

One can hypothesize that an individual decision maker's overall preference or ranking of a choice alternative is a function of the utility which the alternative holds for the individual.

One also can hypothesize that an individual's utility for an alternative is separable into two components: (1) a deterministic component measured in terms of expressed attitudes toward that alternative, and (2) an unobserved random component. The source of the deterministic component is consistent with rational choice theories in psychology and economics (Manski, 1973) and requires no elaboration here. The source of the random component, however, is different from the "repeated measurements" source of error in psychological studies (Bock and Jones, 1968). Manski (1975) lists "omitted structure," the need to make measurement in terms of proxy or "instrumental variable," and "cross-sectional preference variation" as logical bases for such a concept (which he refers to as "stochastic utility").

In essence the assumptions underlying the error term in logit analysis reflect the complexity and richness of the choice process by recognizing that a model of the choice process seldom will be fully specified in terms that can be measured accurately and which identify all of the current and historical attributes that really influence the choice process. *In reality, most models of choice are underspecified and this fact should be taken into account in the analysis.*

Utility is thus written

$$U_i^k = V_i^k + \varepsilon_i^k \tag{1}$$

where:

U_i^k = the utility of alternative k to individual i,
V_i^k = the deterministic component, and
ε_i^k = the random component, which is assumed to be independent and identically distributed across all individuals i.

Consistent with the majority of other multiattribute models (Turban and Metersky, 1971), a form for the deterministic component which is linear and additive in terms of the attribute scores can be assumed:

$$V_i^k = \sum_{j \in S^k} a_j^k x_{ij}^k + \sum_{j \in S} b_j x_{ij}^k \tag{2}$$

where:

x_{ij}^k = score given by individual i to the kth alternative on the jth attribute,
a_j^k = utility weight reflecting the importance of the jth attribute defined uniquely for the kth alternative,
b_j = utility weight reflecting the importance of the jth generic attribute defined consistently for all alternatives,
S^k = set of attributes relevant to alternative k, which are not common to all other alternatives,
S = set of attributes common to the description of all available alternatives.

It is postulated that an individual will *prefer* the choice alternative perceived to have the greatest utility. The probability that individual i will prefer alternative k from a set of available alternatives A_i, denoted by $P_i(k:A_i)$, consequently can be written in utility terms as

(3) $P_i(k:A_i) = \text{Prob}\{U_i^k > U_k^l \quad \text{for all } l \in A_i, l \neq k\}.$

In light of the division of utility in expression 1 into random and deterministic components, the preference probability can be rewritten

$$(4) \qquad P_i(k:A_i) = \text{Prob}\{(V_i^k + \varepsilon_i^k) > (V_i^l + \varepsilon_i^l) \quad \text{for all } l \in A_i, l \neq k\}$$

or

$$(5) \qquad P_i(k:A_i) = \text{Prob}\{(V_i^k - V_i^l) > (\varepsilon_i^l - \varepsilon_i^k) \quad \text{for all } l \in A_i, l \neq k\}.$$

This specification of choice probability in terms of utility differences for each individual automatically takes care of the scale differences problem reflected by differences in scale means across individuals.

If it is assumed that an individual, in making decisions so as to maximize the overall utility of his or her choice, is concerned with maximum values of the unobserved variables contained in the random component of utility, as well as with such values in the deterministic component, then Gumbel (1954) has shown that for a class of distributions (including the normal distribution) the random terms ε_i^l are independently identically distributed with the Weibull (Gnedenko extreme value) distribution, i.e.,

$$(6) \qquad \text{Prob}\{\varepsilon_i^l \geq w\} = \exp(-\exp(-w)).$$

With the assumption represented by equation 6, it is easily shown that the probabilistic choice model, equation 5, takes the form:

$$(7) \qquad P_i(k:A_i) = \exp(V_i^k) \Big/ \sum_{l \in A_i} \exp(V_i^l).$$

A detailed derivation of this type of strict utility model, called the multinomial logit model, is provided by Thiel (1969) and discussions of the rationale for and properties of such models are provided by McFadden (1968, 1972, 1973) and Thiel (1971).

A specific structure of perceptual comparison among choice alternatives is implied by the multinomial logit model. To better visualize this structure, rewrite expression 7 as

$$(8) \qquad P_i(k:A_i) = 1 \Big/ \left(1 + \sum_{\substack{l \in A_i \\ l \neq k}} \exp(V_i^k - V_i^l)\right),$$

where V_i^k and V_i^l are defined in expression 2.

The a_i^k and b_i attribute rating coefficients in the multinomial logit choice model can be estimated by using maximum likelihood (McFadden, 1968) or maximum score (Manski, 1975) techniques. McFadden (1968) has demonstrated that the maximum likelihood estimators are consistent, asymptotically efficient, and are unique under very general conditions. Furthermore, the asymptotic normality of these estimators allows the use of t-statistics for asymptotic tests of coefficient significance. Currently several user-oriented maximum likelihood multinomial logit computer programs are available, such as the one used in the present research (Cambridge Systematics, Inc., 1974).

Logit Related to Other Techniques

There are several basic approaches to choice modeling. Lexigraphic (Russ, 1971) and hierarchical (Recker et al.) approaches attempt to consider the sequence in which attributes enter the decision process. Multidimensional scaling attempts to map the entire preference space (Lehmann, 1971). Choice usually is determined in terms of a metric distance from an "ideal point." Recently linear programming has been suggested as means of relating alternatives within the preference space (Pekelman and Sen, 1974; Shocker and Srinivasan, 1974). A third basic approach is a covariance approach that attempts to relate attribute scores to preference measures of the alternatives. The most commonly used of these techniques are regression, multiple discriminant analysis, and logit and probit analysis. A comprehensive discussion of the relative merits and the situational appropriateness of the basic approaches would be worthwhile, but is beyond the scope of this article. Rather than compare the covariance approach with alternative forms of choice modeling, the authors briefly differentiate the logit approach from the other commonly used covariance techniques.

The basic structure of the multinomial logit model can be used for a number of purposes; for example, a logit formulation has been shown to be one method of providing "logically consistent" explanatory variables for an econometric model of market share where the explanatory variables were product ratios (McGuire and Weiss, 1976). However, the logit approach is particularly well suited for choice models. Within this general framework, the authors argue that logit is the most appropriate technique for cross-sectional multiattribute modeling using a covariance approach. Logit and probit are virtually identical for a dichotomous dependent variable; logit can be expanded to more than two values on the dependent variable, whereas probit is strictly limited to a two-value dependent variable. Recently approximation techniques for expanding probit to multiple choice situations have been proposed (Lerman and Manski, 1976). The computer codes are complex and not generally available; furthermore, it is not clear whether the more general form of the error term in the multinomial probit will actually lead to substantially different or better predictions than those of the logit.

Multiple discriminant analysis (MDA) is a fundamentally different type of model in that it is a *classification* rather than a choice model. The other techniques basically assume one population making choices based on their evaluation of the independent variables. MDA assumes *several distinct populations,* each having a different pattern of scores on the independent variables. Further distinctions between the fundamentally very different multinomial logit and MDA approach are well articulated for the two-group case by Westin and Watson (1975, p. 283). Extensions of their arguments to the general multigroup case are straightforward.

Gensch et al. (1975) give a detailed discussion of four reasons why regression is conceptually incompatible with cross-sectional multiattribute data. The following empirical section shows that because the multinomial logit model is conceptually a statistical technique derived from an underlying behavioral model of choice, it has predictive and diagnostic superiority over a regression model for the data set used.

EMPIRICAL RESULTS: LOGIT VS. REGRESSION

The empirical results presented for model comparison are related to choice of store for grocery shopping. The same data have been analyzed by using different formulations of regression and logit models. Gensch et al. (1975) present more than one formulation of both the regression and logit model. Here, one formulation of each model is considered sufficient to convey the differences in empirical results. Though comparison of model performance is emphasized, the model results also offer insights into the store selection process underlying most brand choice and product purchase models. Researchers working on problems of estimating brand or product purchasing decisions have stated that considerably more work must be done on understanding store preferences *before* meaningful work on brand or product purchasing decisions can proceed (Carman, 1970; Rao, 1969).

The data analyzed were collected from a mail survey sent to a random sample of 1500 households in Buffalo, New York. The return rate was 22.5%. For each household, descriptions of grocery stores visited most often and attitudes toward these stores were elicited. The attitudinal data included satisfaction ratings on a set of prespecified attributes and evaluations of up to four frequently visited stores with respect to each of the attributes. The attitudinal data were in the form of 7-point semantic differentials. The respondent also was asked to indicate the frequency of shopping at each store mentioned and the time required for the trips to each store (as well as the return travel time, if different). Attribute ratings were elicited by asking the respondents to mark a 7-point scale with descriptors ranging from "excellent" to "extremely poor" for each store on each attribute. The attributes are listed in Table 1.

Table 1
LIST OF ATTRIBUTES

1.	Easy to find a parking spot
2.	Easy to get home from store
3.	Easy to get to store from work
4.	Easy to get to store from home
5.	It is near other shops I use
6.	They have convenient hours
7.	They have reasonable prices
8.	They have a good variety of items
9.	The meat quality is good
10.	The produce quality is good
11.	Easy to find things in store
12.	Store has large selection of goods
13.	Store accepts credit cards
14.	It is easy to cash checks there
15.	Easy to return or exchange goods there
16.	Store has items others don't

The grocery stores were classified according to brand name for nine major chain supermarkets. In addition two categories, "small independent market" and "neighborhood store," were used to classify other "nonchain" stores.

Regression Model

Several regression models were estimated to serve as bases for comparison with the logit estimations. These estimations were obtained by using the "screen" regression approach of Furnival and Wilson (1971) which finds the optimal subsets of explanatory variables for increasing numbers of explanatory variables *without* the constraint that the optimal subset at any level contain the optimal subset at the next lowest level as in stepwise regressions. It also lists the R^2 values for the "next best" subsets which usually reveal the somewhat arbitrary nature of the optimal subset. The decision of how many variables to include in the model was made on the basis of adjusted R^2 values. For cases in which the adjusted R^2 were virtually identical, the t-statistic was used as a criterion and the set in which the t-values were most significant was chosen.

The dependent variable in the regression models (and also in the logit models) was related to the actual frequencies of trips to the stores. The reason for selection of this dependent variable is twofold. First, it is well known that the relationships found in relating attributes to consumer intentions are often very different from the relationships found in relating the same attributes to *actual* decisions. Second, the frequencies contain more interval information about the store visits than does a rank order. Other formulations of the models using alternative dependent variables, such as dollars spent per store, could be analyzed in a manner analogous to that used for the trip frequency dependent variable.

In the present case a regression model using a dichotomous dependent variable has a substantially better R^2 value than alternative regression formulations tested (Gensch et al., 1975). This regression formulation is also similar in structure and thus most directly comparable to the logit model. In the questionnaire, each respondent gave frequencies for up to four stores; thus, for each respondent and for each pair of stores with different trip frequencies reported (up to $(4 \cdot 3)/2 = 6$ pairs per respondent), a 1-0 dependent variable was created where the 1 was assigned to the store with the higher frequency and 0 to the other. The independent variables consisted of differences between the satisfaction ratings for the two stores on the attributes of Table 1 and between the perceived times required to get to the stores. The model thus has the form of

$$(9)\quad y_{ik} \text{ is } \begin{Bmatrix} 1 \text{ if } k > l \\ 0 \text{ if } k < l \end{Bmatrix} = \beta_1(x_{k1} - x_{l1}) + \beta_2(x_{k2} - x_{l2}) + \ldots + \beta_n(x_{kn} - x_{ln}) + \alpha$$

where k and l are the shopping frequencies associated with alternatives k and l. Table 2 shows the results for the model defined in equation 9 for a subset of five variables and, though low, the R^2 values obtained were significantly greater than those obtained in the previous two regression models.

Unfortunately, the beta coefficients (diagnostic information) really should not be interpreted because the dichotomous dependent variable forces the error term to violate two of the assumptions underlying the linear model. As Goldberger (1964, p. 249) points out, it is inherent in the model using a dichotomous dependent variable that the classical assumption of homoscedasticity is violated. More important, Thiel (1971, p. 628–30) illustrates that in order for the error term to have an expected value of zero it would have to take on specific values with probabilities greater than one or less than zero. Thus, though one may use the foregoing model for predictive purposes (R^2), an interpretation of the beta coefficients is not advisable because they were generated in a manner that violates assumptions underlying the linear model.

Table 2

REGRESSION MODEL

$R^2 = .282$
Adjusted $R^2 = .271$

Variable	*Coefficient (B)*	*Coefficient (beta)*	*t*
Perceived time to store	−.109	−.325	−5.99
Easy to get to store from home	.046	.146	2.62
They have convenient hours	.047	.126	2.68
Easy to find things in store	.042	.115	2.44
Easy to return or exchange goods there	.048	.136	2.32
Constant	.460		

Multinomial Logit Models

The utility weights (i.e., a_j) in the deterministic component of utility specified by equation 2 were estimated by using maximum likelihood techniques for the probabilistic choice model in the form of equation 8. Because in this application all stores were evaluated on the same set of attributes, the sets of alternative-specific attributes, S^k, for all k, are null sets. The dependent variable was the probability that an individual would shop *most* frequently at store chain k. The set of relevant alternatives for each individual consisted of only the stores where the individual actually shopped. Because this logit formulation uses differences in attribute perceptions, observations where the individual shopped at only one store, only at stores of the same chain, or at stores belonging to different chains but with the same frequency were not used in the model estimation. These restrictions and the withholding of some observations because of missing data reduced the sample size to just over 100 individuals.

Presented in Table 3 are the b_j coefficients for all attributes j for which the coefficients are significantly different from zero at the 95% confidence level; all attributes with coefficients not significantly different

Table 3

LOGIT MODEL 1

(SAMPLE SIZE = 96)

Variable	*Coefficient estimate*	*t*
Perceived time to store	−1.486	−4.23
Easy to return or exchange goods there	0.842	2.57
Easy to get to store from home	1.336	2.92
Easy to find things in store	0.546	2.29
The meat quality is good	0.342	1.93

Ratio of choices predicted correctly = 0.87.
Ratio of individuals predicted correctly = 0.81.

Store	*Percent of choices store was used most frequently*	*Prediction ratio*
1	6.2	0.89
2	21.2	0.77
3	2.7	1.00
4	9.6	0.93
5	2.1	1.00
6	9.6	0.86
7	4.1	0.83
8	21.9	0.94
9	2.1	0.67
10	13.0	0.84
11	7.5	0.91

from zero were excluded in the estimations. The coefficient values are listed in order of their t-statistics.

Although the dichotomous regression model did not yield interpretable diagnostic data, its goodness-of-fit was significantly better than that of other regression formulations tested. The authors therefore attempt to relate the goodness-of-fit achieved by the logit model to that of the dichotomous regression model.

Because the R^2 coefficient of determination goodness-of-fit measure is inappropriate for nonlinear models, reliance must be placed on other goodness-of-fit indices to validate model results. The result of a chi square test ($\chi^2 = 84.4$ for 5 d.f.) offers firm rejection of the joint null hypothesis that all coefficients of the logit models presented herein are equal to zero. In addition, two measures based on the percentage of actual choices predicted "correctly" by the model are provided.

The first measure, the ratio of choices predicted correctly, is the proportion of times the individuals' predicted probability of the chosen alternative was greater than the predicted probability of a nonchosen alternative. As is shown in Table 3, the model correctly predicted the choice between the observed chosen alternative and a nonchosen alternative in 87% of such choice pairings. This same measure of performance, when computed for the dichotomous regression model, was only 71%. Thus the logit provided a 22.5% (16/71) improvement in prediction. This measure also was disaggregated by alternative chosen and the results are shown in Table 3. In this case the disaggregate prediction ratios indicate a uniformly high predictive power across all alternatives. In practice, the finding of a specific alternative with a relatively high frequency and relatively low predictive ratio often will suggest to the researcher a unique attribute of the alternative currently unspecified by the logit model.

The second measure, the ratio of individuals predicted correctly, is the proportion of individuals for which the predicted probability of the chosen alternative was greater than that of every other relevant alternative. The results in Table 3 indicate that the model correctly predicted the total choice set of 81% of the sample. In fact, even when restricted to only those variables included in the regression model, the logit model maintains its high prediction ratios, predicting 87% of the choices and 80% of the individuals correctly. These results again indicate 22.5% and 27% improvements in prediction by the logit. This performance is all the more impressive in light of the insignificance of the coefficient associated with the rating of one of the predictor variables, parking facilities ($t = 0.61$).

Management policy questions relating to what impact a change in an independent variable can be expected to have on the probability of a particular store being the most frequently visited receive considerable guidance from an examination of the elasticities and cross-elasticities associated with the predictor variables for each alternative. An elasticity is a dimensionless quantity defined by economists as the percentage change in the dependent variable which would result from a 1% change in an independent variable:

$$E_{ij}^{kl} = \frac{\partial P_i(k:A_i)}{\partial X_{ij}^l} \frac{|X_{ij}^l|}{P_i(k:A_i)} \tag{10}$$

where:

E_{ij}^{kl} = elasticity of the probability that alternative k is chosen from set A_i by individual i with respect to variable j of alternative l.

By calculating the deviations of the choice probabilities in equation 7 and substituting into equation 10, one can write the individual elasticities of the probability of choice as

$$E_{ij}^{kl} = |X_{ij}^l| \sum_{q \varepsilon A} P_i(q:A) \frac{\partial V_i^k}{\partial X_{ij}^l} - \frac{\partial V_i^q}{\partial X_{ij}^l} \tag{11}$$

The elasticities for $l = k$ are referred to as direct elasticities, or simply elasticities, because they represent the changes in probability of choosing an alternative with respect to perceptions toward the attributes of the alternative itself; the elasticities for $l \neq k$ are referred to as cross-elasticities, and can be interpreted as the sum of the changes in the probabilities of choosing any of the other stores with respect to changes in perceptions. The distribution of these changes in probabilities among the remaining stores is not determined.

Aggregate elasticities can be developed from the individual elasticities to measure the overall sensitivities of choice probabilities to uniform percentage changes in explanatory variables for all individuals. It is easily shown that these aggregate elasticities are given by

$$E_j^{kl} = \frac{\sum_{j=1}^{M} [P_i(k:A_i)\, E_{ij}^{kl}]}{\sum_{i=1}^{M} P_i(k:A_i)} \tag{12}$$

where:

E_j^{kl} = aggregate elasticity of the probability of choosing alternative k with respect to uniform changes in the perceived evaluation of alternative l on attribute j for all $i = 1, \ldots, M$ individuals.

As can be seen in the foregoing formulas, the logit model implies that the magnitude of the effect from the particular predictor variable depends on the level of the dependent choice variable and not solely on the estimated coefficients. This is a more realistic representation of the choice process than the regression approach which ignores the level of the variables (Gensch et al., 1975).

Table 4 provides the actual elasticities associated with store 2 (the major supermarket chain in the survey area) and store 6 (a chain of "discount" supermarket/department stores typically located in the suburban fringes of a city).

A first observation is that the results are intuitively satisfying for several reasons which include: knowledge of the relative locations, store 2 has a typical grocery store inventory layout whereas store 6 has a mixture of food and nonfood goods in the same floorspace, and returning goods at store 2 is relatively quick at an office adjacent the checkout counters whereas returns at store 6 are accomplished at a centralized "customer service" counter and require the completion of forms detailing the return.

The elasticities indicate that store 6 will increase its probability of becoming the most frequented store more than store 2 will, for the same percentage increase in any of the five attributes listed in Table 4. This pattern again appears to be a realistic representation of the choice environment. Table 3 indicates that currently store 2 is the first choice of 21.2% of the sample compared with 9.6% for store 6. Obviously, it should be easier to get a 10% improvement on a current level of 9.6% than on a current level of 21.2%. As previously noted, the logit elasticities, in contrast to the regression elasticities, take into account the current level of the dependent variable and thus in the authors' opinion provide the model user with more realistic information. From *a priori* knowledge of the choice situation, the logit model appears to be providing reasonable results.

A second observation is related to the influence of a 10% increase or decrease in the ease of getting to the store from home. A 10% increase for store 2 is associated with a 9% increase in the probability store 2 will be most frequently visited; similarly, a 10% increase for store 6 is associated with a 19% increase in the probability. However, the cross-elasticities indicate a 10% decrease is associated with a 60–70% reduction in the probability of being visited most frequently. In a wide variety of regression and logit runs the ease of getting to the store was a significant independent variable. Indeed, this finding is generally provided as empirical justification for gravity models for assessing new store location potential. The foregoing elasticity results suggest that the attribute "ease of access" and, to a lesser degree, the attribute "perceived time to store," are very important in determining whether the store is in the feasible set an individual will consider visiting, *but* these two attributes in relation to other attributes are less important in determining store choice within the feasible set.

This finding seems to indicate that consumers tend to treat travel time as a satisficing criterion. If travel time is within a certain tolerance the store is considered in the decision set; the decision as to which store within the decision set to frequent seems then to be reached on the basis of other variables. Thus gravity models would be most efficient when there are minimum competitive store locations within the same threshold travel time overlay. Use of a linear function of time or distance to closest store stocking each brand as a means of attempting to account for differences in availability prior to an analysis of brand purchase data is probably an incorrect procedure.

To derive specific managerial implications in terms of actions that a manager of store 6 could take to make his store more competitive with store 2, one would need an estimate of the costs and savings involved in changing the samples' perception of a given attribute by one rating unit from its current level. Shocker and Srinivasan (1974) provide a good discussion of techniques for managerially operationalizing a consumer perception space. For example, assume that the manager of store 6 estimated that by cutting back his meat counter by 50% he could install a more convenient counter for exchanging goods. He estimates over the long run he will operate the return counter and reduced meat counter at a lower cost than the current meat counter. He estimates that this change will lower consumers' perception of meat quality by one unit but increase their perception of

Table 4

ELASTICITIES AND CROSS-ELASTICITIES FOR TWO STORES CALCULATED FROM LOGIT MODEL 1

	Store 2		*Store 6*	
Variable	*Elasticity*	*Cross-elasticity*	*Elasticity*	*Cross-elasticity*
Perceived time to store	−0.327	2.34	−0.404	1.31
Easy to get to store from home	0.922	−7.24	1.93	−6.10
The meat quality is good	0.229	−1.59	0.377	−1.23
Easy to find things in store	0.366	−2.84	0.789	−2.38
Easy to return or exchange goods there	0.532	−4.18	1.30	−3.75

return convenience by 1.5 units. The elasticities suggest that this move would be associated with an increase in store 6's probability by about 9%.

CONCLUSIONS

Multinomial logit analysis has been proposed as a more appropriate structure for the multiattribute analysis of the choice behavior of *populations* of individuals. On a theoretical basis, the multinomial logit formulation is purported to be superior to linear approaches in that: (1) it can be developed from a behavioral utility theory framework, (2) the bounds on choice are implicitly incorporated in the model form, (3) differences among individuals in terms of alternatives available to them are considered, (4) it allows individuals to consider unique attributes per alternative, (5) the elasticities of demand are consistent with accepted tests of diminishing marginal utility, threshold, and saturation, and (6) the error term recognizes that the choice model is probably underspecified.

In terms of applications, multinomial logit analysis considers the multichoice case as well as the binary choice case, and its estimation eliminates problems of scale differences and unique attribute meanings among choice alternatives. Empirically it has been shown to result in better fit than the regression approach. In addition, the diagnostic information obtained is judged to be in a form that is useful to the decision maker by being disaggregate by attribute and choice alternative.

REFERENCES

Bass, Frank M. and William L. Wilkie. "A Competitive Analysis of Attitudinal Predictions and Brand Preference," *Journal of Marketing Research,* 10 (August 1973), 262–9.

Bettman, James R., Noel Capon, and Richard J. Lutz. "Cognitive Algebra in Multi-Attribute Attitude Models," *Journal of Marketing Research,* 12 (May 1975), 151–64.

Bock, R. and L. Jones. *Measurement and Prediction of Judgment and Choice.* San Francisco: Holden Day, 1968.

Cambridge Systematics, Inc. "Multinomial Logit Estimation Package: Program Documentation," Version 2, Mod. 1, Cambridge, Massachusetts, 1974.

Carman, James M. "Correlates of Brand Loyalty: Some Positive Results," *Journal of Marketing Research,* 7 (February 1970), 67–76.

Dawes, R. M. "A Case Study of Graduate Admissions: Applications of Three Principles of Human Decision Making," *American Psychologist,* 26 (1971).

Fishbein, Martin. "The Search for Attitudinal-Behavioral Consistency," *in* Joel B. Cohen, ed., *Behavioral Science Foundations of Consumer Behavior.* New York: Free Press, 1972, 245–52.

Fishburn, Peter. "Methods of Estimating Additive Utilities," *Management Science,* 13 (March 1967).

———. "Utility Theory," *Management Science,* 14, (January 1968).

Furnival, George M. and Robert W. Wilson. "Regression by Leaps and Bounds," presented at Joint Meeting of the Institute of Mathematical Statistics and Biometrics Society at the Pennsylvania State University, University Park, Pennsylvania, April 21–23, 1971.

Gensch, Dennis H., Thomas F. Golob and Wilfred W. Recker. "A Multinomial, Multi-Attribute Logit Choice Model," working paper 197, School of Business, University of Wisconsin–Milwaukee, August 1975.

Goldberger, Arthur S. *Econometric Theory.* New York: John Wiley & Sons, Inc., 1964.

Gumbel, E. J. "Statistical Theory of Extreme Values and Some Practical Applications," *National Bureau of Standards Applied Mathematics,* Series 20, No. 33, 1954.

Gustafson, D. H., G. K. Pai, and G. C. Kramer. "A Weighted Aggregate Approach to R & D Project Selection," *AIEE Transactions,* 3 (March 1971).

Huber, George. "Multiplicative Utility Models in Cost Effectiveness Analyses," *Journal of Industrial Engineering,* 19 (March 1968).

——— V. Sahney, and D. Ford. "A Study of Subjective Evaluation Models," *Behavioral Science,* 14 (November 1969).

Keeley, S. M. and M. E. Doherty. "Bayesian and Regression Modeling of Graduate-Admission Policy," *Organizational Behavior and Human Performance,* 8 (October 1972).

Lehmann, Donald R. "Television Show Preference: Application of a Choice Model," *Journal of Marketing Research,* 8 (February 1971), 47–55.

Lerman, Steven R. and Charles F. Manski. "An Estimator for the Generalized Multinomial Probit Choice Model," paper presented at 56th Annual Meeting, Transportation Research Board, Washington, D.C., August 1976.

Luce, R. Duncan and P. Suppes. "Preference, Utility, and Subjective Probability," *in* R. D. Luce, ed., *Handbook of Mathematical Psychology,* Vol. 3. New York: John Wiley & Sons, Inc., 1965, 249–410.

MacCrimmon, Kenneth R. "An Overview of Multiple Objective Decision Making," *in* J. L. Cochrane and M. Zeleny, eds., *Multiple Criteria Decision Making.* Columbia: University of South Carolina Press, 1973.

Manski, Charles F. "A Stochastic Utility Model of Choice," unpublished paper, School of Urban and Public Affairs, Carnegie-Mellon University, 1973.

———. "Maximum Score Estimation of the Stochastic Utility Model of Choice," *Journal of Econometrics,* 3 (August 1975), 205–28.

McFadden, Daniel. "Conditional Logit Analysis of Qualitative Choice Behavior," *in* P. Zarenlka, ed., *Frontiers in Economics.* New York: Academic Press, 1973.

———. "Quantal Choice Analysis: A Survey," presented at NSF-NBER Conference on Decision Rules and Uncertainty, March 22–23, 1972, University of California, Berkeley. Unpublished paper, Department of Economics, University of California, Berkeley.

———. "Revealed Preferences of a Government Bureaucracy," unpublished paper, Department of Economics, University of California, Berkeley, 1968.

McGuire, Timothy W. and Doyle L. Weiss. "Logically Consistent Market Share Models," *Journal of Marketing Research,* 13 (August 1976), 296.

Pekelman, Dov and Subrata K. Sen. "Mathematical Programming Models for the Determination of Attribute

Weights," *Management Science,* 20 (April 1974), 1217–29.
Rao, Tanniru R. "Consumer's Purchase Decision Process: Stochastic Models," *Journal of Marketing Research,* 6 (August 1969), 321–9.
Recker, W. W., D. H. Gensch, and T. F. Golob. "SEQUEL: A Sequential Model of Choice Behavior," submitted to *Management Science.*
Rosenberg, Milton J. "Cognitive Structure and Attitudinal Affect," *Journal of Abnormal and Social Psychology,* 53 (November 1956), 368–72.
Russ, F. A. "Evaluation Process Models and the Prediction of Preference," *in* D. M. Gardner, ed., *Proceedings of the Second Annual Conference,* Association for Consumer Research, 1971, 256–61.
Sheth, Jagdish N. and Wayne W. Talarzyk. "Perceived Instrumentality and Value Importance as Determinants of Attitudes," *Journal of Marketing Research,* 9 (February 1972), 6–9.
Shocker, Allan D. and V. Srinivasan. "A Consumer-Based Methodology for the Identification of New Product Ideas," *Management Science,* 20 (February 1974), 921–37.
Slovic, P., D. Fleisnner, and W. S. Bauman. "Analyzing the Use of Information in Investment Decision Making: A Methodological Proposal," *Journal of Business,* 45 (April 1972).
Thiel, Henri. "A Multinomial Extension of the Linear Logit Model," *International Economic Review,* 10 (October 1969), 251–9.
———. "On the Estimation of Relationships Involving Qualitative Variables," *American Journal of Sociology,* 76 (1970), 103–54.
———. *Principles of Econometrics.* New York: John Wiley & Sons, Inc., 1971.
Turban, E. and M. L. Metersky. "Utility Theory Applied to Multi-Variable System Effectiveness Evaluation," *Management Science,* 17 (August 1971).
Westin, Richard B. and Peter L. Watson. "Reported and Revealed Preferences as Determinants of Mode Choice Behavior," *Journal of Marketing Research,* 12 (August 1975), 282–9.
Wilkie, William L. and Edgar A. Pessemier. "Issues in Marketing's Use of Multi-Attribute Attitude Models," *Journal of Marketing Research,* 10 (November 1973), 428–41.

PAUL E. GREEN*

A two-step procedure is described in which AID is applied first to a multiway contingency table to isolate those variables (and levels within variable) that best account for variance in the criterion. A logit analysis follows for estimating parameters for prediction purposes. The method is described and applied illustratively to a set of data on usage of an AT&T telecommunications service.

An AID/Logit Procedure for Analyzing Large Multiway Contingency Tables

Since its introduction in the mid-1960's [8], the Automatic Interaction Detector has received wide attention by marketing researchers. Unfortunately, its disarming simplicity of application has prompted a variety of abuses and overselling. A recent article by Doyle and Fenwick [3] describes AID's limitations and puts the technique in a more proper perspective.

What many of the initial users failed to do was follow the advice of AID's developers—namely, to consider AID as a *preliminary* search tool, to be followed up by a more explicit model, such as Multiple Classification Analysis or MCA [1, 10]. However, a significant marketing application of the combined use of AID and MCA has been reported by Newman and Staelin [9] and the present report owes much to this earlier contribution.

If the dependent variable is a more or less continuous variable, the dummy-variable regression followup (MCA) is reasonable. In many marketing studies, however, one is dealing with a dichotomous dependent variable, such as heavy versus light user, brand loyal versus switcher, private brand versus national brand purchaser, and so on. In these cases, the structure of the problem can be construed as involving a multiway contingency table (with a dichotomous dependent variable).

In this case the dummy-variable regression approach of MCA has several limitations—for example, the error term meets neither normality nor constant variance assumptions and the regression model's predictions can fall outside the range of 0 to 1. For these reasons the *logit model* [2, 4, 5, 11] appears to be a superior statistical alternative to dummy-variable regression involving a 0–1 dependent variable. Moreover, the logit model provides probability estimates as part of its regular output. This feature can be a useful bonus in marketing research applications.

*Paul E. Green is the S.S. Kresge Professor of Marketing, Wharton School, University of Pennsylvania. Appreciation is extended to Frank J. Carmone, Drexel University, for computer assistance and to D. P. Wachspress, R. B. Ellis, and W. R. Reiss, all of AT&T, for supplying data on which the analysis is based.

THE AID/LOGIT PROCEDURE

The approach proposed entails the following steps.

1. Assume that the researcher is faced with a problem involving a relatively large number of predictor variables, all expressed categorically, and a single dichotomous criterion variable. (The categories within the various predictors need not be ordered.)
2. AID is applied as a screening procedure prior to a second-stage analysis by the logit model.
3. After use of the preliminary AID results to suggest (a) the predictors to be included, (b) the categories to be used within each predictor, and (c) the explicit interaction terms to be entered, the logit model is applied to obtain explicit parameter estimates for each predictor or predictor combination.
4. The logit technique then is used to test alternative models (by chi square) and to develop probability estimates for the dichotomous criterion variable.

In short, the author believes that AID and the logit model can serve complementary functions. The former technique provides guidance on which predictors, which categories within predictor, and which types of interactions appear useful to include in the second-stage (logit) analysis. The logit model provides an explicit parameterization of the problem, appropriate significance tests, and estimated probabilities for the criterion variable.

Reprinted from *Journal of Marketing Research,* 15 (February 1978), 132-36, published by the American Marketing Association.

AN ILLUSTRATIVE APPLICATION

To illustrate the AID/logit approach, consider an actual problem that arose in the analysis of heavy versus light users of an AT&T telecommunications service.[1] The analysis was based on a total sample of 12,432 respondents obtained from a 1975 mail survey.

In addition to the designation of whether the respondent was a heavy or light user of the service, data were available on the six demographic variables shown in Table 1. Each characteristic is described categorically. If one were to construct a multiway contingency table from the coded variables as they stand (including the dichotomous dependent variable), a total of

$$2 \times 8 \times 4 \times 8 \times 7 \times 4 \times 3 = 43{,}008$$

cells would be entailed, which is a prohibitively large number.

The first problem, then, was how the various categories of the predictor variables could be recombined so as to provide a more reasonable number of categories per variable. Other problems involved which variables should be included in the second-stage logit analysis and what type of model should be fitted.

Table 1

PREDICTOR VARIABLES AND ORIGINAL CODES USED IN AID ANALYSIS

Income	*Age*
1 < \$3,000	1 < 18 years
2 \$ 3,000– 4,999	2 18–24
3 \$ 5,000– 7,499	3 25–34
4 \$ 7,500– 9,999	4 35–44
5 \$10,000–14,999	5 45–54
6 \$15,000–19,999	6 55–64
7 \$20,000–29,999	7 65 or over
8 \$30,000 or more	
Number of extensions	*Number of moves during the past five years*
1 None	1 None
2 One	2 Once
3 Two	3 Twice
4 Three or more	4 Three times or more
Education	*Residence location*
1 Some grade school	1 Urban location
2 Grade school graduate	2 Suburban location
3 Some high school	3 Rural
4 High school graduate	
5 Some college	
6 College graduate	
7 Some graduate work	
8 Graduate degree(s)	

[1] Heavy users were defined as those respondents whose expenditures for the telecommunications service were above a company-determined value of \$X per month.

The AID Analysis

AID first was applied to the data using the original variable codes of Table 1. Because six potential predictor variables were involved the output became rather voluminous. Figure 1 shows a partial description of the AID tree diagram that emerged from the first stage of the analysis.

Note that the sample is first split on the respondent income variable as follows:

incomes up to \$14,999 (N = 9,617)
versus
incomes of \$15,000 or more (N = 2,815).

As observed from the tree diagram, the proportion in the total sample who are heavy users of the service is 0.33. However, if income is less than \$15,000, Figure 1 shows that the proportion of heavy users drops to 0.28. If the income is \$15,000 or more, the proportion who are heavy users increases to 0.50.

The next predictor to enter is the number of extension phones already installed in the respondent's residence. AID produced a binary split of no extensions versus one or more extensions. In the lower income group the change in the proportion $\bar{Y}$ due to one or more extension phones is 0.36 − 0.22 or 14 percentage points. This compares with 0.68 − 0.45 or 23 percentage points for the higher income group.

Age and education are the next predictor variables to enter. Note that education is split between high school graduate and some college. In all cases the higher education category is associated with a higher proportion of heavy users. The age variable is split by AID into under 54 years of age and 55 years or over. In this case, Figure 1 shows that older respondents include a lower proportion of heavy users.

Not shown in Figure 1 are the remaining predictors, number of moves during the past five years and residence location. These variables did not show up in the AID tree diagram because the between-groups sums of squares associated with the best splits on these variables were still less than the program's initial cutoff value.[2]

A relaxation of the cutoff (to two-thirds of its initial value) indicated that the best split for the first variable was no moves versus one or more moves during the past five years. The splitting character of the residence location variable suggested that all three categories—urban, suburban, rural—should be kept. That is, this variable was first split on urban versus other, then other was split into suburban and rural.[3]

[2] One of AID's control parameters specifies that no group be split if the resulting between-groups sum of squares is less than some decimal fraction Q of the total sum of squares. Q was initially set at 0.006.

[3] Relaxation of the initial control parameter was motivated by other corporate research findings which suggested that mobility and residence location might be useful predictor variables.

Figure 1
TREE DIAGRAM FROM AID PROGRAM
(Partial Analysis—See Table 1 for Code Interpretations)

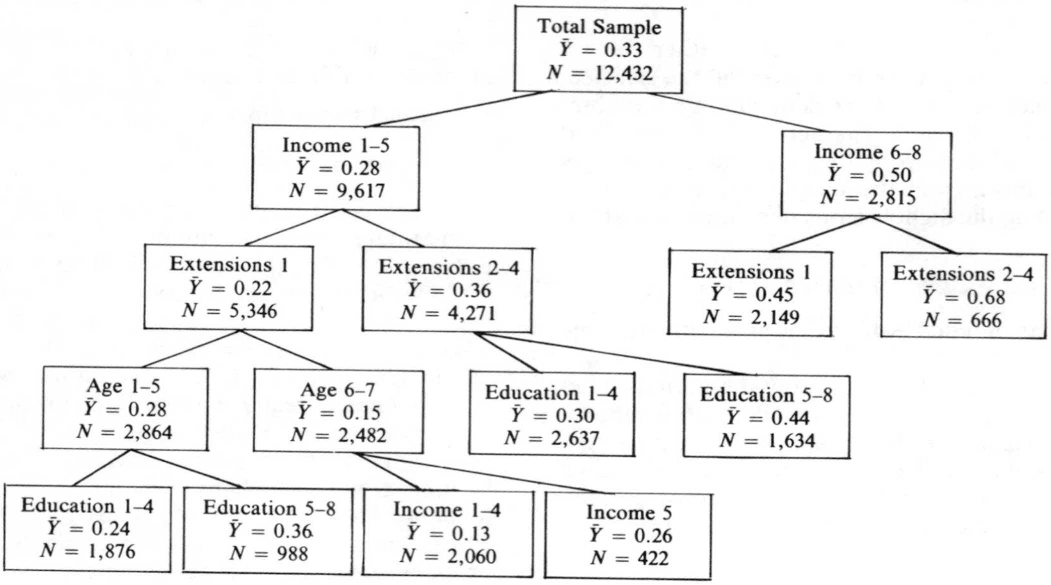

$\bar{Y}$ = Proportion who are heavy users.
N = Number of cases in group.

At this point, the AID analysis indicated that income, number of extensions, education, and age were important variables, whereas number of moves during the past five years and residence location were not. Moreover, AID produced a much more tractable set of categories within each predictor variable than those appearing in Table 1. The AID-produced categories were:

Income
- $9,999 and below
- $10,000–14,999
- $15,000 and above

Number of extensions
- None
- One or more

Education
- High school graduate or less
- Some college or more

Age
- 54 years or less
- 55 years or more

Number of moves during the past five years
- None
- One or more

Residence location
- Urban
- Suburban
- Rural

The tree diagram of Figure 1 provided less guidance on the interaction terms; indeed, the branching was fairly symmetric, suggesting the possibility that an *additive* model (with no interaction terms) might be appropriate.

Further support for an additive model was suggested by making a series of two-factor interaction plots, e.g., income versus extensions, age versus education, age versus income, and so on. Though some departures from parallelism were noted, no serious disordinal interactions were found. However, such two-factor plots are a tedious procedure at best. Accordingly, it was decided to make a more precise test of interaction in terms of the second-stage logit model.

The Logit Analysis

Because strong evidence of predictor-variable interaction was *not* apparent from Figure 1, one of the logit models that was tested consisted of a simple main effects, additive model.[4] For comparison a second logit model was fitted which included all 15 of the possible two-factor interaction terms.

The simple additive model resulted in a chi square value with an associated probability value of over 0.15, whereas (predictably) the more comprehensive model that included all two-factor interactions resulted in a chi square value with an associated probability of over 0.5 [6]. However, because the chi square

---

[4] As reported elsewhere [6], the logit $\psi_{i,j,\ldots,n}$ is defined as the natural log odds:

$$\psi_{i,j,\ldots,n} = \ln\left[P_{i,j,\ldots,n}/(1 - P_{i,j,\ldots,n})\right]$$

where $P_{i,j,\ldots,n}$ is the proportion of *original* cases in the $i,j,\ldots,n$th cell of the multiway table who are heavy users.

produced by the additive model was not significant at the 0.05 level, this considerably simpler model was adopted as being consistent with the data.

Table 2 shows the parameter estimates—*all* of which were significant at the 0.05 level—that were obtained from the additive logit model. As was earlier suggested by AID, the range of the coefficients for income, number of extensions, education, and age shows that these predictors (particularly income) *are* important variables in estimating the probability that a respondent will be a heavy user of the telecommunications service. Moreover, the small range associated with the number of moves during the past five years also supports the AID findings.

The principal anomaly is the residence location variable, whose range of coefficients is 0.428. As recalled, this predictor did *not* enter the AID splitting process until the between-groups sum of squares cutoff value was relaxed from the program's default level. As it turned out, the reason for this is that residence location is highly correlated with both income and education. Therefore its shared variation was lost to these variables in the earlier steps of the AID analysis.

Fitted Values

The coefficients of Table 2 can be easily used to compute any logit of interest [6]. The logit, in turn, can be transformed to an *estimated* probability that the respondent is a heavy user by the equation:

Table 2

PARAMETER VALUES COMPUTED FROM LOGIT ANALYSIS BASED ON MAIN EFFECTS, ADDITIVE MODEL

Variable	*Coefficient*	*Coefficient range*
Constant (intercept)	−0.544	
Income		
$9,999 or below	−0.474	
$10,000–14,999	−0.102	1.050
$15,000 or above	0.576	
Number of extensions		
None	−0.286	0.572
One or more	0.286	
Education		
High school graduate or less	−0.256	0.512
Some college or more	0.256	
Age		
54 years or less	0.224	0.448
55 years or more	−0.224	
Number of moves during the past five years		
None	−0.100	0.200
One or more	0.100	
Residence location		
Urban	0.262	
Suburban	−0.166	0.428
Rural	−0.096	

$$(1) \qquad \hat{P}_{i,j,\ldots,n} = \frac{1}{1 + e^{-\hat{\Psi}_{i,j,\ldots,n}}}$$

where $\hat{P}_{i,j,\ldots,n}$ denotes the estimated probability of being a heavy user, as associated with the i, j, ... nth cell, and $\hat{\Psi}_{i,j,\ldots,n}$ denotes the corresponding logit ($i = 1,2,3$; $j = 1,2$; ...; $n = 1,2,3$)

For example, to find the estimated probability that a respondent is a heavy user, given:

—an income of $15,000 or above,
—one or more extensions,
—some college or more,
—54 years of age or less,
—one or more moves during the past five years, and
—urban location,

one substitutes the appropriate parameter values of Table 2 in the linear equation:

$$\hat{\Psi}_{3,2,2,1,2,1} = -0.544 + 0.576 + 0.286 + 0.256 + 0.224 + 0.1 + 0.262 = 1.16.$$

This value is, in turn, substituted in equation 1 to obtain:

$$\hat{P}_{3,2,2,1,2,1} = \frac{1}{1 + e^{-1.16}} = 0.761.$$

The actual proportion, computed from the original data, is 0.771; hence, the residual error is only one percentage point.

Similarly, the estimated probability under the "worst" conditions of:

—an income of $9,999 or below,
—no extensions,
—high school graduate or less,
—55 years of age or more,
—no moves during past five years, and
—suburban location

is calculated as 0.114. The actual proportion, computed from the original data, is 0.095, an error of 1.9 percentage points.

Estimated probabilities were computed for each of the 144 cells of the $3 \times 2 \times 2 \times 2 \times 2 \times 3$ predictor design matrix. The mean absolute error turned out to be only 1.3 percentage points, indicating that the main effects, additive model of Table 2 performed very well.

Finally, it is of interest to note from Figure 1 that the largest proportion ($\bar{Y}$) obtained from AID was 0.68 for the highest income group who also had one or more extensions. The lowest proportion obtained from AID was 0.13, involving the lowest income, older age group with no extensions. Note that this range ($0.68 - 0.13 = 0.55$) is substantially less than the range ($0.76 - 0.11 = 0.65$) estimated by the logit model. In brief, the logit model found more "extreme" groups than emerged from the AID analysis.[5]

DISCUSSION

The author has tried to illustrate how AID and the logit model can be used profitably in sequence in analyzing multiway contingency tables with a dichotomous criterion variable. AID performs the job of finding appropriate category breaks, as well as screening the candidate predictors and suggesting possible interaction terms.

The logit model, in turn, provides a parameterization of the predictor variables that can be used to estimate probabilities for the dependent variable in *any cell* of the multiway contingency table.

However, as the illustration showed, AID must be used with the prudence suggested by its developers and more recently echoed by Doyle and Fenwick. As was noted in the case of the residence location variable, a useful predictor may fail to enter the AID analysis if it shows substantial correlations with one or more other important variables. Indeed, the following potential problems in using AID should always be kept in mind.

1. Predictors that are correlated with other strong predictors may either enter spuriously or, conversely, fail to enter even though they may be useful in themselves.
2. Variables with small but persistent effects (e.g., the number of moves in the past five years) may fail to enter AID even though they later turn out to be statistically significant. The reason is that AID selects variables on the basis of reduction of error variance, not statistical significance.
3. The appearance of a "symmetric" tree suggests an additive model, but is no guarantee of one [10].
4. Conversely, interaction terms suggested by the AID analysis may *not* turn out to be either statistically significant or operationally useful from an estimation viewpoint, when later incorporated in the logit model.

Despite the preceding limitations, a preliminary AID analysis can be useful.[6] In field survey work it is not unusual to have 20 or more candidate predictors, each at several levels. Clearly, in almost all cases the resulting cell frequencies would be much too small to fit a logit model at the outset. It is in these circumstances that a preliminary AID analysis can both screen the candidate predictors and determine the category breaks within each variable.[7]

Finally, if the AID results are taken only as a rough guide, the tree diagram can be suggestive of possible interaction terms that then can be tested rigorously by the second-stage logit model.

[5]Of course, the estimates of the logit model are limited to the 144 cases that were developed from the category breaks of the preliminary AID analysis.

[6]Though the topic is not pursued here, the AID/logit approach of this report could be generalized to a polytomous (three or more categories) variable. This can be done by applying THAID [7], followed by a multinomial generalization of the logit model [11].

[7]It should be mentioned that other approaches [4] can be used to find category breaks. However, compared with AID, they are considerably more complex (although more consistent with the logit approach).

REFERENCES

1. Andrews, Frank J., James N. Morgan, and John A. Sonquist. *Multiple Classification Analysis.* Ann Arbor, Michigan: Survey Research Center, University of Michigan, 1967.
2. Bishop, Yvonne M. M. "Full Contingency Tables, Logits and Split Contingency Tables," *Biometrics,* 25 (June 1969), 383–400.
3. Doyle, Peter and Ian Fenwick. "The Pitfalls of AID Analysis," *Journal of Marketing Research,* 12 (November 1975), 408–13.
4. Duncan, Otis D. "Partitioning Polytomous Variables in Multiway Contingency Analysis," *Social Science Research,* 4 (September 1975), 167–82.
5. Goodman, Leo A. "A General Model for the Analysis of Surveys," *American Journal of Sociology,* 77 (1971), 1035–86.
6. Green, Paul E., Frank J. Carmone, and David P. Wachspress. "On the Analysis of Qualitative Data in Marketing Research," *Journal of Marketing Research,* 14 (February 1977), 52–9.
7. Morgan, James N. and Robert C. Messenger. *THAID: A Sequential Analysis Program for the Analysis of Nominal Scale Dependent Variables.* Ann Arbor, Michigan: Survey Research Center, University of Michigan, 1973.
8. ——— and John A. Sonquist. "Problems in the Analysis of Survey Data and a Proposal," *Journal of the American Statistical Association,* 58 (September 1963), 415–34.
9. Newman, Joseph W. and Richard Staelin. "Multivariate Analysis of Differences in Buyer Decision Time," *Journal of Marketing Research,* 8 (May 1971), 192–8.
10. Sonquist, John A. *Multivariate Model Building.* Ann Arbor, Michigan: Survey Research Center, University of Michigan, 1970.
11. Theil, Henri. "On the Estimation of Relationships Involving Qualitative Variables," *American Journal of Sociology,* 76 (1970), 103–54.

WILLIAM R. DILLON

This study discusses a simple variable selection procedure, similar in nature to the "F-to-enter" criterion used in stepwise multiple regression, suitable for multidimensional contingency tables having one criterion variable. The procedure is applied to an illustrative set of marketing data and contrasted with other, better-known methods.

ANALYZING LARGE MULTIWAY CONTINGENCY TABLES: A SIMPLE METHOD FOR SELECTING VARIABLES

EVEN in today's era of rapid advances in data analysis sophistication, the preparation and analysis of cross-classified frequency data is still an important activity for many marketing analysts. Often cross-tabulations are useful in summarizing complex marketing relationships. It is difficult to imagine any study in which the data are not displayed in frequency form at some point in the analysis.

The simple two-way contingency table remains the most common type of cross-tabulation. However, restricting attention to only the pairwise relationships between variables may be naive, or even inappropriate, in many situations; rather, the marketing analyst faced with large numbers of variables may wish to focus on the structure of simultaneous relationships among three or more variables. When three or more variables are cross-tabulated, the table formed by combinations of these variables is called a multidimensional contingency table.

Due in large part to the work of Green and his colleagues (1977, 1978), loglinear modeling techniques suitable for analyzing multidimensional contingency tables have received more prominent attention in the marketing literature. Though such techniques are applicable to a wide variety of marketing problems, they have, for the most part, been illustrated and applied in the context of the segmentation problem, and a thorough review of their uses can be found elsewhere (see Wind 1978).

The availability of multivariate frequency data presents a number of interesting challenges for, as those of us who have attempted to use loglinear modeling techniques know all too well, the analysis of multiway contingency tables is often plagued by the nagging problem of cell sparseness. That is, the marketing analyst is frequently faced with analyzing a multiway table having a large number of cells relative to the sample sizes available. For example, in a recent study reported by Green (1978), the multiway table formed from the original coded variables generated 43,008 cells, clearly an unwieldy number. The problem here is that many of the cells are empty or contain too few observations to allow for effective parameter estimation. Consequently, the marketing analyst may wish to reduce the number of variables

William R. Dillon is Assistant Professor of Marketing, School of Business Administration, University of Massachusetts, Amherst, MA. The author thanks the anonymous reviewers for their valuable comments on an earlier draft of this paper.

Reprinted from *Journal of Marketing,* 43 (Fall 1979), 92-102, published by the American Marketing Association.

prior to the model building stage of analysis.

A potential remedy to this problem was suggested by Green (1978) in the form of a two-step model which combined AID (Automatic Interaction Detector—Sonquist 1970) and logit analysis (Green, Carmone, and Wachpress 1977). Essentially, the novelty of his approach was to use AID prior to a logit analysis in order to (1) collapse individual variables—i.e., provide category breaks, (2) screen variables for possible entry, and (3) suggest which interaction terms should be included in a subsequent logit. In assessing this approach, Green fully discussed the problems and pitfalls of AID, and concluded that while a preliminary AID analysis may be insightful, it must be used with extreme prudence. Of particular concern is AID's ability to identify "good" predictors.[1] For example, as Green states, useful (statistically significant) predictors may fail to enter the AID analysis due to substantial correlation with other predictors, or because the between-groups sums of squares associated with the best splits of these variables are less than some arbitrary and predetermined fraction of the total sum of squares.

This report does not consider the issue of collapsing the levels within each variable, but rather the equally important problem of variable selection. The purpose of the study is to present a simple variable selection procedure useful in identifying good predictor variables. The procedure is applicable to the case where interest centers on the analysis of dependence structures involving multiway tables with one dependent variable. Compared to alternative approaches, the procedure to be discussed can provide the marketing analyst with time and cost savings and the following attractive features:

- It is consistent in a fundamental sense with the model building approach taken in a subsequent logit analysis in that it relies on a class of tests which utilize independence arguments.
- It selects variables on the basis of statistical significance and not on ad hoc stopping rules such as the error variance reduction criterion employed in AID analysis.
- It is similar to the well-known "F-to-enter" criterion used in forward stepwise regression and provisions can be made for deleting variables which have already been made part of the system.
- It can easily be operationalized with currently available canned computer software packages suitable for analyzing multiway contingency tables.

[1]It should be noted that the main motivating force behind Green's use of AID was to determine how the various categories of the predictor variables could be collapsed so as to provide a more reasonable number of categories per variable. For this purpose, a preliminary AID analysis may be quite effective.

The Approach

The approach to be taken essentially involves a two-stage process: the first stage entails the selection of good predictor variables, and the second stage involves finding a good-fitting logit model. Note that the selection procedure described below is restricted to the case of one criterion variable and multiple predictors.

Rationale

For ease of discussion let us initially consider a three dimensional $i \times j \times k$ contingency table with $i=2$, $j=2$, and $k=2$, generated by three variables Z_0, Z_1, Z_2, where Z_0 is the response (dependent) measure and Z_1 and Z_2 are potential predictors. (While we illustrate the method with binary predictors all results and ideas are easily extended to the more general case where the predictor variables have more than two categories.) Let f_{ijk} and P_{ijk} denote the observed frequency and probability corresponding to cell *(ijk)* respectively. If the frequencies are summed over all values of Z_0, the result will be the *marginal* total of the jth column and k^{th} layer; hereafter we will denote marginal totals with a "+" so that f_{+jk} means

$$\Sigma_i f_{ijk} = f_{+jk}.$$

In a similar fashion we can define f_{i+k}, f_{ij+}, f_{i++}, f_{+j+}, f_{++k}, and $f_{+++} = N$, where N is the total sample size.

Suppose that we are concerned with the relationships between Z_0 and Z_1, and Z_0 and Z_2—that is, the first-order relationship between each explanatory variable and the response measure. The relative degree of association between the dependent variable and the two predictors can be assessed by computing the Pearson goodness-of-fit chi-square statistic for each 2×2 table corresponding to the hypothesis of complete independence; viz:

$$\begin{aligned} &\text{for } Z_1 \quad H_{Z_1}: \boldsymbol{P}_{ij} = \boldsymbol{P}_{+j} \boldsymbol{P}_{i+} \\ &\text{for } Z_2 \quad H_{Z_2}: \boldsymbol{P}_{ik} = \boldsymbol{P}_{+k} \boldsymbol{P}_{i+} \end{aligned} \qquad (1)$$

Consider next the relationship between Z_0 and both explanatory variables; here we have a $2 \times 2 \times 2$ multiway table and suppose we restrict our attention to hypotheses of the form

$$H_{Z_1 Z_2}: \boldsymbol{P}_{ijk} = \boldsymbol{P}_{i++} \boldsymbol{P}_{+jk}. \qquad (2)$$

This class of hypotheses states that the dependent variable is independent of the explanatory variable taken jointly. If this is true, then the observed odds ratios—the relative odds of finding $Z_0 = 1$ when $Z_1 = j$ and $Z_2 = k$—are homogeneous. The null hypothesis given in (2) can easily be tested with either the Pearson goodness-of-fit chi-square statistic or the likelihood ratio criterion chi-square statistic.[2]

The first hypothesis, H_{Z_1}, is *simple* in that it postulates that Z_0 and Z_1 are completely independent. The second hypothesis, $H_{Z_1Z_2}$, is more complex in that it postulates *partial* independence of Z_0 and the two predictors, Z_1 and Z_2, taken jointly. If Z_2, the second variable to enter, is statistically independent of both Z_0 and Z_1 then Lachin (1973) has shown that

$$\chi^2 H_{Z_1} = \chi^2 H_{Z_1Z_2}. \tag{3}$$

The partial independence hypothesis, $H_{Z_1Z_2}$, has associated with it two components; namely, H_{Z_1} and $H_{Z_2|Z_1}$, where by $H_{Z_2|Z_1}$ we mean the *conditional* independence hypothesis which states that Z_0 and Z_2 are statistically independent given the levels of Z_1. Hence, the equality of the partial and simple independence hypotheses exists in the case where $H_{Z_2|Z_1}$ is true. This means that if Z_1 shows strong association with Z_0, then the decision whether to include Z_2 clearly rests on the chi-square value associated with $H_{Z_2|Z_1}$. If the likelihood ratio criterion chi-square statistic is used, then the partitioning of the partial independence hypothesis is exact so that

$$\chi^2 H_{Z_1Z_2} = \chi^2 H_{Z_1} + \chi^2 H_{Z_2|Z_1}. \tag{4}$$

The relationships among the various hypotheses and the method of testing is developed in the appendix.

In summary, we can determine the merits of Z_2 in an analysis given that Z_1 has already been included by examining $\chi^2 H_{Z_2|Z_1}$. If, for example, $\chi^2 H_{Z_2|Z_1}$ is nonsignificant, then the dependent measures Z_0 and Z_2 are independent given the level of Z_1. In other words, Z_2 should not be included since its association with Z_0 is weak in the presence of Z_1. Suppose, however, that $\chi^2 H_{Z_2Z_1}$ is significant and consider whether to include yet another predictor Z_3. The decision as to whether Z_3 should be included rests on the chi-square value associated with ($H_{Z_1Z_2Z_3} - H_{Z_1Z_2}$), or equivalently $H_{Z_3|Z_2Z_1}$; e.g., if $\chi^2 H_{Z_3|Z_1Z_2}$ is significant, then Z_0 and Z_3 show strong association in the presence of Z_1 and Z_2 and, therefore, it warrants inclusion. If, on the other hand, $\chi^2 H_{Z_3|Z_1Z_2}$ is nonsignificant we accept the hypothesis of conditional independence of Z_0 and Z_3 given the level of Z_1 and Z_2, and Z_3 should not be included. Therefore, the process would stop with two predictors having been selected—assuming, of course, that we have exhausted the available set of predictors.

In essence, this process is similar to the "F-to-enter" criterion used in forward stepwise multiple regression. Assuming the availability of m-predictors, the first variable selected is the one with the largest probability level with regard to its first-order relationship to the dependent measure—i.e., the variable which allows us to reject the hypothesis of no relationship with the greatest degree of confidence. Other variables are included by applying a similar selection rule expressed in terms of conditional independence arguments for successively higher-order relationships. In such cases, we choose that variable which most rejects the hypothesis of conditional independence between the dependent measure and itself given the levels of those predictors already made part of the system. In this way both the main effects of a specific variable and its interaction with previously selected variables are considered in the inclusion decision. In addition, variables can be deleted in a similar fashion. For example, suppose at some step, t-variables have been included with a chi-square value denoted by $\chi^2 H_{Z_1Z_2 \ldots Z_t}$. To determine whether any previously selected variable Z_l, $l = 1,2,\ldots,t\text{-}1$, should be removed, we compute

$$\chi^2 H_{Z_l|Z_1Z_2 \ldots Z_{t-1}} = \chi^2 H_{Z_1Z_2 \ldots Z_l . Z_t} - \chi^2 H_{Z_1Z_2 \ldots Z_{t-1}} \tag{5}$$

(with corresponding d.f. found by subtraction), and if any $\chi^2 H_{Z_l|Z_1Z_2 \ldots Z_{t-1}}$ is nonsignificant, then that variable would be removed from the predictor set and the next step begun.

Operationalization

Another attractive feature of this approach is the ease in which it can be operationalized. The marketing analyst need not develop new computer software since the selection procedure can be easily implemented with readily available programs, such as the BMDP3F program (Dixon 1973), suitable for analyzing multi-way contingency tables via loglinear models.

To illustrate the procedure assume the situation of one dependent measure and m-explanatory variables. Let α_I and α_D be the critical probability levels for including and deleting a variable, respectively. A feature common to most loglinear modeling programs, including BMDP3F, is the use of standard bracket notation which describes a model in terms of the minimal set of marginal totals needed to define (i.e., fit) the requested model. Fortunately, the use of bracket notation simplifies the selection process since at each step the user can test the goodness-of-fit of various hypotheses by merely specifying the corresponding loglinear models; consequently, all relevant

[2]Both statistics are asymptotically distributed as chi-square with d.f. $= (ik - 1)\,(j - 1)$. The exact form of both test statistics can be found in Bishop, Fienberg, and Holland (1975).

hypotheses at any given step can be quickly assessed, and the appropriate variable selected. For example, if we wanted to decide which of two variables Z_1 and Z_2 should be included first (note that the relevant hypotheses are H_{Z_1} and H_{Z_2}), then we would request two models expressible in terms of marginal totals as $[Z_0][Z_1]$ and $[Z_0][Z_2]$, respectively. On the other hand, assuming that Z_1 has already been included, the relevant hypothesis, $H_{Z_2|Z_1}$, of conditional independence of Z_0 and Z_2 given the level of Z_1 can be tested by fitting the model corresponding to $[Z_0Z_1][Z_1Z_2]$.

The selection procedure suggested translates in practice into the following steps:

1. Request the following models corresponding to the hypothesis of complete independence of Z_0 and each Z_m, viz:

$$[Z_0][Z_1]$$
$$[Z_0][Z_2]$$
$$\vdots$$
$$[Z_0][Z_m]$$

On the basis of the individually calculated chi-square values choose that variable Z_j with the largest chi-square per d.f. If the probability level, denoted hereafter by p, associated with the largest chi-square per d.f., is nonsignificant ($p>\alpha_I$), then the process would stop with no variables having been included. This is similar in spirit to the "F-to-enter" criterion used in stepwise multiple regression wherein that variable with the largest univariate F-value is selected first.

2. For each of the remaining $t=m-1$ variables, test the goodness-of-fit of the following models

$$[Z_oZ_j][Z_jZ_1] \text{ and } [Z_o][Z_jZ_1]$$
$$[Z_oZ_j][Z_jZ_2] \text{ and } [Z_o][Z_jZ_2]$$
$$\vdots$$
$$[Z_oZ_j][Z_jZ_t] \text{ and } [Z_o][Z_jZ_t]$$

and select that variable Z_k which most rejects the hypothesis of conditional independence of Z_o and Z_k given the level of Z_j; that is, examine each $[Z_oZ_j][Z_jZ_t]$, $t=1,2,\ldots,m-1$, and select that variable with the smallest p. If this $p>\alpha_I$, then the process would stop with one variable having been selected.

3. Before proceeding to the next step, a test of whether Z_j should be deleted given that Z_k is included can be accomplished by computing $\chi^2[Z_oZ_k][Z_kZ_j]$, where

$$\chi^2[Z_oZ_k][Z_kZ_j]=\chi^2[Z_o][Z_jZ_k]-\chi^2[Z_o][Z_k].$$

If it happens that any value is nonsignificant ($p>\alpha_D$), this implies that the relative contribution of Z_j given the presence of Z_k is not sufficient to warrant its retention in the selected set of predictors.

4. The process continues in a similar fashion and we would test the goodness-of-fit of the following models

$$[Z_oZ_jZ_k][Z_jZ_kZ_1] \text{ and } [Z_o][Z_jZ_kZ_1]$$
$$[Z_oZ_jZ_k][Z_jZ_kZ_2] \text{ and } [Z_o][Z_jZ_kZ_2]$$
$$\vdots$$
$$[Z_oZ_jZ_k][Z_jZ_kZ_r] \text{ and } [Z_o][Z_jZ_kZ_r]$$

where r is the number of predictors not yet included. The variable with the smallest probability level is determined and, again, if this $p>\alpha_I$ the process would stop with m-r variables having been selected.

Use of existing computer software, while extremely helpful, nevertheless has its liabilities. In particular, implementation of the selection procedure with use of the BMDP3F program will require a number of successive computer runs. In general, one run is necessary for each step. However, if the user wishes to check for the deletion of a variable, two runs may be needed for each step after the second since the decision to delete a variable may rest on evaluating specific combinations of the selected variables not tested at a previous step. While this feature is an obvious limitation, the approach suggested here will generally require less *effort* than alternative methods currently in use. In the section to follow, we investigate this issue further.

Alternative Approaches

By reducing the number of variables under consideration prior to the model building stage, the number and form of possible loglinear/logit models that can be fitted is severely restricted. Alternatively, one may argue that a more appropriate strategy would be to work off the complete multiway table generated by all of the available predictors and utilize techniques and methods of model selection to decide whether some variables can be safely collapsed. While it is clearly not possible to fully discuss all the methods which have been proposed for this purpose, the following briefly sketches three of the more popular alternatives. (A complete and detailed discussion of these and other model selection strategies is discussed in Bishop,

Fienberg, and Holland 1975.)

Use of Standardized Parameter Estimates. With this approach, the user would examine the standardized U-terms derived from the saturated model with the view of identifying those variables which generate the largest standardized values; these U-terms then define the minimum hierarchical model that should be fitted, and U-terms are added on the basis of their standardized values.

Measures of Marginal and Partial Association—Brown (1976). Essentially, this approach allows for a screening of U-terms so that only a limited number of loglinear models need to be considered in the second stage model building process. For each U-term effect, two test statistics are computed; these tests, called marginal and partial association, indicate the order of magnitude of the change in the goodness-of-fit produced by entering a given effect into the model. From this process, it is possible to categorize U-terms into (1) those which should be included (both test statistics are significant), (2) those which warrant further examination (only one test statistic is significant), and (3) those which need not be included (both test statistics are nonsignificant).

Stepwise Selection Procedures—Goodman (1970, 1971). This procedure starts with fitting models of uniform order such that we seek a model with terms of order r-l that fits poorly and a model with terms of order r that fits very well. At this point, we consider models based on configurations of order r-l and order r, and utilize either one of the following two approaches: *Forward selection:* start by considering the model containing terms of order r-l and at each step add that U-term of order r that provides the most significant change in the goodness-of-fit test statistic. The process terminates when no further terms can be added which significantly improve the fit. *Backward elimination:* start by considering the model of order r and at each step delete the single term of order r that has the least significant effect. The process terminates when no further term of order r can be deleted on the basis of lack of fit.

Note that the stepwise approaches can be easily modified to yield a "stepwise-up" or "stepwise-down" procedure such that the inclusion or exclusion of a specific term is not irreversible.

It is well-known that the number of hierarchical models that can be fitted increases dramatically as the number of dimensions grows (e.g., there are 166 different hierarchical models in a four-way table and over one thousand in a five-way table). Hence, model selection strategies, such as those described above, which limit the number of models to be evaluated are immensely helpful; unfortunately, no "best" strategy exists since, in large part, a choice depends on (our) a priori knowledge of the interrelationships among the variables.

In field survey work, where a large number of candidate predictors are generally available, the resulting multiway table is likely to be extremely sparse and strategies that use the full table may not be useful, or indeed appropriate. For example, use of standardized parameters (U-terms) is only appropriate when *all* cells have positive observed counts; similarly, the marginal and partial association test statistics are of questionable validity and consistency for higher-order effects. In cases where no a priori ordering of models is available, and little is known about the interrelationships among the variables, the use of stepwise procedures is likely to require a considerable amount of time and computation and cannot be thought of as an automatic device for finding the best loglinear model. In the application section to follow, we will see that these more standard procedures may require the evaluation of an inordinate number of models and may not yield the most parsimonious one. However, it should be noted that while these alternative methods can be used in the context of the general loglinear model, the proposed stepwise procedure is most relevant when one variable has been singled out as the dependent measure.

An Illustrative Example

To illustrate the selection procedure and the subsequent model building stage, we use a set of data previously analyzed elsewhere (Dillon, Goldstein, and Shiffman 1978; Goldstein and Dillon 1977) which originally arose in the analysis of heavy versus light usage of a major household service product. This analysis was based on a total sample size of $N = 464$ respondents obtained from a 1975 mail survey. For the purposes of illustration, six out of the nine previously analyzed predictors were chosen for analysis. The independent variables are:[3]

Z_1 Length of Residence
1. Less than 5 years
2. At least 5 years

Z_2 Location of Previous Home
1. Within the same town or county
2. Outside of county, state, or U.S.A.

Z_3 Head of Household's Occupation
1. Sales, craftsman, clerical worker, or below
2. Professional or manager

[3]The category descriptions for each of the predictors listed below were adopted from Dillon, Goldstein, and Shiffman (1978). With the exception of Z_1—length of residence—all of the variables comprising this subset had previously been determined as useful with respect to usage.

Z_4 Head of Household's Education
1. No college
2. Some college or above

Z_5 Family Income
1. Less than $11,000 a year
2. At least $11,000 a year

Z_6 Stage in Family Life Cycle
1. Less than 55 years old
2. 55 years or older, employed or unemployed

Table 1 shows the first-order relationships of all these variables to heavy and light usage.

TABLE 1
First-Order Relationships Between Predictor Variables and Usage Behavior

Variable	Light	Heavy	Total
Z_1 Length of Residence			
<5 years	111	132	243
	(46%)	(54%)	(100%)
≥5 years	119	103	221
	(54%)	(46%)	(100%)
Z_2 Location of Previous Home			
Same county or town	202	180	382
	(53%)	(47%)	(100%)
Outside of county	28	54	82
	(34%)	(66%)	(100%)
Z_3 Head of Household's Occupation			
Sales or below	130	84	214
	(61%)	(39%)	(100%)
Professional or manager	100	150	250
	(40%)	(60%)	(100%)
Z_4 Head of Household's Education			
No college	105	75	180
	(58%)	(42%)	(100%)
Some college or above	125	159	284
	(44%)	(56%)	(100%)
Z_5 Family Income			
<$11,000 a year	98	42	140
	(70%)	(30%)	(100%)
≥$11,000 a year	132	192	324
	(41%)	(59%)	(100%)
Z_6 Stage in Family Life Cycle			
<55 years old	166	187	353
	(47%)	(53%)	(100%)
≥55, employed or unemployed	64	47	111
	(58%)	(42%)	(100%)

Selection of Variables

The selection process begins by examining the first-order relationship between the dependent measure—usage—and each explanatory variable. Table 2 indicates the relative first-order importance of the predictors in terms of the likelihood ratio chi-square for the hypothesis of complete independence. Family income has the largest chi-square per d.f., and it is our first selection for inclusion since the corresponding p value is highly significant ($p<.01$).

The next step is to determine which of the remaining variables, if any, should be selected given that Z_5—family income—has been included. Therefore, we are considering which of the remaining five variables is most important with respect to usage once family income has been adjusted for. Part B of Table 2 shows the results of testing the hypothesis that usage is independent of each of the remaining variables and family income taken jointly. The cross-tabulations of Z_3—head of household's occupation—and Z_5—family income—shows the largest chi-square per d.f. (13.91); however, the criterion for inclusion at this step rests on the test of conditional independence of usage and head of household's occupation given the level of family income; i.e., $H_{Z_3|Z_5}$. The table shows that a test of this hypothesis yields a significant chi-square value ($p<.05$). This makes Z_3 our next choice for inclusion.

Before proceeding to the next step, however, two points warrant discussion. First, from (4) we see that conditional independence χ^2 values can be computed by taking the difference between the two appropriate joint independence chi-square values; for example

$$\chi^2 H_{Z_3|Z_5} = \chi^2 H_{Z_3Z_5} - \chi^2 H_{Z_5} = 41.72 - 34.18 = 7.54,$$

which is exactly the value shown in Part B of Table 2. Secondly, we can address the issue of whether Z_5 may be dropped given that Z_3 is included. This test rests on $\chi^2 H_{Z_5|Z_3}$ where

$$\chi^2 H_{Z_5|Z_3} = \chi^2 H_{Z_5Z_3} - \chi^2 H_{Z_3} = 41.72 - 20.00 = 21.72,$$

with 2 d.f. Because this value is highly significant ($p<.01$), we can conclude that family income warrants retention in the predictor set which includes head of household's occupation.

The next step is to include both family income and head of household's occupation and compute the relative importance of the remaining four variables. Part C of Table 2 shows that Z_2—location of previous home—has the largest chi-square per d.f. (6.99), and the corresponding conditional independence hypothesis, $H_{Z_2|Z_5Z_3}$, is rejected at the $p=.15$ level. At this point, a decision has to be made as to whether the process should continue. That is, if we had set $\alpha_1=.05$, the process would stop at this step with two predictors having been selected. In general, the setting of an "effective" stopping rule (i.e., critical α-level) is a particularly difficult issue. This is due partly to the paucity of published research on the subject, and because the general area of selecting "good" subsets of variables is inherently problematical. However, in the context of usual forward stepwise multiple

TABLE 2
Hypotheses Tested and Likelihood Ratio Chi-Square Values

Hypothesis[a]		χ^2	d.f.
A. Complete Independence			
(Hz_1)	Usage[b] × Length of Residency	3.09	1
(Hz_2)	Usage × Location of Previous Home	9.62	1
(Hz_3)	Usage × Head of Household's Occupation	20.00	1
(Hz_4)	Usage × Head of Household's Education	9.07	1
(Hz_5)	Usage × Family Income	34.18	1
(Hz_6)	Usage × Stage in Family Life Cycle	3.83	1
B. Family Income Included			
Joint Independence			
(Hz_1z_5)	Usage × Length of Residence, Family Income	38.00	3
(Hz_2z_5)	Usage × Location of Previous Home, Family Income	41.56	3
(Hz_3z_5)	Usage × Head of Household's Occupation, Family Income	41.72	3
(Hz_4z_5)	Usage × Head of Household's Education, Family Income	36.50	3
(Hz_6z_5)	Usage × Stage in Family Life Cycle, Family Income	34.94	3
Conditional Independence			
$(Hz_1\|z_5)$	Usage × Length of Residence|Family Income	3.82	2
$(Hz_2\|z_5)$	Usage × Location of Previous Home|Family Income	7.38	2
$(Hz_3\|z_5)$	Usage × Head of Household's Occupation|Family Income	7.54	2
$(Hz_4\|z_5)$	Usage × Head of Household's Education|Family Income	2.31	2
$(Hz_6\|z_5)$	Usage × Stage in Family Life Cycle|Family Income	0.76	2
C. Family Income and Head of Household Occupation			
Joint Independence			
$(Hz_1z_5z_3)$	Usage × Length of Residence, Family Income, Head of Household's Occupation	46.18	7
$(Hz_2z_5z_3)$	Usage × Location of Previous Home, Family Income, Head of Household's Occupation	48.90	7
$(Hz_4z_5z_3)$	Usage × Head of Household's Education, Family Income, Head of Household's Occupation	43.77	7
$(Hz_6z_5z_3)$	Usage × Stage in Family Life Cycle, Family Income, Head of Household's Occupation	48.98	7
Conditional Independence			
$(Hz_1\|z_5z_3)$	Usage × Length of Residence|Family Income, Head of Household's Occupation	4.45	4
$(Hz_2\|z_5z_3)$	Usage × Location of Previous Home|Family Income, Head of Household's Occupation	7.18	4
$(Hz_4\|z_5z_3)$	Usage × Head of Household's Education|Family Income, Head of Household's Occupation	2.05	4
$(Hz_6\|z_5z_3)$	Usage × Stage in Family Life Cycle|Family Income, Head of Household's Occupation	7.15	4
D. Family Income and Location of Previous Home			
Joint Independence			
$(Hz_1z_5z_2)$	Usage × Length of Residence, Family Income, Location of Previous Home	42.46	7
$(Hz_4z_5z_2)$	Usage × Head of Household's Education, Family Income, Location of Previous Home	45.79	7
$(Hz_6z_5z_2)$	Usage × Stage in Family Life Cycle, Family Income, Location of Previous Home	47.67	7
Conditional Independence			
$(Hz_1\|z_5z_2)$	Usage × Length of Residence|Family Income, Location of Previous Home	0.90	4
$(Hz_4\|z_5z_2)$	Usage × Head of Household's Education|Family Income, Location of Previous Home	4.23	4
$(Hz_6\|z_5z_2)$	Usage × Stage in Family Life Cycle|Family Income, Location of Previous Home	6.11	4

[a]All of the tests of hypotheses are implemented with use of the BMDP3F program.
[b]Usage, the dependent measure, has two levels: light and heavy.

regression problem, Bendel and Afifi (1977) have presented evidence which suggests that rather liberal inclusion levels, in the range of .15 to .25, should be used. Because the main purpose of this section is to illustrate the selection process, we set $\alpha_I = .15$ and $\alpha_D = .05$, and include Z_2 in the predictor set.

Given that location of previous home is included, we can question whether both family income and head of household's occupation should be retained. Let us first consider the relative importance of Z_5—family income—given the levels of Z_3—head of household's occupation—and Z_2—location of previous home. The relevant hypothesis can be easily assessed by examining $\chi^2 H_{Z_5|Z_3Z_2}$ where

$$\chi^2 H_{Z_5|Z_3Z_2} = \chi^2 H_{Z_5Z_3Z_2} - \chi^2 H_{Z_3Z_2} = 48.90 - 27.54 = 21.36$$

with 4 d.f. Since this value is highly significant ($p < .01$), Z_5 should be retained. Similarly, for Z_3 we compute

$$\chi^2 H_{Z_3|Z_2Z_5} = \chi^2 H_{Z_3Z_2Z_5} - \chi^2 H_{Z_2Z_5} = 48.90 - 41.56 = 7.34$$

with 4 d.f. In this case, however, we conclude that head of household's occupation should be dropped given that Z_5 and Z_2 are included since $p > \alpha_D$.

A fourth step in this process is not productive. We see from Part D of Table 2 that each of the remaining variables (Z_1-length of residence, Z_4-head of house-

TABLE 3
Incidence of Heavy Usage for Two Variable Model

Family Income	Location of Previous Home	Total Respondents	Heavy Users	Observed Proportion
<$11,000 a year	Within same county	122	34	.279
	Outside same county	18	8	.444
≥$11,000 a year	Within same county	260	146	.562
	Outside same county	64	46	.719

hold's education, and Z_6-stage in family life cycle) yields a goodness-of-fit chi-square value for the hypothesis of conditional independence which is nonsignificant—indicating a good fit. This means that none of the remaining variables is statistically important when the variables already included in the system are controlled for.

In conclusion, the selection procedure terminates with two variables, Z_5-family income and Z_2-location of previous home, having been included. We now proceed to the second stage of analysis—model building.

Logit Analysis

The second phase of analysis involves fitting a model, and as an initial step consider Table 3 and Figure 1 which show the observed heavy usage prevalences for the two explanatory variables (Z_2 and Z_5) chosen by the selection procedure. Each vertical bar in the figure represents one of the groups of respondents defined according to the two variables previously determined as important. Note that the height of the bars rises from left to right moving from a family income of less than $11,000 a year to family income of at least $11,000 a year. From the table and figure, a number of observations can be offered:

- In general, the likelihood that the respondent is a heavy user is relatively low, about 28%, if family income is less than $11,000 a year and the previous move was within the same county.
- Within each income group, the likelihood of heavy usage is increased if the location of the respondent's previous home was outside the county.
- Respondents who have family incomes of at least $11,000 a year (regardless of their previous home) have a fairly high chance, about 59%, of being a heavy user.
- Regardless of family income, respondents who have previously moved outside of the county have about a 66% chance of being heavy users.
- If the location of the respondent's previous home was in the same county, there is only about a 50-50 chance of heavy usage.

FIGURE 1
Proportion of Total Respondents Who Have Heavy Usage Rates Grouped by Family Income and Location of Previous Home.

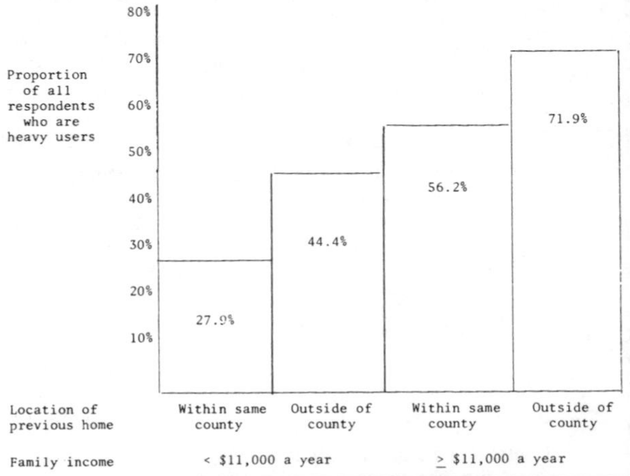

The search for a good fitting loglinear model relating Z_0-usage and the two explanatory variables, Z_2 and Z_5 yielded two potential candidates:

Model 1 $[Z_0Z_2][Z_0Z_5]$ $(p = .57)$

Model 2 $[Z_0Z_2][Z_0Z_5][Z_2Z_5]$ $(p = .97)$

Note that both models provide good fits and will yield logit models (see Green, Carmone, and Wachpress 1977) having identical parameters except their estimates will be slightly different since the margin total $[Z_2Z_5]$ is assumed fixed in Model 2.[4] However, given

[4]Specification of Z_0—usage as the dependent measure—and variables Z_2 and Z_5 as explanatory factors means that the four sampling strata are considered fixed and determined by these two factors. Therefore "permissible" logits must retain the margin total $[Z_2Z_5]$ so that the estimated margin totals equal the observed margin totals. However, as Bishop (1969) has argued, if there is no good rationale for treating the margin totals as fixed, then this customary practice should not be blatantly evoked; furthermore, in certain instances "better" parameter estimates may be obtained from not including the highest-order margin total relating to the explanatory variables.

that there is no reason to believe the margin totals for Z_2-location of previous home and Z_5-family income were fixed in advance, we choose Model 1 as being consistent with the data. Finally, it should be noted that all parameter estimates from the selected model were significant at the p = .01 level, and the signs of the coefficients indicated that the characteristics location of previous home outside of county and family income of at least $11,000 a year had a "negative" effect on the log odds of being a light user.

In closing this section, we attempt to get a fix on how well our two-stage process has explained usage behavior by modifying a statistic recommended by Goodman (1972). If we let $\chi^2(M0)$ be the goodness-of-fit chi-square value corresponding to Model-M0 with fitted margin $[Z_0]$, then the statistic,

$$V = [\chi^2(M0) - \chi^2(M1)]/\chi^2(M0) \qquad (6)$$

measures the relative increase in weighted "accounted for" variation obtained from the case where the additive effects of Z_0, Z_2, and Z_5 are taken into account (Model-M1) vis-à-vis the case where only the main effect of the general mean on Z_0 is taken into account (Model-M0). Using (6), we calculate the proportion of variation accounted for by Model-M1 *given the choice of variables* as 99.7%.

As Goodman (1972) states, this measure is somewhat analogous to R^2, the coefficient of multiple determination, used in multiple regression analysis. However, to derive a measure of the proportion of variation accounted for by the variables *and* the model we need to weight this measure by the proportion of variation accounted for by the two selected variables. To accomplish this, we use a procedure suggested by Light and Margolin (1971). Consider a contingency table in which there are $J = 2$ columns representing usage and I rows, one for each possible combination of values of the selected variables—in our case $I = 4$ since there are two variables under consideration, each having two levels. A measure of accounted for variation by the explanatory variables is given by

$$Q = 1 - \frac{\text{WSS}}{\text{TSS}}, \qquad (7)$$

where

$$\underset{\text{of squares}}{\underset{\text{total sum}}{\text{TSS}}} = \frac{N}{2} - \frac{1}{2N} \sum_{j=1}^{J} (f_{+j})^2$$

$$\underset{\text{of squares}}{\underset{\text{within sum}}{\text{WSS}}} = \frac{N}{2} - \frac{1}{2} \sum_{i=1}^{I} \frac{1}{f_{i+}} \sum_{j=1}^{J} f^2_{ij}$$

For the data of Table 3, $Q = .087$ which means that 8.7% of the variation in usage is accounted for by knowledge of Z_2-location of previous home and Z_5-family income.

To compute an overall measure of accounted for variation (i.e., the variation attributable to the two selected variables *and* Model-M1), we multiply 8.7% by 99.7% and obtain 8.6%. Obviously, a large proportion of variation remains unaccounted for; however, this is not too surprising, or uncommon, given the complexity of the phenomenon under study. Furthermore, the relatively low "adjusted R^2" is neither due to selecting ineffective variables nor from fitting a misspecified model.[5] On the contrary, if all six predictors were brought into the analysis, they would account for only about 16% *(Q = .159)* of the variation in usage behavior. Therefore, we see that the selected variables Z_2 and Z_5 account for over 50% of the total possible accounted for variation.

Comparison with Alternative Methods

As we discussed earlier, a number of alternative model selection procedures are currently in use, all of which work off the complete table. By way of summary, Table 4 presents results for each of three alternative methods in terms of (1) the number of models evaluated, (2) the final model selected, (3) the corresponding p-value, (4) central processing unit time (CPU), (5) the total number of parameters estimated in the final model, (6) the mean absolute error, and (7) the overall accounted for variation. Since nearly one-half of the 2^7 cells of the multiway table formed by the seven variables was empty, the quantity one-half (½) was added to each cell prior to analysis. All results are based on use of the BMDP3F program.

Notice first the number of models that needed evaluation with use of the alternative methods ranged from a low of seven to an unwieldy high of 175. In addition, while the alternative methods yielded final loglinear models having better goodness-of-fit statistics (as evinced in the associated p-values), they required the estimation of a far greater number of parameters since *all* six predictors were included with each method. In terms of the predictors utilized in a subsequent logit analysis, the standardized U-terms method would include Z_3 and Z_5, whereas the marginal/partial association and Goodman's stepwise methods would include Z_2, Z_3, and Z_5. While the

[5]In standard multiple regression analysis, it is well-known that R^2 can be greatly inflated by simply including additional explanatory variables, whether or not these have substantial relationship to the dependent measure. Consequently, larger R^2 does not unequivocably imply a better model. In the case of discrete variables, the extreme case occurs when so many variables are included, and so many cells result, that the observed frequency for specific combinations of variables is either zero or one.

TABLE 4
Comparative Analysis

Method	Number of Models Evaluated	Final Model	p value	CPU[a] Time	Total Number of Parameters Loglinear	Logit	Mean Absolute Error	Accounted for Variation[b]
Stepwise Prior to Logit	3	$[Z_0Z_2]^*[Z_0Z_5]^*$	.57	62.44	6	3	.020	.086
Alternative Methods								
Standardized U-Terms	15	$[Z_0Z_3Z_5]^*[Z_1Z_6][Z_3Z_6]$ $[Z_5Z_6][Z_1Z_2Z_5][Z_3Z_4Z_5]$	.99	100.43	20	4	.017	.086
Marginal/Partial Association	7	$[Z_0Z_2]^*[Z_0Z_3]^*[Z_0Z_5]^*$ $[Z_1Z_2][Z_1Z_6][Z_2Z_4][Z_5Z_6]$ $[Z_3Z_4Z_5][Z_3Z_4Z_6]$	.99	187.03	21	4	.018	.097
Goodman's Stepwise	175	$[Z_0Z_2]^*[Z_0Z_3]^*[Z_0Z_5]^*$ $[Z_1Z_2][Z_1Z_5][Z_1Z_6]$ $[Z_3Z_4][Z_3Z_5][Z_3Z_6]$ $[Z_4Z_5][Z_5Z_6]$	.99	265.10	19	4	.019	.097

*Margins which include the dependent measure.
[a]CPU time is in seconds.
[b]Accounted for variation is the overall variation attributable to the model and the variables included in the logit specification—see text.

alternative methods yield logit models which do not differ greatly from the stepwise procedure with regard to the number of parameters, their estimates did vary considerably since the margins fitted in each final model were rather different. Note also that the use of the stepwise selection approach prior to logit analysis yields a final model that fares well in terms of mean absolute error (as compared to the alternative methods which utilize all six predictors) and accounted for variation.

Finally, inspection of the CPU time used shows the stepwise prior to logit method to be superior to the other approaches. Those approaches require that more computer runs be initiated; furthermore, more complex models need evaluation and the corresponding fitting process consumes more machine time. In short, the procedure described here appears to give relatively good results with less effort than the other approaches.

Concluding Remarks

In cases where a large number of predictors are available, the multiway table formed by all the variables is likely to have a great deal of empty cells. In such circumstances, the practitioner may not wish to fit a logit model at the outset, but rather utilize a variable selection procedure to reduce the number of candidate predictors to a more manageable set.

However, care and good judgment on the part of the practitioner are essential in the intelligent application to any stepwise selection procedure. While pockets of cell sparseness in a data set are often the motivating force leading one to consider variable selection schemes, this same problem is likely to reappear when applying such procedures. Unfortunately, the selection procedure discussed here, as well as other methods, is likely to suffer from difficulties of reliability when cell frequencies are so small as to make chi-square statistics of questionable validity.

While these issues should be kept in mind, the selection procedure discussed here appears potentially useful to practitioners who desire to select good explanatory variables prior to a logit analysis. As we hopefully demonstrated, the selection procedure has the ability to (1) select potential predictors in terms of statistical significance which is consistent with the second stage logit analysis, (2) add or delete variables at any given step, and (3) be implemented with readily available computer software packages.

Appendix

To clearly see the relationship among the hypotheses consider the following. If $H_{Z_1Z_2}$ is true, i.e.,

$$P_{ijk} = P_{i++}\, P_{+jk} \tag{A1}$$

then this implies (by summing over k) H_{Z_1}

$$P_{ij+} = P_{i++}\, P_{+j+} \tag{A2}$$

which also implies $H_{Z_2|Z_1}$; viz:

$$P_{ijk} = P_{ij+} \; P_{+jk}/P_{+j+} \qquad \text{(A3)}$$

Therefore, if we now introduce the notation of Goodman (1970), the hypothesis $H_{Z_1Z_2}$ can be expressed as (Z_0 **x** Z_1Z_2) where **x** means "independent of," and it can be partitioned as

$$(Z_0 \mathbf{x} Z_1Z_2) = (Z_0 \mathbf{x} Z_1) \cap (Z_0 \mathbf{x} Z_2|Z_1). \qquad \text{(A4)}$$

In terms of the hypotheses $H_{Z_1Z_2}$, H_{Z_1}, and $H_{Z_2|Z_1}$ we have the following relationship

$$H_{Z_1Z_2} = H_{Z_1} + H_{Z_2|Z_1}. \qquad \text{(A5)}$$

The chi-square values associated with the two components do not sum to the chi-square value associated with the original hypothesis if the Pearson goodness-of-fit statistic is used. However, the likelihood ratio criterion chi-square statistic does possess an additive property under partitioning in the sense that if two models M_1 and M_2 have the property that the marginals fitted with M_1 are a subset of those fitted by M_2, then

$$\chi^2_{LR}(M1) = \chi^2_{LR}(M1|M2) + \chi^2_{LR}(M2). \qquad \text{(A6)}$$

Accordingly, for the hypothesis statements considered here, we may write

$$\chi^2 H_{Z_1Z_2} = \chi^2 H_{Z_1} + \chi^2 H_{Z_2|Z_1} \qquad \text{(A7)}$$

and, therefore,

$$\chi^2 H_{Z_2|Z_1} = \chi^2 H_{Z_1Z_2} - \chi^2 H_{Z_1}. \qquad \text{(A8)}$$

REFERENCES

Bendel, Robert B. and A. A. Afifi (1977), "Comparison of Stopping Rules in Forward 'Stepwise' Regression," *Journal of the American Statistical Association,* 72 (March), 46-53.

Bishop, Yvonne M. M. (1969), "Full Contingency Tables, Logits, and Split Contingency Tables," *Biometrics,* 25 (June), 383-400.

———, Stephen E. Fienberg, and Paul W. Holland (1975), *Discrete Multivariate Analysis: Theory and Practice,* Cambridge, MA: The MIT Press.

Brown, Morton B. (1976), "Screening Effects in Multi-Dimensional Contingency Tables," *Applied Statistics,* 25, 37-46.

Dillon, William, Matthew Goldstein, and Leon Shiffman (1978), "Appropriateness of Linear Discriminant and Multinomial Classification Analysis in Marketing Research," *Journal of Marketing Research,* 15 (February), 103-112.

Dixon, Wilfred J., editor (1973), *BMD: Biomedical Computer Programs,* Berkeley: University of California Press.

Goldstein, Matthew and William R. Dillon (1977), "A Stepwise Discrete Variable Selection Procedure," *Communications in Statistics,* A6 (14), 1423-1436.

Goodman, Leo G. (1970), "The Multivariate Analysis of Qualitative Data: Interactions Among Multiple Classifications," *Journal of the American Statistical Association,* 65 (March), 226-256.

——— (1971), "The Analysis of Multidimensional Contingency Tables: Stepwise Procedures and Direct Estimation Methods for Building Models for Multiple Classifications," *Technometrics,* 13 (February), 33-61.

——— (1972), "A Modified Multiple Regression Approach to the Analysis of Dichotomous Variables," *American Sociological Review,* 37 (February), 28-46.

Green, Paul E. (1978), "An AID/Logit Procedure for Analyzing Large Multiway Contingency Tables," *Journal of Marketing Research,* 15 (February), 132-136.

———, Frank J. Carmone, and David P. Wachspress (1977), "On the Analysis of Qualitative Data in Marketing Research," *Journal of Marketing Research,* 14 (February), 52-59.

Lachin, John (1973), "On a Stepwise Procedure for Two Population Bayes Decision Rules Using Discrete Variables," *Biometrics,* 29 (September), 551-564.

Light, R. J. and B.H. Margolin (1971), "An Analysis of Variance for Categorical Data," *Journal of the American Statistical Association,* 66 (September), 534-544.

Sonquist, John A. (1970), *Multivariate Model Building.* Ann Arbor, MI: Survey Research Center, University of Michigan.

Wind, Yoram (1978), "Issues and Advances in Segmentation Research," *Journal of Marketing Research,* 15 (August), 317-337.

JOHN R. HAUSER and FRANK S. KOPPELMAN *

Perceptual mapping is widely used in marketing to analyze market structure, design new products, and develop advertising strategies. This article presents theoretical arguments and empirical evidence which suggest that factor analysis is superior to discriminant analysis and similarity scaling with respect to predictive ability, managerial interpretability, and ease of use.

Alternative Perceptual Mapping Techniques: Relative Accuracy and Usefulness

Perceptual mapping has been used extensively in marketing. This powerful technique is used in new product design, advertising, retail location, and many other marketing applications where the manager wants to know (1) the basic cognitive dimensions consumers use to evaluate "products" in the category being investigated and (2) the relative "positions" of present and potential products with respect to those dimensions. For example, Green and Wind (1973) use similarity scaling to identify the basic dimensions used in conjoint analysis. Pessemier (1977) applies discriminant analysis to produce the joint-space maps that are used in his DESIGNR model for new product design. Hauser and Urban (1977) use factor analysis to identify consumer perceptions and innovation opportunities in their method for modeling consumer response to innovation. All of these researchers report empirical applications in a number of product and service categories. When used correctly perceptual mapping can identify opportunities, enhance creativity, and direct marketing strategy to the areas of investigation most likely to appeal to consumers.

Perceptual mapping has received much attention in the literature. Though varied in scope and application, this attention has been focused on refinements of the techniques, comparison of alternative ways to use the techniques, or application of the techniques to marketing problems.[1] Few direct comparisons have been made of the three major techniques—similarity scaling, factor analysis, and discriminant analysis. In fact, most of the interest has been in similarity scaling because of the assumption that similarity measures are more accurate measures of perception than direct attribute ratings despite the fact that similarity techniques are more difficult and more expensive to use than factor or discriminant analyses.

In practice, a market researcher has neither the time nor the money to simultaneously apply all three techniques. He/she usually selects one method and uses it to address a particular marketing problem. The market researcher must decide whether the added insight from similarity scaling is worth the added expense in data collection and analysis. Furthermore, if the market researcher selects an attribute-based method such as factor analysis or discriminant analysis he/she wants to know which method is better for perceptual mapping and how such maps compare with

*John R. Hauser is Assistant Professor of Marketing, Graduate School of Management, and Frank S. Koppelman is Associate Professor of Civil Engineering and Transportation, Technological Institute, Northwestern University.

The authors thank Bruce Bagamery, Yosy Prashker, Steve Shugan, and Ken Wisniewski for their extensive technical assistance. Richard Johnson, Dennis Gensch, William Moore, Edgar Pessemier, Glen Urban, Paul Green, Allan Shocker, Subrata Sen, Brian Sternthal, Lou Stern, Steven Lerman, and Philip Kotler provided useful comments, criticisms, and suggestions.

The data for the study were collected under a University Research Grant, DOT-OS-4001, from the U.S. Department of Transportation, Peter Stopher and Peter Watson, principal investigators. The authors thank the Transportation Center at Northwestern University for the use of these data.

[1]See for example Best (1976), Cort and Dominguez (1977), Day, Deutscher, and Ryans (1976), Etgar (1977), Gensch and Golob (1975), Green and Carmone (1969), Green, Carmone, and Wachspress (1977), Green and Rao (1972), Green and Wind (1973), Hauser and Urban (1977), Heeler, Whipple, and Hustad (1977), Jain and Pinson (1976), Johnson (1970, 1971), Pessemier (1977), Singston (1975), Summers and MacKay (1976), Urban (1975), and Whipple (1976).

Reprinted from *Journal of Marketing Research,* 16 (November 1979), 495-506, published by the American Marketing Association.

those from similarity scaling. To answer these questions, one must compare the alternative mapping techniques.

One way to compare these techniques is theoretically. Each technique has theoretical strengths and weaknesses and the choice of technique depends on how consumers actually react to the alternative measurement tasks. Theoretical hypotheses are established in the next section.

Another comparison approach is Monté Carlo simulation. This useful investigative tool has been employed by researchers to explore variations in similarity scaling and other techniques (Carmone, Green and Jain 1978; Cattin and Wittink 1976; Pekelman and Sen 1977). In perceptual mapping Monté Carlo simulation can compare the ability of various techniques to reproduce a hypothesized perceptual map, but it requires that the researcher assume a basic cognitive structure of the individual. Monté Carlo simulation leaves unanswered the empirical question of whether the analytic technique can adequately describe and predict an actual consumer's cognitive structure.

The comparison procedure we use is practical and is based on theoretical arguments and empirical analyses to identify which procedures yield results most useful for marketing research decisions. If the theoretical arguments are supported, researchers can continue to subject a technique to empirical tests in alternative product categories. In this way, one gains insight about the techniques by learning their strengths and weaknesses. If and when the hypotheses are falsified new theories will emerge.

We chose the following guidelines for the comparison.

1. The marketing research environment should be representative of the way the techniques are used empirically.
2. The sample size and data collection should be large enough to avoid exploiting random occurrences and should have no relative bias in favor of the techniques identified as superior.
3. The use of the techniques should parallel as closely as possible the recommended and common usage.
4. The criteria of evaluation should have managerial and research relevance.

To fulfill these criteria, we chose an estimation sample and a saved data sample of 500 consumers each, drawn from residents of Chicago's northern suburbs. The application area is perceptions of the attractiveness of shopping areas in the northern suburbs and the criteria are the ability to predict consumer preference and choice, interpretability of the solutions, and ease of use.

HYPOTHESES: THEORETICAL COMPARISON

We begin with a brief synopsis of the techniques. Because this synopsis is not a complete mathematical description, we have indicated the appropriate references.

Similarity scaling develops measures of consumers' perceptions from consumer judgments with respect to the relative similarity between pairs of products. Though consumers are asked to judge similarity between products, the definition of similarity usually is left unspecified. The statistical techniques select relative values for two, three, or four perceptual dimensions such that distance between products best corresponds to measured similarity. Green and Rao (1972) and Green and Wind (1973) provide mathematical details.

For empirical studies with large sample sizes, common space representations are developed such that each consumer's i perception $\tilde{x}_{ijd}$ of product j along dimension d is a "stretching" of the common representation $\tilde{x}_{jd}$. The technique, INDSCAL (Carroll and Chang 1970), simultaneously estimates the common space $\tilde{x}_{jd}$ for all i and estimates individual weights v_{id} to "stretch" these dimensions. Effectively, $\tilde{x}_{ijd} = v_{id}^{1/2}\, \tilde{x}_{jd}$. For details see Carroll and Chang (1970).

The dimensions are named by judgment or by a regression-like procedure called PROFIT (Carroll and Chang 1964). In PROFIT, consumers are asked to rate each product on specific attributes, e.g., "atmosphere" for shopping centers. The ratings are dependent variables in a regression (possibly monotonic) on the perception measures, $\tilde{x}_{ijd}$, which serve as explanatory variables. The regression weights, called directional cosines, indicate how strongly each perception measure relates to each attribute rating. For details see Carroll and Chang (1964).

Factor analysis begins with the attribute ratings. The assumption is that there are really a few basic perceptual dimensions, x_{ijd}. Many of the attribute ratings are related to each perceptual dimension. Factor analysis examines the correlations among the attributes to identify these basic dimensions. For statistical details see Harmon (1967) and Rummel (1970). Because concern is with the basic structure of perception, the correlations between attribute ratings are computed across products and consumers (sum over i and j). The perceptions of products are measured by "factor scores" which are based on the attribute ratings. The dimensions are named by examining "factor loadings" which are estimates of the correlations between attribute ratings and perception measures. In applications, attribute ratings are first standardized by individual to minimize scale bias.

Discriminant analysis also begins with the attribute ratings, but rather than examining the structure of attribute correlations, discriminant analysis selects the (linear) combinations of attributes that best discriminate between products. See Cooley and Lohnes (1971) and Johnson (1970) for mathematical details. Because concern is with the ability to differentiate products, the dependent measure is "product rated" and the explanatory variables are the attribute ratings. The analysis is run across consumers to find a common structure. The perceptions are measured by "discriminant scores" which are estimates, based on the attribute ratings, of the perceptual dimensions, $\tilde{x}_{ijd}$, that best distinguish products. The dimensions are named by examining "discriminant scores" which are the weightings of the attributes that make up a discriminant dimension or by computing correlations that are equivalent to factor loadings. In applications, the discriminant dimensions are constrained to be uncorrelated (also called orthogonal).

Comparison of Similarity Scaling and Attribute-Based Techniques

A major difference between similarity scaling and the attribute-based techniques is the consumer task from which the perceptual measures are derived. Attribute ratings are more direct measures of perceptions than similarity judgments, but may be incomplete if the set of ratings is not carefully developed. Similarity judgments introduce an intermediate construct (similarity) but the judgments are made with respect to the actual product rather than specific attribute scales. *A priori,* if the set of attributes is relatively complete there is no theoretical reason to favor one measure over the other.

Another difference is the treatment of variation among consumers. In the attribute-based techniques a common structure is assumed, but the values of individual measures (x_{ijd} or x_{ijd}') are not restricted. In similarity scaling (INDSCAL) $\tilde{x}_{ijd}$ is restricted to be at most a stretching of the common measure, $\tilde{x}_{jd}$. This means that although complete reversals are allowed, no other change in rank order is allowed. For example, INDSCAL will not allow one consumer to evaluate relative sweetness in the order Pepsi, Coke, Royal Crown while another evaluates sweetness as Coke, Royal Crown, Pepsi. This restriction limits the applicability of the similarity scaling.

Finally, similarity scaling is limited by the number of products. At least seven or eight are needed for maps in two or three dimensions (Klahr 1969). There are no such restrictions for factor analysis. The restriction for discriminant analysis is the number of products minus one. This argument favors attribute-based techniques if the number of products in a consumer's evoked set is small; it favors neither technique if the number of products is large. In practice, the evoked set averages about three products (Silk and Urban 1978).

On the basis of these arguments, if the attribute set is reasonably complete, attribute-based techniques should provide better measures of consumer perception than similarity scaling (as implemented by INDSCAL).

Comparison of Factor Analysis and Discriminant Analysis

Factor analysis is based on the correlations across consumers *and* products. Discriminant analysis is limited to dimensions that, on average, distinguish among products. Thus factor analysis should use more attributes than discriminant analysis in the dimensions and therefore produce richer solutions. For example, consider Mercedes Benz and Rolls Royce. Suppose that the true perceptual dimensions are country of origin and reliability and that only reliability affects preference and choice. Suppose that perceptions of country of origin differ among products. Suppose that average perceptions of reliability are the same for both cars but individual perceptions differ among consumers. Discriminant analysis will identify only country of origin. Factor analysis will identify both dimensions.

On the basis of this type of argument, one expects factor analysis to provide a richer perceptual structure than discriminant analysis. It should be able to use more of the attribute ratings and should identify perceptual dimensions that predict preference and choice better than discriminant analysis dimensions.

EMPIRICAL SETTING: SHOPPING LOCATIONS

The empirical setting is north suburban Chicago and the "product" category is overall image of shopping locations, an increasingly important area of investigation in marketing. From the perspective of retailers, shopping center managers, and community planners, the sensitivity of destination choice behavior to the image or attractiveness of the shopping location provides an important opportunity to develop strategies to attract shoppers.

In terms of an empirical comparison of perceptual techniques, shopping location choice provides a strong test of the model's explanatory and predictive capabilities. Shopping location choice is a complex phenomenon, difficult to model and difficult to understand. If a perceptual technique does well in this category, it is likely to do well in a less complex category. (The complexity of the category should introduce no *relative* bias in the model comparisons.)

We develop models based on seven shopping areas including downtown Chicago and six suburban shopping centers of very different characteristics. The locations represent the types of shopping locations available to the residents of the suburbs north of Chicago including large, medium, and small shopping areas with exclusive, general merchandise, or discount orientations.

The data were collected by a self-administered questionnaire. (For details see Stopher, Watson, and Blin 1974.) The attributes were measured by 16 five-point rating scales chosen in an attempt to get as complete a list as possible without causing consumer wearout. (They were selected and refined on the basis of literature reviews, preliminary surveys, and qualitative research.) The similarity judgments were measured by pairwise comparisons on a seven-point scale. The respondent judged all pairs of the products in his/her evoked set (measured by a knowledge question). Table 1 contains example instructions for the attribute ratings and similarity judgments.

The dependent measures for predictive testing were obtained in the same survey. Choice was self-reported frequency of visits. Preference, also called "attractiveness," was rank-order preference in which availability/accessibility was held constant. (Pretests indicated consumers were comfortable with this task.) Availability/accessibility was measured as map distance from the consumer's residence to the shopping location. The model (explained in the next section) was drawn from the retailing and transportation literature and is given as follows.

Perceptions ⟶ Preference ⟶ Frequency of Visits
Availability / Accessibility ↗

This two-stage model allows managers and researchers to measure the "attractiveness" of a shopping center independently of its location. Thus one can readily investigate strategies, such as improving the atmosphere of a shopping center, that may be more cost effective than relocation strategies. This ability is especially useful when relocation is not an option as is the case in many downtown shopping areas.

In the original data set, 37,500 mailback questionnaires were distributed at four of the shopping locations. Of these, 6,000 were returned as complete and usable questionnaires. Although this low return rate may cause some nonresponse bias, the bias should not affect relative comparisons. Because similarity scaling requires at least seven stimuli, the data were screened to select those consumers who indicated

Table 1
EXAMPLE QUESTIONS FOR ATTRIBUTE SCALES AND SIMILARITY JUDGMENTS

In this question, we would like you to rate each of the shopping centers on these characteristics. We have provided a range from good to poor for each characteristic. We would like you to tell us where *you* feel each shopping center fits on this range.

For example:

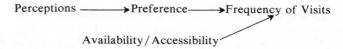

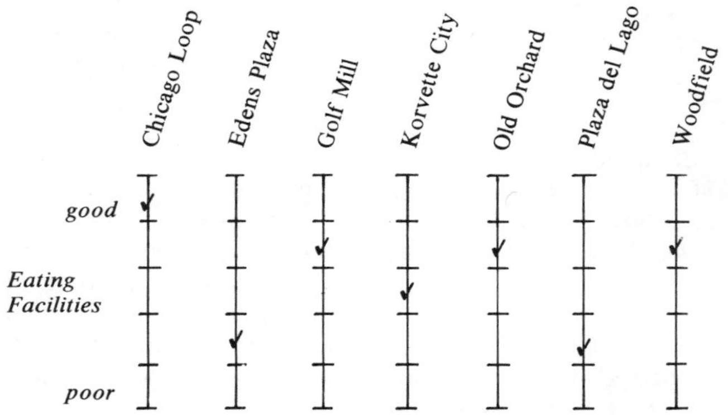

RATINGS OF THE ATTRIBUTES OF SHOPPING LOCATIONS

Again, if all the shopping centers were equally easy to get to, how similar do you think they are to each other? In answering this question, please think about your preference to shop at them for the goods you came to buy. Check the box which best describes how similar they are. Please be sure to do this for *all* pairs of shopping centers.

			Completely similar (identical) 1	2	3	4	5	6	Completely different 7
Woodfield	*and*	*Chicago Loop*	[ ]	[ ]	[ ]	[ ]	[ ]	[ ]	[ ]
Edens Plaza	*and*	*Golf Mill*	[ ]	[ ]	[ ]	[ ]	[ ]	[ ]	[ ]
Woodfield	*and*	*Plaza del Lago*	[ ]	[ ]	[ ]	[ ]	[ ]	[ ]	[ ]

SIMILARITY JUDGMENTS

knowledge of and who rated all seven stimuli (1,600 consumers). Any bias introduced by this screening should favor similarity scaling and thus favor falsifying our hypotheses. Finally, 500 of these consumers were randomly selected for an estimation sample and 500 others for saved data testing.

One source of bias is that samples were taken at four locations but judgments were made for seven locations. This sampling technique should produce no bias in the relative predictive ability of the perceptual techniques but could bias the coefficients in the preference and choice models. Fortunately, this bias can be corrected with choice-based sampling (CBS) estimation procedures. Manski and Lerman (1977) give theoretical proofs and Lerman and Manski (1976) provide intuitive arguments. To test CBS empirically for the data, parallel analyses were performed using only the four sampled shopping locations. Consistent with the theory, all models were statistically equivalent. Koppelman and Hauser (1977) give details of these comparisons.

EMPIRICAL PROCEDURE

So that other researchers can replicate the tests, we describe in this section how the measures were developed. In selecting procedures an attempt was made to follow common and recommended usage as closely as possible. When potential variations occurred (rotation vs. nonrotation, direct vs. indirect similarities, three vs. four dimensions) sensitivity tests were performed.

Similarity Scaling

Pairwise similarities were changed to rank order similarities and input to INDSCAL. Three dimensions were selected on the basis of an elbow in stress values. Four dimensions were not possible with the limited number of products.

Factor Analysis

The attributes were standardized by individual. Correlations were computed across consumers and products. Four dimensions were selected by using elbow and interpretability criteria on the common factor solution with varimax rotation. Limited testing was done with three dimensions for comparability to similarity scaling.

Discriminant Analysis

The attributes were standardized by individual. A discriminant analysis was run with the product rated as the dependent variable and the 16 attributes as explanatory variables. The elbow rule and significance statistics suggested at least three dimensions (97.5% of trace), possibly four because the chi square test was still significant. Most analyses were done with four dimensions although limited analyses were done with three dimensions. Varimax rotation improved the interpretations slightly. Dimensions are constrained to be orthogonal.

Preference

The linear compensatory form was chosen because of its widespread use in marketing (Wilkie and Pessemier 1973), because Monté Carlo simulation has shown it reasonably representative of more complex forms such as disjunctive, conjunctive, and additive (Carmone, Green, and Jain 1978), and because many of the nonlinear models such as conjoint analysis (Green and Srinivasan 1978, Green and Wind 1975) require (more intensive) personal interviews rather than the mailback format used by Stopher, Watson, and Blin (1974).

Mathematically, this model is given by:

$$p_{ij} \sim \sum_{l=1}^{m} w_l d_{ijl} \qquad (1)$$

where p_{ij} is individual i's rank for product j, $\sim$ indicates monotonic, d_{ijl} is i's perception of j along the lth dimension, and w_l is the importance weight of the lth dimension. (For similarity scaling $d_{ijl} \equiv \tilde{x}_{ijd}$, for factor analysis $d_{ijl} \equiv x_{ijd}$, for discriminant analysis $d_{ijl} \equiv x'_{ijd}$.)

Because there is a possibility that any single preference estimation procedure for the w_l's will favor one or another perceptual model, two estimation procedures were simultaneously tested: preference regression and first preference logit. Preference regression is a metric technique which replaces monotonicity ($\sim$) by equality ($=$) and uses ordinary least squares with equation 1. First preference logit is a monotonic technique based on estimating the probability that a consumer will rank a product as first preference. In logit, maximum likelihood techniques are used to determine w_l. For a more complete description, see McFadden (1970). In both models, choice-based sampling variables are used to provide consistent estimates of w_l (Manski and Lerman 1977).

Choice

The multinomial logit model is used to predict choice. (The logit model is based on a probabilistic interpretation of choice. For estimation and prediction equations, see McFadden 1970.) The dependent variable is frequency of visits and the explanatory variables are distance and estimated preference, $\hat{p}_{ij}$, where $\hat{p}_{ij}$ is generated by equation 1 and the estimates, $\hat{w}_l$, of the importance weights. That is, $\hat{p}_{ij} = \Sigma_l \hat{w}_l d_{ijl}$.

Finally, we chose to test the assumption of a two-stage model by using a revealed preference logit model. The dependent variable was frequency and the explanatory variables were distance and the perceptual measures, d_{ijl}. Choice-based sampling variables were included for consistent estimates.

Saved Data Predictions

One begins with the standardized attribute ratings and similarity judgments from the saved data sample. Factor score coefficients from the estimation sample and the attribute ratings from the saved data are used to create factor scores, x_{ijd} (see Rummel 1970). Discriminant score coefficients from the estimation sample and the attribute ratings from the saved data are used to create discriminant scores, x_{ijd}' (see Cooley and Lohnes 1971). INDSCAL is run on the saved data similarity judgments to create similarity scores, $\tilde{x}_{ijd}$. If anything, this procedure should favor similarity scaling. Indeed, an alternative procedure of generating the similarity scores from the attribute ratings provided poorer predictive results for similarity scaling and thus is even stronger support for the hypotheses.

For each combination of models (perception, preference, choice) the estimated importance weights, $\hat{w}_l$, from the estimation sample are applied to the d_{ijl}'s to create $\hat{p}_{ij}$. These are rank ordered and compared with the actual p_{ij}. The estimated relative weights of $\hat{p}_{ij}$ and distance then are used (with the relevant logit equation) to estimate the relative frequency of visits. These predictions are compared with reported frequency of visits.

Predictive Tests

Preference prediction was measured by the percentage of consumers who ranked first the shopping center that the model predicted as first. This measure is straightforward and is commonly reported in the literature.

Choice prediction is more difficult to measure. First, the models predict the probability of choice which must be compared with frequency of choice. This problem is resolved by using percentage uncertainty which is an information theoretic statistic that measures the percentage of uncertainty (entropy) explained by the probabilistic model (see Hauser 1978; McFadden 1970; Silk and Urban 1978). The second problem arises because both accessibility and the perceptual dimensions (through preference) are used to predict choice. Only the incremental gains in uncertainty due to the perceptual measures are of interest. Because the information measure is additive, we use the gain in percentage uncertainty achieved by adding the perceptual dimensions to a model based on distance alone.

Other measures including rank order preference recovery, percentage of consumers choosing the maximum probability shopping location, and mean absolute error in market share prediction are not reported here because each of these measures ranked the perceptual model *in the same relative order* as do the reported measures. For these statistics see Koppelman and Hauser (1977).

EMPIRICAL RESULTS

Predictive Tests

The results of the predictive tests are reported in Table 2. Preference recovery was not computed for revealed preference logit which is estimated directly on choice. Table 2 also reports preference and choice prediction for models using distance and the 16 standardized attribute scales as explanatory variables. These statistics are computed to examine whether the perceptual dimensions provide more or less information than a full set of attribute ratings.

To better understand Table 2, it is useful to consider some base level values. The maximum value for preference recovery is 100%, but most empirical models do not obtain values even near 100%. Rather these measures should be compared with that attainable by purely random assignment, i.e., all locations equally likely to be chosen, and that attainable by assigning consumers to shopping centers in proportion to market share. These values are 14.3% preference recovery for the equally likely model and 26.7% preference recovery for the market share model. Rigorous statistical tests are not applicable in comparing one perceptual technique with another because the preference models are based on different explanatory variables. But, intuitively, differences in preference recovery can be compared via the maximum standard deviation, 2.2, which would result under the assumption that for a given model each observation (consumer) has an equal probability of being correctly classified.

The significance of the choice models can be tested because the uncertainty explained is proportional to a chi square statistic (Hauser 1978). All models are significant at the .01 level.[2] The chi square's cutoff, which is less than 0.4, can also be taken as an intuitive measure in comparing the alternative perceptual techniques.

First examine the predictive tests. Factor analysis is superior to similarity scaling and discriminant analysis for all preference models and both prediction measures. This evidence supports the hypotheses. These results are particularly significant because any incompleteness in the attribute scales would favor similarity scaling over discriminant analysis and factor analysis. Furthermore, the sample was screened to favor similarity scaling.

The fact that factor analysis does well in comparison with models based on attribute scales indicates that

[2] After frequency adjustment, $2N$ * relative percentage uncertainty is a chi square statistic if the null model, i.e., distance alone, is a special case of the tested model, i.e., perceptions and distance. The degrees of freedom equals the difference in the number of variables. For the three similarity dimensions the cutoff is .031. For the other models which contain four dimensions, the cutoff is .037.

Table 2
PREDICTIVE TESTS[a]

	Goodness of fit tests		Saved data tests	
	Preference recovery	*% uncertainty explained (choice)*	*Preference recovery*	*% uncertainty explained (choice)*
Similarity scaling				
Preference regression	36.6	0.9	23.1	−32.4
1st preference logit	34.8	1.1	22.7	−41.3
Revealed preference logit	—	1.5	—	−69.5
Factor analysis				
Preference regression	50.6	3.8	47.3	4.3
1st preference logit	55.0	4.7	50.8	5.3
Revealed preference logit	—	5.9	—	6.0
Discriminant analysis				
Preference regression	35.5	1.7	38.1	1.9
1st preference logit	35.3	1.9	40.3	2.0
Revealed preference logit	—	2.9	—	3.0
Attribute scales				
Preference regression	39.6	3.2	41.4	−3.9
1st preference logit	55.6	5.2	51.6	6.4
Revealed preference logit	—	6.6	—	6.9

[a]The preference test is ability to recover first preference, the choice test is percentage of uncertainty explained relative to a model with distance alone. To get total uncertainty, add 32.6 to these measures. All uncertainty measures are significant at the .01 level.

very little information is lost by using the reduced factors rather than the full set of attributes. The poor showing of preference regression on the attribute scales is the result of multicollinearity. The poor showing of discriminant analysis in relation to the attribute scales supports the hypothesis that concentrating on variations between products neglects dimensions that are important in preference and choice.

Next, examine the saved data test. Factor analysis is still superior to both discriminant analysis and similarity scaling. Both of the attribute-based measures hold up well. The small improvement in the statistics may be attributed to random variation between data sets. Similarity scaling predicts poorly on saved data, doing worse than the naïve model which assigns consumers proportional to market share (26.7% preference recovery). The model does so poorly in relation to distance alone that it adds large amounts of uncertainty (negative uncertainty explained) in choice prediction.

Thus the saved data tests support the hypotheses.

Table 2 is one empirical comparison. Replications, sensitivity, and threats to validity are examined in the next section, but first a more qualitative analysis is used to determine whether these comparisons are consistent with managerial interpretations of the techniques.

Interpretability

First examine how the perceptual dimensions from each technique relate to the attribute scales. These relationships are reported in Table 3. The underlined numbers (directional cosines, factor loadings, or discriminant coefficients) indicate a strong relationship between the underlined attribute (row) and the dimension (column). The dimension names are composites of the underlined attributes.

Despite marked superficial similarities, the different models demonstrate striking differences in interpretation. Factor analysis uses all the attribute scales whereas discriminant analysis uses only 10 of the 16 scales, and only five of those 10 have discriminant scores greater than 0.5. This outcome is consistent with the theoretical hypothesis that concentrating on variance between products neglects information. Note also that the third discriminant dimension, "value vs. satisfaction," is a mixed dimension positively related to value but negatively related to satisfaction. Compare this to the factor analysis solution which has no positive/negative mixed dimension. This difference probably arises because value and satisfaction may be negatively correlated among existing shopping locations (discriminant analysis) but not in the way consumers rate these locations (factor analysis).

These differences are important to the manager who wants as much control over the market as possible. For example, many of the variables left out of the discriminant solution (e.g., "layout of the store," "return and service," "sales assistants") could be affected by relatively low-cost changes in shopping center operation. Because discriminant analysis uses fewer variables the manager can analyze fewer strate-

Table 3
STRUCTURAL COMPARISON OF PERCEPTUAL MODELS

FACTOR ANALYSIS—FACTOR LOADINGS

Fundamental attributes	Variety	Quality and satisfaction	Value	Parking
1. Layout of store	.267	.583	.156	.200
2. Return and service	.095	.528	.343	.255
3. Prestige of store	.338	.822	−.001	−.058
4. Variety of merchandise	.665	.327	.309	−.185
5. Quality of merchandise	.307	.810	.037	−.074
6. Availability of credit	.159	.337	.487	.049
7. Reasonable price	.067	−.063	.599	.113
8. "Specials"	.223	.074	.739	.008
9. Free parking	−.15	.068	.043	.811
10. Center layout	.03	.308	.074	.560
11. Store atmosphere	.080	.658	.034	.400
12. Parking available	.145	.105	.108	.841
13. Center atmosphere	.244	.694	.040	.404
14. Sales assistants	.173	.561	.147	.319
15. Store availability	.619	.320	.204	.034
16. Variety of stores	.829	.288	.160	−.173

DISCRIMINANT ANALYSIS—DISCRIMINANT COEFFICIENTS

Fundamental attributes	Variety	Quality and satisfaction	Value vs. satisfaction	Parking
1. Layout of store	.067	−.110	−.085	−.023
2. Return and service	−.094	.254	.287	.134
3. Prestige of store	.156	.366	−.318	−.137
4. Variety of merchandise	.335	.153	.295	−.042
5. Quality of merchandise	−.196	1.114	.020	−.216
6. Availability of credit	−.008	.170	.352	.025
7. Reasonable price	−.108	−.008	.586	−.009
8. "Specials"	−.101	−.171	.225	−.115
9. Free parking	.065	−.066	−.007	1.714
10. Center layout	−.065	−.233	−.334	.082
11. Store atmosphere	−.158	.087	−.055	−.053
12. Parking available	−.288	−.020	.018	.171
13. Center atmosphere	.109	−.123	−.510	.284
14. Sales assistants	−.138	.015	−.168	−.084
15. Store availability	.089	.035	.084	−.065
16. Variety of stores	1.291	−.123	−.022	.145

SIMILARITY SCALING-DIRECTIONAL COSINES

Fundamental attributes	Variety and value	Quality vs. value	Parking and satisfaction
1. Layout of store	.217	.497	.840
2. Return and service	.318	.122	.940
3. Prestige of store	.297	.804	.515
4. Variety of merchandise	.929	.360	.084
5. Quality of merchandise	.295	.811	−.505
6. Availability of credit	.880	−.085	−.468
7. Reasonable price	.485	−.853	.192
8. "Specials"	.786	−.594	.173
9. Free parking	−.294	−.550	.782
10. Center layout	−.447	.036	.894
11. Store atmosphere	−.199	.452	.869
12. Parking available	−.463	−.478	.747
13. Center atmosphere	−.099	.480	.872
14. Sales assistants	−.052	.411	.910
15. Store availability	.872	.429	−.236
16. Variety of stores	.921	.385	−.054

gies. Also, because of the mixed dimension it is difficult to evaluate strategies that increase both satisfaction and value.

Comparing factor analysis with similarity scaling, one again sees a mixed dimension, "quality vs. value," but the similarity scaling solution uses all 16 attributes. This mixed dimension probably results from the INDSCAL assumption which concentrates on differences between products at the expense of variations in consumer perceptions. But in this case the "quality vs. value" is easier to understand and operate on than "satisfaction vs. value."

Thus, of the three models, factor analysis has the most managerially useful structure. Because all models have strong face validity and all use the basic five constructs—variety, quality, satisfaction, value, and

Figure 1
COMPARISON OF PERCEPTUAL MAPS

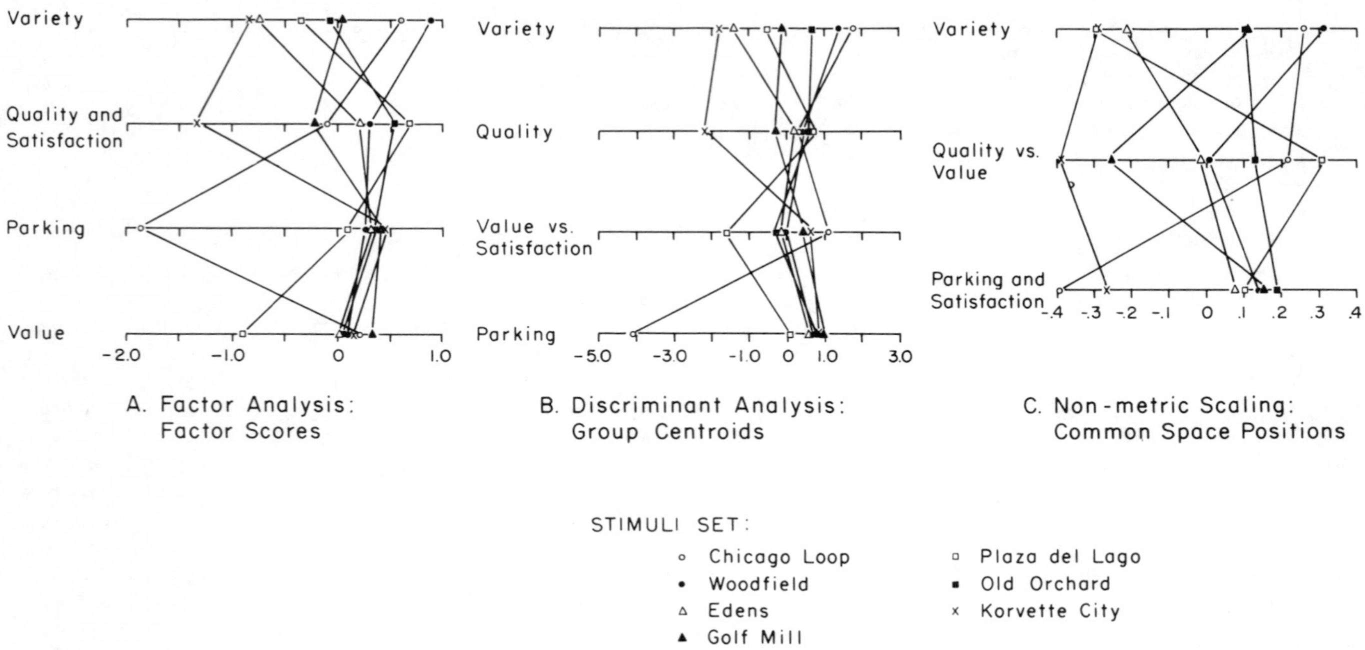

parking—we believe that the predictive and saved data superiority of factor analysis is due to better structure in identifying dimensions.

The second test of interpretability is the visual maps produced by each method (see Figure 1). These maps help managers identify how each shopping location is "positioned" in the marketplace. Thus a manager can know the relative strengths and weaknesses of each shopping location and can identify opportunities in the market.

Careful inspection of Figure 1 shows consistency among the models when the measured constructs are the same. For example, note the low scores for Korvette City on quality (satisfaction) and for Chicago Loop on parking or the high scores for Woodfield on variety and for Plaza del Lago on quality (satisfaction). These and many other "positionings" have strong face validity and are consistent with prior beliefs about the images of the seven shopping locations. But there is an important difference. Factor analysis is better for strategy development because it separates the dimensions in such a way that ambiguous interpretations ("quality vs. value" and "satisfaction vs. value") are avoided.

Ease of Use

A final consideration is the investment in analysis time required by the techniques. Managers and researchers may be willing to accept more approximate models if the approximations allow great cost savings. Our experience indicates that the attribute-based techniques are relatively easy to use whereas similarity scaling is somewhat more difficult with respect to both data collection and data analysis. Both factor and discriminant analyses use only the attribute ratings whereas similarity scaling requires, in addition, judged similarities which can be a difficult consumer task. Once the data have been collected, factor and discriminant analyses are readily available on standard statistical packages (e.g., BMDP, SPSS), cost[3] about \$10–20 to run, and require little professional time. In sharp contrast, the special programs for similarity scaling require many exploratory runs, special FORTRAN programs for data transfer, and a series of statistical manipulations and data handling to develop a common space, estimate individual weights, and compute directional cosines. A single set of runs costs about \$40 in computer time, but because various starting configurations and dimensions must be checked, the effective cost is about \$150. Though the added direct computer costs are acceptable, the programming and analysis require significant professional time and could be very costly to organizations not familiar with the programs.

[3]Costs vary by computer. These costs represent \$510 per cpu hour on a CDC 6400. See Dixon (1975) for BMDP and Nie et al. (1975) for SPSS.

Table 4
SUMMARY OF THE RESULTS OF EMPIRICAL COMPARISON[a]

Criteria	*Results*				
Theory	Factor analysis	>	Discriminant analysis	≥	Similarity scaling
Goodness of fit	Factor analysis	>	Discriminant analysis	~	Similarity scaling
Prediction (saved data)	Factor analysis	>	Discriminant analysis	>	Similarity scaling
Interpretation	Factor analysis	≥	Discriminant analysis	~	Similarity scaling
Ease of use	Factor analysis	~	Discriminant analysis	>	Similarity scaling

[a] > indicates superior, ≥ indicates probably superior, ~ indicates no major difference.

Summary

In this section representative attribute-based and similarity scaling techniques are compared to determine which perceptual mapping technique is most appropriate for marketing research applications. The empirical results, which support the hypotheses, suggest that the most popular technique, similarity scaling, may not be the best; rather, factor analysis may be better on predictability, interpretability, and ease of use (see Table 4). These results are subject to confirmation or qualification in other empirical applications but, at the very least, this empirical test raised issues worth further investigation by other marketing researchers.

THREATS TO VALIDITY, SENSITIVITY, AND REPLICATIONS

Empirical comparisons are difficult. Only by using the state of the art in each technique can one be fair to that technique. To attempt to extrapolate these comparisons, one must examine causes that threaten to make the results specific to the empirical sample.

Threats to Validity

Nonresponse bias, choice-based sampling, representativeness of the set of attributes, and screening on the seven stimuli in the evoked set have been discussed. They should introduce no relative bias favoring the hypotheses.

One threat to the hypotheses is potential halo effects in the attribute scales, i.e., the attribute scales may contain an affective as well as a cognitive component (Beckwith and Lehmann 1975). This threat is minimized by standardization of the attribute scales prior to analysis and by using attribute scles designed to measure only the cognitive component. Another threat is that the stimuli set contained at most seven products. Although this constraint is typical of real-world applications, it does suggest future comparisons with larger stimuli sets.

Sensitivity

The comparisons among techniques are found to remain consistent when limited changes are made in each technique. Rotation of discriminant solutions improved interpretability but not predictive ability (the rotated solution is reported). Use of indirect similarity measures did not improve either interpretability or predictive ability. The factor and discriminant analyses used four dimensions whereas similarity scaling was limited to three dimensions. Though this is a minor change in the degrees of freedom in the preference and choice models (490 vs. 489), it could have an effect. Limited testing showed that dropping the least significant dimension in the four-dimensional solutions caused very little shrinkage in prediction. (For example, with preference regression and discriminant analysis the shrinkage was about one-tenth of one percent in preference recovery.) Finally, use of alternative factor analysis solutions such as principal components or three-way analyses might improve prediction, but such improvement would only add support to the hypotheses.

Replications

Since the orignal study, the hypotheses have been tested on two other data sets. Using a sample of 120 graduate students, Simmie (1978 found preference recoveries of 67.4% for factor analysis, 51.9% for discriminant analysis, and 14.0% for similarity scaling. Simmie also found greater consistency across groups of students with factor analysis than with similarity scaling. Her product category was management schools. Using a random sample of Evanston residents, Englund, Hundt, and Lee (1978) found preference recoveries of 67.1% with factor analysis and 48.6% with discriminant analysis. Their product category was transportation mode choice (bus, walk, or car). The implications of both studies are consistent with our results.

IMPLICATIONS AND FUTURE RESEARCH

Perceptual mapping is an important marketing research tool used in new product planning, advertising development, product positioning, and many other areas of marketing. Strategies based on perceptual maps have led to increased profits, better market control, and more stable growth. Furthermore, much research is based on implications of market structure as identified by perceptual maps. Because of this interest and use, it is crucial that the best mapping technique available be employed in these applications.

We provide and support hypotheses that factor analysis is superior to both similarity scaling and discriminant analysis for developing measures of consumer perceptions. In particular, factor analysis is likely to be superior in categories where:

1. The number of products in the average consumer's evoked set is relatively small (seven stimuli or less).
2. There is variation in the way consumers perceive products in the category.
3. Qualitative research has identified a set of attributes likely to represent the product category.

The presence or absence of these characteristics does not ensure the superiority of one technique, but without evidence to the contrary they can serve as guidelines.

The results of this one theoretical and empirical comparison are hoped to raise the issue of and the need for continued research to identify whether factor analysis is always superior or, if not, under what conditions the alternative mapping techniques should be used.

Confirmation of these comparisons awaits replication in other categories. In addition, further exploration may be appropriate for other preference models. For example, nonlinear models such as conjoint analysis should theoretically order the perceptual models in the same way, but empirical tests are warranted. We have used disaggregate preference models, i.e., models based on individual consumers (p_{ij} rather than p_j, d_{ijk} rather than d_{jk} where i indexes consumers). In most applications these disaggregate models have proven superior to aggregate models which blur individual differences. Because aggregate models still are used in some marketing applications, these might be tested. For example, PREFMAP, which is a form of preference regression, can be used at both the aggregate (Pessemier 1977) and disaggregate level (Beckwith and Lehmann 1975). We hypothesize that because the superiority of factor analysis over discriminant analysis is based on individual differences, predictive comparisons might shift and discriminant analysis might do as well as factor analysis when analyses are limited to the aggregate level.

Other research might be of a more proactive nature, searching for improvements for the weaknesses of each technique. Theoretical developments might make it practical to relax the INDSCAL assumption. Further research could expand the similarity scaling solutions to more stimuli via use of concept statements. Segmentation on perceptions could be used prior to similarity scaling or discriminant analysis to ensure that there is little variation among consumers. These and other methodological developments are suggested by the examination and comparison of the alternative perceptual mapping techniques.

This area of comparative model development is important to marketing and deserves attention from marketing researchers.

REFERENCES

Beckwith, N. E. and D. R. Lehmann (1975), "The Importance of Halo Effects in Multi-Attribute Attitude Models," *Journal of Marketing Research,* 12 (August), 265–75.

Best, R. J. (1976), "The Predictive Aspects of a Joint Space Theory of Stochastic Choice," *Journal of Marketing Research,* 13 (May), 198–204.

Carmone, F. J., P. E. Green, and A. K. Jain (1978), "The Robustness of Conjoint Analysis: Some Monté Carlo Results," *Journal of Marketing Research,* 15 (May), 300–3.

Carroll, J. D. and J. J. Chang (1964), "A General Index of Nonlinear Correlation and Its Application to the Interpretation of Multidimensional Scaling Solutions," *American Psychologist,* 19.

——— and——— (1970), "Analysis of Individual Differences in Multidimensional Scaling via an N-way Generalization of the Eckart-Young Decomposition," *Psychometrika,* 35, 283–319.

Cattin, P. and D. R. Wittink (1976), "A Monté Carlo Study of Metric and Nonmetric Estimation Methods for Multiattribute Models," Research Paper No. 341, Graduate School of Business, Stanford University (November).

Cooley, W. W. and P. R. Lohnes (1971), *Multivariate Data Analysis.* New York: John Wiley & Sons, Inc.

Cort, S. G. and L. V. Dominguez (1977), "Cross Shopping and Retail Growth," *Journal of Marketing Research,* 14 (May), 187–92.

Day, G. S., T. Deutscher, and A. B. Ryans (1976), "Data Quality, Level of Aggregation, and Nonmetric Multidimensional Scaling Solutions," *Journal of Marketing Research,* 13 (February), 92–7.

Dixon, W. J. (1975), *BMDP: Biomedical Computer Programs.* Los Angeles: University of California Press.

Englund, D., F. Hundt, and Y. Lee (1978), "An Empirical Comparison of Factor Analysis and Discriminant Analysis for Non-Work Trips in Evanston," Technical Report, Transportation Center, Northwestern University (August).

Etgar, M. (1977), "Channel Environment and Channel Leadership," *Journal of Marketing Research,* 14 (February), 69–76.

Gensch, P. H. and T. F. Golob (1975), "Testing the Consistency of Attribute Meaning in Empirical Concept Testing," *Journal of Marketing Research,* 12 (August), 348–54.

Green, P. E. (1975), "On the Robustness of Multidimensional Scaling Techniques," *Journal of Marketing Research,* 12 (February), 73–81.

——— and F. J. Carmone (1969), "Multidimensional Scaling: An Introduction and Comparison of Nonmetric Unfolding Techniques," *Journal of Marketing Research,* 7 (August), 330–41.

———, ———, and D. D. Wachspress (1977), "On the Analysis of Qualitative Data in Marketing Research," *Journal of Marketing Research,* 14 (February), 52–9.

——— and V. Rao (1972), *Applied Multidimensional Scaling.* New York: Holt, Rinehart and Winston, Inc.

——— and V. Srinivasan (1978), "Conjoint Analysis in Consumer Behavior; Status and Outlook," *Journal of Consumer Research,* 5 (September), 103–23.

——— and Yoram Wind (1973), *Multiattribute Decisions in Marketing.* Hinsdale, Illinois: The Dryden Press.

——— and ——— (1975), "New Way to Measure Consumer's Judgments," *Harvard Business Review* (July–August).

Harmon, H. H. (1967), *Modern Factor Analysis.* Chicago: University of Chicago.

Hauser, J. R. (1978), "Testing the Accuracy, Usefulness, and Significance of Probabilistic Choice Models: An Information Theoretic Approach," *Operations Research,* 26 (May–June), 406–21.

——— and G. L. Urban (1977), "A Normative Methodology for Modeling Consumer Response to Innovation," *Operations Research,* 25 (July–August), 579–619.

Heeler, R. M., T. W. Whipple, and T. P. Hustad (1977), "Maximum Likelihood Factor Analysis of Attitude Data," *Journal of Marketing Research,* 14 (February), 42–51.

Jain, A. K. and C. Pinson (1976), "The Effect of Order of Presentation of Similarity Judgments on Multidimensional Scaling Results: An Empirical Comparison," *Journal of Marketing Research,* 13 (November), 435–9.

Johnson, R. M. (1971), "Market Segmentation: A Strategic Management Tool," *Journal of Marketing Research,* 8 (February), 13–18.

——— (1970), "Multiple Discriminant Analysis Applications to Marketing Research," Market Facts, Inc. (January).

Jolson, Marvin A. and Walter F. Spath (1973), "Understanding and Fulfilling Shoppers' Requirements," *Journal of Retailing,* 49 (Summer).

Klahr, David (1969), "A Monté Carlo Investigation of the Statistical Significance of Kruskal's Non-metric Scaling Procedure," *Psychometrika,* 34 (September), 319–30.

Koppelman, Frank S. and John Hauser (1977), "Consumer Travel Choice Behavior: An Empirical Analysis of Destination Choice for Non-Grocery Shopping Trips," Technical Report, Transportation Center, Northwestern University (March).

Lerman, S. R. and C. F. Manski (1976), "Alternative Sampling Procedure for Disaggregate Choice Model Estimation," *Transportation Research Record,* 592, Transportation Research Board.

MacKay, David B. and Richard W. Olshavsky (1975), "Cognitive Maps of Retail Locations; An Investigation of Some Basic Issues," *Journal of Consumer Research,* 2 (December).

Manski, C. F. and S. R. Lerman (1977), "The Estimation of Choice Probabilities from Choice Based Samples," *Econometrica,* 45 (November).

McFadden, Daniel (1970), "Conditional Logit Analysis of Qualitative Choice Behavior," in *Frontiers in Econometrics,* P. Zaremblea, ed. New York: Academic Press, 105–42.

Nie, N. H., G. H. Hull, J. G. Jenkins, K. Steinbrenner, and D. H. Bent (1975), *SPSS: Statistical Package for the Social Sciences,* 2nd edition. New York: McGraw-Hill Book Company.

Pekelman, D. and S. Sen (1977), "Improving Prediction in Conjoint Measurement," Working Paper, Graduate School of Management, University of Rochester (January).

Pessemier, E. A. (1977), *Product Management: Strategy and Organization.* New York: Wiley/Hamilton.

Rummel, R. J. (1970), *Applied Factor Analysis.* Evanston, Illinois: Northwestern University Press.

Silk, A. J. and G. L. Urban (1978), "Pretest Market Evaluation of New Packaged Goods: A Model and Measurement Methodology," *Journal of Marketing Research,* 15 (May), 171–91.

Simmie, Patricia (1978), "Alternative Perceptual Models: Reproducibility, Validity, and Data Integrity," *Proceedings* of the American Marketing Association Educators Conference, Chicago (August).

Singston, Ricardo (1975), "Multidimensional Scaling Analysis of Store Image and Shopping Behavior," *Journal of Retailing,* 51, 2.

Stopher, P. R., P. L. Watson, and J. J. Blin (1974), "A Method for Assessing Pricing and Structural Changes on Transport Mode Use," Interim Report to the Office of University Research, U.S. Department of Transportation, Transportation Center, Northwestern University (September).

Summers, J. O. and D. B. MacKay, (1976), "On the Validity and Reliability of Direct Similarity Judgments," *Journal of Marketing Research,* 13 (August), 289–95.

Urban, G. L. (1975), "PERCEPTOR: A Model for Product Positioning," *Management Science,* 8 (April), 858–71.

Whipple, T. W. (1976), "Variation Among Multidimensional Scaling Solutions: An Examination of the Effect of Data Collection Differences," *Journal of Marketing Research,* 13 (February), 98–103.

Wilkie, W. L. and E. A. Pessemier (1973), "Issues in Marketing's Use of Multi-Attribute Attitude Models," *Journal of Marketing Research,* 10 (November), 428–41.

ROGER M. HEELER, THOMAS W. WHIPPLE, and THOMAS P. HUSTAD*

Maximum likelihood factor analysis is a useful technique for analyzing attitude data. The solution can be tested statistically for goodness of fit. Companion procedures for restricting the factor solution permit the testing of hypothesized factor structures. Thus the technique can be used to construct solutions that are more clearly interpretable while still providing adequate fit to the data. A case example is given to illustrate the use of the technique.

Maximum Likelihood Factor Analysis of Attitude Data

INTRODUCTION

Exploratory factor analysis procedures have been used to analyze attitude data in marketing since about 1960. Typically, principal components analysis has been used to extract sequential factors which are rotated to enhance their interpretability. In performing the analysis, the investigator must decide on the number of factors to extract that will provide an adequate representation of the data.

Often this decision is subjective (a sudden drop in proportion of variance explained by an added factor) or is guided by a sound decision rule (eigenvalue must exceed 1.0), but more flexible tests are available. Bartlett [1] presents a statistic (approximately chi-square distributed) which permits testing the significance of roots remaining after the largest ones have been extracted. He stresses that statistical significance does not necessarily imply that a factor will account for a very large fraction of the variance. With large samples, a large number of statistically significant factors may result. Apart from "numeric" importance, there is also no guarantee that a significant factor has any theoretical basis. Alternatively, Horn [4] presents a procedure for estimating the degree to which the "real" latent roots have been inflated by sampling error. Roots obtained by analyzing normally distributed random data are compared with those from the "real" data. Factors are extracted for all roots that are greater than the corresponding root from the random data. This procedure is more restrictive than the "eigenvalue exceeding one" decision rule, which does not allow for sampling error.

Decisions concerning the number of factors to rotate, the nature of the rotation, and the termination of the rotation also must be made. Often the solution is orthogonally or obliquely rotated to obtain arbitrary "simple" structure. Because each rotated solution is not unique, but merely an alternative expression of the unrotated factors, it is difficult to know whether a reasonable depiction of the true underlying structure has been achieved. This issue becomes crucially important when the investigator is formulating hypotheses for future testing and eventual incorporation into a larger body of theory.

In exploratory analysis, the researcher imposes no restrictions on the data or analysis procedures. This condition is necessary if there is no body of relevant theory to be used as a guide. If there is prior theory, exploratory factor analysis procedures are not sufficient. Confirmatory analyses must be performed to test the appropriateness of a hypothesized model. As a first step, it may be useful for the researcher to assume control over the rotational process as an alternative to seeking an arbitrary simple solution. Available procrustean transformations [6, 17] permit linear transformation of a principal components solution into congruence with a hypothesized pattern. Jöreskog [9] developed a technique to use in fitting a specific simple structure based on a specification of zero coefficients of the reference pattern matrix.

There are alternatives to principal components anal-

*Roger M. Heeler, Thomas W. Whipple, and Thomas P. Hustad are Associate Professors of Marketing in the Faculty of Administrative Studies, York University. The writers thank John Pummel for his computing assistance, and the Associates Workshop, University of Western Ontario, for partial funding of the research.

Reprinted from *Journal of Marketing Research,* **14 (February 1977), 42-51, published by the American Marketing Association.**

ysis. Jöreskog was able to build on this work with procrustean transformations to obtain estimates of the parameters of maximum likelihood factor analysis (MLFA). These developments made hypothesis testing possible in factor analysis [17, p. 372]. In other words, MLFA permits further refinement of confirmatory factor analysis. Applications involving MLFA have been used increasingly in the social sciences [13, 15]. Statistical tests for goodness of fit are available and factor solutions can be restricted to provide tests of hypothesized factor structures. In contrast to principal components analysis, however, all estimates produced possess the desirable properties of maximum likelihood estimates, namely sufficiency and efficiency.

A discussion of the use of MLFA in the development of marketing theory follows. A case example is provided to highlight the use of the technique.

METHODOLOGY

Factor analysis is a series of procedures for summarizing the linear relationships among variables. The basic model is:

$$x = \Lambda f + e \tag{1}$$

where:

- x is a column vector of p variates,
- f is a vector of k common factors,
- e is a vector of p residuals, and
- Λ is a $p \times k$ matrix of factor loadings.

The objective is to summarize the information contained in the p variates in a parsimonious set of k factors. Thus, if a comprehensive set of variates is measured, factor analysis can be used to test for the existence of a smaller set of dimensions underlying the larger set of measurements.

The computational procedure commonly used in marketing applications of factor analysis is principal components analysis. The computational procedure used in this report is maximum likelihood factor analysis [14], which has the advantage of providing a χ^2 measure of fit of the reduced factor model to the raw data. An additional extension of the procedure, restricted maximum likelihood factor analysis, permits the testing of prespecified factor structures. This procedure only recently has been applied to marketing problems [2, 16].

Exploratory Factor Analysis

From the basic equation of factor analysis (1), a statistically testable relationship can be derived if it is assumed that: (1) the residuals e are independent of each other and of the common factors f and (2) the elements of f, e, and x are multivariate normally distributed with zero means. The relationship is:

$$\Sigma = \Lambda \Phi \Lambda' + \Psi \tag{2}$$

where the dispersion or covariance matrices of f, e, and x are denoted respectively by Φ, Ψ, and Σ. The assumption of multivariate normality is not necessary for exploratory factor analysis. Howe [5] showed that the maximum likelihood estimates could be derived from a model which made no assumptions about the distributions of the observed variables. Use of the statistical test does require, however, that the observed variables be multivariate normally distributed.

The information contained in S, an estimate of Σ derived from a random sample of observations of x, can be summarized in a log-likelihood function L. Efficient estimates (for large n) of all unknown parameters can be obtained by maximizing L with respect to the parameters. The maximization (actually conducted as a more convenient equivalent minimization) yields a constant which can be used as a χ^2 goodness-of-fit criterion. An efficient routine for performing the analysis was derived by Jöreskog and programmed as UMLFA (unrestricted maximum likelihood factor analysis). A computer program listing is provided in [8]. For exploratory factor analysis, it provides a series of factor solutions with varying dimensionality. In addition, the χ^2 statistic obtained from UMLFA assists in selecting the appropriate dimensionality [13]. Jöreskog [10] notes that the sequential testing for significance of added factors violates the rules of a probability measure and has the effect of compounding the alpha risk.

Confirmatory Factor Analysis

Restricted maximum likelihood factor analysis, programmed by Jöreskog and Gruvaeus as RMLFA, is an extension of maximum likelihood factor analysis which permits the experimenter to test a factor structure hypothesis. A computer listing is provided in [12]. The hypothesis must specify certain elements of Λ, Φ, and Ψ. In practice, values for Ψ seldom are specified. Φ usually is defined so that either its diagonal values are unity and other values are unspecified (oblique, correlated factor solution), or its diagonal values are unity and other values are zero (orthogonal solution). The fixed values for Λ usually are set at zero. This is equivalent to specifying which variables will not contribute to a particular factor. The free, unspecified values then, by analogue, become the hypothesized factor structure. Unlike the case of exploratory analysis (UMLFA), the distribution-free justification for maximum likelihood estimators may not exist. In other words, it has not been shown that the assumption of multivariate normality of observed variables can be relaxed (Jöreskog, cited in [17, p. 382-3]).

Thus the investigator can test an orthogonal or oblique factor solution with prespecified constraints that uniquely restrict the contribution of certain variables to certain factors. In some cases, these restrictions can be used to *clarify* a factor structure obtained by UMLFA or some other factor analytic procedure. The

χ^2 statistic provides an indication of the fit of the clarified structure to the data. In other cases, the investigator may wish to test explicitly whether a hypothesized structure is consistent with the data or even to make an explicit comparison of factor structures for different samples or sample partitions. In the extreme case when the researcher is guided by a considerable body of prior theory, it may be possible to fix all parameters of the RMLFA model and test the model for fit to the data. This would be confirmatory factor analysis rather than exploratory analysis which fixes few if any parameters.

In either case, the analytical focus of the iterative procedure is on building better theory. Figure 1 depicts how UMLFA and RMLFA can be used jointly to form, refine, and test hypotheses. A crucial part of the exploratory analysis involves clarifying the underlying structure in a way consistent with maintaining reasonable goodness of fit to the data. If hypotheses already are well formulated, the investigator can proceed directly to the validation stage.

There are several restrictions on the number and location of the values specified [12, 13]. Because RMLFA is not simply a rotational procedure, the specified values restrict the whole factor space, creating a unique solution. It is not possible to rotate an unrestricted solution into congruence with a uniquely derived solution. The restrictions typically affect the unique variance for each original variable and also (for oblique solutions) may affect the factor intercorrelations. Defining conditions leading to a unique

Figure 1
ILLUSTRATIVE METHODOLOGY FOR JOINT USE OF UMLFA AND RMLFA IN AN EXPLORATORY ANALYSIS

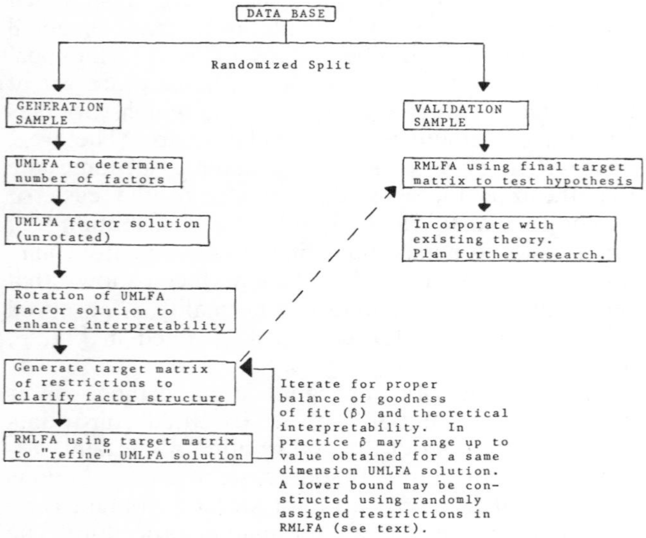

factor solution is not possible with principal components analysis. Hypothesis testing of a principal component solution is limited to various rotational or transformational procedures, a much less powerful approach.

There are certain theoretical advantages for restricting the factor analysis solution in advance. First, a researcher may wish to test his preconceptions about the structure of the data. Second, it would be possible to examine the data in light of relationships detected in other studies. Thus such restriction facilitates the desirable process of linking related studies together in a more unified body of knowledge. In general, both of these advantages of RMLFA relate to the ability to test hypotheses concerning the data rather than merely to observe an unrestricted solution. The third advantage is that, because a prior theoretical structure is imposed, the solution is less likely to be dominated by measurement problems that could cause spurious results.

Data Requirements

With the one exception discussed heretofore, the maximum likelihood method is based on the assumption that variables are multivariate normally distributed. The method therefore should not be used when the data indicate that one or more variables have non-normal distributions. Satisfying this assumption is often possible for sum score attitude scales. However, responses to single questionnaire items often are skewed, bimodal, or otherwise non-normal. Sometimes the assumption of normality still can be fulfilled by a transformation of the data. But in general, considerable caution should be exercised before single questionnaire items are used in maximum likelihood factor analysis. Failure to meet the assumption of multivariate normality may have substantial impact on the computation of the χ^2 statistic.

The Goodness-of-Fit Statistic

The χ^2 statistic indicates the goodness of fit between the factor model and the data. Computational procedures and appropriate degrees of freedom are presented in [13]. Theoretically, the statistic can be used in a conventional statistical null hypothesis testing mode. In practice, however, this usage is only possible with extremely well defined factors. Because the statistic is χ^2, its computation and interpretation are very dependent on sample size. With a large sample size the null hypothesis is seldom accepted. Typically, there is a significant but trivial difference between the factor structure and the data. This problem was discussed in conjunction with principal components analysis.

The Reliability Index

For most practical data bases, a reliability index, $\hat{\rho}$, developed by Tucker and Lewis [19], is more appropriate. Its use is analogous to variance components analysis for assessing whether the variance accounted for by a theory is large or small in relation to the total variance in the data. The index, $\hat{\rho}$, is estimated from the χ^2 statistic by:

$$\text{(3)} \qquad \hat{\rho} = \frac{M_o - M_k}{M_o - 1}$$

where $M_o = \chi_o^2/\text{df}_o$ and $M_k = \chi_k^2/\text{df}_k$. χ_o^2 and df_o are the chi-square statistic and degrees of freedom obtained with a zero factor solution (base case with no factors extracted). χ_k^2 and df_k are the chi-square statistic and degrees of freedom obtained with a k factor solution. The index is unity when χ_k^2 is equal to its expected value.

Use of the index requires an element of subjective judgment. The acceptable level of $\hat{\rho}$ will vary with the study data and purpose. A large value of $\hat{\rho}$ always can be achieved by the use of a large number of k factors. However, as with principal components analysis, scientific parsimony and management practicality usually will suggest the acceptance of fewer factors and a correspondingly lower $\hat{\rho}$. The acceptable level of $\hat{\rho}$ thus will depend on a balancing of the objectives of explanation and parsimony, an exercise often necessary in multivariate analysis. Jöreskog [11] states that ultimately the criteria for goodness of a model depend on its usefulness and the results it produces.

Used in conjunction with RMLFA, the $\hat{\rho}$ has some resemblance to an unadjusted R^2. Both statistics indicate the proportion of total data variation explained by the model being evaluated. However, the apparent degree of explanation may owe much to chance. Model testing with RMLFA is accomplished by specifying certain factor parameters to be fixed and allowing others to be free. Virtually any set of fixed and free parameters for a given data set will yield a RMLFA value of $\hat{\rho}$ greater than zero because some degree of fit will be achieved. However, the RMLFA value of $\hat{\rho}$ can never exceed the value obtained for a same-dimension UMLFA solution. Nevertheless, with fewer parameters to be estimated, the RMLFA solution is more parsimonious [15]. Thus, to assess the performance of RMLFA results, $\hat{\rho}$ comparisons must be made with the corresponding upper-bound UMLFA statistics to judge how much explanation has been lost through restriction. In addition, comparisons must be made with some benchmark measure of RMLFA performance using randomly assigned fixed and free values. The benchmark will be specific to the data base, dimensionality, and proportion of fixed to free values [3].

APPLICATION OF UMLFA AND RMLFA PROCEDURES

The use of maximum likelihood factor analysis to analyze attitudinal data is explored further in the context of a specific marketing example. A conveniently available large data base was chosen. It contained 21 sum score attitude measures which were obtained from 115 items included in a survey of 1,813 adults [18]. The 21 variables span many dimensions of consumers' attitudes toward business and marketing practices. Each score summed response to several 6-point component scales. These variables were part of the female data from a representative sample of an up-scale midwestern community previously reported in [7]. This example includes the male data for the first time in addition to the female data previously reported.

The frequency distributions of the 21 scores conformed closely to the normal distribution, as predicted by the central limit theorem when several items are averaged together. In addition, responses to many socioeconomic, consumer value, market behavior, and media exposure variables were available for segmenting respondents. The use of two segmenting variables, sex and attitudes toward business, is illustrated. They were selected arbitrarily to determine whether there were differences in factor structures among these respondent subsamples.

The data analysis started with a prehypothesized factor structure. Subsequently, an improved posthypothesized model was developed on one split-half (generation sample) of the data. Both pre- and posthypothesized factor structures were tested on the other split-half (validation sample). Other posthypothesized structures then were developed for selected sex and attitudes toward business segments. All analyses used correlation matrices as input data. This procedure, whereby a hypothesized pattern is tested and then improved and retested, is consistent with Figure 1.

Test of Prehypothesized Factor Structure

The prehypothesized three-dimensional factor structure (pattern A), generated by one of the survey's research designers, is shown on the left in Table 1. The zeros correspond to fixed factor loadings specified as zero. The ones correspond to free factor loadings not specified as to value, which are expected to "load" on the factors and form the factor structure. The sum scores had not been factor analyzed, but the researcher believed that responses to the scores were influenced by attitudes toward advertising (hypothesized factor 2) and more general attitudes toward business and the environment (factor 1). Factor 3 was hypothesized to account for the set of attitudes toward specific industries, which in some cases were thought to overlap with factors 1 and 2.

Before pattern A was tested, the respondents were divided by a random process into two split-halves to obtain a hypothesis-generation sample and a validation sample. Then pattern A was RMLFA analyzed on the validation sample, yielding a $\hat{\rho}$ of .54. To

Table 1
TEST OF PREHYPOTHESIZED FACTOR STRUCTURE (PATTERN A)

	Prehypothesized factor structure (pattern A)			*RMLFA prehypothesized factor loadings*			*UMLFA varimax factor loadings*		
Title of sum score	*1*	*2*	*3*	*1*	*2*	*3*	*1*	*2*	*3*
1. Pollution is a serious problem	1	0	0	.426	0	0	−.119	−.067	.924
2. "Other people" do not care about pollution	1	0	0	.281	0	0	−.151	−.173	.078
3. Advertisements and promotions are truthful	0	1	0	0	1.00	0	.742	.495	−.134
4. Advertising is a desirable institution	0	1	0	0	.893	0	.825	.185	−.154
5. Advertising is a good source of consumer information	1	1	0	.605	.320	0	.571	.278	−.102
6. Advertising and promotional practices are not objectionable	0	1	0	0	1.00	0	.936	.324	−.140
7. Products-services are of high quality	1	0	0	.844	0	0	.384	.713	−.281
8. There are too many brands and products available today	1	0	0	.246	0	0	−.103	−.163	.069
9. Business pricing practices are fair and honest	1	0	0	.597	0	0	.244	.565	−.066
10. Retailing/selling practices are in the consumer's best interest	1	0	0	.491	0	0	.318	.416	−.009
11. Businesses are concerned about the public they serve	1	0	0	.743	0	0	.333	.695	−.145
12. Business is responsive to the consumer	1	0	0	.170	0	0	−.041	−.007	.390
13. American businesses are honest	1	0	0	.873	0	0	.602	.679	−.162
14. Consumers need more government control of business practices	1	1	0	.410	.217	0	−.244	−.281	.192
15. Auto industry does a "good job"	0	0	1	0	0	.911	.290	.599	−.283
16. Breakfast cereal industry does a "good job"	0	0	1	0	0	.856	.490	.354	−.209
17. Detergent industry does a "good job"	1	0	1	.632	0	.370	.310	.326	−.612
18. Drug industry does a "good job"	0	0	1	0	0	.692	.209	.542	−.094
19. Newspaper industry does a "good job"	0	1	1	0	.255	.153	.104	.168	.039
20. Television industry does a "good job"	0	1	1	0	.378	.227	.183	.181	−.105
21. Magazine industry does a "good job"	0	1	1	0	.101	.061	−.008	.120	.077

estimate the maximal fit possible, the corresponding three-dimensional unrestricted solution for the validation sample was used for comparison. The UMLFA run yielded a $\hat{\rho}$ of .73. Thus, the prehypothesized structure achieved a respectable 74% of the explanation possible in three dimensions. The relative performance of pattern A is open to judgment, however, until the basic random level of fit is measured [3].

To examine the level of $\hat{\rho}$ obtainable by chance, 40 supplementary three-dimensional runs were derived for the validation sample. The particular model was oblique (all factor correlations are specified as free) and imposed no restrictions on the unique variances. The distribution of $\hat{\rho}$ values obtained for the 40 benchmark runs is shown in Figure 2. The median value of $\hat{\rho}$ of .42 clearly indicates that the prehypothesized model did achieve more of the explanation possible (74%) than would be expected by chance (58%). In fact, none of the Monté Carlo $\hat{\rho}$ values exceeded the $\hat{\rho}$ of .54 obtained from the prehypothesized model. It should be noted, however, that pattern A's improvement over the basic random level was only 16 percentage points of a theoretically possible 42 percentage points. Thus, there is still room for significant improvement (26 percentage points) with a posthypothe-

Figure 2
CUMULATIVE DISTRIBUTION OF $\hat{\rho}$ VALUES DERIVED FROM 40 RMLFA RUNS WITH RANDOM PLACEMENT OF SPECIFIED FACTOR LOADINGS

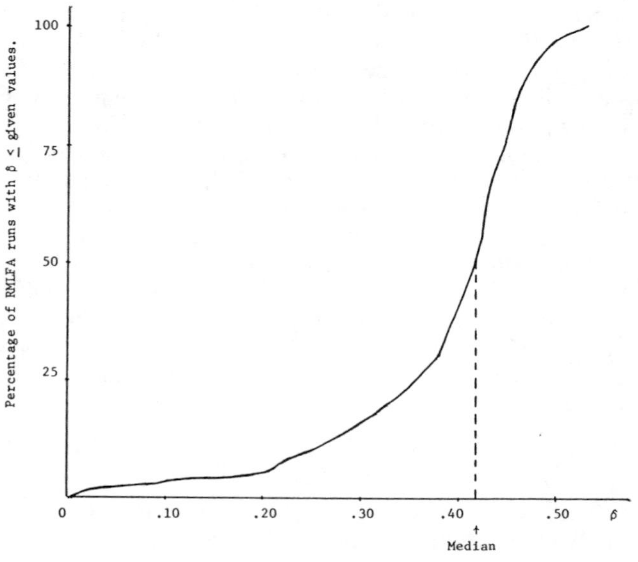

Table 2

RELIABILITY INDEX, $\hat{\rho}$, OF EXPLAINED χ^2 FOR UMLFA RUNS OF VARIED DIMENSIONALITY AND DATA BASE

Dimension	*Split-half samples*		*Respondent segments*			
	Generation	*Validation*	*Female*	*Male*	*Critical of business*	*Not critical of business*
1	.567	.611	.577	.607	.407	.398
2	.673	.696	.685	.694	.563	.536
3	.699	.728	.716	.719	.606	.609
4	.747	.755	.755	.755	.670	.654
5	.799	.785	.812	.795	.747	.710
6	.839	.833	.863	.829	.784	.771

sized factor structure. This conclusion is supported by the difference in the factor loading between the RMLFA and UMLFA solutions shown in Table 1. Prehypothesized factors 1 and 2 are somewhat comparable to UMLFA factors 2 and 1, respectively. Prehypothesized factor 3 is not represented by the UMLFA solution in any way.

Test of Posthypothesized Factor Structure

After the limited success of the prehypothesized factor structure, a factor structure hypothesis was generated from the split-half hypothesis-generation sample. Thus the data *per se* were used to refine the hypothesis and contribute to the formulation of theory. The first step was to determine an appropriate dimensionality. The values of $\hat{\rho}$ corresponding to UMLFA runs of varying dimensionality are shown in Table 2. Three dimensions were chosen as a compromise between explanation and parsimony, the latter being given more weight.

The factor loadings resulting from the UMLFA analysis of the generation sample are shown on the left side of Table 3. For comparison, a principal components and a factor analysis with the diagonal replaced by communalities, estimated by squared multiple correlation coefficients, were computed and also are shown in Table 3. There are some similarities of structure between the UMLFA and traditional procedures, particularly between UMLFA and the factor solution. The traditional solutions account for only 51% of the variance in three factors.

The generation sample UMLFA factor loadings in Table 3 were used to derive the adjacent posthypothe-

Table 3

COMPARISON OF FACTOR ANALYSIS METHODS[a]

Variable number	*UMLFA* 1	2	3	*Principal components* 1	2	3	*Factor analysis* 1	2	3
1	−.22	−.22	.80	−.26	.17	.75	.01	−.24	.79
2	−.07	−.18	.02	−.12	−.37	.23	−.25	−.09	.10
3	.75	.49	−.01	.83	.16	−.16	.42	.74	−.15
4	.83	.24	−.06	.70	.19	−.21	.45	.58	−.19
5	.55	.32	−.02	.60	.26	−.18	.44	.47	−.14
6	.95	.32	−.03	.82	.20	−.20	.52	.69	−.19
7	.33	.80	−.21	.80	−.08	−.29	.06	.82	−.31
8	−.10	−.19	.18	−.27	.37	.20	.16	−.29	.18
9	.26	.57	.02	.68	.00	.03	.10	.63	−.02
10	.28	.48	.10	.68	−.11	.20	.01	.64	.10
11	.34	.70	.02	.79	.09	−.03	.21	.74	−.05
12	−.05	−.07	.44	.04	.07	.70	.00	−.02	.47
13	.55	.72	−.01	.83	.23	−.20	.43	.76	−.17
14	−.32	−.32	.14	−.57	.38	.04	.14	−.56	.13
15	.21	.67	−.23	.57	.05	−.36	.14	.55	−.31
16	.45	.35	−.15	.57	−.05	−.23	.16	.50	−.23
17	.36	.34	−.50	.41	.15	−.63	.31	.33	−.58
18	.17	.57	−.08	.57	−.12	−.10	.00	.54	−.13
19	.09	.13	.13	.13	.58	.11	.34	.05	.11
20	.17	.08	−.05	.05	.53	−.33	.39	.00	−.14
21	.04	.05	.23	.03	.62	.22	.33	−.04	.20

[a] All based on generation sample, all varimax rotated, $n = 907$.

Table 4

TEST OF GENERATION SAMPLE'S POSTHYPOTHESIZED FACTOR STRUCTURE (PATTERN B)

Variable number	*Posthypothesized factor structure (pattern B)*			*RMLFA factor loadings*					
				Generation sample			*Validation sample*		
	1	*2*	*3*	*1*	*2*	*3*	*1*	*2*	*3*
1	0	0	1	0	0	.973	0	0	.977
2	0	1	0	0	−.172	0	0	−.225	0
3	1	1	0	.675	.241	0	.666	.266	0
4	1	0	0	.838	0	0	.825	0	0
5	1	0	0	.626	0	0	.647	0	0
6	1	0	0	.970	0	0	.958	0	0
7	0	1	0	0	.853	0	0	.853	0
8	0	1	1	0	−.194	.122	0	−.216	.010
9	0	1	0	0	.599	0	0	.598	0
10	0	1	0	0	.525	0	0	.507	0
11	0	1	0	0	.737	0	0	.753	0
12	0	0	1	0	0	.374	0	0	.370
13	1	1	0	.322	.607	0	.370	.583	0
14	1	1	0	−.179	−.308	0	−.066	−.361	0
15	0	1	0	0	.683	0	0	.709	0
16	1	1	0	.346	.264	0	.405	.262	0
17	0	0	1	0	0	−.621	0	0	−.650
18	0	1	0	0	.561	0	0	.568	0
19	0	1	1	0	.161	.104	0	.186	.065
20	1	0	0	.192	0	0	.256	0	0
21	0	0	1	0	0	.160	0	0	.058

sized factor structure target matrix (pattern B) shown in Table 4. Pattern B was hypothesized to clarify the underlying structure. In general low UMLFA loadings were restricted to a value of zero. The three resulting business practice factors were labeled (1) advertising value, (2) business standards, and (3) pollution awareness. It should be noted that patterns A and B differ in their specifications for 20 of the 63 values of Λ; however, 13 of the 20 differences are for the final six sum scores which do not load highly on any of the three factors. Thus pattern A was successful in describing much of the factor structure. The refinements in pattern B primarily affect the treatment of the final six sum scores which were hypothesized incorrectly to load on a separate factor.

First, pattern B was RMLFA analyzed on the generation sample split-half. The RMLFA $\hat{\rho}$ of .67 nearly matched the UMLFA $\hat{\rho}$ of .70 (Table 2), indicating that the posthypothesized factor structure successfully represented the generation sample data and that little goodness of fit had been sacrificed to improve the clarity of the factors. Then pattern B was tested on the validation sample, producing a $\hat{\rho}$ of .69, compared with $\hat{\rho}$ of .54 for the prehypothesized model, the validation benchmark value of .42, and the validation sample UMLFA $\hat{\rho}$ of .73. Not only was substantial explanation (95%) achieved within the three-dimensional constraint, but the improvement on chance ($\Delta\hat{\rho} = .27$) was more than twice that achieved with the prehypothesized model ($\Delta\hat{\rho} = .12$). Of the 42 percentage points possible for improvement over the basic random level of fit, pattern B accounted for 37% in contrast to 16% for pattern A. These findings strongly confirm the goodness of fit of the posthypothesized factor structure.

In certain situations, it may be advisable to clarify the factor structure further by eliminating cross-loadings and, subsequently, testing the revised hypothesized structure on fresh data.

All factor structures were tested by imposing no restrictions on the factor correlations and unique variances. Thus, the apparently equivalent factor

Table 5

FACTOR CORRELATIONS FOR POSTHYPOTHESIZED (PATTERN B) GENERATION AND VALIDATION SAMPLE SOLUTIONS

Sample	*Factor*	*Factor 1*	*2*	*3*
	1			
Generation	2	.742		
	3	.006	−.028	
	1			
Validation	2	.733		
	3	−.005	.016	

structures for the generation and validation subsamples could be different if the factor intercorrelations varied between the oblique solutions for the two subsamples. However, this concern can be dismissed as the intercorrelations in Table 5 are clearly very similar for the two solutions. In addition, the unique variances for both solutions are identical to one decimal place accuracy.

The analysis was repeated with pattern B, but the factor intercorrelations were restricted to have fixed values of zero. This orthogonal factor structure was tested on the validation sample, producing a $\hat{\rho}$ of .60. The reduction of $\Delta\hat{\rho}$ = .09 or 13 percentage points in explained variation indicates that the orthogonal solution is inferior to the oblique solution. Even though the factor loadings in the two models are similar, the advantage of a simpler structure with the orthogonal model is outweighed by the higher explained variation and observed significant correlation between factors 1 and 2 in the oblique model.

Segment Testing of Hypothesized Factor Structures

Factor structures appropriate for one market segment may be inappropriate for another. This discrepancy has implications in the area of scale validation as well as for the formulation of managerial strategy. For instance, one segment of toothpaste users may have a factor structure which shows high correlation between perceived tooth whitening power and overall quality, whereas another may link cavity protection with quality.

Analysis of subsamples was examined for two potential segmenting variables, sex and attitudes toward business. The sex variable provided two groups consisting of 912 females and 901 males. The attitudes toward business variable was used to provide two extreme groups, 398 who were labeled critical of business practices and 489 who were labeled not critical of business practices.

The first sequence of analysis consisted of testing the goodness of fit of pattern B on each of the four segments. Table 6 compares the $\hat{\rho}$ values obtained from the RMLFA runs with the Monté Carlo benchmark measures and the upper-bound UMLFA values. These results indicate that pattern B fits the four segments reasonably well. Even though the RMLFA $\hat{\rho}$'s are very similar for all segments, the UMLFA $\hat{\rho}$'s in Table 2 indicate that the factor structures for the critical and not critical of business segments are more complex. It would be very difficult to improve the fit of a three-dimensional factor structure for the critical and not critical of business segments unless more dimensions were included, whereas there is some room for improvement for the female and male segments in three dimensions.

The possibility of fitting unique factor structures to the different segments then was investigated. For the female and male segments, three dimensions were judged to be appropriate. Because of the comparatively slower increase in $\hat{\rho}$ with dimensionality, five dimensions were required to explain a similar amount of variation in the more complex critical and not critical of business segments (Table 2).

The results of the female UMLFA were used to generate a new posthypothesized factor structure (pattern C), which, in fact, differed from pattern B in the specification of only five of the possible 63 factor loadings. When the representativeness of this new model was checked on the generation sample data, the female data RMLFA produced a $\hat{\rho}$ of .63, which was only a slight improvement over pattern B. Except for the few differences in loadings, the only other noticeable difference was the slight positive correlation between factors 1 and 2.

Pattern C then was tested against the male data. The RMLFA test indicated that there was a good fit, $\hat{\rho}$ = .67, compared with a benchmark value of .40 and the .72 UMLFA $\hat{\rho}$. Except for some differences in factor correlations, the generation, validation, female, and male samples all have very similar three-dimensional factor structures. These findings indicate that no set of dimensions is unique to either the female or male segments, and that pattern C is not a worthwhile improvement. This finding, too, contributes to the evolution of theory, suggesting a similar factor structure for both sexes.

A similar sequence of analysis was carried out in five dimensions for the critical and not critical of business segments to determine whether the factor structures were similar and to assign labels to the five factors. The critical of business UMLFA results were used to generate a factor structure (pattern D) for testing on the not critical of business data. The five-dimensional model first was checked against the critical of business data, producing a RMLFA $\hat{\rho}$ of .67, which is a very respectable 91% explained compared with the corresponding UMLFA $\hat{\rho}$ value of .74.

Table 6

RELIABILITY INDEX, $\hat{\rho}$, OF EXPLAINED χ^2 FOR FOUR MARKET SEGMENTS

	Analysis					
	Pattern B hypothesis					
	RMLFA		*Benchmark*		*UMLFA*	
Market segment	$\hat{\rho}$	%	$\hat{\rho}$	%	$\hat{\rho}$	%
Females	.61	85	.37	51	.72	100
Males	.60	83	.40	56	.72	100
Critical of business	.61	100	.26	43	.61	100
Not critical of business	.57	93	.26	43	.61	100

Pattern D then was tested against the not critical of business data. The RMLFA test indicated that there was a reasonable fit, $\hat{\rho} = .61$ or 86%, compared with the UMLFA $\hat{\rho}$ value of .71. Both solutions were essentially orthogonal except for the slight positive correlation between factors 2 and 4.

Much similarity is apparent between the three-dimensional and five-dimensional solutions for two factors, advertising value and pollution awareness. The third three-dimensional solution factor, business standards, however, appears to have split into separate factors in the two five-dimensional solutions. They were labeled business ethics and product/service quality. Thus four of the five factors are very similar for the two groups, even though the critical and not critical of business partitions scored differently on these common dimensions. The fifth factor, however, differed for the two groups. For the critical of business group, the fifth factor was labeled business-consumer relations, whereas the not critical of business group's dimension was named government/media.

The analysis shows that maximum likelihood factor analysis can be used to discern the similarities and differences among sample partitions with respect to their perspectives for viewing business-related issues. A marketing strategist concerned with improving his company's overall image among consumers next would examine the response levels of each group to each factor as a guide to making recommendations. Some factors may be seen to be of more concern than others for a particular segment. In communicating with the group critical of business, the strategist might allow for the emergence of business-consumer relations as a separate factor not included in the other "topic areas." If this factor emerged as an important dimension, it might warrant explicit treatment. In general, the use of such results is similar to the use of those from several multivariate analyses applied in market segmentation research.

CONCLUSION

In this report, concentration is on one set of techniques for developing and testing appropriate factor structures for different population groups. An example applying published data is shown to guide researchers in the joint use of UMLFA and RMLFA. Both techniques require more caution in data selection and use than principal components analysis, but otherwise can be used easily and economically. The χ^2 goodness-of-fit criterion and the measures derived from it, the capability for model specification, and the resultant ability to test hypothesized structures, plus the desirable properties of maximum likelihood estimates, give maximum likelihood factor analysis a considerable range of application. The original marketing applications were both in measure validation [2, 16]. Multiple measurement scales were investigated for establishing concurrent validity and/or ascertaining underlying dimensionality. The present application is in the wider field of attitude structure and subsample analysis. Areas for further applications could include both panel and repeated cross-sectional survey studies. Factor structures at one point in time could be compared with those at other points in time, or, alternatively, after respondents have been exposed to new stimuli.

REFERENCES

1. Bartlett, M. S. "Tests of Significance in Factor Analysis," *British Journal of Psychology, Statistics Section*, 3 (June 1950), 77–85.
2. Heeler, Roger M. and Michael L. Ray. "Measure Validation in Marketing," *Journal of Marketing Research*, 9 (November 1972), 361–70.
3. ——— and Thomas W. Whipple. "A Monte Carlo Aid to the Evaluation of Maximum Likelihood Factor Analysis Solutions," *The British Journal of Mathematical and Statistical Psychology*, 29 (November 1976).
4. Horn, John L. "A Rationale and Test for the Number of Factors in Factor Analysis," *Psychometrica*, 30 (June 1965), 179–85.
5. Howe, W. G. "Some Contributions to Factor Analysis," Report No. ONRL-1919. Oak Ridge, Tennessee: Oak Ridge National Laboratory, 1955. Cited in [17].
6. Hurley, J. R. and R. B. Cattell. "The Procrustes Program: Producing Direct Rotation to Test a Hypothesized Factor Structure," *Behavioral Science*, 7 (July 1962), 258–62.
7. Hustad, Thomas P. and Edgar A. Pessemier. "Will the Real Consumer Activist Please Stand Up: An Examination of Consumers' Opinions About Marketing Practices," *Journal of Marketing Research*, 10 (August 1973), 319–24.
8. Jöreskog, Karl G. "UMLFA—A Computer Program for Unrestricted Maximum Likelihood Factor Analysis," Research Memorandum 66-30. Princeton, New Jersey: Educational Testing Service, 1966.
9. ———. "Testing a Simple Structure Hypothesis in Factor Analysis," *Psychometrica*, 31 (June 1966), 165–78.
10. ———. "Some Contributions to Maximum Likelihood Factor Analysis," *Psychometrica*, 32 (December 1967), 443–82.
11. ———. "Simultaneous Factor Analysis in Several Populations," *Psychometrica*, 36 (December 1971), 409–26.
12. ——— and G. Gruvaeus. "RMLFA—A Computer Program for Restricted Maximum Likelihood Factor Analysis," Research Memorandum 67-21. Princeton, New Jersey: Educational Testing Service, 1967.
13. ——— and D. N. Lawley. "New Methods in Maximum Likelihood Factor Analysis," *The British Journal of Mathematical and Statistical Psychology*, 21 (May 1968), 85–96.
14. Lawley, D. N. "The Estimation of Factor Loadings by the Method of Maximum Likelihood," *Proceedings of the Royal Society Edinburgh (A)*, 60 (1940), 64–82.
15. McGaw, Barry and Karl G. Jöreskog. "Factorial Invariance of Ability Measures in Groups Differing in Intelligence and Socioeconomic States," *The British Journal of Mathematical and Statistical Psychology*, 24

(1971), 154-68.
16. Mitchell, Andrew A. and Jerry C. Olson. "Use of Restricted and Unrestricted Maximum Likelihood Factor Analysis to Examine Alternative Measures of Brand Loyalty," *Proceedings*, Fall Conference, American Marketing Association, 1975 181-6.
17. Mulaik, Stanley A. *The Foundations of Factor Analysis*. New York: McGraw-Hill Book Co., 1972.
18. Pessemier, Edgar A., F. Stewart De Bruicker, and Thomas P. Hustad. "The 1970 Purdue Consumer Behavior Research Project," unpublished paper, Krannert Graduate School of Industrial Administration, Purdue University, 1971.
19. Tucker, L. R. and C. Lewis. "A Reliability Coefficient for Maximum Likelihood Factor Analysis," *Topics in Factor Analysis II*, Technical Report, U.S. Office of Naval Research, 1971.

DAVID A. AAKER and RICHARD P. BAGOZZI*

Structural equation models which include unobservable variables permit theoretical constructs to be represented by multiple indicators. The use and evaluation of such models are illustrated in an industrial salesforce study.

Unobservable Variables in Structural Equation Models with an Application in Industrial Selling

An econometric model consists of a set of independent variables and one or more dependent variables. The relationships between the variables are normally specified by an equation for each dependent variable. These relationships can represent empirical associations or causal links. When causal links are involved, the econometric model is termed a "structural equation model" (Goldberger 1973, p. 2). In such models each variable represents a theoretical construct. The assumption is that the theoretical construct is measured without error by a single variable or indicator. Such an assumption seems naïve on its face.[1] In most contexts any single indicator will be biased, and multiple indicators are a logical means of reducing the biasing effect of any one indicator (Campbell and Fisk 1959). Further, econometricians have shown that even if an indicator is an unbiased representation of a theoretical construct, measurement error can still lead to biased conclusions (Griliches 1974).

The assumption of single indicators without measurement error may be justified under some conditions. In particular, in some situations only one indicator is available, the indicator has a high degree of validity and reliability, and problems of construct and relationship specification dominate. In many situations, however, such an assumption is not justified, but is made because there is no perceived alternative.

One purpose of this article is to present an alternative: the use of unobservable variables to represent theoretical constructs in structural equation models. This approach allows the use of multiple indicators of the theoretical constructs. Further, it explicitly introduces measurement error and formally specifies the relationship between the theoretical construct and the observable indicators. A second purpose of this article is to show how competing structural equation models can be evaluated and to explain how a hypothesis test can be used to help compare them. A third purpose is to illustrate this methodology in the context of a study on an industrial salesforce.

The use of unobservable variables in structural equation models and the associated statistical methodology can be credited to a variety of disciplines including sociology, statistics, econometrics, and psychometrics. It can be viewed as a synthesis of econometrics and factor analysis. In the first section the approach is described, and in the second section it is examined in terms of factor analysis. The third section sets forth several examples of how it can be used in the context of a personal selling study. Parameter estimation and identification are addressed in the fourth section. The model testing and theory development issues are discussed in the fifth section. Finally, alternative approaches to the measurement error problem are considered.

[1]Griliches (1974) notes that econometricians have largely ignored the errors in variables problem. He hypothesizes that the reasons are, among others, that economic data tend to be aggregated (so that random errors will cancel) and collected by others (so responsibility is not felt), that identification and simultaneity have been the major intellectual problems, that the theoretical constructs have been somewhat fuzzy, and that there has been no perceived cure.

*David A. Aaker is Professor and Richard P. Bagozzi is Assistant Professor, School of Business Administration, University of California, Berkeley.

The authors acknowledge the helpful comments of Ronald S. Burt, James M. Carman, and Robert A. Meyer.

Reprinted from *Journal of Marketing Research,* 16 (May 1979), 147-58, published by the American Marketing Association.

STRUCTURAL EQUATIONS AND UNOBSERVABLE VARIABLES

In Figure 1A, a simple model is shown where a single dependent variable, y, is affected by two independent variables, x_1 and x_2. This model can be written mathematically through the well known linear regression model as:

$$y = \beta_1' x_1 + \beta_2' x_2 + \varepsilon' \qquad (1)$$

where β_i' is a standardized regression coefficient (termed a beta weight) and is interpreted as the change in standard deviations of y that would result from a change in one standard deviation of x_i. Throughout this article, the authors adopt the path analysis assumption that all variables are standardized.[2] The error term, ε', represents the amount of variance in y not explained by the independent variables.

Figure 1
AN ECONOMETRIC PERSPECTIVE

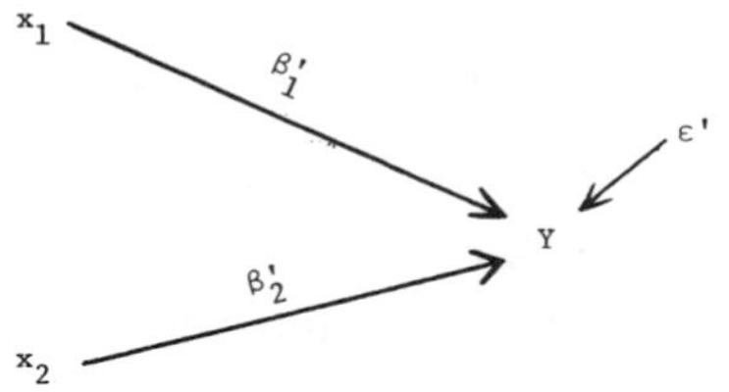

A. A Simple Structural Equation Model

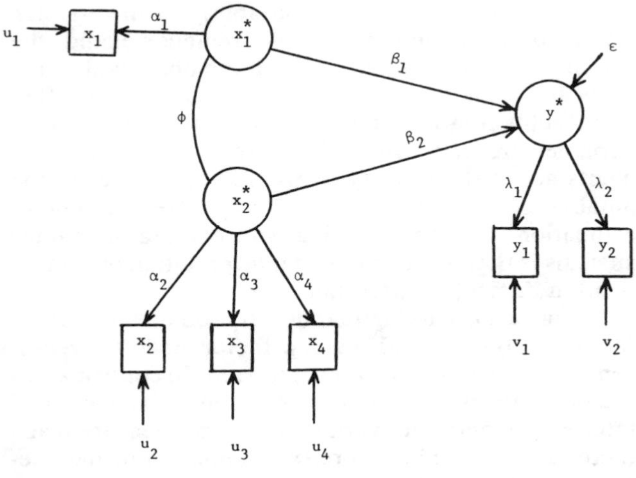

B. A Structural Equation Model with Unobservable Variables

Notice that the model is limited to a system of relationships between observable variables because y, x_1, and x_2 are actual measurements performed on some population. In effect, the model assumes that all variables are measured without error and that the parameters represent relationships between empirical observations. The example could, of course, include additional dependent (and independent) variables. The result would be a system of equations representing a set of cause-effect relationships. Several researchers in marketing have worked with such models (cf. Aaker and Day 1974; Bagozzi 1977b; Bass 1969; Farley, Howard, and Lehmann 1976).

In Figure 1B, a model is portrayed in which two independent unobservable variables, x_1^* and x_2^*, impact on the dependent unobservable variable, y^*. In this figure and succeeding ones, the unobservable variables (except error terms) are indicated by circles, observable variables (i.e., indicators, measurements, operationalizations) are shown as squares, and causal relationships are depicted as straight-line segments with arrowheads. The curved line between x_1^* and x_2^* indicates that they may be correlated. The causal relationships in the model can be represented by two sets of equations.

The first set of equations represents the hypothesized relationships in one's theory:

$$y^* = \beta_1 x_1^* + \beta_2 x_2^* + \varepsilon \qquad (2)$$

Notice that this equation expresses relationships only among unobservable variables (or theoretical constructs) and thus contrasts to the model of equation 1 which is limited exclusively to relationships among observable variables. Notice further that the coefficients and error term in equation 2—β_1, β_2, and ε—will, in general, differ from those in equation 1—i.e., β_1', β_2', and ε'.

The second set of equations captures the relationships between theoretical constructs and their indicators (the observable variables):

$$y_1 = \lambda_1 y^* + v_1 \qquad x_2 = \alpha_2 x_2^* + u_2$$
$$y_2 = \lambda_2 y^* + v_2 \qquad x_3 = \alpha_3 x_2^* + u_3$$
$$x_1 = \alpha_1 x_1^* + u_1 \qquad x_4 = \alpha_4 x_2^* + u_4$$

The linking parameters (i.e., λ_i and α_i) are measures of the degree of correspondence between the theoretical constructs and their indicators or measurements. When an λ_i or α_i is less than one in magnitude (given the standardization convention adopted before), the indicator will be an imperfect measure of the theoretical construct, and the corresponding error term (v_i or u_i) will formally reflect other sources of variation in the respective indicator. The error terms for the indicators are known as "errors in variables."

In effect there are now two "theories." The first is the theory providing causal links between the theoretical constructs. The second is what Blalock

[2]For an introduction to path analysis, see Blalock (1967a), Duncan (1975), and Land (1969). For a discussion of the tradeoffs for using standardized versus unstandardized coefficients, see Kim and Mueller (1976), Lawley and Maxwell (1971), and Tukey (1954). One result of standardization is that there is no intercept term in the linear model.

(1968) terms the "auxiliary" theory which defines the rules of correspondence between the theoretical constructs and their indicators.

THE FACTOR ANALYSIS PERSPECTIVE

Unlike econometrics, in which the use of multiple indicators of unobservable variables is rare (see Goldberger 1974), factor analysis began with the concept of an unobservable variable as a central part of its model. Factor analysis has evolved in two directions. Early work in factor analysis had as its goal the extraction of a small number of "theoretical" constructs from a larger set of observed variables. Typically, the researcher had no theoretical hypothesis in mind when using factor analysis in this sense, but was searching for a structure underlying the data. This type of factor analysis, termed "exploratory factor analysis" in the literature, is the type most frequently used by marketers.

A newer model of factor analysis—termed "confirmatory factor analysis"—has been developed in recent years as a means of discovering an underlying structure in one's data, given some prior theoretical or empirical information. To date, this method has been used in at least three marketing studies (Bagozzi 1977a,b; Mitchell and Olson 1975). Confirmatory factor analysis is described here because it provides the reader, especially one familiar with exploratory factor analysis, with some insight into unobservable variables in structural equation models, because of its methodological relevance, and because it illustrates the role of prior theory specification.

Figure 2
A FACTOR ANALYTIC PERSPECTIVE

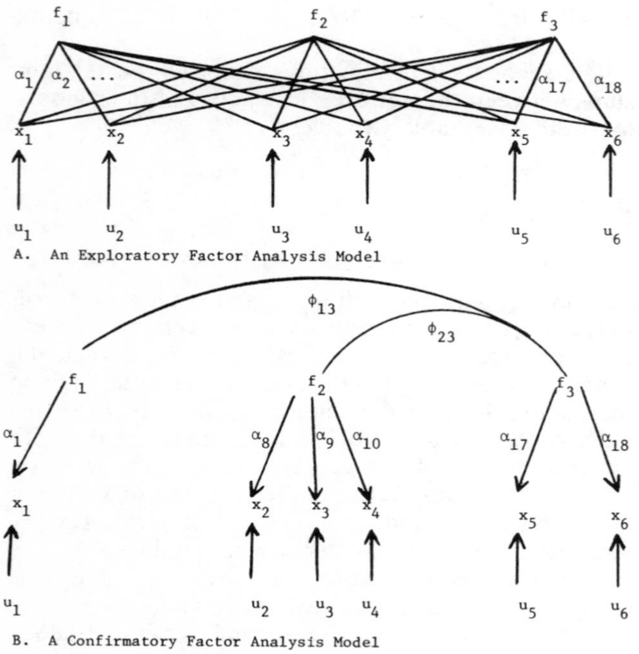

It is useful to begin by reviewing the exploratory factor analysis model shown in Figure 2A. The terms f_1, f_2, and f_3 represent uncorrelated (orthogonal) factors which are unobservable. One also could consider an exploratory factor analysis model in which the factors are permitted to be correlated (oblique). Correlated factors would be linked by a curved line in the representation. In Figure 2A each x is an observable variable which measures to some extent the three factors. Because their variance is not entirely due to the three factors, an error term is included to account for the remaining part of their variance. The error terms are assumed to be independent. Algebraically the model is represented by equations such as:

$$x_1 = \alpha_1 f_1 + \alpha_7 f_2 + \alpha_{13} f_3 + u_1$$
$$x_2 = \alpha_2 f_1 + \alpha_8 f_2 + \alpha_{14} f_3 + u_2$$
$$x_3 = \alpha_3 f_1 + \alpha_9 f_2 + \alpha_{15} f_3 + u_3$$
$$x_4 = \alpha_4 f_1 + \alpha_{10} f_2 + \alpha_{16} f_3 + u_4$$
$$x_5 = \alpha_5 f_1 + \alpha_{11} f_2 + \alpha_{17} f_3 + u_5$$
$$x_6 = \alpha_6 f_1 + \alpha_{12} f_2 + \alpha_{18} f_3 + u_6$$
$$\phi_{12} = \phi_{13} = \phi_{23} = 0$$

where ϕ_{ij} = the correlation between factor i and factor j.

A factor analysis program can estimate the α's, the factor loadings. The loading of x_1 on factor 1, for example, reflects the degree to which x_1 is a measure of the unobservable variable f_1. If all variables are standardized and the factors are uncorrelated, the loadings are correlations between the observable variables and the factors. After the estimation, and often after factor rotation, judgments are made as to which variables are measuring which factors. In fact, judgments about the identity of the factors and even the number of factors are made only after parameter estimation. One shortcoming with exploratory factor analysis is that the meaning or interpretation of factors is often difficult to ascertain.

In contrast to this familiar description of exploratory factor analysis, confirmatory factor analysis represents a completely different approach. In confirmatory factor analysis the factors are conceptualized and interpreted and the variables which measure each factor are identified before the estimation of parameters. Theory thus is employed prior to the estimation phase to impose structure. In practice, this usually means that some of the factor loadings and some (but not necessarily all) of the correlations between factors are set equal to zero. These restrictions are not *ad hoc*, but rather reflect one's theory, past research, or methodology and in any case are hypotheses to be tested on data.

Figure 2B is an example of confirmatory factor

analysis. The factor f_1 is shown as being measured by the observable variable x_1. The links between f_1 and the other observable variables are set equal to zero. Similarly, the factor f_2 is measured only by the observable variables x_2, x_3, and x_4 and the factor f_3 is measured only by x_5 and x_6. Further, the factor f_3 is permitted to be correlated (denoted by the curved lines) with both f_1 and f_2. The α_i coefficients linking the theoretical constructs and the observable variables still have the familiar interpretation of factor loadings. The error terms are assumed uncorrelated. Algebraically the model of Figure 2B is represented by:

$$\begin{aligned}
x_1 &= \alpha_1 f_1 &&&& + u_1 \\
x_2 &= && \alpha_8 f_2 && + u_2 \\
x_3 &= && \alpha_9 f_2 && + u_3 \\
x_4 &= && \alpha_{10} f_2 && + u_4 \\
x_5 &= &&& \alpha_{17} f_3 & + u_5 \\
x_6 &= &&& \alpha_{18} f_3 & + u_6 \\
\phi_{12} &= 0.
\end{aligned}$$

Even in exploratory factor analysis it is common to consider correlated factors. In fact, one can conduct factor analysis of factors, which is termed "second order factor analysis" (Gorsuch 1974, ch. 11). However, it is not natural to think of factors as being causally related. The focus is on operationalizing constructs rather than exploring causal relationships. However, to extend the confirmatory factor analysis to a structural equation with unobservables is actually a rather small step methodologically. The factors are simply considered to be causally related instead of being correlated and an errors-in-equations term is added. Note the similarity between Figures 2B and 1B where f_1, f_2, and f_3 correspond to x_1^*, x_2^*, and y^*, respectively.

The authors have attempted to make a clear distinction between exploratory and confirmatory factor analysis in order to explicate Figure 2B which is closely related methodologically and conceptually to unobservable variables in structural equations. However, the reader should be aware that there is actually a continuum from exploratory to confirmatory factor analysis that is analogous to the process of science moving from the exploration of phenomena to the confirmation of general hypotheses. Pure exploratory factor analysis is represented by the researcher who collects a set of variables and subjects them to factor analysis with no knowledge of what to expect. Pure confirmatory factor analysis might be represented by the researcher who can, from prior theory, specify the exact structure and all the parameters and is only interested in finding out, as an hypothesis, whether the model fits a particular data set. Actually the pure forms are very rare. The exploratory factor analyst usually has some idea of appropriate theoretical constructs when selecting variables, and the conformatory factor analyst usually can specify only some of the parameter restrictions (Mulaik 1972, p. 361–4).

APPLYING THE MODEL IN INDUSTRIAL SELLING

In this section three models are introduced to illustrate the use of unobservable variables in structural equation models.

The theoretical and empirical setting is a study of the industrial salesforce of a company which sells steel and plastic strapping tools and materials (Bagozzi 1976). Each of the 106 salespeople participating in the study has a selling position requiring considerable skill, initiative, and product knowledge. Table 1 defines 10 variables from the study that are used in the models presented in this section and in the rest of the article. The first variable, dollar sales, was determined from internal records. The other variables were obtained from a self-administered questionnaire. A correlation matrix is shown as an appendix.

Consider first Figure 3 which illustrates a multiple-indicator/multiple-cause (MIMIC) model (Aaker et al. 1978; Hauser and Goldberger 1971; Jöreskog and Goldberger 1975). The unobservable variable y^* has three causes (x_1, x_3, and x_5) and three indicators (y_1, y_2, and y_3). The indicators are dollar sales and two measures of self-satisfaction. The unobservable variable is conceptualized as self-fulfillment because it includes sales performance which is hypothesized to be a surrogate for self-performance appraisals as well as two measures of job satisfaction. The three causes are job tension (x_1), specific self-esteem (x_3), and role ambiguity (x_5).

The diagram shows the estimated coefficients and their standard errors. The estimation method is discussed in another section, as is the interpretation of the chi square statistic also shown in Figure 3.

Consider the indicator coefficients. The indicators y_2 and y_3 have about equal coefficients whereas the indicator y_1 has a smaller coefficient. Thus the indicator y_1 has a smaller role in indicating y^* than the other two. These indicator coefficients are interpreted just like factor loadings. The difference is that factor loadings are based only on the intercorrelations among the indicators whereas these indicator coefficients are also based on the links to the causal variables.

The causal coefficients can be used to explore specific causal hypotheses. The significant x_1 coefficient (with a t-value of 5.5) supports the hypothesis of an inverse relationship between felt job tension and self-fulfillment. Further, the hypothesis of a positive relationship between specific self-esteem and self-fulfillment is supported by the significant x_3 coefficient. Finally, the x_5 coefficient does not support the hypothesis of an inverse relationship between role ambiguity and self-fulfillment. For a more detailed discussion of these hypotheses and others introduced

Table 1
DEFINITIONS OF VARIABLES USED IN ANALYSES

Symbol	*Name*	*Description*
y_1	Sales	*Dollar sales*: Dollar volume of sales achieved by each salesperson for year following administration of questionnaire. Steps were taken to adjust for salespeople who quit or were transferred, changes in territory size, shifts in accounts between territories, windfall accounts, and other confounds.
y_2	SAT 1	*Job satisfaction #1:* Four six-point Likert items measuring degree of satisfaction with promotion, pay, and the overall work situation.
y_3	SAT 2	*Job satisfaction #2:* Four six-point Likert items measuring degree of satisfaction with opportunity to demonstrate ability and initiative, job security, belief that work is challenging and gives one a sense of accomplishment, and felt degree of control over aspects of job.
y_4	SAT	*Job satisfaction #1 & #2:* Composite of job satisfaction #1 and job satisfaction #2.
x_1	TEN 1	*Job tension #1:* Eight five-point Guilford self-rating items indicating how frequently the salesperson feels bothered with limits of authority, opportunities for advancement, supervisor demands and decisions, how the amount of work interferes with its quality, and how work interferes with family life.
x_2	TEN 2	*Job tension # 2:* Seven five-point Guilford items indicating how frequently the salesperson feels bothered with the scope and responsibilities of the job, work load, the qualifications required for the job, difficulty of obtaining information necessary to perform the job, relations with coworkers, and decisions conflicting with one's values.
x_3	EST 1	*Specific self-esteem #1*: Two nine-point and one five-point self-rating scales measuring each salesperson's attributions (in relation to other salespeople in the company) of the quantity of sales they achieve, their potential for achieving the top 10% in sales in their company, and the quality of their performance with regard to planning and management of time and expenses.
x_4	EST 2	*Specific self-esteem #2:* Three nine-point self-rating scales measuring each salesperson's ability to reach quota, feeling as to the quality of customer relations, and self-regard as to knowledge of own products and company, competitors' products, and customers' needs.
x_5	RA1	*Role ambiguity #1* Six five-point Likert items indicating degree of uncertainty with limits of authority, call norms, supervisor expectations for management of time and activities, customer expectations on frequency of calls, and family expectations on time to spend on job.
x_6	RA2	*Role ambiguity #2:* Six five-point Likert items indicating degree of uncertainty with freedom to negotiate on price, power to modify delivery schedules, evaluation of supervisor, overall expectations and satisfaction of customers, and family expectations with respect to performance.

in this article, see Bagozzi (1976, 1978) and Churchill, Ford, and Walker (1976).

A second model, shown in Figure 4, is the two-indicator/two-construct model. In this model the unobservable variable role ambiguity, x^*, measured by x_5 and x_6, is hypothesized to have an inverse influence on self-fulfillment measured by y_1 (sales) and y_4 (job satisfaction). The significant coefficient between x^* and y^* supports the hypothesis. Note that x_6 is the superior indicator of x^* in the context of this model.

Figure 3
A MIMIC MODEL

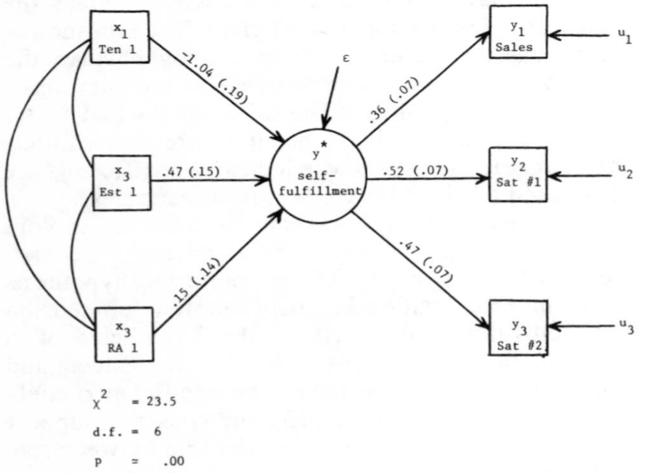

Note: Standard errors are in parentheses.

Figure 4
A TWO-INDICATOR/TWO-CONSTRUCT MODEL

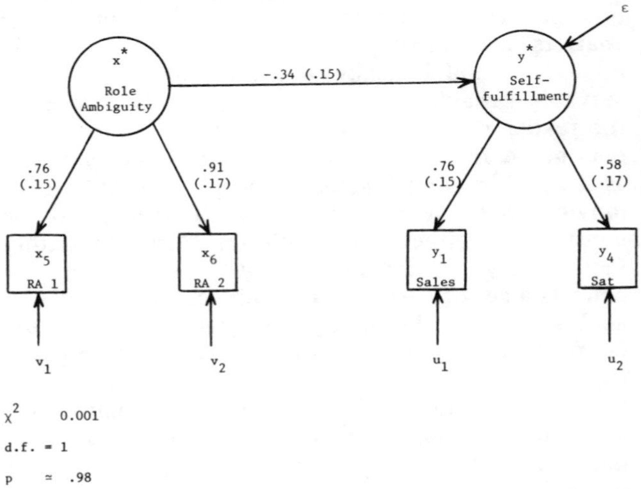

Note: Standard errors are in parentheses.

Figure 5
A FOUR-CONSTRUCT MODEL

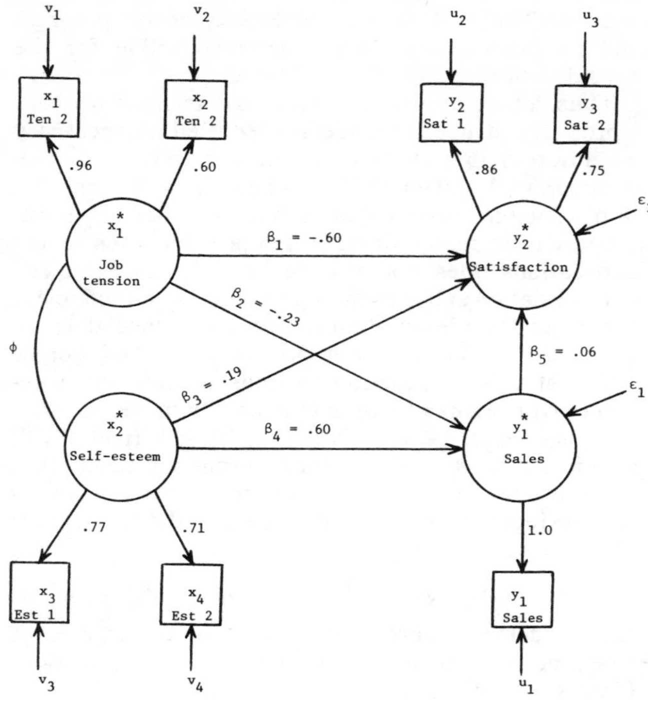

χ^2 13.3

d.f. = 8

p $\simeq$ .10

Note: All coefficients are significant at the .05 level except that
      of β_5

Similarly, y_4 is the better indicator of y^*. Again the chi square statistic is discussed in another section.

The third model, shown in Figure 5, is more complex, containing four constructs. The self-fulfillment construct has now been broken into two constructs, sales and job satisfaction. Further, a model hypothesis that is only very weakly supported is that sales influences job satisfaction. An hypothesis that is supported is that job tension (x_1^*) has a negative influence on job satisfaction and on sales. Another supported hypothesis is that the other independent variable, self-esteem (x_2^*), influences both job satisfaction and sales. Again, the indicator coefficients reflect the relative ability of the indicator to measure the unobservable construct.

IDENTIFICATION AND THE ESTIMATION OF PARAMETERS

The first step in constructing structural equation models is to propose relevant theoretical constructs, their indicators, and the structure or pattern of relationships. This set of procedures is known as specification. Specification depends fundamentally on the

theory one hopes to develop and test, the observable variables available, the results of past research, the creativity and acumen of the researcher, and other factors. Once a theory has been specified, two additional steps are *identification* and *estimation*.

To illustrate identification, consider the simple system consisting of one unobservable variable, y^*, and two indicators, y_2 and y_3, as shown in Figure 6A. The unobservable variable might now represent overall

Figure 6
ONE-CONSTRUCT MODELS

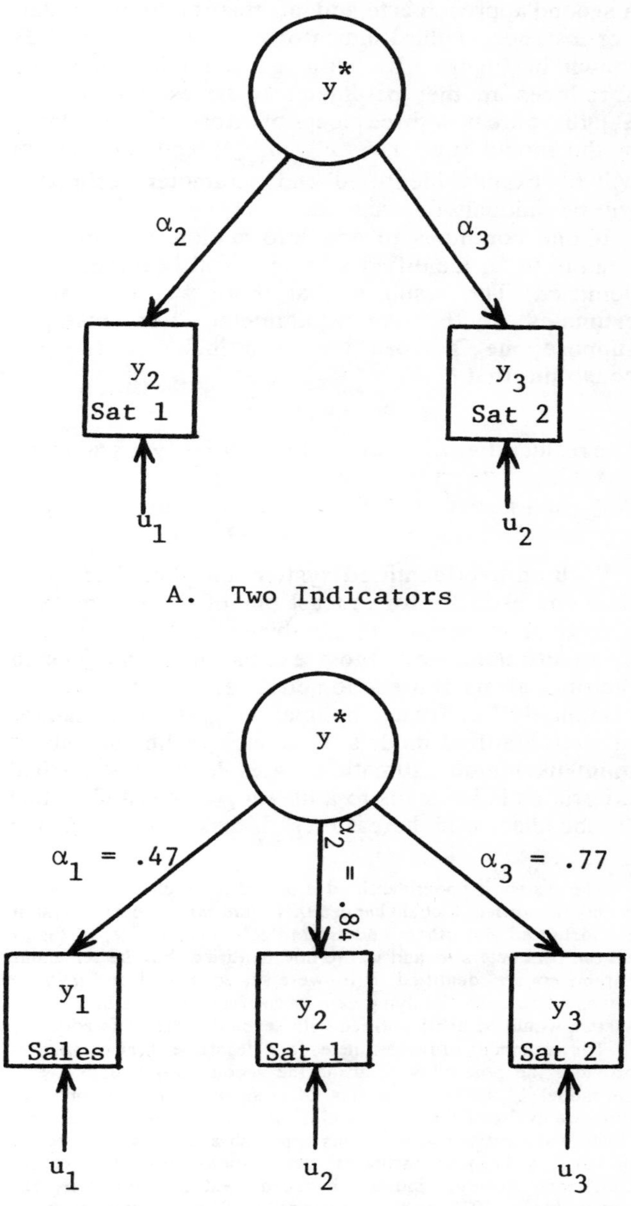

A.   Two Indicators

B.   Three Indicators

job satisfaction which is used here for discussion. In this simple model, only one piece of information—the sample correlation $r_{y_2y_3}$ between y_2 and y_3—is provided, yet two parameters (i.e., α_2 and α_3) are to be estimated. Because unique solutions of the parameters cannot be found without making further assumptions, the system is termed "underidentified."[3]

Two methods can be used to achieve identification for the model of Figure 6A. First, constraints can be added to the system. For example, if one has reason to believe that $\alpha_2 = \alpha_3 = \alpha$, then the model will be exactly identified with

$$\alpha = \sqrt{r_{y_2y_3}} = .80.$$

A second approach is to add information to the model. For instance, a third indicator of y^* can be used as shown in Figure 6B. Although the addition of y_1 introduces another parameter to be estimated (i.e., α_1), there are now three pieces of information available in the model (i.e., $r_{y_1y_2}$, $r_{y_1y_3}$, $r_{y_2y_3}$), and the system will be exactly identified and parameters estimates will be uniquely determined.

If one continues to add information and/or constraints to an identified system it will become overidentified. The result is that there will be several estimates of the same parameter. For example, suppose one included the third indicator and the constraint that

$$\alpha_2 = \alpha_3 = \alpha.$$

The result is two different estimates of the α parameter:

$$\alpha_2 = \sqrt{\frac{r_{y_1y_2}r_{y_2y_3}}{r_{y_1y_3}}} = .77 \quad \alpha_3 = \sqrt{\frac{r_{y_1y_3}r_{y_2y_3}}{r_{y_1y_2}}} = .84$$

With an overidentified system and therefore more than one estimate for at least one of the parameters, a method is needed to combine the two estimates in an efficient way. Most estimation techniques in factor analysis and econometrics are techniques that "implicitly" construct optimal weights for estimates in overidentified models. One such technique, maximum likelihood estimation, rates high on statistical criteria and also leads to a useful goodness-of-fit test (to be discussed hereafter.)[4] Jöreskog developed a practical maximum likelihood estimation program, LISREL, which can handle the most general structural equation problem including both errors in equations and errors in variables (1969, 1970, 1973; Jöreskog and Van Thillo 1972). The availability of this program and its predecessors is in part responsible for the consideration of this class of model.

Thus, a first step of analysis is to determine whether a proposed structural model is identified. A necessary condition is that the number of correlations (which is equal to $1/2\ (w)\ (w-1)$, where w is the number of observable variables) exceed the number of parameters. Unfortunately it could happen that each of the correlations does not provide an independent piece of information and thus this condition is not a sufficient condition for identifiability. For some special cases such as the MIMIC model (Jöreskog and Goldberger 1975), structural equation systems without measurement error (Fisher 1966), and a small number of other models (Geraci 1974; Hsiao 1976, 1979; Wright 1970), general rules are available for determining identifiability. For example, in the MIMIC model with q causes and p effects, the model will be identified if the degrees of freedom are nonnegative:

$$\text{d.f.} = q(p-1) + p(p-3)/2 \geq 0.$$

The model of Figure 3 therefore has six degrees of freedom or six overidentifying pieces of information. Unless one of the special cases is involved, the only sure way to prove identifiability is to show algebraically that each parameter can be estimated. Because such an approach can become involved for a complex model, identification can be a practical problem. However, some diagnostic information can be obtained from the LISREL program to help discover underidentifiability.

MODEL TESTING AND THEORY DEVELOPMENT

Ideally, one's theory will dictate a unique structural equation model, and a program such as LISREL can be used to estimate parameters. In practice, however, the researcher will more often begin with a tentative model as an hypothesis which then needs to be tested, refined, and retested before a satisfactory model can emerge. Further, a researcher also is likely to have several structural equation models to investigate as rival hypotheses. This likelihood is partly a result of the immaturity of theory in marketing and the social sciences and partly a consequence of the complexity of marketing problems and the uncertainty inherent in all phases of the research process. The researcher thus would like to know which, if any, of the models are or are not supported by the data.

An overall goodness-of-fit test of any structural equation model is provided by the maximum likelihood estimation procedure. To describe this test, it is useful to explain the estimation procedure from another

[3]The system is underidentified if one or more of the parameters is underidentified. It could happen that some parameters in a system are identified and others underidentified. For example, in Figure 1B the parameters α_1 and u_1 are not identified, but the remaining parameters are identified. If α_1 were set equal to 1 and u_1 were set equal to zero (implying zero measurement error in x_1^*), the system would be overidentified with seven degrees of freedom.

[4]The availability of two estimates for at least one of the parameters provides the possibility of using the second estimate to "test" the model. If the two estimates differ significantly, this outcome provides evidence that the model is false in some respect. Costner (1969) discusses the logic of this approach and shows how it can be used to diagnose particular specification errors. Hauser and Goldberger, however, indicate that such a test has some interpretation problems (1971, p. 83). A discussion of another type of model test is presented elsewhere in the article.

perspective. Start with **R**, the sample correlation matrix of observable variables.[5] Corresponding to **R** is a true population correlation matrix Σ. Each element in the true correlation matrix can be determined (if the system is identified) from the model parameters. Maximum likelihood estimation effectively attempts to find parameter estimates which will generate an estimated correlation matrix, $\hat{\Sigma}$, that will come as close as possible to the actual sample correlation matrix, **R**. If the model is just identified, there will be a perfect match. If, however, the model has one or more overidentifying restrictions, the match probably will not be perfect in the presence of sample errors. A chi square statistic is generated in the maximum likelihood estimation procedure that provides the probability that the differences between **R** and $\hat{\Sigma}$ would be that large under the null hypothesis that the specified model is correct.[6] The alternative hypothesis is that there are no restrictions on the matrix Σ.[7]

The test is thus whether the hypothesized model fits the data. Like most hypothesis tests, it is sensitive to sample size. Further, it does not provide any indication why the model does not fit the data, only that it does not fit. Similarly, if the model fits the data, it does not by itself suggest which other models might also fit the data. Such a test is most important because in a general structural equation model there is no commonly used statistic like R^2 in a regression context to evaluate the overall model.[8]

The chi square statistics presented in Figures 3, 4, and 5 now can be examined. The chi square value for the MIMIC model of Figure 3, 23.5, indicates a poor fit or a very large sample. As the sample size, 106, is not excessive and the p value is so low, a judgment that the model did not fit these data is appropriate. The interpretation of the various model coefficients presented heretofore should be tempered with the knowledge of the poor fit and the implication that the model structure is faulty. One way the structure could be faulty is by the omission of constructs and/or indicators.

The chi square value for the model in Figure 4, in contrast, suggests an extremely good fit and tends to confirm and support the judgments made about the model coefficients. The chi square value for the Figure 5 model, 13.3, is more borderline. The p-value of about 0.10 means that chi square value of over 13.3 would appear about one time in 10 if the proposed structure is true. To illustrate an important use of the chi square goodness-of-fit measure in hypothesis testing and theory construction, the analysis of the Figure 5 model is continued in the next section.

Exploring Nested Models

One model is said to be nested or contained within a second if the latter can be obtained by adding causal paths to the former. By continuing to add paths, one can obtain a sequence of nested models. Nested models provide a mechanism for exploring alternative theories. A researcher can begin with a model that is most consistent with theory. If this model is not compatible with the data (i.e., is rejected), causal paths can be added to the inadequate model to construct a better performing model. If, in contrast, the original model performs adequately, causal paths might be deleted to determine whether a more parsimonious model might also fit the data. The particular deletion or addition should be theoretically justifiable, of course. The adequacy of the new model(s) so constructed can be determined from the comparison of the individual chi square statistics.

To illustrate, assume that in the Figure 5 model the strongest theoretical evidence is only for the β_4 and β_5 links. Thus the researcher begins with a Figure 5 model in which:

$$\beta_1 = \beta_2 = \beta_3 = 0.$$

The resulting model, as noted in Table 2, has a chi square value at 45.84, indicating an extremely poor fit to the data and suggesting that the model is incorrectly specified. Perhaps needed constructs were omitted, the indicators were invalid, the errors were not independent (to be considered hereafter), or relevant causal paths were omitted. The last possiblility is now explored.

The procedure is to add a set of paths, thereby specifying a new model. The usefulness of the additional paths can be judged by the difference in the chi square statistics. The difference for large samples is, in fact, also distributed as a chi square distribution with degrees of freedom equal to the number of added

Table 2

SUMMARY OF HYPOTHESIS TESTS FOR SELECTED NESTED MODELS OF FIGURE 5

Model	χ^2	*d.f.*	*p-value*	*Change in* χ^2
1. $\beta_1 = \beta_2 = \beta_3 = 0$	45.84	11	.00	—
2. $\beta_2 = \beta_3 = 0$	19.45	10	.03	26.39
3. $\beta_3 = 0$	14.57	9	.10	4.88
4. Full model of Figure 5	13.33	8	.10	1.24
5. $\beta_5 = 0$	13.47	9	.14	.14
6. $\beta_3 = \beta_5 = 0$	16.25	10	.10	2.78

[5]Or the sample variance-covariance matrix if the variables are not standardized.

[6]Lawley and Maxwell indicate that the chi square test probably can be trusted when the sample size exceeds the number of observable variables by about 50 although they do recommend that a correction factor be applied to improve the chi square approximation (1971, p. 36).

[7]The matrix does have to be positive semidefinite.

[8]In the MIMIC model several useful statistics are available, one of which has an interpretation similar to R^2 in regression (Aaker et al. 1978; Jöreskog and Goldberger 1975).

paths.[9] A large chi square value (and small p-value) provides evidence that the paths should be included.

To continue the example, suppose that of the omitted paths β_1 had the greatest theoretical support. Adding β_1 provides Model 2 in Table 2 which generates a reduction in chi square from Model 1 of 26.39. This chi square value has one degree of freedom associated with it because one path was added. Thus, strong evidence that the β_1 path should be included is provided.

Model 2 still has an unsatisfactory fit so it may be useful to add another causal path if it would be theoretically justified. In fact, there is theoretical support for a negative link between job tension and sales represented by β_2 (Bagozzi 1976, 1978). Adding the link yields Model 3 which is shown in Table 2 to generate further chi square reduction of 4.88, a reduction which is significant at the .02 level. Thus, empirical support is provided for the inclusion of the β_2 link.

Finally, the inclusion of β_3, generating the complete Figure 5 model, provides an insignificant improvement in chi square, 1.24. Thus, one can conclude that without strong theoretical support for the β_3 link, it should be omitted.

The use of hypothesis tests to explore nested models can also proceed in the other direction (see Nan and Burt 1975 for an example). If a model fits well it might be possible to delete paths to generate a more parsimonious model that will also fit the data. Thus, the researcher will attempt to justify theoretically the elimination of some model paths to see whether the model performance will be affected. Paths which have small or nonsignificant coefficients associated with them (the standard t-test applies) are candidates for omission, if their presence is not mandated by theory.

For an illustration, consider again the Figure 5 model. Given the relatively low β_5 path magnitude, it seems appropriate to consider a model with it deleted. Such a model, termed Model 5 in Table 2, barely increases the chi square statistic. The next candidate for deletion is the β_3 link. The resulting Model 6 in Table 2 increases the chi square by 2.78. Because a chi square value of 2.78 with one degree of freedom is just significant at the 0.10 level, the empirical conclusion on the marginal inclusion of the β_3 link, given that the β_5 link is deleted, is not definitive.[10] Of course, the researcher can remove more than one path at a time. If both the β_3 and β_5 links were removed together, the chi square difference would be 2.92 and the appropriate degrees of freedom would be two.

A few additional comments are in order. First, if the researcher selects in advance a particular nested model to test, the theory is relatively clear. Suppose, however, a series of models are tested and then, after the results are examined, one hypothesis test is selected to support a particular model. The researcher should know that the selected hypothesis test may appear impressive in part because it was selected from a group of tests, and it should be interpreted accordingly. A second and related comment is that this procedure (like stepwise regression) is not a mechanism to mechanically generate a theory, although it can suggest hypotheses. There should be competing theories which are being evaluated at each step. Third, because the p-level is sensitive to sample size, it is often difficult to interpret when large sample sizes are present. Further, the maximum likelihood estimation approach is best suited for large samples and thus the large sample case should be the norm. A solution is to work with the chi square statistic. Although it will not have any meaning in an absolute sense, it will provide a good indication of the relative fit of the various submodels and can thus be used as an aid in theory construction.

MEASUREMENT ERRORS

In the foregoing discussion an assumption is made that the measurement errors are independent. In some situations it is appropriate and useful to relax that assumption.

Consider the two-construct models in Figure 7A, with job tension as the independent variable and self-fulfillment as the dependent variable. The chi square value indicates a marginal fit ($p \cong .07$). There are a variety of possible reasons why the model did not fit better. One possibility is that self-fulfillment needs to be divided into two constructs as was done in the Figure 5 model. Another is that the error terms of y_2 and y_3 are correlated. Correlated errors within constructs arise from the presence of some unmeasured third variable causing an association between y_2 and y_3. Perhaps y_2 and y_3 are indicators of not only self-fulfillment but also some other unobservable not in the model. In any case, the Figure 7B model with correlated errors can be tested formally and compared with the model without correlated errors. The reduction in the chi square value is 3.30 which (with one degree of freedom) is significant at the 0.10 level and provides empirical support (but does not prove) that a link should be made between u_2 and u_3.

Errors can also be correlated across constructs (e.g., v_1 and u_1). Such an occurrence is particularly common in longitudinal studies (Jöreskog and Sörbom 1977). Suppose two unobservable constructs are attitude and lagged attitude. The attitude indicators may have

---

[9]This test is based on the likelihood ratio test. See Mood and Graybill (1963, p. 298).

[10]For Model 6 the revised path coefficients are:

$$\beta_1 = -.751$$
$$\beta_2 = -.260$$
$$\beta_3 = .570.$$

Figure 7
MODELING CORRELATED ERRORS

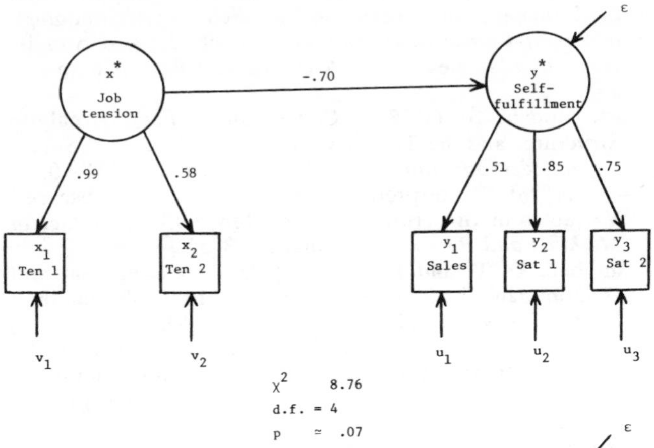

A. Uncorrelated Errors

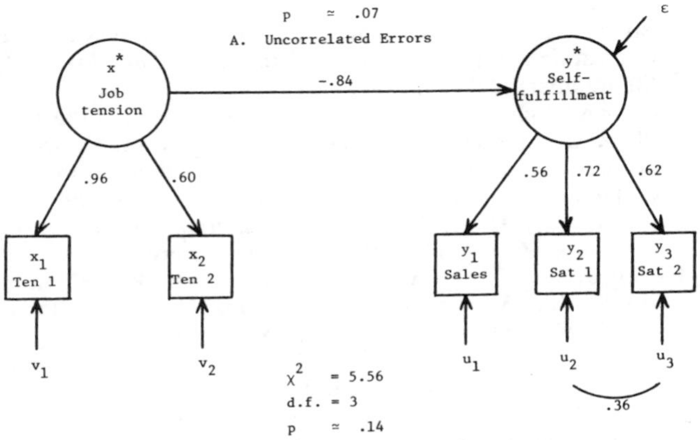

B. Correlated Errors Within Constructs

correlated errors due to the use of a common scale, common response sets, or memory effects. Costner and Schoenberg (1973) show how in some models the presence of correlated errors across constructs can be detected. Still another possibility is a path between an unobservable construct (i.e., x^* in Figure 7) and an error term associated with another construct (i.e., u_1). If an observable variable were an indicator of two constructs in the model, such a link would be appropriate (Jöreskog and Sörbom 1977).[11]

ALTERNATIVE APPROACHES TO UNOBSERVED VARIABLES

Several alternatives are available other than the structural equation approach to unobserved variables. As noted at the outset, a common and often inappropriate approach is simply to assume that the unobserved variable is measured without error by a single indicator.

Another approach is to build an index of an unobservable construct based on indicators that are considered relevant and to use this index in the structural equation. The index might be a simple sum or it could be more complex, involving weights and a nonadditive structure. The internal consistency of the index can be measured by a reliability coefficient such as the Cronbach α (Jöreskog 1973). Hopefully, the index will serve to cancel the effects of nonrandom errors associated with the various indicators. However, the use of an index requires the *a priori* establishment of the weighting scheme and functional form, a demanding task in many contexts. An index will also tend both to create and obscure specification errors. Further, in part because the error terms are not explicitly introduced, the resulting interpretation of the system is less precise and complete than it might be.

Still another approach involves conducting a factor analysis and then using the resulting factor scores in the structural model (Jöreskog and Goldberger 1975). Such an approach contains all the characteristics of exploratory factor analysis. The constructs and their indicators are not specified from prior theory and experience but rather are generated by the data which contain sampling and nonsampling errors. Often this can be a relatively subjective and unreliable procedure. If the analyst has any prior information whether from theory, past research, or the particular research design at hand, the use of unobservable variables in the structure equation context should be more appropriate.

It is possible to decompose the parameter estimation procedure and obtain prior estimates of the "factor loadings" in a multiple indicator model. For example, in Figure 1B the terms λ_1 and λ_2 and ν_1 and ν_2 can be estimated in a confirmatory factor analysis sense by using only the correlations between the two indicator variables for y^*. Then the other model parameters can be estimated with λ_1 and λ_2 and ν_1 and ν_2 prespecified. Burt (1976) points out that such an approach often can result in different estimates of the "factor loadings." When the complete model is estimated the other exogenous and endogenous variables help to define the y^* construct and therefore influence λ_1, λ_2, ν_1, and ν_2. If the rest of the model is ignored, y^* must be defined solely in terms of its indicators. If the analyst has more confidence and knowledge about the indicators than about the total model structure, this decomposition approach might be reasonable.

CONCLUSIONS

It will be useful in conclusion to highlight some of the assumptions and limitations of the approach described. First, the relationships are postulated to be linear and additive although suitable transforma-

[11]The researcher normally will strive to have each measurement be an indicator for only a single theoretical construct, however, to avoid ambiguities in interpretation.

tions can relax this assumption in some contexts. Second, the variables are assumed to be intervally scaled (see Goldberger 1964, p. 248) and normally distributed. The use of nominally scaled dependent variables can cause substantial problems. Third, the maximum likelihood estimate and the goodness-of-fit test based on it may not perform well if a small sample is used (i.e., for $n \lesssim 50$). Fourth, in contrast, the chi square statistic on which the goodness-of-fit test is based has no clear interpretation by itself and its associated significance level will not be useful when the sample size is so large that all results are "significant." Finally, although the approach does provide ways to guide theory development, it is predicated on the researcher starting with some theory to specify and test.

The use of unobservable variables in structural equations seems to have exceptional potential to help marketing researchers. The reality is that, for marketing problems, single indicators of theoretical constructs tend often to be biased and unreliable. A reasonable solution is to use multiple indicators and to model the errors in variables explicitly rather than have them confounded with errors in equations resulting from a misspecified theory.

REFERENCES

Aaker, David A., Richard P. Bagozzi, James M. Carman, and James M. MacLachlan (1979), "On Using Response Latency," working paper, University of California (February).

———and George S. Day (1974), "A Dynamic Model of Relationships Among Advertising, Consumer Awareness, Attitudes and Behavior," *Journal of Applied Psychology*, 59, 281–6.

Bagozzi, Richard P. (1976), "Toward a General Theory for the Explanation of the Performance of Salespeople," unpublished doctoral dissertation, Northwestern University.

———(1977a), "Convergent and Discriminant Validity by Analysis of Covariance Structures: The Case of the Affective Behavioral, and Cognitive Components of Attitude," in *Advances in Consumer Research*, W. D. Perreault, Jr., ed., Volume 4, Association for Consumer Research.

———(1977b), "Structural Equation Models in Experimental Research," *Journal of Marketing Research*, 14 (May), 209–26.

———(1978), "Salesforce Performance and Satisfaction as a Function of Individual Difference, Interpersonal, and Situational Factors," *Journal of Marketing Research*, 15 (November), 517–31.

Bass, Frank M. (1969), "A Simultaneous Equation Regression Study of Advertising and Sales of Cigarettes," *Journal of Marketing Research*, 6 (August), 291–300.

Bielby, William T. and Robert M. Hauser (1977), "Structural Equation Models," *Annual Review of Sociology*, Volume 2. Palo Alto: Annual Reviews.

Blalock, Hubert M., Jr. (1967a) "Causal Inferences, Closed Populations, and Measures of Associations," *American Political Science Review*, 61, 130–6.

———(1967b), "Path Coefficients Versus Regression Coefficients," *American Journal of Sociology*, 72, 675–6.

———(1968), "The Measurement Problem: A Gap Between the Languages of Theory and Research," in *Methodology in Social Research*, Hubert M. Blalock, Jr. and Ann B. Blalock, eds. New York: McGraw-Hill Book Company, 5–27.

Burt, Ronald S. (1973), "Confirmatory Factor-Analytic Structures and the Theory Construction Process," *Sociological Methods and Research*, 2 (November), 131–90.

———(1976), "Interpreting Confounding of Unobserved Variables in Structural Equation Models," *Sociological Methods and Research*, 5 (August), 3–52.

Campbell, D. T. and J. D. Fisk (1959), "Convergent and Discriminant Validation by the Multitrait-Multimethod Matrix," *Psychological Bulletin*, 56, 81–105.

Churchill, G. A., Jr., N. M. Ford, and O. C. Walker, Jr. (1976), "Organizational Climate and Job Satisfaction in the Salesforce," *Journal of Marketing Research*, 13 (November), 323–32.

Costner, H. L. (1969), "Theory, Deduction and Rules of Correspondence," *American Journal of Sociology*, 75 (September), 245–63.

———and Schoenberg, R. (1973), "Diagnosing Indicator Ills in Multiple Indicator Models," in *Structural Equation Models in the Social Sciences*, A. S. Goldberger and O. D. Duncan, eds. New York: Seminar Press, 167–99.

Duncan, Otis Dudley (1975), *Introduction to Structural Equation Models*. New York: Academic Press.

Farley, John U., John A. Howard, and Donald R. Lehmann (1976), "A 'Working' System Model of Car Buyer Behavior," *Management Science*, 23 (November), 235–47.

Fisher, F. M. (1966), *The Identification Problem in Econometrics*. New York: McGraw-Hill Book Company.

Geraci, V. J. (1974), "Simultaneous Equation Models with Measurement Error," unpublished doctoral dissertation, Department of Economics, University of Wisconsin.

Goldberger, Arthur S. (1964), *Econometeric Theory*. New York: John Wiley & Sons, Inc.

———(1973), "Structural Equation Models: An Overview," in *Structural Equation Models in the Social Sciences*, A. S. Goldberger and O. D. Duncan, eds. New York: Seminar Press, 1–18.

———(1974), "Unobservable Variables in Econometrics," in *Frontiers in Econometrics*, P. Zarembka, ed. New York: Academic Press. 193–213.

Gorsuch, Richard L. (1974), *Factor Analysis*. Philadelphia: W. B. Saunders Company.

Griliches, A. (1974), "Errors in Variables and Other Unobservables," *Econometrica*, 42 (November), 971–98.

Hauser, R. M. and Arthur S. Goldberger (1971), "The Treatment of Unobservable Variables in Path Analysis," in *Sociological Methodology 1971*, H. L. Costner, ed. San Francisco: Jossey-Bass, 81–117.

Hsiao, C. (1976), "Identification for a Linear Dynamic Simultaneous Error-Shock Model," working paper, Department of Economics, University of California.

———(1979), "Identification and Estimation of Simultaneous Equation Models with Measurement Error," *International Economic Review*, forthcoming.

Jacobson, Alvin L. and N. M. Lalu (1974), "An Empirical and Algebraic Analysis of Alternative Techniques for Measuring Unobserved Variables," in *Measurement in the Social Sciences*, H. M. Blalock, Jr., ed. Chicago: Aldine, 215–42.

Jöreskog, Karl G. (1969), "A General Approach to Confirmatory Maximum Likelihood Factor Analysis," *Psychometrika*, 34, 183–202.

———(1970), "A General Method of Analysis of Covariance Structures," *Biometrika*, 57, 239–51.

———(1973), "A General Method for Estimating a Linear Structural Equation System," in *Structural Equation Models in the Social Sciences*, A. S. Goldberger and O. D. Duncan, eds. New York: Seminar Press, 85–112.

———and Arthur S. Goldberger (1975), "Estimation of a Model with Multiple Indicators and Multiple Causes of a Single Latent Variable," *Journal of the American Statistical Association*, 70 (September), 631–9.

———and D. Sörbom (1977), "Statistical Models and Methods for Analysis of Longitudinal Data," in *Latent Variables in Socioeconomic Models*, D. J. Aigner and A. S. Goldberger eds. Amsterdam: North-Holland.

———and M. van Thillo (1972), "LISREL: A General Computer Program for Estimating a Linear Structural Equation System Involving Multiple Indicators of Unmeasured Variables," RB-72-56. Princeton, New Jersey: Educational Testing Service.

Kim, J. and C. W. Mueller (1976), "Standardization and Unstandardized Coefficients in Causal Analysis," *Sociological Methods and Research*, 4 (May), 423–38.

Land, K. C. (1969), "Principles of Path Analysis," in *Sociological Methodology 1969*, E. F. Borgatta, ed. San Francisco: Jossey-Bass, 3–37.

Lawley, D. N. and A. E. Maxwell (1971), *Factor Analysis as a Statistical Method*. London: Butterworth.

Lord, F. C. and M. R. Novick (1968), *Statistical Theories of Mental Test Scores*. Reading, Massachusetts: Addison-Wesley.

Massy, William F. (1969), "What is Factor Analysis?" in *Proceedings of the 1964 Conference of the American Marketing Association*. Chicago: American Marketing Association, 291–307.

Mitchell, A. A. and J. C. Olson (1975), "The Use of Restricted and Unrestricted Maximum Likelihood Factor Analysis to Examine Alternative Measures of Brand Loyalty," Working Paper No. 29, Pennsylvania State University.

Mood, Alexander M. and Franklin A. Graybill (1963), *Introduction to the Theory of Statistics*. New York: McGraw-Hill Book Company.

Mulaik, Stanley A. (1972), *The Foundations of Factor Analysis*. New York: McGraw-Hill Book Company.

Nan, Lin and Ronald S. Burt (1975), "Differential Effects of Information Channels in the Process of Innovation Diffusion," *Social Forces*, 54 (September), 256–74.

Tukey, J. W. (1954), "Causation, Regression and Path Analysis," in *Statistics and Mathematics in Biology*, O. Kempthorne, T. A. Bancroft, J. W. Gowen, and J. L. Lush, eds. Ames, Iowa: Iowa State College Press, 35–66.

Werts, C. E., K. G. Jöreskog, and R. L. Linn (1973), "Identification and Estimation in Path Analysis with Unmeasured Variables," *American Journal of Sociology*, 78, 1469–84.

Wright, Sewall (1970), "Path Coefficients and Path Regressions: Alternatives or Complementary Concepts?" *Biometrics*, 16, 189–202.

APPENDIX

PEARSON PRODUCT-MOMENT CORRELATIONS FOR OBSERVATIONS OF VARIABLES USED IN ANALYSES

Variables	y_1	y_2	y_3	y_4	x_1	x_2	x_3	x_4	x_5	x_6
Dollar sales, y_1	1.000									
Job satisfaction #1, y_2	.395	1.000								
Job satisfaction #2, y_3	.364	.647	1.000							
Job satisfaction #1 and #2, y_4	.420	.929	.884	1.000						
Job tension #1, x_1	−.438	−.589	−.491	−.600	1.000					
Job tension #2, x_2	−.383	−.290	−.324	−.337	.572	1.000				
Specific self-esteem #1, x_3	.536	.297	.288	.322	−.273	−.392	1.000			
Specific self-esteem #2, x_4	.494	.254	.284	.294	−.248	−.267	.548	1.000		
Role ambiguity #1, x_5	−.187	−.134	−.137	−.149	.307	.260	−.294	−.289	1.000	
Role ambiguity #2, x_6	−.222	−.139	−.191	−.179	.293	.391	−.364	−.425	.696	1.000

$n = 106$

Conjoint Analysis in Consumer Research: Issues and Outlook

PAUL E. GREEN
V. SRINIVASAN*

Since 1971 conjoint analysis has been applied to a wide variety of problems in consumer research. This paper discusses various issues involved in implementing conjoint analysis and describes some new technical developments and application areas for the methodology.

The modeling of consumer preferences among multiattribute alternatives has been one of the major activities in consumer research for at least a decade. Undoubtedly, the expectancy-value class of attitude models (Fishbein 1967; Rosenberg 1956) has occupied more researchers' time and journal pages than any other approach. However, a more recent contender, conjoint analysis, shows indications of coming into its own as a practical set of methods for predicting consumer preferences for multiattribute options in a wide variety of product and service contexts.

The purpose of this paper is to trace the development of conjoint methodology and relate it to relevant topics in applied psychology, decision theory, and economics. We then discuss the merits and demerits of the alternatives that have been proposed for implementing the different steps in conjoint analysis. Next, we focus on reliability and validity testing of the methodology. The discussion then proceeds to applications of conjoint analysis to the evaluation of products and services in the public and private sectors. The paper concludes with a brief discussion of some new developments in methodology and application areas.

Readers who are unfamiliar with conjoint analysis may want to read Green and Wind (1975) before attempting a detailed study of this paper.[1]

CONJOINT ANALYSIS IN REVIEW

While the foundations of the field go back to at least the 1920s, it is generally agreed that 1964 marks the start of conjoint measurement, with the seminal paper by Luce, a mathematical psychologist, and Tukey, a statistician (Luce and Tukey 1964). Shortly thereafter, a number of theoretical contributions (Krantz 1964; Tversky 1967) and algorithmic developments (Kruskal 1965; Carroll 1969; Young 1969) appeared.

Conjoint measurement, as practiced by mathematical psychologists, has primarily been concerned with the conditions under which there exist measurement scales for both the dependent and independent variables, given the order of the joint effects of the independent variables and a prespecified composition rule. Computer programs have been developed and applied in examining whether a set of data meets the necessary conditions for applying various composition rules (e.g., additive) hypothesized by the researcher (Ullrich and Painter 1974; Barron 1977). However, applications by psychometricians and consumer researchers have emphasized the scaling aspects—finding specific numerical scale values, *assuming* that a particular composition rule applies, possibly with some error. Accordingly, it now seems useful to adopt the name, "conjoint analysis," to cover models and techniques that emphasize the transformation of subjective responses into estimated parameters.

While conjoint methodology was discussed briefly in the working paper by Green and Rao (1969) and the book by Green and Carmone (1970), the first detailed, consumer-oriented paper did not appear until 1971 (Green and Rao). Following this, a spate of papers dealing with either algorithms or applications (Green, Carmone, and Wind 1972; Srinivasan and Shocker 1973b; Johnson 1974; Westwood, Lunn, and Beazley 1974) appeared in a variety of journals. Theoretical justification for the multiattribute modeling of consumer preferences was provided in the growing literature on

* Paul E. Green is S.S. Kresge Professor of Marketing, Wharton School, University of Pennsylvania, Philadelphia, PA 19104, and V. Srinivasan is Professor of Marketing and Management Science, Graduate School of Business, Stanford University, Stanford, CA 94305. The authors wish to thank all those contributors to the field who were kind enough to send various bibliographic materials relating to conjoint analysis. The authors also extend their appreciation to John Hauser, Subrata Sen, and the referees for helpful comments on an earlier version of this paper.

[1] For a technical description of parameter estimation algorithms with illustrations, the reader is urged to see the excellent review of conjoint analysis by Rao (1977). A monograph-length treatment of conjoint analysis and related procedures for analyzing multiattribute data can be found in the text by Green and Wind (1973).

Reprinted with permission from *Journal of Consumer Research,* 5 (September 1978), 103-23.

the Fishbein-Rosenberg class of expectancy-value models and the new economic theory of consumer choice (Lancaster 1971; Ratchford 1975). However, economists have generally been most interested in the aggregate implications of multiattribute utility structures and less concerned with estimation of individual utility functions per se.

As Wilkie and Pessemier (1973) have observed, expectancy-value models draw upon a *compositional* or build-up approach in which the total utility for some multiattribute object is found as a weighted sum of the object's perceived attribute levels and associated value ratings, as *separately* (and explicitly) judged by the respondent. In contrast, conjoint methodology is based on a *decompositional* approach, in which respondents react to a set of "total" profile descriptions. It is the job of the analyst to find a set of *part worths* for the individual attributes that, given some type of composition rule (e.g., an additive one), are most consistent with the respondent's overall preferences. Furthermore, a key distinction between these two approaches lies in the predominant purpose for which each approach is used. Users of conjoint analysis have generally emphasized predictive validity and regarded explanation largely as a desirable (but secondary) objective, while the converse has generally been true for the expectancy-value theorists.

Conjoint analysis, both in spirit and computational detail, is closely related to two other developments in applied psychology—the modeling of clinical judgments and functional measurement.

Since 1960, the modeling of clinical judgments has been the principal pursuit of a group of behavioral scientists initially identified with the Oregon Research Institute (Dawes and Corrigan 1974). This approach has involved decompositional modeling of subjects' responses to profile descriptions representing such diverse topics as gastric ulcer symptoms (Hoffman, Slovic, and Rorer 1968), psychological test scores (Goldberg 1968), and student applications for graduate study (Dawes 1971). Multiple regression has been the main technique for parameter estimation in these models, although analysis of variance (ANOVA) has been applied occasionally.

In clinical judgment modeling the dependent variable is, for instance, an admissions officer's overall evaluation of the likelihood of success in graduate study of an applicant described in terms of the predictors: individual Graduate Record Examination score, undergraduate grade-point average, and rating of the undergraduate institution's quality. The standardized partial regression coefficients (or beta weights) are often interpreted as measures of the relative importance of predictors in estimating the dependent variable.

Functional measurement, as originally proposed by Anderson (1970), also employs a decompositional approach utilizing, in this case, ANOVA and full factorial designs. Functional measurement has been used for both parameter estimation and model testing (e.g., to see if certain theoretically predicted interaction effects occur) in such content areas as information integration, attitude change theory, person perception, decision theory, and consumer behavior.

In terms of methodology, functional measurement proceeds similarly to clinical judgment modeling and conjoint analysis. For example, a researcher may be interested in how a subject judges the friendliness of a person described in terms of levels on two factors, say, boldness and laziness. Each of the two factors in the experiment would consist of a set of levels, and all levels of the first factor would be crossed with all levels of the second. Overall friendliness ratings are then decomposed by ANOVA procedures to yield a scale value for each level of each of the two factors. Moreover, assuming that replicate judgments are available, the researcher can check for the significance of interaction effects.

A very different set of procedures has been developed by Keeney and Raiffa (1976) for multiattribute utility estimation in normative contexts. The form of the utility function is derived deductively from a set of assumptions. The parameters of the utility function are obtained from tradeoff judgments and from preferences for alternative gambles (lotteries). The data collection is considerably more complex than conjoint analysis. Although the utility function approach employs decompositional modeling in several parts of its implementation (Hauser and Urban 1977), it is not an estimation procedure in that virtually no measurement error is assumed (in contrast to the just described statistical approaches).

In what follows, we use the term conjoint analysis broadly to refer to any decompositional method that estimates the *structure* of a consumer's preferences (e.g., part worths, importance weights, ideal points) given his/her overall evaluations of a set of alternatives that are prespecified in terms of levels of different attributes. This type of estimation has been referred to as "external analysis" in the psychometric literature (Carroll 1972).

ISSUES IN IMPLEMENTING CONJOINT ANALYSIS

Because of the substantial amount of among-person variation in consumer preferences, conjoint analysis is usually carried out at the individual level. The form of the preference model (composition rule) is generally assumed to be the same for all individuals, but the parameters of the model are permitted to vary across the sample of individuals from the relevant target population.

Several alternate means exist for identifying the attributes which are relevant to consumers in forming their preferences (Alpert 1971). A preliminary data collection effort, questioning consumers regarding attributes important to them, usually helps in identifying those attributes that are most frequently regarded as relevant (Braun and Srinivasan 1975). Kelly's (1955) repertory grid, focus group interviews, or judgments of product managers, retailers and others knowledgeable about the product/service and its uses can be used for this purpose. The more difficult and often subjective task is to reduce the number of attributes to a manageable size so that the estimation procedures are reliable while at the same time accounting for consumer preferences sufficiently well.

The various steps in conjoint analysis and the alternative methods of implementing each of the steps are summarized in the table. We discuss each of these steps in turn and indicate the empirical results, if any, that are available for comparing the alternatives. There is considerable scope for empirical research in this area to determine the methods that are most appropriate for each of the steps.

Among the numerous combinations of methods that can be chosen for the different steps, some of the combinations are not feasible and these will be pointed out in the ensuing discussion. To date, most applications of conjoint analysis have utilized only a few of the many possible combinations. By focusing attention on the steps themselves, better overall combinations may emerge. A worthwhile goal for empirical research is to identify the combination of methods that provides the maximum predictive validity for a given amount of respondent time (or research budget). Of course, the best combination will probably depend on factors such as the type of product/market, the number of relevant attributes, the type of respondent, and so on. Future studies might entail several combinations, each dealing with a separate part of the data collection and analysis.

TABLE

STEPS INVOLVED IN CONJOINT ANALYSIS

Step	Alternative methods
1. Selection of a model of preference	Vector model, ideal-point model, part-worth function model, mixed model
2. Data collection method	Two-factor-at-a-time (trade-off analysis), full-profile (concept evaluation)
3. Stimulus set construction for the full-profile method	Fractional factorial design, random sampling from multivariate distribution
4. Stimulus presentation	Verbal description (multiple cue, stimulus card), paragraph description, pictorial or three-dimensional model representation
5. Measurement scale for the dependent variable	Paired comparisons, rank order, rating scales, constant-sum paired comparisons, category assignment (Carroll, 1969)
6. Estimation method	MONANOVA, PREFMAP, LINMAP, Johnson's nonmetric tradeoff algorithm, multiple regression, LOGIT, PROBIT

Preference Models

First, let

$$p = 1, 2, \ldots, t \tag{1}$$

denote the set of t attributes or factors that have been chosen. Next, let y_{jp} denote the level of the pth attribute for the jth stimulus. We first consider the case where y_{jp} is inherently a continuous variable (e.g., travel time or price). The case of categorical (or polytomous) attributes will be considered later. The vector model of preference, referred to as the Composite Criterion Model by Srinivasan and Shocker (1973b) and Parker and Srinivasan (1976), posits that the preference s_j for the jth stimulus is given by

$$s_j = \sum_{p=1}^{t} w_p y_{jp}, \tag{2}$$

where the $\{w_p\}$ are the individual's weights for the t attributes. Thus, the vector model is identical in mathematical form to the Fishbein-Rosenberg class of multiattribute models. As remarked earlier, the weights $\{w_p\}$ will, in general, be different for different individuals in the sample. Geometrically, the preference s_j can be represented as the projection of the stimulus point $\{y_{jp}\}$ on the vector $\{w_p\}$ in the t-dimensional attribute space.

The *ideal-point model* posits that the preference s_j is negatively related to the squared (weighted) distance d_j^2 of the location $\{y_{jp}\}$ of the jth stimulus from the individual's ideal point $\{x_p\}$, where d_j^2 is defined as

$$d_j^2 = \sum_{p=1}^{t} w_p(y_{jp} - x_p)^2. \tag{3}$$

Thus, stimuli which are closer to the ideal point (smaller d_j^2) will be the more preferred ones (larger s_j). It turns out that the simultaneous estimation of $\{w_p\}$ and $\{x_p\}$ is feasible for the weighted Euclidean measure of distance as specified in equation (3). If, however, the exponent 2 in equation (3) is replaced by a general Minkowski metric r, the estimation of $\{x_p\}$ becomes very difficult. Fortunately, however, the Euclidean metric is often a close enough approximation to the general Minkowski metric (Green 1975).

The *part-worth function* model posits that

$$s_j = \sum_{p=1}^{t} f_p(y_{jp}), \tag{4}$$

where f_p is the function denoting the part worth of different levels of y_{jp} for the pth attribute. In practice, $f_p(y_{jp})$ is estimated only for a selected set of levels for y_{jp} (usually three or four), with the part worth for intermediate y_{jp} obtained by linear interpolation. Thus the

FIGURE

ALTERNATIVE MODELS OF PREFERENCE

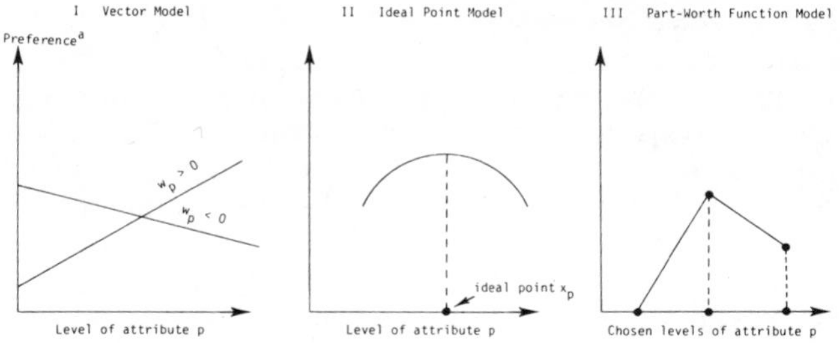

[a] Preference for different levels of attribute p while holding the values for the other attributes constant.

part-worth function is represented as a piecewise linear curve. To determine the part worth for a value of y_{jp} outside the range of estimation, extrapolation of the piecewise linear function would be needed and the validity of this procedure is questionable. (Hence, the researcher should try to employ the full range of the attribute, wherever practical.) Still, the part-worth function approach has received wide acceptance due, in part, to the ready interpretability of the graphicelly displayed attribute part-worth functions. The three models of preference are illustrated in the figure.

The part-worth function model provides the greatest flexibility in allowing different shapes for the preference function along each of the attributes. In particular, by defining $f_p(y_{jp}) = -w_p(y_{jp} - x_p)^2$ we get the ideal-point model and by setting $f_p(y_{jp}) = w_p y_{jp}$ we obtain the vector model. Similarly, the ideal-point model is more flexible than the vector model since it can be shown (Carroll 1972) that the vector model is a special case of the ideal-point model as $x_p \rightarrow \pm \infty$. Intuitively, as $x_p \rightarrow +\infty$, preference along the pth dimension increases as y_{jp} increases (since the ideal is at plus infinity) and this is essentially the same as the vector model with $w_p > 0$.

Although the part-worth function model seems to be the most attractive in terms of being compatible with any arbitrary shape for the preference function, this benefit comes at the cost of having to estimate additional parameters (thereby lowering their reliability) and the need to approximate intermediate values by linear interpolation. In particular, estimation of the vector model involves only the t parameters $\{w_p\}$. For the ideal-point model, $2t$ parameters have to be estimated, namely $\{w_p\}$ and $\{x_p\}$. If there are q levels, say, for each of the t attributes then $(q - 1)t$ parameters have to be estimated for the part-worth function model. Replacing $f_p(y_{jp})$ by $f_p(y_{jp}) + a_p$ does not alter the model in equation (4) in any essential way so that the part worth for level 1, say, can be taken to be zero without any loss of generality. Consequently, only $(q - 1)$ parameters need to be estimated for the pth attribute.

To summarize the discussion so far, the flexibility of the shape of the preference model is greater as we go from the vector to the ideal point to the part-worth function models; however, the reliability of the estimated parameters is likely to improve in the reverse order. Consequently, from the point of view of predictive validity, the relative desirability of the three models is not clear. Thus a priori notions of the shape of the part-worth function could help us in the choice of an appropriate model. One may always prefer greater durability (vector), smaller waiting time (vector), but may prefer moderate levels of sweetness or size of automobile (ideal point). However, one may prefer maximum temperature levels for both iced and hot tea (Carroll 1972) and have a lower preference for in-between temperature levels (part-worth function). If the attribute is categorical, (e.g., mode of travel—auto versus carpool versus public transit; type of educational institution—junior college, private university, state university), we are forced to use the part-worth function model. It is, of course, probable that for some attributes the vector model would be the best while for some others the ideal-point or part-worth models may be more appropriate.

We may combine the features of the three models to formulate a *mixed model*. It is well known (e.g., Green and Tull 1978, pp. 297–8) that a polytomous attribute with k levels can be converted into $(k - 1)$ dummy variables, where the ith dummy variable takes the value 1 for the ith level and 0 otherwise. (The kth level serves as the reference.) Thus the part-worth model can be converted to the vector model with the use of dummy variables. (The situation is analogous to the analysis of factorial experiments through multiple regression.) Similarly, if we consider the component of the ideal-point model along the pth attribute and relate the squared distance to preference by a negative sign, we obtain

$$f_p(y_{jp}) = -w_p(y_{jp}^2 - 2x_p y_{jp} + x_p^2). \quad (5)$$

Equation (5) may be rewritten as,

$$f_p(y_{jp}) = a_p + b_p y_{jp}^2 + c_p y_{jp}, \quad (6)$$

where $a_p = -w_p x_p^2$, $b_p = -w_p$ and $c_p = 2w_p x_p$. Thus, the essential nature of the ideal-point model can be captured in the vector model by considering the pseudo-attribute y_{jp}^2 in addition to y_{jp} (Carroll 1972). Furthermore, if $f_p(y_{jp})$ is substantially nonlinear (convex or concave), it may also be capable of being parsimoniously represented by equation (6). It may also be worthwhile to consider higher order polynomial terms, such as y_{jp}^3. Pekelman and Sen (1978) show that if the utility function has the form given in equation (6), then the estimation of that function would give better predictive results than a part-worth function approach combined with linear interpolation. However, if the functional form is likely to be very different from equation (6), the part-worth function approach may be appropriate.

A mixed model that may capture the advantages of all three models can be implemented by the notation,

$$s_j = \sum_{q=1}^{T} v_q z_{jq}, \tag{7}$$

where T is the total number of pseudo-attributes (also the total number of estimated parameters) and the $\{z_{jq}\}$ are defined from the y_{jp}, as follows:

1. attributes where the preference is expected to be monotone and approximately linear: z_j is defined to be equal to y_j;
2. attributes for which the preference is expected to be either substantially nonlinear (convex or concave) or of the ideal-point type: for each attribute p, two z variables, one equal to y and the other equal to y^2, are defined;
3. attributes which are categorical, or the preference function is not well approximated by equation (6): for each attribute p with k levels, $(k - 1)$ dummy variable would be defined.

If the dependent variable (overall preference) is measured on an interval scale and multiple regression is used as the estimation procedure, then statistical testing of equation (7) could guide us in the choice of vector versus ideal point versus part-worth model for the pth attribute, e.g., if the coefficient of the y^2 term is not significant then the vector model could be chosen over the ideal-point model.

Much empirical research has examined whether consumers actually use the linear-compensatory model (i.e., the vector model) rather than the seemingly simpler evaluation models such as the lexicographic and conjunctive (cut-off) rules (Russ 1971; Wright 1975; Hansen 1976). (Actually, the lexicographic model is a special case of the vector model in equation (2) where the weight for the most important attribute is considerably larger than the second most important attribute whose weight, in turn, is considerably larger than the third most important attribute, etc.) This research has found that some consumers use each of the models, but generally prefer those requiring simpler processes. However, for predictive validity this problem is not as serious as it may initially seem. This is because the compensatory model of conjoint analysis can approximate the outcomes of other kinds of decision rules quite closely. In fact, a recent study by Berl, Lewis, and Morrison (1976) of high school seniors' choice of colleges showed that the linear compensatory model was more consistent with the respondents' actual behavior than the lexicographic and conjunctive rules.

Dawes and Corrigan (1974), Rorer (1971), and Green and Devita (1975b) discuss the general conditions under which linear-compensatory models perform well. Three of these conditions prevail in many situations in the context of modeling preferences for real brands/services: (i) the preference function is monotone (increasing or decreasing) over increasing levels of an attribute while holding other attributes constant, (ii) there are errors in the measurement of attribute levels (possibly because of perceptual differences across consumers), and (iii) the attributes tend to be correlated. Thus, even if the respondent's information processing strategy and decision model are complex, the compensatory model can usually produce good *predictions*, assuming that this is the main concern of the researcher. Furthermore, the ideal-point and the part-worth function models are more general than the linear-compensatory model, in that only additivity, not linearity, is assumed (i.e., only interaction terms are omitted). Consequently the predictive validity of these models can be expected to be very good.

In situations where specific interaction effects can be expected a priori, these could be captured in the mixed model by adding pseudo-attributes of the form $z = y_1 y_2$. In some other situations, interaction effects can be taken into account by combining two categorical attributes into one. For example, the researcher may believe that car roominess and gas mileage may interact in the following way:

- A respondent generally prefers a roomier car to a cramped one.
- A respondent generally prefers higher gas mileage to lower gas mileage.
- However, a roomy car *with* high gas mileage is evaluated much higher than the sum of the separate part worths.

If so, the researcher can construct a four-level factor from the two two-level factors and test his surmise using the *main-effect* estimates of the four-level superfactor.

Data Collection Alternatives

Data collection procedures in conjoint analysis have largely involved variations on two basic methods:

- the two-factor-at-a-time procedure, and
- the full-profile approach.

The two-factor-at-a-time procedure, also referred to as the "trade-off procedure" (Johnson 1974), considers factors (attributes) on a two-at-a-time basis. The respondent is asked to rank the various combinations of each pair of factor levels from most preferred to least preferred. Panel I of the exhibit shows an illustration of the approach, as applied to consumer evaluations of steel-belted radial replacement tires.

The two-factor-at-a-time procedure is simple to apply and reduces information overload on the part of the respondent. It also lends itself easily to mail questionnaire form, since no special props are needed. However, in actual problems, it displays a number of limitations:

EXHIBIT

ALTERNATIVE DATA COLLECTION METHODS

I. Two-Factor-at-a-Time Approach

Tire brand	Tread life: 30,000 miles	40,000 miles	50,000 miles
Goodyear	8	4	1[a]
Goodrich	12	9	5
Firestone	11	7	3
Sears	10	6	2

[a] 1 denotes the best-liked combination and 12 denotes the least-liked combination for a hypothetical respondent.

II. Full-Profile Approach (Sample stimulus card)

Brand
SEARS
Tread Life
50,000 MILES
Sidewall
WHITE
Price
$55

- By decomposing the overall set of factors to two-at-a-time combinations, there is some sacrifice in realism. Moreover, respondents are usually unclear as to what should be assumed about the *t*-2 factors that are *not* being considered in a specific evaluation task. For instance, in Panel I of the exhibit it is reasonable to expect that as the tread life increases the price of the tire is also likely to increase. Consequently, when the attributes of a product or service are correlated (e.g., for technological reasons) what the rank order in a particular table corresponds to is not clear.
- With, say, only six factors, each at four levels, the respondent could be asked to fill out 15 tables, each consisting of 16 cells. While partially balanced incomplete block designs (Green 1974) or related procedures (Johnson and VanDyk 1975) can be used to reduce the number of two-way tables, the total number of required judgments is still quite large.
- There is some tendency for respondents either to forget where they are in the table or to adopt patternized types of responses, such as always attending to variations in one factor before considering the other (Johnson 1976).
- The procedure appears to be most suited to *verbal* descriptions of factor combinations, rather than pictorial or other kinds of iconic representations. For example, a study of package designs in which color, logo, size, and shape can be simultaneously varied and portrayed graphically would not lend itself well to this approach.

The full-profile approach (also referred to as the concept evaluation task) utilizes the complete set of factors, as shown by the illustrative stimulus card for a four-factor design in Panel II of the exhibit. The major limitation of this approach is the possibility of information overload and the resulting temptation on the part of the respondent to simplify the experimental task by ignoring variations in the less important factors or by simplifying the factor levels themselves. The conjoint results obtained under such conditions may not be representative of the real life behavior of the individual where he/she may have more time and motivation to deliberate on the choice from among a small set of alternatives.

Because of the information overload problem, the full-profile procedure is generally confined to, at most, five or six factors in any specific sort. If a larger number of factors is entailed—some industrial studies have included 25 or more factors, each at from two to six levels—the analyst is more or less forced to incorporate "bridging-type" factors. The idea here is to prepare several card decks in which the full set of factors is first split into subsets of five or six factors each. Each card deck is then composed of factor combinations that involve, say, five factors, only. In each case one or two factors are common across decks so that they provide a basis for linking part-worth functions across the various subsets of factors. (For an illustration, see Hopkins, Larréché, and Massy 1977, p. 371.)

The full-profile approach—when implemented by various kinds of fractional factorial designs (to be discussed later)—entails fewer judgments to be made by the respondent, although each single judgment is more complex. As per later discussion on response (or dependent) variable data, the two-factor-at-a-time procedure provides only a set of rank orders while the full-profile approach can employ either a rank order or ratings (e.g., on a seven-point scale from "least liked" to "most liked"). Such flexibility in scaling seems desirable. In the full-profile approach, each stimulus card can potentially be assigned any level on a continuous attribute. However, in the two-factor-at-a-time approach, each continuous attribute is assigned only a few levels because of the need to construct manageable trade-off tables. (This is also true for the full-profile approach using fractional factorial designs.)

The main argument that seems to favor the full-profile approach is that it gives a more realistic description of stimuli by defining the levels of each of the factors and possibly taking into account the potential environmental correlations between factors in real stimuli. On the other hand, it has the disadvantage of making the task difficult for the respondent by having to consider several factors at one time. Based on these two considerations, we would speculate that in contexts where the environmental correlation between factors is large and the number of factors on the stimulus card is small (but greater than two), the full-profile approach is likely to be better in terms of predictive validity. However, if the environmental correlation between the factors is small and the number of factors on the stimulus card is large, the two-factor-at-a-time approach is likely to be better.

Four empirical studies have compared the two approaches to data collection. Montgomery, Wittink, and Glaze (1977), in a study of job choice by MBAs, found that the two-factor-at-a-time approach yielded higher predictive validity than the full-profile approach.

Similarly, Alpert, Betak, and Golden (1978) found that the goodness-of-fit to input data was better for the two-factor-at-a-time approach in their study of commuters' choice of transportation modes. However, Jain, Acito, Malhotra, and Mahajan (1978) found that the two methods yielded approximately the same level of cross-validity in the context of choosing checking accounts offered by various banks. Also, Oppedijk van Veen and Beazley (1977) found that the utilities determined by the two methods were roughly similar in the context of a durable good product class.

The first two studies used eight and nine attributes, respectively, and the resulting information overload may have biased the results against the full-profile approach. In comparison, the third and fourth studies used five and three attributes respectively. In all four studies, the problem contexts were such that there were no substantial environmental correlations across factors. (In any event, the full-profile approaches used orthogonal designs that exhibited no interattribute correlations.) Thus the results are not inconsistent with the conjecture advanced earlier comparing the effectiveness of the two alternative data collection procedures.

Stimulus Set Construction for the Full-Profile Method

The number of brands in a product class that a respondent may be familiar with is usually small. Furthermore, real brands and services are usually not distinctive enough to provide reliable estimates of parameters. For these reasons, conjoint analysis is usually done with hypothetical stimulus descriptions. This has the additional advantage of enabling us to compare predicted behavior with the actual behavior of the respondents towards real brands or services. In constructing the stimulus profiles for the full-profile approach several questions arise:

1. How many stimuli do we need to use?
2. What should be the range of attribute variation and interattribute correlation in constructing the stimuli?
3. How should the stimuli themselves be constructed?

The number of stimuli should obviously depend on the number of estimated parameters. From multiple regression theory (Darlington 1968), we know that the expected mean squared error of prediction is given by $(1 + T/n)\sigma^2$ where T is the number of estimated parameters, n is the number of stimuli to be evaluated, and σ^2 is the unexplained (error) variance in the model. Thus the ratio (n/T) should be as large as possible to minimize the increment to prediction error over and above the error (σ^2) that is unavoidable. For a given T, as n increases from $2T$ to $5T$ the prediction error decreases by 20 percent. (As the formula indicates, it is more appropriate to think in terms of the n/T ratio rather than $n - T$, the degrees of freedom.) However, a respondent typically takes about 20–30 minutes for $n = 25$ in a five attribute, full-profile rank ordering task. Given the usual considerations of maintaining the respondent's interest in the task, it is often difficult to increase n much above 30.

In deciding the range of variation of attribute levels and interattribute correlation (e.g., between auto versus bus and travel time to work, or between horsepower rating and gas mileage of cars), two conflicting considerations are relevant. The use of stimulus descriptions similar to those that currently exist (similar in terms of ranges of attribute levels and environmental correlations) will increase believability and hence validity of the preference judgments. On the other hand, if we make the ranges for attribute levels much larger than reality and/or decrease the magnitude of interattribute correlations to zero (as is implied by orthogonal designs), we may decrease believability and hence validity. But orthogonal designs and/or larger ranges for attribute values have the advantage of improving the accuracy of the parameter estimates for a given level of validity for the preference judgments. Thus, the extreme strategy of using descriptions similar to those that exist has the disadvantage of loss of accuracy in estimation while the alternate extreme strategy of using an orthogonal design and/or ranges for attribute values much larger than reality has the disadvantage of decreasing the validity of the respondent's preference judgments.

We would recommend, therefore, that the ranges be made larger than reality, but not so large as to be unbelievable. Further, we would recommend making interattribute correlations in the hypothetical descriptions smaller (in absolute value) than the environmental correlations that exist in real stimuli, but not to make them so small as to be unbelievable. However, if the environmental interattribute correlations are small to start with, there will be virtually no loss in believability by using orthogonal designs, and there is everything to gain in terms of accuracy of the estimated parameters.

The hypothetical stimulus descriptions can be constructed in either of two ways. The more popular method has been to define a number of levels (say, three or four) for each of the attributes over the range of attribute variation. The researcher should pretest the levels of the continuous factors to insure that they are far enough apart to be considered as realistically distinct. For categorical attributes the feasible levels are readily available but the selection of which levels are "representative" of the factor often requires careful study. If a full factorial design is used, the number of possible stimuli quickly becomes very large (e.g., with three attributes at three levels each and two attributes at two levels each, the total number of possible descriptions is $3^3 \times 2^2 = 108$). Green (1974) has suggested the use of various types of *fractional factorial designs* to reduce the number of combinations to a manageable size while at the same time maintaining orthogonality. These types of designs assume away most (sometimes all) interaction effects, which is realistic given the type of preference models discussed earlier. For instance, the preceding numerical example with five attributes can be reduced to an orthogonal main-effects plan with only 18 stimuli (Green and Wind 1975, p. 108).

A discussion of various kinds of fractional factorials, including both orthogonal and nonorthogonal designs, can be found in the paper by Green, Carroll, and Carmone (1978). This paper describes both main-effects plans, in which no interactions can be separately estimated, and less restrictive plans (such as Resolution IV and Compromise designs) that permit estimation of all main effects *and* selected two-factor interactions, without an inordinate increase in the number of stimuli. This paper also shows how various basic designs can be modified to handle different combinations of factor levels. In addition, a number of references to the specialized literature in this area are included.

If there is a substantial amount of environmental correlation between some of the attributes, an orthogonal design can produce some stimuli which may not be believable. If the environmental correlations are very high (e.g., 0–55 mph acceleration time, gas mileage, horsepower rating, and top speed), the researcher may wish to prepare a composite factor covering all four subfactors whose separate levels show various gradations of performance-mileage. Each level of the composite would reflect the subfactor correlations that exist technologically so that a 300 hp engine does not coexist with a 35 mpg fuel consumption. However, with this approach, it is no longer possible to separate the effects of the subfactors contained in the composite.

If one wishes to capitalize on the high efficiency of orthogonal arrays and other fractional factorials, factor independence is to be sought wherever possible. If some of the profiles turn out to be unbelievable, other orthogonal displays can be tried by permuting sets of factor levels. Finally, if worse comes to worst, a few profiles may have to be deleted or modified to incorporate correlated factor levels. However, methods such as the two-factor-at-a-time approach are less amenable to the correlated-factor approach, since all combinations of factor levels are typically displayed for evaluation.

An alternate procedure for creating the stimulus descriptions is that of random sampling from a multivariate distribution. Assuming for the moment that all the attributes are continuous, a multivariate distribution can be defined given the means, standard deviations (derived from the ranges), and interattribute correlations. The stimulus descriptions could then be randomly drawn from a multivariate normal distribution (Naylor, Balintfy, Burdick, and Chu 1966, pp. 97–9). Dichotomous attributes (e.g., auto versus bus as mode of travel) could also be handled in the above framework by defining a proxy continuous random variable and a cut-off value (e.g., if $x \geq 0$, then auto, if $x < 0$, then bus). For categorical variables with more than two categories, the values could be randomly drawn from a discrete distribution. If this categorical attribute is to be correlated with other continuous attributes, different sets of parameters for the multivariate distribution would have to be defined, depending on the value assigned to the categorical attribute.

Thus, if the attributes are to be correlated in the stimulus set, the random sampling procedure just described provides a systematic, although cumbersome procedure. By creating random descriptions in excess of the required number n, it is possible to delete descriptions which are dominated (i.e., have a less desirable attribute level on each of the attributes) by other stimuli. By trial and error, it is generally possible to construct the n descriptions so that none of the stimuli dominates any of the remaining $(n - 1)$ descriptions (Parker and Srinivasan 1976). Although this procedure is time consuming, it may still be desirable from the point of view of getting maximum potential information from the respondent's evaluative judgments.

To illustrate this point, consider a two-attribute product class with three levels for each attribute. Assume that the part-worth function is monotone (increasing or decreasing) over the three levels, e.g., as might be the case with attributes such as tread mileage, price, or waiting time. Without loss of generality, let us assume that greater levels are preferred to smaller levels on the attribute. Then in the (3×3) orthogonal design with nine descriptions it can be shown that only nine of the 36 potential paired comparisons have any information content. For example, the (1,1) and (3,3) descriptions provide no information at all; they are, by the monotonicity assumption, the worst and the best stimuli. Furthermore, the pairs comparing, say, the stimulus (3,2) to the stimuli (3,1), (2,2), (2,1), (1,2) and(1,1) also convey no information.

The random sampling procedure seems to be well suited to estimating ideal-point type models, as portrayed by equation (3). For example, in the fractional-factorial type approach, that uses only a few levels for each attribute, it is difficult to distinguish well between alternative ideal-point locations that lie between the adjacent levels used in the design. In the random sampling procedure, many levels of the attribute are likely to be used so that a finer discrimination regarding the ideal-point location can be made.

The fractional-factorial type design, on the other hand, is considerably easier to develop. If no attribute correlations are desired, it is likely to produce more accurate parameter estimates. It involves no limiting assumption such as multivariate normality which needs to be assumed in the random sampling approach. Finally, if the relative importances of the attributes are to be obtained, the orthogonal design produces less ambiguous answers than the correlated factors approach.

Based on these considerations, we would speculate that the fractional-factorial designs are better (in terms of predictive power) than the random sampling approach if the environmental interattribute correlations are not high. The random sampling approach is likely to be better if the attribute correlations are high or if most of the attribute part-worth functions are monotone with changes in attribute levels and ordinal overall preference judgments are obtained.

Stimulus Presentation

To date, the presentation of the hypothetical stimuli in the full profile approach has involved variations and combinations of three basic approaches:

- verbal description (multiple cue stimulus card),
- paragraph description, and
- pictorial representation.[2]

The two-factor-at-a-time approach has primarily used the verbal description approach. However, pictorial representation has been used in a few cases. For instance, Alpert, Betak, and Golden (1978) use pictures with different numbers of drops of gasoline to indicate the different levels of gasoline consumption of alternative modes of transportation.

Panel II of the exhibit illustrates the verbal description approach. In a typical task, the respondent is given n stimulus cards, each card defining the levels of each of the t attributes. The respondent is asked to either rank order them or rate them on a scale. The main advantage with this procedure is its simplicity and the efficiency with which the data can be collected.

Acito (1977) has found that the measured importance of an attribute is to some extent affected by the order or position of the attribute on the stimulus card. To reduce this potential bias, the order of the attributes is usually randomized over respondents. To reduce confusion, the order of attributes is kept the same for all the stimulus cards given to any one respondent. Of course, the stimulus cards themselves are shuffled thoroughly before giving them to a respondent.

Some researchers, such as Hauser and Urban (1977), have adopted the paragraph description approach. The advantage of this approach is that it provides a more realistic and complete description of the stimulus (similar to concept testing in new product development) and has the advantage of simultaneously testing advertising claims. A significant drawback of this procedure is that it limits the total number of descriptions to a small number, so that parameter estimates are likely to be very inaccurate when estimated at the individual level.

Pictorial representation using various kinds of visual props or three dimensional models provides several important advantages over verbal profiles:

- Information overload is reduced since the respondent is not required to read and then visualize large quantities of information.
- Higher homogeneity of perceptions of such things as car roominess or trunk capacity is obtained across respondents.
- The task itself is more interesting and less fatiguing.
- The stimuli are more realistic.

Alpert, Betak, and Golden (1978) report that a combination of pictures and words produced roughly the same results as the purely verbal approach, but the respondents took less time to complete the pictorial task. The primary disadvantage of the pictorial approach is the increased cost and time on the part of the researcher in preparing the stimulus descriptions. Furthermore, there is a danger in the picture displaying information different than the researcher intended (e.g., styling of the car may be conveyed in addition to roominess). The pictorial approach is usually administered by mail or personal interview. Data collection by time-shared computer terminals cannot, in general, employ this approach except through the use of sketches in cathode ray terminals or by providing the pictures to the respondents as props to be used in conjunction with a time-shared terminal. However, the pictorial approach has been successfully used on several occasions involving mailed props, followed by telephone interviews.

Based on these considerations, we feel that the verbal and, particularly, the pictorial approaches are likely to be the best methods of presenting stimulus descriptions, assuming individual-level parameter estimates are to be obtained. Choice of the pictorial approach depends upon the nature of the product class (the importance of imagery) and cost considerations.

Measurement Scale for the Dependent Variable

The various alternatives for defining a measurement scale for the dependent variable can be roughly classified as nonmetric (paired comparisons, rank order) or metric (rating scales assuming approximately interval scale properties, or ratio scales obtained by constant-sum paired comparisons [Torgerson 1958, pp. 105–12]). Depending on the purpose of the study, the measurement can be either in terms of overall preference or intention to buy (likelihood of purchase). The latter criterion is particularly suited to studies of new product classes and services that consumers do not purchase currently.

[2] We expect, however, that future applications of conjoint analysis, particularly in packaged goods (such as foods and beverages), will increasingly employ *actual* products, factorially composed using fractional designs from a set of physical/chemical attributes.

In comparing the metric with the nonmetric measurement scales, it should be noted that even though the dependent variable is nonmetric, the estimated parameters tend to satisfy close to interval-scaled properties, for typical values of n and T, the number of estimated parameters (Colberg 1978). The main advantage of the metric methods is the increased information content potentially present in these scales. However, based on results in nonmetric multidimensional scaling (Green and Carmone 1970, p. 36) we would expect the differential advantage of the metric scale to diminish as the n/T ratio becomes large. The nonmetric methods, on the other hand, have the following advantages:

- Ranked data are likely to be more reliable, since it is easier for a respondent to say which he/she prefers more as compared to expressing the magnitude of his/her preference.
- Data analysis based on a nonmetric dependent variable allows the part-worth functions to be combined in either an additive or multiplicative manner. This is because estimation of an additive model with a nonmetric dependent variable is also consistent with a multiplicative model, since the logarithmic transformation is just one of the permissible monotone transformations of the dependent variable.
- With the two-factor-at-a-time approach the nonmetric method is more appropriate than the metric method. The metric scale value for the dependent variable will necessarily depend on the levels of the $(t - 2)$ missing factors, whereas the rank order of the cells in a tradeoff table need not depend on the levels of the missing factors, except if the attributes are correlated.

The paired-comparison approach is the least efficient, in terms of information obtained per unit time, of all the methods. Its only advantages seem to be the increased reliability of the averaged rank order and the ability to test for intransitivities in the respondent's expressed preferences. All things considered, however, we conjecture that the rank-order approach will fare better in terms of predictive validity than the direct paired-comparisons approach for a given amount of the respondent's time.

In collecting data by means of paired comparisons, one generally collects more data than needed. Recognizing the potential redundancy of paired-comparisons data, a number of researchers (Johnson 1976; Shugan and Hauser 1977) have proposed interactive computer approaches for obtaining preference data. Johnson's procedure, in particular, has been designed to obtain conjoint analysis data from computer terminals placed in shopping malls and other high density locations. This proprietary procedure, the technical details of which are not available, is a sequential method in that it uses the results of earlier evaluations to select subsequent stimulus pairs, so that redundancy is kept to a minimum. Based on still early results, it appears that the number of paired comparisons may be reduced by as much as 25–30 percent without appreciable loss in accuracy. While practical experience with the method is still meager, it looks potentially promising for applications amenable to this type of data collection procedure. However, the relative efficiency of the interactive paired-comparison methods vis-a-vis the rank-order procedure is still not known.

One of the advantages of the rating-scale approach is that it can potentially be administered by mail. On the other hand, the rank-ordering task usually entails a personal interview since the procedure requires a considerable amount of explanation (such as first sorting the cards into two or more piles, corresponding to the more preferred versus the less preferred ones; then sorting the cards in each pile from most preferred to least preferred; and finally merging the different piles of cards and checking the final rank order).

Another way of obtaining interval-scale judgments is the so-called "dollar metric" approach (Pessemier, Burger, Teach, and Tigert 1971). In this method, the respondent compares stimuli A and B and if he/she prefers A to B, states how much the price of A has to increase until he/she will be indifferent between A and B. The results of such paired comparisons are aggregated to obtain an intervally scaled dollar metric of preference. This is a very slow procedure compared to the rating method; furthermore, the results may be influenced by the social biases involved in using dollar differences as a response measure.

The constant-sum method of obtaining ratio-scaled judgments in an interactive mode with a time-shared terminal has been compared (Hauser and Shugan 1977) to simply using the ordinal component of data obtained from paired comparisons. As might be expected, the ratio-scaled data provided better predictive results than the paired comparisons per se. However, this comparison is misleading. For a given amount of respondent's time, a very large number of paired comparisons can be obtained (e.g., by the use of rank order) as compared to the small number of constant-sum paired comparisons. Consequently, for a given amount of respondent's time, the relative desirability of the two methods is still unclear.

Given the conflicting considerations involved in the choice of a metric versus nonmetric dependent variable, additional empirical studies are needed to compare these alternative methods.

Estimation Methods

Parameter estimation methods in conjoint analysis can be roughly classified into three categories:

1. Methods which assume that the dependent variable is, at most, ordinally scaled. Methods in this class are MONANOVA (Kruskal 1965), PREFMAP (Carroll 1972), Johnson's nonmetric tradeoff procedure (Johnson 1973; Nehls, Seaman, and Montgomery 1976), and LINMAP (Srinivasan and

Shocker 1973a, 1973b; Pekelman and Sen 1974). For a more exhaustive list of this class of algorithms, see Rao (1977).

2. Methods which assume that the dependent variable is intervally scaled. Methods in this class are ordinary least squares (OLS) regression (Johnston 1972, Chap. 5), and minimizing sum of absolute errors (MSAE) regression (Srinivasan and Shocker 1973a, pp. 358–60).
3. Methods which relate paired-comparison data to a choice probability model. Methods in this class are LOGIT (McFadden 1976; Ben-Akiva 1973; Gensch, Golob, and Recker 1976; Green and Carmone 1977; Punj and Staelin 1978) and PROBIT (Goldberger 1964, pp. 250–1; Rao and Winter 1977).

In the class of algorithms designed for an ordinal-scaled dependent variable, MONANOVA is restricted to the part-worth function model (equation 4). The remaining approaches can be used for the vector or part-worth function models. For the ideal-point model, LINMAP is best suited since the use of other approaches may lead to negative weights and resulting interpretation difficulties (Srinivasan and Shocker 1973a, p. 338). The algorithms differ from each other in their operational definitions of the poorness-of-fit index, analogous to $(1 - R^2)$ in multiple regression studies, and the optimization method used to determine parameter estimates to achieve the minimum poorness-of-fit. While there is no a priori way to choose between the different poorness-of-fit definitions, empirical predictive validity tests could guide us in this direction.

LINMAP differs from the others in that it uses linear programming as compared to classical calculus methods employed by the other approaches. The use of linear programming enables LINMAP to obtain global optimum parameter estimates, while the other approaches cannot be guaranteed to achieve global optimums. In LINMAP, attribute weights can be constrained to be nonnegative, part-worth functions can be constrained to be monotone or of the ideal-point type, while such constraints cannot be imposed for the other approaches. Such constraints, as imposed on the basis of prior knowledge, can be useful in improving the accuracy of the parameter estimates when the (n/T) ratio is small—assuming, of course, that the prior knowledge is correct. Finally, the usage of sum-of-absolute-errors as the poorness-of-fit measure, rather than the sum-of-squared-errors, tends to produce more robust estimates, i.e., the estimated parameters are not as much affected by outliers or large errors in the input data (Blattberg and Sargent 1971). On the other hand, when the n/T ratio is small, the use of linear programming sometimes produces alternate optimums (i.e., different sets of estimated parameters have the same minimal poorness-of-fit), which is intuitively unappealing.

Among the metric methods, the OLS procedure has the important advantage of providing standard errors for the estimated parameters. None of the procedures in (1) has this advantage. However, the overall statistical significance of MONANOVA can be roughly ascertained using the computer simulation results obtained under the assumption of a random rank order for the dependent variable (Acito 1978). The MSAE procedure, on the other hand, is more robust than the OLS method (Blattberg and Sargent 1971) and, furthermore, permits us to impose a priori constraints on the estimated parameters.

The probabilistic approaches, (3), explicitly model the errors that may be present in the preference functions, thereby leading to a deductive development of the choice model. The LOGIT approach has the advantage that the estimation procedure produces global maximum likelihood estimates (McFadden 1976). However, the use of the LOGIT model involves the "independence of irrelevant alternatives" assumption, which may not be a realistic assumption in many consumer behavior contexts. Briefly, if two substantially different services, say automobiles (A) and public transit (B), have choice probabilities of 0.75 and 0.25, respectively, and another mode of public transit (C), very similar to B, is introduced, then the LOGIT model leads to choice probabilities of 0.6, 0.2, and 0.2, respectively, for A, B, and C. Thus the *total* probability for public transit has risen which is intuitively unappealing. Since the two transit modes, B and C, are very similar, the introduction of C should draw its choice probability largely from B rather than A.

The PROBIT procedure is particularly suited to cases where a dichotomous intention-to-buy scale is used as the dependent variable (Rao and Winter 1977). The estimation procedure, however, cannot guarantee global maximum likelihood estimates.

The probabilistic choice models such as LOGIT and PROBIT assume that the paired comparisons are probabilistically independent. If the dependent variable data are obtained directly as paired comparisons, this may be a realistic assumption. (However, we have argued earlier that this is an inefficient way of collecting data.) If the data are obtained as a rank order and then converted to the equivalent $n(n - 1)/2$ paired comparisons, this assumption is not realistic.[3] The asymptotic estimates of standard errors are not likely to be valid either. (In any event, the limited number of stimuli usually used in consumer research studies casts doubt on the appropriateness of such asymptotic statistics.) Despite these limitations, however, the probabilistic choice models appear to have substantial predictive validity.

The choice between the nonmetric, (1) and (3), and metric methods, (2), should logically depend on the

[3] However, Punj and Staelin (1978) utilize a procedure based only on the $n - 1$ *independent* choices that mitigates this problem.

scale properties of the dependent variable. The simulation studies by Cattin and Wittink (1976) and Carmone, Green, and Jain (1978) have found that the OLS regression applied to integer ranks (the rank ordered dependent variable is redefined as a pseudo-interval-scaled variable, taking values 1, 2, . . . , n depending on the rank given that stimulus) produces solutions that are very close, in terms of predictive validity, to those obtained by the more expensive nonmetric algorithms. However, by employing integer ranks as the dependent variable, the usual standard errors and statistical tests are not strictly valid.

Cattin and Wittink (1976) report that the results from OLS and MONANOVA are virtually indistinguishable: the difference in predictive validity is, at most, 0.003 in terms of Pearson's rho. In other words, because of local optimum problems with MONANOVA, it may produce solutions which are only marginally different from OLS. The difference between OLS on the one hand and LOGIT and LINMAP on the other is about 0.03 units in terms of Pearson's rho, with OLS being the better approach when the attribute weights are normally distributed (compensatory model) and LINMAP and LOGIT being the preferred methods when the attribute weights exhibit a lexicographic structure. In general, this simulation study found that the methods differed by only *very small amounts* in their predictive validities.

A few empirical (as opposed to simulation) studies have compared alternative estimation procedures. Hauser and Urban (1977, p. 600) report that the monotonic methods have a slightly better fit to saved data than OLS. (The dependent variable was a rank order.) Hauser and Shugan (1977) state that the MSAE regression performs better than OLS because of its ability to incorporate constraints on the estimated parameters. (The dependent variable in this case was intervally scaled.) Montgomery, Wittink, and Glaze (1977) report that the predictive validity of OLS was better than that of MONANOVA. The dependent variable was a rank order but the small $n/T = 32/19$ ratio is likely to have biased this result in favor of OLS. Fidler and Thompson (1977) report that LINMAP and a PROBIT-like procedure yielded roughly the same validity and substantive conclusions. McCullough (1978) reports that Johnson's nonmetric procedure and MONANOVA predict at roughly the same level of validity and better than a Fishbein-Rosenberg type multiattribute model. Rao and Solgaard (1977) report that MONANOVA, Johnson's nonmetric procedure, LINMAP, and CCM (Carroll 1969) yield roughly the same level of cross validity. Jain et al. (1978) report that MONANOVA, Johnson's nonmetric procedure, LINMAP, LOGIT, and OLS yield roughly the same level of cross-validity, with LOGIT and LINMAP being the slightly preferred procedures.

Overall, the estimation methods do not seem to differ very much in their predictive validities. The metric procedures (2) seem to perform slightly better if the preference model is approximately compensatory. If the model is approximately lexicographic, the nonmetric methods seem to do slightly better. Based on these results, we would recommend that researchers estimate parameters using both a metric and a nonmetric method as a rough check on the robustness of their results, at least until more empirical evidence on their correspondence has been assembled.

RELIABILITY AND VALIDITY TESTS

While some researchers have been careful to test the reliability and/or validity of conjoint analysis, a large number of applications of conjoint analysis have ignored these issues. We will now discuss methods for assessing reliability and validity with the hope that future applications will incorporate at least some of these tests.[4]

Tests of Reliability

Tests of reliability can be carried out either at the level of input judgments of the respondent or at the level of estimated parameters. To obtain the reliability of a respondent's input judgments, the researcher can ask for preference judgments on a second set of stimulus cards which contain a subset of the original set of stimulus cards. This needs to be done only for a subsample of the respondents after the respondent has completed some intervening task, such as supplying a set of demographic data. The repeated evaluations can be used in determining the *test-retest reliability of the input preference judgments*.

If we view conjoint analysis as an instrument to measure the parameters of the preference model, then the *alternate forms method with spaced testing* may be more appropriate (Parker and Srinivasan 1976). After completing a conjoint analysis task, a subset of the respondents can be approached after a period of time and asked to perform the rank ordering or rating task on a second set of stimuli. The second stimulus set ("alternate form") would also have n descriptions from the same factor levels as the first set but would avoid duplication of stimuli from the initial set. This could be done by using a second fractional-factorial design from the same factor levels or by randomly drawing a second set of n descriptions from the multivariate distribution. Product moment correlations of the estimated parameters from the two tasks provides a measure of reliability, sometimes referred to as the *coefficient of equivalence*.

The second method of reliability testing is more rigorous than the first one, in that it takes into account

[4] Our discussion emphasizes predictive validity rather than validation of the actual decision process which, in large measure, is not known.

four sources of error: inaccuracies in the input data, variability in the set of constructed stimuli, errors in the estimation procedure, and lack of stability (variations from one time period to another). By contrast, the first method focuses only on the first source of error.

Tests of Validity

The *internal validity* of conjoint analysis can be reported in terms of the correlation (Pearson's or Spearman's rho depending on the scale properties of the dependent variable) between the input versus estimated values of the dependent variable. If Pearson's rho is used, it is desirable to adjust the correlation for the number of estimated parameters, as in the coefficient of multiple determination (R^2) adjusted for degrees of freedom.

Data used for the reliability tests also provide a method of cross-validation. The parameters of the preference function estimated from the first set of preference data can be used to predict the preferences for the second set. The predicted preferences can be correlated to the actual to obtain a measure of cross-validity. The procedure can then be reversed by predicting from set 2 to set 1, thus completing a double cross-validation.

While internal validity tests the goodness of the model, cross-validation also takes into account the predictive ability of the model. But neither method tests the *external validity* of the model. Since conjoint analysis studies are usually carried out using hypothetical stimulus descriptions, we can test for external validity by comparing predictions against a respondent's actual behavior with respect to real stimuli. This method, referred to as *predictive validity* by Parker and Srinivasan (1976, p. 1,017), involved predicting the respondent's rank order of the n real stimuli (choice set) using the estimated preference function. The respondent's actual choices will fall somewhere in this rank order (1 to n). The closer the number is to 1, the better is the external validity for that respondent. By repeating the predictions for each of the respondents in the sample, we obtain a frequency distribution of the number of respondents choosing the first, second, . . . , nth most preferred stimuli. The median of the distribution can be compared to 1 (best) and $(n + 1)/2$ (random model) to get a measure of the external validity. The obtained frequency distribution (which should be skewed positively) can be tested for statistical significance against a uniform distribution (random model) by the Kolmogorov-Smirnov statistic.

One of the important uses of conjoint analysis is to predict the behavior of the respondents toward *new* stimuli. The most rigorous tests for conjoint analysis predict the reaction of a respondent toward a new stimulus and compare it with actual behavior. However, since conjoint analysis is, at best, a static analysis, it can only be expected to predict responses in "steady state," assuming that consumers become knowledgeable about the new stimulus.

Additional Considerations in Reliability/ Validity Testing

If paired comparison preference judgments are obtained directly, one can also test for intransitivities. Hauser and Shugan (1977) have developed measures of intransitivity for interval and ratio-scaled preference data obtained through constant-sum paired comparisons. In addition, consistency can be tested at the aggregate level in terms of market shares. For example, in a conjoint analysis study designed by one of the authors for a large transportation company, data were available on market share, by supplier, for various pairs of cities served by the company. Shares of choices, estimated at the individual level and then aggregated, agreed closely enough with the actual market share data to provide reasonable assurance of the model's validity in the aggregate. Similar tests have been carried out by Fiedler (1972), Davidson (1973), and Punj and Staelin (1978).

Scott and Wright (1976) suggest some additional consistency checks to test whether the estimated parameters make sense. First, the signs of the estimated parameters should agree with a priori expectations, based on prior theory or reasoning. Second, the parameters derived for different subpopulations should differ in the direction that would be expected from prior theory or reasoning. In addition, the "face validity" of the results can be checked by comparing a respondent's subjective estimates (self-reports) with estimated parameters. A somewhat unobtrusive method of testing for face validity is to aggregate respondents' spontaneous verbalizations during the interview regarding the factors or attributes important to them and comparing them against aggregated results from estimated model parameters (Parker and Srinivasan 1976, p. 1,013).

To get some feel for the cost/benefit of conjoint analysis, its predictions can be compared against "naive" models which do not involve any data collection. For instance, if the vector model of preference is a reasonable approximation and the attributes are reoriented, if necessary, so that higher attribute levels are more preferred, and the attributes are standardized to unit standard deviation, then a *unit weighting model* (i.e., each weight w_p in equation (2) is set equal to unity) is often a good contender for a naive model (Dawes and Corrigan 1974). Alternately, the most important attribute from a priori considerations (e.g., price) can be used to define a naive preference model in which the weight for the most important attribute is unity, while all other attributes are assigned zero weights. An extension of this would be a lexicographic naive model with the ordering of attributes obtained from prior judgments.[5] For an illustration of these tests against naive models, see Parker and Srinivasan (1976, pp. 1,015–17).

Published empirical results on the predictive validity of conjoint analysis are encouraging (e.g., Fiedler 1972, condominiums; Davidson 1973, air transportation; Parker and Srinivasan 1976, primary health care facilities; Montgomery, Wittink, and Glaze 1977, job choice by MBAs; Scott 1977, solar heating for homes). Furthermore, the reliability and cross validity reported by Parker and Srinivasan (1976) are high. The only reported study we know of which showed extremely poor predictions is that by Bither and Wright (1977) in the context of selection of a set of movies dealing with golfing demonstrations.

APPLICATIONS OF CONJOINT ANALYSIS

The typical output from conjoint analysis is a set of estimated parameters of the preference model for each individual in the sample. A direct use of these results is to describe the degree to which each of the attributes is considered important by the respondent sample. If the vector model of equation (2) or ideal-point model of equation (3) is used, the weights $\{w_{ip}\}$ for individual i are first standardized by multiplying w_{ip} by the standard deviation s_p for attribute p—similar to the determination of standardized regression weights (beta weights) in multiple regression—and then normalized so that the attribute importances sum to unity. If the part-worth function model of equation (4) is used, the range of the values for the part-worth function over the levels of attribute p serves as a measure of importance for attribute p. Again, the ranges are normalized so that the t attribute importances sum to unity. The resulting distributions (over the respondent sample) of importances may be summarized in terms of the means and standard deviations for each of the t attributes. If the ideal-point model of equation (3) is used, the distribution of ideal points can be plotted for each of the attributes.

In addition to this "descriptive" use of conjoint analysis, its "normative" uses are described next for both public and private sector applications.

Public Sector Applications

Conjoint analysis offers a tremendous potential for conducting cost/benefit analysis for many public policy decisions. We discuss this here in the contexts of planning rural primary health care delivery and evaluating the implications of energy policies for work-trip gasoline conservation. For additional applications in the public sector area, see McClain and Rao (1974), Whitmore and Cavadias (1974), Wind and Spitz (1976), and Hopkins, Larréché, and Massy (1977).

Parker and Srinivasan (1976) address the problem of determining the number, locations, and physical and operational characteristics of a set of health care facilities to be added to an existing health care delivery system so as to maximize the incremental benefit to the community, subject to a cost (budget) constraint. The conjoint analysis study used the mixed model of equation (7) with travel time (hours) to the facility as one of the attributes. Each respondent's estimated preference function was then transformed into a benefit function expressing the individual's benefit in dollars/year for an existing or potential health care facility. Briefly, this involved multiplying each of the estimated weights $\{v_q\}$ in equation (7) by a common positive number, chosen so that the transformed weight for the travel time attribute coincides with the annual dollar cost for the respondent's household to travel to a health facility that is one hour away.

For example, suppose there are currently only three facilities in the area with benefits for individual i of \$50/year, \$200/year, and \$150/year. Then assuming that individual i chooses the most preferred facility, his/her benefit from the existing system is \$200/year, corresponding to his/her choosing Facility 2. If we now add a fourth facility whose benefit for this individual is \$275/year, then his/her incremental benefit is \$75/year (i.e., he/she would, in "steady state," choose Facility 4 so that the new benefit is \$275/year). If, however, Facility 4's benefit was only \$175/year then the incremental benefit for this individual is zero—he/she would stay with Facility 2 so that his/her benefit has not changed. The total incremental benefit for adding Facility 4 to the community can be obtained by aggregating the individual incremental benefits, after differentially weighting different socioeconomic segments of the population, and then multiplying by the population/sample size ratio. Some optimization procedure can then be used to determine a set of additional facilities that would be feasible (i.e., total cost stays within the budget) and would maximize the total incremental benefit to the community.

In an ongoing study by one of the authors, potential energy policies (such as gasoline surcharges, transit subsidies) are being evaluated in terms of their impact on gasoline conservation. By developing a conjoint analysis model with mode of travel (car versus carpool versus public transit), time of travel, gasoline price, etc. as attributes, it is possible to predict whether changes in attributes, such as gasoline cost increased by a gas tax or waiting time decreased by transit improvements, would change the modal choice of the respondent, and if so, what the resulting gasoline conservation would be. The social costs of such policies can also be evaluated by a procedure similar to that in the health care study.

In short, conjoint analysis offers an excellent oppor-

[5] For an illustration of these tests against naive models, see Parker and Srinivasan (1976, pp. 1015–17).

tunity for consumer researchers to provide valuable cost/benefit analysis inputs for public policy decisions.

Private Sector Applications

While no precise figures are available, it is estimated that several hundred conjoint analysis studies have been conducted by corporate marketing research groups and consulting firms. The applications have spanned a wide variety of products/services: consumer nondurables and durables, industrial goods, financial and other services, transportation, etc.

In most private sector applications of conjoint analysis, some type of consumer choice simulation is carried out to see what share of choices would be generated by each of several product/service profiles if they were competing with each other in the market place. (The word "simulation" is used here to mean prediction of individual choices under hypothetical scenarios and subsequent aggregation of choices—it does not necessarily mean Monte-Carlo probabilistic simulation.)

The typical consumer choice simulator is quite simple in construction. Each individual's utility function and background description (current purchase behavior, socioeconomic, demographic, and psychographic characteristics) are entered into the simulator. Each of, say, six competitive products or services is entered as a full-profile description. Then, for each individual, in turn, a utility is computed for each of the competing items. The individual is assumed to choose that item displaying the highest utility to him. Elaborations on this theme incorporate various probability-of-choice rules, based on the utilities of all contending items. (See Shocker and Srinivasan 1977b for a detailed discussion.) The first-choice frequencies for each item are then simply added and expressed relatively.

Many variations on this simple procedure have been used in proprietary studies. For example, one may wish to employ the respondents' background data to obtain consumer segments; shares of choices are then cross-classified by these prior-defined segments. If profile data on current market brands are also available, it is a simple matter to examine brand switching behavior as new items are entered into the existing array, either as replacements for current items or as net additions to the product/service set.

More sophisticated choice simulators can also be constructed with additional features, such as:

- a provision for describing new item profiles in terms of probability distributions over factor levels, rather than as a deterministic level for each factor;
- a provision for simulating trial and repeat purchase, conditioned on assumptions about the relative amounts of sales effort and consumer satisfaction-in-use associated with each item.

Not surprisingly, one of the more important uses of conjoint analysis in the private sector has been in the evaluation of new product or service concepts. If augmented by cost data, this approach can also be extended to determine "optimal" new product/service ideas by searching the product space, taking into account existing brands/services in the market place and the possible effect of the cannibalization of one's own brands by the new entry. Shocker and Srinivasan (1977b) have reviewed such approaches and their applications to product concept evaluation and generation.

Another important use of conjoint analysis is in the context of guiding strategies for market communication. For instance, an analysis of the attribute importances and the relative position of the firm's brand vis-a-vis the firm's competitors can help in the development of suitable advertising strategies (Boyd, Ray, and Strong 1972).

Conjoint analysis is also useful in market segmentation. The idea is to divide a heterogenous population of consumers into more homogenous segments so that different marketing strategies can be tailored to different segments of consumers to achieve maximum marketing results. Cluster analysis can be employed to group respondents with similar "importances," for t attributes, into clusters. The clusters, in turn, can be cross-tabulated against various background variables, such as demographics, psychographics, product and media usage. Alternatively, the "importances" can be employed as a set of predictor variables in a multiple discriminant analysis in which subjects have been previously classified into groups on the basis of some other criterion, such as brand choice or product-class consumption levels.

For such market segmentation studies, one could also use the predicted, or input, preferences for the n stimuli as the segmentation variables instead of "importances." However, we have found that in many applications it is the importances rather than the preferences which are more discriminating. The reason for this is that *within* a specific attribute, e.g., tread life or price, there is often high agreement on at least the ordering of levels, e.g., more tread life is preferred to less. However, the importance of the factor, tread life, i.e., the relative part-worth range, is often more sensitive to individual variation.

NEW DEVELOPMENTS

In the relatively short time that conjoint analysis has been in use, a number of new developments have already appeared. Some of these are briefly described here.

Preference Models for Collections of Items

Most of the conjoint methodologies and their applications have been in the context of choosing a single item from a product (service) class. However, Green,

Wind, and Jain (1972) have examined whether the total preference for, say, an entree-dessert combination can be decomposed, via an additive model, into the preference for an entree plus the preference for a dessert. Green and Devita (1974, 1975a) discuss a method of taking into account two-factor interaction effects in the context of menu choice through MDPREF (Carroll 1972). Farquhar and Rao (1976)—see also Rao (1973)—consider the choice of subsets such as TV programs, liquor assortments, etc., by their "balance model." They model the utility for a set of n stimuli as composed of (i) preference components relating to *total* attribute level (over the n stimuli) on each of the t attributes and (ii) preference components relating to the standard deviation of attribute levels (within the n stimuli) for each of the t attributes. The latter terms correspond to the preference for "balance" or "counterbalance," depending on whether variability is desirable or undesirable.

McAlister (1978) considers the same problem of choice of subsets but models the overall preference for a set of magazines (say) using a part-worth function approach, where the argument in the part-worth function for attribute p is its *total* attribute level over the subset of magazines. By assuming that the part-worth function is approximated by linear and quadratic terms (to model attribute satiation), she is able to use LINMAP to estimate the parameters. McAlister (1978) also examines a second context of choice of subsets where the consumption is limited to only one of the elements in the subset (e.g., a student may apply to several universities but enrolls in only one of the schools which offer admission). She models this context by embedding preferences for individual items in a decision tree.

Incorporating Interaction Effects in Preference Models

Green, Carroll, and Carmone (1978) have developed an algorithm that incorporates selected interaction terms after main effect terms have been estimated. This algorithm appears to be most useful in cases involving a large number of factors, thus precluding the use of full factorial designs.

The authors use various kinds of fractional factorials that permit the researcher to estimate all main effects at the individual level and selected two-factor interactions at the group (or subgroup) level, without necessitating an unwieldy number of stimuli for respondent evaluation. The assumption is that the researcher will be primarily interested in interaction effects at the group (rather than individual) level. Under this assumption, the algorithm is able to take advantage of the additional degrees of freedom gained by pooling over groups of respondents.

Multi-Stage Consumer Decision Processes

Srinivasan (1978) observes that protocol analyses of consumer decision processes indicate that for many respondents the processing strategy seems to change during the task, starting from an initial strategy aimed at narrowing the choice to a small subset (through processes approximating conjunctive type rules) and ending in a detailed examination to choose the most preferred item through processes approximating compensatory rules. He models a multi-stage decision process as a sequence of linear models of the form of equation (7), where the weights change from one stage to the next (several of the weights in each stage may be zero). In an m-stage model, the ith stage preference function ($i = 1,2, \ldots, m$) discriminates only among stimuli which are tied by each of the previous stages $1,2, \ldots, i - 1$. Assuming that each attribute has only a small number of levels, this model includes the compensatory ($m = 1$), lexicographic (each stage has only one weight positive with all other weights equal to zero), conjunctive and disjunctive rules, and any combination thereof as special cases. Srinivasan provides a procedure to estimate the stage weights from rank-order preference judgments using LINMAP (Shocker and Srinivasan 1977a). The multi-stage model seems to offer the potential of taking us one step closer to actual consumer decision processes.

Componential Segmentation

As remarked earlier in the context of private sector applications, one of the uses of conjoint analysis has been in the development of market segments. A recent development, known as componential segmentation (Green 1977; Green, Carroll, and Carmone 1976, 1977; Green and DeSarbo 1977), takes a further step in this direction. Traditionally, market segments have been defined as groups of consumers whose responses to some market stimulus exhibit relatively little within-group variation but considerable among-groups variation. In contrast, componential segmentation places emphasis on the *interaction of a stimulus profile with a person profile*; that is, the concern here is less with market partitioning and more with predicting how a respondent, characterized by a particular set of attribute levels, will respond to a set of stimuli, each of which represents a particular profile of factor levels. It is the joint effect of the two sets of attribute and factor levels that results in response.

As an illustration, consider the earlier example in which consumers are choosing among alternative steel-belted replacement tires, varying by brand, tread life, price, and sidewall color. Illustratively, the consumers are assumed to vary by sex, type of car ownership, and age of car owned. Traditional segmentation procedures might first group the consumers by type of tire owned and then see (e.g., by means of discriminant analysis) whether the a priori defined segments differ in terms of other consumer background variables. In contrast, componential segmentation decomposes total variability in preferences for alternative product descriptions (each involving a profile of brand, tread life, price, and sidewall color) by alternative respondents (each involving a profile of sex, type of car, and age of car) into three components: (i) variability due to product attributes, (ii) variability due to person attributes and (iii) variability due to interaction between person and product attributes. The first component, in a sense, explains the variation in preference for different levels of product attributes for the average respondent and should be of interest in product planning. The second component is usually not of interest, since it is simply due to different respondent profiles having a different mean scale value for preferences. (Thus, if the data were standardized so that each respondent gave the same average preference rating for the *n* profiles, this component would be zero.) The third component is due to interaction effects between stimulus and respondent profiles and, therefore, provides a direct measure of segmentability of the market. It may show, for instance, that compact car owners attach more importance to tire price than owners of medium and big cars. This could suggest that a firm has to be considerably more price competitive in the compact car segment, but could use a product differentiated, high-price strategy for the medium and big car segment.

Extensions of componential segmentation to three-way (respondents by scenarios by products) and higher-way matrices are also possible, thus providing a means for operationalizing the concept of situation dependence (Belk 1975) as it may interact with the stimulus attributes under evaluation by different types of respondents.

Preferences for Alternative Allocations of Scarce Resources

Recently conjoint analysis has been applied to study consumers' preferences for alternative allocations of some scarce resource, such as money or time. One pilot study (Carroll, Green, and DeSarbo 1978) considered preferences for alternative allocations of leisure time for different levels of (i) watching TV, (ii) recreational reading, (iii) sports activity, (iv) hobbies, and (v) socializing. The same type of approach can also be used to find consumer utilities for such things as alternative household budget allocations, or allocations of household savings across such investments as insurance, common stocks, municipal bonds, etc. If time (rather than money) is the scarce resource, possible applications can involve such things as preferences for TV news shows regarding the amount of time spent on national news, local news, weather, sports, and the like, or allocations of magazine space to various kinds of editorial matter and advertisements.

Conjoint Analysis in the Modeling of Perceptions Data

Until recently conjoint analysis has been restricted to the analysis of preference (and other kinds of dominance) data. If the analyst wished to explore consumers' *perceptions* of products or services, he/she usually fell back on the apparatus of multidimensional scaling, with its associated problems of dimension interpretation and the like.

More recently, conjoint analysis has been extended to the modeling of similarities data (Green and DeSarbo 1978). To illustrate the approach, assume that a researcher is interested in consumers' perceptions of various vacation sites, e.g., London, Bermuda, Las Vegas, Honolulu, etc. A set of six factors (say) are selected that are capable of describing vacation sites in general, such as (i) food quality, (ii) sightseeing opportunities, (iii) outdoor sports, (iv) night life/entertainment, (v) chance to meet new friends, and (vi) trip cost. Next assume that each factor is described in terms of three levels (e.g., superb, good, or fair food quality). An orthogonal main effects plan of 18 stimulus cards can be constructed from the 3^6 full factorial. The respondent is then shown a card on which each reference site, such as London, appears and is asked to sort the profiles along, say, a 9-point scale according to how similar each of the profiles is to each selected location (e.g., London). The similarities data are analyzed for each site separately via some type of nonmetric or metric conjoint algorithm. However, in this situation the analysis produces *part-similarity* functions (analogous to part-worth functions) and factor saliences (relative ranges of the part-similarity functions).

The results from such an analysis can be pooled over those who chose London (based on an earlier question) as the most preferred place to visit versus those who chose some other vacation site. Green and DeSarbo (1978) found, for instance, that London choosers attached higher salience to sightseeing, while others attached higher salience to outdoor sports and total trip cost.

Although not described here, the part-similarity functions can, in turn, be transformed into respondents' subjective probability distributions relating to the uncertainty of perceptions of London along each of the factors. This information together with the respondent's preference function (as developed from a conjoint analysis of the respondent's preference data) could be valuable in developing communication campaigns to correct misperceptions and attract more visitors to London. The implications of this extended conjoint methodology should be of considerable interest in positioning products and services.

CONCLUDING REMARKS

The wide support by academic and industry researchers over a relatively short time (since 1971) is an indication of the potential of conjoint analysis in providing a useful methodology for representing the structure of consumer preferences and some ability for predicting consumers' behavior towards new stimuli. Much empirical work needs to be done to identify the combination of alternatives in each of the various steps of conjoint analysis to achieve maximum predictive validity for a given problem definition and research budget. The answers could, of course, depend on situational factors such as type of product-market, number of relevant attributes, etc. Researchers are urged to pay considerably greater attention to testing reliability and validity in their applications. Although conjoint analysis has been extensively applied mainly in the private sector, it has a large potential for public sector applications as well. As the last section of the paper indicated, conjoint analysis is far from being a settled, cut-and-dried methodology. Many opportunities still exist for extending present techniques and applying them to a greater variety of substantive problems in consumer behavior.

[*Received August 1977. Revised March 1978.*]

REFERENCES

Acito, Franklin (1977), "An Investigation of Some Data Collection Issues in Conjoint Measurement," in *1977 Educators' Proceedings,* Chicago: American Marketing Association, 82–5.

——— (1978), "A Monte Carlo Investigation of Conjoint Measurement Under Random Data Conditions for Various Orthogonal Designs," Working Paper, School of Business, Indiana University.

Alpert, Mark I. (1971), "Definition of Determinant Attributes: A Comparison of Methods," *Journal of Marketing Research,* 8, 184–91.

———, Betak, John F., and Golden, Linda, L. (1978), "Data Gathering Issues in Conjoint Measurement," Working Paper, Graduate School of Business, The University of Texas at Austin.

Anderson, Norman H. (1970), "Functional Measurement and Psychophysical Judgment," *Psychological Review,* 77, 153–70.

Barron, F. Hutton (1977), "Axiomatic Conjoint Measurement," *Decision Sciences,* 8, 48–59.

Belk, Russell W. (1975), "Situational Variables and Consumer Behavior," *The Journal of Consumer Research,* 2, 157–64.

Ben-Akiva, Moshe (1973), "Program for Maximum Likelihood Estimation of the Multinomial Logit Model," Cambridge, MA: Massachusetts Institute of Technology, Department of Civil Engineering.

Berl, Janet, Lewis, Gordon, and Morrison, Rebecca Sue (1976), "Applying Models of Choice to the Problem of College Selection," in *Cognition and Social Behavior,* eds. J. S. Carroll and J. W. Payne, Hillsdale, NJ: Lawrence Elbaum Associates, 203–19.

Bither, Stewart W., and Wright, Peter (1977), "Preferences Between Product Consultants: Choices vs. Preference," *The Journal of Consumer Research,* 4, 39–47.

Blattberg, Robert, and Sargent, Thomas (1971), "Regression with Non-Gaussian Stable Disturbances: Some Sampling Results," *Econometrica,* 39, 501–10.

Boyd, Harper W., Jr., Ray, Michael L., and Strong, Edward C. (1972), "An Attitudinal Framework for Advertising Strategy," *Journal of Marketing,* 36, 27–33.

Braun, Michael A., and Srinivasan, V. (1975), "Amount of Information as a Determinant of Consumer Behavior Towards New Products," *1975 Combined Proceedings,* Chicago: American Marketing Association, 373–8.

Carmone, Frank J., Green, Paul E., and Jain, Arun K. (1978), "The Robustness of Conjoint Analysis: Some Monte Carlo Results," *Journal of Marketing Research,* 15, 300–3.

Carroll, J. Douglas (1969), "Categorical Conjoint Measurement," Meeting of Mathematical Psychology, Ann Arbor, MI.

——— (1972), "Individual Differences and Multidimensional Scaling," in *Multidimensional Scaling: Theory and Applications in Behavioral Sciences, Vol. I,* eds. R. N. Shepard, et al., New York: Seminar Press, 105–55.

———, Green, Paul E., and DeSarbo, Wayne S. (1978), "Optimizing the Allocation of a Fixed Resource: A Simple Model and Its Experimental Test," Working Paper, Bell Laboratories, Murray Hill, NJ.

Cattin, Philippe, and Wittink, Dick R. (1976), "A Monte-Carlo Study of Metric and Nonmetric Estimation Methods for Multiattribute Models," Research Paper No. 341, Graduate School of Business, Stanford University.

Colberg, Roger T. (1978), "A Monte Carlo Evaluation of Metric Recovery of Conjoint Measurement Algorithms," Research Paper, College of Business Administration, University of Nevada-Reno.

Darlington, Richard B. (1968), "Multiple Regression in Psychological Research and Practice," *Psychological Bulletin,* 69, 161–82.

Davidson, J. D. (1973), "Forecasting Traffic on STOL," *Operational Research Quarterly,* 24, 561–9.

Dawes, Robyn M. (1971), "A Case Study of Graduate Admissions: Application of Three Principles of Human Decision Making," *American Psychologist,* 26, 180–8.

———, and Corrigan, Bernard (1974), "Linear Models in Decision Making," *Psychological Bulletin,* 81, 95–106.

Farquhar, Peter H., and Rao, Vithala, R. (1976), "A Balance Model for Evaluating Subsets of Multiattributed Items," *Management Science,* 22, 528–39.

Fidler, Eduard, J., and Thompson, Gerald L. (1977), "An Experiment on Executive Decision Making," Management Science Research Report No. 407, Graduate School of Industrial Administration, Carnegie-Mellon University.

Fiedler, John A. (1972), "Condominium Design and Pricing: A Case Study in Consumer Trade-off Analysis," in *Proceedings (Third Annual Conference),* ed. M. Venkatesan, Chicago: Association for Consumer Research, 279–93.

Fishbein, Martin (1967), "A Behavior Theory Approach to the Relations between Beliefs about an Object and the Attitude towards the Object," in *Readings in Attitude and Theory Measurement,* ed. M. Fishbein, New York: John Wiley & Sons, Inc., 389–99.

Gensch, Dennis H., Golob, Thomas F., and Recker, Wilfred W. (1976), "Regression is Inappropriate for Analyzing Cross-Sectional Data," in *1976 Educators' Proceedings,* Chicago: American Marketing Association, 120–4.

Goldberg, Lewis R. (1968), "Simple Models or Simple Processes? Some Research on Clinical Judgments," *American Psychologist,* 23, 483–96.

Goldberger, Arthur S. (1964), *Econometric Theory,* New York: John Wiley & Sons, Inc.

Green, Paul E. (1974), "On the Design of Choice Experiments Involving Multifactor Alternatives," *The Journal of Consumer Research,* 1, 61–8.

——— (1975), "Marketing Applications of MDS: Assessment and Outlook," *Journal of Marketing,* 39, 24–31.

——— (1977), "A New Approach to Market Segmentation," *Business Horizons,* 20, 61–73.

———, and Carmone, Frank J. (1970), *Multidimensional Scaling and Related Techniques in Marketing Analysis,* Boston: Allyn and Bacon.

———, and Carmone, Frank J. (1977), "A BIB/Logit Approach to Conjoint Analysis," Working Paper, Wharton School, University of Pennsylvania.

———, Carmone, Frank J., and Wind, Yoram (1972), "Subjective Evaluation Models and Conjoint Measurement," *Behavioral Science,* 17, 288–99.

———, Carroll, J. Douglas, and Carmone, Frank J. (1976), "Superordinate Factorial Designs in the Analysis of Consumer Judgments," *Journal of Business Research,* 4, 281–95.

———, Carroll, J. Douglas, and Carmone, Frank J. (1977), "Design Considerations in Attitude Measurement," in *Moving A Head with Attitude Research*, eds. Y. Wind and M. G. Greenberg, Chicago: American Marketing Association, 9–18.

———, Carroll, J. Douglas, and Carmone, Frank J. (1978), "Some New Types of Fractional Factorial Designs for Marketing Experiments," in *Research in Marketing, Vol. I,* ed. J. N. Sheth, Greenwich, CT: JAI Press.

———, and DeSarbo, Wayne S. (1977), "Demographic Stereotypes and Brand Preferences: An Application of Componential Segmentation," Working Paper, Wharton School, University of Pennsylvania.

———, and DeSarbo, Wayne S. (1978), "Additive Decomposition of Perceptions Data Via Conjoint Analysis," *The Journal of Consumer Research*, 5, 58–65.

———, and Devita, Michael T. (1974), "A Complementarity Model of Consumer Utility for Item Collections," *The Journal of Consumer Research,* 1, 56–67.

———, and Devita, Michael T. (1975a), "An Interaction Model of Consumer Utility," *The Journal of Consumer Research,* 2, 146–53.

———, and Devita, Michael T. (1975b), "The Robustness of Linear Models Under Correlated Attribute Conditions," *1975 Educators' Conference,* Chicago: American Marketing Association, 108–11.

———, and Rao, Vithala R. (1969), "Nonmetric Approaches to Multivariate Analysis in Marketing," Working Paper, Wharton School, University of Pennsylvania.

———, and Rao, Vithala R. (1971), "Conjoint Measurement for Quantifying Judgmental Data," *Journal of Marketing Research,* 8, 355–63.

———, and Tull, Donald S. (1978), *Research for Marketing Decisions (4th Edition),* Englewood Cliffs, NJ: Prentice-Hall, Inc.

———, and Wind, Yoram (1973), *Multiattribute Decisions in Marketing: A Measurement Approach,* Hinsdale, IL: The Dryden Press.

———, and Wind, Yoram (1975), "New Way to Measure Consumers' Judgments," *Harvard Business Review*, 53, 107–17.

———, Wind, Yoram, and Jain, Arun K. (1972), "Preference Measurement of Item Collections," *Journal of Marketing Research,* 9, 371–7.

Hansen, Fleming (1976), "Psychological Theories of Consumer Choice," *The Journal of Consumer Research,* 3, 117–42.

Hauser, John R., and Shugan, Steven M. (1977), "Efficient Measurement of Consumer Preference Functions: A General Theory for Intensity of Preference," Working Paper 602-001, Graduate School of Management, Northwestern University.

———, and Urban, Glen L. (1977), "A Normative Methodology for Modeling Consumer Response to Innovation," *Operations Research,* 25, 579–619.

Hoffman, Paul J., Slovic, Paul, and Rorer, L. G. (1968), "An Analysis of Variance Model for the Assessment of Configural Cue Utilization in Clinical Judgment," *Psychological Bulletin,* 69, 338–49.

Hopkins, David S. P., Larréché, Jean-Claude, and Massy, William F. (1977), "Constrained Optimization of a University Administrator's Preference Function," *Management Science,* 24, 365–77.

Jain, Arun K., Acito, Franklin, Malhotra, Naresh, and Mahajan, Vijay (1978), "A Comparison of Predictive Validity of Alternative Methods for Estimating Parameters in Preference Models," Working Paper, School of Management, State University of New York, at Buffalo.

Johnson, Richard M. (1973), "Varieties of Conjoint Measurement," Working Paper, Market Facts, Inc., Chicago.

——— (1974), "Trade-off Analysis of Consumer Values," *Journal of Marketing Research,* 11, 121–7.

——— (1976), "Beyond Conjoint Measurement: A Method of Pairwise Tradeoff Analysis" in *Advances in Consumer Research, Vol. III,* ed. B. B. Anderson, Proceedings of Association for Consumer Research, Sixth Annual Conference, 353–8.

———, and VanDyk, Gerald J. (1975), "A Resistance Analogy for Efficiency of Paired Comparison Designs," unpublished paper, Market Facts, Inc., Chicago.

Johnston, J. (1972), *Econometric Methods* (2nd Edition), New York: McGraw-Hill Book Co.

Keeney, Ralph L., and Raiffa, Howard (1976), *Decisions with Multiple Objectives: Preferences and Value Tradeoffs,* New York: John Wiley & Sons, Inc.

Kelly, George A. (1955), *The Psychology of Personal Constructs,* New York: W. W. Norton & Co., Inc.

Krantz, David H. (1964), "Conjoint Measurement: The Luce-Tukey Axiomatization and Some Extensions," *Journal of Mathematical Psychology,* 1, 248–77.

Kruskal, Joseph B. (1965), "Analysis of Factorial Experiments by Estimating Monotone Transformations of the Data," *Journal of the Royal Statistical Society, Series B,* 27, 251–63.

Lancaster, Kelvin (1971), *Consumer Demand: A New Approach,* New York: Columbia University Press.

Luce, R. Duncan, and Tukey, John W. (1964), "Simultaneous Conjoint Measurement: A New Type of Fundamental Measurement," *Journal of Mathematical Psychology,* 1, 1–27.

McAlister, Leigh (1978), "Choosing Multiple Items from a Homogenous Product Class," unpublished doctoral dissertation, Graduate School of Business, Stanford University.

McClain, John O., and Rao, Vithala R. (1974), "Trade-offs and Conflicts in Evaluation of Health Systems Alternatives: A Methodology for Analysis," *Health Services Research,* 9, 35–52.

McCullough, James M. (1978), "Identification of Preference Through Conjoint Measurement: A Comparison of Data Collection and Analytical Procedures," Working Paper, College of Business Administration, The University of Arizona.

McFadden, Daniel (1976), "Quantal Choice Analysis: A Survey," *Annals of Economic and Social Measurement,* 5, 363–90.

Montgomery, David B., Wittink, Dick R., and Glaze, Thomas (1977), "A Predictive Test of Individual Level Concept Evaluation and Trade-off Analysis," Research Paper No. 415, Graduate School of Business, Stanford University.

Naylor, Thomas, H., Balintfy, Joseph L., Burdick, Donald S., and Chu, Kong (1966), *Computer Simulation Techniques,* New York: John Wiley & Sons, Inc.

Nehls, Lyle, Seaman, Bruce, and Montgomery, David B. (1976), "A PLI Program for Trade-Off Analysis," Cambridge, MA: Marketing Science Institute.

Oppedijk van Veen, Walle M., and Beazley, David (1977), "An Investigation of Alternative Methods of Applying the Trade-off Model," *Journal of the Market Research Society,* 19, 2–9.

Parker, Barnett R., and Srinivasan, V. (1976), "A Consumer Preference Approach to the Planning of Rural Primary Health Care Facilities," *Operations Research,* 24, 991–1025.

Pekelman, Dov, and Sen, Subrata (1974), "Mathematical Programming Models for the Determination of Attribute Weights, *Management Science,* 20, 1217–29.

———, and Sen, Subrata (1978), "Improving Prediction in Conjoint Measurement," Working Paper, Graduate School of Management, The University of Rochester.

Pessemier, Edgar A., Burger, Philip, Teach, Richard, and Tigert, Douglas (1971), "Using Laboratory Brand Preference Scales to Predict Consumer Brand Purchases," *Management Science,* 17, B371–85.

Punj, Girish N., and Staelin, Richard (1978), "The Choice Process for Graduate Business Schools," *Journal of Marketing Research,* 15 (forthcoming).

Rao, Vithala R. (1973), "On Models for Scaling Second Choice Data," Working Paper, Graduate School of Business and Public Administration, Cornell University.

——— (1977), "Conjoint Measurement in Marketing Analysis," in *Multivariate Methods for Market and Survey Research,* ed. J. N. Sheth, Chicago: American Marketing Association, 257–86.

———, and Solgaard, Hans S. (1977), "An Empirical Evaluation of Alternative Multiattribute Utility Models," Working Paper, Graduate School of Business and Public Administration, Cornell University.

———, and Winter, Frederick W. (1977), "Application of the Multivariate Probit Model for Market Segmentation and Product Design," Working Paper 388, School of Business Administration, University of Illinois at Urbana.

Ratchford, Brian T. (1975), "The New Economic Theory for Consumer Behavior: An Interpretive Essay," *The Journal of Consumer Research,* 2, 65–78.

Rorer, Leonard G. (1971), "A Circuitous Route to Bootstrapping," in *Conference on Personality Measurement in Medical Education,* eds. H. B. Haley, A. G. D'Costa, and A. M. Schafer, Washington, D.C.: Association of American Medical Colleges.

Rosenberg, Milton J. (1956), "Cognitive Structure and Attitudinal Affect," *Journal of Abnormal and Social Psychology,* 53, 367–72.

Russ, Frederick A. (1971), "Consumer Evaluation of Alternative Product Models," unpublished doctoral dissertation: Carnegie-Mellon University.

Scott, Jerome E. (1977), "Demand Curve and Utility Estimation in Industrial Markets," Paper MPB 18.4, Atlanta: Joint National ORSA/TIMS meeting.

———, and Wright, Peter (1976), "Modeling an Organizational Buyer's Product Evaluation Strategy: Validity and Procedural Considerations," *Journal of Marketing Research,* 13, 211–24.

Shocker, Allan D., and Srinivasan, V. (1977a), "LINMAP (Version II): A FORTRAN IV Computer Program for Analyzing Ordinal Preference (Dominance) Judgments via Linear Programming Techniques and for Conjoint Measurement," *Journal of Marketing Research,* 14, 101–3.

———, and Srinivasan, V. (1977b), "Multi-Attribute Approaches for Product Concept Evaluation and Generation: A Critical Review," Research Paper No. 326 (Rev.), Graduate School of Business, Stanford University.

Shugan, Steven M., and Hauser, John R. (1977), "P.A.R.I.S.: An Interactive Market Research Information System," Working Paper 602-002, Graduate School of Management, Northwestern University.

Srinivasan, V. (1978), "A Model and Estimation Procedure for Multi-Stage Decision Processes," Working Paper, Graduate School of Business, Stanford University.

———, and Shocker, Allan D. (1973a), "Linear Programming Techniques for Multidimensional Analysis of Preferences," *Psychometrika,* 38, 337–69.

———, and Shocker, Allan D. (1973b), "Estimating the Weights for Multiple Attributes in a Composite Criterion Using Pairwise Judgments," *Psychometrika,* 38, 473–93.

Torgerson, Warren S. (1958), *Theory and Methods of Scaling,* New York: John Wiley & Sons, Inc.

Tversky, Amos (1967), "A General Theory of Polynomial Conjoint Measurement," *Journal of Mathematical Psychology,* 4, 1–20.

Ullrich, James R., and Painter, John R. (1974), "A Conjoint Measurement Analysis of Human Judgment," *Organizational Behavior and Human Performance,* 12, 50–61.

Westwood, Dick, Lunn, Tony, and Beazley, David (1974), "The Trade-off Model and Its Extensions," *Journal of the Market Research Society,* 16, 227–41.

Whitmore, G. A., and Cavadias, G. S. (1974), "Experimental Determination of Community Preferences for Water Quality-Cost Alternatives," *Decision Sciences,* 5, 614–31.

Wilkie, William L., and Pessemier, Edgar A. (1973), "Issues in Marketing's Use of Multi-Attribute Attitude Models," *Journal of Marketing Research,* 10, 428–41.

Wind, Yoram, and Spitz, Lawrence, K. (1976), "An Analytical Approach to Marketing Decisions in Health Care Organizations," *Operations Research,* 24, 973–90.

Wright, Peter (1975), "Consumer Choice Strategies: Simplifying vs. Optimizing," *Journal of Marketing Research,* 12, 60–7.

Young, Forrest W. (1969), "Polynomial Conjoint Analysis of Similarities: Definitions for a Special Algorithm," Research Paper No. 76, Psychometric Laboratory, University of North Carolina.

DONALD G. MORRISON

This paper provides a framework for collecting, analyzing, and interpreting purchase intentions data.

PURCHASE INTENTIONS AND PURCHASE BEHAVIOR

MANY surveys contain purchase intentions questions on such items as new food products, frequently purchased package goods, appliances, automobiles, and capital equipment. The time frame may range from one week to 24 months or more. Although these purchase intentions data are used, there has not been much work done on evaluating the accuracy of these data—neither at the individual nor aggregate levels. In particular, there has been little follow-up to see if individuals surveyed actually purchased the product of interest over the specified time periods. One purpose of this paper is to stimulate such follow-up procedures.

Purchase intentions continue to be an important concept in marketing. The published literature contains a very small fraction of the actual studies which have used purchase intentions; nevertheless, the quantity of literature is quite large. Axelrod (1968) analyzes purchase intentions along with other attitude measures used for predicting actual purchase behavior. Smith (1965) presents a highly readable and interesting discussion on the use of purchase intentions in evaluating the effectiveness of automobile advertising. Silk and Urban (1978) have purchase intentions as one input for a new product model. Bass, Pessemier, and Lehmann (1972) use purchase intentions in their well-known soft drink study. Sewall (1978) uses purchase intentions to segment markets for proposed new (redesigned) products. In spite of this heavy use of purchase intentions data, there has been little effort to construct a formal mathematical model that establishes the intermediate links between stated purchase intentions and actual purchase behavior. This paper is an attempt at building such a model which will make purchase intentions a better understood and more useful concept.

First, a general framework for analyzing purchase intentions data is presented. This model focuses attention on three very different phenomena that often are implicitly and confusingly combined. Then within this overall framework a specific, mathematically tractable and statistically testable model is developed. Some actual data from the well-known study by Juster (1966) is analyzed.

The data used are purchase intentions for automobiles and household appliances. The data fit the

Donald Morrison is Professor of Business at Columbia University, New York. The work reported here was supported by the Center for Food Policy Studies at the Graduate School of Business, Columbia University.

Reprinted from *Journal of Marketing,* 43 (Spring 1979), 65-74, published by the American Marketing Association.

model quite well, but this is not the important point. Rather the model highlights the differences between intentions data for a major purchase of an automobile and a still substantial, but less major purchase of an appliance.

In the automobile study, only 53% of those who said that they were certain to buy a new automobile actually did so. How can we assess this statistic? By itself not much can be said; however, within the context of our model the 53% statistic appears to be quite "good." We will now proceed to develop the model that allows us to make this evaluation.

The General Model

The overall model uses a three-step transformation to transform stated intention, I_s, into a purchase probability estimate, $\hat{p}$.

Step 1. Stated intention, I_s, is transformed into an estimate of the true intention, $\hat{I}_t$, by the True Intention Model (TIM). This procedure has a long history in the psychometric literature where an observed score on, for example, a multiple choice test is used to estimate the subject's true ability. The driving force for all of this work is that the observed score may be written as

$$\text{Observed Score} = \text{True Ability} + \text{Error} \qquad (1)$$

The obvious analog for intentions is

$$\text{Stated Intention} = \text{True Intention} + \text{Error}$$

This literature is well summarized in the book by Lord and Novick (1968) and articles by Lord (1959; 1965), Keats and Lord (1962), and Duncan (1974). A less mathematically demanding article which illustrates the basic notion can be found in Morrison (1973). Briefly expressed, the TIM deflates the high stated intentions and inflates the low stated intentions in an effort to more accurately represent true intention *at the time of the survey*. This type of adjustment, known as "regression to the mean" is required in all situations where the observed phenomena can be expressed qualitatively by (1). This regression to the mean effect will be quantitatively developed in (7) within the context of a specific TIM.

Step 2. The estimated true intention, $\hat{I}_t$, is transformed into an unadjusted purchase probability estimate, $\hat{p}_u$, by the Exogenous Events Model (EEM). An individual may not expect to buy a new appliance during the next year and accurately state this fact on the survey. However, six months later the dishwasher motor may burn out leaving the individual with a buy or repair decision. At this point in time he or she may elect to buy. Similarly, an individual may truly plan to buy a new car during the next year. However, a subsequent sudden loss of income may make such a purchase infeasible. The EEM allows for such changes in circumstances—albeit in a very simple manner in the specific model.

Step 3. The estimated unadjusted purchase probability, $\hat{p}_u$, is transformed into the estimated purchase probability, $\hat{p}$, by the Probability Adjustment Model (PAM). There is no reason to believe that the average stated purchase intention will equal the proportion that actually buy the product for all products and all time frames. Hence, some transformation will be needed to adjust for this bias. There are many possible adjustment formulas and, again in our specific model, we use an extremely simple adjustment.

The general model can be summarized by

*S*tated Intention
↓ TIM
*T*rue Intention
↓ EEM
*U*nadjusted Purchase Probability
↓ PAM
*P*urchase Probability

The reader may have noticed the first letter of each of the two intentions and two probabilities. However, we will resist the temptation to call this the Three Step STUP Model.

Each of the three transformation models will now be given a well-defined and quite simple mathematical structure. The resulting aggregate model will then be fitted to some of Juster's data. The research implications of this approach will be discussed in the final section.

A Specific Model

A Beta Binomial True Intentions Model

Probably the simplest model one could construct would be a linear relation between stated intention, I_s, and average true intention, I_t.
Namely,

$$I_t = a + k\, I_s. \qquad (2)$$

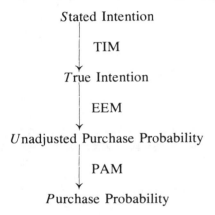

The regression to the mean notion implies $a > 0, k > 0$, and $a + k < 1$. Graphically, this implies that (with I_t on the vertical axis) equation (2) is a straight line with a positive intercept and a slope of less than 1, or equivalently, the straight line makes an angle of less than 45 degrees with the horizontal axis.

We could leave the model at this level of justification (i.e., mere simplicity), but there is, in fact, good reason for such a formulation. At the individual level, the stated intention is a random variable—recall equation (1)—with a mean at or near the true intention. If the individual is responding on an n+1 point scale which we can label 0,1,2, . . . ,n, then the most natural individual model will be that I_s is distributed according to the binomial distribution with parameters n and I_t. More formally,

$$P(I_s = r;\, n,\, I_t) = \binom{n}{r} I_t^r (1-I_t)^{n-r}, \qquad r = 0, 1, \ldots, n. \tag{3}$$

An underlying and untestable model that generates (3) is that an individual with true intention I_t responds 1 or 0 in an independent fashion to each point on the scale with probabilities I_t and 1 - I_t, respectively. The stated intention then is the sum of these 0,1 responses (i.e., a binomial random variable). This process that yields a binomially distributed stated intention may sound a little strange, but it is in the same spirit of many of the mathematical psychology models of attitude formation where subjects pick up cues in a probabilistic manner. In any event, we are not interested in the detailed micro process of forming the stated intentions. Rather, we only need (3) to be a reasonably specific representation of the general model: Stated Intention = True Intention + Error.

No direct evidence for or against (3) as a model of stated purchase intention is in the literature, but Juster (1966) does give some data that support the within individual variability that the binomial model yields. He cross classifies individuals by their responses on a 10 point intention probability scale and a five point "definitely will" to "definitely will not" scale (p. 677). The individuals show sufficient inconsistency to make our binomial model at least a good starting point. More will be said on this issue in the Discussion section.

Whatever individual stated intentions model is used, it is clear that true intention will vary across the population of respondents. Letting $g\,(I_t)$ represent the probability density function of I_t, then the aggregate distribution of I_s is well-known mixed binomial

$$P(I_s = r) = \int_0^1 P(I_s = r;\, n,\, I_t)\, g(I_t)\, dI_t, \qquad r = 0, 1, \ldots, n. \tag{4}$$

There is a vast statistical and psychometric literature on this general mixed binomial model (4). The first n moments of the unobservable distribution $g\,(I_t)$ can be estimated from the first n moments of the observable distribution on I_s. (See Skellam 1948; Keats and Lord 1962.) An estimate of I_t from I_s can be obtained for this general mixture model. (See Lord and Stocking 1976.) However, for our purposes we will restrict $g\,(I_t)$ to being a beta distribution

$$g(I_t;\alpha,\beta) = \frac{\Gamma(\alpha+\beta)}{\Gamma(\alpha)\,\Gamma(\beta)}\, I_t^{\alpha-1}\,(1-I_t)^{\beta-1}, \qquad 0 < I_t < 1. \tag{5}$$

The beta is a flexible distribution that takes on unimodal, U, J, and reverse J shapes. Using (5), the mixed binomial (4) becomes the well-known beta binomial model

$$P(I_s = r;\, n, \alpha, \beta) = \binom{n}{r} \frac{B(\alpha + r, \beta + n - r)}{B(\alpha,\beta)}, \qquad r = 0, 1, \ldots, n. \tag{6}$$

where $B\,(\alpha,\beta) = \dfrac{\Gamma(\alpha)\,\Gamma(\beta)}{\Gamma(\alpha+\beta)}$.

This beta binomial model has been used extensively in branch switching models (e.g., Kalwani and Morrison 1977) and in advertising reach and frequency models (e.g., Greene 1970). Furthermore, (6) is the unique aggregate distribution that (assuming a binomially distributed I_s at the individual level) will yield a linear relationship between the expected value I_t and I_s. This is proved in Keats and Lord (1962) where they refer to the beta binomial as the negative hypergeometric distribution.

If we divide the stated intention by n (so it now takes on values 0, $1/n$, $2/n$, . . . ,1), the linear relation shown in (2) becomes[1]

$$\hat{I}_t = \frac{\alpha}{\alpha+\beta+1} + \left(\frac{1}{\alpha+\beta+1}\right) I_s. \tag{7}$$

For the beta distribution (5) the parameters α, $\beta >$ 0. Hence, when $\alpha+\beta$ approaches 0, the slope of (7) approaches 1. That is, stated intention is very close to true intention. This is intuitively appealing because when $\alpha+\beta \rightarrow 0$ the beta distribution has virtually all of its mass near 0 or 1. For most people the binomial variance in (3) will be near 0. Hence, the stated intention is very close to the true intention.

At the other extreme, when $\alpha+\beta$ becomes large the slope in (7) approaches 0. This implies that stated intention has very little relationship to true intention.

[1]Originally we have the stated purchase intention take on the $n + 1$ integer values between 0 and n. This allows us to make the binomial assumption at the individual level. However, when we compare stated intentions with actual purchase probabilities it is natural to transform these stated intentions into the interval 0 and 1. Therefore, the transformed stated intentions which take on values 0, $1/n$, $2/n$, . . . , 1 are not strictly binomially distributed at the individual level since the range of this random variable is no longer 0, 1, 2,

Again this is intuitively appealing since the beta distribution becomes a "spike" at its mean $\alpha/(\alpha+\beta)$ when $\alpha + \beta \rightarrow \infty$. Hence, all individuals have virtually the same true intention. The variation in stated intention is all "noise"—i.e., the "Error" component in (1)—and accordingly the true intention estimate is not influenced by the observed stated intention.

A detailed discussion of these two special cases and situations in between can be found in Sabavala and Morrison (1977). In most purchase intention settings, the case of a small value of $\alpha+\beta$ will prevail. This will lead to a steep slope for a graph of true purchase intention versus stated purchase intention. Notice in (7) when $\alpha+\beta = ½$ the slope of the graph is $1/(½ + 1) = ⅔$. Equivalently, this straight line makes a 34 degree angle with the horizontal axis. The Juster data yield values of $\alpha+\beta$ in the neighborhood of ½.

However, when the graph uses *actual* purchase probabilities on the vertical axis instead of the estimated $\hat{I}_t$, a much flatter curve usually results. (See Figures 1-4 which will be discussed when Juster's data are analyzed.) If $\hat{I}_t$ is really a good estimate of the true intention, why is there this apparent discrepancy between true intention and actual behavior? This leads us to Step 2.

A New Draw Exogenous Events Model

As mentioned in the introduction, many things can happen to change an individual's purchase intentions during the time frame of interest. These exogenous events could be modeled in a variety of ways. In particular, we could segment the individuals by their stated intentions and model each class separately. However, it seems much more appropriate to begin with a simple model.

The spirit of this model will be to obtain a graph of p_u, the unadjusted purchase probability, versus I_s where this graph has a smaller slope than $\hat{I}_t$ versus I_s. If we also can retain a linear relation, so much the better.

A model that accomplishes this reduced slope, linear relationship is as follows:

- With probability $1-\rho$ the individual has no change in true intention and this true intention is in fact the unadjusted purchase probability.
- With probability ρ the individual has a change in true intention. When this change occurs a new value for I_t is drawn from the original beta distribution (5). This new value I_t then becomes the unadjusted purchase probability.

Basically, all this model is saying is that when a change occurs it is as if the individual is being replaced by a randomly chosen, new individual from a population with I_t distributed according to (5). This model will yield a $\hat{p}_u$ which is a simple weighted average of (7) ($\hat{I}_t$ if no change occurs) and $\alpha/(\alpha+\beta)$, the expected value of I_t, if a change does occur. This results in

$$\hat{p}_u = \frac{\rho\alpha}{\alpha+\beta} + \frac{(1-\rho)\alpha}{\alpha+\beta+1} + \left(\frac{1-p}{\alpha+\beta+1}\right) I_s \qquad (8)$$
$$= \rho\, E(I_t) + (1-\rho)\hat{I}_t.$$

Note that the slope in (7) is reduced by a factor of $1-\rho$. When $\rho = 0$, there is no change and (8) reduces to (7) as it should. When $\rho = 1$, everyone changes so that stated intention at the time of the survey has no effect on actual purchase probability.

Since the probability of change ρ is independent of I_s, the population average for $\hat{p}_u$ will equal the population average of I_t which is in turn the population average of I_s (rescaled to take on values $0, 1/n, 2/n, \ldots, 1$). This average is, of course, the average of the beta distribution (5)—namely, $\alpha/(\alpha+\beta)$.

If there does exist some systematic bias in I_t (i.e.. on average it over or understates p, the average actual purchase probability), then some form of adjustment to (8) is required. This brings us to Step 3.

A Constant Bias Adjustment Model

The overall bias in (8) will be

$$b = \bar{I}_s - \bar{p} \qquad (9)$$

where $\bar{I}_s$ is the average stated intention and $\bar{p}$ is the proportion that actually purchase.

Again, there are numerous ways to adjust (8). However, with simplicity in mind, we merely subtract b from each estimate $\hat{p}_u$ yielding a purchase probability estimate for each individual of

$$\hat{p} = \hat{p}_u - b,$$

or

$$\hat{p} = \frac{\rho\alpha}{\alpha+\beta} + \frac{(1-\rho)\alpha}{\alpha+\beta+1} + \left(\frac{1-\rho}{\alpha+\beta+1}\right) I_s - b. \qquad (10)$$

While (8) produces estimates that are constrained to lie in the acceptable range of 0 to 1, (10) can yield values of $\hat{p}$ outside of this range. However, this will only happen when α, β, and ρ are small (i.e., initial true intentions are concentrated near either 0 or 1 and few changes take place) and/or b, the bias, is very large. This disadvantage of (10) is balanced by the retained linearity between $\hat{p}$ and I_s.

Some Empirical Examples

The Juster (1966) paper is one of the few published

works where both purchase intention and actual purchase behavior have been obtained on the same sample of individuals. For both automobiles and household appliances, individuals responded to the following question:

> Taking everything into account, what are the prospects that some member of your family will buy a —— sometime during the next —— months; between now and ——?

The time frames were six, 12, and 24 months for both automobiles and appliances. The respondent chose a number on a flash card which contained the following statements.

Certain, practically certain (99 in 100)	10
Almost sure (9 in 10)	9
Very probably (8 in 10)	8
Probably (7 in 10)	7
Good possibility (6 in 10)	6
Fairly good possibility (5 in 10)	5
Fair possibility (4 in 10)	4
Some possibility (3 in 10)	3
Slight possibility (2 in 10)	2
Very slight possibility (1 in 10)	1
No chance, almost no chance (1 in 100)	0

Juster then calculates the actual purchase probability for each intentions class. However, because of relatively small sample sizes he only presents the results for the following five aggregate intention groups:

$$10, \{9, 8, 7\}, \{6, 5, 4\}, \{3, 2, 1\}, 0.$$

Juster's actual purchases were in a six month

TABLE 1
Automobiles: 6 and 12 Month Intentions vs. 6 Month Purchases

Intention Scale	No. with 6 Month Intention		Intention Group Purchase Probability	Purchase Probability Sample Size
0.0	345	(347)	.10	300
0.1	29	(27)		
0.2	16	(15)	.30	53
0.3	14	(11)		
0.4	3	(9)		
0.5	10	(7)	.65	17
0.6	6	(7)		
0.7	6	(6)		
0.8	6	(6)	.36	14
0.9	5	(6)		
1.0	11	(9)	.55	11
	Total: 451		Mean: .17	395

$\alpha = .074, \quad \beta = .67, \quad \overline{I}_s = .099, \quad \rho = .37, \quad b = -.071$

Intention Scale	No. with 12 Month Intention		Intention Group Purchase Probability	Purchase Probability Sample Size
0.0	293	(288)	.07	256
0.1	26	(35)		
0.2	21	(20)	.19	57
0.3	21	(15)		
0.4	10	(13)		
0.5	9	(11)	.41	32
0.6	12	(11)		
0.7	13	(10)		
0.8	11	(11)	.48	31
0.9	10	(12)		
1.0	21	(20)	.53	19
	Total: 447		Mean: .17	395

$\alpha = .12, \quad \beta = .56 \quad \overline{I}_s = .17 \quad \rho = .22, \quad b = 0$

TABLE 2
Appliances: 12 and 24 Month Intentions vs. 6 Month Purchases

Intention Scale	No. with 12 Month Intention	Intention Group Purchase Probability	Purchase Probability Sample Size
0.0	2377 (2386)	.017	2111
0.1	87 (84)		
0.2	57 (45)	.053	150
0.3	29 (32)		
0.4	23 (25)		
0.5	22 (21)	.111	63
0.6	21 (19)		
0.7	14 (18)		
0.8	11 (17)	.184	38
0.9	17 (18)		
1.0	30 (24)	.105	19
	Total: 2688	**Mean:** .026	2381

$\alpha = .034, \quad \beta = .69, \quad \overline{I}_s = .047, \quad \rho = .79, \quad b = .021$

Intention Scale	No. with 24 Month Intention	Intention Group Purchase Probability	Purchase Probability Sample Size
0.0	2174 (2177)	.015	1429
0.1	95 (115)		
0.2	99 (64)	.034	206
0.3	41 (46)		
0.4	38 (38)		
0.5	28 (34)	.045	206
0.6	30 (31)		
0.7	29 (31)		
0.8	36 (32)	.084	83
0.9	24 (39)		
1.0	80 (69)	.215	65
	Total: 2674	**Mean:** .026	1989

$\alpha = 0.05, \quad \beta = .51, \quad \overline{I}_s = 0.90, \quad \rho = .74, \quad b = .064$

period—December 1964 to June 1965. Yet, he used these same purchase data for assessing six, 12, and 24 month intentions. When the 12 and 24 month intentions are compared to six month purchases we seem to be comparing apples to oranges. However, as the automobile data will show there is some advantage to doing these differing time frame comparisons.

Table 1 gives the results for automobiles. The sample histogram for both six and 12 month intentions are presented. The numbers in parentheses are the fitted beta binomial expected values (rounded to the nearest integer). The beta binomial parameters α and β are estimated by the method of moments while ρ is estimated by a simple regression of intention versus actual purchase probability for the intention group.[2] When the $\{1, 2, \text{and } 3\}$ group was used, the middle value of 2 was the value used in the regression, and similarly for $\{4, 5, \text{and } 6\}$ and $\{7, 8, \text{and } 9\}$. The bias is, of course, the difference between the mean intention and the total sample purchase proportion. Finally, some of the purchase data were not collected so that the two sample sizes differ somewhat. Juster doesn't explain why he kept some of the intention data that had no corresponding purchase data. In any event we had no way of correcting this difference.

Table 2 contains analogous results for six household appliances (air conditioners, refrigerators, washing machines, clothes dryers, television sets, and dishwashers). Juster does not present data for the individual appliances. That is, each individual represents six data points—an intention, purchase pair for each of the six appliances. In addition, only 12 and 24 month

[2]Scaling the stated intentions 0, 1, . . . , 10 the sample mean, $\overline{X}$, and sample variance, S^2, of these intentions are calculated. We then solve for the values $\widehat{\alpha}$ and $\widehat{\beta}$ that make the theoretical mean $10\alpha/(\alpha+\beta)=\overline{X}$ and the theoretical variance $10\alpha\beta\,(\alpha+\beta+10)/(\alpha+\beta)^2(\alpha+\beta+1)=S^2$. The theoretical slope of actual purchase probability versus stated intentions is $(1-\rho)/(\alpha+\beta+1)$. Since we previously calculated $\widehat{\alpha}$ and $\widehat{\beta}$ we now find $\widehat{\rho}$ which makes the observed slope equal $(1-\widehat{\rho})/(\widehat{\alpha}+\widehat{\beta}+1)$.

intentions were collected. Of course, they are both being compared to the six month purchase data.

Since we are grouping all six appliances together, the resulting parameter values are an approximate average across all six appliances. We could make the rather heroic assumption of common parameters for each appliance, but that would be stretching a little too far. Therefore, we will use the average parameter interpretation. The next section will show that the behavior of the purchase intentions for this "average appliance" differs considerably from the behavior of the automobile purchase intentions.

Figures 1-4 plot the stated purchase intentions versus the intention group purchase probabilities. The straight line in each graph represents equation (10).

Summary of Empirical Findings

A number of points emerge from Tables 1 and 2, Figures 1-4, and the summary results in Table 3.

- The beta binomial fits the stated intentions histogram quite well in all four cases. This only implies that the *composite* hypothesis of individual binomial responses and beta distributed true intentions is a good approximation. Nevertheless, these results are encouraging for the beta binomial true intentions model.
- The six month automobile intentions data are not very good. They exhibit a large downward bias and they are not at all monotonically related to actual purchase probabilities.
- The 12 month automobile intentions fit the six month purchase data very well. There is no bias and the intentions are linearly related to purchase probabilities.
- Both 12 and 24 month appliance intentions have the positive bias that is expected. The purchases only cover a six month period—leaving six or 18 months in which to fulfill the intention by actually buying.
- Both appliance figures show a much flatter relationship between actual purchases and stated intentions. This implies a higher ρ value (see Table 3) which in turn implies a greater influence of unexpected exogenous effects.
- The quantity $1/(1+\alpha+\beta)$ is an index that varies between 1 (when $\alpha + \beta \rightarrow 0$ and all of the true intentions are concentrated at the extreme values of 0 and 1) and 0 (when $\alpha + \beta \rightarrow \infty$ and all of the true intentions are the same). Hence, $1/(1+\alpha+\beta)$ can be called a polarization index of true intentions. In all four cases, the polarization is about the same. See Sabavala and Morrison (1977) for a more detailed description of this index.
- The parameter estimates for α and β are quite good since large sample sizes are involved. The estimate of ρ is somewhat more suspect since only five points (albeit each point is an average of a large number of other data points) are used. In addition, both variables are subject to error so that the usual least square assumptions don't apply. Nevertheless, the slopes for the automobile curves are clearly much greater than those of the appliance curves.

Discussion

The three-step model presented here focuses attention on a number of important issues that tend to be overlooked when stated purchase intentions are compared to actual purchase behavior. Our model forces the researcher to explicitly consider:

- The number of scale points
- The numerical value of each point on the scale
- The adjectives associated with each point on the scale
- Whether a direct probability response scale should be used
- The reliability of stated intentions

TABLE 3
Summary Statistics

Category	Time Frame	α	β	$\frac{1}{1+\alpha+\beta}$	ρ	b
Automobile	6 months	.074	.67	.57	.37	−.071
Automobile	12 months	.120	.56	.60	.22	0
Appliances	12 months	.034	.69	.58	.79	.021
Appliances	24 months	.050	.51	.64	.74	.064

FIGURE 1

Automobiles: 6 Month Intentions

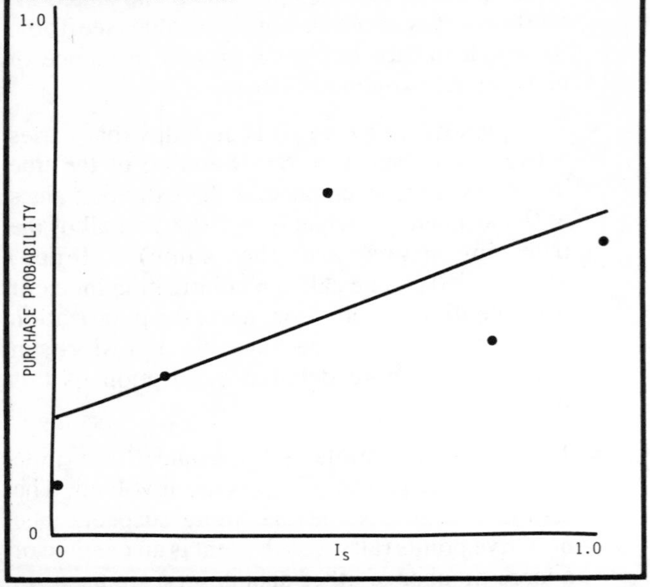

FIGURE 2

Automobiles: 12 Month Intentions

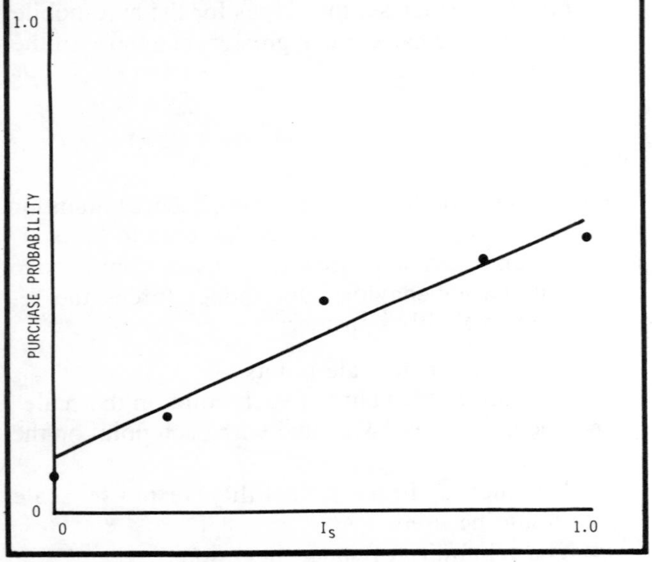

- The transformation from stated intentions to true intentions
- The distribution of true intentions across the population of consumers
- The appropriate time frame for the intentions
- The effect of ''unexpected'' events over the time frame
- Systematic discrepencies between average intentions and average purchase probabilities

This list could go on, but the 10 items mentioned will suffice.

Table 1 shows that 12 month intentions are better (both in terms of bias and monotonicity) in predicting six month automobile purchases than are the corresponding six month intentions. This may be an isolated case, but it is a concept worth studying further. Perhaps better estimates of actual purchases over x months can be obtained by having stated intentions over y months.

Clearly, automobile intentions are more stable over time than appliance intentions. This would lead one to conjecture that purchase intentions for low cost, low involvement items are even less stable—yielding an even smaller slope in the purchase probability versus purchase intentions graphs. However, since the time frame for these low cost product intentions data is often two weeks, the slopes are not comparable unless some adjustment is made for the differing time scales.

The model also directs attention to the ''yea sayer''—''nea sayer'' issue. Clearly, the absolute purchase probability for the ''certain to purchase'' group tells us nothing. Figure 3 shows that this group actually purchases less than the .8 intention group. This non-monotonicity implies a ''yea sayer'' effect, but the other three graphs do not indicate such an effect. Recall that in the introduction we posed the question of whether a 53% purchase probability for a ''definitely will buy'' group was a ''good'' value. We really can't say for sure, but by looking at Figure 2 we do see that this 53% value is ''consistent'' with the model. Hence, it is a ''good'' value.

Our model suggests some natural ways of segmenting intentions data into meaningful categories. When sufficient data have been gathered, we could separate products along the following dimensions.

- Reliability of stated intentions
- Slope of $\widehat{p}$ vs. I_s (i.e., the stability of true intentions)
- Linearity of $\widehat{p}$ vs. I_s
- Difference between $\widehat{p}$ and $\bar{I}_s$ (i.e., the bias in the stated intentions)
- The most appropriate time frames

Other dimensions come to mind, but again this list will suffice.

We need to make some comments on empirically assessing the model. Most data sets will contain only stated intentions and actual purchase behavior.[3] Therefore

[3]At the individual level, we could test the model by correlating the estimated purchase probability p with the actual binary purchase variable (the individual did or did not purchase) across all individuals in the sample. However, the resulting empirical correlation would need to be interpreted carefully. A ''low'' value of r (or r^2) may not be quite so low. (see Morrison 1972.) Alternatively, we might wish to classify the individuals as buyers or nonbuyers based on stated intentions. Again the resulting 2 × 2 classification table would need to be interpreted with care. (See Beckwith and Morrison 1977.)

fore, the three steps of the model are not tested individually. (Studies aimed at determining the reliability and stability of purchase intentions will help determine the validity of the first two steps in the model.) Any Juster type data where purchase probabilities are linearly related to stated purchase intentions are consistent with our model if the stated purchase intentions have a beta binomial distribution. The advantage of the formal three-step model is that the resulting parameters decompose the empirical slope of this linear relationship into the component due to the heterogeneity of the true purchase intentions (determined by α and β) and that due to the propensity of individual purchase intentions to change (determined by ρ).

Finally, we must discuss the key issue of parameter stationarity over time. The beta distribution parameters α and β are estimated from the histogram of stated intentions so they pose no stationarity problem. That is, they are estimated at the current point in time. However, in projecting these intentions into actual purchasing behavior, ρ, the stability of the individual true intentions, and b, the bias, are obviously crucial. For a new product the problem is even more severe. Namely, we have to first ascertain the appropriate product category and/or identify past new products that were similar to the proposed new product. Then, the parameters estimated for these appropriate past products must be assumed valid for the current new product so that equation (10) type forecasts can be made.

At the moment there is not an adequate set of purchase intentions with follow up purchase behavior studies in the literature to make the above type of forecast. Hopefully, this paper will supply a unifying framework for the design of such studies and that the researchers involved will be motivated to publish their findings. If this is done the probability is very high that empirical regularities will emerge that will make purchase intentions data much more useful to the marketing community.

FIGURE 3

Appliances: 12 Month Intentions

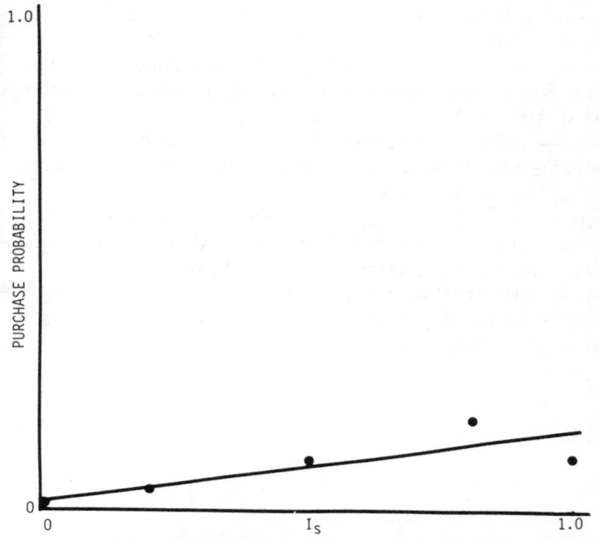

FIGURE 4

Appliances: 24 Month Intentions

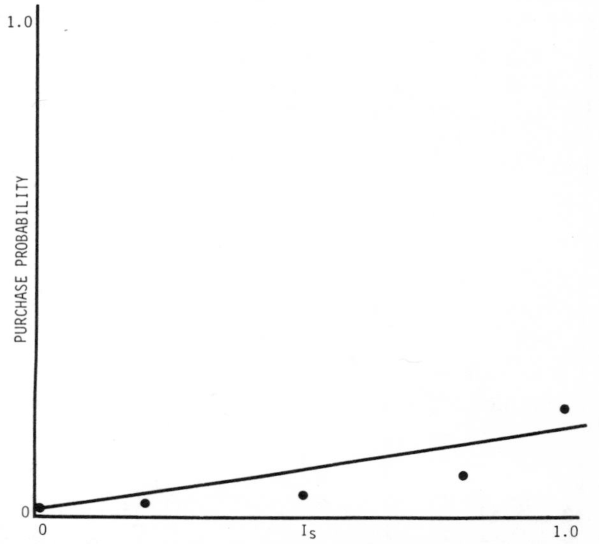

REFERENCES

Axelrod, J.N. (1968), "Attitude Measures that Predict Purchase," *Journal of Advertising Research,* 8 (March), 3-18.

Bass, F.M., E.A. Pessemier, and D.R. Lehmann (1972), "An Experimental Study of the Relationship Between Attitudes, Brand Preferences and Choice," *Behavioral Science,* 17 (November), 532-541.

Beckwith, N.E. and D.G. Morrison (1977), "Stochastic Interpretation of 2x2 Classification Tables," *Journal of the American Statistical Association,* 72 (June), 303-308.

Duncan, G.T. (1974), "An Empirical Bayes Approach to Scoring Multiple Choice Tests in the Misinformation Model," *Journal of the American Statistical Association,* 69 (March), 50-57.

Greene, J.D. (1970), "Personal Media Probabilities," *Journal of Advertising Research,* 5 (October), 12-18.

Juster, F.T. (1966), "Consumer Buying Intentions and Purchase Probability: An Experiment in Survey Design," *Journal of the American Statistical Association,* 61 (September), 658-696.

Kalwani, M.U. and D.G. Morrison (1977), "A Parsimonious Description of the Hendry System," *Management Science,* 23 (January), 467-477.

Keats, J.A. and F.M. Lord (1962), "A Theoretical Distribution for Mental Test Scores," *Psychometrika,* 27 (March), 59-72.

Lord, F.M. (1959), "An Approach to Mental Test Theory," *Psychometrika,* 24 (December), 283-302.

——— (1965), "A Strong True-Score Theory with Applications," *Psychometrika,* 30 (September), 239-270.

——— and M.R. Novick (1968), *Statistical Theories of Mental Test Scores,* with contributions by Allen Birnbaum. Reading, MA: Addison-Wesley.

——— and M.L. Stocking (1976), "An Interval Estimate for Making Statistical Inferences about True Scores," *Psychometrika,* 41 (March), 79-87.

Morrison, D.G. (1972), "Upper Bounds for Correlations Between Binary Outcomes and Probabilistic Predictions," *Journal of the American Statistical Association,* 67 (March), 68-70.

——— (1973), "Reliability of Tests: A Technique Using the 'Regression to the Mean' Fallacy," *Journal of Marketing Research,* 10 (February), 91-93.

Sabavala, D.J. and D.G. Morrison (1977), "A Model of TV Show Loyalty," *Journal of Advertising Research,* 17 (December), 35-43.

Sewall, A. (1978), "Market Segmentation Based on Ratings of Proposed Product Designs," *Journal of Marketing Research,* 15 (November), 557-564.

Silk, A.J. and G.L. Urban (1978), "Pre-Test-Market Evaluation of New Packaged Goods: A Model and Measurement Methodology," *Journal of Marketing Research,* 15 (May), 171-191.

Skellam, J.G. (1948), "A Probability Distribution Derived from the Binomial Distribution by Regarding the Probability of Success as a Variable Between Sets of Trials," *Journal of the Royal Statistical Association,* B10, 257-265.

Smith, G. (1965), "How GM Measures Ad Effectiveness," *Printer's Ink,* (May 14), 19-29.

FRANK M. BASS AND DICK R. WITTINK*

The existence of multiple observations within several cross sections gives rise to both opportunities and problems in the application of regression analysis. In this article the issues associated with the decision of whether or not to pool the data for purposes of estimation are explored and examples of marketing applications are provided.

Pooling Issues and Methods in Regression Analysis with Examples in Marketing Research

The existence of multiple observations within several cross sections gives rise to both opportunities and problems in the application of regression analysis. In this article we shall explore and discuss the issues associated with the decision of whether or not to pool the data for purposes of estimation and we shall provide examples of marketing applications of the most modern estimation methods for pooled data.

A major opportunity arises in conjunction with the gain in degrees of freedom when pooling is appropriate. Suppose, for example, that there are 18 time-series observations available for each of 25 sales districts. A separate regression for each of the districts would involve only 18 observations for a single district, while a pooled regression over observations from all districts and time periods would yield estimates based on 450 observations. Moreover, since cross-sectional variation is ordinarily substantially greater than time-series variation, the pooled estimates would have the desirable property of being derived from a wider space of variation than estimates based solely on time-series data.

MAJOR POOLING ISSUES

Although pooling offers advantages over separate regressions, major decisions must be made before the development of pooled estimates. These decisions are: (1) whether or not pooling is appropriate, and (2) how to pool the data. If there are N cross sections of time-series observations involving the same dependent and independent variables of the conventional form:

$$\mathbf{Y}_i = \mathbf{X}_i\beta_i + \epsilon_i \qquad i = 1, 2, \ldots, N \tag{1}$$

where $\mathbf{Y}_i$ is $T_i \times 1$, $\mathbf{X}_i$ is $T_i \times k$, β_i is a fixed $k \times 1$ vector, and ϵ_i is a $T_i \times 1$ random vector, a test of the hypothesis that $\beta_i = \beta_j$, any or all $i \neq j$ may be developed very easily on the basis of a comparison of the error sum of squares from the separate regressions with the error sum of squares from pooled ordinary least squares estimates.

If the homogeneity hypothesis is rejected, then the estimates based on the pooled model:

$$\begin{bmatrix} \mathbf{Y}_1 \\ \mathbf{Y}_2 \\ \vdots \\ \mathbf{Y}_N \end{bmatrix} = \begin{bmatrix} \mathbf{X}_1 \\ \mathbf{X}_2 \\ \vdots \\ \mathbf{X}_N \end{bmatrix} \beta + \begin{bmatrix} \epsilon_1 \\ \epsilon_2 \\ \vdots \\ \epsilon_N \end{bmatrix} = \mathbf{X}\beta + \epsilon \tag{2}$$

will, in a strict sense, lack meaning. Nevertheless, if the differences between the β_i's, though significant, are thought to be small, Wallace [14] has argued that one should consider the possibility of a tradeoff, accepting some bias in order to reduce variances, and he has suggested weaker criteria in terms of a mean square error criterion than the conventional significance tests. There are instances when the departure from homogeneity is so great that pooling will seriously distort the conclusions about the nature of the rela-

*Frank M. Bass is Ford Foundation Visiting Professor of Marketing, Graduate School of Business, University of Chicago; Dick R. Wittink is Assistant Professor of Business Administration, Graduate School of Business, Stanford University.

Reprinted from *Journal of Marketing Research,* 12 (November 1975), 414-25, published by the American Marketing Association.

tionships among the variables. Thus it is important to estimate the relationships separately for each cross section and to test the homogeneity hypothesis instead of accepting the pooled estimates uncritically.

If a decision is made to pool the data for estimation purposes, there remains the issue of how this should be done. Three major methods (sets of assumptions) present themselves. The first involves an assumption that the regression coefficients are fixed parameters. The assumption of fixed coefficients is, of course, the conventional regression assumption, and the most common historical pooling methods, pooling under complete homogeneity and pooling with dummy variable intercepts for each cross section, are associated with this assumption. Equation (2) represents the format for pooling under fixed coefficients and complete homogeneity. Pooling with common slope coefficients and with intercepts which vary by cross section is but one possible form of mixed pooling methods. A second major method of pooling involves the assumption of fixed and common slope coefficients and intercepts which are not fixed, but random. This method, as we shall see, represents something of a compromise between pooling under complete homogeneity and pooling with common slope coefficients but with intercepts which vary by cross section. The third major pooling method may be accomplished on the basis of the assumption that all of the elements in the coefficient vector, slopes as well as intercepts, are random variables rather than fixed parameters. The choice among possible methods of pooling is not always simple. While hypothesis tests may conclusively rule out some assumptions as inappropriate, frequently the choice of method will rest primarily on judgment or theory about the process as well as upon the intended application of the regression results. In the remaining sections of this article we shall discuss in detail the assumptions associated with the major pooling methods and we shall compare and illustrate different estimation methods with marketing research applications.

VARIANCE COMPONENT POOLING

Under the assumption of intercepts for the cross sections which are random variables and slope coefficients which are fixed parameters, the vector β_i in (1) would represent slopes only while the random disturbance term would have two components. Thus

$$(3) \qquad \epsilon_i = \begin{bmatrix} u_i + v_{i1} \\ u_i + v_{i2} \\ \vdots \\ u_i + v_{iT_i} \end{bmatrix},$$

and u_i represents randomness which is due to the choice of the cross section (the random intercept), while v_{it} represents the random influence which stems from cross section and time period. The v_{it}'s represent the conventional random disturbance elements in regression models. The u_i's represent what Maddala [4] has referred to as "specific ignorance"[1] as opposed to the "general ignorance" represented by the v_{it}'s. In those cases in which the homogeneity of slope coefficients has been accepted but overall homogeneity (slopes and intercepts) has been rejected, pooling under the assumption of fixed intercepts is possible and ordinary least squares with dummy variable intercepts (OLSDV) would be an appropriate procedure for estimation. The assumption of fixed intercepts, however, would not always appear to be appropriate since it would seem to imply systematic variation in the intercepts as, for example, when larger cross sections have greater intercepts. In many cases, however, the intercept variation does not have an apparent logical basis and thus the "specific ignorance" assumption seems appropriate.

Employing the pooled model shown in (2) along with the assumption about random disturbances indicated by (3), we also assume that $E(u_i) = E(v_{it}) = 0$ and that the disturbance components are independent so that:

$$E(\epsilon_i \epsilon_i') = \begin{bmatrix} \sigma_u^2 + \sigma_v^2 & \sigma_u^2 & \cdots & \sigma_u^2 \\ \sigma_u^2 & \sigma_u^2 + \sigma_v^2 & \cdots & \sigma_u^2 \\ \vdots & \vdots & \cdot & \vdots \\ \sigma_u^2 & \sigma_u^2 & \cdots & \sigma_u^2 + \sigma_v^2 \end{bmatrix} \text{ and}$$

$$E(\epsilon\epsilon') = E\begin{bmatrix} \epsilon_1\epsilon_1' & \epsilon_1\epsilon_2' & \cdots & \epsilon_1\epsilon_N' \\ \epsilon_2\epsilon_1' & \epsilon_2\epsilon_2' & \cdots & \epsilon_2\epsilon_N' \\ \vdots & \vdots & \cdot & \vdots \\ \epsilon_N\epsilon_1' & \epsilon_N\epsilon_2' & \cdots & \epsilon_N\epsilon_N' \end{bmatrix}$$

$$= \sigma^2 \begin{bmatrix} \mathbf{A}_1 & \mathbf{0} & \mathbf{0} & \cdots & \mathbf{0} \\ \mathbf{0} & \mathbf{A}_2 & \mathbf{0} & \cdots & \mathbf{0} \\ \vdots & \vdots & \vdots & \cdot & \vdots \\ \mathbf{0} & \mathbf{0} & \mathbf{0} & \cdots & \mathbf{A}_N \end{bmatrix},$$

where $\mathbf{A}_i$ is the $T_i \times T_i$ matrix:

$$\begin{bmatrix} 1\,\rho \ldots \rho \\ \rho\,1 \ldots \rho \\ \cdots\cdots \\ \rho\,\rho \ldots 1 \end{bmatrix}$$

and $$\sigma^2 = \sigma_u^2 + \sigma_v^2, \; \rho = \frac{\sigma_u^2}{\sigma^2}.$$

It is convenient to write $\mathbf{A}_i = (1 - \rho)I + \rho e_i e_i'$ where $\mathbf{e}_i$ is a $T_i \times 1$ vector of 1's. It is then possible to show (see Appendix A) that:

[1] We shall follow closely the notation and the logical development of Maddala in [4].

$$(4)\quad \mathbf{A}_i^{-1} = \frac{1}{(1-\rho)} I - \frac{\rho}{(1-\rho)(1-\rho+T_i\rho)} e_i e_i' = \lambda_2 \mathbf{I} + \lambda_{1i}\mathbf{e}_i\mathbf{e}_i'.$$

If ρ is known, and if there are no lagged endogenous variables, the generalized least squares estimator will be efficient. Thus

$$(5)\quad \hat{\beta} = \left[\sum_{i=1}^{N} \mathbf{X}_i' \mathbf{A}_i^{-1} \mathbf{X}_i\right]^{-1} \left[\sum_{i=1}^{N} \mathbf{X}_i' \mathbf{A}_i^{-1} \mathbf{Y}_i\right].$$

Defining

$$\mathbf{T}_{xx} = \sum_{i=1}^{N} \mathbf{X}_i'\mathbf{X}_i,$$

$$\mathbf{B}_{xx} = \sum_{i=1}^{N} \left(\frac{\mathbf{X}_i'\mathbf{e}_i\mathbf{e}_i'\mathbf{X}_i}{T_i}\right) = \sum_{i=1}^{N} T_i \bar{\mathbf{x}}_i \bar{\mathbf{x}}_i',$$

$$\mathbf{W}_{xx} = \mathbf{T}_{xx} - \mathbf{B}_{xx},$$

$$\mathbf{T}_{xy} = \sum_{i=1}^{N} \mathbf{X}_i'\mathbf{Y}_i,$$

$$\mathbf{B}_{xy} = \sum_{i=1}^{N} \left(\frac{\mathbf{X}_i'\mathbf{e}_i\mathbf{e}_i'\mathbf{Y}_i}{T_i}\right) = \sum_{i=1}^{N} T_i \bar{\mathbf{x}}_i \bar{\mathbf{y}}_i,$$

$$\mathbf{W}_{xy} = \mathbf{T}_{xy} - \mathbf{B}_{xy},$$

$$\mathbf{T}_{yy} = \sum_{i=1}^{N} \mathbf{Y}_i'\mathbf{Y}_i,$$

$$\mathbf{B}_{yy} = \sum_{i=1}^{N} \left(\frac{\mathbf{Y}_i'\mathbf{e}_i\mathbf{e}_i'\mathbf{Y}_i}{T_i}\right) = \sum_{i=1}^{N} T_i \bar{\mathbf{y}}_i^2,$$

$$\mathbf{W}_{yy} = \mathbf{T}_{yy} - \mathbf{B}_{yy},$$

where $\bar{\mathbf{x}}_i$ is the mean vector of independent variables in the ith cross section and $\bar{\mathbf{y}}_i$ is the mean of the dependent variable in the ith cross section, the **B**'s contain the sums of squares and cross products between cross sections, the **W**'s contain the corresponding within terms and the **T**'s represent total variation.

Using (4) in the terms found in (5) we have:

$$(6)\quad \sum_{i=1}^{N} \mathbf{X}_i'\mathbf{A}_i^{-1}\mathbf{X}_i = \sum_{i=1}^{N} \lambda_{1i}\mathbf{X}_i'\mathbf{e}_i\mathbf{e}_i'\mathbf{X}_i + \lambda_2 \sum_{i=1}^{N} \mathbf{X}_i'\mathbf{X}_i = \sum_{i=1}^{N} \lambda_{1i} T_i^2 \bar{\mathbf{x}}_i\bar{\mathbf{x}}_i' + \lambda_2 \mathbf{T}_{xx}, \text{ and}$$

$$(7)\quad \sum_{i=1}^{N} \mathbf{X}_i'\mathbf{A}_i^{-1}\mathbf{Y}_i = \sum_{i=1}^{N} \lambda_{1i}\mathbf{X}_i'\mathbf{e}_i\mathbf{e}_i'\mathbf{Y}_i + \lambda_2 \sum_{i=1}^{N} \mathbf{X}_i'\mathbf{Y}_i = \sum_{i=1}^{N} \lambda_{1i} T_i^2 \bar{\mathbf{x}}_i\bar{\mathbf{y}}_i + \lambda_2 \mathbf{T}_{xy}.$$

If we let $\Theta_i = 1 + (\lambda_{1i} T_i/\lambda_2)$ and employ this along with earlier definitions in (6) and (7) we find:

$$(8)\quad \sum_{i=1}^{N} \mathbf{X}_i'\mathbf{A}_i^{-1}\mathbf{X}_i = \lambda_2\left[\mathbf{W}_{xx} + \sum_{i=1}^{N} \Theta_i T_i \bar{\mathbf{x}}_i\bar{\mathbf{x}}_i'\right] \text{ and}$$

$$(9)\quad \sum_{i=1}^{N} \mathbf{X}_i'\mathbf{A}_i^{-1}\mathbf{Y}_i = \lambda_2\left[\mathbf{W}_{xy} + \sum_{i=1}^{N} \Theta_i T_i \bar{\mathbf{x}}_i\bar{\mathbf{y}}_i\right].$$

Using (8) and (9) in (5), we find

$$(10)\quad \hat{\beta} = \left[\mathbf{W}_{xx} + \sum_{i=1}^{N} \Theta_i T_i \bar{\mathbf{x}}_i\bar{\mathbf{x}}_i'\right]^{-1} \times \left[\mathbf{W}_{xy} + \sum_{i=1}^{N} \Theta_i T_i \bar{\mathbf{x}}_i\bar{\mathbf{y}}_i\right] \text{ and therefore}$$

$$(11)\quad \mathrm{var}(\hat{\beta}) = \sigma^2 \frac{1}{\lambda_2}\left[\mathbf{W}_{xx} + \sum_{i=1}^{N} \Theta_i T_i \bar{\mathbf{x}}_i\bar{\mathbf{x}}_i'\right]^{-1}.$$

If the number of time-series observations in each cross section is the same so that $T_i = T$ and $\Theta_i = \Theta$, then (10) becomes:

$$(12)\quad \hat{\beta} = [\mathbf{W}_{xx} + \Theta\mathbf{B}_{xx}]^{-1}[\mathbf{W}_{xy} + \Theta\mathbf{B}_{xy}]$$

and (11) becomes:

$$(13)\quad \mathrm{var}(\hat{\beta}) = \frac{\sigma^2}{\lambda_2}[\mathbf{W}_{xx} + \Theta\mathbf{B}_{xx}]^{-1}.$$

If $\Theta = 1$, (12) becomes $\hat{\beta} = \mathbf{T}_{xx}^{-1}\mathbf{T}_{xy}$. This estimate corresponds to ordinary least squares under the assumption that the slope coefficients are homogeneous and the intercept zero. Since the estimate involves the total sums of squares and cross products matrix, it is referred to as the "Total" regression. If $\Theta = 0$, (12) becomes $\hat{\beta} = \mathbf{W}_{xx}^{-1}\mathbf{W}_{xy}$. The "Within" estimate corresponds to the OLSDV estimate of the slope coefficients.

Thus since Θ lies between 0 and 1, the GLS (generalized least squares) indicated by (12) is in some sense a compromise between the "Total" and the "Within" regressions. The OLSDV estimate ignores the between-group variation and the "Total" estimate gives a weight of unity to the between variation, while the GLS estimate gives a weight to between variation which depends on the variance components σ_u^2 and σ_v^2. Since $\Theta = 1 + (\lambda_1 T/\lambda_2) = (1 - \rho)/(1 - \rho + T\rho)$, as $\sigma_u^2 \to 0$, $\Theta \to 1$ and $\hat{\beta} \to \mathbf{T}_{xx}^{-1}\mathbf{T}_{xy}$, while as $\sigma_v^2 \to 0$, $\Theta \to 0$ and $\hat{\beta} \to \mathbf{W}_{xx}^{-1}\mathbf{W}_{xy}$. The ratio ρ, involving the variance components, determines the weight to be accorded to the between-group variation in the GLS regression.

In practice, of course, the variance components are unknown and must be estimated. Nerlove [8] in Monte Carlo experiments of a model with a lagged endogenous variable and a model with one exogenous variable and a lagged endogenous variable found that a two-step procedure called 2RC was superior on the basis of mean square error and relative bias when compared to other estimation methods including maximum likelihood. Maddala and Mount [5] in Monte Carlo experiments with a model with only an exogenous variable found that on a mean square error basis several two-step GLS estimators, including 2RC, perform equally well. In addition, when Θ is close to 0, the ordinary least squares estimates are substantially inferior to GLS estimates and when Θ is not close to 0, OLSDV estimates are inferior to the GLS estimates.

Since Nerlove's procedure appears to be in no case inferior and in some cases superior to other estimation methods for the random intercept model, a computer program, GENCROST, has been written at Purdue University for the purpose of developing regression estimates of pooled cross-sectional and time-series data on the basis of Nerlove's 2RC procedure.[2] The first step in Nerlove's procedure is an OLSDV regression for the purpose of estimating the variance components. Thus $\hat{\sigma}_v^2 = 1/\Sigma T_i[\mathbf{W}_{yy} - \mathbf{W}'_{xy}\mathbf{W}_{xx}^{-1}\mathbf{W}_{xy}]$, the mean of the squared residuals of the "Within" regression, is taken as the estimate of the variance of "general ignorance" while $\hat{\sigma}_u^2 = (1/\Sigma T_i)\ \Sigma T_i\ [\bar{\mathbf{y}}_i - \bar{\mathbf{y}} - \mathbf{W}'_{xy}\mathbf{W}_{xx}^{-1}(\bar{\mathbf{x}}_i - \bar{\mathbf{x}})]^2$, the variance of the estimates of the coefficients of the dummy variables, is taken as estimate of the variance of cross-sectional randomness or "specific ignorance." The second step in Nerlove's 2RC method is the utilization of the estimates of the variance components in estimating ρ and thus Θ in the GLS estimate indicated by (12). Since Θ lies in the interval between 0 and 1, computer programs such as GENCROST may be easily adjusted to include a sensitivity analysis feature, in order to study the sensitivity of the estimates to the unknown Θ.

ILLUSTRATION OF TESTING AND POOLING CROSS-SECTIONAL AND TIME-SERIES DATA

Data from *Sales Management*'s Survey of Buying Power [10] for the years 1948-1970 and for the 48 adjacent states have been used in developing examples of pooling issues and methods. Thus the examples involve 48 cross sections and 23 time periods. Two different models and data sets are utilized as examples. The first is:

$$FHA_{it} = \beta_1 P_{it} + \beta_2 R_{it} + u_i + v_{it} \tag{14}$$

where:

FHA_{it} = furniture and household appliance sales in state i at year t in millions of dollars,
P_{it} = population in state i at year t in millions,
R_{it} = total retail sales in state i at year t in millions of dollars.

The second example involves the model:

$$F_{it} = \beta_1 P_{it} + \beta_2 I_{it} + u_i + v_{it} \tag{15}$$

where:

F_{it} = food store sales in state i at year t in millions of dollars,
P_{it} = population in state i at year t in millions,
I_{it} = effective buying income in state i at year t in millions of dollars.

[2] Mark Moriarty, John McCann, Lynn McKell, and Terry Cooper contributed to the development of GENCROST.

Table 1

ORDINARY LEAST SQUARES TIME-SERIES ESTIMATES BY STATES OF RELATIONSHIPS BETWEEN FURNITURE AND HOUSEHOLD APPLIANCE SALES AND POPULATION AND TOTAL RETAIL SALES, FIXED INTERCEPT

	Estimates					
Cross sections	$\hat{\beta}_1$	$\sigma_{\hat{\beta}_1}$	$\hat{\beta}_2$	$\sigma_{\hat{\beta}_2}$	*Intercept*	R^2
Connecticut	−91.46	(28.08)	.072	(.009)	158.75	.938
Maine	−115.98	(30.23)	.031	(.004)	115.41	.785
Massachusetts	−194.14	(38.24)	.072	(.006)	811.11	.974
New Hampshire	−117.29	(51.58)	.047	(.011)	63.76	.824
Rhode Island	−116.98	(33.29)	.057	(.006)	89.71	.924
Vermont	−69.36	(37.64)	.033	(.005)	29.65	.896
New Jersey	55.89	(33.82)	.023	(.011)	−85.93	.962
New York	−40.76	(41.49)	.050	(.009)	756.48	.935
Pennsylvania	−126.80	(33.03)	.048	(.005)	1454.43	.924
Illinois	−5.46	(30.73)	.038	(.006)	148.90	.953
Indiana	−39.72	(15.63)	.044	(.003)	198.30	.977
Michigan	22.78	(12.31)	.036	(.003)	−62.21	.977
Ohio	−19.08	(15.27)	.043	(.005)	230.81	.960
Wisconsin	−3.06	(15.25)	.045	(.004)	10.65	.977
Iowa	−22.05	(28.43)	.030	(.002)	104.99	.958
Kansas	−.26	(34.73)	.032	(.007)	40.06	.864
Minnesota	−28.02	(13.05)	.046	(.003)	74.11	.986
Missouri	−104.25	(33.91)	.043	(.005)	459.52	.961
Nebraska	−16.18	(49.48)	.040	(.006)	33.76	.923
North Dakota	80.55	(21.93)	.033	(.003)	−47.78	.931
South Dakota	5.21	(32.26)	.032	(.005)	−1.09	.792
Delaware	−53.92	(17.69)	.064	(.007)	15.81	.972
Florida	15.16	(9.95)	.037	(.004)	30.53	.988
Georgia	−42.19	(15.50)	.049	(.004)	160.05	.991
Maryland	−14.79	(8.89)	.040	(.003)	49.34	.990
North Carolina	−55.93	(29.45)	.055	(.007)	246.00	.966
South Carolina	−34.60	(21.14)	.050	(.006)	90.54	.943
Virginia	−12.16	(11.74)	.043	(.004)	66.81	.990
West Virginia	48.93	(13.81)	.047	(.004)	−85.91	.937
Alabama	−3.96	(18.35)	.047	(.004)	30.00	.985
Kentucky	71.27	(24.68)	.032	(.003)	−179.11	.985
Mississippi	51.25	(17.76)	.032	(.002)	−92.95	.972
Tennessee	−104.98	(48.97)	.060	(.009)	336.98	.965
Arkansas	34.99	(9.86)	.035	(.001)	−49.66	.976
Louisiana	−19.27	(11.17)	.043	(.004)	83.11	.980
Oklahoma	−67.67	(25.31)	.046	(.003)	161.70	.964
Texas	−42.65	(14.41)	.050	(.005)	344.14	.975
Arizona	48.66	(12.94)	.017	(.006)	−8.56	.975
Colorado	3.10	(17.95)	.043	(.006)	6.27	.967
Idaho	−9.39	(28.33)	.039	(.006)	10.26	.936
Montana	20.37	(12.55)	.030	(.004)	−7.02	.942
Nevada	96.07	(21.16)	.003	(.009)	−8.62	.974
New Mexico	23.46	(11.95)	.029	(.005)	−6.06	.971
Utah	−135.24	(24.59)	.106	(.009)	65.71	.963
Wyoming	11.84	(21.59)	.031	(.005)	.69	.878
California	51.60	(27.24)	.027	(.010)	−91.50	.959
Oregon	−82.99	(21.14)	.054	(.005)	123.54	.971
Washington	2.21	(16.54)	.040	(.004)	14.57	.984

All values of the variables are measured on the basis of *Sales Management* estimates. The term u_i may be regarded as fixed or random to correspond with the assumption employed. Tables 1 and 2 show the ordinary least squares estimates for each state on the 23 time-series observations for a fixed intercept model. Pooling would increase the number of observations

Table 2

ORDINARY LEAST SQUARES TIME-SERIES ESTIMATES BY STATES OF RELATIONSHIPS BETWEEN FOOD STORE SALES AND POPULATION AND EFFECTIVE BUYING INCOME, FIXED INTERCEPT

	Estimates					
Cross sections	$\hat{\beta}_1$	$\sigma_{\hat{\beta}_1}$	$\hat{\beta}_2$	$\sigma_{\hat{\beta}_2}$	*Intercept*	R^2
Connecticut	55.04	(95.29)	.087	(.013)	194.56	.979
Maine	169.41	(137.58)	.112	(.009)	−33.30	.955
Massachusetts	150.63	(185.42)	.077	(.013)	83.02	.974
New Hampshire	348.71	(123.50)	.089	(.015)	−92.25	.990
Rhode Island	129.62	(128.54)	.073	(.011)	17.12	.952
Vermont	−6.76	(146.90)	.129	(.010)	40.87	.981
New Jersey	139.82	(83.10)	.072	(.011)	173.01	.979
New York	457.35	(148.04)	.045	(.013)	−3688.28	.946
Pennsylvania	75.44	(137.43)	.085	(.008)	521.63	.964
Illinois	449.04	(81.61)	.051	(.008)	−2620.89	.983
Indiana	203.83	(54.64)	.081	(.006)	−417.48	.990
Michigan	235.89	(49.39)	.074	(.006)	−582.95	.988
Ohio	221.05	(64.66)	.071	(.009)	−609.62	.974
Wisconsin	218.61	(60.52)	.068	(.007)	−266.70	.983
Iowa	799.30	(131.58)	.066	(.005)	−1816.49	.978
Kansas	395.47	(82.48)	.055	(.007)	−500.73	.968
Minnesota	269.37	(86.74)	.062	(.009)	−405.73	.973
Missouri	345.04	(112.24)	.083	(.008)	−1002.11	.993
Nebraska	227.45	(104.11)	.077	(.006)	−163.89	.979
North Dakota	43.95	(97.27)	.077	(.006)	26.46	.909
South Dakota	331.36	(105.03)	.082	(.007)	−163.24	.920
Delaware	120.27	(117.63)	.082	(.022)	−2.23	.981
Florida	210.19	(45.01)	.091	(.012)	−256.67	.986
Georgia	356.43	(62.31)	.066	(.009)	−894.84	.992
Maryland	210.82	(45.77)	.070	(.008)	−169.26	.992
North Carolina	442.31	(49.86)	.068	(.006)	−1493.48	.993
South Carolina	230.24	(45.22)	.093	(.006)	−352.96	.989
Virginia	283.17	(42.21)	.074	(.007)	−661.98	.993
West Virginia	33.93	(109.94)	.149	(.016)	−56.20	.935
Alabama	443.05	(107.98)	.080	(.012)	−1093.32	.974
Kentucky	411.66	(151.76)	.098	(.009)	−1005.35	.981
Mississippi	−59.78	(98.27)	.130	(.007)	198.44	.979
Tennessee	737.59	(102.62)	.049	(.011)	−2061.53	.989
Arkansas	−328.34	(51.54)	.135	(.004)	669.80	.982
Louisiana	197.11	(78.31)	.098	(.013)	−389.91	.974
Oklahoma	−402.64	(130.93)	.135	(.009)	1009.78	.975
Texas	330.55	(31.34)	.057	(.005)	−1501.53	.994
Arizona	102.86	(41.19)	.101	(.011)	−2.62	.985
Colorado	138.43	(60.66)	.085	(.012)	−26.68	.982
Idaho	317.27	(68.61)	.083	(.009)	−120.34	.978
Montana	90.91	(52.57)	.107	(.009)	−5.49	.958
Nevada	−41.47	(113.51)	.131	(.027)	17.96	.968
New Mexico	186.04	(37.66)	.074	(.009)	−63.89	.982
Utah	264.76	(38.56)	.066	(.008)	−111.66	.991
Wyoming	164.27	(126.19)	.114	(.015)	−29.96	.903
California	175.02	(51.24)	.070	(.010)	16.42	.988
Oregon	441.98	(113.66)	.056	(.014)	−426.36	.976
Washington	536.57	(77.44)	.042	(.010)	−890.94	.984

from 23 to 1,104 and thus could greatly increase the reliability of the estimates. Pooling is, however, in a strict sense appropriate only when the homogeneity hypothesis can be accepted. The test of the hypothesis of equality of intercepts and slopes (overall homogeneity) for all of the cross sections is accomplished on the basis of an F test with degrees of freedom of $k(N - 1)$ and $N(T - k)$. The critical value of $F_{.01, 141, 960}$ is approximately 1.2. The computed value of F with the fixed intercept assumption is 26.12 for (14) and 15.26 for (15). Thus the assumption of overall homogeneity is conclusively rejected. The test of the hypothesis of equality of the slope coefficients alone is based on an F test with degrees of freedom of $(N - 1)(k - 1)$ and $N(T - k)$. The critical value of $F_{.01, 94, 960}$ is approximately 1.4. The computed value of F for the Furniture-Household Appliance equation in testing the equality of slopes is 3.56 and for the Food Store equation the computed value is 5.66. Therefore, the hypothesis of equality of slope coefficients is also rejected for both the Furniture-Household Appliance regression and for the Food Store regression.

Although pooling of the observations for all states and years for the purpose of estimating a common vector of slope coefficients is not in a strict sense appropriate for (14) and (15), an argument can be made for pooling to estimate slope coefficients on the basis of Wallace's tradeoff argument. Thus pooling for the purpose of estimating slope coefficients is defensible. The question remains, however, as to which method of pooling to employ. The evidence indicates that the intercepts for the different cross sections are not equal. The question is whether to treat the intercepts as fixed or random. If they are assumed to be fixed, then OLSDV is the procedure to follow in developing the pooled estimates. But if the intercepts are random, then the variance component procedure should be followed.

If an assumption of random intercepts is made, then testing of the hypothesis of homogeneity of slope coefficients should proceed on the basis of that assumption. The assumption implies that a zero intercept model should be employed in estimation. Table 3 shows the ordinary least squares estimates for each state on the 23 time-series observations for a random intercept model. The test of the hypothesis of the equality of slope coefficients is accomplished on the basis of an F test with degrees of freedom of $k(N - 1)$ and $N(T - K)$. The critical value of $F_{.01, 94, 1008}$ is approximately 1.4. The computed value of F for the Furniture-Household Appliance equation is 39.02. Thus the homogeneity hypothesis for slope coefficients is clearly rejected if an assumption of random intercepts is employed.

The evidence indicates that if a fixed intercept assumption is made, pooling is appropriate and OLSDV is the correct method of estimation. If the

Table 3

ORDINARY LEAST SQUARES TIME-SERIES ESTIMATES BY STATES OF RELATIONSHIPS BETWEEN FURNITURE AND HOUSEHOLD APPLIANCE SALES AND POPULATION AND TOTAL RETAIL SALES, RANDOM INTERCEPT

	Estimates				
Cross sections	$\hat{\beta}_1$	$\sigma_{\hat{\beta}_1}$	$\hat{\beta}_2$	$\sigma_{\hat{\beta}_2}$	R^2
Connecticut	13.92	(8.44)	.042	(.006)	.891
Maine	21.82	(4.72)	.017	(.004)	.558
Massachusetts	4.18	(4.11)	.042	(.003)	.939
New Hampshire	29.87	(5.31)	.016	(.004)	.752
Rhode Island	14.69	(5.06)	.035	(.004)	.863
Vermont	18.57	(3.36)	.023	(.002)	.867
New Jersey	31.66	(4.34)	.031	(.003)	.961
New York	22.49	(4.92)	.037	(.003)	.927
Pennsylvania	23.57	(4.31)	.030	(.003)	.844
Illinois	15.04	(3.73)	.034	(.002)	.952
Indiana	17.94	(2.82)	.033	(.002)	.962
Michigan	11.18	(2.98)	.039	(.002)	.976
Ohio	16.97	(3.85)	.033	(.003)	.948
Wisconsin	0.82	(2.79)	.044	(.002)	.977
Iowa	20.05	(2.12)	.027	(.001)	.953
Kansas	23.26	(4.55)	.028	(.004)	.861
Minnesota	1.39	(2.17)	.040	(.002)	.982
Missouri	25.22	(2.78)	.025	(.002)	.937
Nebraska	11.58	(3.92)	.037	(.003)	.922
North Dakota	−2.36	(4.58)	.038	(.003)	.881
South Dakota	3.47	(5.09)	.032	(.004)	.792
Delaware	18.96	(7.58)	.040	(.005)	.946
Florida	28.50	(3.76)	.032	(.002)	.987
Georgia	12.84	(1.55)	.036	(.001)	.986
Maryland	11.36	(2.09)	.032	(.002)	.986
North Carolina	13.26	(2.67)	.040	(.003)	.956
South Carolina	13.30	(2.92)	.039	(.003)	.928
Virginia	12.31	(1.59)	.036	(.001)	.988
West Virginia	11.77	(1.88)	.038	(.002)	.914
Alabama	7.16	(1.41)	.045	(.001)	.985
Kentucky	6.66	(1.34)	.039	(.001)	.980
Mississippi	5.90	(1.44)	.036	(.002)	.962
Tennessee	11.22	(2.56)	.039	(.002)	.956
Arkansas	7.57	(1.57)	.036	(.002)	.966
Louisiana	18.02	(2.22)	.032	(.002)	.969
Oklahoma	10.57	(2.59)	.037	(.002)	.947
Texas	14.99	(3.66)	.033	(.003)	.955
Arizona	34.02	(4.83)	.023	(.003)	.973
Colorado	9.57	(4.94)	.041	(.003)	.966
Idaho	12.02	(4.12)	.035	(.003)	.934
Montana	5.47	(4.12)	.033	(.003)	.937
Nevada	20.54	(11.82)	.032	(.007)	.953
New Mexico	11.65	(3.23)	.034	(.003)	.970
Utah	−5.60	(8.57)	.060	(.007)	.909
Wyoming	14.50	(5.03)	.030	(.003)	.878
California	39.30	(7.19)	.031	(.005)	.958
Oregon	13.19	(3.98)	.034	(.003)	.940
Washington	9.84	(2.35)	.038	(.002)	.984

intercepts are assumed to be random and slopes fixed, pooling is questionable and should not be done at all unless, using Wallace's argument, one is willing to accept a great deal of bias in exchange for reduced variance. Although a comparison of the estimates in Table 1 with those in Table 3 does indicate substantial correlation between the intercept and the population coefficient, there is some indication of a tendency toward systematic variation in the estimate of the intercept. Although there are exceptions, the intercept estimates tend to be larger for larger states than for smaller states. Systematic variation in the intercepts would suggest that the assumption of random coefficients is inappropriate and thus, on balance, pooled estimates are probably most appropriately developed with OLSDV.

Since the GENCROST program's Within regression estimates of slope coefficients are equivalent to OLSDV estimates and since the program produces estimates for Total, Between, as well as GLS with variance component estimates according to Nerlove's method, it is convenient to employ this program in studying the sensitivity of the parameter estimates to the pooling method. Table 4 shows the estimates and explained variance by slope variables. The Between estimates correspond to cross-sectional regression estimates on aggregated time-series data. The Total, Within, and Variance Components estimates utilize within and/or between variation with weight given to between variation of Θ as previously explained.

A comparison of the estimates in Table 4 indicates that the estimate of the coefficient for the population variable is most sensitive to the method of pooling. Excluding the Between estimates, the estimates of β_2 do not vary greatly over the different methods of pooling. In Table 4, the estimated value of Θ is close to 0, and the OLSDV estimate of β_1 is not very different from the variance component estimate of this parameter. Thus the assumption about whether the intercept is fixed or random does not greatly influence the interpretation one would give to the influence of population on furniture and household appliance sales. The sensitivity analysis in Table 5 shows that as Θ departs from 0 the parameter estimates are not very sensitive to the departure for values of Θ close to the estimated value. Hence the distinction in terms of parameter estimates between OLSDV and

Table 4

POOLED CROSS-SECTIONAL AND TIME-SERIES ESTIMATES OF THE RELATIONSHIP BETWEEN FURNITURE AND HOUSEHOLD APPLIANCE SALES AND POPULATION AND TOTAL RETAIL SALES

	Pooling method				
Parameters	*Between*	*Total*	*Within (OLSDV)*	*Variance components*	*OLS with intercept*
$\hat{\beta}_1$	−25.19	9.73	22.07	20.10	16.14
$\sigma_{\hat{\beta}_1}$	(8.10)	(1.16)	(2.65)	(1.47)	(1.23)
$\hat{\beta}_2$	.070	.043	.035	.036	.040
$\sigma_{\hat{\beta}_2}$	(.006)	(.001)	(.001)	(.001)	(.001)
$\hat{\rho}$	—	0	1	.731	—
$\hat{\Theta}$	—	1	0	.016	—
R^2	.952	.978	.978	.978	.980

Table 5

SENSITIVITY ANALYSIS OF PARAMETER ESTIMATES FROM GENCROST ON THE RELATIONSHIP BETWEEN FURNITURE AND HOUSEHOLD APPLIANCE SALES AND POPULATION AND TOTAL RETAIL SALES

Parameters	*Estimates*													
ρ	0	.005	.010	.050	.100	.200	.500	.700	.731	.800	.900	.950	.980	1.0
θ	1.0	.896	.811	.452	.281	.148	.042	.018	.016	.011	.005	.002	9.001	0
$\hat{\beta}_1$	9.73	10.55	11.26	14.57	16.38	17.93	19.42	20.00	20.10	20.36	20.90	21.35	21.73	22.07
$\sigma_{\hat{\beta}_1}$	(1.16)	(0.60)	(0.61)	(0.66)	(0.71)	(0.79)	(1.09)	(1.40)	(1.47)	(1.64)	(2.00)	(2.26)	(2.47)	(2.65)
$\hat{\beta}_2$	.043	.042	.042	.039	.038	.037	.036	.036	.036	.035	.035	.035	.035	.035
$\sigma_{\hat{\beta}_2}$	(.001)	(.001)	(.001)	(.001)	(.001)	(.001)	(.001)	(.001)	(.001)	(.001)	(.001)	(.001)	(.001)	(.001)
R^2	.978	.978	.978	.978	.978	.978	.977	.978	.978	.978	.978	.978	.978	.978

variance components pooling is not great in the Furniture-Household Appliance regression.

In a strict sense, the estimates in all of the pooling methods are biased. However in the case of a fixed intercept model we are willing to accept a relatively small amount of bias resulting from the assumption of homogeneous slope coefficients. Nevertheless, the estimates from other pooling methods do provide some information when compared to the OLSDV estimates of the possible range of the parameter values. Since the percentage of explained variance is large for all of the pooling methods and does not vary greatly with the pooling method, there is not much to choose from among the methods if the purpose of the analysis is forecasting. Interpretation of the meaning of the estimated relationship is, however, somewhat sensitive to the method of pooling. In general it is wise when analyzing cross-sectional and time-series data to: (1) test the homogeneity hypothesis before pooling the data and (2) estimate pooled data with a variety of methods in order to determine the sensitivity of the estimates to underlying assumptions.

In addition to the results from time-series analyses, interest may focus on estimates obtained from cross-sectional regressions. While the time-series analyses provide the relationship for each state separately, by performing cross-sectional regressions we can make inferences about the extent to which the relationships are constant over time. In fact, when performing regressions based on time-series observations, the assumption is made that the relationship is homogeneous over time. We have argued that OLSDV, with separate intercepts for each of the states, is probably the best method of pooling for these data. This implies that for a cross-sectional analysis we should allow for a separate intercept for each state, which is impossible in a conventional cross-sectional analysis due to a lack of degrees of freedom. To estimate with intercepts, we have subtracted the intercepts, estimated by performing OLSDV on (14) and (15), from the actual values for the dependent variable for each of the 23 years. Tables 6 and 7 show the results for the two models.

An inspection of Table 6 indicates that there exists an inverse relationship between the coefficients of the two independent variables, and that the magnitudes are very similar for the first and last year for which data have been included in the analysis. The same inverse relationship appears to exist for the second model as evidenced by the results shown in Table 7. Here, however, the magnitude of the coefficients appears to change more systematically over time ending at approximately twice the level for $\hat{\beta}_1$, and half the level for $\hat{\beta}_2$ in 1970 compared with 1948. Pooling the data does not provide any insight into these trends, and long-term forecasts from pooled

Table 6

ORDINARY LEAST SQUARES CROSS-SECTIONAL ESTIMATES BY YEARS OF RELATIONSHIPS BETWEEN FURNITURE AND HOUSEHOLD APPLIANCE SALES AND POPULATION AND TOTAL RETAIL SALES

	Estimates					
Year	$\hat{\beta}_1$	$\sigma_{\hat{\beta}_1}$	$\hat{\beta}_2$	$\sigma_{\hat{\beta}_2}$	*Intercept*	R^2
1948	33.19	(4.63)	.020	(.005)	4.38	.987
1949	32.51	(5.03)	.017	(.005)	5.78	.982
1950	27.85	(4.48)	.031	(.004)	0.63	.994
1951	26.58	(4.49)	.030	(.004)	1.14	.994
1952	28.07	(3.90)	.033	(.003)	−0.40	.997
1953	30.07	(3.23)	.031	(.003)	−1.69	.998
1954	26.86	(3.11)	.033	(.003)	−0.74	.998
1955	20.39	(2.30)	.038	(.002)	−2.29	.999
1956	16.71	(2.37)	.042	(.002)	−1.36	.999
1957	17.05	(2.43)	.043	(.002)	−3.17	.999
1958	18.66	(2.44)	.040	(.002)	−2.06	.999
1959	11.88	(2.43)	.043	(.002)	2.41	.999
1960	14.50	(2.48)	.039	(.002)	2.04	.999
1961	15.04	(2.36)	.038	(.002)	1.88	.999
1962	12.04	(2.39)	.039	(.002)	2.06	.999
1963	10.22	(3.80)	.042	(.003)	−0.56	.998
1964	4.41	(4.27)	.047	(.003)	3.01	.997
1965	9.72	(4.86)	.041	(.003)	0.69	.997
1966	9.50	(5.81)	.043	(.004)	−0.49	.997
1967	9.58	(6.51)	.044	(.004)	−1.34	.996
1968	5.11	(7.82)	.047	(.004)	−2.94	.995
1969	39.46	(8.72)	.025	(.005)	0.08	.995
1970	47.72	(9.52)	.020	(.005)	−0.64	.996

Table 7

ORDINARY LEAST SQUARES CROSS-SECTIONAL ESTIMATES BY YEARS OF RELATIONSHIPS BETWEEN FOOD STORE SALES AND POPULATION AND EFFECTIVE BUYING INCOME

	Estimates					
Year	$\hat{\beta}_1$	$\sigma_{\hat{\beta}_1}$	$\hat{\beta}_2$	$\sigma_{\hat{\beta}_2}$	*Intercept*	R^2
1948	151.55	(32.04)	.097	(.021)	15.75	.984
1949	172.44	(29.23)	.074	(.019)	5.62	.984
1950	163.84	(9.11)	.088	(.006)	−8.62	.999
1951	159.64	(14.49)	.102	(.009)	−16.95	.998
1952	154.64	(14.41)	.114	(.008)	−14.70	.998
1953	151.00	(15.21)	.112	(.008)	−19.19	.998
1954	133.41	(16.67)	.121	(.009)	−13.85	.998
1955	179.31	(8.68)	.084	(.005)	−11.27	.999
1956	173.47	(12.26)	.088	(.006)	−4.22	.999
1957	178.79	(10.76)	.091	(.005)	0.62	.999
1958	179.52	(11.06)	.094	(.005)	2.88	.999
1959	202.94	(6.35)	.072	(.003)	2.43	.999
1960	217.09	(6.27)	.065	(.003)	1.65	.999
1961	213.96	(7.96)	.069	(.003)	−3.73	.999
1962	210.73	(6.92)	.071	(.003)	3.23	.999
1963	214.32	(7.74)	.068	(.003)	−0.21	.999
1964	237.46	(7.07)	.055	(.003)	12.72	.999
1965	264.61	(11.74)	.048	(.004)	7.96	.999
1966	263.55	(12.23)	.051	(.004)	15.29	.999
1967	260.41	(15.86)	.048	(.005)	20.91	.999
1968	279.41	(13.14)	.045	(.004)	7.68	.999
1969	270.29	(12.59)	.051	(.004)	13.55	.999
1970	303.10	(14.14)	.045	(.004)	11.81	.999

estimates are not very useful. However, cross-sectional regressions do provide a basis for estimating such long-term effects.

RANDOM COEFFICIENT REGRESSION

There are instances when the variation of regression coefficients from one cross section to another appear in theory or in practice to be unsystematic, or random. Although conventional regression model assumptions require fixed coefficients, recent theoretical contributions by Swamy [11, 12] and others [3, 9] have provided the framework for estimating relationships between variables from pooled cross-sectional data under the assumption that regression coefficients are random. Special assumptions are required, of course, about the covariance structure of disturbances and the random regression coefficient vectors. We shall outline the assumptions suggested by Swamy and the estimating procedure which flows from them.

We begin with the cross-sectional model indicated by (1) with the understanding that β_i is a random variable vector. The additional assumptions are:

$$E(\epsilon_i) = 0,\ E(\epsilon_i \epsilon_j') = \begin{cases} \sigma_{ii}\mathbf{I} & \text{if } i = j \\ 0 & \text{if } i \neq j \end{cases}, \tag{16}$$

$$E(\beta_i) = \bar{\beta}, \tag{17}$$

$$E[(\beta_i - \bar{\beta})(\beta_j - \bar{\beta})'] = \begin{cases} \Delta & \text{if } i = j \\ 0 & \text{if } i \neq j \end{cases}, \tag{18}$$

(19) β_i and ϵ_j are independent,

(20) β_i and β_j for $i \neq j$ are independent.

If $\beta_i = \bar{\beta} + \delta_i$ $(i = 1, 2, \ldots N)$, where δ_i is a $k \times 1$ vector of random elements, then (17) and (18) are equivalent to the assumption $E(\delta_i) = 0$ and

$$E(\delta_i \delta_j') = \begin{cases} \Delta & \text{if } i = j \\ \mathbf{0} & \text{if } i \neq j \end{cases}.$$

Using (17) and (18) it is possible to write (1) as:

$$\begin{bmatrix} \mathbf{Y}_1 \\ \mathbf{Y}_2 \\ \vdots \\ \mathbf{Y}_N \end{bmatrix} = \begin{bmatrix} \mathbf{X}_1 \\ \mathbf{X}_2 \\ \vdots \\ \mathbf{X}_N \end{bmatrix} \bar{\beta} + \begin{bmatrix} \mathbf{X}_1 & \mathbf{0} & \cdots & \mathbf{0} \\ \mathbf{0} & \mathbf{X}_2 & \cdots & \mathbf{0} \\ \vdots & \vdots & \cdot & \vdots \\ \mathbf{0} & \mathbf{0} & \mathbf{0} & \mathbf{X}_N \end{bmatrix} \begin{bmatrix} \delta_1 \\ \delta_2 \\ \vdots \\ \delta_N \end{bmatrix} + \begin{bmatrix} \epsilon_1 \\ \epsilon_2 \\ \vdots \\ \epsilon_N \end{bmatrix}, \tag{21}$$

or, in partitioned matrix notation, as:

$$\mathbf{Y} = \mathbf{X}\bar{\beta} + \mathbf{D}\delta + \epsilon. \tag{22}$$

Using the assumptions, the disturbance vector $\mathbf{D}\delta + \epsilon$ has the covariance matrix $\mathbf{D}E(\delta\delta')\mathbf{D}' + E(\epsilon\epsilon') = \mathbf{D}\Delta\mathbf{D}' + E(\epsilon\epsilon')$, or

$$\mathbf{V}(\Theta) = \begin{bmatrix} \mathbf{X}_1\Delta\mathbf{X}_1' + \sigma_{11}\mathbf{I} & \mathbf{0} & \cdots & \mathbf{0} \\ \mathbf{0} & \mathbf{X}_2\Delta\mathbf{X}_2' + \sigma_{22}\mathbf{I} & \cdots & \mathbf{0} \\ \vdots & \vdots & \cdot & \vdots \\ \mathbf{0} & \mathbf{0} & \cdots & \mathbf{X}_N\Delta\mathbf{X}_N' + \sigma_{NN}\mathbf{I} \end{bmatrix}. \tag{23}$$

The parametric vector Θ contains all the distinct elements of Δ and σ_{ii}, $i = 1, 2, \ldots N$. Assumptions (17) and (18) imply that the random coefficient vectors β_i are uncorrelated across the cross sections but have a common distribution with mean $\bar{\beta}$ and variance-covariance matrix Δ. The distribution is stable over time. Specification of a random coefficient model of the type specified by Swamy is appealing for purposes of estimating relationships with pooled data since there is no requirement that the coefficient vectors for the different cross sections be identical.

If Δ and σ_{ii} were known, then the minimum variance linear unbiased estimator of $\bar{\beta}$ in (22) would be the Aitken generalized least squares estimator:

$$\hat{\bar{\beta}}(\Theta) = [\mathbf{X}'\mathbf{V}(\Theta)^{-1}\mathbf{X}]^{-1}\mathbf{X}'\mathbf{V}(\Theta)^{-1}\mathbf{Y} = \left[\sum_{i=1}^{N} \mathbf{X}_i'(\mathbf{X}_i\Delta\mathbf{X}_i' + \sigma_{ii}\mathbf{I})^{-1}\mathbf{X}_i\right]^{-1} \times \tag{24}$$

$$\sum_{i=1}^{N} \mathbf{X}_i'(\mathbf{X}_i\Delta\mathbf{X}_i' + \sigma_{ii}\mathbf{I})^{-1}\mathbf{Y}_i.$$

It is possible to show that $\hat{\hat{\beta}}(\Theta) = \Sigma_{i=1}^{N} \mathbf{W}_i^* \hat{\hat{\beta}}_i$ where:

$$\mathbf{W}_i^* = \left[\sum_{i=1}^{N} (\Delta + \sigma_{ii}(\mathbf{X}_i'\mathbf{X}_i)^{-1})^{-1}\right]^{-1} \times (\Delta + \sigma_{ii}(\mathbf{X}_i'\mathbf{X}_i)^{-1})^{-1}$$

and $\hat{\hat{\beta}} = (\mathbf{X}_i'\mathbf{X}_i)^{-1}\mathbf{X}_i'\mathbf{Y}_i$, the conventional OLS estimator for the ith cross section. The equation for the ith cross section from (21) is $\mathbf{Y}_i = \mathbf{X}_i\bar{\beta} + \mathbf{X}_i\delta_i + \epsilon_i$. Using only data from the ith cross section the OLS estimator would be $\hat{\hat{\beta}}_i = (\mathbf{X}_i'\mathbf{X}_i)^{-1}\mathbf{X}_i'\mathbf{Y}_i$. Hence $(\hat{\hat{\beta}}_i - \bar{\beta}) = (\mathbf{X}_i'\mathbf{X}_i)^{-1}\mathbf{X}_i'(\mathbf{X}_i\delta_i + \epsilon_i)$ and $(\hat{\hat{\beta}}_i - \bar{\beta})(\hat{\hat{\beta}}_i - \bar{\beta})' = (\mathbf{X}_i'\mathbf{X}_i)^{-1}\mathbf{X}_i'(\mathbf{X}_i\delta_i + \epsilon_i)(\mathbf{X}_i\delta_i + \epsilon_i)'\mathbf{X}_i(\mathbf{X}_i'\mathbf{X}_i)^{-1}$. Then $\mathrm{Var}(\hat{\hat{\beta}}_i) = E[(\hat{\hat{\beta}}_i - \bar{\beta})(\hat{\hat{\beta}}_i - \bar{\beta})'] = (\mathbf{X}_i'\mathbf{X}_i)^{-1}\ \mathbf{X}_i'[\mathbf{X}_i\Delta\mathbf{X}_i' + \sigma_{ii}\mathbf{I}]\mathbf{X}_i(\mathbf{X}_i'\mathbf{X}_i)^{-1} = \Delta + \sigma_{ii}(\mathbf{X}_i'\mathbf{X}_i)^{-1}$. Therefore $\hat{\hat{\beta}}(\Theta)$ is a weighted average of the OLS estimators with the weights proportional to the inverse of the variance-covariance matrices of these estimators. The variance-covariance matrix of the estimator $\hat{\hat{\beta}}(\Theta)$ is:

$$\text{(25)} \qquad \mathbf{C}(\Theta) = \left[\sum_{i=1}^{N} \mathbf{X}_i'(\mathbf{X}_i\Delta\mathbf{X}_i' + \sigma_{ii}\mathbf{I})^{-1}\mathbf{X}_i\right]^{-1} = \left[\sum_{i=1}^{N} (\Delta + \sigma_{ii}(\mathbf{X}_i'\mathbf{X}_i)^{-1})^{-1}\right]^{-1}.$$

In practice, of course, Δ and σ_{ii} will not be known and must be estimated. An unbiased estimator of σ_{ii} is:

$$\text{(26)} \qquad s_{ii} = \frac{\mathbf{Y}_i'\mathbf{M}_i\mathbf{Y}_i}{T_i - k}$$

where $\mathbf{M}_i = \mathbf{I} - \mathbf{X}_i(\mathbf{X}_i'\mathbf{X}_i)^{-1}\mathbf{X}_i'$. An unbiased estimator of Δ is:

$$\text{(27)} \qquad \hat{\Delta} = \frac{\mathbf{S}}{N-1} - \frac{1}{N}\sum_{i=1}^{N} s_{ii}(\mathbf{X}_i'\mathbf{X}_i)^{-1}$$

where:

$$\text{(28)} \qquad \mathbf{S} = \sum_{i=1}^{N} \hat{\hat{\beta}}_i\hat{\hat{\beta}}_i' - \frac{1}{N}\sum_{i=1}^{N}\hat{\hat{\beta}}_i\sum_{i=1}^{N}\hat{\hat{\beta}}_i'.$$

These are the estimators recommended by Swamy and it is possible to use them in (24) to develop the generalized least squares estimator of $\bar{\beta}$.

One possible way around the problem of pooling when coefficients for different cross sections are not homogeneous is the random coefficient model and the method for obtaining estimates of pooled data developed by Swamy.[3] Unfortunately, extensive experience with applications of the model indicates that the variance estimates from (27) are not always positive, possibly an indication of specification error. The Swamy procedure is therefore not feasible in every situation. However, there are many cases where the Swamy procedure is feasible and where the assumptions do not appear to be inappropriate.

AVERAGING AND AGGREGATION

When the cross-sectional coefficients are not homogeneous and when the Swamy method is not feasible, either because the assumption of random coefficients is inappropriate or because of negative variance estimates, a method of averaging does exist which for many applications is very useful. Moreover, extensive experience with this method in comparison to the Swamy method indicates that the averaging method yields estimates which are similar to the Swamy estimates.

Using the cross-sectional relations indicated by (1) and the assumption of fixed coefficients, the arithmetic average of the coefficient is $1/N\ \Sigma_{i=1}^{N}\ \beta_i$ and the weighted average is

$$\text{(29)} \qquad \bar{\beta} = \sum_{i=1}^{N} W_i\beta_i$$

where W_i is the weight for the ith cross section. Suppose, for example, that $\mathbf{Y}_i$ is the time-series vector of market shares for the ith cross section, W_i is the relative size of the ith cross section, and β_i consists of the coefficients of responsiveness of share to advertising, price, and other variables. If the purpose of the analysis is to determine policies for each cross section separately, then β_i contains the information relevant for the ith cross section. If, however, the purpose is to develop strategies such as advertising expenditures, for example, for the market as a whole and ignoring the allocation issue, then the average responsiveness measures reflected in $\bar{\beta}$ are relevant.

If $\hat{\beta}_i$ is an unbiased estimator of β_i, then $\hat{\bar{\beta}} = \Sigma_{i=1}^{N} W_i\hat{\beta}_i$ will be an unbiased estimator of $\bar{\beta}$ and

$$\text{(30)} \qquad \mathrm{Var}(\hat{\bar{\beta}}) = \sum_{i=1}^{N} W_i^2\,\mathrm{Var}(\hat{\beta}_i) + 2\ {}_{\text{all}}\Sigma_{i<j}\ W_i W_j \mathrm{Cov}(\hat{\beta}_i, \hat{\beta}_j).$$

In some instances the disturbances for different cross sections may be independent and the second term on the right-hand side of (30) will vanish. In other cases it may be reasonable to assume that disturbances are contemporaneously correlated between the cross

[3]It may be noted that if the coefficients are random, the OLS estimator is also unbiased. However, OLS would be inefficient and the formula for the variance of the OLS estimator is then incorrect.

sections. In this case if Ω is the covariance matrix of disturbances between cross sections, then an estimator of the *ij*th element of Ω, after the fashion of the typical method of estimating contemporaneous covariance in "seemingly unrelated regression," is:

$$s_{ij} = \frac{\hat{\epsilon}_i' \hat{\epsilon}_j}{T - k} \quad (31)$$

where $\hat{\epsilon}_i$ is the vector of residuals resulting from OLS regression. The estimated variance of $\hat{\bar{\beta}}$ is then:

$$\hat{\text{Var}}(\hat{\bar{\beta}}) = \sum_{i=1}^{N} W_i^2 s_{ii}(\mathbf{X}_i'\mathbf{X}_i)^{-1} + 2_{\text{all}} \Sigma_{i<j} W_i W_j s_{ij} (\mathbf{X}_i'\mathbf{X}_i)^{-1} \mathbf{X}_i'\mathbf{X}_j (\mathbf{X}_j'\mathbf{X}_j)^{-1}. \quad (32)$$

Examples of estimates of average responsiveness and estimated variances of these estimates in a market segmentation study are provided by McCann [6, 7].

If the purpose of the analysis is to gain information about the responsiveness of the whole market, then one might argue for regression analysis based on data aggregated over the cross sections. Thus starting with (1) and an assumption of fixed coefficients if we let:

$$\mathbf{Y} = \sum_{i=1}^{N} \mathbf{Y}_i, \ \mathbf{X} = \sum_{i=1}^{N} \mathbf{X}_i, \ \text{and} \ \epsilon = \sum_{i=1}^{N} \epsilon_i,$$

we have:

$$\mathbf{Y} = \mathbf{X}\beta + \epsilon. \quad (33)$$

The equality expressed in (33) does not follow mathematically unless $\beta_i = \beta_j$ for all *i* and *j*. Ordinary least squares estimation of β in (33) if $\beta_i \neq \beta_j$ results in the well-known "aggregation bias."

$$\hat{\beta} = (\mathbf{X}'\mathbf{X})^{-1}\mathbf{X}'\mathbf{Y} = (\mathbf{X}'\mathbf{X})^{-1}\mathbf{X}' \sum_{i=1}^{N} \mathbf{Y}_i$$

$$= (\mathbf{X}'\mathbf{X})^{-1}\mathbf{X}' \sum_{i=1}^{N} (\mathbf{X}_i\beta_i + \epsilon_i) \quad \text{and}$$

$$E(\hat{\beta}) = \sum_{i=1}^{N} (\mathbf{X}'\mathbf{X})^{-1}\mathbf{X}'\mathbf{X}_i\beta_i$$

and thus the expectation of a single element in $\hat{\beta}$ will depend not only on the corresponding elements in the β_i's, but also on the noncorresponding elements [13, 15]. Fortunately, the dilemma of aggregation bias may be averted if one is willing to assume that the cross-sectional regression coefficient vectors are random and have a common distribution. Thus if the β_i are random and the assumptions indicated by (16), (17), and (18) apply, then (1) may be rewritten as:

$$\mathbf{Y}_i = \mathbf{X}_i(\bar{\beta} + \delta_i) + \epsilon_i. \quad (34)$$

Summing,

$$\sum_{i=1}^{N} \mathbf{Y}_i = \sum_{i=1}^{N} \mathbf{X}_i\bar{\beta} + \sum_{i=1}^{N} \mathbf{X}_i\delta_i + \sum_{i=1}^{N} \epsilon_i, \text{ or} \quad (35)$$

$$\mathbf{Y} = \mathbf{X}\bar{\beta} + \sum_{i=1}^{N} \mathbf{X}_i\delta_i + \sum_{i=1}^{N} \epsilon_i. \quad (36)$$

The OLS estimator of $\bar{\beta}$ in (36) will be $\hat{\bar{\beta}} = (\mathbf{X}'\mathbf{X})^{-1}\mathbf{X}'(\mathbf{X}\bar{\beta} + \Sigma_{i=1}^{N} \mathbf{X}_i\delta_i + \Sigma_{i=1}^{N} \epsilon_i)$ and its expectation will be $\bar{\beta}$. Therefore, under the assumption of random coefficients the aggregation bias vanishes.

ILLUSTRATION OF RANDOM COEFFICIENT ESTIMATION

A computer program, RCR, has been written at Purdue University to estimate pooled cross-sectional and time-series relationships.[4] Utilization of this program in conjunction with the *Sales Management* data provides a basis for a comparison of estimates of the coefficients in (14) under the random coefficient assumption with estimates derived from fixed coefficient assumptions. In addition to pooled estimates, ordinary least squares estimates of data aggregated over cross sections have been developed. Finally, the averages of the regression coefficients for the cross sections have been calculated. Table 8 displays the estimated coefficients.

In both regressions the estimates associated with random coefficients (with intercept) and the average of the OLS estimates for each cross section are similar. The estimated standard errors, however, are smaller for the average than for the random model. This result, in our experience, is typical and is not unexpected since in both cases a mean vector is being estimated. But under the random coefficient model assumptions there is an additional source of randomness in comparison to randomness which arises in averaging estimates of fixed coefficients.

The estimates of β_2 are not very sensitive to underlying assumptions. This is especially true when the standard errors of the estimates of β_2 in Table 8 are taken into account. The estimates, however, of the responsiveness of the dependent variable to changes in population are very sensitive to the method of estimation. Multicollinearity is a factor in each of the estimating methods and the inverse correlation of the estimates β_1 and β_2 is apparent in pairwise comparisons of the numbers in Table 8. For purposes of forecasting it probably would not matter a great deal which of the estimates are used providing the forecast is based on good estimates of the independent variables. Interpretation of the meaning of the relationships and the responsiveness of the dependent variable to changes in population do depend, however, in an important way on underlying assumptions. Taking into account the homogeneity tests reported earlier the OLSDV method is probably, in this case, in closest agreement with the evidence.

[4]The RCR program was developed primarily by John McCann and Terry Cooper.

Table 8

A COMPARISON OF REGRESSION COEFFICIENT ESTIMATES UNDER RANDOM COEFFICIENT ASSUMPTIONS AND FIXED COEFFICIENT ASSUMPTIONS IN THE RELATIONSHIP BETWEEN FURNITURE AND HOUSEHOLD APPLIANCE SALES AND POPULATION AND TOTAL RETAIL SALES

Parameters	*All random with intercept*	*All random zero intercept*	*Fixed, average*	*Random, aggregate*	*Variance components*	*OLSDV*	*Total*
$\hat{\beta}_1$	−15.44	14.17	−23.90	−18.61	20.10	22.07	9.73
$\sigma_{\hat{\beta}_1}$	(9.56)	(2.48)	(3.79)	(16.79)[a]	(1.47)	(2.65)	(1.16)
$\hat{\beta}_2$	.041	.035	.043	.044	.036	.035	.043
$\sigma_{\hat{\beta}_2}$	(.007)	(.005)	(.001)	(.005)[a]	(.001)	(.001)	(.001)
Intercept	81.93	—	122.71	430.24	—	—	—

[a] The standard errors reported here are obtained by applying OLS, and are incorrect.

CONCLUSIONS

Pooling of observations from several cross sections for the purpose of estimating relationships among variables in regression analysis offers the possibility for greatly increasing the reliability of the estimates providing pooling is appropriate. Furthermore, even when the relationships are not precisely homogeneous, there are instances in which one could argue for estimation on the basis of pooled data since the reduced variance of the estimates could be more valuable than small bias resulting from pooling. Before a decision is made to pool, however, it is important to test the homogeneity hypothesis. There are instances in which the structure of relationships varies substantially from one cross section to another [1]. Pooling under these circumstances would be a serious mistake and the biased estimates based on pooled data would be grossly misleading.

In addition to the traditional fixed coefficient assumptions, recent developments have made it possible to estimate relationships on pooled data with the assumption that coefficients are partially or entirely random. The assumption of random coefficients thus extends the conditions under which estimates of pooled or aggregated data are possible and appropriate. The intended application, the background conditions and circumstances of the process being studied, and the empirical evidence and tests of homogeneity should each be considered in deciding whether or not to pool and, if so, how to pool.

APPENDIX A

We start with

$$\mathbf{A} = (1 - \rho)\mathbf{I} + \rho\mathbf{ee}' \tag{37}$$

and find that $[\mathbf{A} - (1 - \rho)\mathbf{I}]\mathbf{e} = \rho T\mathbf{e}$ and hence

$$\frac{\mathbf{ee}'}{(1 - \rho + T\rho)} = \mathbf{A}^{-1}\mathbf{ee}' . \tag{38}$$

From (37) we find $\mathbf{I} = (1 - \rho)\mathbf{A}^{-1} + \mathbf{A}^{-1}\rho\mathbf{ee}'$ and therefore

$$\mathbf{A}^{-1} = \frac{1}{(1 - \rho)}\mathbf{I} - \frac{\rho}{(1 - \rho)}\mathbf{A}^{-1}\mathbf{ee}' . \tag{39}$$

Substituting the equality of (38) in the second term on the right-hand side of (39) we find

$$\mathbf{A}^{-1} = \frac{1}{(1 - \rho)}\mathbf{I} - \frac{\rho}{(1 - \rho)(1 - \rho + T\rho)}\mathbf{ee}' . \tag{40}$$

REFERENCES

1. Bass, Frank M. "Profitability and the A/S Ratio," *Journal of Advertising Research*, 14 (December 1974), 9-20.
2. Fisher, F. M. "Tests of Equality Between Sets of Coefficients in Two Linear Regressions: An Expository Note," *Econometrica*, 38 (March 1970), 361-6.
3. Hsiao, Cheng. "Some Estimation Methods for a Random Coefficient Model," Technical Report No. 77, Institute for Mathematical Studies in the Social Sciences, Stanford University, 1972.
4. Maddala, G. S. "The Use of Variance Components Models in Pooling Cross Section and Time Series Data," *Econometrica*, 39 (March 1971), 341-58.
5. ——— and T. D. Mount. "Comparative Study of Alternative Estimators for Variance Components Models," *Journal of the American Statistical Association*, 68 (June 1973), 324-8.
6. McCann, John M. "Study of Market Segment Response to the Marketing Decision Variables," *Journal of Marketing Research*, 11 (November 1974), 399-412.
7. ———. "Market Segment Response to the Marketing Decision Variables," Working Paper, Graduate School of Business and Public Administration, Cornell University, 1973.
8. Nerlove, Marc. "Further Evidence on the Estimation of Dynamic Economic Relations from a Time Series of Cross Sections," *Econometrica*, 39 (March 1971), 359-82.
9. Rosenberg, Barr. "The Analysis of a Cross Section of Time Series by Stochastically Convergent Parameter Regression," *Annals of Economic and Social Measurement*, 2 (October 1973), 399-428.

10. "Survey of Buying Power," *Sales Management*, special issues. 1949-71.
11. Swamy, P.A.V.B. "Efficient Inference in a Random Coefficient Regression Model," *Econometrica*, 38 (March 1970), 311-23.
12. ______. *Statistical Inference in Random Coefficient Regression Models*. Berlin: Springer-Verlag, 1971.
13. Theil, Henri. "Consistent Aggregation of Micromodels with Random Coefficients," Report 6816, Center for Mathematical Studies in Business and Economics, University of Chicago, 1968.
14. Wallace, T. D. "Weaker Criteria and Tests for Linear Restrictions in Regression," *Econometrica*, 40 (July 1972), 689-98.
15. Zellner, Arnold. "On the Aggregation Problem: A New Approach to a Troublesome Problem," Report 6628 Center for Mathematical Studies in Business and Economics, University of Chicago, 1966.

FREDERICK W. WINTER*

This study investigates the influence of advertising exposure on individual brand attitude change. Results indicate that past exposures, brand familiarity, and prior attitude are significantly related to attitudinal response.

A Laboratory Experiment of Individual Attitude Response to Advertising Exposure

INTRODUCTION AND THEORETICAL FRAMEWORK

One of the most potentially profitable and yet elusive areas of consumer behavior remains the study of advertising's effect on the consumer. Unfortunately, the methodology required in modeling consumer response to advertising exposures is complex. Essentially the problem is to measure the advertising effect in an environment that is "psychologically equivalent," if not physically equivalent, to the real world environment; in addition it is important to measure accurately the number of exposures that each individual receives. Finally, the criterion measure by which advertising is evaluated must be determined and causally related to controllable advertising variables.

Techniques range from econometric analyses [1, 9, 13], to laboratory methods [10]. The argument for one method over another is a familiar one. While the econometric analyses offer realistic criterion measures (such as sales or profits) in a meaningful environment, the methods fall short in terms of causal inference or exposure control; only recently have the simultaneous estimation procedures [1] considered the mutual interdependence between advertising and sales. Critics of econometric methods point out that advertising dollars are only proxy measures of exposure in that dollar measures can be expected to, at best, approximate both reach and frequency. While the environment is certainly realistic, it can be drastically altered by variables beyond the control of the advertiser.

Laboratory methods do offer the degree of control necessary to measure advertising's impact on the consumer. Nevertheless, these studies tend to be small in scope and artificial in nature. Advocates of other methods are quick to note that laboratory research usually involves awareness measures or perhaps attitude measures which may be somewhat removed from decision-making criteria such as sales or profits.

In spite of its shortcomings, attitude change is a particularly appealing measure of advertising effect in laboratory studies because it is possible to control for variables outside of advertising's influence such as economic fluctuations, competitive response, availability, pricing, and retail practices. The brand attitude measures that were used in this research were based on two informational inputs: importance of attribute possession to the consumer and beliefs of the amount of each attribute possessed by the alternative brands. These measures have been used successfully by Lehmann [8] in the prediction of television show preference and are in the class of linear attitude measures [2, 11, 12]. Although the focus here is on attitude change at the "macro" level, an attempt will also be made to explore individual differences in response to advertising exposures.

An interesting finding has been documented by Zajonc [16], who found that mere exposure to nonsense words or photographs produced favorable attitude change; this response was a function of the logarithm of the number of prior exposures. Thus the more familiar the subject was with the exposure material, the smaller the attitude change produced.

In addition to familiarity, it has been a widely held position in the area of social psychology that the attitude prior to exposure greatly affects the manner in which the information is received. Dealing with a low ego involve-

* Frederick Winter is Assistant Professor of Business Administration, University of Illinois at Urbana-Champaign. The author expresses his sincere gratitude to Professor Frank M. Bass for his valuable suggestions. Professors Edgar A. Pessemier, Dan E. Schendel, and William L. Wilkie provided additional assistance. Financial support was furnished by a grant to Professor Bass from the AAAA Educational Foundation. The agency of Batten, Barton, Durstine, and Osborn assisted in obtaining commercial advertisements.

Reprinted from *Journal of Marketing Research,* 10 (May 1973), 130-40, published by the American Marketing Association.

ment issue, Hovland and Pritzker [6] report that the greater the change advocated in a communication, the greater the attitude change in the desired direction. The work of Freedman [3] supports this finding with additional evidence suggesting that under conditions of high ego involvement the relation between change advocated and change produced may be nonmonotonic. The theory of this phenomenon is perhaps best explained by Hovland, Harvey, and Sherif [5]. Under highly involving circumstances the authors hypothesize that the latitude of acceptance for alternative communication positions is narrower than under low involvement conditions. To support the premise that individuals will accept communications that are within their latitudes of acceptance, the study reported that when a large discrepancy exists between the subjects' attitudes and the advocated position, the tendency is to remain unchanged in attitude. A communication that was reasonably close to the subject's initial position often resulted in a positive attitude change.

Although consumer involvement with products can be expected to cover a wide range of values, there is some indication that most products tend to be of low involvement [7]. The type of products that are likely to be of low involvement are frequently purchased consumer nondurables. Both facial tissues and scouring pads, the products considered in this research, would be expected to fit this category. Under these conditions the following hypotheses were selected for testing:

H_1: advertising exposure will have a favorable effect on attitude change.

H_2: individuals for whom the advertising advocates the greatest change (i.e., the group with the most unfavorable initial attitude) will respond with the most favorable attitude change.

H_3: individuals with high brand familiarity will experience less favorable attitude change than individuals with low brand familiarity.

H_4: each additional exposure will have a decreasing effect on favorable attitude change.

H_5: brand familiarity is positively related to the number of previous exposures.

THE DATA COLLECTION PROCEDURES

The data were collected in a laboratory experiment in the Krannert Behavioral Laboratory at Purdue University in the fall of 1970. Product categories included in the study were facial tissues, scouring pads, spray disinfectants, and a common household cleaning product. It has been agreed that neither the brands nor the specific nature of the latter category be divulged. Brands selected for study within each category are shown in Table 1. Facial tissues and scouring pads were studied intensively, and this article is confined to these two product categories.

All of the subjects used in the study were housewives from the Lafayette, Indiana area. Recruiting was done by securing subject lists from presidents of various ladies' organizations in the area, primarily church groups and philanthropic organizations. The fact that the organization would receive the $5 compensation only if all four sessions were attended was very effective in encouraging continued participation. Of the 490 subjects who attended the first week, 453 attended all four weeks, for a 92.4% completion rate.

Table 1

PRODUCT CATEGORIES, BRANDS, AND ATTRIBUTES STUDIED

Product category	*Brand evaluated*	*Salient attributes*
Facial tissues	1. Scott[a]	1. Softness
	2. Kleenex	2. Price
	3. Puffs	3. Strength
	4. Ritz	4. Ease of removal from box
		5. Beauty of box
		6. Pleasantness of odor
Scouring pads	1. SOS	1. Durability of pad
	2. Rescue[a]	2. Durability of soap
	3. Brillo	3. Price
	4. Soettes	4. Rust resistance
		5. Gentleness to hands
		6. Scouring ability
Spray disinfectant	1. Lysol	1. Economy
	2. Staphene	2. Freshness of odor
	3. Dow[a] (new brand)	3. Germ-killing power
		4. Mildew-killing power
		5. Confidence in manufacturer
Household cleaning product[b]	1. Brand A	1. Stain-removing power
	2. Brand B	2. Whitening power
	3. Brand C	3. Sudsiness
	4. Brand D	4. Mildness to skin
	5. Brand X[a] (new brand)	5. Mildness to clothes
		6. Pollution control

[a] Advertised brand.
[b] Product category and brands cannot be disclosed.

Prior to the experiment a videotaped group interview was used to define the salient attributes of brands within the product categories. A review of the videotapes produced five or six relevant brand attributes for each product category which were then pretested in the proposed attitude questionnaire format. With these inputs the final test instruments were formulated.

The data can be segmented in the following way:

1. Pre-session information
   a. demographic data (first week only)
   b. television viewing data
   c. past purchase and usage history

Table 2

CELL DESIGN AND EXPOSURE LEVELS

	Time of treatment	Weekly exposure level			
		Week 1	*Week 2*	*Week 3*	*Week 4*
Treatment I	Monday afternoon or Wednesday morning	Scott Dow Brand X	Scott Dow	Scott	Scott
Treatment II	Wednesday afternoon or Wednesday evening	Dow Rescue Scott	Dow Rescue	Dow	Dow
Treatment IIIA	Monday morning or Monday evening	Rescue Brand X Dow	Rescue Brand X	Rescue	Rescue
Treatment IIIB	Monday evening (no preexposure attitude questionnaire)	Rescue Brand X Dow	Rescue Brand X	Rescue	Rescue
Treatment IIIC	Monday evening (no pre- or post-exposure attitude questionnaire)	Rescue Brand X Dow	Rescue Brand X	Rescue	Rescue
Treatment IV	Thursday morning or Thursday evening	Brand X Scott Rescue	Brand X Scott	Brand X	Brand X
Treatment V	Thursday afternoon	no commercial	no commercial	no commercial	no commercial

2. Pre- and postexposure attitude information (collected twice each session for all four weeks)
   a. importance of attributes in purchase
   b. rank order preference
   c. brand familiarity
   d. "ideal" combinations of attributes
   e. perception of brands' possession of attributes
   f. dollarmetric preferences
3. Product selection data
   a. brands selected for "purchase"
   b. adoption–trial classification of "purchase".

It was necessary to disguise the true nature of the study; therefore, from the initial contact with the subject until the last session ended, the experiment was said to be a television communications study. This guise provided justification for the shows and commercials to which the subjects were exposed. To support the guise, questions about television shows were interspersed throughout the questionnaires.

The television program which the subjects saw was a different episode of the Andy Griffith Show each week. This particular series contained no controversial issues which could arouse strong feelings and affect responses. Each week the subjects viewed a half-hour sequence as it had been taped from the air, complete with commercials.

The only modification made to the program was the substitution of commercials for the brands being studied in place of the commercials originally in those time spots. The same commercial was used for each of the brands throughout the experiment. These commercials were copies of those actually used for the brands, and they were obtained with the assistance of Batten, Barton, Durstine, and Osborne, Inc.

For each of the brands studied, different levels of exposure, which were created with the design shown in Table 2, allowed the effect of the commercials to be examined. The design shows that Group V received no exposures at all, and the assumption of product independence was confirmed by comparing, for each product category, the responses of this group with those of the other nonexposed group. Comparison of the responses of Group IIIB for the postexposure attitude and preference questionnaire with those of Group IIIA indicated that the preexposure questionnaires had no confounding effects until the postexposure measurement of the last week of the study. A comparison of groups IIIC and IIIA responses suggested that all of the attitude and preference questionnaires throughout the study had had no undesirable effects. Group IIIB and Group IIIC met in different rooms and were separated from each other and from Group IIIA.

The laboratory procedure was identical for all four weeks of the study with the exception of the first week during which demographic data were also collected. The following indicates the schedule for each session:

1. arrival, check-in
2. videotaped introduction (3 min.)
3. initial questionnaire (10 min.)
4. preexposure attitude questionnaire (15 min.)
5. television show and advertising exposure (30 min.)
6. television show questionnaire (10 min.)
7. postexposure attitude questionnaire (15 min.)
8. simulated shopping trip (20 min.)

The study sessions began with a short introduction videotaped to insure uniformity of instructions across all subjects. The guise of the study was reinforced by initially describing the focus of the research as the investigation of television shows, and in later weeks the experimenters mentioned fictitious problems certain individuals had in filling out questionnaires pertaining to television shows.

An initial questionnaire followed the introduction each week. The first initial questionnaire provided demographic information, concentration of past purchases among brands, and the level of product usage. The initial questionnaire given during the latter three weeks was used to determine the brands used most during the previous week and television viewing levels.

The second questionnaire the subjects completed each week was the preexposure attitude and preference measurement for each brand in the four product categories. This was the same for all four weeks. Following completion of this questionnaire, subjects were shown the half-hour, videotaped television program. The advertising exposures, as dictated by the experimental design, were inserted at the appropriate time.

Immediately after seeing the television program, subjects were given a questionnaire concerning the program itself to support the claim that the study was concerned with the television programs. The next questionnaire the subjects completed was the postexposure measurement of attitude and preferences. This was identical to the preexposure questionnaire.

The final measuring instrument indicated the subjects' selections of products during a simulated shopping trip. The selection was made in the hall between the viewing room and the room set up as the "store." Some realism was sacrificed by having the subjects indicate their selections on a questionnaire, but the advantages of this system were that the selections were recorded immediately and accurately and that the selections of the later shoppers of each group were not affected by their seeing the proportions of the various brands taken by previous shoppers. All of the brands studied were available every week, and subjects received monetary change resulting from the selection of brands priced less than the maximum spending allowance.

In summary, the data collection procedures involved a large scale laboratory experiment designed to simulate a realistic environment and, at the same time, offer a high degree of control over measurement and experimental procedures. Additional details of the experiment are available from other sources [4, 14, 15].

THE RESEARCH APPROACH

The attitude measurement model that was used in this research is composed of three information components combining to form a "city block" attitude measure:

$$A_j = \sum_{k=1}^{n} b_{kj} v_k$$

where:

A_j = the attitude measurement for brand j (the smaller the value the greater the affect),

b_{kj} = the amount of attribute k that brand j is perceived to possess (beliefs or perceived instrumentalities),

v_k = the importance of a brand possessing the desired amount of attribute k (attribute importances or value importances), and

n = the number of attributes relevant to preference of brand in the product category.

Thus the overall favor in which a brand is regarded is a function of the affect on the relevant attributes; judgments regarding those attributes which are more important than others are weighted more heavily than the relatively unimportant attributes. The model recognizes that although individuals may differ in their values and perceptions, they can still have the same degree of affect for a brand.

Attitude measures reported in this research are normalized by dividing the raw brand attitude score by the sum of the scores for all the brands evaluated by the individual at a particular point in time. Thus a measure of relative attractiveness results:

$$Z_{i,j,t} = A_j / \sum_{j=1}^{m} A_j = \sum_{k=1}^{n} b_{kj,t} v_{k,t} / \sum_{j=1}^{m} \sum_{k=1}^{n} b_{kj,t} v_{k,t}$$

where:

$Z_{i,j,t}$ = the normalized attitude measure of individual i toward brand j at time t,

m = total number of brands evaluated, and

b_{kj}, v_k, A_j are defined as before.

The decision to use normalized measures depends mainly on the measurement assumptions of the researcher. The use of semantic differential scales involves the risk of response bias. This bias becomes a particularly critical issue when attitudes are compared across time. If the nature of the response bias is multiplicative, the normalization will correct for the bias; additive response bias is only partially corrected in such a case.

The normalization procedure can, however, discard valuable information. It is not known if change in the normalized attitude toward a brand is the result of a change in the evaluation of the brand, a reassessment of a competitive brand, or both phenomena. Similarly, in no way can the general level of satisfaction with the brands be derived.

The use of normalized attitudes in this research reflected the researcher's desire to eliminate response bias from the measures which were compared with subsequent measures. The result is a measure of relative favorability which reflects consumers' perceptions of relative differences between brands.

Mean Attitude Change

Before examining possible reasons for attitude change, it is important that we have some confidence in the premise that attitude changes did, in fact, occur. The mean attitude measurements toward Rescue scouring pads appear in Table 3; comparable data for Scott tissues are shown in Table 4. Significance tests of consecutive differences between means are included. The mean attitude level analysis indicates it is difficult to draw conclusions concerning the nature of attitude change. For example, from Table 3, it can be observed that between t_3 and t_4 cell 1 received no exposure and became more favorable; cell 2 was not exposed but became more unfavorable. Cell 3 was exposed and reflected an unfavorable attitude change, while cell 5 (also exposed between t_3 and t_4) became more favorable toward Rescue. The analysis of means, unfortunately, masks individual differences of response.

A Regression Model of Attitude Change

A wide variety of possible regression models could be considered in the modeling of the attitude change processes. The theory indicates that such a model should include change effects resulting from both nonadvertising exposure effects as well as the exposure itself. A naive model of attitude change would be:

$$\Delta Z_{i,t,t+1} = \alpha + B_1 Z_{i,t} + B_2 Z^2_{i,t} + B_3\, exp_{i,t,t+1} + \mu_{i,t,t+1}$$

where:

Table 3

MEAN DISTANCE OF RESCUE FROM IDEAL POINT

		t_1	t_2	t_3	t_4	t_5	t_6	t_7	t_8
Cell 1 (1 Rescue exposure)	$\bar{z}$	.36487	.35021	.28640[a]	.27006	.21426[a]	.23617	.21740	.21151
	σ_z	.11573	.16171	.16163	.16371	.11929	.16287	.12492	.14183
	n	46	45	53	49	52	51	52	51
Cell 2 (No Rescue exposure)	$\bar{z}$	.35510	.35622	.28936[a]	.30155	.21407[a]	.22316	.18929	.19956
	σ_z	.11573	.16171	.16163	.16371	.11929	.16287	.12492	.14183
	n	46	45	53	49	52	51	52	51
Cell 3 (4 Rescue exposures)	$\bar{z}$	.37744	.32860[a]	.26029[a]	.27386	.19141[a]	.23281	.22173	.21793
	σ_z	.11888	.13362	.16941	.20224	.16017	.24238	.23380	.24091
	n	36	37	39	37	38	37	41	40
Cell 4 (0 Rescue exposures)	$\bar{z}$	.31165	.32188	.28875	.29911	.22506[a]	.22098	.17822	.17888
	σ_z	.09090	.10463	.13020	.14652	.12220	.14977	.12435	.13793
	n	54	53	50	52	53	52	52	52
Cell 5 (2 Rescue exposures)	$\bar{z}$	.36161	.33576	.23602	.21645	.16259[a]	.14787	.16389	.15576
	σ_z	.08100	.09553	.10829	.09957	.08500	.10525	.09927	.08790
	n	41	38	40	39	37	38	35	37
Cell 6 (2 Rescue exposures)	$\bar{z}$	.35060	.29764[a]	.24743[a]	.26954	.22170[a]	.23388	.21934	.22655
	σ_z	.13042	.14226	.11578	.14497	.11449	.15591	.12255	.13216
	n	57	57	54	54	51	52	50	51
Cell 7 (1 Rescue exposure)	$\bar{z}$	.33896	.26640[a]	.23261	.23237	.22665	.22193	.19945	.19116
	σ_z	.09439	.10442	.11513	.12080	.10814	.10544	.10785	.10510
	n	40	38	41	42	42	42	40	43
Cell 8 (0 Rescue exposures and no other exposures)	$\bar{z}$	.37983	.39143	.31446[a]	.31454	.23355[a]	.23254	.21444	.22241
	σ_z	.09171	.10296	.17595	.19466	.15918	.15664	.12489	.13858
	n	29	28	28	29	30	28	30	30
Cell 9 (1 Rescue exposure)	$\bar{z}$	.34033	.29140[a]	.26113	.27717	.21501[a]	.22131	.21979	.21330
	σ_z	.09154	.13443	.14294	.15098	.14110	.14857	.15529	.15435
	n	61	59	58	58	60	60	59	61
Cell 10 (4 Rescue exposures, no pre-questionnaire)	$\bar{z}$		.36162		.33325		.30653		.22986
	σ_z		.14669		.15141		.26427		.20080
	n		15		13		15		14
Cell 11 (4 Rescue exposures, only final questionnaire)	$\bar{z}$								.19199
	σ_z								.12620
	n								13

$\bar{z}$ = sample mean attitude (distance of Rescue from ideal point).
σ_z = sample standard deviation of attitude.
n = number of observations in sample.
[a] Difference between previous period's mean is significant at the .05 level.

Table 4

MEAN DISTANCE OF SCOTT FROM IDEAL POINT

		t_1	t_2	t_3	t_4	t_5	t_6	t_7	t_8
Cell 1 (0 Scott exposures)	$\bar{z}$	.20293	.20801	.20170	.18595	.19473	.19512	.21842	.19421
	σ_z	.11860	.10751	.10280	.10377	.11036	.10259	.12894	.10683
	n	49	48	50	50	54	51	53	51
Cell 2 (4 Scott exposures)	$\bar{z}$	.18268	.18019	.18939	.18705	.18382	.18422	.17849	.17049
	σ_z	.09282	.08020	.08005	.08619	.08613	.07888	.08305	.08652
	n	53	48	52	50	53	52	54	54
Cell 3 (0 Scott exposures)	$\bar{z}$	.18493	.17065	.18371	.18468	.18383	.17376	.17170	.17395
	σ_z	.08817	.09045	.09505	.09051	.07553	.09048	.08082	.07265
	n	36	36	39	38	34	35	38	39
Cell 4 (4 Scott exposures)	$\bar{z}$	.20682	.20905	.20275	.20074	.21384	.20589	.21496	.21787
	σ_z	.09238	.07367	.07411	.08173	.07853	.08208	.07530	.08421
	n	55	54	50	53	53	53	53	53
Cell 5 (1 Scott exposure)	$\bar{z}$	.20902	.18156	.19277	.19553	.20590	.21290	.20301	.20928
	σ_z	.09937	.08071	.09083	.07944	.08818	.09285	.08300	.08353
	n	40	41	40	39	38	38	37	37
Cell 6 (1 Scott exposure)	$\bar{z}$	.16751	.16191	.19465[a]	.18604	.18822	.18900	.18711	.18982
	σ_z	.08487	.08760	.07850	.08771	.08926	.08736	.08512	.08384
	n	57	54	55	55	52	51	51	48
Cell 7 (2 Scott exposures)	$\bar{z}$	.19285	.18464	.18072	.17683	.19023	.18419	.20356	.18182
	σ_z	.07772	.08490	.07355	.07978	.06914	.07652	.06960	.08438
	n	41	41	41	41	42	40	40	41
Cell 8 (0 Scott exposures and no other exposures)	$\bar{z}$	.14995	.15666	.16972	.15589	.15487	.14462	.15067	.15147
	σ_z	.08181	.09098	.09898	.10523	.08619	.08455	.08485	.07852
	n	27	23	28	29	29	29	30	29
Cell 9 (2 Scott exposures)	$\bar{z}$	.19012	.15876[a]	.18754[a]	.18417	.18952	.19206	.19402	.18168
	σ_z	.08876	.08161	.09710	.08404	.08712	.09926	.10033	.09066
	n	59	59	59	58	60	57	62	60
Cell 10 (0 Scott exposures, no pre-questionnaire)	$\bar{z}$		.12836		.13573		.16075		.14731
	σ_z		.08237		.08453		.10049		.07347
	n		13		14		15		15
Cell 11 (0 Scott exposures, only final questionnaire)	$\bar{z}$								.21481
	σ_z								.07231
	n								13

$\bar{z}$ = sample mean attitude (distance of Scott from ideal point).
σ_z = sample standard deviation of attitude.
n = number of observations in sample.
[a] Difference between previous period's mean is significant at the .05 level.

$\Delta Z_{i,t,t+1}$ = change in brand attitude of individual i between periods t and $t+1$ (negative change indicates a favorable change),

$Z_{i,t}$ = attitude of individual i at time t (prior to exposure). (Values range between 0 and 1; 0 represents the maximum degree of affect.), and

$exp_{i,t,t+1}$ = dummy variable, where 1 represents an advertising exposure received by individual i between measurements t and $t+1$, 0 otherwise.

Such a model does, in a sense, consider " control group" attitude change effects. Thus the "regression effect" that is often prevalent in attitude change studies can be considered separately from the exposure effect. The model has one fundamental shortcoming; an underlying hypothesis of the model is that exposure has the same effect on all individuals. What is required is a model that considers the basic effect of an exposure that is common to all individuals as well as interaction terms to account for complex differential effects of advertising exposures. A priori, these interactions are expected because of the superficial findings of the mean attitude change analysis.

To capture the interactive nature between exposure, prior attitudes, and brand familiarity, the following model was considered:

$$\begin{aligned}\Delta Z_{i,t,t+1} = \alpha &+ B_1 Z_{i,t} + B_2 Z^2_{i,t} + B_3\, exp_{i,t,t+1} \\ &+ B_4(Z_{i,t})(exp_{i,t,t+1}) \\ &+ B_5(exp_{i,t,t+1})(e^{-fam_{i,t}}) \\ &+ B_6(Z_{i,t})(exp_{i,t,t+1})(e^{-fam_{i,t}}) \\ &+ B_7(exp_{i,t,t+1})(eptd_{i,t}) \\ &+ B_8(Z_{i,t})(exp_{i,t,t+1})(eptd_{i,t}) \\ &+ B_9(exp_{i,t,t+1})(e^{-fam_{i,t}})(eptd_{i,t}) \\ &+ B_{10}(Z_{i,t})(exp_{i,t,t+1})(e^{-fam_{i,t}})(eptd_{i,t}) \\ &+ B_{11}(Z^2_{i,t})(exp_{i,t,t+1}) \\ &+ B_{12}(Z^2_{i,t})(exp_{i,t,t+1})(e^{-fam_{i,t}})\end{aligned}$$

Table 5

ESTIMATES OF SCOTT ATTITUDE CHANGE FUNCTION BY EXPOSURE PERIOD

Independent variables	*Exposure period 1*	*Exposure period 2*	*Exposure period 3*	*Exposure period 4*	*Combined exposure periods*
α (intercept)	.046	.028	.046	.010	.025
$Z_{i,t}$	−.289 (.033)[a]	−.169 (.028)	−.140 (.026)	n.s.	−.117 (.036)
$Z^2_{i,t}$	n.s.[b]	n.s.	n.s.	−.373 (.045)	−.181 (.081)
$(Z_{i,t})\ (exp_{i,t,t+1})\ (e^{-fam_{i,t}})\ (eptd_{i,t})$	—[c]	—	—	—	.287 (.119)
$(Z^2_{i,t})\ (exp_{i,t,t+1})\ (e^{-fam_{i,t}})$	−1.242 (.408)	n.s.	n.s.	n.s.	−1.371 (.313)
N	385	398	396	407	1586
R^2	.209	.082	.066	.144	.127

[a] Values in parentheses represent the standard errors of the estimated coefficients.
[b] Variable is not significant at the .05 level.
[c] Variable not considered since *eptd* is a constant in each given time period.

$$+ B_{13}(Z^2_{i,t})(exp_{i,t,t+1})(eptd_{i,t}) + B_{14}(Z^2_{i,t})(exp_{i,t,t+1})(e^{-\text{fam}_{i,t}})(eptd_{i,t}) + \mu_{i,t,t+1}$$

where:

$\Delta Z_{i,t,t+1}$, $Z_{i,t}$, and $exp_{i,t,t+1}$ are defined as before,

$\text{fam}_{i,t}$ = familiarity of individual i with advertised brand at time t [values range from 1 (lowest familiarity) to 6], and

$eptd_{i,t}$ = the number of previous advertising exposures received by individual i during the experiment.

It can be noted that models which consider the interactive effect of an advertising exposure greatly increase the number of required variables. The influence of demographic variables on the exposure effect has been considered [14] but these variables were noted for their lack of significance.

Table 6

ESTIMATES OF SCOTT ATTITUDE CHANGE FUNCTION BY FAMILIARITY LEVEL

Independent variables	*Low brand familiarity (1, 2)*	*Medium brand familiarity (3, 4)*	*High brand familiarity (5, 6)*
α (intercept)	.005	.073	.209
$Z_{i,t}$	n.s.[a]	−.317 (.042)	−.188 (.016)
$Z^2_{i,t}$	−.317 (.129)[b]	n.s.	n.s.
$(Z^2_{i,t})\ (exp_{i,t,t+1})$	−.785 (.238)	n.s.	n.s.
$(Z^2_{i,t})\ (exp_{i,t,t+1})\ (eptd_{i,t})$	.437 (.165)	n.s.	n.s.
N	38	159	1389
R^2	.422	.264	.089

[a] Variable is not significant at the .05 level.
[b] Values in parentheses represent the standard errors of the estimated coefficients.

THE STATISTICAL RESULTS

Scott Facial Tissue Analysis

Stepwise multiple regression analyses of Scott attitude change as a function of attitude, exposure, and familiarity variables resulted in the empirical models shown in Table 5. The first four analyses represent the data from one exposure period each, and these data were then pooled to form the combined analysis. The positive intercept as well as the negative coefficient of $Z_{i,t}$ and $Z^2_{i,t}$ suggest a "regression effect." Only the first exposure (in exposure period 1) was significant; in this case the exposure effect is interactive with the attitude prior to exposure, as well as brand familiarity prior to exposure.

The combined periods analysis includes a similar exposure effects term that is multiplied by $Z_{i,t}$ and $eptd_{i,t}$, the number of previous exposures. The positive coefficient indicates that each exposure has a decreasing effect on favorable attitude change.

The empirical model predicts that the individuals experiencing the most favorable attitude change are those who are unfamiliar and relatively unfavorable toward the brand prior to their first advertising exposure. It is important to remember that in the regression model there may exist some covariance between variables. Table 6, an analysis of attitude change for individuals in three brand familiarity levels, illustrates this point. The variables in the analysis are the same as before except terms that include the familiarity measure were excluded. Only those who were relatively unfamiliar with Scott tissues were significantly affected by exposure. For those who

Table 7

ESTIMATES OF SCOTT FAMILIARITY FUNCTION

Independent variables	*Combined exposure periods*
α(intercept)	5.9
$Z_{i,t}$	n.s.[a]
$Z^2_{i,t}$	−9.172 (.556)[b]
$eptd_{i,t}$	n.s.
N	1586
R^2	.146

[a] Variable is not significant at the .05 level.
[b] Values in parentheses represent the standard errors of the estimated coefficients.

Table 8

COMPARISON OF PRIOR ATTITUDE AND EXPOSURE EFFECTS ON FIRST AND SECOND PERIOD SCOTT ATTITUDE CHANGE

Prior attitude and exposure group[a]	$\Delta Z \leq -.02$[b]	$\Delta Z > -.02$
$Z_{i,t} \leq .30$[c,e] Exposed	11 (.367)	19 (.633)
$Z_{i,t} > .30$[c,f] Exposed	12 (.706)	5 (.294)
$Z_{i,t} \leq .30$[d,e] Unexposed	100 (.348)	187 (.652)
$Z_{i,t} > .30$[d,f] Unexposed	25 (.595)	17 (.404)

[a] Analysis for individuals with brand familiarity level = 2, 3, or 4.
[b] Negative ΔZ values represent favorable attitude change; positive ΔZ values represent unfavorable attitude change.
[c] χ^2 test significant, $p < .05$.
[d] χ^2 test significant, $p < .01$.
[e] χ^2 test not significant, $p \leq .10$.
[f] χ^2 test not significant, $p \leq .10$.

remained unfamiliar with the brand over several exposures, the term with $eptd_{i,t}$ reflects the decreasing attitude change. The regression result of brand familiarity as a function of brand attitude can be seen in Table 7. As expected, the group that holds the most unfavorable Scott attitude also tends to be the least familiar with the brand.

Another view of the attitude change process is provided by cross-classification analysis. Because of the distributions of the data, it was necessary to collapse the classification categories to yield minimum cell sizes. Table 8 illustrates initial attitude and exposure conditions when cross-classified with attitude change. An attempt was made to hold the previous exposure experience as well as the brand familiarity level constant by confining the analysis to first and second exposure levels and considering only individuals in the middle of the familiarity range (i.e., 2, 3, and 4). As expected, prior attitude interacts with exposure effect on attitude change; those experiencing the greatest favorable attitude change ($\Delta Z \leqslant -.02$) were those with the most unfavorable prior attitude. The exposure effect was significant only for the group with the most unfavorable prior attitude. The significance of prior attitude is particularly important since over 76% of the individuals in the more favorable group ($Z_{i,t} \leqslant .30$) were actually within the range $.20 < Z_{i,t} \leqslant .30$. As suggested by the regression analysis, attitude change of the unexposed group is dependent on prior attitude level. This indicates a strong probability of a measurement "regression effect."

Table 9

COMPARISON OF BRAND FAMILARITY AND EXPOSURE EFFECTS ON FIRST AND SECOND PERIOD SCOTT ATTITUDE CHANGE

Familiarity level prior to exposure[a]	$\Delta Z \leq -.08$[b]	$-.08 < \Delta Z \leq -.02$	$\Delta Z > -.02$
1, 2, 3 (Exposed)[c,d]	5 (.263)	9 (.474)	5 (.263)
4, 5 (Exposed)[c,e]	6 (.097)	18 (.290)	38 (.613)
6 (Exposed)[c,f]	21 (.146)	55 (.382)	68 (.472)
Unexposed group[d,e,f]	14 (.107)	38 (.290)	79 (.603)

[a] Analysis for individuals with prior attitude < .20.
[b] Negative ΔZ values represent favorable attitude change; positive ΔZ values represent unfavorable attitude change.
[c] χ^2 test: significant $p < .10$.
[d] χ^2 test: significant $p < .02$.
[e] χ^2 test: not significant $p \leq .10$.
[f] χ^2 test: significant $p < .10$.

Table 9 indicates the effect of brand familiarity on attitude change when exposure experience and prior attitude are held constant. It can be seen that the group experiencing the most favorable attitude change was the group with the lowest level of brand familiarity; it was this group alone which was significantly different than the unexposed group at the .05 level. The significant (.10 level) reaction of the high familarity group cannot be explained and, therefore, must be attributed to chance.

Table 10

ESTIMATES OF RESCUE ATTITUDE CHANGE FUNCTION BY EXPOSURE PERIOD

Independent variables	*Exposure period 1*	*Exposure period 2*	*Exposure period 3*	*Exposure period 4*	*Combined exposure periods*
α (intercept)	.019	.007	.005	—	.007
$(Z_{i,t})(exp_{i,t,t+1})$	−.191 (.028)[a]	n.s.	n.s.	n.s.	−.144 (.015)
$(Z_{i,t})(exp_{i,t,t+1})(eptd_{i,t})$	—[b]	—	—	—	.064 (.010)
$(Z^2_{i,t})(exp_{i,t,t+1})(e^{-fam_{i,t}})$	n.s.[c]	−.449 (.155)	1.77 (.431)	n.s.	n.s.
N	381	401	406	403	1591
R^2	.107	.021	.040	0	.057

[a] Values in parentheses represent the standard errors of the estimated coefficients.
[b] Variable not considered since *eptd* is a constant in each given time period.
[c] Variable is not significant at the .05 level.

Rescue Scouring Pad Analysis

A similar analysis plan was used to investigate Rescue scouring pads attitude change. The results of attitude change by exposure period can be seen in Table 10. During the first exposure, advertising effects are interactive with attitude prior to exposure; the absence of a significant brand familiarity interactive term is probably due to the fact that the brand was relatively unknown in the Lafayette area resulting in a strong correlation between initial attitude and familiarity. Period 2 analysis reflects the differential familiarity response to exposure and,

Table 11

ESTIMATES OF RESCUE ATTITUDE CHANGE FUNCTION BY FAMILIARITY LEVEL

Independent variables	*Low brand familiarity (1, 2)*	*Medium brand familiarity (3, 4)*	*High brand familiarity (5, 6)*
α (intercept)	.033	.005	—
$Z_{i,t}$	−.080 (.032)[a]	n.s.	n.s.
$(Z_{i,t})(exp_{i,t,t+1})$	−.138 (.023)	n.s.	n.s.
$(Z_{i,t})(exp_{i,t,t+1})(eptd_{i,t})$	.080 (.015)	n.s.	n.s.
$(Z^2_{i,t})\ (exp_{i,t,t+1})$	n.s.[b]	−.261 (.071)	n.s.
N	623	416	552
R^2	.098	.032	0

[a] Values in parentheses represent the standard errors of the estimated coefficients.

[b] Variable is not significant at the .05 level.

therefore, the interaction between prior attitude, exposure, and familiarity is not unexpected. The third exposure yielded a positive coefficient suggesting that those individuals who were exposed two previous times and remained unfavorable, perhaps experience a slight negative reaction to the exposure. In a manner similar to the facial tissue reaction, the fourth exposure produced no significant advertising response. The combined period analysis indicates a favorable response to advertising that decreases significantly with each additional exposure. The absence of the familiarity term suggests that the effect may be generalizable to a greater number of familiarity levels when compared with the corresponding Scott facial tissues analysis. The analysis of individual attitude change while holding brand familiarity level constant appears in Table 11. The results of the low familiarity group are congruent with previous findings, and exposure in this product class did have a significant effect on the medium level familiarity group. The lack of a number of previous exposures term is, most likely, due to the relation between brand familiarity and number of exposures.

Table 12

ESTIMATES OF RESCUE FAMILIARITY FUNCTION

Independent variables	*Combined exposure periods*
α (intercept)	5.458
$Z_{i,t}$	−11.438 (.664)[a]
$Z^2_{i,t}$	7.516 (.987)
$eptd_{i,t}$	.315 (.042)
N	1591
R^2	.375

[a] Values in parentheses represent the standard errors of the estimated coefficients.

It is interesting to note the difference between the two product categories. The facial tissue brands can probably be considered relatively homogeneous; only minute variations existed between the alternative brands. Scouring pads studied, however, included several product variations; two brands were of the conventional steel wool variety. Soettes and Rescue were abrasive "fabrics" cemented to sponge pads. Soettes offered high quantities of low useful life while the Rescue pads were offered with fewer pads per package, each pad being used for a longer duration. Thus it is quite possible that consumers who are familiar with the complex variety of offerings could reflect attitude changes following exposure. The attitude measure used is specifically geared to advertising that may attempt to induce changes in the salience of attributes as well as changes in perceptions of the brands' possessions of these attributes.

An analysis of Rescue brand familiarity appears in Table 12. For this relatively new brand it can be seen that there is significant correlation between familiarity and exposure as well as brand attitude.

In a manner similar to that of the facial tissue analysis, Table 13 indicates a significant interaction between prior attitude and exposure effect on attitude change; as before, the group with the more unfavorable prior attitude tended to experience the most favorable attitude change. Within the relatively favorable group over 70% were between .20 and .30 in prior attitude. Attitude also appears to interact with change for the unexposed group. The outcome of the regression analysis suggests that this may be due to variance differences between groups and not due to mean differences.

Table 14 holds attitude level relatively constant and considers the effect of the first and second exposure levels on attitude change for different familiarity levels. A comparison of exposed groups that differed in familiarity produced no significant difference. It must be noted, however, that the directions of change appear to be in the hypothesized direction. Each of the familiarity levels differed significantly when compared with the unexposed group.

DISCUSSION

The statistical results support the hypothesis that attitude change resulting from exposure is a function of the individual's attitude prior to exposure, the number of previous exposures, and brand familiarity. The validity of these conclusions depends on the validity of the data that were collected in the laboratory experiment.

In spite of attempts to disguise the true nature of the study, it is unlikely that a great many of the subjects did not understand that brand evaluation was an important part of the experiment. A danger of this is that the ex-

Table 13

COMPARISON OF PRIOR ATTITUDE AND EXPOSURE EFFECTS ON FIRST AND SECOND PERIOD RESCUE ATTITUDE CHANGE

Prior attitude and exposure group[a]	$\Delta Z \leq -.08$[b]	$-.08 < \Delta Z \leq -.04$	$-.04 < \Delta Z \leq -.02$	$-.02 < \Delta Z \leq 0$	$0 < \Delta Z \leq .04$	$.04 < \Delta Z$
$Z_{i,t} \leq .30$[c,e] Exposed	17 (.181)	8 (.085)	13 (.138)	11 (.117)	27 (.287)	18 (.191)
$Z_{i,t} > .30$[c,f] Exposed	17 (.279)	9 (.148)	7 (.115)	9 (.148)	6 (.098)	13 (.213)
$Z_{i,t} \leq .30$[d,e] Unexposed	4 (.023)[g]	14 (.080)[g]	17 (.097)	38 (.217)	71 (.406)	31 (.177)
$Z_{i,t} > .30$[d,f] Unexposed	22 (.130)	21 (.124)	13 (.077)	33 (.195)	33 (.195)	47 (.278)

[a] Analysis for individuals with brand familiarity level = 2, 3, or 4.
[b] Negative ΔZ values represent favorable attitude change; positive ΔZ values represent unfavorable attitude change.
[c] χ_2 test: significant at $p < .10$.
[d] χ_2 test: significant at $p < .001$.
[e] χ_2 test: significant at $p < .01$.
[f] χ_2 test: significant at $p < .10$.
[g] Columns 1 and 2 were collapsed for analysis.

posed group may have artificially reflected greater attitude change for the advertised brand. The results suggest that the level of subject compliance may have been low. Exposure effects were primarily significant during the first and second exposures, the periods when subjects were most likely unaware of the nature of the experiment. Secondly, there are no obvious reasons why the effects resulting from compliance would be interactive with brand familiarity and number of exposures; a significant noninteractive term might have suggested compliance. The statistical analysis suggests that if the effect of subject compliance did exist, the magnitude of this factor was small or the variance across respondents was large.

It is not possible to determine exactly the cause for the apparent low level of compliance. It is felt that linear attitude models, in addition to providing explanatory power and more information, may make it more difficult for the subject to artificially alter his attitude. Derived measures are somewhat more complex and require that the individual expend more effort to consciously alter his measurement.

SUMMARY AND CONCLUSIONS

The data from a large scale laboratory experiment, in general, support the research hypotheses of the effect of advertising on consumer brand attitudes. Subjects received a maximum of four advertising exposures in the four-week study, and a cross section analysis of the data revealed that only the first and second exposures provided a significant level of favorable attitude change. A combined analysis of the four exposure periods leads further to the acceptance of the hypotheses of decreasing marginal effectiveness of advertising exposures.

One category, scouring pads, revealed that brand familiarity was significantly related to advertising exposures. A more mature brand in the facial tissue category resulted in an insignificant relation between familiarity and exposures; this is most likely the result of high levels of brand familiarity prior to the experiment.

An attempt was made to hold prior attitudes and number of exposures constant while measuring the effect of attitude change as a function of brand familiarity level prior to exposure. The Scott analysis supported the research hypothesis that high levels of brand familiarity suppress the favorable attitude change produced by exposure. The analysis of Rescue scouring pads, however, resulted in no significant relationship between brand fa-

Table 14

COMPARISON OF BRAND FAMILIARITY AND EXPOSURE EFFECTS ON FIRST AND SECOND PERIOD RESCUE ATTITUDE CHANGE

Familiarity level prior to exposure[a]	$\Delta Z \leq -.08$[b]	$-.08 < \Delta Z \leq -.02$	$-.02 < \Delta Z \leq .02$	$.02 < \Delta Z$
1 (Exposed)[c,d]	67 (.360)	40 (.215)	35 (.188)	44 (.237)
2 (Exposed)[c,e]	11 (.212)	14 (.269)	17 (.327)	10 (.192)
3 (Exposed)[c,f]	11 (.268)	12 (.293)	11 (.268)	7 (.171)
4 (Exposed)[c,g]	9 (.265)	10 (.294)	5 (.147)	10 (.294)
5,6 (Exposed)[c,h]	9 (.180)	14 (.280)	16 (.320)	11 (.220)
Unexposed[d,e,f,g,h]	23 (.084)	52 (.190)	92 (.337)	106 (.388)

[a] Analysis for individuals with prior attitude > .20.
[b] Negative ΔZ values represent favorable attitude change; positive ΔZ values represent unfavorable attitude change.
[c] χ^2 test: not significant at $p \leq .10$.
[d] χ^2 test: significant at $p < .001$.
[e] χ^2 test: significant at $p < .01$.
[f] χ^2 test: significant at $p < .001$.
[g] χ^2 test: significant at $p < .01$.
[h] χ^2 test: significant at $p < .05$.

miliarity and attitude change. One possible explanation might be that the nonhomogeneous nature of the brands in the scouring pad category led to unstable value systems that were altered by advertising. Obviously, a tighter experimental design across many product categories is necessary before a firm conclusion is warranted.

In both product categories, the hypothesis that attitude change is proportional to amount of change advocated cannot be rejected. In terms of this experiment, the more unfavorable the attitude prior to exposure, the greater the favorable attitude change produced by the advertising. These findings are congruent with the theory that when dealing with low involvement issues, the latitude of acceptance for a communication may be so large that there is very little selectivity in the reception or perception of a message. Thus, for many products advertisers may not need to worry about messages being distorted. Further validation across a large number of product categories that span the involvement continuum is required.

This study clearly illustrates the limits of advertising persuasibility. While exposure does alter the values and perceptions of those who are unfamiliar with the brand, it has little effect on those who have been exposed previously or those who are familiar with the brand.

A common implicit assumption is that consumer attitude is positively related to a marketing decision-maker's objective function. If this is true, then new information may be required for effective media selection and advertising budgeting. Advertising copy can be revised when the relationship between component change and attitude change has been established. Nevertheless, the establishment of a link between attitudes and behavior (such as purchase behavior which can be related to objectives) must remain a key area for future effort by attitude researchers.

REFERENCES

1. Bass, Frank M. "A Simultaneous Equation Regression Study of Advertising and Sales of Cigarettes," *Journal of Marketing Research*, 6 (August 1969), 291–300.
2. Fishbein, Martin. "An Investigation of the Relationship Between Beliefs About an Object and the Attitude Toward that Object," *Human Relations*, 16 (August 1963), 233–9.
3. Freedman, Jonathan L. "Involvement, Discrepancy, and Change," *Journal of Abnormal and Social Psychology*, 69 (September 1964), 290–5.
4. Ginter, James L. "An Experimental Study of Attitude Change and Choice of New Brands," unpublished doctoral dissertation, Purdue University, 1972.
5. Hovland, Carl I., O. J. Harvey, and Muzafer Sherif. "Assimilation and Contrast Effects in Reactions to Communication and Attitude Change," *Journal of Abnormal and Social Psychology*, 55 (September 1957), 244–52.
6. Hovland, Carl I. and H. A. Pritzker. "Extent of Opinion Change as a Function of Amount of Change Advocated," *Journal of Abnormal and Social Psychology*, 54 (March 1957), 257–61.
7. Hupfer, Nancy T. and David M. Gardner. "Differential Involvement with Products and Issues: An Exploratory Study," Faculty Working Paper No. 21, College of Commerce and Business Administration, University of Illinois at Urbana-Champaign, 1971.
8. Lehmann, Donald R. "Television Show Preference: Application of a Choice Model," *Journal of Marketing Research*, 8 (February 1971), 47–55.
9. Palda, Kristian S. *The Measurement of Cumulative Advertising Effects*. Englewood Cliffs, N. J.: Prentice Hall, 1964.
10. Ray, Michael L. and Alan G. Sawyer. "Repetition in Media Models: A Laboratory Technique," *Journal of Marketing Research*, 8 (February 1971), 20–9.
11. Rosenberg, Milton J. "An Analysis of Affective-Cognitive Consistency," in M. J. Rosenberg et al., *Attitude Organization and Change: An Analysis of Consistency Among Attitude Components*. New Haven, Conn.: Yale University Press, 1960.
12. Sheth, Jagdish N. and W. Wayne Talarzyk. "Perceived Instrumentality and Value Importance as Determinants of Attitudes," *Journal of Marketing Research*, 9 (February 1972), 6–9.
13. Telser, Lester G. "Advertising and Cigarettes," *Journal of Political Economy*, 70 (October 1962), 471–99.
14. Winter, Frederick W. "A Laboratory Experimental Study of the Dynamics of Attitude and Choice Behavior," unpublished doctoral dissertation, Purdue University, 1972.
15. ——— and James L. Ginter. "An Experiment in Inducing and Measuring Changes in Brand Attitudes," *Proceedings*. Fall Conference, American Marketing Association, 1971, 411–5.
16. Zajonc, Robert B. "Attitudinal Effects of Mere Exposure," *Journal of Personality and Social Psychology*, Monograph Supplement, 9 (June 1968), 1–27.

Impact of Different Comparison Sets on Evaluation of a New Subcompact Car Brand

JOHN U. FARLEY
JERROLD KATZ
DONALD R. LEHMANN*

To reduce the burden on subjects, a five-wave national telephone panel used to track the introduction of a new brand of subcompact automobile evaluated a different subset of competing brands. MANOVA revealed significant differences in the evaluation of both the new brand and an established brand.

Complex longitudinal and cross-sectional research designs may involve subsegments of a sample being asked different questions or only some of the questions in a given study. In the case of attitude items, for example, the number of objects under study and the number of attributes of each object may combine to make a questionnaire burdensome for a subject, especially when remeasurement is involved. In this case a particular subject may be asked to evaluate only a subset of attributes or objects. In longitudinal studies (particularly panel designs), systematic changes in knowledge may be incorporated into a question structure which changes over time with questions added and others dropped as useful information accrues or as new issues become relevant.

This situation may arise in many settings—in market research with changes in a competitive environment, such as with the introduction of the new brand described here, in political polls, as candidates enter or leave races, or in public opinion polling as major external events raise new and important policy issues. As a practical matter, it is usually vital to modify survey instruments to reflect these environmental changes, and it is equally vital to be able to assess any systematic components in responses that can be attributed to changes in the stimulus sets.

This paper investigates systematic patterns in evaluation by potential consumers of a new brand of subcompact automobile when subgroups of a panel are asked to evaluate the new brand with different pairings of seven competing brands. The hypothesis is that evaluation of the new brand is systematically related to the particular groupings of other brands included on a given questionnaire. If such an effect is isolated, adjustment would be required to remove it in developing procedures to track impact of the introduction of the new brand (Farley, Howard, and Lehmann 1976). The results may have broader implications for survey research in fields other than marketing and for other than attitudinal measurements.

MEASUREMENT OF ATTITUDE AND ATTITUDE CHANGE

Attitude and attitude change provide key inputs for major classes of behavioral research. Summaries of attitude research in terms of history, theory, and application cover a wide range of fields (McGuire 1973; Pool and Schramm 1973)—communications, education, marketing and advertising, public opinion polling, politics, safety behavior, race relations, cultural differences and patterns, and family relationships, to name just a few.

In addition to these many substantive areas, measurement issues arise in assessing systematic effects on attitude measurements of concomitant variables often not central to the major purpose of study. Examples which have been reported in a variety of fields (Hovland, Janis, and Kelley 1953) include effects of prestige and credibility of data sources and effects of surroundings or other distractions. Attitude measurements have also been shown to vary systematically due to differences in measurement techniques and in such stimulus set characteristics as the number of scale points and

* John U. Farley is Professor and Donald R. Lehmann is Associate Professor, both at the Graduate School of Business, Columbia University, New York, NY 10027. Jerrold Katz is Associate Professor, Graduate School, Simmons College, Boston, MA 02115. The authors are indebted to John A. Howard for guidance and help.

Reprinted with permission from *Journal of Consumer Research,* 5 (September 1978), 138-42.

order of items on questionnaires (Green and Carmone 1970; Green and Rao 1970; Hulbert and Lehmann 1975).

Method

Measures. For each of eight competing brands of subcompact automobiles, ten-point semantic differential scales were developed using items from an earlier pilot study (Farley, Howard, and Weinstein 1974) to evaluate ten attributes:

1. Resale value
2. Gas economy
3. Value for money
4. Overall appearance of the car's exterior
5. Ease and fun of driving
6. Simplicity of design and easy maintenance
7. Reliability and quality
8. Pickup and acceleration
9. Price
10. Availability of desired special features

In addition, for each brand, measurements were made with ten-point scales of overall attitude, perceived degree of knowledge, intention to buy and confidence in ability to make judgments about each brand. Likelihood of buying any brand of the product class within three months and within two years was similarly measured, and socio-demographic descriptors of each responding family were also collected. The variable set was designed for use in tracking changes in these measurements over the course of the introduction of the new brand.

Subjects. Data were collected in a five-wave national telephone panel. Initial contacts were made to randomly selected telephone numbers, and the panel was composed of persons who responded positively to a screening question about interest in purchasing a subcompact car. The panel was maintained for 18 months, with two waves of data collected before, and three after, the introduction of the new brand. The first wave was used only for benchmark purposes as it was collected before any details about the new brand were available to the public.

In all, 709 respondents completed all five waves of interviewing, representing 44 percent of respondents completing the first wave. The substantial falloff of sample size over waves, caused chiefly by refusals to continue in the panel, constitutes a major problem facing longitudinal studies using multi-wave panels. Sobol (1959) for example, reports a 64 percent survival rate in a five-wave panel study using an instrument much simpler than the one used here.

The amount of information collected on each wave of interviews was considerable, requiring between 50 and 70 minutes per respondent. Interviewee fatigue and high rates of termination were evident in pretesting an even longer instrument in which respondents evaluated each of eight competing brands that constituted the product class. To deal with these problems, the eight brands studied were divided into four groups of three each, with the new brand (Brand H) in each group and the existing brand with largest national sales (Brand A) in two of the four groups.

The result was a five-wave panel design with four groups of brands within each wave as follows:

Group	*Brands*	*Sample size*
1	A, D, H (New)	192
2	A, E, H (New)	171
3	B, F, H (New)	169
4	C, G, H (New)	177

Potential subjects were assigned randomly to each group before the first wave of interviewing. A check on the random group assignment was provided by four-group discriminant analyses performed on two-halves formed by randomly splitting respondents to the first-wave sample. The discriminant functions used six demographic explanatory variables: sex of respondent, age, family income, education of head of household, number of drivers in the household, and a dummy variable, set to one if the principal user of a subcompact car would be a minor. Insignificant Mahalanobis D^2 values of 17.5 and 13.1, respectively, for the two halves of the sample indicate that the assignment of subjects to groups produced comparable subsamples on the basis of these demographic measurements.

Procedure

Because measurements on the individual attributes were found to be correlated in an earlier study (Farley, Howard, and Weinstein 1974), multivariate analysis of variance (MANOVA) was used to assess differences among groups and among waves.

MANOVA resembles analysis of variance (ANOVA), except that the dependent variable for each observation is a vector (in this case, a vector of fourteen scale values) rather than a single number. While the generalization of the ANOVA model is straightforward, special attention must be paid to construction of simultaneous tests for groups of mean differences when elements of the multivariate dependent variable are correlated (Press 1971).

Results

The MANOVA results for Brand H (Table 1) show relatively large differences across waves, significant but smaller differences across groups, and a barely significant interaction between groups and waves. Univariate tests of individual measurements indicate sig-

TABLE 1

MANOVA OF GROUPS, INTERVIEWING WAVES, AND GROUPS × WAVE INTERACTIONS FOR EVALUATION OF TWO BRANDS OF SUBCOMPACT AUTOMOBILE

Item	Brand H (new) Group	Brand H (new) Wave	Brand H (new) Group × wave	Brand A (established) Group	Brand A (established) Wave	Brand A (established) Group × wave
Wilks' lambda criterion on canonical roots:						
F ratio	3.821**	18.987**	1.323*	2.138**	3.919**	1.303
Degrees of freedom	42,8328	42,8328	126,21456	14,1431	42,4246	42,4246
			Univariate *F* ratios			
General						
Perceived knowledge about the brand	7.364**	193.51**	1.647	6.069*	.669	0.978
Overall attitude toward the brand	.741	31.106**	3.148**	4.287*	.423	0.541
Intention to purchase the brand	2.281	.289	1.483	4.106*	1.648	0.901
Confidence in evaluation of the brand	12.408**	90.216**	.859	1.922	.240	1.245
Attributes						
Resale value	2.482	1.181	2.260*	1.215	1.201	0.345
Gas economy	.644	14.643**	4.076**	1.888	2.931*	1.240
Value for money	3.674*	9.923**	2.676**	4.591*	2.426	0.200
Exterior appearance	4.232**	31.698**	3.758**	0.320	0.043	2.098
Ease and fun of driving	1.748	27.582**	1.811	0.393	16.522**	0.720
Simplicity of design and easy maintenance	.676	2.781*	2.722**	1.494	2.005	1.282
Reliability and quality	5.299**	1.625	1.592	1.630	3.061*	0.561
Pickup and acceleration	6.851**	4.193**	1.678	0.152	0.544	1.955
Price	.441	11.514**	1.939*	2.056	0.379	1.577
Availability of desired special features	3.405*	33.573**	2.691**	0.260	2.124	2.773*

Note: * denotes significance at $\alpha = .05$; ** denotes significance at $\alpha = .01$.

nificant inter-group differences for seven variables, but significant inter-wave differences for eleven variables showing impact of the introductory marketing program on the new brand.

The MANOVA on the established brand (Brand A) also has significant intergroup differences, with four significant inter-group differences on individual variables indicated by the univariate tests. Differences over waves, while significant, are traceable almost entirely to changes in the evaluation of the car in terms of "Ease and Fun of Driving." The group-by-wave interaction is not significant.

Mean values (Table 2) show that the established brand outscored the new brand over the course of the entire study on twelve of the fourteen attributes, in seven cases by more than one scale point. In all but one case ("Gas Economy," which was the key marketing feature of the established brand and which had a significantly smaller variance), standard deviations for a given attribute were within 0.6 scale points across brands.

The contrasts for the two MANOVA's show much greater movement in evaluations over time than over groups. In no case does a set of group contrasts span a range greater than a single scale point for either brand, and there is no distinct sign pattern in the inter-group contrasts. The effects of grouping on measurement, while significant, are relatively small. By comparison, in seven cases the wave contrasts for the new brand range more than a scale point. Further, the signs show a consistent inter-wave pattern of increase from Wave 2 to Wave 5, with all Wave 2 contrasts negative and all Wave 5 contrasts positive.

The largest contrasts of all involved increased familiarity with the new brand over the introduction, with gains of more than two scale points over the course of the introduction in perceived knowledge about the new brand and in confidence in the individual's ability to make judgments about the new brand. The smallest inter-wave contrast for the new brand involved the key surrogate for behavior—intention to buy—which was the only individual variable showing no significant differences over groups, waves, or in group-by-wave interaction for that brand. For the established brand, none of the overall measurements were affected significantly by the entry of the competitive brand. Three attributes changed significantly over waves, but only one changed by one full scale point over waves, "Ease and Fun of Driving."

SUMMARY

Members of a five-wave national telephone panel designed to track the introduction of a new brand of subcompact automobile were randomly assigned to one of four groups in order to ease the burden of responding

TABLE 2

GROUP AND WAVE MANOVA CONTRASTS FOR TWO BRANDS OF SUBCOMPACT AUTOMOBILE

Item	Brand	Contrast: Group[a] 1	2	3	4	Wave 2	3	4	5	Mean	Standard deviation
General											
Perceived knowledge about brand	H	−.002	−.164	−.168	.334	−1.716	.101	.657	.958	3.263	2.527
	A	.165	−.165			.152	−.072	−.050	−.030	6.507	2.558
Overall attitude toward brand	H	.047	.094	−.085	.056	−.755	−.026	.275	.506	5.230	2.645
	A	.159	−.159			−.008	−.045	−.089	.142	6.244	2.914
Intention to purchase brand	H	−.100	−.016	−.030	.146	−.015	−.029	.008	.052	1.732	1.844
	A	−.114	.114			2.13	−.070	.123	−.266	1.851	2.137
Confidence in evaluation of brand	H	−.299	−.176	−.156	.571	−1.472	.209	.452	.811	4.154	2.986
	A	.106	−.106			.040	−.075	−.035	.070	6.800	2.896
Attributes											
Resale value	H	−.017	.044	.179	−.206	−.135	.128	−.013	.020	5.746	2.672
	A	.026	−.026			−.008	.175	−.095	−.072	8.267	2.127
Gas economy	H	.034	−.028	−.091	.085	−.538	.179	.223	.136	7.002	2.540
	A	−.049	.049			.049	.133	−.043	−.139	9.033	1.357
Value for money	H	.019	.210	.016	−.245	−.456	.132	.191	.133	6.442	2.602
	A	.124	−.124			.140	.169	−.124	−.185	7.952	2.213
Exterior appearance	H	−.213	.138	.192	−.117	−.789	.099	.302	.388	6.759	2.604
	A	.041	−.041			.001	.004	.020	−.025	5.679	2.379
Ease and fun of driving	H	−.154	.091	.125	−.062	−.780	.262	.155	.363	6.459	2.700
	A	.044	−.044			−.859	.326	.297	.236	6.497	2.701
Simplicity of design and easy maintenance	H	−.048	.105	.015	−.168	−.238	.138	.045	.055	6.568	2.553
	A	.078	−.078			.245	−.001	−.073	−.171	7.245	2.443
Reliability and quality	H	−.052	.104	.233	−.285	−.180	.089	.066	.025	6.330	2.565
	A	.080	−.080			.328	−.097	−.084	−1.97	7.512	2.395
Pickup and acceleration	H	−.094	.083	.304	.293	−.289	.051	1.46	.092	6.240	2.574
	A	.025	−.025			.123	.031	−.079	−.075	5.787	2.425
Price	H	−.081	.068	.031	−.018	−.495	.087	.226	.182	6.810	2.620
	A	−.085	.085			−.013	.097	−.024	−.010	7.720	2.264
Availability of desired special features	H	−.222	.127	.178	−.083	−.886	.212	.338	.518	6.230	2.769
	A	.038	−.038			−.336	.040	.139	.157	6.004	2.878

[a] Brand A not studied in groups 3 or 4.

to a questionnaire. Each group evaluated only the new brand and two of seven other brands in the product category.

Ratings of the new brand changed over time in the expected direction. Moreover, significant differences in evaluation were found among the interviewing groups for both the new and an established brand. This suggests that analysis using the entire sample should use an adjustment procedure, e.g., including group and wave dummy variables in regressions. The magnitudes of the adjustment needed will depend on the relative homogeneity of the comparison brands.

[*Received December 1977. Revised April 1978.*]

REFERENCES

Farley, J. U., Howard, J., and Lehmann, D. R. (1976), "A 'Working' System Model of Car Behavior," *Management Science*, 23, 235–47.

———, Howard, J., and Weinstein, D. (1974), "The Relationship of Liking and Choice to Attributes of an Alternative and their Saliency," *Multivariate Behavioral Research*, 9, 27–36.

Green, P., and Carmone, F. (1970), *Multidimensional Scaling and Related Techniques in Marketing Analysis*, Boston: Allyn & Bacon, Inc.

———, and Rao, V. (1970), Applied Multidimensional Scaling: A Comparison of Approaches and Algorithms, New York: Holt, Rinehart and Winston, Inc.

Hovland, C., Janis, I., and Kelley, H. (1953), *Communication and Persuasion,* New Haven: Yale University Press.

Hulbert, J., and Lehmann, D. (1975), "Assessing the Importance of the Sources of Error in Structured Survey Data," in *Control of "Error" in Market Research Data,* eds. J. Farley and J. Howard, Lexington, MA: Lexington Books, 81–108.

McGuire, W. J. (1973), "The Nature of Attitude and Attitude Change," in *The Handbook of Social Psychology,* eds. G. Lindzey and E. Aronson, Reading, MA: Addison-Wesley Publishing Co., 136–314.

Pool, I. S., and Schramm, W. (1973), *Handbook of Communication,* Chicago: Rand McNally.

Press, S. J., (1971), *Applied Multivariate Analysis,* New York: Holt, Rinehart and Winston, Inc., 239–57.

Sobol, M. (1959) "Panel Mortality and Panel Bias," *Journal of the American Statistical Association,* 54, 52–68.

Consumer Acquisition Patterns for Durable Goods

JACK J. KASULIS
ROBERT F. LUSCH
EDWARD F. STAFFORD, JR.*

Durable goods will be the fastest growing sector of the consumer market in the 1980's. Through Guttman scalogram analysis, consumer acquisition patterns for twelve heterogeneous durables are examined. Ownership patterns are compared through split-half analyses, across data collected in two consecutive years, and between types of dwelling units.

Three families are in the process of purchasing a major consumer durable. What will each purchase—another car, a microwave oven, a freezer, or some other item? Is there some underlying priority schema that consumers use in determining which durables to buy? If a schema exists, does it differ for those who own a home, rent one, or live in an apartment? In this article we examine the extent to which there is a common utility structure for major durables across the population. Priority patterns are assessed for twelve major household durables, and the reliability of the findings are examined through an analysis of split-half samples and data collected from two separate calendar years.

For a variety of reasons, including the increased size of the 18- to 34-year-old age group and the rise of affluence in young adults, the fastest growing sector of the consumer market in the early 1980's will be durable goods (Reynolds and Wells 1977). This situation will attract a great deal of attention by practitioners and academics alike.

This subject is also of interest to researchers who are attempting to understand the consumer behavior process, e.g., home economists, marketers, and social psychologists. In the classical sense, the acquisition of a durable is a discretionary purchase. But in today's society, there is sufficient discretionary income for everyone to be in the market for a durable at one time or another. The examination of priority patterns of acquisition may be viewed as an attempt to determine which durables are perceived more as necessities and which are considered frills, bought only as additional discretionary dollars become available. Beyond the focus on consumption behavior regarding durables are the issues of adoption of innovations, the acquisition patterns of time-saving appliances, and others, which warrant study.

The goal of this research is primarily descriptive, and to a lesser extent, explanatory. Although attempts should be made to explain how consumers accumulate durable goods, it is also important to describe the order in which they are acquired. In science, there is no single correct "logic of discovery." Descriptive research is likely to be just as useful in the discovery process as other available modes (Hunt 1976). However, although our research goal is primarily descriptive, our approach is not totally lacking in explanatory orientation. In fact, the analytical technique used to describe acquisition patterns assumes that all consumers have similar utility structures. If the analytical technique uncovers a common acquisition pattern, then we have an indication that our assumption was reasonable. This being the case, we have the beginning of an explanatory model. Subsequent research can then focus on the explanation of the observed behavior.

THEORETICAL BACKGROUND

Few people in our society are able to acquire all the goods desired at the same time. Income is received over time, and income and credit are limited. Thus, consumers need to prioritize, or order, their acquisition of goods, particularly regarding those that are high priced, such as household durables. In a real sense, particular household durables are competing for a fixed set of consumer dollars. The order in which durables are acquired is an indication of the utility structure for a

*Jack J. Kasulis is MBA Program Director and Assistant Professor, Division of Marketing, Robert F. Lusch is Director of the Division of Marketing and Associate Professor, and Edward F. Stafford, Jr., is Assistant Professor, Division of Management, all at the University of Oklahoma, Norman, OK 73019. The authors gratefully acknowledge the role of Phil Stout and Jim Williams of the Oklahoma Publishing Company in the collection and use of the Continuing Consumer Audit data base.

Reprinted with permission from *Journal of Consumer Research,* 6 (June 1979), 47-57.

particular family. Although classical economic theory does not deal with the consumption of durables over time, one could reasonably hypothesize that consumers acquire goods to maximize the present value of their utility function. Given knowledge of future prices, consumer incomes, and the utility function, one could theoretically determine the order in which consumers will acquire durables in the future. Furthermore, if all consumers had similar utility structures, one could predict the particular order in which *all* consumers acquire goods.

Consider, for example, the existence of k durable goods. Mathematically there would be $k!$ possible patterns of acquisition. However, if one tentatively accepts the notion that there is a common order of acquisition for all consumers, then only one of the possible $k!$ patterns represents the underlying hierarchy for the population. Such a pattern could be represented as: D_1, D_2, D_3, . . . D_k. D_1 would be acquired first, then D_2, and so on, until D_k is acquired. Second or third units of a particular durable may be treated as separate products and designated with their own D_ks.

The necessity of prioritizing the acquisition of durables and the potential value of finding similar utility structures has led to several studies examining whether there is a common order of acquisition for consumer durables (Pyatt 1964; Paroush 1965; McFall 1969; Hebden and Pickering 1974; Lusch, Stafford, and Kasulis 1978). The outcome of this research is somewhat encouraging, and can be summarized as follows:

1. All the preceding research concluded that the populations under study could be characterized as having a common order of acquisition for the durables examined.
2. The pattern of acquisition in some cases varied by population group and in other cases remained consistent across groups. For example, Hebden and Pickering (1974) found that the acquisition pattern for five leisure goods varied by social class, and the pattern for five diverse goods varied by family life cycle. McFall (1969) demonstrated that the pattern for 17 consumer durables varied by income and urban/rural consumers. On the other hand, Paroush (1965) found that for families in Israel, the order of acquiring a set of four durables was identical regardless of the continent of birth and duration of residence.
3. Acquisition patterns have been observed for both homogeneous goods (McFall 1969; Paroush 1965; and Lusch et al. 1978) and heterogeneous goods (Hebden and Pickering 1974). A homogeneous set of goods consists of goods capable of performing similar or highly related functions (e.g., kitchen appliances), whereas a heterogeneous set of goods consists of goods capable of performing quite different and unrelated functions (e.g., TV, car, dryer, stereo, freezer).
4. The underlying priority patterns have been revealed by a variety of analytical techniques. They have included the Guttman coefficient of reproducibility (Paroush 1965; McFall 1969), the point correlation matrix (Paroush 1965), a matrix of conditional probabilities (Hebden and Pickering 1974), a dynamic Bayesian differential equation model (Pyatt 1964), and a multiple criteria evaluation procedure combining the work of Guttman, Loevinger, Kuder-Richardson, and Green (Lusch et al. 1978).

While the contributions of the previously mentioned research are recognized, there is need for more study of consumer durable acquisition patterns. The focus of this article is directed to two broad research hypotheses:

H1: There is an underlying order of acquisition for a large set of heterogeneous durables.

H2: There is a difference in the order of acquisition for a large set of heterogeneous durables across dwelling units.

In examining these hypotheses, this article contributes to the literature in the following ways:

1. The specific set of durables examined have not previously been explored.
2. The data analyzed are a large representative sample of a major metropolitan market not previously examined, except in the Lusch et al. (1978) study of five kitchen durables.
3. Recognizing that prioritization patterns may change over time, the more current data of this study provide additional insight.
4. The impact of a recent innovation on the pattern of acquisition is examined.
5. The impact of second purchase durables (e.g., second vehicles) on the pattern of acquisition is examined.
6. Only one other study examined such a large set of durables, and that study dealt with a more homogeneous set of items (McFall 1969).
7. The relationship of dwelling unit on the priority patterns is examined.
8. The internal validity of the results is examined through an analysis of split-half samples, and the longitudinal reliability is tested across two years of data.

METHODOLOGY

The empirical analysis focuses on the ownership of twelve household durables: (1) clothes dryer, (2) dishwasher, (3) freezer, (4) microwave oven, (5) range, (6) refrigerator, (7) stereo or tape player, (8) first television, (9) second television, (10) first vehicle, (11) second vehicle, and (12) washer. These are common durables acquired by American consumers, and their substantive costs require household prioritization.

Several other factors make this set of items especially interesting. The durables represent three major categories—kitchen durables, entertainment items, and transportation vehicles. The selection of such a diverse group of items probably decreases the likelihood of finding a common priority pattern. However, inasmuch as a consumer's budget is not realistically confined to a subset of the items, it is important to include all of them. One major exclusion is a house. It was excluded because one's dwelling is thought to be a potential determinant of the priority patterns. Therefore, type of dwelling is used as a market segmentation variable wherein prioritization patterns are analyzed.

An additional point of interest is that the set of durables includes a microwave oven. By examining this innovation, one can see the extent to which an innovation cuts across established acquisition patterns or is acquired only by those who own the other eleven items. Finally, multiple ownership of televisions and vehicles was studied. This is the first time multiple ownership has been examined in the literature. It was thought to be appropriate, because second purchases of these items compete for the same scarce consumer resources as the first purchases of other items.

Subjects

The data were obtained from the DRP/OPUBCO Continuing Consumer Audit. The Distribution Research Program (DRP) at the University of Oklahoma and the Oklahoma Publishing Company (OPUBCO) collaborate in the collection of data on the purchasing behavior of individuals in the Oklahoma City Standard Metropolitan Statistical Area (SMSA). Reported in this article are some findings from the 1975 audit, which included 1,747 respondents, and the 1976 audit, which included 2,025 respondents. The sample is a stratified, random cluster, representative of the populations in geographic regions in the Oklahoma City SMSA. Subjects from urban, suburban, and rural areas are included. All types of dwelling units—houses, apartments, condominiums, trailers—are included. New samples are drawn each year with the distribution of the sample reflecting population changes in the strata.

Procedure

The Consumer Audit questionnaire is administered in a personal interview with both the male and female heads of the household responding. The interviewer is directed to a specific address as a starting point in a cluster of three or four residences. The starting point is a randomly selected location within the geographical strata. The interviewer is instructed to obtain a designated number of completed interviews from adjacent residences. Each visit is a "cold" call with no pre-visit contact made to request cooperation; the first contact is when the doorbell is rung. The respondents are told the study is being conducted by the University of Oklahoma and the interview will last at least one hour. If necessary, the interviewer will arrange an appointment for a more convenient time.

"Not-at-home" families are revisited at different hours of the day (three times) before a substitute respondent is designated for the interview. After three not-at-home visits or a refusal, a neighbor's house in the cluster is assigned as a substitute. Approximately 50 percent of the households selected complete the interview. Of the other 50 percent, approximately one-half are refusals and one-half are not-at-home.

The data are collected continuously throughout the year by professional interviewers, under close supervision. Each week completed questionnaires are returned for processing. Telephone callbacks are made within three days of the return to verify the data collection. In addition, subjects may be telephoned again to obtain clarification of responses, if needed.

Analysis

The stock of durables that a household possesses can be characterized by a multivariate distribution of 0's and 1's. A value of "one" would depict possession of the durable and a "zero" nonpossession. If consumers have relatively similar utility structures for a large set of heterogeneous goods, the data on durable ownership can be described in terms of a unidimensional scaling model. For example, if one considers five durables, a logically consistent conceptual model would be theoretically characterized by the pattern exhibited in Table 1. The data in this table indicate the order of acquisition to be D_1, D_2, D_3, D_4, D_5. If it is observed that each consumer fits any one of the patterns (rows), then one could transform the multivariate data into a unidimensional scale. Thus, by only knowing the last durable acquired, one can perfectly predict a consumer's total stock of durables and the durable to be purchased next. In other words, if the last durable added to one's stock of durables was D_3, then one would know that D_1 and D_2 were also owned, but not D_4 and D_5. Furthermore, the next durable to be acquired would be D_4.

Clearly, not all consumers will acquire a set of durables in the same pattern. Deviations will inevitably exist. The task is to determine whether this divergence

TABLE 1

SIX OWNERSHIP SITUATIONS REPRESENTING A PERFECT SCALE PATTERN FOR FIVE DURABLES

	Durables				
Scale score	D_5	D_4	D_3	D_2	D_1
S_5	1	1	1	1	1
S_4	0	1	1	1	1
S_3	0	0	1	1	1
S_2	0	0	0	1	1
S_1	0	0	0	0	1
S_0	0	0	0	0	0

is sufficiently large for the perfect model to be considered unrealistic for the real world. Thus, some measure of scalability is needed to empirically test the appropriateness of the model.

Guttman (1971) developed a scaling model called *scalogram analysis,* which may be applied to this task, even though it was originally devised for a different purpose (attitude measurement). In the discussion of attitudinal dispositions and the role of scalogram analysis, Guttman stated that ". . .the universe is said to be scalable for the population if it is possible to rank the people from high to low in such a fashion that from a person's rank alone we can reproduce his response to each of the items in a simple fashion" (Guttman 1971, p. 188). In this article, Guttman's ranking procedure is used to examine durable priority patterns. Such an approach has been used previously by Paroush (1965), McFall (1969), and Lusch et al. (1978).

Guttman scaling has been traditionally used with cross-sectional data to rank an individual's attitude toward an object. In this study, Guttman scaling is used to model the temporal phenomenon of consumers acquiring discretionary durable goods. Although the data used are cross-sectional, it is possible to scale the underlying temporal phenomenon. As the sample is large and the interviewing procedure is tightly controlled, it is reasonable to assume that the sample represents a true cross section of the entire population of the Oklahoma City SMSA. Therefore, individuals at all stages in the order of the acquisition process will be represented in the sample. And, because this cross section of individuals is at various stages in the acquisition process, conclusions can be drawn about the order of acquisition over time.

The thesis of this paper is that the twelve durables mentioned earlier tend to be acquired in a designated priority pattern, with the "more difficult" durables being acquired only after the "less difficult" items. In this context, a lesser degree of difficulty is synonymous with higher levels of expected utility derived from the ownership of the durables. Among the various scaling techniques available, the Guttman approach is almost unique in its possession of this cumulative property (Nie, Hau, Jenkins, Steinbrenner, and Bent 1975).

The results of the Guttman analysis are tested for statistical significance by using the Green (1956) technique for assessing the quality of Guttman scaling. The ownership patterns are compared for 1975 and 1976, and the reliability of the results are further analyzed by using split-halves. The analyses of priority patterns are also extended to include an assessment of the importance of a respondent's dwelling unit. Priority patterns are examined separately for those who own their dwelling and for those who rent their dwelling. Renters are further analyzed by looking at whether the respondent rents a house or an apartment/duplex.

RESULTS AND ANALYSIS

With twelve durables, there are 4,096 (2^{12}) possible ownership combinations. In the case of 2^k, the k depicts the number of durables and the 2 indicates the class of ownership—own or not own. Of these 4,096 combinations, $k + 1$ or 13 situations would characterize the perfect Guttman scale. If we take any one of these 13 ownership combinations in which i items are owned, these items could have been obtained in any of $i!$ different permutations. Nevertheless, only one of these $i!$ permutations matches the perfect acquisition scale. The Guttman coefficient tests whether the frequency distribution of ownership on the i items reflects a perfect scale when applied to all 13 ownership combinations.

Table 2 presents the underlying priority patterns for each of the analyses performed. The durables are ranked from one to twelve, with a one indicating the first item acquired, a two the second, and so on. The numbers in parentheses below the asset rankings depict the percentage of the sample owning each durable. Table 2 summarizes the 14 separate scalogram analyses performed for this study. (Each row comes from a separate scalogram table.)[1]

The Figure represents a tree diagram of the different analyses performed herein. Thus, one can see that, first, an examination was made of the total sample. The second stage of analysis was to divide the total sample into dwelling owners and renters, as renters may depend on the landlord or furniture rentals for many durables, and therefore their priority patterns may be different. Stage three further segments the study of renters into those who rent a house and those who rent an apartment or duplex. People who rent a house may perceive themselves as being more transient than those who rent an apartment, and the landlord of a house may provide a different set of appliances than a landlord of an apartment. The analysis represented by the tree is duplicated for the 1975 data and the 1976 data. Below each of the nodes of the tree are the measures of scalability. The first number is Green's *index of reproducibility*.[2] Note that in every case the index of reproducibility is significant at the 0.001 level. The bottom number is Green's *index of consistency*.

---

[1]This summary was done for reasons of simplicity. The separate scalogram tables may be obtained from the authors.

[2]Green's approach to establishing the reliability of a scale depends not on the scale item and test variances, as do most other reliability measures, but rather on the summary statistics of the sampling results obtained when a scale is designated. Green's measures, along with other scale reliability measures (Green, Kuder-Richardson, and Loevinger), and the associated statistical equations are described and compared by Lusch, Stafford, and Kasulis (1978). Additionally, a technical appendix that details the calculations necessary to derive these reliability measures is available from these authors.

TABLE 2

OWNERSHIP RANK ORDERS AND FREQUENCIES FOR TWELVE DURABLES BY ANALYSIS GROUP

Stage analyses	Micro-wave oven	Freezer	Second TV	Dish-washer	Second vehi-cle	Dryer	Stereo or tape player	Washer	Range	Refrig-erator	First vehi-cle	First TV
Stage One												
(1) Full Sample (1975) (n = 1747)	12[a] (3)[b]	11 (34)	10 (30)	9 (40)	8 (59)	7 (67)	6 (73)	5 (77)	4 (88)	3 (90)	2 (92)	1 (97)
(2) Split Half I (1975) (n = 867)	12 (3)	11 (34)	10 (33)	9 (42)	8 (59)	7 (69)	6 (73)	5 (79)	4 (89)	3 (90)	2 (93)	1 (97)
(3) Split Half II (1975) (n = 880)	12 (3)	11 (35)	9 (39)	10 (39)	8 (60)	7 (66)	6 (73)	5 (76)	4 (87)	3 (90)	2 (92)	1 (97)
(4) Full Sample (1976) (n = 2025)	12 (5)	11 (38)	9 (49)	10 (40)	8 (60)	7 (63)	6 (74)	5 (77)	4 (88)	3 (90)	2 (92)	1 (97)
(5) Split Half I (1976) (n = 1009)	12 (4)	11 (38)	9 (49)	10 (39)	8 (61)	7 (67)	6 (75)	5 (76)	4 (88)	2 (91)	3 (91)	1 (97)
(6) Split Half II (1976) (n = 1016)	12 (6)	11 (38)	9 (48)	10 (41)	8 (60)	7 (68)	6 (73)	5 (77)	4 (88)	3 (90)	2 (92)	1 (97)
Stage Two												
(7) Owners (1975) (n = 1323)	12 (4)	11 (42)	10 (45)	9 (50)	8 (66)	6 (78)	7 (75)	5 (88)	1 (99)	2 (99)	4 (95)	3 (98)
(8) Owners (1976) (n = 1586)	12 (5)	11 (45)	9 (55)	10 (49)	8 (67)	6 (78)	7 (75)	5 (87)	1 (99)	2 (98)	4 (94)	3 (98)
(9) Renters (1975) (n = 414)	12 (0)	10 (11)	9 (20)	11 (10)	7 (38)	8 (33)	3 (68)	6 (44)	5 (50)	4 (60)	2 (83)	1 (92)
(10) Renters (1976) (n = 439)	12 (2)	10 (13)	9 (27)	11 (7)	7 (38)	8 (31)	3 (70)	6 (38)	5 (51)	4 (61)	2 (83)	1 (92)
Stage Three												
(11) Rent House (1975) (n = 244)	12 (0)	10 (16)	9 (23)	11 (14)	8 (43)	7 (48)	5 (69)	6 (63)	4 (74)	2 (87)	3 (86)	1 (94)
(12) Rent House (1976) (n = 264)	12 (2)	10 (19)	9 (30)	11 (11)	8 (41)	7 (43)	5 (70)	6 (55)	4 (73)	2 (86)	3 (83)	1 (94)
(13) Rent Apt./ Duplex (1975) (n = 162)	12 (1)	11 (4)	6 (17)	10 (4)	4 (33)	9 (9)	3 (67)	7 (15)	8 (15)	5 (22)	2 (80)	1 (91)
(14) Rent Apt./ Duplex (1976) (n = 167)	11 (2)	10 (5)	6 (22)	12 (1)	4 (33)	9 (12)	3 (72)	8 (12)	7 (16)	5 (23)	2 (81)	1 (90)

For each item: [a] = ownership rank order, [b] = percentage owning durable.

Whether the rankings in Table 2 represent priority patterns or merely frequency of ownership without any underlying schema is assessed through the methodology developed by Green (1956). The index of reproducibility measures how successful the Guttman scale is in reproducing an individual's ownership of the twelve durables given knowledge only of an individual's scale score. A value of "one" depicts perfect reproducibility (i.e., all the respondents conformed perfectly to the scale), and a "zero" characterizes perfect

FIGURE

TREE DIAGRAM OF THE STAGES OF ANALYSIS AND THE GREEN STATISTICAL MEASURES OF SCALABILITY

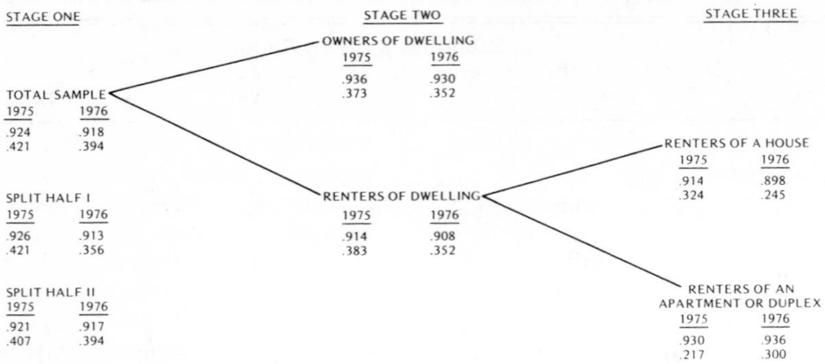

NOTES: All top numbers = index of reproducibility and are significant at the .001 level.
All bottom numbers = index of consistency.

nonreproducibility. Researchers have demonstrated that the index of reproducibility is influenced by the distribution of the scale items. To assess this, the expected coefficient of reproducibility is calculated. It determines the coefficient that could be obtained based only on the item frequencies. Whether or not the index of reproducibility and the expected coefficient of reproducibility are significantly different is assessed through the Student's *t*-test. Finally, the index of consistency provides an additional way of looking at the situation using the same information as above. This measure depicts the percentage of maximum possible improvement in reproducibility that the derived scale actually obtained. Its value also ranges from zero to one.

Stage One: Aggregate Analyses

The results of the Guttman analyses and the Green statistical measures are presented in Table 2 and the Figure. In looking at the total sample (1975 data), one can see the following ownership pattern: (1) first television, (2) first vehicle, (3) refrigerator, (4) range, (5) washing machine, (6) stereo or tape player, (7) dryer, (8) second vehicle, (9) dishwasher, (10) second television, (11) freezer, and (12) microwave oven. Green's statistics suggest that there is a scale or underlying priority pattern. In other words, the order of acquisition tends to follow the ownership frequencies, e.g., the number of people who bought washing machines before ranges is very small. The reproducibility coefficient was 0.924, which is statistically significant from the expected reproducibility coefficient. Additionally, the index of consistency indicates that the Guttman scale achieved 42.1 percent of the improvement in reproducibility that was theoretically possible.

In order to shed light on the quality of the results—an issue previous studies have ignored—both the reliability and validity were assessed. To test the internal validity of the scaling procedure just reported, the 1975 sample of the 1,747 respondents was split into two halves. The respondents were split according to the odd or even last digit of their sequential identification number to provide two subsamples. As the completed questionnaires, gathered over months of 1975, were numbered as they were collected from the interviews, neither split-half sample was biased by seasonal factors.

Both split-halves have very similar Green statistics, and statistics similar to the total sample. The order of acquisition was also similar with exception that the second TV and the dishwasher were reversed in split-half II. This switching is not surprising because in the total sample of 1,747 respondents, 40.3 percent owned a dishwasher and 38.6 percent a second TV. Thus normal sampling variation could be expected to change the positioning in the derived scale for these two durables.

To test the longitudinal reliability of the derived scales, the 1976 DRP/OPUBCO Consumer Audit and the same Guttman and Green techniques were used. The 1976 data were also subjected to a split-half analysis in order to assess the internal validity of the derived scale. The Green statistics are of the same magnitude and statistical significance as in 1975, and the order of acquisition pattern is similar to the previous year (identical to the 1975 split-half II). In addition, the split-halves for 1976 demonstrated that the 1976 scale was also internally valid. It can be concluded, based on both the 1975 and 1976 data, that the population as a whole has a common order of acquisition for a large set of heterogeneous goods.

Stage Two: Owner-Rental Subsample Analyses

Previous research has demonstrated that in selected cases, patterns of acquisition vary by social class and family life cycle (Hebden and Pickering 1974). Although they are important, rather than examining these same variables it was decided to utilize a previously unexamined variable. This variable is type of dwelling. It was postulated that owners and renters are likely to acquire durables in differing patterns. They are likely to differ because: (1) owners are generally more stable and permanent than renters, and (2) owning a home necessitates the acquisition of some durables such as a range and refrigerator, whereas renters frequently have these durables included as part of their rent.

An examination of the Figure shows that the 1975 data on owners and renters resulted in Green reproducibility coefficients that were statistically significant. The index of consistency was 0.373 for the owner subsample, and 0.383 for the renters. Thus, approximately 38 percent of the gain theoretically possible in reproducibility was obtained with the derived scales. While the scalability measures are similar, the order of acquisition is different between owners and renters. For example, Table 2 reveals that the first six items in the acquisition scale for owners are a range, refrigerator, TV-1, vehicle-1, washer, and clothes dryer. The first six items acquired by renters are TV-1, vehicle-1, stereo or tape player, refrigerator, range, and washer.

The longitudinal reliability of the preceding results is quite strong, as shown in Table 2 and the Figure. For home owners, the order of acquisition changed only slightly from 1975 to 1976. During this time span, TV-2 became the ninth durable on the scale and dishwasher the tenth durable, whereas in 1975 the order was reversed. For renters, the only aberration was in regard to clothes dryer and vehicle-2. In 1975 clothes dryer was the seventh item in the acquisition scale and vehicle-2 was the eighth item. During 1976 this order was reversed. As in our preceding analyses, the Guttman Scalogram Analysis for the renters showed that physically and functionally dissimilar goods compete intensively for limited consumer dollars.

Stage Three: House-Apartment/Duplex Renter Subsample Analyses

To further examine the extent to which acquisition patterns vary by market segment, the rental group was subdivided into house renters and apartment/duplex renters. It seemed intuitively appealing to view house renters as being somewhere between a home owner and apartment dweller.

To examine the extent to which acquisition patterns do vary between house renters and apartment/duplex renters, separate Guttman analyses were performed on the two groups. Examination of the Green statistics in the Figure reveals that all Green coefficients of reproducibility (1975 and 1976) are statistically significant. However, the Green index of consistency is the lowest of any of the stages and quite low for the apartment/duplex renters. In 1975 this index was 0.217, revealing that only 21.7 percent of the maximum improvement possible in reproducibility was obtained with the derived scale of acquisition. Obviously, considerable room for improvement exists in scaling the acquisition of durables for apartment/duplex renters.

Although the scale for apartment/duplex renters is weaker than others, it is interesting to compare it to that of all renters and house renters (Table 2). As mentioned previously, the first six durables in the scale for all renters are TV-1, vehicle-1, stereo or tape player, refrigerator, range, and washer. If one looks at the scale for apartment/duplex renters one will notice some shifting among durables. For example, apartment/duplex renters acquire their first six durables in the following order: TV-1, vehicle-1, stereo or tape player, vehicle-2, refrigerator, and TV-2. Most noteworthy about their pattern is their acquisition of two TVs and two vehicles by the time they make their sixth acquisition. Thus, apartment and duplex renters appear to be a lucrative market for second vehicles and TVs.

The longitudinal reliability of the scales for house renters and apartment/duplex renters was also assessed. The acquisition scale for house renters had good reliability, as the Green statistics were similar between years, and the twelve durables maintained identical positions on the 1975 and 1976 scales. Thus, house renters, on the whole, are a stable and predictable segment of the market, at least in relation to their acquisition of the twelve durables under investigation.

The reliability results for apartment/duplex renters were not as encouraging. The Green statistics were weaker and the index of consistency varied considerably between years. Also disheartening were the several changes in the derived acquisition scales for 1975 and 1976 (see Table 2). This suggests that apartment/duplex renters are a less homogeneous group than others studied. Coupled with the smaller sample size, the orders were less stable.

Error Analyses

Predictably, the scale derived for each of the analyses possesses some error. This is represented by indexes of reproducibility and consistency that are less than 1.0. Each of these statistical coefficients is determined directly from the number of deviations, or errors, from the perfect Guttman scale pattern. An examination of these errors should lead to a fuller understanding of the strengths and weaknesses of a particular scale.

Table 3 presents the data necessary to conduct an error analysis of the durables in this study. Included in Table 3 are 10 of the 14 Guttman analyses conducted. The split halves are excluded because their sole purpose was for an internal validity analysis. Each cell in Table 3 consists of four numbers: (1) rank order of ownership, (2) number of skip errors, (3) number of ownership errors, and (4) error percentage.

Because there are differences in the order of acquisition across the analysis groups, the rank order of own-

TABLE 3

OWNERSHIP RANK ORDERS AND ERROR STATISTICS FOR TWELVE DURABLES BY ANALYSIS GROUP

Stage analyses	Microwave	Freezer	Second TV	Dishwasher	Second vehicle	Dryer	Stereo or tape player	Washer	Range	Refrigerator	First vehicle	First TV	Total errors
Stage One													
(1) Full Sample	12[a]	11	10	9	8	7	6	5	4	3	2	1	
1975	0[b]	12	85	153	164	118	249	165	113	134	114	47	1354
	32[c]	414	284	107	194	84	161	27	39	9	3	0	1354
	1.8[d]	24.4	21.1	14.9	20.5	11.6	23.5	11.0	8.7	8.2	6.7	2.7	
(4) Full Sample	12	11	9	10	8	7	6	5	4	3	2	1	
1976	0	15	240	83	221	154	288	217	132	147	157	54	1708
	70	534	265	263	213	90	186	22	57	4	4	0	1708
	3.5	27.1	24.9	17.1	21.4	12.0	23.4	11.8	9.3	7.5	8.0	2.7	
Stage Two													
(7) Owners	12	11	10	9	8	6	7	5	1	2	3	4	
1975	0	12	82	134	151	156	165	106	9	13	46	19	893
	31	369	218	89	95	5	71	13	0	0	2	0	893
	2.3	28.8	22.7	16.9	18.6	12.2	17.8	9.0	0.7	1.0	3.6	1.4	
(8) Owners	12	11	9	10	8	6	7	5	1	2	4	3	
1976	0	15	233	81	205	195	203	126	23	25	69	27	1202
	61	479	179	249	104	17	86	14	0	0	10	3	1202
	3.8	31.1	26.0	20.8	19.5	13.4	18.2	8.8	1.5	1.6	5.0	1.9	
(9) Renters	12	10	9	11	7	8	3	6	5	4	2	1	
1975	0	6	12	0	40	7	86	25	64	73	50	27	390
	1	32	52	36	78	68	7	35	48	30	3	0	390
	0.2	9.2	15.5	8.7	28.5	18.4	22.5	14.5	27.1	24.9	12.8	6.5	
(10) Renters	12	10	9	11	7	8	3	6	5	4	2	1	
1976	0	9	7	0	43	11	89	40	78	77	62	27	443
	9	50	86	26	79	71	11	25	50	32	4	0	443
	2.1	13.4	21.2	5.9	27.8	18.7	22.8	14.8	29.2	23.9	15.0	6.1	
Stage Three													
(11) Rent House	12	10	9	11	8	7	5	6	4	2	3	1	
1975	0	6	12	0	12	17	33	19	43	27	24	14	207
	0	24	26	29	45	23	21	22	14	0	3	0	207
	0.0	12.3	15.6	11.9	23.4	16.4	22.1	16.8	23.4	11.1	11.1	5.7	
(12) Rent House	12	10	9	11	8	7	5	6	4	2	3	1	
1976	0	9	7	0	15	26	31	36	52	35	38	16	265
	6	41	47	25	57	23	15	23	21	0	7	0	265
	2.3	18.9	20.5	9.5	27.3	18.6	17.4	22.3	27.7	13.3	17.0	6.1	
(13) Rent Apart-	12	11	6	10	4	9	3	7	8	5	2	1	
ment	0	0	8	0	34	0	22	1	2	21	17	11	116
1975	1	7	17	7	6	14	5	18	24	16	1	0	116
	0.6	4.3	15.4	4.3	24.7	8.6	16.7	11.7	16.0	22.8	11.1	6.8	
(14) Rent Apart-	11	10	6	12	4	9	3	8	7	5	2	1	
ment	0	0	13	0	31	0	19	1	7	23	20	11	125
1976	3	8	27	1	5	19	10	15	20	14	3	0	125
	1.8	4.8	24.0	0.6	21.6	11.4	17.4	9.6	16.2	22.2	13.8	6.6	

For each item: [a] = rank order, [b] = skip errors, [c] = ownership errors, [d] = error percentage.

ership is presented as the top number in each cell in Table 3. This is the same information as the top line of each of the analyses in Table 2. In studying Table 3, it is particularly important to be aware of the orderings because the incidence of error tends to be less pronounced at the extreme ends of the scale under examination.

The second number represents the respondents that had skip errors. A skip error occurs when a respondent does not own a particular durable, but was predicted to have owned it given his score for the scale. In other words, the individual skipped ownership of the next durable in sequence for a higher order of goods.

For example, let us assume that an individual in the 1975 full sample case owned five different durables: television, motor vehicle, refrigerator, range, and stereo or tape player. By owning five durables, such an individual would be ranked a five. However, if this theoretical person had a perfect scale, he would have owned a washer and not a stereo or tape player. In short, he skipped the washer for the stereo or tape player and, thereby, is recorded as a skip type error.

The third number represents the respondents that had ownership errors. An ownership error is actually the other side of the coin of a skip error. It exists when a respondent does own a particular durable, but should not have owned it given the scale score assigned to him by the scalogram program. The preceding example can also be used to illustrate this point. The same hypothetical respondent owned a stereo or tape player when he should not have had such a durable. Therefore, he was assigned an ownership error.

In summary, the skip and ownership error counting procedure means that every deviation from the perfect scale is double counted. The total skip errors must equal the total ownership errors. This double counting is a major weakness of the classical approach to Guttman scaling.[3]

The column furthest to the right in Table 3 indicates the total number of skip and ownership errors. For example, in the 1975 full sample case, there were 1,354 skip errors and 1,354 ownership errors. Though these numbers may appear to be large relative to the sample size, two issues should be emphasized. First, there is the double counting of errors. Therefore, the first analysis only has 1,354 unique errors. Second, the relevant error comparison is not the sample size, as any person can be assigned more than one error. It is even theoretically possible to have more errors than people. To emphasize this point, consider a hypothetical example of a person in the 1975 full sample scale owning two durables, a TV, and a microwave. This person would be assigned a scale score of 2 and would be predicted to own a TV and a motor vehicle. However, this hypothetical individual skipped the vehicle and nine other durables to get a microwave. S/he has ten skip errors. Moreover, by owning a microwave, this individual should have owned all eleven lower order goods. Since s/he only owned a TV, s/he would be given ten ownership errors.

In conducting an error analysis, the most relevant comparison is the percent of errors for each durable in the scale. This is calculated by summing the total errors for an item and dividing this sum by the number of respondents in the sample. Thus, in the 1975 full sample case, there was never more than 24.4 percent error for any given durable. This means that only 12.2 percent (one-half of 24.4 percent, because errors are double counted) of the people either owned a durable when they did not own all lower order goods or did not own durables while owning higher order goods.

To date, error analysis of scalogram data has been virtually ignored in the literature. Consequently, no guidelines exist for systematically exploring the ten separate groups given in Table 3. However, even a naive analysis reveals some interesting findings.

The data presented in Table 3 indicate that the high frequency of ownership items on each scale have very low error rates associated with them. Even with double counting, these are generally less than 12 percent. Further, as the respondents are segmented into more specialized groups, these low error rates become even more pronounced. The only exception to this is in the second-stage analysis where the renter scales have higher error rates for nearly all of the items. These higher rates should be expected because the renter scales were derived from a subset of the total respondent population that was made up of two different homogeneous populations, each considerably different from the other. The much improved error rates for the stage three analyses (the homogeneous renter groups considered separately) reinforce this argument.

On the other end of the scales, only extremely low frequency of ownership items exhibit low error rates. Items between the scale extremes tend to have higher error rates, with increased error rates as one proceeds from either extreme of a scale to the middle.

As mentioned earlier, the set of durables selected for this study has the advantage of including an innovation (microwave) and second purchase goods (TV-2, vehicle-2). An examination of scale errors gives an indication of the impact these items have on the derived scales. In the case of the 1975 full sample, only three percent (52 households) owned a microwave oven. This small group could be classified as innovators. However, the order of acquisition scale does not do a good job in predicting innovative behavior. Of the 52 households owning a microwave, Table 3 indicates that 32 households or 61.5 percent did not own all lower order durables. Comparable results are found in the other nine analyses. Thus, it appears that ownership of microwaves is cutting across established priority or acquisition patterns in that the innovators are not necessarily households that have accumulated all other durables on the scale. In general, it can be concluded that the derived order of acquisition scale fails to precisely identify the adopters of microwave ovens. Innovators generally came from households that owned several durables. Thus, there is an indication that innovators for durables are people who have already acquired a basic stockpile of durable goods.

In examining the acquisition of second purchase durables, both the multiple purchase items—TV-2 and vehicle-2—have a high number of scale deviates. This suggests, like microwave ovens, that the acquisition of

[3]Chilton (1969) discusses this issue in considerable detail. He further demonstrates the superiority of the Green reproducibility measures to the classical measures. His arguments form the justification for using the Green measures in this current study.

a second vehicle and/or TV cuts across established acquisition patterns. Moreover, by being in the middle or latter part of the scales, they appear to be viewed by society as more discretionary purchases than the earlier items in the scale. Furthermore, the position of vehicle-2 and TV-2 in the scales suggests that second-purchase durables compete with other goods that are physically and functionally dissimilar. For example, the second vehicle is acquired after a clothes dryer, but before a dishwasher in the 1975 full sample. Similarly, a second TV is acquired after a dishwasher, but before a freezer in that same analysis group. This ordering of second TVs and vehicles in the acquisition scale suggests that they are competing with products of quite different form—namely clothes dryers, dishwashers, and freezers. It is likely that most appliance and car dealers do not view their competition so broadly.

The item that generally had the highest rate of errors throughout was the freezer. This is particularly true when the total sample was considered for a single scale (24–27 percent double counted errors) and for the home ownership scales (29–31 percent double counted errors). The error rates for freezers dropped considerably when only the renters were considered. This finding reflects the low incidence of ownership for renter groups. Thus, the home ownership segment needs to be further partitioned in order to better understand the acquisition of freezers. For example, home owners with large families may have considerably different preference patterns for freezers from home owners with small families. Such an analysis represents a fruitful research question; but this and similar questions are beyond the scope of this article.

Finally, the error analysis table indicates that renters have the most heterogeneous utility structures for durable goods. On the average, renters had a higher incidence of error earlier in the acquisition process than did other respondents. This same group, however, tended to have the lowest incidence of error near the latter part of the scales. This finding reflects the general low incidence of durable ownership for renters.

CONCLUSIONS

The results support previous findings and, in addition, shed light on several previously unexamined areas. The following conclusions are suggested:

1. The population has an underlying common order of acquisition for a large set of heterogeneous durables. The magnitude of the indexes of reproducibility and their statistically significant differences from minimally expected reproducibilities demonstrated this. However, the indexes of consistency, particularly regarding renters of apartments or duplexes, point out that the reproducibility coefficients can be improved substantially. This leads one to speculate about additional ways to segment the household durables' market.
2. Meaningful population breakdowns will reveal different patterns of acquisition. For example, home owners, house renters, and apartment/duplex renters all had varying acquisition patterns for the twelve durables examined, although some overlap did exist.
3. The order of acquisition scales generated were internally valid and generally longitudinally reliable. When they lacked some reliability it was attributed to the competitive dynamics of the marketplace. It is speculated that there is strong underlying competition between a dishwasher, freezer, clothes dryer, TV-2, and vehicle-2 for the same consumer dollars.
4. The early adopters of microwave ovens (first three percent of the market) cannot be accurately identified in terms of their stock of the other eleven durables investigated. Although the microwave oven was the twelfth item on the scale, the majority of microwave owners did not possess all other eleven durables. In short, the early adopters of microwave ovens cut across established priority or acquisition patterns.
5. Second TVs and vehicles were two items with considerable error on the derived acquisition scales. The order in which these two durables are acquired is different among home owners, house renters, and apartment/duplex renters. Furthermore, the order varies between 1975 and 1976 for several of the scales. The utility that consumers have for these two durables thus varies considerably.

Naturally, acceptance of these conclusions rests on the study being replicated. Future examination should include studies across different sets of durable goods, within different geographic samples, and between other segmentation variables, such as social class, family life cycle, and income groups.

[*Received April 1978. Revised December 1978.*]

REFERENCES

Chilton, Roland J. (1969), "A Review and Comparison of Simple Statistical Tests for Scalogram Analysis," *American Sociological Review*, 238–45.

Green, Bert F. (1956), "A Method of Scalogram Analysis Using Summary Statistics," *Psychometrica*, 79–88.

Guttman, Louis (1971), "A Cornell Technique for Scale and Intensity Analysis," in *Attitude Measurement*, ed. Gene F. Summers, Chicago: Rand McNally, pp. 187–202.

Hebden, J. J., and Pickering, J. F. (1974), "Patterns of Acquisition of Consumer Durables," *Oxford Bulletin of Economics and Statistics*, 67–94.

Hunt, Shelby D. (1976), *Marketing Theory: Conceptual Foundations of Research in Marketing*, Columbus, OH.: Grid, Inc.

Lusch, Robert F., Stafford, Edward F., Jr., and Kasulis, Jack J. (1978), "Durable Accumulation: An Examination of Priority Patterns," in *Advances in Consumer Research,* Keith H. Hunt ed., vol. 5, Ann Arbor: Association for Consumer Research, pp. 119–25.

McFall, John (1969), "Priority Patterns and Consumer Behavior," *Journal of Marketing,* 50–5.

Nie, Norman J., Hall, C. Hadlai, Jenkins, Jean G., Steinbrenner, Karin, and Bent, Dale H. (1975), *Statistical Package for the Social Sciences,* New York: McGraw-Hill Book Co.

Paroush, Jacob (1965), "The Order of Acquisition of Consumer Durables," *Econometrica,* 225–35.

Pyatt, F. Graham (1964), *Priority Patterns And The Demand For Household Durable Goods,* Cambridge, MA.: Cambridge University Press.

Reynolds, Fred D. and Wells, William D. (1977), *Consumer Behavior,* New York: McGraw-Hill Book Co.